GLIMPSES OF THE
Open Gates of Heaven

GLIMPSES OF THE
Open Gates of Heaven

Martin Klein

Savannah
Pictures

First edition.
Sixth printing.

ISBN: 978-0-9975897-3-3 (Paperback)
Religion: Christian Theology: Eschatology

www.savannahpictures.com

Dedicated to those precious and sincere souls who long for truth, yet remain a part of Babylon, for whom Jesus has reserved a final call: "Come out of her, my people, that ye be not partakers of her sins, and that ye receive not of her plagues."

Table of Contents

Forward

"From the rise and fall of nations as made plain in the books of Daniel and the Revelation, we need to learn how worthless is mere outward and worldly glory. Babylon, with all its power and magnificence, the like of which our world has never since beheld—power and magnificence which to the people of that day seemed so stable and enduring—how completely has it passed away! As 'the flower of the grass,' it has perished. So perished the Medo-Persian kingdom, and the kingdoms of Grecia and Rome. And so perishes all that has not God for its foundation. Only that which is bound up with His purpose, and expresses His character, can endure. His principles are the only steadfast things our world knows.

"When the books of Daniel and Revelation are better understood, believers will have an entirely different religious experience. They will be given such **glimpses of the open gates of heaven** that heart and mind will be impressed with the character that all must develop in order to realize the blessedness which is to be the reward of the pure in heart. The Lord will bless all who will seek humbly and meekly to understand that which is revealed in the Revelation. This book contains so much that is large with immortality and full of glory that all who read and search it earnestly receive the blessing to those 'that hear the words of this prophecy, and keep those things which are written therein.'[1] One thing will certainly be understood from the study of Revelation—that the connection between God and His people is close and decided.

"Let us give more time to the study of the Bible. We do not understand the Word as we should. The book of Revelation opens with an injunction to us to understand the instruction that it contains.... **When we... understand what this book means to us, there will be seen among us a great revival.**"[2]

---

[1] Revelation 1:3

[2] E. G. White, *The Faith I Live By* (Nampa, ID: Pacific Press, 1958), p. 345.2-4.

Introduction

God declared to the beloved prophet, "But thou, O Daniel, shut up the words, and seal the book, even to the time of the end: many shall run to and fro, and knowledge shall be increased."[1] On the authority of the word of God, knowledge of the prophecies of Daniel will increase just prior to the second coming of Jesus. "The prophet of God declares that in the last days knowledge shall be increased. There are new truths to be revealed to the humble seeker. The teachings of God's word are to be freed from the errors and superstition with which they have been encumbered."[2] Therefore, knowledge of the book of Revelation will also be increased, for "The books of Daniel and the Revelation are one. One is a prophecy, the other a revelation; one a book sealed, the other a book opened."[3]

"There is no excuse for any one in taking the position that there is no more truth to be revealed, and that all our expositions of Scripture are without an error. The fact that certain doctrines have been held as truth for many years by our people, is not a proof that our ideas are infallible. Age will not make error into truth, and truth can afford to be fair. No true doctrine will lose anything by close investigation. We are living in perilous times, and it does not become us to accept everything claimed to be truth without examining it thoroughly; neither can we afford to reject anything that bears the fruits of the Spirit of God; but we should be teachable, meek and lowly of heart. There are those who oppose everything that is not in accordance with their own ideas, and by so doing they endanger their eternal interest as verily as did the Jewish nation in their rejection of Christ. The Lord designs that our opinions shall be put to the test, that we may see the necessity of closely examining the living oracles to see whether or not we are in the faith. Many who claim to believe the truth have settled down at their ease, saying, 'I am rich, and increased with goods, and have need of nothing.' But Jesus says to these self-complacent ones, Thou 'knowest not that thou art wretched, and miserable, and poor, and blind, and naked.' Let us

---

[1] Daniel 12:4

[2] E. G. White, *The Spirit of Prophecy* (Nampa, ID: Pacific Press, 1884), Vol. 4, p. 186.3.

[3] E. G. White, *Manuscript Releases*, Vol. 1 (Washington D.C.: Review and Herald Publishing Association, 1981), p. 99.3.

11

individually inquire, Do these words describe my case? If so, the True Witness counsels us, saying, 'Buy of me gold tried in the fire, that thou mayest be rich; and white raiment, that thou mayest be clothed, that the shame of thy nakedness do not appear; and anoint thine eyes with eye-salve, that thou mayest see.'"[4]

"Many refuse to obey the truth through fear that they will lose their standing in the world. They allow the inconveniences in the pathway of truth to prevent them from following the Saviour. They do not realize that to reject truth means to lose eternal life."[5]

"We must have greater wisdom than we have yet manifested in regard to the manner in which we treat those who in some points of faith honestly differ from us. It is unbecoming in anyone who claims to be a follower of Christ to be sharp and denunciatory, to stoop to ridicule the views of another. The spirit of criticism unfits men for receiving the light that God would send them, or for seeing what is evidence of the truth.

"Should the Lord reveal light after His own plan, many would not respect or comprehend it; they would ridicule the bearer of God's message as one who set himself up above those who were better qualified to teach. The papal authorities first ridiculed the reformers, and when this did not quench the spirit of investigation, they placed them behind prison walls.... We should be very cautious lest we take the first steps in this road that leads to the Inquisition. The truth of God is progressive; it is always onward, going from strength to greater strength, from light to greater light. We have much reason to believe that the Lord will send us increased truth, for a great work is yet to be done... Much has been lost because our ministers and people have concluded that we have had all the truth essential for us as a people; but such a conclusion is erroneous and in harmony with the deceptions of Satan; for truth will be constantly unfolding. The greatest care should be exercised lest we do despite to the Spirit of God by treating with indifference and scorn the messenger, and the messages, God sends to His people, and so reject light because our hearts are not in harmony with God."[6]

---

[4] E. G. White, *The Review and Herald*, December 20, 1892 par. 1.

[5] *Ibid.*, November 13, 1900 par. 21.

[6] E. G. White, *The Signs of the Times*, May 26, 1890 par. 2.

Greater light is to shine from the word of God at the end of time, especially from the prophecies of Daniel and Revelation. God pronounced a special blessing on all who read and study the book of Revelation: "Blessed is he that readeth, and they that hear the words of this prophecy, and keep those things which are written therein: for the time is at hand."[7]

The greater light that God has promised to bestow will not contradict the light he has already given. The spirit of prophecy, in these last days, has abundantly clarified large segments of the prophecies of Daniel and Revelation. The historical chapters of Daniel 1, 3, 4, 5, 6 and 10 are frequently referenced. The prophetic chapters of Daniel 2, 7, 8 and 9 are expounded in great detail. Revelation 1, 2, 3, 7, 10, 11, 12, 13, and 14 are thoroughly explained and interpreted. Revelation 18, 19, 20, 21, and 22 are heavily quoted from and elucidated. Surely the greater light that God intends to stream from the prophecies of Daniel and Revelation in these last days will come mostly from those chapters lightly covered and hardly referred to, where large and significant portions are left undefined, rather than from those chapters on which abundant light has already been received.

"In the Scriptures are presented truths that relate especially to our own time. **To the period just prior to the appearing of the Son of man, the prophecies of Scripture point, and here their warnings and threatenings pre-eminently apply. The prophetic periods of Daniel, extending to the very eve of the great consummation, throw a flood of light upon events then to transpire.** The book of Revelation is also replete with warning and instruction for the **last generation.** The beloved John, under the inspiration of the Holy Spirit, portrays the fearful and thrilling scenes connected with the close of earth's history, and presents the duties and dangers of God's people. None need remain in ignorance, none need be unprepared for the coming of the day of God."[8]

The prophecies of Scripture, especially the books of Daniel and Revelation pre-eminently apply to the very eve of Christ's coming and the final generation. Despite such unequivocal definitions, the

---

[7] Revelation 1:3

[8] E. G. White, *The Review and Herald*, September 25, 1883 par. 6.

five major segments[9] of Daniel and Revelation on which the spirit of prophecy is all but silent, have each traditionally been placed almost entirely in the past.

"There are many at the present day thus clinging to the customs and traditions of their fathers. When the Lord sends them additional light, they refuse to accept it, because, not having been granted to their fathers, it was not received by them. We are not placed where our fathers were; consequently our duties and responsibilities are not the same as theirs. We shall not be approved of God in looking to the example of our fathers to determine our duty instead of searching the word of truth for ourselves. Our responsibility is greater than was that of our ancestors. We are accountable for the light which they received, and which was handed down as an inheritance for us, and we are accountable also for the additional light which is now shining upon us from the word of God."[10]

"'Who does not know,' he [Martin Luther] responded, 'that one can seldom advance a new idea without having some appearance of pride, and without being accused of exciting quarrels? Why were Christ and all the martyrs put to death?—Because they appeared proud despisers of the wisdom of the times in which they lived, and because they brought forward new truths without having first consulted the oracles of the old opinions.'
"Again he declared: 'What I am doing will not be effected [sic] by the prudence of man, but by the counsel of God. If the work be of God, who shall stop it? If it be not, who shall forward it? Not my will, not theirs, not ours, but thy will, holy Father who art in Heaven!'"[11]

"We should never let the impression prevail that only a privileged few have a knowledge of the Scriptures and that others must refer to these—one or another of their favorite ministers—as authority for their doctrines. People should be educated to search the Scriptures for themselves, to dare to think for themselves, taking the Bible as their guidebook, their standard of faith. Although heresy may lift its head boldly, and insult the truth by perverted ideas and false

---

[9] Daniel 11; Daniel 12; Revelation 4-6; Revelation 8-9; and Revelation 17.

[10] E. G. White, *The Great Controversy* (Nampa, ID: Pacific Press Publishing Co., 1911), p. 164.1.

[11] E. G. White, *The Spirit of Prophecy* (1884), Vol. 4, p. 106.1-2.

interpretations and misapplication of Scripture, there should be no suppression of religious freedom by reformers."[12]

"But God will have a people upon the earth to maintain the Bible, and the Bible only, as the standard of all doctrines and the basis of all reforms. The opinions of learned men, the deductions of science, the creeds or decisions of ecclesiastical councils, as numerous and discordant as are the churches which they represent, the voice of the majority—not one nor all of these should be regarded as evidence for or against any point of religious faith. Before accepting any doctrine or precept, we should demand a plain 'Thus saith the Lord' in its support.

"Satan is constantly endeavoring to attract attention to man in the place of God. He leads the people to look to bishops, to pastors, to professors of theology, as their guides, instead of searching the Scriptures to learn their duty for themselves. Then, by controlling the minds of these leaders, he can influence the multitudes according to his will."[13]

"The greatest want of the world is the want of men,—men who will not be bought or sold; men who in their inmost souls are true and honest; men who do not fear to call sin by its right name; men whose conscience is as true to duty as the needle to the pole; men who will stand for the right though the heavens fall."[14]

"Let us give more time to the study of the Bible. We do not understand the Word as we should. The book of Revelation opens with an injunction to us to understand the instruction that it contains... *When we... understand what this book means to us, there will be seen among us a great revival.*"[15]

The absence among us of this great revival stands as a silent and embarrassing witness to the fact that we do not understand what Revelation means to us. "Every truly honest soul will come to the light of truth. 'Light is sown for the righteous.' Psalm 97:11. And no

---

[12] E. G. White, *Christ Triumphant* (Hagerstown, MD: Review and Herald Publishing Association,1999), p. 332.5.

[13] E. G. White, *The Great Controversy* (1911), p. 595.1-2.

[14] E. G. White, *Education* (Mt. View, CA: Pacific Press Publishing Co., 1903), p. 57.3.

[15] E. G. White, *The Faith I Live By* (Hagerstown, MD, 1958), p. 345.2-4.

church can advance in holiness unless its members are earnestly seeking for truth as for hid treasure."[16]

"Every mind should turn with reverent attention to the revealed word of God. Light and grace will be given to those who thus obey God. They will behold wondrous things out of his law. Great truths that have lain unheeded and unseen since the day of Pentecost, are to shine from God's word in their native purity. To those who truly love God the Holy Spirit will reveal truths that have faded from the mind, and will also reveal truths that are entirely new. Those who eat the flesh and drink the blood of the Son of God will bring from the books of Daniel and Revelation truth that is inspired by the Holy Spirit. **They will start into action forces that cannot be repressed**. The lips of children will be opened to proclaim the mysteries that have been hidden from the minds of men. The Lord has chosen the foolish things of this world to confound the wise, and the weak things of the world to confound the mighty."[17]

"When God's Word is studied, comprehended, and obeyed, a bright light will be reflected to the world; new truths, received and acted upon, will bind us in strong bonds to Jesus. **The Bible, and the Bible alone, is to be our creed, the sole bond of union; all who bow to this Holy Word will be in harmony.** Our own views and ideas must not control our efforts. Man is fallible, but **God's Word is infallible**. Instead of wrangling with one another, let men exalt the Lord. Let us meet all opposition as did our Master, saying, 'It is written.' Let us lift up the banner on which is inscribed, **The Bible our rule of faith and discipline**."[18]

METHODS OF INTERPRETATION:

"Knowing this first, that no prophecy of the scripture is of any private interpretation."[19] We may not; we dare not, interpret Scripture

---

[16] E. G. White, *The Great Controversy* (1911), p. 521.3.

[17] E. G. White, *The Review and Herald*, August 17, 1897, par. 19.

[18] E. G. White, *The Review and Herald*, December 15, 1885 par. 16.

[19] 2 Peter 1:20

ourselves, but must allow Scripture to be its own interpreter.[20] "For precept must be upon precept, precept upon precept; line upon line, line upon line; here a little, and there a little."[21] The author has placed this principle above all others, and has attempted to always, only, allow the Bible to explain itself.

Secondly, as Martin Luther declared, "We cannot attain to the understanding of Scripture either by study or by the intellect. Your first duty is to begin by prayer. **Entreat the Lord to grant you, of His great mercy, the true understanding of His word. There is no other interpreter of the word of God than the Author of this word**, as He Himself has said, 'They shall be all taught of God.' Hope for nothing from your own labors, from your own understanding: trust solely in God, and in the influence of His Spirit."[22]

Third, the author has also followed the fourteen principles of interpretation[23] outlined by the Protestant American reformer, William Miller, a "man specially chosen of God to lead out in the proclamation of Christ's second coming."[24] "Endeavoring to lay aside all preconceived opinions, and dispensing with commentaries, he compared scripture with scripture by the aid of the marginal references and the concordance. He pursued his study in a regular

---

[20] "The vague and fanciful interpretations of Scripture, and the many conflicting theories concerning religious faith, that are found in the Christian world are the work of our great adversary to confuse minds so that they shall not discern the truth. And the discord and division which exist among the churches of Christendom are in a great measure due to the prevailing custom of wresting the Scriptures to support a favorite theory. Instead of carefully studying God's word with humility of heart to obtain a knowledge of His will, many seek only to discover something odd or original.

"In order to sustain erroneous doctrines or unchristian practices, some will seize upon passages of Scripture separated from the context, perhaps quoting half of a single verse as proving their point, when the remaining portion would show the meaning to be quite the opposite. With the cunning of the serpent they entrench themselves behind disconnected utterances construed to suit their carnal desires. Thus, do many willfully pervert the word of God. Others, who have an active imagination, seize upon the figures and symbols of Holy Writ, interpret them to suit their fancy, with little regard to the testimony of **Scripture as its own interpreter**, and then they present their vagaries as the teachings of the Bible."
E. G. White, *The Great Controversy* (1911), 520.3-521.1.

[21] Isaiah 28:10

[22] E. G. White, *The Great Controversy* (1911), 132.2.

[23] William Miller, *Miller's Works*, Vol. 1: Views of the Prophecies and Prophetic Chronology (Boston, Joshua V. Himes, 1842), p. 20-23.

[24] E. G. White, *The Great Controversy* (1911), p. 317.1.

and methodical manner; beginning with Genesis, and reading verse by verse, he proceeded no faster than the meaning of the several passages so unfolded as to leave him free from all embarrassment. When he found anything obscure, it was his custom to compare it with every other text which seemed to have any reference to the matter under consideration. Every word was permitted to have its proper bearing upon the subject of the text, and if his view of it harmonized with every collateral passage, it ceased to be a difficulty. Thus, whenever he met with a passage hard to be understood he found an explanation in some other portion of the Scriptures. As he studied with earnest prayer for divine enlightenment, that which had before appeared dark to his understanding was made clear. He experienced the truth of the psalmist's words: 'The entrance of Thy words giveth light; it giveth understanding unto the simple.' Psalm 119:130."[25] "Our conclusions have been formed deliberately and prayerfully, as we have seen the evidence in the Scriptures."[26]

Fourth, "As differences of opinion have arisen in reference to interpretations of Scriptures and methods of labor, calculated to unsettle the faith of believers in the message and lead to disunion in the work, the spirit of prophecy has always thrown light on the situation. It has always brought union of thought and harmony of action to the body of believers. In every crisis that has arisen in the development of the message and the growth of the work, those who have stood firmly by the law of God and the light of the Spirit of prophecy have triumphed and the work has prospered in their hands."[27]

"The book of Revelation, in connection with the book of Daniel, especially demands study. Let every God-fearing teacher consider how most clearly to comprehend and to present the gospel that our Saviour came in person to make known to His servant John—'The Revelation of Jesus Christ, which God gave unto Him, to show unto His servants things which must shortly come to pass.' Revelation 1:1. None should become discouraged in the study of the Revelation because of its apparently mystical symbols. 'If any of you lack

---

[25] E. G. White, *The Great Controversy* (1911), p. 320.1.

[26] *Ibid.*, p. 337.2.

[27] E. G. White, *Loma Linda Messages* (1981), p. 34.1.

wisdom, let him ask of God, that giveth to all men liberally, and upbraideth not.' James 1:5.

"'Blessed is he that readeth, and they that hear the words of this prophecy and keep those things which are written therein: for the time is at hand.' Revelation 1:3."[28]

"In view of the testimony of Inspiration, how dare men teach that the Revelation is a mystery beyond the reach of human understanding? It is a mystery revealed, a book opened. The study of the Revelation directs the mind to the prophecies of Daniel, and both present most important instruction, given of God to men, concerning events to take place at the close of this world's history.

"To John were opened scenes of deep and thrilling interest in the experience of the church. He saw the position, dangers, conflicts, and final deliverance of the people of God. He records the closing messages which are to ripen the harvest of the earth, either as sheaves for the heavenly garner or as fagots for the fires of destruction. Subjects of vast importance were revealed to him, especially for the last church, that those who should turn from error to truth might be instructed concerning the perils and conflicts before them. None need be in darkness in regard to what is coming upon the earth.

"Why, then, this widespread ignorance concerning an important part of Holy Writ? Why this general reluctance to investigate its teachings? It is the result of a studied effort of the prince of darkness to conceal from men that which reveals his deceptions. For this reason, Christ the Revelator, foreseeing the warfare that would be waged against the study of the Revelation, pronounced a blessing upon all who should read, hear, and observe the words of the prophecy."[29]

It is my prayer that this volume will unfold to your wondering eyes Glimpses of the Open Gates of Heaven.

---

[28] E. G. White, *Education* (1903), p. 191.2.

[29] E. G. White, *The Great Controversy* (1911), p. 341.3-342.1.

The Prophecy of Daniel

Daniel 1

SUMMARY:
Daniel and his three friends, Hananiah, Mishael, and Azariah are taken captive into Babylon, and made eunuchs by king Nebuchadnezzar. When offered food and wine from the king's table, at the risk of their lives, they purpose to follow God and request pulse and water instead of the king's unwholesome dainties. The prince of the eunuchs is afraid that granting this request might endanger his life. Daniel proposes his famous ten-day clinical trial, complete with control group, study group, and variable. At the end of the trial, Daniel and his three friends are found to be healthier, and ten times wiser than all the wise men in the realm. The wisdom that God blesses them with enables Daniel to interpret the king's vision in Chapter 2, which saves the lives of Daniel and his friends and the rest of the wise-men of Babylon.

For some people, the Biblical book of Daniel would be the last book they would expect to find quoted in scientific circles. Yet some of the most famous scientists in the world, including Sir Isaac Newton, have spent significant portions of their lives studying the amazing prophecies of this book.

The most astonishing prophecies of ancient times are recorded in the book of Daniel. However, to begin our study of ancient prophecies that reveal the future, let us turn to a modern scientific source, *The New England Journal of Medicine,* containing a discussion of the earliest clinical trial ever recorded: "The earliest clinical trial was neither Watson's study of smallpox nor Lind's study of the prevention of scurvy. The first report of a clinical trial has Biblical origins, in the book of Daniel...."[1] This is a very interesting statement to be published in this prestigious medical journal. One of the physicians participating in the discussion replies, "I acknowledge Dr. Lewis's successful search for an earlier clinical trial, one that was

---

[1] Edmund J. Lewis, M.D., "Ancient Clinical Trials," *The New England Journal of Medicine,* Volume 348: 83-8, January 2, 2003.
http://www.nejm.org/doi/full/10.1056/NEJM200301023480120

performed a couple thousand years ago and described in the Book of Daniel."[2]

Let us therefore turn to the book of Daniel and discover to what this medical journal refers—the most ancient clinical trial ever recorded.

Daniel 1:1 In the third year of the reign of Jehoiakim king of Judah came Nebuchadnezzar king of Babylon unto Jerusalem, and besieged it.

Because the Israelite nation had disregarded the commands of God, he promised that he would send the Babylonians against them to punish them for their sins,[3] to turn them to repentance. The Lord, through the prophet Jeremiah, told Israel to submit to Nebuchadnezzar and put their neck under the yoke of the king of Babylon. If they would follow God's instructions, they would be allowed to live peaceably in their land, but if they would not harken, their land would be destroyed, and their people slain or taken captive.[4] Israel and other nations did not harken to the word of the Lord through his prophet and thus the fateful judgment arrived. The Babylonians came against them and besieged Jerusalem.

Though Nebuchadnezzar was "an idolater by birth and training, and at the head of an idolatrous people, he had nevertheless an innate sense of justice and right, and God was able to use him as an instrument for the punishment of the rebellious and for the fulfillment of the divine purpose."[5]

"At the very time messages of impending doom were urged upon princes and people, their ruler, Jehoiakim, who should have been a wise spiritual leader, foremost in confession of sin and in reformation and good works, was spending his time in selfish pleasure. 'I will build me a wide house and large chambers,' he proposed; and this house, 'ceiled with cedar, and painted with vermilion' (Jeremiah

---

[2] Frank J. Lepreau, M.D., "Ancient Clinical Trials," *The New England Journal of Medicine*, Volume 348: 83-8, January 2, 2003.
http://www.nejm.org/doi/full/10.1056/NEJM200301023480120

[3] Jeremiah 25:9

[4] See Jeremiah 27.

[5] G. White, *Prophets and Kings* (Nampa, ID: Pacific Press, 1917), p. 514.2.

22:14), was built with money and labor secured through fraud and oppression."[6]

Daniel 1:2 And the Lord gave Jehoiakim king of Judah into his hand, with part of the vessels of the house of God: which he carried into the land of Shinar to the house of his god; and he brought the vessels into the treasure house of his god.

The king of Jerusalem was taken captive by Nebuchadnezzar and carried into Babylon. "Yet through the very humiliations that Israel's departure from Him had invited, God gave Babylon evidence of His supremacy, of the holiness of His requirements, and of the sure results of obedience. And this testimony He gave, as alone it could be given, through those who were loyal to Him."[7]

Daniel 1:3 And the king spake unto Ashpenaz the master of his eunuchs, that he should bring certain of the children of Israel, and of the king's seed, and of the princes;

This was a direct fulfillment of the prophecy that God had given to Hezekiah, king of Judah, because he had dishonored God by showing the Babylonians all the treasures of his house, rather than pointing them to God as the source of his healing.

"And Isaiah said unto Hezekiah, Hear the word of the LORD. Behold, the days come, that all that is in thine house, and that which thy fathers have laid up in store unto this day, shall be carried into Babylon: nothing shall be left, saith the LORD. And of **thy sons** that shall issue from thee, which thou shalt beget, shall they take away; and they **shall be eunuchs[8] in the palace of the king of Babylon**."[9]

Exactly as the Bible had predicted, some of the king's offspring were carried into exile and became eunuchs in the court of Babylon.

---

[6] E. G. White, *Prophets and Kings* (1917), p. 429.2.

[7] *Ibid.*, p. 479.2

[8] Eunuch: a man who has been castrated.

[9] 2 Kings 20:16-18

Daniel 1:4 Children in whom was no blemish, but well favoured, and skilful in all wisdom, and cunning in knowledge, and understanding science, and such as had ability in them to stand in the king's palace, and whom they might teach the learning and the tongue of the Chaldeans.

Those who were taken captive to serve in the court of Babylon were the most talented and brightest of Israel's youth. Throughout history the youth are the ones targeted for indoctrination programs. The king intended to take these young people and enroll them in the University of Babylon, give them new names as a part of his propaganda program, and brainwash them to believe the religion, culture, politics and thought of the Babylonians so they would be sure to serve faithfully in the court of the king. In this manner he could take advantage of the knowledge of the kingdoms that he conquered.

Daniel 1:5 And the king appointed them a daily provision of the king's meat, and of the wine which he drank: so nourishing them three years, that at the end thereof they might stand before the king.

The young captives were enrolled in the University of Babylon with full scholarships that promised the honor of standing before the king after graduation. In fact, he even honored them with the food from his own table. It would have been easy for them to be flattered by the honor. They were special people, appointed not only a special education, but also a special diet.[10]

This posed a problem, however, because there were at least four young men among those that were taken captive from Jerusalem that would not violate the principles of the word of God.

Daniel 1:6 Now among these were of the children of Judah, Daniel, Hananiah, Mishael, and Azariah:

Since Daniel was of royal lineage, it is possible that he (or one of his friends) would have been a successor to the throne of Judah, had

---

[10] Notwithstanding the fact that they had been subjected to the forced castration procedure.

they not been taken captive. Instead, God saw fit to make Daniel prime minister of two separate world empires—something no other person in history has ever attained.

Daniel 1:7 Unto whom the prince of the eunuchs gave names: for he gave unto Daniel the name of Belteshazzar; and to Hananiah, of Shadrach; and to Mishael, of Meshach; and to Azariah, of Abednego.

As a part of their indoctrination program, they were given new names. This is important because in ancient cultures the meanings of names were considered highly significant.

The children of Israel worshiped the only true God, the Creator of heaven and earth. The ancient Babylonians worshipped all kinds of deities, the chief of which was the sun god, and they denied the God of heaven. The Babylonians assigned the captives new names with new meanings. Daniel means, "God is my judge." Daniel's name gave glory to the Hebrew God, to the one Creator of the universe. The Babylonians gave him the name Belteshazzar—which means, "Bel protects" or "may Bel protect the king."[11] This was a reference to one of the Babylonian deities—the equivalent of Baal. Hananiah's name meant "Jehovah has given" but this they changed to Shadrach which meant "Aku's command" or "Illumined by the sun," giving reference to another Babylonian deity. Mishael, meant "who is like God" or "one who is like God." His name was changed to Meshach "who is like Aku." Notice that the Babylonians obviously knew what the Hebrews' names meant and, as much as possible, gave them similar sounding names, and even names with a similar meaning only twisting them to honor a Babylonian deity. Azariah meant "whom Jehovah helps," while his new name was Abed-Nego, "the servant of Nebo."

It is interesting to note that there is no record in Scripture of the names of any other of the youth with whom Daniel and his friends were taken captive. The names that are recorded are only the four who remained faithful to God.

---

[11] In Daniel 4:8 Nebuchadnezzar mentions the fact that the name Belteshazzar (the Babylonian name given Daniel) was according to the name of his god.

Daniel 1:8 But Daniel purposed in his heart that he would not defile himself with the portion of the king's meat, nor with the wine which he drank: therefore he requested of the prince of the eunuchs that he might not defile himself.

Why was Daniel concerned with defilement from the king's diet? The word of God forbids defilement with several things:

1. Unclean meats.[12]
2. Meat that contains blood or fat.[13]
3. Things sacrificed to idols.[12, 14]

In Leviticus 11, God specifies the animals which were unclean and therefore unfit for consumption.

In Leviticus 3:17 the Scriptures declare, "It shall be a perpetual statute for your generations throughout all your dwellings, that ye eat neither fat nor blood."

Scripture also forbids the drinking of fermented beverages: "Wine is a mocker, strong drink is raging: and whosoever is deceived thereby is not wise."[15] and "Woe unto them that are mighty to drink wine, and men of strength to mingle strong drink:"[16]

The king's food was also offered to idols.

Daniel and his friends knew these Biblical principles and determined that they could not eat the things the king set before them while remaining faithful to God. They well knew that to refuse the king's meat would likely be considered the highest insult, which could cost them their lives. Yet they would not defile their bodies even if it meant risking death.

---

[12] See Leviticus 11; Genesis 7:2-3

[13] The New Testament in Acts 15:28-29 also gives these principles: "For it seemed good to the Holy Ghost, and to us, to lay upon you no greater burden than these necessary things; That ye abstain from meats offered to idols, and from blood, and from things strangled, and from fornication: from which if ye keep yourselves, ye shall do well..."

[14] Revelation 2:14

[15] Proverbs 20:1

[16] Isaiah 5:22

This verse says that Daniel **"purposed in his heart**." In Hebrew the word for "purposed" is שׂוּם (śûm), which is translated twice as "gave" in verse seven. Daniel "gave" his heart; he had surrendered his life to God, and it did not matter what difficulties or trials came or even if he were to lose his life—his faith was in God. Daniel and his companions were true "Christian patriots, men who were as true as steel to principle, who would not be corrupted by selfishness, but who would honor God at the loss of all things. In the land of their captivity these men were to carry out God's purpose by giving to heathen nations the blessings that come through a knowledge of Jehovah. They were to be His representatives. Never were they to compromise with idolaters; their faith and their name as worshipers of the living God they were to bear as a high honor. And this they did. In prosperity and adversity they honored God, and God honored them."[17]

Subjected to forced surgical procedures, attending a pagan university, surrounded by pagan worship, given new names that mocked the God of heaven, they are challenged with a decision regarding their diet that endangers their lives. "Daniel and his companions were captives in a strange land, but God suffered not the envy and hatred of their enemies to prevail against them. The righteous have ever obtained help from above. How often have the enemies of God united their strength and wisdom to destroy the character and influence of a few simple persons who trusted in God. But because the Lord was for them, none could prevail against them."[18]

God's followers today may prevail against the prince of darkness. The Scripture declares "This is the victory that overcometh the world, even our faith."[19] "All things are possible to him that believeth;" and "What things soever ye desire, when ye pray, believe that ye receive them, and ye shall have them."[20] God will do great things for us if we put our trust in him.

---

[17] E. G. White, *Prophets and Kings* (1917), p. 479.1.

[18] E. G. White, *Testimonies for the Church*, Vol. 2 (Mt. View, CA: Pacific Press Publishing Association, 1871), p. 139.2.

[19] 1 John 5:4

[20] Matthew 21:22; 1 John 5:14-15

Daniel 1:9 Now God had brought Daniel into favour and tender love with the prince of the eunuchs.

Despite of the difficult circumstances, God opens the way for Daniel to cultivate friendships with those in charge of the captives.

Daniel 1:10 And the prince of the eunuchs said unto Daniel, I fear my lord the king, who hath appointed your meat and your drink: for why should he see your faces worse liking than the children which are of your sort? then shall ye make me endanger my head to the king.

Even in ancient Babylonian times, people apparently believed that one had to eat meat and drink wine in order be healthy. Perhaps they thought one would be malnourished and become protein deficient: something will be wrong with you; your faces will look worse than the other children and then the king will notice that you are not getting the proper nourishment. Nothing has changed today. There is the same opinion prevailing still but let us consider the testimony of Scripture.

Even though Daniel's request was denied by the prince of the eunuchs, he did not give up; he pressed forward in faith.

Daniel 1:11 Then said Daniel to Melzar, whom the prince of the eunuchs had set over Daniel, Hananiah, Mishael, and Azariah,

Daniel 1:12 Prove thy servants, I beseech thee, ten days; and let them give us pulse to eat, and water to drink.

Daniel then went to Melzar, who the prince of the eunuchs had set over the captives, and proposed the first clinical trial in recorded history. He suggested a scientific experiment in which two groups would be observed; a control group (those eating the king's diet) and an experimental group (Daniel and his three friends who would eat pulse and water), with the trial period lasting ten days.

Daniel asked for pulse. The word pulse in Hebrew is זֵרֹעַ zêrôa'. This word comes from the same root word as the word זֶרַע zera' meaning seed. In Genesis 1:29, the Bible says, "And God said, Behold, I have given you every herb bearing **seed**, which is upon the face of all the earth, and every tree, in the which is the fruit of a tree yielding **seed**; to you it shall be for meat." The word translated seed is zera'.

In the beginning, God told man that he had given for meat all the things bearing seed; thus, Daniel was actually asking for the plant-based diet of Eden—pulse and water. Daniel requested a diet of things bearing seeds—fruits, grains, nuts, and vegetables.

Daniel continues to explain the rest of this oldest recorded clinical trial:

Daniel 1:13 Then let our countenances be looked upon before thee, and the countenance of the children that eat of the portion of the king's meat: and as thou seest, deal with thy servants.

After the ten-day trial period the two different groups were to be compared and evaluated to see if there were any deficiencies. The decision of what the students could eat for the rest of their schooling would be based on objective, scientific findings.

Daniel 1:14 So he consented to them in this matter, and proved them ten days.

Daniel 1:15 And at the end of ten days their countenances appeared fairer and fatter in flesh than all the children which did eat the portion of the king's meat.

They did not appear malnourished; in fact, they looked healthier, stronger, and more fit than those who were eating the king's meat.

Daniel 1:16 Thus Melzar took away the portion of their meat, and the wine that they should drink; and gave them pulse.

Daniel and his companions were allowed to continue their truly special diet—given to them by God.

Daniel 1:17 As for these four children, God gave them knowledge and skill in all learning and wisdom: and Daniel had understanding in all visions and dreams.

If Daniel had not purposed in his heart to avoid defiling his body, then God could not have given him skill and wisdom and understanding in all visions and dreams. According to the context the blessing that God gave them was directly in response to their choice to honor God in their bodies by refusing the king's meat and wine. It was this God-given skill and understanding of visions and dreams that prevents Daniel and his friends from being killed in Daniel 2.

Daniel 1:18 Now at the end of the days that the king had said he should bring them in, then the prince of the eunuchs brought them in before Nebuchadnezzar.

Daniel 1:19 And the king communed with them; and among them all was found none like Daniel, Hananiah, Mishael, and Azariah: therefore stood they before the king.

Daniel 1:20 And in all matters of wisdom and understanding, that the king inquired of them, he found them ten times better than all the magicians and astrologers that were in all his realm.

Not only did they have understanding of dreams and visions, but God gave them temporal knowledge and wisdom as well. When Nebuchadnezzar gave them the examination at the end of their university course, he found them ten times wiser than everyone else in the empire.

You may ask: did not God give people permission to eat meat?

When God created the world in Genesis 1, he gave man everything that bore seed to be their meat. He did not give them permission to eat flesh until nine chapters later. What had happened in the interim? Man had sinned and the earth had become so wicked that God said he was going to destroy the earth with a flood of water. In Genesis 9:3 God gave Noah and his sons and their wives permission to eat flesh because they had just come off the ark after the earth was destroyed by the flood and there were no plants on the planet to eat. They had no other option to sustain life than to eat flesh, so God gave them permission. However, with that permission he gave them some specific parameters: "But flesh with the life thereof, which is the blood thereof, shall ye not eat. And surely your blood of your lives will I require; at the hand of every beast will I require it, and at the hand of man; at the hand of every man's brother will I require the life of man."[21]

God said they were forbidden to eat flesh that contained blood. Additionally, God told them that as a result of eating flesh—even if they followed the prohibition of not eating the blood—their lives would be required; the lifespan would be shortened. Exactly as the Bible outlined, immediately after the flood the longevity of the patriarchs dropped off dramatically.

Notice how the Bible states this principle in Leviticus 3:17, "It shall be a perpetual statute for your generations throughout all your dwellings, that ye eat neither fat nor blood."

God said in effect, I am allowing you to eat flesh under the current conditions, though it is a non-ideal situation, but you must never eat the blood or the fat. Some might object, saying that these were just Old Testament principles—only for the Jews. Is this the case?

In the New Testament book of Acts, God outlines this principle for the Gentiles, "For it seemed good to the Holy Ghost, and to us, to lay upon you no greater burden than these necessary things; That ye abstain from meats offered to idols, and from blood, and from things strangled, and from fornication...."[22]

In the church council recorded in Acts 15, such importance was placed on not eating blood that its consumption was classified with fornication. This is a serious issue in which most Christians do not realize that they are ignoring this explicit Biblical mandate when they eat flesh containing blood.[23] Perhaps you might consider something even better by moving away from flesh foods entirely, like Daniel did. Daniel knew that there was something scientific about the plant-

---

[21] Genesis 9:4-5

[22] Acts 15:28-29

[23] Practically all flesh from the grocery store (unless it is labeled Kosher) contains the blood. Much of the taste of meat comes from the blood. Most people would likely not even like the taste of meat without the blood.

based diet, as given by God in Eden, that would give him wisdom and health.

Today, science is finally catching up with the Bible. Notice the following quote from one of the most famous nutritional scientists in the world, Dr. T. Colin Campbell, director of the China study, the most comprehensive nutritional study ever conducted; (the China study is a 20-year ongoing project, in which he compared disease rates to lifestyle and dietary habits):[24] "We compared the prevalence of Western diseases in each county with diet and lifestyle variables and, to our surprise, we found that one of the strongest predictors of Western diseases was blood cholesterol."[25] Cholesterol is found only in animal products. It is found in all whole animal products. There is no cholesterol in the fattiest plant food you can think of; coconut, avocado, olives—none. No cholesterol occurs in any plant product; it is found only in animal products.

One of the most famous studies in the world by one of the most famous researchers demonstrated exactly what Daniel already knew; that the animal products the king was offering him would not be the best way to preserve health or glorify God.[26]

Daniel 1:21 And Daniel continued even unto the first year of king Cyrus.

God blessed Daniel as a result of his commitment to do nothing that would dishonor God with his body. Not only was he blessed with health and wisdom, but also with long life. He continued even to the first year of Cyrus—well into his eighties.

"The history of Daniel is recorded for the special benefit of those who desire to place themselves in the best condition of physical soundness, that they may reach as high a standard of usefulness as Daniel reached. The first chapter of Daniel is one of the most forcible

---

[24] The China Study was funded by the National Institutes of Health, and was a joint effort between Cornell University, Oxford University, and the Chinese Academy of Sciences, and directed by Dr. T. Colin Campbell.

[25] T. Colin Campbell, Ph.D., *The China Study,* January 2005 ed. (Dallas, TX: BenBella Books, 2004), p. 77.

[26] For more information on reversing diseases through lifestyle see: www.klondikemountainhealthretreat.org

discourses on temperance that could be given. Read it, read it, and as you read, become wise, not in your own conceit, but wise like Daniel and his fellows, whose physical, mental and spiritual understanding increased with their sanctified resolution to adhere strictly to the principles of temperance in eating and drinking. These youth were greatly blessed in their effort to honor and please God by preserving their physical powers so that they would have mental strength, and so that God could mould and fashion them after the divine similitude."[27]

Why not try Daniel's diet for ten days? Try it and see if God will not also give you the same blessing that he gave to Daniel. You will not only will feel better, but your mind will be clearer to understand truth.

You cannot accomplish this on your own, but you can give your heart to God, and he will give you the desire and strength to create new lifestyle habits. Why not repeat the oldest scientific experiment? Let the Lord show himself strong again. Ask the Lord that he would grant to you the wisdom and self-control he gave Daniel. God will bless in this experiment of faith and provide wisdom to understand the things that he has revealed in these ancient prophecies.

---

[27] E. G. White, *Battle Creek Letters* (Nampa, ID: Pacific Press, 1928), p. 11.3.

Daniel 2

SUMMARY:

Daniel and his three friends, Shadrach, Meshach, and Abednego, are sentenced to death along with all the other wise men in Babylon for failure to tell King Nebuchadnezzar the dream he could not remember. The king had dreamed about an image with a head of gold, chest and arms of silver, belly and thighs of brass, legs of iron, and feet part of iron and part of clay. After Daniel's fervent prayer God reveals the king's dream and its meaning to Daniel. The astonishing interpretation is a detailed view of the world's empires covering thousands of years, and an outline of the future that predicts precisely what is now world history. History comes alive as the meaning of this dream unfolds, providing some of the strongest possible evidence that God's word is true, reliable, and infallible.

Daniel 2:1 And in the second year of the reign of Nebuchadnezzar Nebuchadnezzar dreamed dreams, wherewith his spirit was troubled, and his sleep brake from him.

The king is so disturbed by his dream that he cannot sleep.

Daniel 2:2 Then the king commanded to call the magicians, and the astrologers, and the sorcerers, and the Chaldeans, for to show the king his dreams. So they came and stood before the king.

This pagan king thought that the best way to discover the meaning of his dream was to ask the magicians, the astrologers, and the sorcerers.[1]

Daniel 2:3 And the king said unto them, I have dreamed a dream, and my spirit was troubled to know the dream.

---

[1] "It is fondly assumed that today, in the civilization of the twenty-first century, that the heathen superstitions have disappeared. But the word of God and the testimony of facts all around us, show plainly that sorcery is practiced today just as surely as in the days of the old-time magicians. In reality, this same ancient magic is the same as what is now known as modern spiritualism." E. G. White, *Acts of the Apostles* (Boise, ID: Pacific Press Publishing Association, 1911), p. 289.2.

The king knows his dream was important but is unable to recall the details.

Daniel 2:4 Then spake the Chaldeans to the king in Syriack, O king, live for ever: tell thy servants the dream, and we will show the interpretation.

The Old Testament books of the Bible were originally written in Hebrew, while the New Testament books were originally written in Greek. However, a large part of the book of Daniel, and some portions of Ezra, were written in Aramaic rather than Hebrew. This verse contains the transition from Hebrew into Aramaic. Daniel 1:1 through the beginning of 2:4, is written in Hebrew. When this verse says, "**then spake the Chaldeans to the king in Syriac**k," Daniel switches to Aramaic (Aramaic is the same as Syriack). He then continues writing in Aramaic through the end of Daniel 7. In Daniel chapter 8, the prophet transitions back to Hebrew for the remainder of the book.

The magicians assure the king that if he will tell them the dream they will be able to interpret it for him.

Daniel 2:5 The king answered and said to the Chaldeans, The thing is gone from me: if ye will not make known unto me the dream, with the interpretation thereof, ye shall be cut in pieces, and your houses shall be made a dunghill.

Nebuchadnezzar has a temper, and he is deadly serious about recalling his dream. He employed the wise-men and magicians to provide him inside information and is unimpressed that they are unable to deliver.

Daniel 2:6 But if ye show the dream, and the interpretation thereof, ye shall receive of me gifts and rewards and great honour: therefore show me the dream, and the interpretation thereof.

Daniel 2:7 They answered again and said, Let the king tell his servants the dream, and we will show the interpretation of it.

The magicians politely stall for time. They have no idea what the king dreamed and realize there is no way for them to know. If he can at least tell them the dream, perhaps they could manufacture a convincing interpretation.

Daniel 2:8 The king answered and said, I know of certainty that ye would gain the time, because ye see the thing is gone from me.

Daniel 2:9 But if ye will not make known unto me the dream, there is but one decree for you: for ye have prepared lying and corrupt words to speak before me, till the time be changed: therefore tell me the dream, and I shall know that ye can show me the interpretation thereof.

The king accuses the magicians of telling him lies. The Chaldeans reply:

Daniel 2:10 The Chaldeans answered before the king, and said, There is not a man upon the earth that can show the king's matter: therefore there is no king, lord, nor ruler, that asked such things at any magician, or astrologer, or Chaldean.

This is their polite way of saying: king, you're being unreasonable. What else could they say? They know they cannot just make something up, so they are just trying their best to preserve their lives by stalling for time. Perhaps they can convince the king that he is being irrational. The Chaldeans proceed, however, to state something very revealing.

Daniel 2:11 And it is a rare thing that the king requireth, and there is none other that can show it before the king, except the gods, whose dwelling is not with flesh.

These are the magicians and the astrologers who claim to have special ability to communicate with the gods; to discover things that others do not know. But here they admit the fact that they are not able to do this. They betray the inadequacy of their religion by stating that only the gods have this knowledge. The gods, they say, do not dwell with humans.

This statement shows their pagan religion to be contrary to the religion of the Bible: "And let them make me a sanctuary; that I may dwell among them."[2] "Thy way, O God, is in the sanctuary: who is so great a God as our God?"[3] The central and defining theme of the religion of Daniel is the desire of God to dwell with his people. "As God hath said, I will dwell in them, and walk in them; and I will be their God, and they shall be my people."[4]

Daniel 2:12 For this cause the king was angry and very furious, and commanded to destroy all the wise men of Babylon.

Nebuchadnezzar issues the command that all the wise men should be slain.

Daniel 2:13 And the decree went forth that the wise men should be slain; and they sought Daniel and his fellows to be slain.

Obviously, Daniel was not among those who were called in before the king to be asked if they could interpret this vision. Perhaps he was considered a junior wise man. Yet, he and his companions are included in the decree of those who are to be slain.

Daniel 2:14 Then Daniel answered with counsel and wisdom to Arioch the captain of the king's guard, which was gone forth to slay the wise men of Babylon:

One can only imagine Arioch coming to Daniel's house, knocking on his door, and saying, I'm here to kill you. But Daniel answers Arioch with counsel and wisdom. Trusting God to take care of him he has no need to panic.

---

[2] Exodus 25:8

[3] Psalms 77:13

[4] 2 Corinthians 6:16

Daniel 2:15 He answered and said to Arioch the king's captain, Why is the decree so hasty from the king? Then Arioch made the thing known to Daniel.

Apparently, Daniel must have cultivated a good relationship with Arioch, since Arioch allowed him to ask this question and replied with an explanation.

Daniel 2:16 Then Daniel went in, and desired of the king that he would give him time, and that he would show the king the interpretation.

Daniel has great faith in God's ability to reveal this thing to him. God has not done anything for him yet; he has no idea what the dream is, but he goes straight in and tells the king that he will be able to show the interpretation, if given a little time. The king grants him the requested deferment.

Daniel 2:17 Then Daniel went to his house, and made the thing known to Hananiah, Mishael, and Azariah, his companions:

Daniel 2:18 That they would desire mercies of the God of heaven concerning this secret; that Daniel and his fellows should not perish with the rest of the wise men of Babylon.

"Daniel gathers his three companions, and together they take the matter before God, seeking for wisdom from the Source of light and knowledge. Although they were in the king's court, surrounded with temptation, they did not forget their responsibility to God. They were strong in the consciousness that His providence had placed them where they were; that they were doing His work, meeting the demands of truth and duty. They had confidence toward God. They had turned to Him for strength when in perplexity and danger, and He had been to them an ever-present help."[5]

Daniel 2:19 Then was the secret revealed unto Daniel in a night vision. Then Daniel blessed the God of heaven.

---

[5] E.G. White, *The Sanctified Life* (1889), p. 35.1.

41

"The servants of God did not plead with Him in vain. They had honored Him, and in the hour of trial He honored them. The secret was revealed to Daniel, and he hastened to request an interview with the king."[6] Daniel does not forget to praise and thank God when help is given.

Daniel 2:20 Daniel answered and said, Blessed be the name of God for ever and ever: for wisdom and might are his:

Daniel 2:21 And he changeth the times and the seasons: he removeth kings, and setteth up kings: he giveth wisdom unto the wise, and knowledge to them that know understanding:

Daniel 2:22 He revealeth the deep and secret things: he knoweth what is in the darkness, and the light dwelleth with him.

Daniel 2:23 I thank thee, and praise thee, O thou God of my fathers, who hast given me wisdom and might, and hast made known unto me now what we desired of thee: for thou hast now made known unto us the king's matter.

The God of Daniel still lives and reigns. He still reveals the deep and secret things; he still knows what is in the darkness, the light still dwells with him and he still desires to give us wisdom to understand his word.

Daniel 2:24 Therefore Daniel went in unto Arioch, whom the king had ordained to destroy the wise men of Babylon: he went and said thus unto him; Destroy not the wise men of Babylon: bring me in before the king, and I will show unto the king the interpretation.

The dream is revealed to Daniel, and he quickly requests an interview with the king.

Daniel 2:25 Then Arioch brought in Daniel before the king in haste, and said thus unto him, I have found a man of the

---

[6] E.G. White, *The Sanctified Life* (1889), p. 35.2.

captives of Judah, that will make known unto the king the interpretation.

Arioch seemed to want to get some credit for finding the answer the king desired. He said "**I have found a man**," when in reality he did not find him. Arioch was going to execute Daniel, and Daniel brought the matter up. Arioch also makes a somewhat derogatory statement here, "**I have found a man of the captives of Judah**," drawing attention to the fact that Daniel is a prisoner.

Daniel 2:26 The king answered and said to Daniel, whose name was Belteshazzar, Art thou able to make known unto me the dream which I have seen, and the interpretation thereof?

Daniel stands before the monarch of an empire the wealth and power of which the world has never since beheld.[7] The king, surrounded by his riches and glory, in great distress, demands of Daniel: are you able to tell me the dream and give me the interpretation? The exiled youth places his confidence in God rather than himself.

Daniel 2:27 Daniel answered in the presence of the king, and said, The secret which the king hath demanded cannot the wise men, the astrologers, the magicians, the soothsayers, show unto the king;

Daniel politely draws attention to the fact that the king's religion is inadequate.

Daniel 2:28 But there is a God in heaven that revealeth secrets, and maketh known to the king Nebuchadnezzar what shall be in the latter days. Thy dream, and the visions of thy head upon thy bed, are these;

Daniel takes no glory or credit to himself, but exalts God as the source of all wisdom. He says, in essence: Your wise men cannot tell you the dream. No one can tell you the dream, not even myself, but there is a God in heaven who can.

---

[7] E.G. White, *Education* (1903), p. 175.4.

God had revealed future events stretching to the end of time—"**the latter days.**"

Daniel 2:29 As for thee, O king, thy thoughts came into thy mind upon thy bed, what should come to pass hereafter: and he that revealeth secrets maketh known to thee what shall come to pass.

As he drifted to sleep, Nebuchadnezzar was pondering what would happen in the future. The God of heaven saw the yearning heart of that heathen king and stooped low to reveal to him things to come.

Daniel 2:30 But as for me, this secret is not revealed to me for any wisdom that I have more than any living, but for their sakes that shall make known the interpretation to the king, and that thou mightest know the thoughts of thy heart.

Once again, Daniel makes sure it is very clear that it is not his own wisdom; but God who has revealed the secret. As Daniel begins to speak, one can imagine the king sitting there listening; probably skeptically. Perhaps his arms are folded; he is unconvinced that this young Jewish captive will be able to tell him his dream.

Daniel 2:31 Thou, O king, sawest, and behold a great image. This great image, whose brightness was excellent, stood before thee; and the form thereof was terrible.

Daniel 2:32 This image's head was of fine gold, his breast and his arms of silver, his belly and his thighs of brass,

As Daniel continues, we imagine the king's mouth opening and his eyes widening as he leans forward and begins to recall what he had dreamed. Daniel continues recounting the forgotten details.

Daniel 2:33 His legs of iron, his feet part of iron and part of clay.

Nebuchadnezzar had seen a great image composed of four different metals, with feet part of iron and part of clay.

Daniel 2:34 Thou sawest till that a stone was cut out without hands, which smote the image upon his feet that were of iron and clay, and brake them to pieces.

A supernatural stone strikes the image on the feet—not the head, nor the chest, or the legs. This point will be important later.

Daniel 2:35 Then was the iron, the clay, the brass, the silver, and the gold, broken to pieces together, and became like the chaff of the summer threshingfloors; and the wind carried them away, that no place was found for them: and the stone that smote the image became a great mountain, and filled the whole earth.

The mountain would be the final power to rule the earth.

Daniel 2:36 This is the dream; and we will tell the interpretation thereof before the king.

By this time, Daniel certainly has the king's attention as he begins to explain what God is revealing to the king through these symbols.

Daniel 2:37 Thou, O king, art a king of kings: for the God of heaven hath given thee a kingdom, power, and strength, and glory.

Daniel brings the attention of the king to the fact that God was the one who had given him his kingdom.

Daniel 2:38 And wheresoever the children of men dwell, the beasts of the field and the fowls of the heaven hath he given into thine hand, and hath made thee ruler over them all. Thou art this head of gold.

The head of gold represents King Nebuchadnezzar and his kingdom—the empire of Babylon.[8] This might sound like a very nice

---

[8] Nebuchadnezzar is the king of Babylon, Daniel 1:1. Both Nebuchadnezzar and his kingdom are represented by the head of gold, for verse 39 states that another kingdom will arise.

thing to say about Nebuchadnezzar, but Daniel has no flattering words for the king, for he does not stop there. Daniel continues giving exactly what God showed him.

Daniel 2:39 And after thee shall arise another kingdom inferior to thee, and another third kingdom of brass, which shall bear rule over all the earth.

Daniel tells the mightiest king of the known world that his kingdom was to fall to an inferior kingdom. This would not be the best of news, and certainly if the magicians had been able to make up an interpretation for this vision, they would not have included this part.

9

Daniel further reveals three world empires to succeed Babylon. He specifies world empires by the phrase **"which shall bear rule over all the earth**." With one simple vision God declares the scope of

---

9 Prophetic artwork p. 46, 110, 113, 121, 150, 165, 193, 426, 524, 600, 624, 700, 751, 769, and cover.© Steve Creitz, used by permission.

future world history. "Declaring the end from the beginning, and from ancient times the things that are not yet done, saying, My counsel shall stand, and I will do all my pleasure."[10]

The astonishing accuracy of this vision has confounded skeptics and confirmed believers for millennia. Just as the Bible prophesied, the famous empire of Babylon reigned from 605 B.C. to 539 B.C. Attaining unrivaled wealth, Babylon is well represented by the head of gold. But despite its wealth and power and the ambitions of Nebuchadnezzar, Babylon did not last forever. Daniel 5 records that the famed empire was divided, "and given to the Medes and Persians," and "in that night was Belshazzar the king of the Chaldeans slain. And Darius the Median took the kingdom, being about threescore and two years old."[11]

Medo-Persia was not as rich as Babylon, using silver as its currency rather than the gold tender used by Babylon. The Medo-Persians conquered Babylon in 539 B.C. Just as Daniel predicted, the Medo-Persian Empire also did not last forever. Later in the book of Daniel, using different symbols, God reveals the second and third empires, by name: "The ram which thou sawest having two horns are the kings of Media and Persia. And the rough goat is the king of Grecia: and the great horn that is between his eyes is the first king."[12] Just as the Bible predicted, Greece conquered Medo-Persia under the generalship of Alexander the Great.

"The forces which he [Darius III—Medo-Persia's last monarch] collected for the final struggle comprised—besides Persians, Medes, Babylonians, and Susianians from the center of the Empire—Syrians from the banks of the Orontes, Armenians from the neighborhood of Ararat, Cappadocians and Albanians from the regions bordering on the Euxine, Cadusians from the Caspian, Bactrians from the Upper Oxus, Sogdians from the Jaxartes, Arachosians from Cabul, Arians from Herat, Indians from Punjab, and even Sacae from the country about Kashgar and Yarkand, on the borders of the Great Desert of Gobi. Twenty-five nations followed the standard of the Great King,

---

[10] Isaiah 46:10

[11] Daniel 5:28, 30-31

[12] Daniel 8:20-21

and swelled the ranks of his vast army, which amounted (according to the best authorities) to above a million of men."[13]

"For those who looked only to numbers, the host assembled at Arbela might well inspire confidence; for it is said to have consisted of 1,000,000 of infantry—40,000 cavalry—200 scythed chariots—and fifteen elephants; of which animals we now read for the first time in a field of battle."[14]

With Alexander's mere forty-seven thousand men, this created a ratio—Persians to Greeks—of approximately 20 to 1.[15] But God had decreed nearly 300 years before that Greece would conquer the Persian Empire and regardless of the size of their army the Persians could not stand before Alexander's forces. "The prodigious army of Darius was all either killed, taken, or dispersed at the battle of Arbela…. The miscellaneous contingents of this once mighty empire, such at least among them as survived, dispersed to their respective homes and could never be again mustered in mass.
"The defeat of Arbela was in fact the death-blow of the Persian Empire. It converted Alexander into the Great King, and Darius into nothing better than a fugitive pretender."[16]

Thus, the Grecian Empire came to power in 331 B.C. and reigned until 168 B.C.

Daniel 2:40 And the fourth kingdom shall be strong as iron: forasmuch as iron breaketh in pieces and subdueth all things: and as iron that breaketh all these, shall it break in pieces and bruise.

Greece was conquered by the power which we still call today the iron monarchy of Rome. Rome was particularly known for its use of iron, especially for weapons. It was also one of the most cruel powers and ruled with an iron fist. It was under Rome's rule that Christ was born.

---

[13] George Rawlinson, M.A., *The Seven Great Monarchies of the Ancient Eastern World*, Vol. II (New York: John B. Alden, Publisher, 1885) p. 544-545.

[14] George Grote, F.R.S., *A History of Greece: From the Earliest Period to the Close of the Generation Contemporary with Alexander the Great*, Vol. XII (New York: Harper and Brothers, Publishers, 1869) p. 155-156.

[15] *Ibid.*, p. 159.

[16] *Ibid.*, p. 167.

It was a Roman governor who sentenced Christ to death and Roman soldiers who nailed him to a Roman cross. Many of the early Christians were killed by Roman Emperors; the apostle Paul by Nero and many others during the cruel ten-year persecution under the reign of Diocletian.

The pagan Roman Empire held world dominance from 168 B.C. to A.D. 476.

Daniel 2:41 And whereas thou sawest the feet and toes, part of potters' clay, and part of iron, the kingdom shall be divided; but there shall be in it of the strength of the iron, forasmuch as thou sawest the iron mixed with miry clay.

Daniel 2:42 And as the toes of the feet were part of iron, and part of clay, so the kingdom shall be partly strong, and partly broken.

The Bible declared that when the iron monarchy of Rome disintegrated, it would divide into ten major divisions, some strong and others weak. Just as Daniel prophesied, in A.D. 476 the Western Roman Empire broke into ten divisions which formed the countries of the Western Europe of today.

Alemanni	Germans
Burgundians	Swiss
Franks	French
Lombards	Italians
Anglo-Saxon	English
Suevi	Portuguese
Visigoths	Spanish
Heruli	Extinct
Ostrogoths	Extinct
Vandals	Extinct

Another characteristic of the Western European powers was their amalgamation of church and state. "The mingling of churchcraft and statecraft is represented by the iron and the clay. This union is weakening all the power of the churches. This investing the church with the power of the state will bring evil results. Men have almost passed the point of God's forbearance. They have invested their strength in politics,... But the time will come when God will punish those who have made void His law, and their evil work will recoil upon themselves."[17]

Daniel 2:43 And whereas thou sawest iron mixed with miry clay, they shall mingle themselves with the seed of men: but they shall not cleave one to another, even as iron is not mixed with clay.

God decreed that Western Europe would not adhere together regardless of how much they tried to mingle themselves genetically. What could be a more precise description of the monarchies of Western Europe? All of the royal families of Western Europe are related, for they were continually trying to mingle themselves with the seed of men. They would intermarry, attempting to restore unity to Europe and regain the empire that was lost when Rome broke apart. Just as the Bible decreed, this has not been, and never will be, successful.

Charlemagne, Charles V, Louis XIV, Napoleon, Hitler, and Stalin have all sought to reunite divided Rome, but failed. Today the European Union still tries to defy the decree of God. Of course, they have made some strides towards uniting, just as they thought in many cases that one of the new marriages had also made strides in bringing union. But none has yet succeeded in uniting Europe. According to the Bible, **"they shall not cleave one to another."**

Daniel 2:44 And in the days of these kings shall the God of heaven set up a kingdom, which shall never be destroyed: and the kingdom shall not be left to other people, but it shall break in pieces and consume all these kingdoms, and it shall stand for ever.

In the days of the kings of Western Europe the God of heaven will set up a kingdom which shall never be destroyed. The stone which struck the image on the feet represents God's eternal kingdom,

---

[17] E. G. White, *Manuscript Releases*, Vol. 15 (1990) p. 39.2.

which will come in the days of the feet—the days of divided Rome. We are living in the days of Western Europe. This means that God's kingdom is not far distant.

"What power mapped out all this history, that nations, one after another, should arise at the predicted time and fill their appointed place, unconsciously witnessing to the truth of that which they themselves knew not the meaning."[18]

Daniel 2:45 Forasmuch as thou sawest that the stone was cut out of the mountain without hands, and that it brake in pieces the iron, the brass, the clay, the silver, and the gold; the great God hath made known to the king what shall come to pass hereafter: and the dream is certain, and the interpretation thereof sure.

This amazing vision outlines precisely the four empires that would hold sway over the world for thousands of years—centuries before some of these powers existed.

Daniel 2:46 Then the king Nebuchadnezzar fell upon his face, and worshipped Daniel, and commanded that they should offer an oblation and sweet odours unto him.

Daniel 2:47 The king answered unto Daniel, and said, Of a truth it is, that your God is a God of gods, and a Lord of kings, and a revealer of secrets, seeing thou couldest reveal this secret.

In astonishment King Nebuchadnezzar admits that Daniel's God is a God of gods and Lord of kings who only can reveal the future. The king is overwhelmed with this amazing portrayal of the future and Daniel's ability to tell him exactly what he had dreamed and what it meant.

Daniel 2:48 Then the king made Daniel a great man, and gave him many great gifts, and made him ruler over the whole

---

[18] E. G. White, "Lessons From the Life of Daniel—XIII" *The Youth's Instructor*, September 29, 1903, p. 6, 7.

province of Babylon, and chief of the governors over all the wise men of Babylon.

Daniel 2:49 Then Daniel requested of the king, and he set Shadrach, Meshach, and Abednego, over the affairs of the province of Babylon: but Daniel sat in the gate of the king.

Daniel was a humble man, and in his exultation, he did not forget his three faithful friends who had stood with him, risking their lives to honor their God in refusing the king's food, and joining in prayer for God to reveal the king's vision to Daniel.

The accurate fulfillment of prophecy is the Divine signature that authenticates the reliability of Scripture. God has provided incontestable evidence, appealing to the reason of intelligent minds, for the infallibility of his Word.

Daniel 3

SUMMARY:

As Nebuchadnezzar, still unconverted and controlled by worldly ambition and self-exaltation, contemplated the implications of the dream of Daniel 2, he determined that the mighty empire of Babylon should never be succeeded by an inferior kingdom. So, in defiance of the decree of God, he commissions a statue to be made of pure gold—the metal from his dream that had symbolized Babylon. Not only does he create this idol, but he legislates that all the important people and officers of the kingdom must come and bow down and worship the image. Further, there was to be a death penalty for any who would not bow. Nebuchadnezzar's law poses a problem for Daniel's three friends, Shadrach, Meshach, and Abednego, as they will not bow to any other than the God of heaven. As a result, they are thrown into the fiery furnace from which God delivers them before all assembled dignitaries. Nebuchadnezzar then decrees that anyone who speaks against the God of Shadrach, Meshach and Abednego should be cut in pieces and their houses made a dunghill.

"The words, 'Thou art this head of gold,' had made a deep impression upon the ruler's mind. The wise men of his realm, taking advantage of this and of his return to idolatry, proposed that he make an image similar to the one seen in his dream, and set it up where all might behold the head of gold, which had been interpreted as representing his kingdom.

"Pleased with the flattering suggestion, he determined to carry it out, and to go even farther. Instead of reproducing the image as he had seen it, he would excel the original. His image should not deteriorate in value from the head to the feet, but should be entirely of gold—symbolic throughout of Babylon as an eternal, indestructible, all-powerful kingdom, which should break in pieces all other kingdoms and stand forever."[1]

---

[1] E. G. White, *Prophets and Kings* (1917), p. 504.1-2.

Daniel 3:1 Nebuchadnezzar the king made an image of gold, whose height was threescore cubits, and the breadth thereof six cubits: he set it up in the plain of Dura, in the province of Babylon.

Nebuchadnezzar, the king of Babylon, and his counselors of state determine to do everything they can to exalt Babylon and defy the prophetic message from the God of heaven. This action is in direct defiance of what God had revealed. God decreed that there would be three world empires that would succeed the kingdom of Babylon. The golden image is similar to the one in the dream, except that it is made entirely of gold.

The dimensions of this image are six cubits in breadth and threescore cubits in height (a score is twenty, therefore the height is three times twenty, or sixty cubits). The width, when unspecified is assumed to be equal to the breadth. This makes the image sixty cubits high, six cubits wide, and six cubits deep. This appears to be an allusion to that famous number 666 of Revelation.[2]

In the sexagesimal system of numbering (parts of which we use today), which had its origins in the Empire of Babylon, everything is divisible by six. A minute, for example, has 60 seconds. An hour has 60 minutes. The day has 24 hours. The year had 360 days.[3] And a circle has 360 degrees.

The sexagesimal system of numbering was a part of the Babylonian religion and was viewed as sacred, encompassed in the 360 degrees of the circle. When the depth and height of this image are multiplied (60 X 6) the result is 360. In the Babylonian religion each 10 degrees of the circle was ruled by a different Babylonian deity. There were 36 deities to rule over each ten degrees of space and each ten days of time. Adding each number from 36 to one yields 666.

$$36 + 35 + 34 + 33 + 32 + 31 + 30 + 29 + 28 + 27 + 26 + 25 + 24 + 23 + 22 + 21 + 20 + 19 + 18 + 17 + 16 + 15 + 14 + 13 + 12 + 11 + 10 + 9 + 8 + 7 + 6 + 5 + 4 + 3 + 2 + 1 = 666$$

---

[2] The full meaning of the number 666 will be uncovered in Revelation 13.

[3] Until the time of the flood, the year was 360 days in length. See Genesis 7 & 8.

This was known as the number of the sun. The Babylonians believed that one god—the sun god, Marduk—outside of the circle of space and time, ruled over the other 36 deities. Much of this numbering system passed from the Babylonians all the way down through the Medo-Persians, the Greeks and the Romans, into the system which we refer to as Roman numerals.

Adding each of the original six Roman numerals,[4] D, C, L, X, V, and I, yields the same number of the sun god—666.

Nebuchadnezzar is building an image using these numbers and dimensions, exalting the sun god in defiance of the God of heaven.

Thus, the symbolic representation that God had revealed to the king and nations of earth, to show his purposes, is turned into something to glorify human wisdom. Satan is attempting to prevent the fulfillment of God's word.

Daniel's interpretation is rejected, the truth misinterpreted and misapplied, and the symbol that God designed should unfold to the minds of men the events of the future, is turned to hinder the spread of the truth of God to the world.

Daniel 3:2 Then Nebuchadnezzar the king sent to gather together the princes, the governors, and the captains, the judges, the treasurers, the counsellors, the sheriffs, and all the rulers of the provinces, to come to the dedication of the image which Nebuchadnezzar the king had set up.

All the dignitaries and public officials are required to come to this meeting.

Daniel 3:3 Then the princes, the governors, and captains, the judges, the treasurers, the counsellors, the sheriffs, and all the rulers of the provinces, were gathered together unto the dedication of the image that Nebuchadnezzar the king had set up; and they stood before the image that Nebuchadnezzar had set up.

---

[4] M was added later in the Middle Ages.

In Jeremiah 51:59 we are told that "Zedekiah the king of Judah {went} into Babylon in the fourth year of his reign." Most likely, he went to Babylon in response to this command. He was, therefore, probably standing in this vast assembly, and when the order came to bow down to the image, he apparently complied. What a blessing he missed by not standing with Daniel's three friends. His fame would have glorified God to the ends of the earth. Instead, his trip to Babylon is briefly mentioned in one sentence of Scripture.

Daniel 3:4 Then an herald cried aloud, To you it is commanded, O people, nations, and languages,

Daniel 3:5 That at what time ye hear the sound of the cornet, flute, harp, sackbut, psaltery, dulcimer, and all kinds of music, ye fall down and worship the golden image that Nebuchadnezzar the king hath set up:

Music has always been, in all pagan religions, a very important part of getting people into the mode of worship. Here it is used very effectively to cause everyone to worship the image which Nebuchadnezzar had set up instead of worshipping the Creator of heaven and earth.

Daniel 3:6 And whoso falleth not down and worshippeth shall the same hour be cast into the midst of a burning fiery furnace.

A death penalty is instituted for further incentive to worship Nebuchadnezzar through his image.

Daniel 3:7 Therefore at that time, when all the people heard the sound of the cornet, flute, harp, sackbut, psaltery, and all kinds of music, all the people, the nations, and the languages, fell down and worshipped the golden image that Nebuchadnezzar the king had set up.

The threat of death; the music; and the peer pressure are enough to cause the entire assembly, in one accord, to fall down and worship this image, just as Nebuchadnezzar had commanded—or so it seems. Yet there, at the edge of that vast prostrate throng, are three men who had firmly resolved that they would not dishonor the God of heaven. Their God is the King of kings and Lord of lords, and they will not bow to another; they will not disobey the commandment of God.[5] They could have compromised, pretended to bow, bent to tie their shoe; but no, they stand straight and tall for the God of heaven; regardless of the consequences.

In the book of Revelation, in the chapter revealing the cryptic number 666,[6] there is outlined an event still in the future, when people will once more be asked to worship an image, with a death penalty for those who do not obey. Will we bow to the pressure of the world, or obey the commandments of God?

Daniel 3:8 Wherefore at that time certain Chaldeans came near, and accused the Jews.

Among the bowing assembly are scores, perhaps hundreds, of Jews which had been taken captive with Daniel and his friends. It is not these Jews who are accused. Apparently, these are all in obeisance before the pagan idol.

Daniel 3:9 They spake and said to the king Nebuchadnezzar, O king, live for ever.

Daniel 3:10 Thou, O king, hast made a decree, that every man that shall hear the sound of the cornet, flute, harp, sackbut, psaltery, and dulcimer, and all kinds of music, shall fall down and worship the golden image:

Daniel 3:11 And whoso falleth not down and worshippeth, that he should be cast into the midst of a burning fiery furnace.

Daniel 3:12 There are certain Jews whom thou hast set over the affairs of the province of Babylon, Shadrach, Meshach, and Abednego; these men, O king, have not regarded thee: they

---

[5] Exodus 20:3-6

[6] Revelation 13

serve not thy gods, nor worship the golden image which thou hast set up.

The accusation of refusing to bow is only against three specific Jews—Shadrach, Meshach, and Abednego.[7]

The accusation states, **"There are certain Jews that thou has set over the affairs of the province of Babylon."** There is clearly jealousy over the high position to which these men had attained in the government of Babylon, and this situation provides an opportunity for the Chaldeans to rid themselves of these competitors. The accusations brought against the three Hebrews imply that they are guilty of treason.

"This scheme, devised in the counsel of Satan, was made in order to compel the three Hebrew children to obey human laws in direct opposition to the laws of Jehovah. The most learned of the nation, men who were noted for their aptness and educational advantages, thus worked to form a confederacy that would exalt the king of Babylon and excite enmity against the Hebrew captives. They prevailed upon the king to enact certain laws which these youth could not consent to respect.

"The worship of the image which the king had set up, was made the established religion of the country. But the Hebrew children were determined not to dishonor the God of heaven, who made the world, and all things that are therein. Their God was the King of kings and Lord of lords, and they would serve him, at whatever cost."[8]

Daniel 3:13 Then Nebuchadnezzar in his rage and fury commanded to bring Shadrach, Meshach, and Abednego. Then they brought these men before the king.

Daniel 3:14 Nebuchadnezzar spake and said unto them, Is it true, O Shadrach, Meshach, and Abednego, do not ye serve my gods, nor worship the golden image which I have set up?

---

[7] Apparently, Daniel was sent on official business to absent him from this event, as the king well knew he would not bow, and apparently did not want to execute the one who had revealed the meaning of his dream. Perhaps he thought Daniel would be influenced by his friends if they could be induced to bow.

[8] E. G. White, "A Lesson from the Three Hebrew Children," *Signs of the Times, September 2, 1897* par. 2-3.

Daniel 3:15 Now if ye be ready that at what time ye hear the sound of the cornet, flute, harp, sackbut, psaltery, and dulcimer, and all kinds of music, ye fall down and worship the image which I have made; well: but if ye worship not, ye shall be cast the same hour into the midst of a burning fiery furnace; and who is that God that shall deliver you out of my hands?

Nebuchadnezzar is ready to give them a second chance. Despite his fury at being defied, perhaps he is reluctant to execute Daniel's friends. The king boasts that if they do not take the second chance he is providing, not even the God of heaven will be able to deliver them. His compromise in exalting himself against the revealed Word of God led to open defiance of the God of heaven.

Daniel 3:16 Shadrach, Meshach, and Abednego, answered and said to the king, O Nebuchadnezzar, we are not careful to answer thee in this matter.

The young men place their faith in God. They reply to the king that they do not need time to think about what they will do. They are not afraid of the king and his threats. Their reply to the king is decided.

Daniel 3:17 If it be so, our God whom we serve is able to deliver us from the burning fiery furnace, and he will deliver us out of thine hand, O king.

Daniel 3:18 But if not, be it known unto thee, O king, that we will not serve thy gods, nor worship the golden image which thou hast set up.

The three Hebrews tell the king that their God is able, not only to deliver them out of the fiery furnace, but he would certainly deliver them out of the king's hand. But, even if God chose not to deliver them from the fiery furnace, they refuse to worship Nebuchadnezzar's image for they know who is their God. They trust him. They know that God has told them that they should not worship any other God nor bow to an image. They are willing to risk their lives to follow the commandments of God.

Today we are to firmly maintain this principle still. The banner of truth and religious liberty held aloft by the founders of the gospel church and by God's witnesses during the centuries, has, in this last conflict, been committed to our hands. The responsibility for this great gift rests with those whom God has blessed with a knowledge of his Word. We are to receive this Word as the supreme authority.

Why were Shadrach and his companions so stubborn? Was it not the ruling power that God had set up issuing this command? We are commanded by God to respect kings and governments as an ordinance of God, and we should obey their commands, as a sacred duty, in their proper sphere.[9] But, when their commands conflict with the commands of God, we are to "obey God rather than men."[10] God's word is above all human legislation. We must take a "thus saith the Lord" rather than set it aside for a "thus saith the church" or "thus saith the state." The crown of Christ is above all earthly crowns. Therefore, these three Hebrews said, even if our God does not save us, be it known unto you that we will not serve your gods. They were not seeking to defy authority, but they could not consent to sacrifice freedom of conscience in worship, even in the face of death.

Daniel 3:19 Then was Nebuchadnezzar full of fury, and the form of his visage was changed against Shadrach, Meshach, and Abednego: therefore he spake, and commanded that they should heat the furnace one seven times more than it was wont to be heated.

The face of the king contorts with rage; his fury knows no limits. At the very height of his glory and pride, he is being defied by three captives. This is an insult that his proud heart cannot take. He commands that the furnace be made seven times hotter.

Daniel 3:20 And he commanded the most mighty men that were in his army to bind Shadrach, Meshach, and Abednego, and to cast them into the burning fiery furnace.

---

[9] See Romans 13.

[10] Acts 5:29

He must have been afraid that something might happen to deliver them for he orders his most powerful soldiers to throw them in the furnace.

Daniel 3:21 Then these men were bound in their coats, their hosen, and their hats, and their other garments, and were cast into the midst of the burning fiery furnace.

Daniel 3:22 Therefore because the king's commandment was urgent, and the furnace exceeding hot, the flame of the fire slew those men that took up Shadrach, Meshach, and Abednego.

The fire is so hot that the strongest men of Nebuchadnezzar's army are killed by throwing the three protesters into the furnace.

Daniel 3:23 And these three men, Shadrach, Meshach, and Abednego, fell down bound into the midst of the burning fiery furnace.

As the youth fall bound into the midst of that raging fire, all seems over. All the officials of the realm have witnessed the execution.

Daniel 3:24 Then Nebuchadnezzar the king was astonied, and rose up in haste, and spake, and said unto his counsellors, Did not we cast three men bound into the midst of the fire? They answered and said unto the king, True, O king.

You can imagine the king almost leaping out of his throne in astonishment. He sees movement in the inferno. He asks his counsellors, did we not put three men in the furnace? They assure him that it was so.

Daniel 3:25 He answered and said, Lo, I see four men loose, walking in the midst of the fire, and they have no hurt; and the form of the fourth is like the Son of God.

They were loose. The only thing that has burned are the Babylonian fetters that had bound them, for One greater than Nebuchadnezzar is with them in the furnace. This pagan king acknowledges that the fourth being in the fire had the form of the Son of God.[11] This is none other than Jesus Christ, the Creator of the universe, walking in the midst of the fire with these three young men. Nebuchadnezzar is given the privilege of seeing the Lord of creation.

The three Hebrews did not stop to weigh the consequences. They did not stop to ask, What will all the people think of me if I don't bow to this image? or, how will this affect my worldly prospects? At the risk of their lives they desired to glorify God. They had talent, intellectual ability, and positions of honor; but they did not forget God. They had surrendered their lives to the Lord and by their steadfastness they showed "forth the praises of him" who had called them "out of darkness into his marvellous light."[12] By their amazing deliverance the power and glory of God was displayed before that vast multitude. The three Hebrews walked and talked with Christ. By the glory of his presence the proud king Nebuchadnezzar was convinced that he could be none other than the Son of God. Daniel's three companions had allowed God to shine out of their lives and all their associates knew of the faith which they possessed.

By this incredible story of the Lord's deliverance of his faithful ones, we know that today God will walk with us through oppression or persecution. In the final days of this earth's history, the Son of God will ultimately overthrow all earthly powers that seek to trample upon his authority.

Daniel 3:26 Then Nebuchadnezzar came near to the mouth of the burning fiery furnace, and spake, and said, Shadrach, Meshach, and Abednego, ye servants of the most high God, come forth, and come hither. Then Shadrach, Meshach, and Abednego, came forth of the midst of the fire.

Forgetting his own dignity and greatness, Nebuchadnezzar descends his throne and approaches as near as he dares to the mouth of the furnace. When he called the three Hebrews out, he did

---

[11] Many modern Bibles remove this reference to the divinity of Christ by translating this verse as "a son of the gods." For more on this subject see, Martin Klein, *Thou Hast Magnified Thy Word Above All Thy Name* (2016).

[12] 1 Peter 2:9

not call them, you Jews or you captives; instead he says, "**Ye servants of the most high God.**"

It is interesting that they just stayed in the fire until he called them out. They were apparently aware of the presence of the Son of God, and were content to commune with him in the flames.

Daniel 3:27 And the princes, governors, and captains, and the king's counsellors, being gathered together, saw these men, upon whose bodies the fire had no power, nor was an hair of their head singed, neither were their coats changed, nor the smell of fire had passed on them.

To the astonishment of the dignitaries gathered from all the civilized world, three men walk out of the furnace unharmed. The imposing golden image still stands in the midst of the plain of Dura, its grandeur completely forgotten.

"In every age God's chosen messengers have been reviled and persecuted, yet through their affliction the knowledge of God has been spread abroad. Every disciple of Christ is to step into the ranks and carry forward the same work, knowing that its foes can do nothing against the truth, but for the truth. God means that truth shall be brought to the front and become the subject of examination and discussion, even through the contempt placed upon it. The minds of the people must be agitated; every controversy, every reproach, every effort to restrict liberty of conscience, is God's means of awakening minds that otherwise might slumber."[13]

Every dignitary of the empire watches in rapt silence as Shadrach, Meshach, and Abednego come out of the fire. Skeptics claim that the book of Daniel is a fraud. But the very fact that the entire Babylonian empire's officials were assembled there, make the story irrefutable. Daniel's account was recorded and widely circulated. If it had been a fraud someone would have written a protest. All had seen the mighty power of God. This story was certainly on the front page of the local newspapers when the officials arrived back at their homelands. Likely, the greater part of the inhabited globe heard the story of the

---

[13] E. G. White, *Thoughts from the Mount of Blessings* (Boise, ID: Pacific Press Publishing Association, 1896), p. 33.2.

deliverance of Daniel's three friends. This miraculous occurrence also carried the prophecy of four world empires, followed by the kingdom of the Son of God, to all nations and languages.

Daniel 3:28 Then Nebuchadnezzar spake, and said, Blessed be the God of Shadrach, Meshach, and Abednego, who hath sent his angel, and delivered his servants that trusted in him, and have changed the king's word, and yielded their bodies, that they might not serve nor worship any god, except their own God.

Nebuchadnezzar recognizes that they had been willing to die rather than transgress the commandment of God; and that God had honored their faith by preserving their lives. The king admits that their God is stronger than his decree.

Daniel 3:29 Therefore I make a decree, That every people, nation, and language, which speak any thing amiss against the God of Shadrach, Meshach, and Abednego, shall be cut in pieces, and their houses shall be made a dunghill: because there is no other God that can deliver after this sort.

Once again Nebuchadnezzar is constrained by the circumstances to admit that the God of heaven is stronger than his gods. But that knowledge still has not changed his heart. He still does not understand the principles of religious freedom for which Shadrach and his companions are standing. It was right for the king to make a public confession of his conviction that God was above all other gods, but for him to try to force his subjects to confess the same conviction violates the principles of the government of heaven. God never compels men's minds nor forces their wills. He leaves all free to choose whom they will serve.[14]

Daniel 3:30 Then the king promoted Shadrach, Meshach, and Abednego, in the province of Babylon.

---

[14] Joshua 24:15

The deliverance of Shadrach, Meshach, and Abednego is a promise that God will be with us in all troubles and that he is greater than all earthly powers. The three Hebrews proclaimed to the whole Babylonian Empire that they believed the promises of the God who declared, "When thou passest through the waters, I will be with thee; and through the rivers, they shall not overflow thee: when thou walkest through the fire, thou shalt not be burned; neither shall the flame kindle upon thee."[15] In an amazing manner God honored their faith in the living Word before all nations.

May God give us a faith that will not falter, even under trying circumstances. May we, by his strength and righteousness, remain steadfast to his eternal word, instead of the commands of men. May we receive a love of the truth[16] and surrender to it no matter the cost.

"God never leads His children otherwise than they would choose to be led, if they could see the end from the beginning, and discern the glory of the purpose which they are fulfilling as coworkers with Him. Not Enoch, who was translated to heaven, not Elijah, who ascended in a chariot of fire, was greater or more honored than John the Baptist, who perished alone in the dungeon. 'Unto you it is given in the behalf of Christ, not only to believe on him, but also to suffer for his sake' (Philippians 1:29). And of all the gifts that Heaven can bestow upon men, fellowship with Christ in His sufferings is the most weighty trust and the highest honor."[17]

---

[15] Isaiah 43:2

[16] 2 Thessalonians 2:10

[17] E. G. White, *Desire of Ages* (1898), p. 224.5.

Daniel 4

SUMMARY:
God communicates a second message, by dream, to
Nebuchadnezzar. This time the king remembers the dream but again
turns to the magicians, sorcerers, and astrologers, for the
explanation. After the magicians, sorcerers, and astrologers are
unable to give an interpretation, Daniel is finally called. After hearing
the dream, Daniel tells the king that the interpretation is for his
enemies. The sentence comes from heaven that Nebuchadnezzar
will be exiled to the pasture to eat grass like an ox and live with the
beasts of the earth for seven years, until his pride is humbled.
Finally, the mercy and might of the God of heaven converts the
proud heart of the king of Babylon. In humble praise to the Creator of
the universe, Nebuchadnezzar testifies to his entire empire of the
wonders the God of heaven has wrought toward him.

***Daniel 4:1 Nebuchadnezzar the king, unto all people, nations,
and languages, that dwell in all the earth; Peace be multiplied
unto you.***

The story is given by Daniel in the king's own words, quoted from the
letter Nebuchadnezzar sent to all nations of the earth. This is the
only chapter in Scripture written by a secular monarch.

***Daniel 4:2 I thought it good to show the signs and wonders that
the high God hath wrought toward me.***

Nebuchadnezzar wishes to declare to his whole realm what God has
done for him.

***Daniel 4:3 How great are his signs! and how mighty are his
wonders! his kingdom is an everlasting kingdom, and his
dominion is from generation to generation.***

The king is finally convinced that only the kingdom of the God of
heaven is to last forever.

Daniel 4:4 I Nebuchadnezzar was at rest in mine house, and flourishing in my palace:

With Babylon prosperous and beautiful, his wars and conquest over, Nebuchadnezzar now stood as king of the most powerful nation on earth and ruler of the world.

The king begins to relate the events that led to this proclamation of what God had done.

Daniel 4:5 I saw a dream which made me afraid, and the thoughts upon my bed and the visions of my head troubled me.

This is the second dream that God gave to Nebuchadnezzar. This time, he does not forget his dream.

Daniel 4:6 Therefore made I a decree to bring in all the wise men of Babylon before me, that they might make known unto me the interpretation of the dream.

Daniel 4:7 Then came in the magicians, the astrologers, the Chaldeans, and the soothsayers: and I told the dream before them; but they did not make known unto me the interpretation thereof.

Nebuchadnezzar still turns first to human counsel and pagan wisdom. His pride prevents him from consulting the God of heaven through Daniel. Perhaps he is not sure he wants to hear what God intends to communicate. The magicians, the Chaldeans, the astrologers and soothsayers, could not interpret the dream.

Daniel 4:8 But at the last Daniel came in before me, whose name was Belteshazzar, according to the name of my god, and in whom is the spirit of the holy gods: and before him I told the dream, saying,

The king turns to Daniel and the God of heaven last of all. How often today do we consult doctors, lawyers, counsellors, astrologers, friends, family, the internet, or a radio talk-show host first and as a last resort turn to God? God says, "Seek ye first the kingdom of God, and his righteousness; and all these things shall be added unto you."[1]

The names that had been given to Daniel and his friends were names of pagan gods[2] as we are told here by Nebuchadnezzar himself. The king admits that Daniel has the spirit of the holy gods in him. Referring to gods plural shows that he has still not extricated himself fully from his pagan ideas, but he is admitting that there is a God greater than the Babylonian gods.

Daniel 4:9 O Belteshazzar, master of the magicians, because I know that the spirit of the holy gods is in thee, and no secret troubleth thee, tell me the visions of my dream that I have seen, and the interpretation thereof.

The king still classifies Daniel among the magicians, despite the fact that when the magicians were called, Daniel was not summoned. He is still distinguished from the others; though Nebuchadnezzar calls him master of the magicians. Daniel is not a magician in the same sense as were the pagans. In Nebuchadnezzar's mind, he is a magician because he can interpret dreams.

Daniel 4:10 Thus were the visions of mine head in my bed; I saw, and behold, a tree in the midst of the earth, and the height thereof was great.

Nebuchadnezzar begins to describe his vision—a mighty tree in the midst of the earth.

Daniel 4:11 The tree grew, and was strong, and the height thereof reached unto heaven, and the sight thereof to the end of all the earth:

---

[1] Matthew 6:33

[2] See comments for Daniel 1:7.

Daniel 4:12 The leaves thereof were fair, and the fruit thereof much, and in it was meat for all: the beasts of the field had shadow under it, and the fowls of the heaven dwelt in the boughs thereof, and all flesh was fed of it.

This tree nourished and protected all the fowls and beasts of the world, indeed, "**all flesh was fed of it**," indicating that the people of the world gained sustenance from its abundance.

Daniel 4:13 I saw in the visions of my head upon my bed, and, behold, a watcher and an holy one came down from heaven;

God sees all things—nothing is hid from him, his eyes "run to and fro throughout the whole earth."[3] Jesus Christ is called the Holy One in Scripture.[4]

"As the king gazed upon that lofty tree, he beheld a 'watcher, even a holy one,—a divine messenger, similar in appearance to the One who walked with the three Hebrews in the fiery furnace. This heavenly being approached the tree, and in a loud voice cried..."[5]

Daniel 4:14 He cried aloud, and said thus, Hew down the tree, and cut off his branches, shake off his leaves, and scatter his fruit: let the beasts get away from under it, and the fowls from his branches:

Daniel 4:15 Nevertheless leave the stump of his roots in the earth, even with a band of iron and brass, in the tender grass of the field; and let it be wet with the dew of heaven, and let his portion be with the beasts in the grass of the earth:

Despite the punishment decreed, God promised to secure for him the kingdom. The king was to be be wet with the dew of heaven and consigned to dwell in the grass with the beasts of the field.

---

[3] 2 Chronicles 16:9

[4] Psalm 71:22; Luke 4:34

[5] E. G. White, "The Life of Daniel an Illustration of True Sanctification," *The Review and Herald*, February 1, 1881 par. 25.

Daniel 4:16 Let his heart be changed from man's, and let a beast's heart be given unto him: and let seven times pass over him.

It was decreed that seven years[6] must pass with Nebuchadnezzar having the heart (or mind) of a beast.

Daniel 4:17 This matter is by the decree of the watchers, and the demand by the word of the holy ones: to the intent that the living may know that the most High ruleth in the kingdom of men, and giveth it to whomsoever he will, and setteth up over it the basest of men.

The discipline decreed was to bring to the empire the knowledge that the God of heaven is he that rules over the kingdoms of men. The purpose of the punishment was for the salvation of the ruler of Babylon. "As many as I love, I rebuke and chasten."[7]

Daniel 4:18 This dream I king Nebuchadnezzar have seen. Now thou, O Belteshazzar, declare the interpretation thereof, forasmuch as all the wise men of my kingdom are not able to make known unto me the interpretation: but thou art able; for the spirit of the holy gods is in thee.

Nebuchadnezzar remembers that Daniel had interpreted the previous dream, and he believes by faith that Daniel can do the same with this dream.

Daniel 4:19 Then Daniel, whose name was Belteshazzar, was astonied for one hour, and his thoughts troubled him. The king spake, and said, Belteshazzar, let not the dream, or the interpretation thereof, trouble thee. Belteshazzar answered and said, My lord, the dream be to them that hate thee, and the interpretation thereof to thine enemies.

---

[6] In Bible prophecy a time is equivalent to a year. See also comments on Daniel 7:25.

[7] Revelation 3:19

Daniel stands transfixed in silence and astonishment for an hour. One can only imagine Daniel standing there before the king, while Nebuchadnezzar patiently waits. For a whole hour, Daniel grapples with the implications of this vision. He knows exactly what the dream means and its significance startles him so much that he is initially unable to speak.

Seeing Daniel's hesitation and distress Nebuchadnezzar, in sympathy, tells Daniel not to allow the dream to trouble him.

Finally, Daniel answers the king that the dream would please those who hated him and satisfy his enemies. Daniel realizes that God had laid on him the important responsibility of revealing to king Nebuchadnezzar the judgments that God was about to bring on him because of his pride and self-exaltation. Although, the dreadfulness of the interpretation made him hesitate in dumb amazement, he knows that he must tell the king the truth, no matter the cost to himself. Thus, Daniel begins to interpret the vision.

Daniel 4:20 The tree that thou sawest, which grew, and was strong, whose height reached unto the heaven, and the sight thereof to all the earth;

Daniel 4:21 Whose leaves were fair, and the fruit thereof much, and in it was meat for all; under which the beasts of the field dwelt, and upon whose branches the fowls of the heaven had their habitation:

Daniel 4:22 It is thou, O king, that art grown and become strong: for thy greatness is grown, and reacheth unto heaven, and thy dominion to the end of the earth.

The mighty tree represents king Nebuchadnezzar, his kingdom and its power.

Daniel 4:23 And whereas the king saw a watcher and an holy one coming down from heaven, and saying, Hew the tree down, and destroy it; yet leave the stump of the roots thereof in the earth, even with a band of iron and brass, in the tender grass of the field; and let it be wet with the dew of heaven, and let his

portion be with the beasts of the field, till seven times pass over him;

Daniel 4:24 This is the interpretation, O king, and this is the decree of the most High, which is come upon my lord the king:

God decrees a punishment upon Nebuchadnezzar, which Daniel begins to explain.

Daniel 4:25 That they shall drive thee from men, and thy dwelling shall be with the beasts of the field, and they shall make thee to eat grass as oxen, and they shall wet thee with the dew of heaven, and seven times shall pass over thee, till thou know that the most High ruleth in the kingdom of men, and giveth it to whomsoever he will.

Daniel 4:26 And whereas they commanded to leave the stump of the tree roots; thy kingdom shall be sure unto thee, after that thou shalt have known that the heavens do rule.

Daniel assures him that his kingdom would be secure; that during this period of trial when he is banished from among men, God would keep his kingdom safe until he admits that God rules from heaven.

Daniel 4:27 Wherefore, O king, let my counsel be acceptable unto thee, and break off thy sins by righteousness, and thine iniquities by showing mercy to the poor; if it may be a lengthening of thy tranquillity.

God communicated the consequences that Nebuchadnezzar might avoid the pending judgment, if he would.

"Having faithfully interpreted the dream, Daniel urged the proud monarch to repent and turn to God, that by right doing he might avert the threatened calamity....
"For a time the impression of the warning and the counsel of the prophet was strong upon Nebuchadnezzar; but the heart that is not transformed by the grace of God soon loses the impressions of the Holy Spirit. Self-indulgence and ambition had not yet been eradicated from the king's heart, and later on these traits

reappeared. Notwithstanding the instruction so graciously given him, and the warnings of past experience, Nebuchadnezzar again allowed himself to be controlled by a spirit of jealousy against the kingdoms that were to follow. His rule, which heretofore had been to a great degree just and merciful, became oppressive. Hardening his heart, he used his God-given talents for self-glorification, exalting himself above the God who had given him life and power.

"For months the judgment of God lingered. But instead of being led to repentance by this forbearance, the king indulged his pride until he lost confidence in the interpretation of the dream, and jested at his former fears."[8]

Daniel 4:28 All this came upon the king Nebuchad-nezzar.

Daniel 4:29 At the end of twelve months he walked in the palace of the kingdom of Babylon.

Daniel 4:30 The king spake, and said, Is not this great Babylon, that I have built for the house of the kingdom by the might of my power, and for the honour of my majesty?

The capital of Babylon was one of the seven wonders of the ancient world. Nebuchadnezzar took all the glory for the impressive architecture, the hanging gardens, the palaces, and the fortifications. His heart was lifted up in boasting, **"Is not this great Babylon that I have built**...." He forgot that it was the Lord who had lent him the crown and given him his power.

Daniel 4:31 While the word was in the king's mouth, there fell a voice from heaven, saying, O king Nebuchadnezzar, to thee it is spoken; The kingdom is departed from thee.

Daniel 4:32 And they shall drive thee from men, and thy dwelling shall be with the beasts of the field: they shall make thee to eat grass as oxen, and seven times shall pass over thee, until thou know that the most High ruleth in the kingdom of men, and giveth it to whomsoever he will.

---

[8] E. G. White, *Prophets and Kings* (1917), p. 518.2-519.2.

The message that had been given in warning had commenced.

Daniel 4:33 The same hour was the thing fulfilled upon Nebuchadnezzar: and he was driven from men, and did eat grass as oxen, and his body was wet with the dew of heaven, till his hairs were grown like eagles' feathers, and his nails like birds' claws.

Nebuchadnezzar loses his reasoning abilities and begins behaving like a beast. The monarch is a maniac and commences eating grass like the cows. He is exiled to the royal pastures for seven years.

The God who gave Nebuchadnezzar his reason was able to remove it if the gift was misused. What a lesson for us today. God does not endow us with reasoning ability so that we may oppress our fellows. God can remove just as surely as he gives. May we humble ourselves before God, plead for his righteousness, and use his gifts for his honor and glory.

Yet even in punishment God's mercy is displayed. How could the kingdom of this powerful monarch be kept safe for him for seven years if he has gone crazy, living in the fields? Surely someone would attempt to seize the kingdom. God had promised that the kingdom would be preserved for him. Daniel had been made the prime minister of Babylon and certainly functioned in the place of the king for seven years. The kingdom was kept safe by the hand of God until the king returned to his senses.

Daniel 4:34 And at the end of the days I Nebuchadnezzar lifted up mine eyes unto heaven, and mine understanding returned unto me, and I blessed the most High, and I praised and honoured him that liveth for ever, whose dominion is an everlasting dominion, and his kingdom is from generation to generation:

For seven long years Nebuchadnezzar, the great monarch, was an astonishment to his whole realm and was humbled before the entire world. But at the end of seven years, just as God promised, he returned the special gift of reasoning to the king. Nebuchadnezzar realized that this was exactly what God had predicted would happen to him. He knew he had been humbled by the Lord of heaven, whose kingdom was forever.

Nebuchadnezzar humbled himself before the monarch of the universe, and was saved by faith in the righteousness of Jesus Christ, who revealed himself personally to the king.[9] The love of heaven knew no bounds, as Christ stooped to save even a proud pagan king and through him to distribute, by letter, the gospel, to the entire planet: "Nebuchadnezzar the king, unto all people, nations, and languages, that dwell in all the earth; Peace be multiplied unto you. I thought it good to show the signs and wonders that the high God hath wrought toward me. How great are his signs! and how mighty are his wonders! his kingdom is an everlasting kingdom, and his dominion is from generation to generation."[10]

Daniel 4:35 And all the inhabitants of the earth are reputed as nothing: and he doeth according to his will in the army of heaven, and among the inhabitants of the earth: and none can stay his hand, or say unto him, What doest thou?

Daniel 4:36 At the same time my reason returned unto me; and for the glory of my kingdom, mine honour and brightness returned unto me; and my counsellors and my lords sought unto me; and I was established in my kingdom, and excellent majesty was added unto me.

Daniel 4:37 Now I Nebuchadnezzar praise and extol and honour the King of heaven, all whose works are truth, and his ways judgment: and those that walk in pride he is able to abase.

The kingdom is restored and Nebuchadnezzar praises and honors the God of heaven. He is finally a converted man. Doubtless, untold millions in the Babylonian empire came to a saving knowlege of God through this monarch's witness.

No more terrible threats are made for those who will not listen. He does not try to legislate that all the people are to worship only the

---

[9] Daniel 3:25

[10] Daniel 4:1-3

God of heaven; rather he simply says, "**I Nebuchadnezzar praise... the King of heaven.**" There are no more boasts about his kingdom; he has sunk into insignificance in his own mind. The Lord is the king and all the inhabitants of the earth are as nothing.

Nebuchadnezzar then wrote this letter and sent it throughout his kingdom. In a public proclamation he acknowledges his guilt and the wonderful mercy that God has showed him—evidence of a true change in heart.

"The once proud monarch had become a humble child of God; the tyrannical, overbearing ruler, a wise and compassionate king. He who had defied and blasphemed the God of heaven, now acknowledged the power of the Most High and earnestly sought to promote the fear of Jehovah and the happiness of his subjects. Under the rebuke of Him who is King of kings and Lord of lords, Nebuchadnezzar had learned at last the lesson which all rulers need to learn—that true greatness consists in true goodness. He acknowledged Jehovah as the living God, saying, 'I Nebuchadnezzar praise and extol and honor the King of heaven, all whose works are truth, and His ways judgment: and those that walk in pride He is able to abase.'

"God's purpose that the greatest kingdom in the world should show forth His praise was now fulfilled. This public proclamation, in which Nebuchadnezzar acknowledged the mercy and goodness and authority of God, was the last act of his life recorded in sacred history."[11]

---

[11] E. G. White, *Prophets and Kings* (1917), p. 521.2-3

Daniel 5

SUMMARY:
King Belshazzar, grandson of Nebuchadnezzar, calls an impious feast for all the lords of his realm. He calls for the sacred vessels taken from the temple at Jerusalem to be brought to his feast for use in the drunken revelry. Suddenly in the midst of the merrymaking, a bloodless hand appears and begins writing a mysterious phrase on the wall. Terrified, Belshazzar calls the magicians and astrologers, but they are unable to explain the meaning. The queen mother suggests that Daniel, who had interpreted Nebuchadnezzar's dreams over a half century earlier, would be able to interpret the writings. Daniel is summoned and tells Belshazzar that the cryptic Mene, Mene, Tekel, Upharsin means that God hath numbered his kingdom, and brought it to an end. He is weighed in the balances, and found wanting; his kingdom is divided and given to the Medes and Persians. That very night the Medo-Persians, under the command of Cyrus, invaded Babylon exactly as predicted by the prophet Isaiah.[1]

After Nebuchadnezzar's death, there was a time of turmoil and a succession of rulers in the empire of Babylon. In 561 B.C., "on the death of this great prince [Nebuchadnezzar], Evilmerodach[2] his son succeeded him in the Babylonish empire; and, as soon as he was settled in the throne, he released Jehoiachin, the king of Judah, out of prison, after he had lain there near thirty-seven years, and promoted him to great honour in his palace."[3]

"When Evilmerodach had reigned two years at Babylon, his lusts, and his other wickedness, made him so intolerable, that at length even his own relations conspired against him, and put him to death,

---

[1] Isaiah 44:24 - 45:5

[2] Evilmerodach is mentioned in 2 Kings 25:27-30; Jeremiah 52:31-34.

[3] Humphrey Prideaux, D.D., *The Old and New Testament Connected, in the History of the Jews and Neighboring Nations,* Vol. I (London: Thomas Tegg and Son, 1839), p. 101-102.

and Neriglissar, his sister's husband, who was the head of the conspiracy against him, reigned in his stead."[4]

There was war brewing between the Babylonians and the Persians and "after both parties had now been for three years together forming their alliances, and making their preparations for the war, in the fourth year of Neriglissar, the confederates on both sides being all drawn together, both armies took the field, and it came to a fierce battle between them; in which Neriglissar being slain, the rest of the Assyrian army was put to the rout, and Cyrus had the victory."[5]

"The death of Neriglissar was a great loss to the Babylonians; for he was a very brave and excellent prince.... But nothing made the loss of Neriglissar more appear, than the succeeding of Laborosoarchod [or Labashi-Marduk] his son in the kingdom after him; for he was in every thing the reverse of his father, being given to all manner of wickedness, cruelty, and injustice; to which, on his advancement to the throne, he did let himself loose in the utmost excess, without any manner of restraint whatsoever, as if the regal office which he was now advanced to, were for nothing else but to give him a privilege of doing without control all the vile and flagitious things that he pleased.... [Therefore] his own people conspired against him and slew him, after he had reigned only nine months,"[6] in the end of the year 556 B.C. "After him succeeded Nabonidus, and reigned seventeen years."[7]

The Bible prophesied that Babylon was to continue from Nebuchadnezzar to his son and grandson: "And now have I given all these lands into the hand of Nebuchadnezzar the king of Babylon, my servant; and the beasts of the field have I given him also to serve him. And all nations shall serve him, and his son, and his son's son, until the very time of his land come: and then many nations and great kings shall serve themselves of him."[8]

---

[4] Humphrey Prideaux, D.D., *The Old and New Testament Connected, in the History of the Jews and Neighboring Nations,* Vol. I, (1839), p. 103.

[5] *Ibid.,* p. 107.

[6] *Ibid.,* p. 108-109.

[7] *Ibid.,* p. 109.

[8] Jeremiah 27:6-7

Evilmerodach was Nebuchadnezzar's son, which fulfilled the prophecy that Nebuchadnezzar's son would reign. But Neriglissar was the husband of Nebuchadnezzar's daughter and therefore the son-in-law of Nebuchadnezzar. Neriglissar's son, Laborosoarchod, having only reigned nine months within the last year of his father was not reckoned in the Canon of Ptolemy as reigning at all.[9] In addition, although a grandson, Laborosoarchod, was Nebuchadnezzar's daughter's son, not his son's son, as Jeremiah predicted. Nabonidus was not a son of Nebuchadnezzar, and although a skilled soldier, disclaimed royal lineage. Yet, Nabonidus refers to Belshazzar as his son. Apparently, the murder by Neriglissar of Evilmerodach, left a widow and a young son of royal lineage—Belshazzar. The trusted soldier Nabonidus became the husband of Evilmerodach's widow, and therefore the step-father of Belshazzar. This would explain his detachment from the court, and the installment of Belshazzar at such a young age. Nabonidus was simply training Belshazzar for the throne, and managing the affairs of state until Belshazzar was old enough to manage on his own. Belshazzar—the last king of Babylon, whom Nabonidus made co-ruler with himself, was the grandson of the great king Nebuchadnezzar. Thus, the prophecy was fulfilled exactly. All nations were given to Babylon to serve Nebuchadnezzar, his son, and his son's son. Belshazzar reigned about eleven years.

Belshazzar soon showed himself to be proud, arrogant, and licentious. "Admitted to a share in kingly authority at fifteen years of age, Belshazzar gloried in his power, and lifted up his heart against the God of heaven. He despised the One who is above all rulers, the General of all the armies of heaven."[10]

---

[9] "He [Laborosoarchod] is not named in the Canon of Ptolemy; for it is the method of that Canon to ascribe all the year to him that was king in the beginning of it, how soon soever he died after, and not to reckon the reign of the successor, but from the first day of the year ensuing; and therefore, if any king reigned in the interim, and did not live to the beginning of the next year, his name was not put into the Canon at all. And this was the case of Laborosoarchod: for Neriglissar his father being slain in battle in the beginning of the spring, the nine months of his son's reign ended before the next year began; and therefore, the whole of that year is reckoned to the last of Neriglissar, and the beginning of the next belonged to his successor: and this was the reason that he is not at all mentioned in that Canon."
Humphrey Prideaux, D.D., *The Old and New Testament Connected, in the History of the Jews and Neighboring Nations*, Vol. I, (1839), p. 109.

[10] E. G. White, "The Unseen Watcher.—No. 1," *The Youth's Instructor, May 19, 1898,* par 4.

Daniel 5:1 Belshazzar the king made a great feast to a thousand of his lords, and drank wine before the thousand.

At the time of this feast Babylon was under siege by the Persians, but because Babylon stockpiled enough food to survive a twenty-year siege, the king and his subjects reveled in their presumed security. They were confident in their impregnable walls. The Euphrates River ran through the middle of the city, under the city wall, thus providing an unlimited supply of water.

Cyrus, [the nephew and Persian general of Darius the Mede[11]] "marched on toward Babylon, that being the only place in all the east which now held out against him: and… he… besieged him [Belshazzar].… But this siege proved a very difficult work: for the walls were high and impregnable, the number of men within to defend them very great, and they were fully furnished with all sorts of provisions for twenty years, and the void ground within the walls was able both by tillage and pasturage to furnish them with much more. And therefore, the inhabitants, thinking themselves secure in their walls and their stores, looked on the taking of the city by a siege as an impracticable thing; and therefore, from the top of their walls, scoffed at Cyrus, and derided him for every thing he did towards it.… "But after near two years had been wasted this way, and nothing effected, he at length lighted on a stratagem, which, with little difficulty, made him master of the place."[12]

"When all was prepared, Cyrus determined to wait for the arrival of a certain festival, during which the whole population were wont to engage in drinking and revelling [sic] and then silently in the dead of night to turn the water of the river and make his attack.… The festival was held with even greater pomp and splendor than usual; for Belshazzar, with the natural insolence of youth, to mark his contempt of the besieging army, abandoned himself wholly to the delights of the season, and himself entertained a thousand lords in his palace. Elsewhere the rest of the population was occupied in feasting and dancing. Drunken riot and mad excitement held possession of the

---

[11] "Babylon was besieged by Cyrus, nephew of Darius the Mede, and commanding general of the combined armies of the Medes and Persians."
E. G. White, *Prophets and Kings* (1917), p. 523.1.

[12] Humphrey Prideaux, D.D., *The Old and New Testament Connected, in the History of the Jews and Neighboring Nations*, Vol. I, (1839), p. 115.

town; the siege was forgotten; ordinary precautions were neglected. Following the example of their king, the Babylonians gave themselves up for the night to orgies in which religious frenzy and drunken excess formed a strange and revolting medley."[13]

Daniel 5:2 Belshazzar, whiles he tasted the wine, commanded to bring the golden and silver vessels which his father Nebuchadnezzar had taken out of the temple which was in Jerusalem; that the king, and his princes, his wives, and his concubines, might drink therein.

Belshazzar revels in his power and his heart is lifted up against the God of heaven. Impaired by the influence of alcohol, his actions are no longer controlled by reason. He follows his passions and impulses. He is the king of the world; and his kingdom is invincible. To show his contempt for the sacred things of God, Belshazzar commands that the sacred vessels which had been taken from the temple of the Lord in Jerusalem be brought to his sacrilegious feast.

This verse calls Nebuchadnezzar Belshazzar's father, which is a typical way that the Bible often refers to an ancestor even from a previous generation. This does not mean he was his immediate father, for Nebuchadnezzar was his grandfather.

Daniel 5:3 Then they brought the golden vessels that were taken out of the temple of the house of God which was at Jerusalem; and the king, and his princes, his wives, and his concubines, drank in them.

Three times, the text draws attention to the fact that the wives and concubines were participating in this feast. "But the women were not in the habit of feasting with men—how is this? An account, by Cyrus himself, of his capture of Babylon... declares that Babylon was captured 'without fighting,' on the fourteenth day of the month Tammuz. Now the month Tammuz was named in honor of the god Tammuz, the Babylonian Adonis, who married their Venus, or Ishtar;

---

[13] George Rawlinson, M.A., *The Seven Great Monarchies of the Ancient Eastern World*, Vol. II (New York: John B. Alden, 1885), p. 256.

and the fourteenth of Tammuz was the regular time to celebrate their union, with lascivious orgies. On this day of all days the women took part in the horrible rites.... The Bible is here fully and wonderfully corroborated."[14]

Daniel 5:4 They drank wine, and praised the gods of gold, and of silver, of brass, of iron, of wood, and of stone.

Belshazzar thinks he can boast of his greatness above the God of heaven, but an uninvited guest is at his drunken feast. This is to be the last feast of proud boasting that Babylon holds. God has borne long with Belshazzar, desiring just as much to see him saved as his grandfather. But Belshazzar's probation has closed. The unseen Watcher is witness to the king's idolatrous revelry.

Daniel 5:5 In the same hour came forth fingers of a man's hand, and wrote over against the candlestick upon the plaster of the wall of the king's palace: and the king saw the part of the hand that wrote.

Suddenly, the wild orgy comes to an abrupt halt as giant fingers trace figures of flaming fire, left luminous on the palace plaster. "Little did Belshazzar think that there was a heavenly Witness to his idolatrous revelry; that a divine Watcher, unrecognized, looked upon the scene of profanation, heard the sacrilegious mirth, beheld the idolatry. But soon the uninvited Guest made His presence felt. When the revelry was at its height a bloodless hand came forth and traced upon the walls of the palace characters that gleamed like fire—words which, though unknown to the vast throng, were a portent of doom to the now conscience-stricken king and his guests."[15]

Daniel 5:6 Then the king's countenance was changed, and his thoughts troubled him, so that the joints of his loins were loosed, and his knees smote one against another.

---

[14] Wm. Hayes Ward, D.D., *Sunday-School Times,* Vol. XXV. No. 42, p. 659, 660, as cited in A. T. Jones, *The Great Empires of Bible Prophecy: from Babylon to the Fall of Rome* (Battle Creek, MI: Review and Herald Publishing Co., 1898), p. 44.1.

[15] E. G. White, *Prophets and Kings* (1917), p. 524.1.

"Hushed was the boisterous mirth, while men and women, seized with nameless terror, watched the hand slowly tracing the mysterious characters. Before them passed, as in panoramic view, the deeds of their evil lives; they seemed to be arraigned before the judgment bar of the eternal God, whose power they had just defied. Where but a few moments before had been hilarity and blasphemous witticism, were pallid faces and cries of fear. When God makes men fear, they cannot hide the intensity of their terror.

"Belshazzar was the most terrified of them all. He it was who above all others had been responsible for the rebellion against God which that night had reached its height in the Babylonian realm. In the presence of the unseen Watcher, the representative of Him whose power had been challenged and whose name had been blasphemed, the king was paralyzed with fear. Conscience was awakened. 'The joints of his loins were loosed, and his knees smote one against another.' Belshazzar had impiously lifted himself up against the God of heaven and had trusted in his own might, not supposing that any would dare say, 'Why doest thou thus?' but now he realized that he must render an account of the stewardship entrusted him, and that for his wasted opportunities and his defiant attitude he could offer no excuse.

"In vain the king tried to read the burning letters. But here was a secret he could not fathom, a power he could neither understand nor gainsay. In despair he turned to the wise men of his realm for help. His wild cry rang out in the assembly, calling upon the astrologers, the Chaldeans, and the soothsayers to read the writing."[16]

Daniel 5:7 The king cried aloud to bring in the astrologers, the Chaldeans, and the soothsayers. And the king spake, and said to the wise men of Babylon, Whosoever shall read this writing, and show me the interpretation thereof, shall be clothed with scarlet, and have a chain of gold about his neck, and shall be the third ruler in the kingdom.

Belshazzar had not learned from the experience of his grandfather, Nebuchadnezzar, for he summons the astrologers and wise men of Babylon to read the writing.

---

[16] E. G. White, *Prophets and Kings* (1917), p. 524.2-524.4.

Belshazzar promises to make the person who can interpret the writing the third ruler in the kingdom. The reason for offering the position of third ruler is because he could not make him the second ruler in the kingdom for Nabonidus, Belshazzar's father,[17] was still the king. Belshazzar was made co-regent, because Nabonidus did not like the politics or the limelight of the throne; so he lived in his summer palace by himself, placing Belshazzar in charge of Babylon.

Daniel 5:8 Then came in all the king's wise men: but they could not read the writing, nor make known to the king the interpretation thereof.

Daniel 5:9 Then was king Belshazzar greatly troubled, and his countenance was changed in him, and his lords were astonied.

Daniel 5:10 Now the queen by reason of the words of the king and his lords came into the banquet house: and the queen spake and said, O king, live for ever: let not thy thoughts trouble thee, nor let thy countenance be changed:

The queen mother, Amytis,[18] wife of Nebuchadnezzar, was not attending the feast, but upon hearing of the commotion arrived at the banquet house. "There was in the palace a woman who was wiser than them all,—the queen of Belshazzar's grandfather. In this emergency she addressed the king in language that sent a ray of light into the darkness. 'O king, live forever,' she said, 'let not thy thoughts trouble thee, nor let thy countenance be changed. There is a man in thy kingdom....'"[19]

Daniel 5:11 There is a man in thy kingdom, in whom is the spirit of the holy gods; and in the days of thy father light and understanding and wisdom, like the wisdom of the gods, was found in him; whom the king Nebuchadnezzar thy father, the

---

[17] Nabonidus was apparently Belshazzar's stepfather. See introductory comments for Daniel 5.

[18] Amytis was a Median princess who was given as wife to Nebuchadnezzar to stabilize relations with Media. She was the aunt (or possibly the great aunt) of Cyrus the Great—the general who conquered Babylon for the Medes and Persians.

[19] E. G. White, "The Unseen Watcher," The Bible Echo, May 2, 1898, p. 138.

king, I say, thy father, made master of the magicians, astrologers, Chaldeans, and soothsayers;

Daniel 5:12 Forasmuch as an excellent spirit, and knowledge, and understanding, interpreting of dreams, and showing of hard sentences, and dissolving of doubts, were found in the same Daniel, whom the king named Belteshazzar:[20] now let Daniel be called, and he will show the interpretation.

The queen mother knew Daniel. She was present when Nebuchadnezzar received the dream he could not remember. She was there when the king went mad as a result of his pride. She had seen how Daniel's God had taken away Nebuchadnezzar's reason and restored it; she had witnessed the king's confession that God was above all. The queen mother clearly retains high regard for Daniel.

Daniel 5:13 Then was Daniel brought in before the king. And the king spake and said unto Daniel, Art thou that Daniel, which art of the children of the captivity of Judah, whom the king my father brought out of Jewry?

"'Then was Daniel brought in before the king.' Making an effort to brace himself and to show his authority, Belshazzar said, 'Art thou that Daniel which art of the children of the captivity of Judah, which the king, my father, brought out of Jewry? I have even heard of thee, that the spirit of the gods is in thee....'"[21]

Daniel 5:14 I have even heard of thee, that the spirit of the gods is in thee, and that light and understanding and excellent wisdom is found in thee.

Daniel 5:15 And now the wise men, the astrologers, have been brought in before me, that they should read this writing, and make known unto me the interpretation thereof: but they could not show the interpretation of the thing:

---

[20] Not to be confused with Belshazzar. Belteshazzar was the name that Nebuchadnezzar had given to Daniel to honor the pagan deities. Belshazzar, Nebuchadnezzar's grandson, is now the king.

[21] E. G. White, *The Bible Echo*, May 2, 1898 par. 2.

Belshazzar is forced to admit that his wise men are powerless to interpret the writing.

Daniel 5:16 And I have heard of thee, that thou canst make interpretations, and dissolve doubts: now if thou canst read the writing, and make known to me the interpretation thereof, thou shalt be clothed with scarlet, and have a chain of gold about thy neck, and shalt be the third ruler in the kingdom.

Notice the doubt in Belshazzar's words, "**if thou canst read the writing, and make known to me the interpretation**...." Contrast this to his grandfather's words of faith, "because I **know** that the spirit of the holy gods is in thee, and no secret troubleth thee...declare the interpretation thereof, forasmuch as all the wise men of my kingdom are not able to make known unto me the interpretation: but **thou art able**; for the spirit of the holy gods is in thee."[22]

Daniel 5:17 Then Daniel answered and said before the king, Let thy gifts be to thyself, and give thy rewards to another; yet I will read the writing unto the king, and make known to him the interpretation.

"Daniel was not awed by the king's appearance, nor confused or intimidated by his words. 'Let thy gifts be to thyself,' he answered, 'and give thy rewards to another.'"[23]

Daniel has the same confidence as an old man that he had when young—that the God of heaven will reveal to him the secret.

Daniel 5:18 O thou king, the most high God gave Nebuchadnezzar thy father a kingdom, and majesty, and glory, and honour:

Daniel 5:19 And for the majesty that he gave him, all people, nations, and languages, trembled and feared before him: whom

---

[22] Daniel 4:9-18

[23] E. G. White, *The Bible Echo*, May 2, 1898 par. 3.

he would he slew; and whom he would he kept alive; and whom he would he set up; and whom he would he put down.

Daniel 5:20 But when his heart was lifted up, and his mind hardened in pride, he was deposed from his kingly throne, and they took his glory from him:

Daniel 5:21 And he was driven from the sons of men; and his heart was made like the beasts, and his dwelling was with the wild asses: they fed him with grass like oxen, and his body was wet with the dew of heaven; till he knew that the most high God ruled in the kingdom of men, and that he appointeth over it whomsoever he will.

Daniel 5:22 And thou his son, O Belshazzar, hast not humbled thine heart, though thou knewest all this;

Daniel 5:23 But hast lifted up thyself against the Lord of heaven; and they have brought the vessels of his house before thee, and thou, and thy lords, thy wives, and thy concubines, have drunk wine in them; and thou hast praised the gods of silver, and gold, of brass, iron, wood, and stone, which see not, nor hear, nor know: and the God in whose hand thy breath is, and whose are all thy ways, hast thou not glorified:

Daniel 5:24 Then was the part of the hand sent from him; and this writing was written.

"The prophet first reminded Belshazzar of matters with which he was familiar, but which had not taught him the lesson of humility that might have saved him. He spoke of Nebuchadnezzar's sin and fall, and of the Lord's dealings with him—the dominion and glory bestowed upon him, the divine judgment for his pride, and his subsequent acknowledgment of the power and mercy of the God of Israel; and then in bold and emphatic words he rebuked Belshazzar for his great wickedness. He held the king's sin up before him, showing him the lessons he might have learned but did not. Belshazzar had not read aright the experience of his grandfather, nor heeded the warning of events so significant to himself. The opportunity of knowing and obeying the true God had been given him, but had not been taken to heart, and he was about to reap the consequence of his rebellion."[24]

Then Daniel begins to interpret the dramatic writing on the wall that none could understand.

Daniel 5:25 And this is the writing that was written, MENE, MENE, TEKEL, UPHARSIN.

Daniel 5:26 This is the interpretation of the thing: MENE; God hath numbered thy kingdom, and finished it.

Daniel 5:27 TEKEL; Thou art weighed in the balances, and art found wanting.

Daniel 5:28 PERES; Thy kingdom is divided, and given to the Medes and Persians.

With this terrible sentence, the king must have been even more afraid than when he first saw the handwriting upon the wall.

The succinct statement, which Daniel interpreted without any hesitation, was actually a fulfillment of a prophecy made over 170 years before in the book of Isaiah. "Thus saith the LORD, thy redeemer, and he that formed thee from the womb, I am the LORD that maketh all things; that stretcheth forth the heavens alone; that spreadeth abroad the earth by myself; That frustrateth the tokens of the liars, and maketh diviners mad; that turneth wise men backward, and maketh their knowledge foolish;"[25]

Notice, as a part of this prophecy, God said he makes the diviners mad. He turns the knowledge of the magicians into foolishness, for they cannot interpret these things.

Isaiah continues, "That confirmeth the word of his servant, and performeth the counsel of his messengers; that saith to Jerusalem, Thou shalt be inhabited; and to the cities of Judah, Ye shall be built,

---

[24] E. G. White, *Prophets and Kings* (1917), p. 529.2.

[25] Isaiah 44:24-25

and I will raise up the decayed places thereof: That saith to the deep, Be dry, and I will dry up thy rivers: That saith of Cyrus, He is my shepherd, and shall perform all my pleasure: even saying to Jerusalem, Thou shalt be built; and to the temple, Thy foundation shall be laid. Thus saith the LORD to his anointed, to Cyrus, whose right hand I have holden, to subdue nations before him; and I will loose the loins of kings, to open before him the two leaved gates; and the gates shall not be shut; I will go before thee, and make the crooked places straight: I will break in pieces the gates of brass, and cut in sunder the bars of iron: And I will give thee the treasures of darkness, and hidden riches of secret places, that thou mayest know that I, the LORD, which call thee by thy name, am the God of Israel."[26]

This prophecy mentions by name the person who would overthrow the kingdom of Babylon over 170 years before it happened. In fact, this prophecy was written before Babylon became an empire.
The prophecy specified that the loins of kings would be loosed. This was fulfilled exactly for the Bible says, "Then the king's countenance was changed, and his thoughts troubled him, so that the joints of his loins were loosed, and his knees smote one against another."

Cyrus had been besieging Babylon for two years. Feeling secure with their fortifications and supplies, Belshazzar ignored the siege.

"But after near two years had been wasted this way, and nothing effected, he [Cyrus] at length lighted on a stratagem, which, with little difficulty, made him master of the place; for understanding that a great annual festival was to be kept at Babylon on a day approaching, and that it was usual for the Babylonians on that solemnity to spend the whole night in revelling, drunkenness, and all manner of disorders, he thought this a proper time to surprise them; and, for the effecting of it, he had this device: he sent up a party of his men to the head of the canal leading to the great lake... with orders, at a time set, to break down the great bank or dam, which was between the river and that canal, and to turn the whole current that way into the lake. In the interim, getting all his forces together, he posted one part of them at the place where the river ran into the city, and the other where it came out, with orders to enter the city that night by the channel of the river, as soon as they could find it

---

[26] Isaiah 44:26-45:3

fordable. And then, toward the evening, he opened the head of the trenches on both sides the river above the city, to let the water of it run into them. And, by this means, and the opening of the great dam, the river was so drained, that, by the middle of the night, it being then in a manner empty...."[27]

God had said of Cyrus, that the deep would "be dry, and I will dry up thy rivers."[28] That is exactly what Cyrus did, when he diverted the river Euphrates and his men marched underneath the city wall.

As Daniel was interpreting the writing on the wall, which proclaimed the doom of the empire, "outside the city, in silence and darkness, the Persians watched at the two points where the Euphrates entered and left the walls. Anxiously they noted the gradual sinking of the water in the river-bed; still more anxiously they watched to see if those within the walls would observe the suspicious circumstance, and sound an alarm through the town. Should such an alarm be given, all their labors would be lost. If, when they entered the river-bed, they found the river-walls manned and the river-gates fast-locked, they would be indeed 'caught in a trap.' Enfiladed on both sides by an enemy whom they could neither see nor reach, they would be overwhelmed and destroyed by his missiles before they could succeed in making their escape. But, as they watched, no sounds of alarm reached them—only a confused noise of revel and riot, which showed that the unhappy townsmen were quite unconscious of the approach of danger."[29]

Ordinarily, even the draining of the river would not have caused the fall of Babylon. Alongside the river on the inside of the city there were also walls with gates to prevent anyone who might get under the outside wall via the river channel, from being able to gain entrance to the city. But when Cyrus and his army marched underneath the wall on the river bed they found "the gates leading

[27] Humphrey Prideaux, D.D., *The Old and New Testament Connected, in the History of the Jews and Neighboring Nations,* Vol. I, (1839), p. 115-116.

[28] Isaiah 44:27

[29] George Rawlinson, M.A., *The Seven Great Monarchies of the Ancient Eastern World,* Vol. II (New York: John B. Alden, 1885), p. 256.

down to the river, which used all other nights to be shut, then all left open, through the neglect and disorder of that time of looseness."[30]

The prophecy of Isaiah, given 170 years before had declared that God would go before Cyrus "to open before him the two leaved gates; and the gates shall not be shut."

These amazing prophecies have been recorded for us to give us confidence in the word of God. The fact that God can foretell these things hundreds and thousands of years before they happen, and have them happen exactly as prophesied, gives us hope for our future. We know that the other things that he has said will be fulfilled and will happen also exactly as he has decreed. Prophecy is the Divine signature authenticating Scripture.

Daniel 5:29 Then commanded Belshazzar, and they clothed Daniel with scarlet, and put a chain of gold about his neck, and made a proclamation concerning him, that he should be the third ruler in the kingdom.

Daniel's message does not seem to register in Belshazzar's mind. Daniel has just pronounced that his kingdom is given to the Medes and Persians and Belshazzar arrays him in scarlet and makes a proclamation to make him the third ruler in the kingdom. As Belshazzar speaks these words regarding Daniel, the armies of the Medes and Persians are marching into the capital city of Babylon. "At last shadowy forms began to emerge from the obscurity of the deep river-bed, and on the landing-places opposite the river-gates scattered clusters of men grew into solid columns—the undefended gateways were seized—a war-shout was raised[31]—the alarm was spread—and swift runners started off to 'show the King of Babylon that his city was taken at one end.'[32] In the darkness and confusion of the night a terrible massacre ensued.[33] The drunken revelers

---

[30] Humphrey Prideaux, D.D., *The Old and New Testament Connected, in the History of the Jews and Neighboring Nations,* Vol. I, (1839), p. 116.

[31] Jeremiah 51:14

[32] Jeremiah 51:31-32

[33] Jeremiah 50:30, 35-37; 51:3-4, 58

could make no resistance.[34] The king paralyzed with fear at the awful handwriting upon the wall, which too late had warned him of his peril, could do nothing even to check the progress of the assailants, who carried all before them everywhere."[35]

The prophet Jeremiah declared, "In their heat I will make their feasts, and I will make them drunken, that they may rejoice, and sleep a perpetual sleep, and not wake, saith the LORD. Because the spoiler is come upon her, even upon Babylon, and her mighty men are taken, every one of their bows is broken: for the LORD God of recompenses shall surely requite. And I will make drunk her princes, and her wise men, her captains, and her rulers, and her mighty men: and they shall sleep a perpetual sleep, and not wake, saith the King, whose name is the LORD of hosts."[36]

Daniel 5:30 In that night was Belshazzar the king of the Chaldeans slain.

The Medes and Persians arriving at the palace "surprised the guards, and slew them all: and when, on the noise, some that were within opened the gates to know what it meant, they rushed in upon them, and took the place; where, finding the king, with his sword drawn, at the head of those who were at hand to assist him, they slew him, valiantly fighting for his life, and all those that were with him. After this, proclamation being made, of life and safety to all such as should bring in their arms, and of death to all that should refuse so to do, all quietly yielded to the conquerors, and Cyrus, without any further resistance, became master of the place."[37]

God protected Daniel for even though he had been made the third ruler of the kingdom for a matter of minutes, he became a high ruler in the Medo-Persian Empire. Apparently the Medo-Persians had

---

[34] Jeremiah 51:30

[35] George Rawlinson, M.A., *The Seven Great Monarchies of the Ancient Eastern World,* Vol. II (New York: John B. Alden, 1885), p. 256-257.

[36] Jeremiah 51:39, 56-57

[37] Humphrey Prideaux, D.D., *The Old and New Testament Connected, in the History of the Jews and Neighboring Nations,* Vol. I, (1839), p. 116.

some intelligence on the matter, and saw the importance to their empire of the man who could foretell their victory.

Thus, perished the Empire of Babylon. "For to be carnally minded is death; but to be spiritually minded is life and peace."[38]

Daniel 5:31 And Darius the Median took the kingdom, being about threescore and two years old.

The morning sun arose with Darius the Mede emperor of the world at 62 years of age, just as God had specified.

May we humble ourselves before God and accept his gift of mercy and life, as Nebuchadnezzar, rather than resisting and rejecting his infinite gift as did Belshazzar.

---

[38] Romans 8:6

Daniel 6

SUMMARY:
The princes of Medo-Persia become jealous of Daniel and plot to overthrow him. Since they cannot find anything to accuse in his character, they plot to create legislation against Daniel's religion by flattering the king with a law requiring all requests of the empire come only to the king for thirty days. As before, Daniel prays to the God of heaven. The punishment is to be thrown into a den of lions. The king realizes that he has been tricked and labors till sundown to deliver Daniel. But, the law of the Medes and Persians cannot be altered. So, Daniel is thrown to the lions, while Darius expresses his faith that God can deliver him.

Daniel 6:1 It pleased Darius to set over the kingdom an hundred and twenty princes, which should be over the whole kingdom;

Daniel 6:2 And over these three presidents; of whom Daniel was first: that the princes might give accounts unto them, and the king should have no damage.

In Daniel 5 the Babylonian empire fell and Belshazzar the king was slain. Now Daniel, the captive from Judah, is quickly elevated to one the highest positions in the palace of the new Medo-Persian empire. He is placed at the head of three presidents, who managed 120 princes, who would administrate the new Babylonian acquisition.

Daniel 6:3 Then this Daniel was preferred above the presidents and princes, because an excellent spirit was in him; and the king thought to set him over the whole realm.

Daniel lived the life of a true servant of God; his life had been transformed by the grace of God; he was pure and holy, and he put God first in everything he did. This made a powerful impact on Darius, for he could see that Daniel was filled with the Spirit of God. We too may be transformed by the grace of God to live pure and holy lives, that others may see the evidence of the power of God in our lives.

Satan knew the influence that Daniel would have in the court of the king and especially on the king himself. This would be a severe blow to the devil's kingdom and so he sought to turn the men in the realm against Daniel. In the same manner, whenever we seek to serve the Lord with our whole heart and take him at his word, we will come under fire.

Because of Daniel's excellent spirit, king Darius decides to place him over the entire empire, making Daniel the only man in the world's history to serve as prime minister of two subsequent world super-powers. This proposition provokes the jealousy of the presidents and princes.

Daniel 6:4 Then the presidents and princes sought to find occasion against Daniel concerning the kingdom; but they could find none occasion nor fault; forasmuch as he was faithful, neither was there any error or fault found in him.

Daniel's blameless life makes it difficult, even for his enemies, to find fault with him. The princes can find nothing in which they can accuse Daniel. In exasperation they counsel together.

Daniel 6:5 Then said these men, We shall not find any occasion against this Daniel, except we find it against him concerning the law of his God.

"The life of Daniel is an inspired illustration of what constitutes a sanctified character. It presents a lesson for all, and especially for the young. A strict compliance with the requirements of God is beneficial to the health of body and mind. In order to reach the highest standard of moral and intellectual attainments, it is necessary to seek wisdom and strength from God and to observe strict temperance in all the habits of life.
"The more blameless the conduct of Daniel, the greater was the hatred excited against him by his enemies. They were filled with madness, because they could find nothing in his moral character or in the discharge of his duties upon which to base a complaint against him. '**Then said these men, We shall not find any occasion**

against this Daniel, except we find it against him concerning the law of his God' Daniel 6:5."[1]

"There is another... question that should engage the attention of the churches of today.... 'All that will live godly... shall suffer persecution...' Why is it, then, that persecution seems in a great degree to slumber? The only reason is that the church has conformed to the world's standard and therefore awakens no opposition.... It is only because of the spirit of compromise with sin, because the great truths of the word of God are so indifferently regarded, because there is so little vital godliness in the church, that Christianity is apparently so popular with the world. Let there be a revival of the faith and power of the early church, and the spirit of persecution will be revived, and the fires of persecution will be rekindled."[2]

Daniel 6:6 Then these presidents and princes assembled together to the king, and said thus unto him, King Darius, live for ever.

The salutation, **"King Darius, live for ever,"** is not a statement of belief that the king will really live forever, but was a term used in ancient cultures to wish the king a long life—until his life was completed.

Daniel 6:7 All the presidents of the kingdom, the governors, and the princes, the counsellors, and the captains, have consulted together to establish a royal statute, and to make a firm decree, that whosoever shall ask a petition of any God or man for thirty days, save of thee, O king, he shall be cast into the den of lions.

The first sentence out of the prince's mouths is a lie, for Daniel was one of the presidents, and he was not invited to this meeting. These men are going to extreme lengths to flatter the king, and satisfy their jealous revenge. What they are proposing is really an administrative nightmare. Would the king really want everyone in his kingdom to

---

[1] E. G. White, *Counsels for the Church* (1991), p. 52.3.

[2] E. G. White, *The Great Controversy* (1911), p. 48.3.

petition only him for everything? Does he really want to replace God and man, even for just one month? Despite the logistical challenges, the flattery works—the king falls for the trap.

"You should be guarded against flattery. Whoever is foolish enough to flatter you cannot be your true friend. Your true friends will caution, entreat, and warn you, and reprove your faults."[3]

Daniel 6:8 Now, O king, establish the decree, and sign the writing, that it be not changed, according to the law of the Medes and Persians, which altereth not.

The Medes and Persians had a legal statute that no law they made could ever be reversed. This was clearly the reason for the time limit on the proposed thirty-day edict.

Daniel 6:9 Wherefore king Darius signed the writing and the decree.

The king allows pride to overcome reason, and by accepting flattery, signs away the life of his most trusted president. Satan is working for the destruction of God's faithful servant, and yet the Lord is working for the salvation of another pagan king. Just as in the case of Nebuchadnezzar, God is seeking the redemption of Darius and his subjects.

Daniel 6:10 Now when Daniel knew that the writing was signed, he went into his house; and his windows being open in his chamber toward Jerusalem, he kneeled upon his knees three times a day, and prayed, and gave thanks before his God, as he did aforetime.

Daniel well knew that if he changed his habit of praying by his window toward Jerusalem, he would be obeying the king's decree thereby giving his allegiance to someone besides God. This would have been a violation of the first commandment to have no other

---

[3] E. G. White, *Testimonies for the Church,* Vol. 3, (1875), p. 225.2.

gods before the Creator.[4] He knew what would happen if he was caught praying to the God of heaven, yet he chose to surrender to God's will and trust him fully, rather than violate the ten-commandments.

Daniel 6:11 Then these men assembled, and found Daniel praying and making supplication before his God.

Are we surprised that they discover him praying? They are ready and waiting—this is the whole point of the law. They made this law, affecting the whole realm, simply because of their jealousy of one person. We will find that Revelation 13 predicts a similar scenario— at the end of time, a few people will make a law that affects everyone because a little group will not go along with their program.

Daniel 6:12 Then they came near, and spake before the king concerning the king's decree; Hast thou not signed a decree, that every man that shall ask a petition of any God or man within thirty days, save of thee, O king, shall be cast into the den of lions? The king answered and said, The thing is true, according to the law of the Medes and Persians, which altereth not.

The trap is almost sprung. First, they induce the king to admit that he had written the law.

Daniel 6:13 Then answered they and said before the king, That Daniel, which is of the children of the captivity of Judah, regardeth not thee, O king, nor the decree that thou hast signed, but maketh his petition three times a day.

Here is a familiar theme occurring throughout the book of Daniel— **"that Daniel, which is of the children of the captivity of Judah."** In Daniel 2, when Arioch brought Daniel before Nebuchadnezzar, he reminded the king—"this is that captive out of the land of Judah." When Daniel's three companions would not bow to the golden image it was again those Jews of the captivity. When Daniel went in before

---

[4] Exodus 20:2-3

Belshazzar to interpret the writing on the wall, Belshazzar said, are you that captive? Once again, these presidents and princes refer to Daniel derogatorily as that captive from Judah, despite the fact that he was their boss, and prime minister elect of the empire.

Daniel 6:14 Then the king, when he heard these words, was sore displeased with himself, and set his heart on Daniel to deliver him: and he laboured till the going down of the sun to deliver him.

The king immediately realizes what this whole thing has been about. He now knows exactly why they had flattered him, and he is very upset with himself. He knows that he has unknowingly signed Daniel's death warrant, and he "**set his heart on Daniel to deliver him.**" He retrieves the legal books and begins pouring over the constitutional documents. Desperately he searches for some legal loophole to save Daniel. He works until sundown, but he can find nothing; no legal way to extricate himself from this predicament. The princes wait and wait and finally in exasperation, at sunset, they approach to the king to remind him of his law.

Daniel 6:15 Then these men assembled unto the king, and said unto the king, Know, O king, that the law of the Medes and Persians is, That no decree nor statute which the king establisheth may be changed.

Reluctantly the king is constrained to implement the punishment of placing Daniel in the lion's den.

Daniel 6:16 Then the king commanded, and they brought Daniel, and cast him into the den of lions. Now the king spake and said unto Daniel, Thy God whom thou servest continually, he will deliver thee.

What amazing faith in the God of Daniel is expressed by this pagan king. He appreciates Daniel; he has learned to know him, to love him, and to respect him. But more than this, he has seen a glimpse of God through Daniel's life, and realizes that Daniel's faithfulness and purity of life is attended by the blessing of God. Daniel has witnessed faithfully to the king of the wonders and power of the true God of heaven. Faith in the king of the universe has kindled hope in the heart of Darius that the God of heaven will be able to deliver Daniel.

Daniel 6:17 And a stone was brought, and laid upon the mouth of the den; and the king sealed it with his own signet, and with the signet of his lords; that the purpose might not be changed concerning Daniel.

The king no longer trusts his princes. They have conspired to bring an end to one of the most faithful and accomplished statesmen in the empire. He does not trust that they will not try to bring an end to Daniel themselves, if the lions do not, so he seals the top of the lion's den.

Daniel 6:18 Then the king went to his palace, and passed the night fasting: neither were instruments of music brought before him: and his sleep went from him.

Though he may not have known the principle from Scripture of fasting and praying,[5] he intuitively decides to do this.

Daniel 6:19 Then the king arose very early in the morning, and went in haste unto the den of lions.

Daniel 6:20 And when he came to the den, he cried with a lamentable voice unto Daniel: and the king spake and said to Daniel, O Daniel, servant of the living God, is thy God, whom thou servest continually, able to deliver thee from the lions?

The king returns the next morning to the lions' den, weeping as his quivering voice wails a stammering expression of faith in Daniel's God into the dark and silent pit below him: "**is thy God, whom thou servest continually, able to deliver thee**?" We imagine him waiting with bated breath to see if there will be a reply, when suddenly he hears from the bottom of the den, "O king, live for ever."

---

[5] Nehemiah 1:4; Acts 13:3; 1 Corinthians 7:5; etc.

Daniel 6:21 Then said Daniel unto the king, O king, live for ever.

One can only imagine the joy of the king at the sound of Daniel's voice as Daniel continues to explain the reason he is still alive.

Daniel 6:22 My God hath sent his angel, and hath shut the lions' mouths, that they have not hurt me: forasmuch as before him innocency was found in me; and also before thee, O king, have I done no hurt.

Daniel 6:23 Then was the king exceeding glad for him, and commanded that they should take Daniel up out of the den. So Daniel was taken up out of the den, and no manner of hurt was found upon him, because he believed in his God.

Daniel emerges from the den of lions completely unscathed. Sometimes these kinds of jealousies and conspiracies seem to go undetected for a time. But eventually, they will always be found out, and they will be dealt with. For the princes and presidents who originated this conspiracy, retribution comes rapidly.

Daniel 6:24 And the king commanded, and they brought those men which had accused Daniel, and they cast them into the den of lions, them, their children, and their wives; and the lions had the mastery of them, and brake all their bones in pieces or ever they came at the bottom of the den.

Before the conspirators hit the bottom of the den, all their bones were broken. There were one hundred and twenty princes and two presidents involved in this conspiracy. Counting wives and children there could have been 400 or 500 people. To take down that many people, that quickly, the lion's den must have been much larger than the children's books picture, with perhaps more than fifty lions participating in the carnage.

Daniel 6:25 Then king Darius wrote unto all people, nations, and languages, that dwell in all the earth; Peace be multiplied unto you.

Darius does not send threats, but peace to all his people. This is the same language that Nebuchadnezzar used, when after his conversion he sent to all the provinces: "Nebuchadnezzar the king, unto all people, nations, and languages, that dwell in all the earth; Peace be multiplied unto you."[6]

Daniel 6:26 I make a decree, That in every dominion of my kingdom men tremble and fear before the God of Daniel: for he is the living God, and stedfast for ever, and his kingdom that which shall not be destroyed, and his dominion shall be even unto the end.

Darius makes no legislation violating his subjects' religious freedom. The decree of Darius is unlike Nebuchadnezzar's pre-conversion decree of Daniel 3, in which he declared that if any one spoke any thing against the God of heaven, he should be cut in pieces, and his house made a dunghill. Darius does not say everyone must worship only Daniel's God. He simply declares that all should tremble before the God of heaven because he is the one true God. Darius proclaims that Daniel's God is the God whose dominion shall never end. Daniel must have told the king the prophecy of Daniel 2; of the four world empires that would extend through history, and of the stone that would break all the others in pieces, standing forever; for he uses some of the same language.

Daniel 6:27 He delivereth and rescueth, and he worketh signs and wonders in heaven and in earth, who hath delivered Daniel from the power of the lions.

Daniel 6:28 So this Daniel prospered in the reign of Darius, and in the reign of Cyrus the Persian.

Because of his faithfulness to God in this severe trial, God blessed Daniel with long life and he was prospered into the reign of Cyrus.

---

[6] Daniel 4:1

Daniel 7

SUMMARY:

In Daniel 7 some of the most amazing details of Bible prophecy unfold and a most astonishing and universal deception is unmasked. This time, Daniel has the dream rather than Nebuchadnezzar. Daniel first sees a lion with eagle's wings emerge from the waves of the sea, then a bear with three ribs in its mouth, followed by a leopard with four heads and four wings, and finally a terrible beast with great iron teeth and ten horns. As Daniel watches in speechless awe, another little horn comes up among the ten, uprooting three. This little horn has eyes like the eyes of a man, and a mouth speaking great words against God. As the angel presents the interpretation, Daniel discovers that he has been transported far into the future through the four major world empires to come: Babylon, Medo-Persia, Greece, and Rome. Daniel is then carried through the 1,260-year reign of the little horn power, past the judgment, all the way to the second coming of the Messiah. Daniel has many questions, especially about the mysterious little horn. Ten distinguishing marks, in this chapter alone, identify the little horn power—a force that would "think to change times and laws."

Daniel 7:1 In the first year of Belshazzar king of Babylon Daniel had a dream and visions of his head upon his bed: then he wrote the dream, and told the sum of the matters.

As this vision occurs in the first year of king Belshazzar, it is received prior to Daniel 5 where the Babylonian kingdom fell and Belshazzar was killed. That Daniel wrote this dream means that by the time of Belshazzar's impious feast, the king knew about the information reveal in this vision.

Daniel 7:2 Daniel spake and said, I saw in my vision by night, and, behold, the four winds of the heaven strove upon the great sea.

Daniel sees a pictorial scene given in spectacular symbolic imagery. Allowing the Bible to interpret itself, we find what the waters of the sea symbolize: "And he saith unto me, The waters which thou sawest, where the whore sitteth, are peoples, and multitudes, and nations, and tongues."[1] Daniel saw the winds striving upon the nations. As defined in this verse, winds represent strife among the peoples and nations of the earth.[2]

Daniel 7:3 And four great beasts came up from the sea, diverse one from another.

Scripture defines its own symbols: "These great beasts, which are four, are four kings…. Thus he said, The fourth beast shall be the fourth kingdom upon earth…."[3] From the strife of nations four kingdoms surface, ascending to pre-eminence above the rest of the teeming masses. Four world empires would conquer, attaining world dominance with super-power status.

The dream given by God to Nebuchadnezzar in Daniel 2 also revealed four future world empires. The stunning revelation given by four symbolic metals provides a template for understanding Daniel 7.

Daniel 7:4 The first was like a lion, and had eagle's wings: I beheld till the wings thereof were plucked, and it was lifted up from the earth, and made stand upon the feet as a man, and a man's heart was given to it.

In Scripture, the kingdom of Babylon is likened to both a lion and an eagle. Through the prophet Jeremiah, God warned Israel of the coming destruction from the nation of Babylon, if they did not repent: "The lion is come up from his thicket, and the destroyer of the Gentiles is on his way; he is gone forth from his place to make thy land desolate; and thy cities shall be laid waste, without an inhabitant."[4] Through the prophet Habakkuk, the Lord described the Babylonians flying like eagles: "For, lo, I raise up the Chaldeans, that bitter and hasty nation, which shall march through the breadth of the

---

[1] Revelation 17:15

[2] See also Jeremiah 25:31-33 and Revelation 7:1-3.

[3] Daniel 7:17, 23

[4] Jeremiah 4:7
See also Jeremiah 50:17, 43-44.

land, to possess the dwelling places that are not theirs.... their horsemen shall spread themselves, and their horsemen shall come from far; they shall fly as the eagle that hasteth to eat."[5]

For anyone in the ancient world, the symbol of a lion with eagle's wings would immediately bring to mind Babylon, for it was the symbol of the empire.

The head of gold in Daniel 2 represented Nebuchadnezzar, and the kingdom which he had made great. Each successive kingdom was symbolized by increasingly inferior metals. The gold was the most

---

[5] Habakkuk 1:6-8
See also Ezekiel 17:3, 12 and Lamentations 4:19.

valuable. Nebuchadnezzar was referred to as a "king of kings."[6] The lion is the king of beasts.

The wings of this lion were to be plucked; then he would be lifted up and made to stand on his feet like a man, and would receive a man's heart. In Daniel 4, Nebuchadnezzar was filled with pride by his wealth and power. In conquest he had the power of a lion and the speed of an eagle. But the wings of the eagle were plucked, and he was given the heart of a beast. "Let his heart be changed from man's, and let a beast's heart be given unto him: and let seven times pass over him."[7] He became like a beast for seven long years, till he knew that the God of heaven ruled. "The same hour was the thing fulfilled upon Nebuchadnezzar: and he was driven from men, and did eat grass as oxen, and his body was wet with the dew of heaven, till his hairs were grown like eagles' feathers, and his nails like birds' claws."[8] At the end of those seven years of insanity, he said, "I Nebuchadnezzar lifted up mine eyes unto heaven, and mine understanding returned unto me, and I blessed the most High, and I praised and honoured him that liveth for ever, whose dominion is an everlasting dominion, and his kingdom is from generation to generation:"[9]

Nebuchadnezzar had the proud and ferocious character of a lion, but God took away his reasoning powers and he became like a beast. Then the Lord in his mercy reached down, when there was none that could save the king from himself, and lifted him up causing him to stand upon his feet, giving him a new heart—the heart of a man. No longer was he a raging, brutal tyrant, but a humble, human servant of the God of heaven.

Daniel 7:5 And behold another beast, a second, like to a bear, and it raised up itself on one side, and it had three ribs in the mouth of it between the teeth of it: and they said thus unto it, Arise, devour much flesh.

---

[6] Daniel 2:37

[7] Daniel 4:16

[8] Daniel 4:33

[9] Daniel 4:34

Just as the chest of silver of Daniel 2 had two arms representing the Medes and Persians, so the bear has two front feet, one of which was longer and stronger raising him up asymmetrically, depicting the Persians as stronger than the Medes.

A beast in Bible prophecy represents a kingdom, as we have seen. A rib is a part of a dead beast; in particular one that has been devoured by another beast. Therefore, the three ribs in the bear's mouth represent three kingdoms that were conquered as Medo-Persia rose to power. Exactly as the Bible predicted, Medo-Persia devoured the kingdoms of Babylon, Lydia, and Egypt.

Daniel 7:6 After this I beheld, and lo another, like a leopard, which had upon the back of it four wings of a fowl; the beast had also four heads; and dominion was given to it.

The third beast corresponds to the third metal—the belly and thighs of brass on the image of Daniel 2.

The leopard is a very swift beast and this feline has four wings of a fowl making it even faster. Alexander the Great overtook the Medo-Persian Empire with lightning speed. Within less than a decade he had conquered the world, defeating Medo-Persia at the striking young age of 25.[10]

The head is the part that guides and controls the body. Thus, a head represents a ruler of the kingdom from which it emanates. After the Greek Empire took over the world, Alexander the Great died suddenly at 33 years of age, and his kingdom was eventually divided between four of his generals. These four generals, Cassander, Seleucus, Lysimachus, and Ptolemy divided the Greek Empire among themselves and ruled. The four-headed leopard perfectly symbolizes the empire of Greece.

Daniel 7:7 After this I saw in the night visions, and behold afourth beast, dreadful and terrible, and strong exceedingly;

---

[10] Alexander was born in 356 B.C., began his conquest in 334 .B.C. and conquered Medo-Persia in 331 B.C. (see Daniel 2:39). His conquest lasted ten years, at which point he died in 323 B.C. at the age of 33.
https://en.wikipedia.org/wiki/Alexander_the_Great Retrieved: 03-02-2016.

and it had great iron teeth: it devoured and brake in pieces, and stamped the residue with the feet of it: and it was diverse from all the beasts that were before it; and it had ten horns.

Daniel can think of no animal on earth to use to describe the fourth beast. He simply calls it dreadful, terrible, and exceedingly strong. It was different from all the other beasts and devoured and broke in pieces the nations it conquered. What remained after it had devoured and broken, was stamped with its feet.

There are striking parallels between this fourth beast and the fourth metal—the iron legs of Daniel 2: "And the fourth kingdom shall be strong as iron: forasmuch as iron breaketh in pieces and subdueth all things: and as iron that breaketh all these, shall it break in pieces and bruise."[11]

The fourth beast is described as much stronger and more terrible than the previous beasts. Therefore, since this fourth power subjugates Greece, it could not be of less magnitude than its predecessor. "History may allow us to think that Alexander and a Roman ambassador did meet at Babylon; that the greatest man of the ancient world saw and spoke with a citizen of that great nation, which was destined to succeed him in his appointed work, and to found a wider and still more enduring empire."[12]

The great iron teeth remind us of the legs of the fourth kingdom in Daniel 2. Today we still refer to the iron monarchy of Rome. Rome was indeed a terrible nation. One need only read the works of history on the Roman Empire to discern the dreadful deeds done in the centuries of its dominion.

The fourth beast has ten horns: "And the ten horns out of this kingdom are ten kings that shall arise...."[13] This is directly parallel to the ten toes of the image of Daniel 2. Rome was not conquered by a

---

[11] Daniel 2:40

[12] Thomas Arnold, D.D., *History of Rome,* 3 Vol. in 1 (New York: D. Appleton & Company, 1866), p. 277; emphasis supplied.

[13] Daniel 7:24

succeeding empire, rather it was carved into ten divisions which became the nations of Europe today.[14]

Daniel 7:8 I considered the horns, and, behold, there came up among them another little horn, before whom there were three of the first horns plucked up by the roots: and, behold, in this horn were eyes like the eyes of man, and a mouth speaking great things.

This dramatic vision portrays a little horn arising in the midst of the previous ten. Who is this little horn with the mouth and eyes like a man, speaking great things, who plucked up three of the other horns by their roots? Later in the chapter is given: "and another shall rise after them; and he shall be diverse from the first, and he shall subdue three kings."[15] This little horn will be identified in subsequent verses, but for now we see that it is a kingdom arising from the Roman Empire, among the first ten horns, with a man at its head who speaks blasphemies.[16]

As Daniel continues watching the vision unfold, his attention is directed heavenward where he beholds the Supreme Court of the Universe.

Daniel 7:9 I beheld till the thrones were cast down, and the Ancient of days did sit, whose garment was white as snow, and the hair of his head like the pure wool: his throne was like the fiery flame, and his wheels as burning fire.

The Aramaic word translated "cast down" is a single word, and can mean placed or set[17] rather than overturned as some might assume.

---

[14] See the comments on Daniel 2:41-43.

[15] Daniel 7:24

[16] Revelation 13:5

[17] "'I beheld,' says the prophet Daniel, '**till thrones were placed**, and One that was Ancient of Days did sit: His raiment was white as snow, and the hair of His head like pure wool; His throne was fiery flames, and the wheels thereof burning fire.'"
E. G. White, *The Great Controversy* (1911), p. 479.1.

David declares that in the house of God "there are set thrones of judgment, the thrones of the house of David."[18]

The sitting of the ancient of days, or God the Father, signifies the opening of the investigative session of the Supreme Court of the Universe (as indicated in the following verse).

His throne is described as having wheels of burning fire indicating that it is able to move from place to place.[19]

Daniel 7:10 A fiery stream issued and came forth from before him: thousand thousands ministered unto him, and ten thousand times ten thousand stood before him: the judgment was set, and the books were opened.

As the court convenes the heavenly judgment begins with the opening of the books of record. The prophet Malachi records, "...and a book of remembrance was written before him for them that feared the LORD, and that thought upon his name."[20] The Psalmist laments "Thou tellest my wanderings: put thou my tears into thy bottle: are they not in thy book?"[21] Isaiah prophesies, "Behold, it is written before me.... Your iniquities, and the iniquities of your fathers together, saith the LORD,"[22] and Solomon concludes, "Let us hear the conclusion of the whole matter: Fear God, and keep his commandments: for this is the whole duty of man. For God shall bring every work into judgment, with every secret thing, whether it be good, or whether it be evil."[23]

Daniel 7:11 I beheld then because of the voice of the great words which the horn spake: I beheld even till the beast was slain, and his body destroyed, and given to the burning flame.

---

[18] Psalms 122:5

[19] See Ezekiel 1; and comments on Revelation 4.

[20] Malachi 3:16

[21] Psalms 56:8

[22] Isaiah 65:6-7

[23] Ecclesiastes 2:13-14

One of the most infamous cases to be decided in the court of heaven is that of the little horn that took control of the fourth beast. The sentence is pronounced that this power should be **"slain, and his body destroyed, given to the burning flame.**"

Daniel 7:12 As concerning the rest of the beasts, they had their dominion taken away: yet their lives were prolonged for a season and time.

Exactly as the Bible described, history has been fulfilled. These four beasts are four world empires, and as each subsequent power came on the scene of world dominion the previous beast lost its dominion. But their lives were prolonged. There was a country of Babylonia after Persia became a world empire. Even today, Iraq corresponds to the country of Babylon. There was a country of Persia, centuries after it was no longer an empire. Persia still exists as the country of Iran, speaking a national language—Persian. Today there is still a country of Greece, even though it is no longer a world empire. Italy is the remainder of the country of Rome, though it fragmented into pieces.

The influence of these nations has also lived beyond their world dominance. Each subsequent power adopted some of the customs and beliefs of the powers before it. "Each one, before being destroyed, was merged into the succeeding one, and its characteristic principles are represented in succession until the end of time. This is clearly shown in the second chapter of Daniel, where the gold, silver, brass, iron, and clay are broken to pieces together and blown away like the chaff, when all earthly nations are destroyed. The same truth was represented in the fourth chapter, when the tree representing Babylon was cut down, but the roots remained in the ground. The roots represented the foundation principles upon which Babylon was built, and they have remained in the earth ever since. When Medo-Persia fell, she left her principles of government, education, and religion still alive, transmitting them to her posterity, the nations of earth. Greece did likewise, and with each succeeding empire those foundation principles, so clearly portrayed in Babylon, which were placed there by the prince of the power of the air, instead of appearing in a weakened state, sprang into life with renewed vigor. So, it was that when the fourth kingdom appeared, those same principles of government, which were the counterfeit of heaven's underlying principles, were so strong that no natural beast could symbolize even pagan Rome.

"Rome in religion renewed all the religious errors of Babylon, and in education she perpetuated the errors of Greece, while in cruelty she followed in the footsteps of Media and Persia..."[24]

Daniel 7:13 I saw in the night visions, and, behold, one like the Son of man came with the clouds of heaven, and came to the Ancient of days, and they brought him near before him.

Daniel sees the Son of man himself, coming with the clouds of heaven. It may seem at first that this is a reference to his second coming, but a careful reading of Scripture is important, for it says he is coming, not to the world the second time to get his people, but to the Ancient of days before the Supreme Court of Heaven. The description of the heavenly judgment scene continues:

Daniel 7:14 And there was given him dominion, and glory, and a kingdom, that all people, nations, and languages, should serve him: his dominion is an everlasting dominion, which shall not pass away, and his kingdom that which shall not be destroyed.

The final ruling given in the investigative judgment is that the eternal dominion of this world is legally transferred to Christ. "The kingdoms of this world are become the kingdoms of our Lord, and of his Christ; and he shall reign for ever and ever."[25] This is once more parallel to Daniel 2, where the stone becomes an everlasting kingdom that would never be destroyed.

In the book of Ezekiel is given a most significant prophecy. Israel had become corrupt before God. He had borne long with her, but she would not repent; so he is about to allow her to be overcome and taken into captivity by the Babylonian Empire. Of this God says: "Therefore thus saith the Lord GOD; Because ye have made your iniquity to be remembered, in that your transgressions are discovered, so that in all your doings your sins do appear; because, I

---

[24] Stephen N. Haskell, The *Story of Daniel the Prophet* (South Lancaster, MA: Bible Training School, 1908), p. 106-107.

[25] Revelation 11:15

say, that ye are come to remembrance, ye shall be taken with the hand. And thou, profane wicked prince of Israel, whose day is come, when iniquity shall have an end, Thus saith the Lord GOD; Remove the diadem, and take off the crown: this shall not be the same: exalt him that is low, and abase him that is high. I will overturn, overturn, overturn, it: and it shall be no more, until he come whose right it is; and I will give it him."[26]

The crown of Israel would be given to Babylon. That crown was to be overturned three times. Just as he prophesied, Medo-Persia overturned Babylon, receiving Israel's crown; Greece overturned Medo-Persia, obtaining Israel's crown, and finally Rome overturned Greece to acquire the crown of Israel. Rome is the last one to hold the crown, until he come whose right it is—then Christ receives the crown of David. The Son of God, at the conclusion of this judgment scene, comes near before the Ancient of days to receive "**dominion, and glory, and a kingdom, that all people, nations, and languages, should serve him: his dominion is an everlasting dominion, which shall not pass away, and his kingdom that which shall not be destroyed.**"

Daniel 7:15 I Daniel was grieved in my spirit in the midst of my body, and the visions of my head troubled me.

Daniel 7:16 I came near unto one of them that stood by, and asked him the truth of all this. So he told me, and made me know the interpretation of the things.

Daniel, distressed by the dramatic events of the vision approaches the angel and asks what it all means. The initial interpretation the angel gives to Daniel is only two verses long:

Daniel 7:17 These great beasts, which are four, are four kings, which shall arise out of the earth.
Daniel 7:18 But the saints of the most High shall take the kingdom, and possess the kingdom for ever, even for ever and ever.

---

[26] Ezekiel 21:24-27

Essentially the angel's reply to Daniel's question was that there would be four world empires, and then God's eternal kingdom. This was not news to the prophet as God had already revealed this basic outline of history to Daniel for King Nebuchadnezzar.[27]

Sometimes the Lord does not tell us everything at once, but waits for us to ask: "ye have not, because ye ask not."[28] Daniel pressed the matter and asked for further explanation.

Daniel 7:19 Then I would know the truth of the fourth beast, which was diverse from all the others, exceeding dreadful, whose teeth were of iron, and his nails of brass;[29] which devoured, brake in pieces, and stamped the residue with his feet;

Daniel 7:20 And of the ten horns that were in his head, and of the other which came up, and before whom three fell; even of that horn that had eyes, and a mouth that spake very great things, whose look was more stout than his fellows.

Daniel understood that the four beasts were four world empires; he knew that those details had already been given to him, but he realized that in the fourth beast there were more details than had been given in the previous vision of Daniel 2. He saw that there was something that made this beast different than the others and describes it as "**exceeding dreadful.**"

Daniel also wanted to know the meaning of the ten horns, which corresponded to the toes of Nebuchadnezzar's image. Especially he wanted to know about the little horn, arising among the ten, with eyes and the mouth speaking great things, being more stout than the others.

---

[27] See Daniel 2.

[28] James 4:2

[29] Here Daniel also adds another detail which he did not mention in his initial description of the vision. The beast has nails of brass. This parallels closely to the third kingdom of brass of Daniel 2. This shows that of all the kingdoms before it, Rome would especially adopt characteristics and culture of Greece. History has conformed to every detail of this prophecy.

Daniel 7:21 I beheld, and the same horn made war with the saints, and prevailed against them;

Daniel 7:22 Until the Ancient of days came, and judgment was given to the saints of the most High; and the time came that the saints possessed the kingdom.

In answer to Daniel's question the angel continues, revealing more details. The little horn would make war with God's people and overcome them, continuing the war against the people of God until the Messiah returns to reward his people with the inheritance of his eternal kingdom.

From this we see that this little horn power cannot be one person for it would last through many centuries, to the end of time.

Daniel 7:23 Thus he said, The fourth beast shall be the fourth kingdom upon earth, which shall be diverse from all kingdoms, and shall devour the whole earth, and shall tread it down, and break it in pieces.

The angel tells Daniel that this fourth beast will be the fourth kingdom to rule, showing that the others must also be kingdoms. It is clearly a world empire for it would "**devour the whole earth**." As we have seen earlier, Rome fits this description perfectly. Rome was the fourth world empire, and was the most cruel of the four.

Daniel 7:24 And the ten horns out of this kingdom are ten kings that shall arise: and another shall rise after them; and he shall be diverse from the first, and he shall subdue three kings.

The ten horns arising from the fourth beast represent ten kingdoms. History confirms that the pagan Roman Empire fragmented into the ten divisions of Western Europe in A.D. 476. They were the Anglo-Saxons (who became the English), the Franks (French), the Suevi (Portuguese), Visigoths (Spanish), the Burgundians (Swiss), Alemanni (Germans), and the Lombards (Italians). The remaining three powers, the Ostrogoths, the Heruli, and the Vandals do not correspond to any Western European nation today, because they do not exist. These three were uprooted by the little horn power.

"The three divisions which were plucked up were the Heruli in 493, the Vandals in 534, and the Ostrogoths in 538 A.D."[30] The Ostrogoths were the last ones to be uprooted in the year A.D. 538. This is an important date as we shall soon discover.

Daniel 7:25 And he shall speak great words against the most High, and shall wear out the saints of the most High, and think to change times and laws: and they shall be given into his hand until a time and times and the dividing of time.

What is meant by this little horn speaking "**great words against the most High**?" When Sennacherib king of Assyria came against Israel the Bible records that he scoffed at the Lord God, saying that the other gods were not able to deliver their people "how much less shall your God deliver you out of mine hand?"[31] "He wrote also letters to **rail on the LORD God** of Israel, and to **speak against him**, saying,

---

[30] Stephen N. Haskell, *The Story of Daniel the Prophet* (1908), p. 109.

[31] 2 Chronicles 32:15

As the gods of the nations of other lands have not delivered their people out of mine hand, so shall not the God of Hezekiah deliver his people out of mine hand."[32] Here we see two parallel phrases, "rail on the Lord God" and "speak against him." These two are the same thing; the one defines the other. The Hebrew word for "rail" is, חָרַף châraph: reproach, taunt, defy, blaspheme. To speak against God is to blaspheme. There are two definitions given in Scripture of what constitutes blasphemy:

1. A man claiming to be God:
"The Jews answered him, saying, For a good work we stone thee not; but for blasphemy; and because that thou, being a man, makest thyself God."[33]

2. A man claiming to forgive sins:
"But there were certain of the scribes sitting there, and reasoning in their hearts, Why doth this man thus speak blasphemies? who can forgive sins but God only?"[34] The little horn would speak words of blasphemy, or great words against God.

The little horn would speak blasphemy (claim to be the representative of God on earth, and claim the power to forgive sins); persecute and wear out God's people; and he would attempt to change God's times and laws.

God's people would be given into his hand for a "time and times and the dividing of time." The angel reveals a cryptic time period during which God's people would be persecuted by this little horn power. A "time" is one year;[35] therefore, "times" are two years, and "the dividing of time" is half a year. This totals three and a half times or

---

[32] 2 Chronicles 32:17

[33] John 10:30
The pharisees had a correct definition of blasphemy, but did not have a correct understanding of Christ's divinity. Therefore, the accusation was false, because Jesus was God.

[34] Mark 2:6-7
In this Scripture Jesus was being accused of blasphemy. For Jesus this was a false accusation because Jesus is God (see John 1:1-3, 14; 1 Timothy 3:16, etc.).

[35] See Daniel 4:16. Nebuchadnezzar made to eat grass as an ox for seven times or seven years.

three and a half years. One Biblical year is 360 days.[36] Therefore, three and a half years contain 1,260 days. Considering the fact that the preceding four world empires each reigned much longer than three and a half years literal years, and that this power is said to exist until the second coming of Jesus,[37] three and a half literal years is too short a time. This is a prophetic number. In symbolic Bible prophecy a day represents a year. "After the number of the days in which ye searched the land, even forty days, **each day for a year**, shall ye bear your iniquities, even forty years, and ye shall know my breach of promise."[38] "And when thou hast accomplished them, lie again on thy right side, and thou shalt bear the iniquity of the house of Judah forty days: **I have appointed thee each day for a year**."[39] Therefore 1,260 prophetic days represent 1,260 literal years.

Whenever God mentions something in Scripture more than one time, it is especially important. This time-prophecy is so important that God caused it to be repeated seven different times in Scripture. No other prophetic time period is presented so often.

1. Daniel 7:25 "time, times, and a dividing of time"
2. Daniel 12:7 "time, times, and an half"
3. Revelation 11:2 "forty-two months."
4. Revelation 11:3 "a thousand two hundred and sixty days"
5. Revelation 12:6 "a thousand two hundred and sixty days"
6. Revelation 12:14 "time, and times, and half a time"

---

[36] Until the time of the flood, according to Scripture, there were 360 days in a year. Counting 150 days from the seventeenth day of the second month to the seventeenth day of the seventh month, makes each month 30 days in length. Therefore, the length of a year before the flood was 360 days. Apparently, the violence of the flood actually altered the earth's course around the sun.

Genesis 7:11 "In the six hundredth year of Noah's life, **in the second month, the seventeenth day of the month**, the same day were all the fountains of the great deep broken up, and the windows of heaven were opened."
Genesis 7:24 "And the waters prevailed upon the earth **an hundred and fifty days**."
Genesis 8:3 "And the waters returned from off the earth continually: and after the **end of the hundred and fifty days** the waters were abated."
Genesis 8:4 "And the ark rested **in the seventh month, on the seventeenth day of the month**, upon the mountains of Ararat."

[37] Daniel 7:11; Daniel 7:26-27; 1 Thessalonians 2:8

[38] Numbers 14:34

[39] Ezekiel 4:6

7. Revelation 13:5 "forty-two months"[40]

1,260 days, forty-two months, and time, times and half a time all delineate the same time period. This little horn power would rule for 1,260 years.

From the evidence given to Daniel by the angel in this vision there are at least ten marks revealing the identity of the little horn power:

1. It would arise out of the fourth beast or fourth world power—the pagan Roman Empire. Daniel 7:7,8
2. It would arise among the ten divisions of the Roman Empire, therefore would be located geographically in Western Europe. Daniel 7:8
3. It would arise after the other ten horns, therefore gaining its political power after A.D. 476 (before which the ten divisions of Europe did not exist). Daniel 7:24
4. It was to be different from the other ten horns; it would not be just a political power like the other kingdoms. Daniel 7:24
5. Although described as a little horn, it would be more stout (strong) than the other ten horns. Daniel 7:20
6. It would uproot three of the previous ten horns; the Heruli, Vandals, and Ostrogoths. Daniel 7:8, 20, 24
7. It would have a prominent man—eyes and mouth—speaking great and blasphemous words against the Most High, claiming the attributes of deity, and the ability to forgive sins. Daniel 7:8, 25
8. It would wear out and persecute God's saints. Daniel 7:25.
9. It would think to change God's laws; specifically, his laws having to do with time. Daniel 7:25

---

[40] The way in which the Bible presents this time period in so many forms helps us to verify any of the assumptions we might have made. For example, someone might say, Well, you're making an assumption to say a dividing of times is a half a time. No, for in one place it mentions it as a "dividing of time," but in the other place it mentions it as "half a time." Others might say, you are making an assumption to say that there are 360 days in a year. The fact is that 360 days in a year, times three and a half, comes out to exactly 1,260 days; therefore, we know that we were correct in the conclusion that a Biblical year is 360 days. The time period is also presented as 42 months, which if you multiply by 30 days (in a 360-day year every month has 30 days) it comes to 1,260 days. The various presentations of the same information provide validation, allowing Scripture to interpret itself. The different passages in which these time periods are given were written in three different languages—Aramaic for the first passage, Hebrew for the second, and Greek for the last five—yet it all matches perfectly so that we do not misunderstand or misinterpret.

10. It would reign for 1,260 years.[41] Daniel 7:25

One, and only one power in all of history can answer to these detailed descriptions. If you still have not guessed the power the Bible is warning us about, let us allow history to make the identification. Speaking of the little horn of Daniel 7, Sir Isaac Newton[42] writes: "Kings are put for kingdoms, as above; and therefore the little horn is a little kingdom. It was a horn of the fourth beast... and therefore we are to look for it among the nations of the Latin Empire [Western Europe], after the rise of the ten horns. But, it was a kingdom of a different kind from the other ten kingdoms, having a life or soul peculiar to itself, with eyes and a mouth. By its eyes it was a seer; and by its mouth speaking great things and changing times and laws, it was a Prophet as well as a King. And such a Seer, a Prophet and a King, is the church of Rome."[43]

Does the church of Rome fit these ten identifying marks?

1. The church of Rome arose out of the pagan Roman Empire (the fourth beast). This is why it is still called today, the Roman Catholic Church.

2. The papacy is located in the midst of Western Europe; in the heart of Italy.

3. The papacy gained its political power in A.D. 538 when it took control of Rome from the Ostrogoths, just after the disintegration of the Roman Empire in A.D. 476.

---

[41] Daniel 7:25 – Reign for a time, times, and dividing of times. A time is a year (Daniel 4:16). A Biblical year is 360 days (see the story of the flood and calculate from the dates given). Therefore, we have here $3^{1/2}$ times or $3^{1/2}$ years. In symbolic Biblical prophecy a day represents a year – Numbers 14:34 and Ezekiel 4:6. Therefore we have 1260 days, representing 1,260 years. This prophecy is repeated seven times in Scripture.
Daniel 7:25 ...time, times, and a dividing of time
Daniel 12:7 ...time, times, and an half
Revelation 11:2 ...forty-two months
Revelation 11:3 ...a thousand two hundred and sixty days
Revelation 12:6 ...a thousand two hundred and sixty days
Revelation 12:14 ...time, and times, and half a time
Revelation 13:5 ...forty-two months

[42] Sir Isaac Newton (1642-1727), the famous scientist who first quantified the laws of gravity, and arguably the most brilliant mind of modern times, actually wrote more about the Bible than about science. The books of Daniel and Revelation were his particular interest.

[43] Isaac Newton, *Observations upon the Prophecies of Daniel, and the Apocalypse of St. John* (London: J. Darby and T. Browne, 1733), p. 74, 75.

4. The ten kingdoms of Western Europe among which it rose were all strictly political in nature. The papacy, on the other hand, was a religio-political power—very different from the other ten.

5. Although it is small (today being only 110 acres, and the smallest internationally recognized independent state) it is stronger (more stout) than the nations of Europe.

6. Just as the Bible prophesied, it was the church of Rome that annihilated three of the tribes of Western Europe. This identifying mark alone would be sufficient. "The three divisions which were plucked up were the Heruli in 493, the Vandals in 534, and the Ostrogoths in 538 A.D."[44]

7. None speak more blasphemous words against God than the pope. In the Ferrari's Ecclesiastical Dictionary (originally written in Latin, the official language of the papacy), under the heading of "Papa" is the following: "The Pope is of so great dignity that he is not a man, but as it were, God, and the Vicar of God. The Pope is called Most Holy because he is rightfully presumed to be such. The Pope alone is deservedly called Most Holy because he alone is the Vicar of Christ, and the fountain and source of all fullness and holiness. He is likewise the Divine Monarch and Supreme Emperor and King of Kings. Hence the Pope is crowned with the Triple Crown as king of the heavens, and of the earth, and of the lower regions. Moreover, the superiority and power of the Roman pontiff but by no means pertain only to Heavenly things, to earthly things and to things under the earth, but even over angels, of whom he is greater. So that if it were possible that angels might err in the faith, or might think contrary to the faith, they could be judged and excommunicated by the Pope. The Pope is as it were, God on earth, sole sovereign of the faithful of Christ, chief King of Kings, having plentitude of power.... The Pope is of so great authority and power, that he is able to modify, declare, or interpret even divine laws.... The Pope can modify divine law, since his power is not of man but of God, and he acts as

---

44 S. N. Haskell, *The Story of Daniel the Prophet* (Nashville, TN: Southern Publishing Association, 1905), p. 94.

vicegerent of God upon earth with most ample power of binding and loosing his sheep."[45]

Great words indeed against the most high God. The Bible tells us there is only one God.[46] The Ten Commandments stipulate having no other gods beside the God of heaven,[47] the Creator of the universe. Certainly, we may not worship a sinful mortal. Scripture says, "As it is written, There is none righteous, no, not one."[48]

In Pope Gregory's XIII *Decretum Gratiani* it says, "But to believe that **our Lord God the Pope,** the establisher of the said decretal, and of this, could not decree, as he did decree,

---

[45] Lucii Ferraris, *Prompta Bibliotheca Canonica, Juridica, Moralis, Theologica, nec non Ascetica, Polemica, Rubristica, Historica,* Editio Quarta, Superiorum Permissu, AC Privilegio (Paris: J. P. Migne, 1858), p. 1827-1828.
http://biblelight.net/1827r.gif. Retrieved 3-15-2017.
http://biblelight.net/prompta-cover.gif. Retrieved 3-15-2017.

[46] See Deuteronomy 4:35; 2 Samuel 7:22; 1 Chronicles 17:20; Isaiah 44:6; Isaiah 45:5; Isaiah 45:21-23; Hosea 13:4, etc.

[47] Exodus 20:3-6

[48] Romans 3:10; See also the passage quoted in Isaiah 41:26.

should be accounted heretical."[49] In other words, if anybody believes that the pope could not decree this decree, they should be counted a heretic. In this official document he is specifically called "our Lord God the Pope."

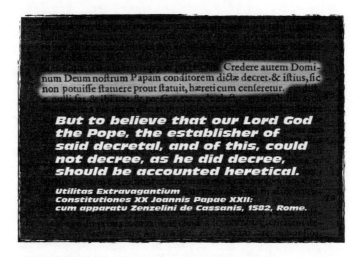

> Credere autem Domi-num Deum noftrum Papam conditorem dictæ decret. & iftius, fic non potuiffe ftatuere prout ftatuit, hæreti cum cenferetur.

> **But to believe that our Lord God the Pope, the establisher of said decretal, and of this, could not decree, as he did decree, should be accounted heretical.**

> *Utilitas Extravagantium*
> *Constitutiones XX Joannis Papae XXII:*
> *cum apparatu Zenzelini de Cassanis, 1582, Rome.*

Pope Nicholas I wrote: "'You affirm that you are submissive to your sovereign.... But you appear to forget that we, as the vicar of Christ, have the right to judge all men....

"'We alone have the power to bind and to loose, to absolve Nero, and to condemn him; and Christians cannot, under penalty of excommunication, execute other judgment than ours, which alone is infallible....

"'Know, prince, that the vicars of Christ are above the judgment of mortals; and that the most powerful sovereigns have no right to punish the crimes of popes, how enormous soever they may be. ...for no matter how scandalous or criminal may be the debaucheries of the pontiffs, you should obey them, for they are seated on the chair of St. Peter....'

"'Fear, then, our wrath, and the thunders of our vengeance; for Jesus Christ has appointed us with his own mouth

---

[49] Gregorii XIII. Pont. Max., *Decretvm Gratiani Emendatvm et Notationibvs Illvstratvm Vna cum glofsis, Gregorii XIII. Pont. Max. iussu editum.* (Rome: In Aedibus Populi Romani, 1582), p. 153. Latin: "Credere autem Dominum Deum noftrum Papam conditorem dictae decret & iftius, fic non poruiffe ftatuere prout ftatuit, haereti cum cenferetur."
http://biblelight.net/Extravagantes.htm. Retrieved: 03-04-2016.

absolute judges of all men; and kings themselves are submitted to our authority. The power of the Church has been consecrated before your reign, and it will subsist after it...."[50]

Blasphemous words indeed.

The Bible tells us exactly where God dwells: "O LORD of hosts, God of Israel, that dwellest between the cherubims, thou art the God, even thou alone, of all the kingdoms of the earth: thou hast made heaven and earth."[51] The only true God, Creator of the universe, dwells between the cherubims in the most holy place of the heavenly sanctuary. Between these two cherubims God sits on a great white throne.[52]

Notice the symbolism portrayed in this picture. Here you see Pope Francis sitting on a white throne between two golden angels. By this symbolism the papacy is claiming to sit in the temple of God.

The Bible predicted that this is precisely where this power would sit. "Let no man deceive you by any means: for that day {the second coming} shall not come, except there come

---

[50] Louis Marie de Cormenin, *A Complete History of the Popes of Rome,* Vol. 1 (Philadelphia: James L. Gihon, 1851), p. 242-244.

[51] Isaiah 37:16

[52] Revelation 20:11

a falling away first, and that man of sin be revealed, the son of perdition; Who opposeth and exalteth himself above all that is called God, or that is worshipped; so that he as God sitteth in the temple of God, showing himself that he is God."[53]

Not only does the papacy claim that the pope is God on earth, but the priest is also considered to be God. The catechism of the Council of Trent says, "Bishops and priests being, as they are, God's interpreters and ambassadors, empowered in His name to teach mankind the divine law and the rules of conduct, and holding, as they do, His place on earth, it is evident that no nobler function than theirs can be imagined. Justly, therefore, are they called not only Angels, but even gods, because of the fact that they exercise in our midst the power and prerogatives of the immortal God."[54] "Priests and bishops are, as it were, the interpreters and heralds of God, commissioned in his name to teach mankind the law of God, and the precepts of a Christian life—they are the representatives of God upon earth. Impossible, therefore, to conceive a more exalted dignity, or functions more sacred. Justly, therefore, are they called not only 'angels,' but gods, holding, as they do, the place and power and authority of God on earth."[55]

The papacy claims: "And God himself is obliged to abide by the judgment of his priests, and either not to pardon or to pardon, according as they refuse or give absolution, provided the penitent is capable of it...The sentence of the priest precedes, and God subscribes to it....
"Were the Redeemer to descend into a church, and sit in a confessional to administer the sacrament of penance, and a priest to sit in another confessional, Jesus would say over each penitent, 'Ego te absolve,' the priest would likewise say

---

[53] 2 Thessalonians 2:3-4

[54] *The Catechism of the Council of Trent* (The Roman Catechism) (Rockford, IL: Tan Books and Publishers, Inc., 1992), trans. John A. MecHugh, O.P., S.T.M., Litt.D. and Charles J. Callan, O.P., S.T.M., Litt.D., p. 318.

[55] *Catechism of the Council of Trent, published by command of Pope Pius the Fifth* (Dublin: Richard Coyne, 1829), trans. Rev. J. Donovan, p. 304-305.

over each of his penitents, 'Ego te absolve,' and the penitents of each would be equally absolved."[56]

It is hard to imagine anything more blasphemous.

8. How does this power wear out the saints of the most high? "It is estimated by careful and credible historians, that more than FIFTY MILLIONS of the human family, have been slaughtered for the crime of heresy by popish persecutors, an average of more than forty thousand religious murders for every year of the existence of Popery."[57]

Protestants have frequently repeated the conservative estimate of fifty million killed by the papacy. However, there is good evidence that the documented numbers may be higher than two hundred million.[58] If the truth would be known, as recorded in the books of God's record, the numbers could very well be much higher. Records of these atrocities were systematically destroyed. The Catholic Church continually sought out and persecuted anyone who disagreed with it, even those whose crime was nothing more than reading the Bible. The most inhumane tortures were invented to root out the hated sects who wanted to follow God's Word alone. Putting to death heretics was not only pardonable, but commendable. In a letter to the king of Bulgaria, Pope Nicholas I writes: "'You advise us,' he says,

---

[56] St. Alphonsus de Liguori, *The Complete of Saint Alphonsus de Ligouri: The Ascetical Works,* Vol. 12: Dignity and Duties of the Priest, The Centenary ed. (New York: Benziger Brothers, 1889), trans. from Italian, ed. by Rev. Eugene Grimm, p. 27-28.

[57] John Dowling, A.M., *The History of Romanism: From the Earliest Corruptions of Christianity to the Present Time* (New York: Edward Walker, 1845), p. 541-542.

"No computation can reach the numbers who have been put to death, in different ways, on account of their maintaining the profession of the Gospel, and opposing the corruptions of the Church of Rome. A MILLION of poor Waldenses perished in France; NINE HUNDRED THOUSAND orthodox Christians were slain in less than thirty years after the institution of the order of the Jesuits. The Duke of Alva boasted of having put to death in the Netherlands, THIRTY-SIX THOUSAND by the hand of the common executioner during the space of a few years. The Inquisition destroyed, by various tortures, ONE HUNDRED AND FIFTY THOUSAND within thirty years. These are a few specimens, and but a few, of those which history has recorded; but the total amount will never be known till the earth shall disclose her blood, and no more cover her slain (Scott's Church History)."
John Dowling, A.M., *The History of Romanism: From the Earliest Corruptions of Christianity to the Present Time* (New York: Edward Walker, 1845), p. 542.

[58] David A. Plaisted, "Estimates of the Number Killed by the Papacy in the Middle Ages and Later," 2006, p. 7, 41.
http://www.cs.unc.edu/~plaisted/estimates.html#_Toc135810590 Retrieved: 03-10-2016.

to the Bulgarian king, that 'you have caused your subjects to be baptized without their consent, and that you have exposed yourself to so violent a revolt as to have incurred the risk of your life. I glorify you for having maintained your authority by putting to death those wandering sheep who refused to enter the fold; and you not only have not sinned, by showing a holy rigor, but I even congratulate you on having opened the kingdom of heaven to the people submitted to your rule. A king need not fear to command massacres, when these will retain his subjects in obedience, or cause them to submit to the faith of Christ, and God will reward him in this world, and in eternal life, for these murders."[59]

"There perished under pope Julian 200,000 christians: and by the French massacre, on a moderate calculation, in 3 months, 100,000. Of the Waldenses there perished 150,000; of the Albigenses 150,000. There perished by the Jesuits in 30 years only, 900,000. The Duke of Alva destroyed by the *common hangman* alone, 36,000 persons; the amount murdered by him is set down, by Grotius, at 100,000! There perished by the fire, and by the tortures of the Inquisition in Spain, Italy, and France, 150,000…In the Irish massacres…there perished 150,000 Protestants!…
"To sum up the whole, the Roman catholic church has caused the ruin, and destruction of a million and a half of Moors in Spain; nearly two millions of Jews, in Europe! In Mexico, and South America, including the islands of Cuba and St. Domingo, fifteen millions of Indians, in 40 years, fell victim to popery. And in Europe, and the East Indies, and in America, 50 millions of Protestants at least have been murdered by it!
"Thus the church of Rome stands forward before the world, 'the woman in scarlet, on the scarlet colored Beast!' A church claiming to be *christian*, drenched in the blood of *sixty-eight millions, and five hundred thousand human beings!*"[60]

---

[59] Louis Marie de Cormenin, *Complete History of the Popes of Rome,* Vol. 1 (1857), p. 244.

[60] W.C. Brownlee, D.D., *Letters in the Roman Catholic Controversy* 2nd ed., (New York: The Author, 1834), p. 348.

"And, O merciful Father in heaven, this does not include the millions of their own people, and her enemies, which fell in her crusades, and wars, and massacres! Here thirty millions and a half would be a moderate calculation! Thus, Rome papal has hurried into eternity A HUNDRED MILLION OF THE HUMAN RACE, by her bloody religion!"[61]

Exactly as the Bible prophesied, this power would wear out the saints of the most high. This terrible persecuting power would try to root out all Bibles, for they hated the Scriptures. They burned the Bibles and their owners at the stake.

9.   How does this power think to change God's times and laws? Ferraris Ecclesiastical Dictionary, under the heading of the Pope claims, "The Pope is of so great authority and power, that he is able to modify, declare, or interpret even divine laws.... The Pope can modify divine law, since his power is not of man but of God, and he acts as vicegerent of God upon earth with most ample power of binding and loosing his sheep."[62] If we compare the Ten Commandments as originally given by God in the Bible with the ones in Roman Catholic catechisms, we see that they have indeed attempted to change God's law.

Aside from being dramatically abbreviated, the second commandment, which forbids the worship of images, is completely gone from the Catholic catechism. It should be obvious that the reason for removal of the second commandment is that Catholicism requires the violation of this command of God. Since everyone knows that there are ten commandments, they split the tenth commandment in two, to preserve the number.

The papacy has also changed God's time—the sabbath—which is the heart of God's law and the only commandment that has to do with time. This, Catholicism boldly asserts:

---

[61] W.C. Brownlee, *Romanism in the Light of Prophecy and History: Its Final Downfall, and the Triumph of the Church of Christ* (New York: American and Foreign Christian Union, 1854), p. 58.

[62] Lucii Ferraris, *Prompta Bibliotheca Canonica, Juridica, Moralis, Theologica, nec non Ascetica, Polemica, Rubristica, Historica*, Editio Quarta, Superiorum Permissu, AC Privilegio (Paris: J. P. Migne, 1858), p. 1827-1828.

10 COMMANDMENTS AS FOUND IN SCRIPTURE	10 COMMANDMENTS AS COMMONLY ABBREVIATED IN A ROMAN CATHOLIC CATECHISM
1. I am the LORD thy God, which have brought thee out of the land of Egypt, out of the house of bondage. Thou shalt have no other gods before me.	1. I am the LORD thy God. Thou shalt have no strange gods before Me.
2. Thou shalt not make unto thee any graven image, or any likeness of any thing that is in heaven above, or that is in the earth beneath, or that is in the water under the earth: Thou shalt not bow down thyself to them, nor serve them: for I the LORD thy God am a jealous God, visiting the iniquity of the fathers upon the children unto the third and fourth generation of them that hate me; And showing mercy unto thousands of them that love me, and keep my commandments.	Removed.
3. Thou shalt not take the name of the LORD thy God in vain; for the LORD will not hold him guiltless that taketh his name in vain.	2. Thou shalt not take the name of the LORD thy God in vain.
4. Remember the sabbath day, to keep it holy. Six days shalt thou labour, and do all thy work: But the seventh day is the sabbath of the LORD thy God: in it thou shalt not do any work, thou, nor thy son, nor thy daughter, thy manservant, nor thy maidservant, nor thy cattle, nor thy stranger that is within thy gates: For in six days the LORD made heaven and earth, the sea, and all that in them is, and rested the seventh day: wherefore the LORD blessed the sabbath day, and hallowed it.	3. Remember to keep holy the Sabbath day.
5. Honour thy father and thy mother: that thy days may be long upon the land which the LORD thy God giveth thee.	4. Honour thy father and thy mother.
6. Thou shalt not kill.	5. Thou shalt not kill.
7. Thou shalt not commit adultery.	6. Thou shalt not commit adultery.
8. Thou shalt not steal.	7. Thou shalt not steal.
9. Thou shalt not bear false witness against thy neighbor.	8. Thou shalt not bear false witness against thy neighbor.
10. Thou shalt not covet thy neighbor's house, thou shalt not covet thy neighbor's wife, nor his manservant, nor his maidservant, nor his ox, nor his ass, nor any thing that is thy neighbor's.	9. Thou shalt not covet thy neighbor's wife.
	10. Thou shalt not covet thy neighbor's goods.

"The Bible says, 'Remember that thou keep holy the Sabbath day.' The Catholic Church says: 'No! By my divine power I abolish the Sabbath day, and command you to keep holy the first day of the week.' And lo! the entire civilized world bows down in reverent obedience to the command of the holy Catholic Church."[63]

By her power, not the power of God, the "change" is made. And the whole world bows, not in reverent obedience to God's commands, but to the command of the Roman church.

"Sunday is a Catholic institution, and its claims to observance can be defended only on Catholic principles... From the beginning to the end of Scripture there is not a single passage that warrants the transfer of weekly public worship from the last day of the week to the first."[64]

Catholic authors tell us frankly that there is not a single passage in Scripture to warrant the change from Saturday to Sunday. How can they make this change when it is not found in the Scriptures? The claim is made that:

"The Church is above the Bible; and this transference of Sabbath observance from Saturday to Sunday is proof positive of that fact."[65]

"If protestants would follow the Bible, they should worship God on the Sabbath day. In keeping the Sunday, they are following a law of the Catholic church."[66]

---

[63] Fr. Enright, CSS. R. to E.E. Franke, January 11, 1892, in "An Adventist Minister on Sunday Laws," *American Sentinel,* June 1, 1893, p. 173.

[64] M. Long, "Rampant Sabbatarianism," *Catholic Press,* August 25, 1900, p. 22, biblelight.net/Catholic Press.jpg Retrieved: 01-31-2016.

[65] "Sabbath Observance," *The Catholic Record,* September 1, 1923, p. 4, http://www.biblelight.net/c-record.htm Retrieved 02-09-2016.

[66] Albert Smith, Chancellor of Archdiocese of Baltimore, replying for the Cardinal in a letter dated February 10, 1920.

"Protestantism, in discarding the authority of the Roman Catholic Church, has no good reason for its Sunday theory, and ought, logically, to keep Saturday as the Sabbath."[67]

The little horn power would think to change God's times and laws.

"Since the Catholic Church, probably influenced by Constantine, made the day Sunday a holiday, it can claim the honor of having granted man a rest from his labors every seven days."[68]

Great words against the most High God.

"Reason and common sense demand the acceptance of one or the other of these alternatives: either Protestantism and the keeping holy of Saturday, or Catholicity and the keeping holy of Sunday. Compromise is impossible."[69]

Modern Protestantism is being inconsistent; more than that, they have apostatized, becoming drunk with the wine of her fornication, returning to the whoredoms of their mother.[70] In order to be Protestant, they must accept Sola Scriptura, the Bible and the Bible only as their rule of faith and doctrine. This would necessitate a return to the sabbath of Scripture, and a rejection of the papal sabbath—the day of the sun.

In a Catholic work entitled *Plain Talk About the Protestantism of Today,* they says: "It is worth its while to remember that this observance of [Sunday as] the Sabbath,—in which, after all, the only Protestant *worship* consists,—not only has no

---

[67] John Gilmary Shea, L.L.D, *American Catholic Quarterly Review,* Vol. 8 –January, 1883– No. 29 (Philadelphia: Hardy & Mahony, Publishers and Proprietors, 1883), p. 152.

[68] C. S. Mosna, S.C.J., *Storia della Domenica Dalle Origini Fino Agli Inizi del v Secolo [History of Sunday From its Origins to the Early Fifth Century]* (Rome: Libreria Editrice dell'Universita Gregoriana, 1969), p. 366, http://biblelight.net/Sources.htm Retrieved: 03-13-2016.
Italian: "Avendo la Chiesa influito probabilmente su Costantino per rendere la domenica giorno <<festivo>>, Essa può rivendicarsi l'onore di aver voluto concedere all'uomo una pausa alle sue fatiche ogni sette giorni."

[69] "The Christian Sabbath," *The Catholic Mirror,* December 23, 1893, p. 8-9.

[70] Scripture also prophesied this in Revelation 17.

foundation in the Bible, but it is in flagrant contradiction with its letter, which commands rest on the Sabbath, which is Saturday. It was the Catholic Church which, by the authority of Jesus Christ, has transferred this rest to the Sunday in remembrance of the resurrection of our Lord. Thus the observance of Sunday by the Protestants is an homage they pay, in spite of themselves, to the authority of the Church."[71]

"Perhaps the boldest thing, the most revolutionary change the Church ever did, happened in the first century. The holy day, the Sabbath, was changed from Saturday to Sunday. "The Day of the Lord" (dies Dominica) was chosen, not from any directions noted in Scripture, but from the Church's sense of its own power. The day of the resurrection, the day of Pentecost, fifty days later, came on the first day of the week. So this would be the new Sabbath. People who think that the Scriptures should be the sole authority, should logically become 7th Day Adventists, and keep Saturday holy."[72]

The Scriptures declare: "Remember the sabbath day, to keep it holy. Six days shalt thou labour, and do all thy work: But **the seventh day is the sabbath of the LORD thy God**: in it thou shalt not do any work, thou, nor thy son, nor thy daughter, thy manservant, nor thy maidservant, nor thy cattle, nor thy stranger that is within thy gates: For in six days the LORD made heaven and earth, the sea, and all that in them is, and rested the seventh day: wherefore the LORD blessed the sabbath day, and hallowed it."[73]

If Jesus had wanted to change the day from the seventh day to the first day, he would have had to do it in no less of a dramatic manner as the presentation of the law on Sinai.

---

[71] Louis Gaston de Segur, *Plain Talk About the Protestantism of Today,* from the French of Mgr. Segur (Boston: Patrick Donahoe, 1868), p. 225.

[72] Fr. Leo Broderick, "Pastor's Page," *The Sentinel,* May 21, 1995, biblelight.net/st-cath.htm Retrieved: 03-13-2016.

[73] Exodus 20:8-11

The sabbath is a commemoration of his creation of the world.[74] It was the day upon which he rested from his work of creation and sanctified. No other day has he hallowed in such a manner. For "I know that, whatsoever God doeth, it shall be for ever: nothing can be put to it, nor any thing taken from it: and God doeth it, that men should fear before him."[75] There is not a single word in Scripture for him hallowing the first day of the week. "Jesus Christ the same yesterday, and to day, and for ever."[76] "For I am the LORD, I change not; therefore ye sons of Jacob are not consumed."[77]

All throughout the Bible, the followers of God: patriarchs and prophets, in the Old Testament, and Jesus and his disciples in the New Testament, kept the seventh-day sabbath holy.[78]

Jesus himself said, "Think not that I am come to destroy the law, or the prophets: I am not come to destroy, but to fulfil. For verily I say unto you, Till heaven and earth pass, one jot or one tittle shall in no wise pass from the law, till all be fulfilled."[79] "And hereby we do know that we know him, if we keep his commandments. He that saith, I know him, and keepeth not his commandments, is a liar, and the truth is not in him.... Brethren, I write no new commandment unto you, but an old commandment which ye had from the beginning. The old commandment is the word which ye have heard from the beginning."[80]

God did not change the Ten Commandments in the New Testament. There is no mention of any such thing. In fact, the Bible specifically states the very opposite. "For he spake

---

[74] Genesis 2:1-3

[75] Ecclesiastes 3:14

[76] Hebrews 13:8

[77] Malachi 3:6

[78] See Exodus 16:28; Nehemiah 13:15-21; Isaiah 58:13-14; Jeremiah 17:21-27; Luke 4:16; Matthew 24:20; Acts 17:2; 13:42-44; Isaiah 66:22-24.

[79] Matthew 5:17-18
"Whosoever therefore shall break one of these least commandments, and shall teach men so, he shall be called the least in the kingdom of heaven: but whosoever shall do and teach them, the same shall be called great in the kingdom of heaven." Matthew 5:19

[80] 1 John 2:3-4, 7

in a certain place of the seventh day on this wise, And God did rest the seventh day from all his works. And in this place again, If they shall enter into my rest. Seeing therefore it remaineth that some must enter therein, and they to whom it was first preached entered not in because of unbelief: Again, he limiteth a certain day, saying in David, To day, after so long a time; as it is said, To day if ye will hear his voice, harden not your hearts. For if Jesus[81] had given them rest, then would he not afterward have spoken of another day. There **remaineth** therefore a rest to the people of God. For he that is entered into his rest, he also hath ceased from his own works, as God did from his. Let us labour therefore to enter into that rest, lest any man fall after the same example of unbelief."[82] If Jesus brought a different rest, would he not have spoken of another day? But he did not. The rest that remains for the people of God is the same rest which remains from creation.

The understanding that it was the Catholic Church who claims responsibility for changing the sabbath of the fourth commandment is not new. Individuals who accepted God's word above ecclesiastical decrees or the traditions of men understood these issues very clearly. Thomas Tillam boldly risked his life to publish the following in 1657:

"The first Royal Law that ever Jehovah instituted, and for our Example celebrated, (namely his blessed Seventh-day Sabbath,) is in these very last days become the last great controversy between the Saints and the Man of sin, The Changer of Times and Laws....
"Therefore rouse up yourselves, ye spirited Citizens of Zion; shake off the dust and trash of beastly Babylon; and whiles that imperious Harlot shames not to assert that Ignorance is the Mother of Devotion, let heavenly wisdom be your sole design, with raised expectations of his faithful performance; who has promised, That the earth shall be filled with the

---

[81] Most modern bibles inaccurately translate Jesus as Joshua. Most modern versions also say that Jesus did speak of another day, making the verse say the exact opposite as the King James Version. For more on why this is the case, and which versions to trust, see Martin Klein, *Thou Hast Magnified Thy Word Above All Thy Name.*

[82] Hebrews 4:4-11

knowledge of the glory of the Lord, as the waters cover the Sea.

"You are assured Christians the Horn has changed the Laws, and he cannot be that Horn unless he change your Times also; will you therefore wisely weigh that he had no Times to change, save the Lord's Sabbath time, and the Lord's Supper time, and these he and none but he changed...."[83]

10. In A.D. 538, Justinian, the Emperor of Rome, declared the bishop of Rome—Vigilius—to be the head of all churches and the corrector of all heretics.[84] Pope Pius IX said that "To act with freedom, as it is just she should, she has always needed the assistance which was suitable to the conditions and the necessities of the age. It is, therefore, by a particular decree of Divine Providence that, at the fall of the Roman Empire and its partition into separate kingdoms, the Roman Pontiff, whom Christ made the head and center of his entire Church, acquired civil power."[85] It was also in A.D. 538 that the bishop of Rome was actually allowed to take control of Rome, by the destruction of the Ostrogoths, the third kingdom to be uprooted. Up until that time the Ostrogoths had control of Rome. The Ostrogoths were the last of the three European powers to be wiped off the face of the earth by this power. The bishop of Rome could not begin a temporal reign until they gained control of their capital city.

Exactly 1,260 years from A.D. 538, the papacy's political power was "as it were wounded to death"[86] by Napoleon's General Berthier, who imprisoned the Pope and confiscated the Vatican property in 1798.

---

[83] Thomas Tillam, *The Seventh-Day Sabbath Sought out and Celebrated* (London: printed for the author, 1657), p. 1-5.

[84] http://biblelight.net/jus-code.htm. Retrieved: 01-31-2016.

[85] Benedictine Monks of Solesmes, *Papal Teachings: The Church*, St. Paul ed., trans. Mother E. O'Gorman, R.S.C.J. (Boston: Manhattanville College of the Sacred Heart, 1962), p. 160. Italian: "quando l'Impero Romano si dissolse e fu diviso in vari regni, il Romano Pontefice, costituito da Cristo capo e centro di tutta la Chiesa, ottenne un Principato civile." Pope Pius, IX, *Cum Catholica Ecclesia,* March 26, 1860. http://biblelight.et/1260years.htm. Retrieved: 03-03-2016.

[86] Revelation 13:3

So explicit was this Bible prophecy, that in 1689, 109 years before its fulfillment, Drue Cressener, vicar of the Church of England, pronounced almost to the year, when it would be fulfilled. "For if the first time of the Beast was at Justinian's recovery of the City of Rome, then must not it end till a little before the year 1800."[87]

"Concerning this we find an interesting extract in a work written by Edward King, Esq., F.R.S.A.S., and published in London, A.D. 1798. 'Is not the papal power at Rome, which was once so terrible and so domineering, at an end? But let us pause a little. Was not the end, in another part of the holy prophecies, foretold to be at the end of the 1,260 years? And was it not foretold by Daniel to be at the end of a time, times and a half, which computation amounts to the same period?' 'And now let us see, hear, and understand. This is the year 1798—and just 1,260 years ago, in the very beginning of the year 538, Belisarius put an end to the empire and dominion of the Goths at Rome. He had entered the city on the 10th of the preceding December, in triumph, in the name of Justinian, the emperor of the East, and soon after made it tributary to him; **leaving thenceforward, from A.D. 538, no power in Rome that could be said to rule over the earth, excepting the ecclesiastical, pontifical power.**' 'We have reason to apprehend, then, that the 1,260 years are now completed, and that we may venture to date the commencement of that period... from the end of the Gothic power at Rome.'"[88] "Justinian... enriched himself with the property of all 'heretics'—that is non-Catholics, and gave all their churches to the Catholics; published edicts in 538 compelling all to join the Catholic Church in ninety days or leave the empire, and confiscated all their goods."[89]

This little horn power can be none other than the papacy.

---

[87] Drue Cressener, D.D., *The Judgments of God upon the Roman-Catholick Church, From its First Rigid Laws for Universal Conformity to it, Unto its Last End* (London: Rose and Crown, 1689), p. 312.

[88] Edward King, Esq., F.R.S.A.S., *Hales Manuel,* (London: 1798), p. 91, 92. As cited in J. G. Matteson, *Prophecies of Jesus or The Fulfillment of the Predictions of Our Saviour and His Prophets* (Battle Creek, MI: International Tract Society, 1895), p. 354-355.

[89] N. Summerbell, D.D., History of the Christian Church (Cincinnati: The Christian Pulpit, 1873), p. 310-311.

Jesus declared, "And other sheep I have, which are not of this fold: them also I must bring, and they shall hear my voice; and there shall be one fold, and one shepherd."[90] God wants to call His people from all these deceptive errors to the truth of his word and into his fold. Revelation 18 predicts a time when a very specific message will go to all the world, "And I heard another voice from heaven, saying, Come out of her, my people, that ye be not partakers of her sins, and that ye receive not of her plagues." God will call his people to come out of the confusion of papal doctrines into the light of the gospel of his word, that they might not receive the plagues decreed to fall on Babylon. "And the times of this ignorance God winked at; but now commandeth all men every where to repent:"[91]

"It is true that there are real Christians in the Roman Catholic communion. Thousands in that church are serving God according to the best light they have. They are not allowed access to his Word, and therefore they do not discern the truth. They have never seen the contrast between a living heart-service and a round of mere forms and ceremonies. God looks with pitying tenderness upon these souls, educated as they are in a faith that is delusive and unsatisfying. He will cause rays of light to penetrate the dense darkness that surrounds them. He will reveal to them the truth, as it is in Jesus, and many will yet take their position with his people. "But Romanism as a system is no more in harmony with the gospel of Christ now than at any former period in her history. The Protestant churches are in great darkness, or they would discern the signs of the times. The Roman Church is far-reaching in her plans and modes of operation. She is employing every device to extend her influence and increase her power in preparation for a fierce and determined conflict to regain control of the world, to re-establish persecution, and to undo all that Protestantism has done. "Catholicism is gaining ground upon every side. See the increasing number of her churches and chapels in Protestant countries. Look at the popularity of her colleges and seminaries in America, so widely patronized by Protestants. Look at the growth of ritualism in England, and the frequent defections to the ranks of the Catholics. These

---

[90] John 10:16

[91] Acts 17:30

things should awaken the anxiety of all who prize the pure principles of the gospel."[92]

Daniel 7:26 But the judgment shall sit, and they shall take away his dominion, to consume and to destroy it unto the end.

God has promises that the injustices, massacres, deception and cruelty of the papacy will someday be brought to justice. The judgment will adjourn and the sentence of destruction be carried out.

Daniel 7:27 And the kingdom and dominion, and the greatness of the kingdom under the whole heaven, shall be given to the people of the saints of the most High, whose kingdom is an everlasting kingdom, and all dominions shall serve and obey him.

God promises a day when his eternal kingdom will conquer every earthly kingdom bringing an end to wars, sin, suffering and death. The people of God inherit the eternal kingdom of Jesus Christ.

Daniel 7:28 Hitherto is the end of the matter. As for me Daniel, my cogitations much troubled me, and my countenance changed in me: but I kept the matter in my heart.

When Daniel saw the amazing things outlined and the terrible ordeal God's people would pass through for so many centuries, he was very disturbed.

---

[92] E. G. White, *The Great Controversy* (1911), p. 565.2-3.

"There are many souls in the Roman Catholic faith who are looking with interest to this people; but the power of the priest over his charges is great, and if he can prejudice the people by his stay-away arguments, so that when the truth is uttered against the fallen churches they may not hear it, he will surely do it. But as laborers together with God, we are provided with spiritual weapons, mighty to the pulling down of the strongholds of the enemy."
E. G. White, *Evangelism* (Nampa, ID: Pacific Press Publishers Co., 1946), p. 574.2.

"There are many who are reading the Scriptures who cannot understand their true import. All over the world men and women are looking wistfully to heaven. Prayers and tears and inquiries go up from souls longing for light, for grace, for the Holy Spirit. Many are on the verge of the kingdom, waiting only to be gathered in."
E. G. White, *The Acts of the Apostles* (1911), p. 109.1.

With exact precision, the progression of history has been just as God revealed. The prophecies of Scripture are the divine signature of authenticity. They demonstrate that more than human wisdom originated the words of Scripture. "And ye shall know the truth, and the truth shall make you free."[93] May the truth of God's word, set you free.

---

[93] John 8:32

Daniel 8

SUMMARY:
In Daniel 8, the prophet receives a second vision. This time he sees a ram with two horns, one of which is higher than the other, followed by a goat, with a notable horn, which attacks the ram, throwing him to the ground and trampling him. None were able to deliver the ram from the goat. The goat's horn is then broken, and in its place, four horns arise toward the four winds. After this, a little horn appears (just as in Daniel chapter 7), which magnifies himself against God. This power takes away the daily [sacrifice] and sets up the transgression of desolation. When the question is asked, "How long shall be the vision concerning the daily [sacrifice], and the transgression of desolation, to give both the sanctuary and the host to be trodden under foot?," the angel replies, "Unto two thousand and three hundred days; then shall the sanctuary be cleansed." The angel Gabriel tells Daniel exactly what world powers are represented by the ram and the goat: Medo-Persia and Greece. The first king of Greece, Alexander the Great, is specified by the notable horn that is broken. Daniel is so overwhelmed by the time period presented, that he faints and was sick certain days. Unfortunately, he fainted in the middle of the angel's explanation, therefore he does not understand the vision. Gabriel must return (in chapter 9) to finish the explanation.

Daniel 8:1 In the third year of the reign of king Belshazzar a vision appeared unto me, even unto me Daniel, after that which appeared unto me at the first.

Like Daniel 7 this vision takes place before the fall of Babylon in 539 B.C. This vision occurs during the third year of Belshazzar, the last king of Babylon, therefore the kingdom of Babylon is not far from its end.

Daniel 1-2:4a is written in Hebrew, while 2:4b-7:28 is written in Aramaic. In **Daniel 8:1** the prophet switches back to writing in Hebrew.

The prophecies of Daniel 2 and 7 reveal that the kingdom of Babylon would be succeeded by three other world empires. Daniel 8 is parallel to Daniel 2 and 7, covering the same history, but adding greater detail to the later events.

Daniel 8:2 And I saw in a vision; and it came to pass, when I saw, that I was at Shushan in the palace, which is in the province of Elam; and I saw in a vision, and I was by the river of Ulai.

Daniel was physically located in Babylon, but in this vision, he is transported into the future to a place called Shushan, where he sees himself in the palace. The fact that he is taken in vision to the palace of the Medo-Persian Empire sets the stage for what is to be revealed next. Shushan was to be the capital and house the palace of the upcoming kingdom—the Medo-Persian Empire. Once Babylon fell, Daniel served in the courts of the palace at Shushan, just as he had seen in vision.

Daniel 8:3 Then I lifted up mine eyes, and saw, and, behold, there stood before the river a ram which had two horns: and the two horns were high; but one was higher than the other, and the higher came up last.

All the beasts in the previous vision were predatory animals (unclean animals), while in this vision we see a ram and goat (clean animals). The ram and goat are also both sanctuary animals, used in the sacrificial services. This will become significant later in the chapter.

The ram represents the Medo-Persian Empire. Of the two horns, one is higher than the other, signifying that one would be stronger or greater than the other. This is directly parallel to the bear of Daniel 7 which was raised up on one side. Indeed, the Persians were the stronger of the two nations that composed the Medo-Persian Empire. The Persians rose to their ultimate power after the Medes just as the Bible predicted—"**the higher came up last**."

Daniel 8:4 I saw the ram pushing westward, and northward, and southward; so that no beasts might stand before him, neither was there any that could deliver out of his hand; but he did according to his will, and became great.

If the ram is pushing westward, northward, and southward, it is therefore coming from the east. This fits precisely the Medo-Persian Empire which indeed came from the east.

The empire of Medo-Persia is described as becoming "great." Take notice of this word "great," for an interesting pattern becomes apparent. The empire became great particularly during the reign of Xerxes or the Ahasuerus of the book of Esther, "Now it came to pass in the days of Ahasuerus, (this is Ahasuerus which reigned, from India even unto Ethiopia, over an hundred and seven and twenty provinces:)"[1]

Daniel 8:5 And as I was considering, behold, an he goat came from the west on the face of the whole earth, and touched not the ground: and the goat had a notable horn between his eyes.

The he goat came from the west so rapidly that he is portrayed as not even touching the ground. The Greeks, from the west, under the command of Alexander the Great conquered Persia, taking over the world almost overnight.

Daniel 8:6 And he came to the ram that had two horns, which I had seen standing before the river, and ran unto him in the fury of his power.

Daniel 8:7 And I saw him come close unto the ram, and he was moved with choler against him, and smote the ram, and brake his two horns: and there was no power in the ram to stand before him, but he cast him down to the ground, and stamped upon him: and there was none that could deliver the ram out of his hand.

The Hebrew for choler is מרר mârar which means bitter, vexed, grieved, sorely provoked. This goat came so fast, with such great power, that nothing could stand in his way; he mowed down the ram and no one could deliver the Medo-Persian Empire from the power of Greece. At the Battle of Arbela, in 331 B.C., the ratio of soldiers

---

[1] Esther 1:1

between Darius[2] and Alexander the Great[3] was approximately 20:1. But God had decreed that nothing would stand in the way of the Grecian Empire and no matter how large the Persian's army was **"there was none that could deliver the ram out of his hand."**

"The prodigious army of Darius was all either killed, taken, or dispersed at the battle of Arbela…. The defeat of Arbela was in fact the death-blow of the Persian Empire. It converted Alexander into the Great King, and Darius into nothing better than a fugitive pretender."[4]

---

[2] "For those who looked only to numbers, the host assembled at Arbela might well inspire confidence; for it is said to have consisted of 1,000,000 of infantry—40,000 cavalry—200 scythed chariots—and fifteen elephants; of which animals we now read for the first time in a field of battle." George Grote, F.R.S., *A History of Greece: From the Earliest Period to the Close of the Generation Contemporary with Alexander the Great,* Vol. XII (1867) p. 155-156.

[3] Alexander had only forty-seven thousand men. See George Grote, F.R.S., *A History of Greece: From the Earliest Period to the Close of the Generation Contemporary with Alexander the Great,* Vol. XII (1867), p. 159.

[4] George Grote, F.R.S., *A History of Greece: From the Earliest Period to the Close of the Generation Contemporary with Alexander the Great,* Vol. XII, A New ed. (1867) p. 167.

Daniel 8:8 Therefore the he goat waxed very great: and when he was strong, the great horn was broken; and for it came up four notable ones toward the four winds of heaven.

Remember, the Scriptures said the ram **"became great,"** but now notice that the goat **"waxed very great."** The Grecian Empire was indeed greater than the Persian kingdom.

In prophecy a horn represents a king.[5] The goat's identification as Greece[6] requires the first notable horn to represent Alexander the Great, who conquered the world and set up the Grecian Empire. But when he became strong, he was broken. History reveals that after his rapid conquest of the world, Alexander the Great died at a young age—unable to conquer self.

After the empire had been secured, Alexander travelled to the city of Babylon for the funeral of his friend Hephaestion. "The sacrifices connected with these obsequies were on the most prodigious scale. Victims enough were offered to furnish a feast for the army, who also received ample distributions of wine. Alexander presided in person at the feast, and abandoned himself to conviviality like the rest. Already full of wine, he was persuaded by his friend Medius to sup with him, and to pass the whole night in yet farther drinking, and with the boisterous indulgence called by the Greek Kômus or Revelry. Having slept off his intoxication during the next day, he in the evening again supped with Medius, and spent a second night in the like unmeasured indulgence. It appears that he already had the seeds of fever upon him, which was so fatally aggravated by this intemperance that he was too ill to return to his palace."[7] Eight days later he had "become incapable of utterance. One of his last words spoken is said to have been, on being asked to whom he bequeathed his kingdom, '*To the strongest.*'"[8] Two days later "In the afternoon he expired—June 323 B.C.—after a life of thirty-two years and eight months—and a reign of twelve years and eight months."[9] Alexander was a man who could rule the world but could not rule

---

[5] Daniel 7:24

[6] Daniel 8:21 identifies the goat by name leaving no room for any other conclusion.

[7] George Grote, F.R.S., *A History of Greece,* Vol. XII (1867), p. 76-78.

[8] *Ibid.*

[9] *Ibid.*

himself; he could conquer nations and cause kingdoms to tremble, but he could not conquer his own passions and fell for a glass of wine. Scripture declares: "Wine is a mocker, strong drink is raging: and whosoever is deceived thereby is not wise."[10]

"For it" or in the place of the first horn **"came up four notable ones** {horns} **toward the four winds of heaven."** From the turmoil of Alexander's death four of his generals eventually emerged victorious—Cassander, Lysimachus, Seleucus, and Ptolemy—dividing the empire.

Daniel 8:9 And out of one of them came forth a little horn, which waxed exceeding great, toward the south, and toward the east, and toward the pleasant land.

In language distinctly parallel to the symbols of Daniel 7 the **"little horn"** arises **"out of one of them."** At first glance, verse nine appears to have the little horn coming forth out of one of the other four horns. But, we must ask the question to what does "them" refer? There are two sets of four items mentioned in verse eight—four horns ("notable ones") and "four winds." The closest antecedent in the passage is the winds. Also, the Hebrew word "them," in this passage, םהhêm, has a masculine gender. This matches the gender of the winds and not the horns, because the winds can be either masculine or feminine, but horns are only feminine. Therefore, the grammar of this passage reveals that the little horn comes out of one of the winds and not out of one of the horns. In other words, it arises from the strife of nations rather than emanating from a division of the Greek empire.

Much of the Christian world today has interpreted this little horn to be Antiochus Epiphanes, a Greek king. Allowing the language of the Bible in these verses to speak for themselves makes this interpretation impossible. The ram or Medo-Persian Empire, **"became great."**[11] The he goat, or Greece, was described as **"very great"**[12] In this verse, the little horn arose and **"waxed exceeding**

---

[10] Proverbs 20:1

[11] Daniel 8:4

[12] Daniel 8:8

great."[13] The little horn must be a power that is greater than the entire empire of Medo-Persia and greater than Greece. Antiochus Epiphanes being one of many Greek kings was certainly not greater than the entire kingdom of Greece, nor was he greater than the succeeding empire.

"Was Antiochus exceeding great when compared with Alexander, the conqueror of the world? Let an item from the *Encyclopedia of Religious Knowledge* answer: 'Finding his resources exhausted, he resolved to go into Persia, to levy tributes and collect large sums which he had agreed to pay to the Romans.' Surely we need not question which was exceeding great, the Roman power which exacted the tribute, or Antiochus who was compelled to pay it."[14] The Bible says that the little horn, **"waxed exceeding great, toward the south, and toward the east, and toward the pleasant land."** This must specify a power greater than either Medo-Persia or Greece, as shown by the succession of terms.

Rome is the only historical contender that could possibly meet the criteria of "exceeding great." Verse nine describes the horizontal conquest of Rome of the nations of the earth. It conquered the south, the east and toward the pleasant land; Egypt and Africa, Greece and Asia Minor, and Judah. But, the power symbolized extends its conquests further.

Daniel 8:10 And it waxed great, even to the host of heaven; and it cast down some of the host and of the stars to the ground, and stamped upon them.

Now the little horn begins vertical conquest; this power would generate a powerful attack against the host of heaven. It would attack God himself. We have already seen the haughty words, from the little horn, claiming dominance over angels[15]—casting the stars to the ground. We saw that the little horn power of Daniel 7 also spoke great blasphemous words against God. Therefore, the little horn here also represents papal Rome, just as in Daniel 7.

---

[13] Daniel 8:9

[14] J. N. Andrews, *The Sanctuary and Twenty-three Hundred Days* (Rochester, NY: James White, 1853), p. 8-9.

[15] See comments on Daniel 7:25.

Daniel 7 is parallel to Daniel 8. Chapter 7 deals with the secular or political nature of the empires, which are therefore represented by unclean beasts. Chapter 8 deals with the religious nature of the empires presented and their impact on the religion of the Bible, therefore sanctuary animals are used as symbols in Daniel 8. In Daniel 7, partially separate symbols are used for pagan and papal Rome. Politically, pagan and papal Rome are somewhat separate entities, hence the employment of separate (though connected) symbols in chapter seven. Religiously, pagan and papal Rome are the same, hence the employment of the one symbol for both powers in chapter eight—the Catholic Church today is, in fact, called the **Roman** Catholic Church.

"No saying of ecclesiastical history is more pregnant than that in which Hobbes declares that 'the Pope is the ghost of the deceased Roman Empire, sitting crowned upon the grave thereof.' This is the true original basis of his dignity and power, and it appears even in the minutest details."[16]

Daniel 8:11 Yea, he magnified himself even to the prince of the host, and by him the daily [sacrifice] was taken away, and the place of his sanctuary was cast down.

The little horn would wax great against the host of heaven and magnify himself against the prince of the host. The Hebrew word for "host" is צבא tsâbâ' which can also refer to an appointed time.[17] This power would actually fight against the appointed time of heaven, and trample it in the dust. The little horn magnifies himself against the Creator of the universe. He dares to supplant the prince of the host— the prince of the appointed time—the Lord of the Sabbath. "For the Son of man is Lord even of the sabbath day."[18] All the titles and prerogatives of Jesus, the papacy claims to possess.[19]

---

[16] Arthur P. Stanley, Dean of Westminster, "Some Characteristics of the Papacy: Part 1," May 1, 1868, in Norman Macleod, D.D., *Good Words for 1868* (London: Strahan & Co., Magazine Publishers, 1868), p. 307.

[17] Tsâbâ is translated "appointed time" elsewhere in Scripture. See Job 7:1; 14:14; Daniel 10:1.

[18] Matthew 12:8

[19] See comments on Daniel 7:25.

"By him the daily [sacrifice] was taken away, and the place of his sanctuary was cast down." The papacy casts down the place of the sanctuary of the prince of the host.

"And the LORD spake unto Moses, saying... And let them make me a sanctuary; that I may dwell among them."[20] The sanctuary of God in the wilderness was used as a system to demonstrate, in pictorial language, the plan of salvation; a plan which was instituted in heaven itself before the world began, for Christ is "the Lamb slain from the foundation of the world."[21] The earthly sanctuary was but a small scale replica—a pattern—of the sanctuary in heaven. For "Thy way, O God, is in the sanctuary: who is so great a God as our God?"[22] "Now of the things which we have spoken this is the sum: We have such an high priest, who is set on the right hand of the throne of the Majesty in the heavens; A minister of the sanctuary, and of the true tabernacle, which the Lord pitched, and not man."[23]

The true tabernacle, which the Lord pitched, is in heaven itself. The heavenly sanctuary is the throne room of the Majesty of heaven. "And the temple of God was opened in heaven, and there was seen in his temple the ark of his testament."[24] It provided the template after which the earthly tabernacle was patterned. "Who serve unto the example and shadow of heavenly things, as Moses was admonished of God when he was about to make the tabernacle: for, See, saith he, that thou make all things according to the pattern showed to thee in the mount."[25] "It was therefore necessary that the patterns of things in the heavens should be purified with these {the blood of goats and calves}; but the heavenly things themselves with better sacrifices than these {the blood of Christ}."[26] "Thus the eternal throne room of God himself is a depiction of the plan of salvation—

---

[20] Exodus 25:1, 8

[21] Revelation 13:8

[22] Psalm 77:13

[23] Hebrews 8:1-2

[24] Revelation 11:19

[25] Hebrews 8:5

[26] Hebrews 9:23

each item representing different aspects of the design to rescue the fallen race."[27]

The door represents Jesus.[28] The lamb represents Jesus the "Lamb of God, which taketh away the sin of the world."[29] The altar of burnt offering represents the sacrifice of Jesus in our behalf.[30] The laver represents Jesus, the water of the Word by which we are washed.[31] Entering into the holy place the table of showbread containing two stacks of six loaves each of unleavened bread, represent Jesus—the bread of life.[32] At the altar of incense the righteousness of Christ ascends "with the prayers of the saints"[33] making them acceptable to God;[34] making the incense a symbol of Jesus. The light of the seven-branched candlestick represents Jesus, the Word[35]—the light of the world.[36] The oil, which also represents the Holy Spirit, was to be pure oil made by beating the olives representing the fact the Jesus was

[37]

---

[27] Martin Klein, *Thou Hast Magnified Thy Word Above All Thy Name*, (Savannah Pictures, 2016) p. 230.

[28] John 10:9, 1

[29] John 1:29

[30] 1 Corinthians 5:7

[31] Ephesians 5:25-26; John 1:1, 14; John 7:37

[32] John 6:51

[33] Revelation 8:4

[34] Ephesians 5:2

[35] John 1:1, 14; Psalm 119:105

[36] John 8:12

[37] Tabernacle in the wilderness, p. 156, 206, © Doris Parrett, used by permission.

"bruised for our iniquities."[38] The veil separating the holy from the most holy represents Christ's humanity. "By a new and living way, which he hath consecrated for us, through the veil, that is to say, his flesh."[39] "He veiled his divinity in the flesh of humanity, so that we could behold him. When Christ died, the veil between the holy and most holy place was rent showing that his death was the ultimate revelation of divinity."[40] Inside the most holy place, the ark of the covenant contained the law of God, above which was the covering or mercy seat—the very throne of God. "Being justified freely by his grace through the redemption that is in Christ Jesus: Whom God hath set forth to be a propitiation through faith in his blood...."[41] Christ is the propitiation for our sins. The Greek word for propitiation is ἱλαστήριον hilastērion which is translated "mercy seat" in Hebrews 9:5. The mercy seat symbolizes Jesus, whose sacrifice shields us from the condemnation of the law which we have transgressed.[42] Every part of the tabernacle services pointed to Jesus.

The sanctuary also outlines the path which Jesus followed in the plan of salvation. The courtyard, made all of brass, represents the earth[43] and portrays symbolically the events in the plan of salvation which would occur in reality on this earth. The holy and most holy places of the earthly sanctuary, being made of gold, represent the heavenly throne rooms and the events to be literally fulfilled in heaven.

Jesus came from heaven and the first thing he did as he entered his earthly ministry, at age thirty, was to be washed at his baptism,[44] symbolized by the laver. The next event outlined in the sanctuary was his death on the cross, at the altar of sacrifice. After, his death he was buried and resurrected to new life, back at the laver. Still he

[38] Isaiah 53:5

[39] Hebrews 10:20

[40] Martin Klein, *Thou Hast Magnified Thy Word Above All Thy Name* (2016), p. 233.

[41] Romans 3:24-25

[42] 1 John 3:4

[43] Revelation 11:2 "But the court which is without the temple leave out, and measure it not; for it is given unto the Gentiles: and the holy city shall they tread under foot forty and two months." In order for the court to be given unto the Gentiles for a specified time period, it must be on this earth, as the Gentile could not tread heaven under foot.

[44] Baptism represents death, burial, and resurrection to new life. See Romans 6:3-8.

walked on the earth for a short time (forty days) after his resurrection, before returning to heaven – entering first the holy place and second the most holy. "For Christ is not entered into the holy places made with hands, which are the figures of the true; but into heaven itself, now to appear in the presence of God for us:"[45] The whole sanctuary is a revelation of the plan of salvation.

So, God, in his mercy is warning us that the little horn would cast Christ's sanctuary to the ground. This fourth world empire (in both its phases) would attack the foundation and methods through which God ordained that man should be saved.

The Scriptures declare: "Seeing then that we have a great high priest, that is passed into the heavens, Jesus the Son of God, let us hold fast our profession. For we have not an high priest which cannot be touched with the feeling of our infirmities; but was in all points tempted like as we are, yet without sin. Let us therefore come boldly unto the throne of grace, that we may obtain mercy, and find grace to help in time of need."[46]

Pope John Paul II, in an apostolic exaltation, contradicts the Scriptures by asserting, "For the sacrament of confession is indeed being undermined,... by the sometimes widespread idea that one can obtain forgiveness directly from God, even in a habitual way, without approaching the sacrament of reconciliation."[47] John Paul II is claiming that you cannot get forgiveness directly from God—that you must go through the priest or the sacrament.

The place of God's sanctuary is cast down by the papal power replacing heaven's plan of salvation with an earthly one. The Bible says we can come boldly before the throne of grace through Jesus alone—the one who was tempted in all points, like as we are, yet without sin. Earthly priests are not without sin.

---

[45] Hebrews 9:24

[46] Hebrews 4:14-16

[47] Pope John Paul II, *Post-Synodal Apostolic Exhortation: Reconciliation and Penance, of John Paul II to the Bishops, Clergy, and Faithful on Reconciliation and Penance in the Mission of the Church Today,* Chap. 2 "The Sacrament of Penance and Reconciliation," http://w2.vatican.va/content/john-paul-ii/en/apost_exhortations/documents/hf_jp-ii_exh_02121984_reconciliatio-et-paenitentia.html Retrieved: 03-17-2016.

John Paul II agrees in his contradiction of the word of God, with a similar declaration by Pope Leo the Great, "'the pardon of God can only be obtained by sinners through the prayers of the priests. Jesus Christ Himself has conferred upon the rulers of the Church the power of imposing canonical penance upon sinners who confess their sins...'"[48]

The Bible says, "For there is one God, and one mediator between God and men, the man Christ Jesus; Who gave himself a ransom for all...."[49]

The papacy has erected an earthly sanctuary, with human priests, altars, candles, incense, sacrifices, penance, confessionals, adoration of images, and the seeking of forgiveness from many mediators—dead saints, Mary, and the priest—thereby removing from the minds of the people the ministration of Christ for their forgiveness in the sanctuary of heaven. No truer picture can be had of the sanctuary of the prince of heaven being cast down to the ground.

Daniel 8:12 And an host was given him against the daily [sacrifice] by reason of transgression, and it cast down the truth to the ground; and it practiced, and prospered.

The Hebrew word for **"host"** (צבא tsâbâ') is also translated in other places as "appointed time."[50] So verse 12 might read: "**And an appointed time was given him against the daily...**" In fact, the only other place in the book of Daniel—outside of Daniel 8:10-13—where this word צבא tsâbâ' is used is in Daniel 10:1. "In the third year of Cyrus king of Persia a thing was revealed unto Daniel, whose name was called Belteshazzar; and the thing was true, but the **time appointed {צבא tsâbâ'} was long**: and he understood the thing, and had understanding of the vision." An "appointed time" of 1,260 years is given for the papacy to fight against the "daily [sacrifice]."

[48] Rev. Bertrand L. Conway, *The Question Box,* New ed. (New York: The Paulist Press, 1929), p. 284.

[49] 1 Timothy 2:5-6

[50] Job 7:1; 14:14; Daniel 10:1

What is the "daily [sacrifice]" that the little horn fights by sin,[51] or transgression of the law? The word for "the daily" in this passage is התמיד ha tâmîyd. In most of the other passages where this word is used in Scripture, outside the book of Daniel, only the word תמיד tâmîyd is used, not התמיד ha tâmîyd. In a few passages the word התמיד ha tâmîyd is used,[52] but in these instances there is a noun following, making התמיד ha tâmîyd into an adjective. Daniel uses the phrase התמיד ha tâmîyd five times and in every place, he uses it as a proper noun, "the daily." Because Daniel uses "the daily" as a noun, adding the noun "sacrifice," would turn "the daily" into an adjective, violating Daniel's usage. Therefore, the supplied word [sacrifice][53] does not belong in the text.[54]

Why is this understanding important? Historically there are two primary interpretations for the phrase "the daily." One view is that "the daily" represents pagan Romanism which must be taken out of the way in order for this little horn power to arise. The second view is that "the daily" refers to Jesus' continual ministration, on our behalf, in the heavenly sanctuary. These two views are clearly quite opposite to each other.

As always, allowing the Bible to interpret itself is the only safe course. Considering the meaning of this word, gives us powerful evidence as to whether these views are correct, or not. The word תמיד tâmîyd means: continual, perpetual, always, ever, and ever more. The term "the daily," therefore, could be written "the perpetual," or "the continual."

Can the phrase "the perpetual" or "the continual" apply to pagan Romanism? The answer is no. Praise the Lord that pagan Romanism is not continual or perpetual. The Bible says in many

---

[51] "...Sin is the transgression of the law." 1 John 3:4.

[52] See Numbers 4:7, 16; 28:10, 15, 23, 24, 31; 29:6, 11, 16, 19, 22, 25, 28, 31, 34, 38.

[53] The King James Version either puts brackets around that word, or italicizes the word, to indicate the fact that the word was supplied by the translators. This occurs in many places, most of which require the supplied word for the sense to be rendered correctly in English.
In one language, a single word might require multiple words to express in proper English. For example, the English phrase "let us go" uses three words whereas in Spanish only one word "vamos" supplies the same meaning.

[54] "Then I saw in relation to the 'daily' (Daniel 8:12) that the word 'sacrifice' was supplied by man's wisdom, and does not belong to the text."
E. G. White, *Early Writings* (1892), p. 74.2.

places that pagan Romanism would be superseded by another power.[55] The pagan Roman Empire disintegrated in A.D. 476. Therefore, one cannot reasonably apply the meaning of this word—"the daily"—to pagan Romanism.

On the other hand, does the meaning of "the daily" or "the perpetual" fit Jesus' ministry in the heavenly sanctuary? The fact is, the Bible tells us that Jesus' ministry in the heavenly sanctuary is not perpetual. It will not continue forever. Praise the Lord, there will be a point at which Christ will finish the ministration in the heavenly sanctuary, for that ministry must come to an end for sin to be eradicated. "For Christ is not entered into the holy places made with hands, which are the figures of the true; but into heaven itself, now to appear in the presence of God for us: Nor yet that he should offer himself often, as the high priest entereth into the holy place every year with blood of others; For then must he often have suffered since the foundation of the world: **but now once in the end of the world hath he appeared to put away sin by the sacrifice of himself**. And as it is appointed unto men once to die, but after this the judgment: So Christ was once offered to bear the sins of many; and unto them that look for him shall he appear the second time **without sin unto salvation**."[56] When Christ appears the second time it will be without sin. The heavenly sanctuary will be cleansed of even the record of sin, and sin will be no more. Christ's intercession in the heavenly sanctuary will cease at the close of probation, when every case has been decided. Therefore, Christ's ministry in the heavenly sanctuary also cannot be called "the daily."[57]

What then is "the daily?" The Bible defines its own meaning, with the sanctuary service providing the answers. "And upon the table of showbread they shall spread a cloth of blue, and put thereon the dishes, and the spoons, and the bowls, and covers to cover withal: and the **continual** bread shall be thereon:"[58] Upon the table of showbread was placed the "continual bread." The Hebrew word translated continual bread is tâmîyd—the perpetual bread. "And thou

---

[55] See Daniel 2:40-41; 7:17-18.

[56] Hebrews 9:24-28

[57] This will be covered in more depth in Daniel 8:14.

[58] Numbers 4:7

shalt set upon the table showbread before me **alway**."[59] The Hebrew word translated "alway" is tâmîyd. "During the sojourn in the wilderness the kindling of fires upon the seventh day had been strictly prohibited.[60] The prohibition was not to extend to the land of Canaan, where the severity of the climate would often render fires a necessity; but in the wilderness, fire was not needed for warmth."[61] This would preclude the baking of bread on the sabbath. In fact, the Israelites were specifically instructed to accomplish any food preparation, even of the manna that God provided by miracle, on Friday before the sabbath began.[62] However, the bread which was placed upon the table of showbread was baked fresh, once a week, on the sabbath![63] This is the reason why Jesus said, "Have ye not read what David did, when he was an hungred, and they that were with him; How he entered into the house of God, and did eat the showbread, which was not lawful for him to eat, neither for them which were with him, but only for the priests? Or have ye not read in the law, how that on the sabbath days the priests in the temple profane the sabbath, and are blameless? But I say unto you, That in this place is one greater than the temple."[64] Christ, the bread of life, was David's salvation. The priests profaned the sabbath by baking bread on that day, yet they were blameless because that bread represented the fresh serving of the bread of life that was to be given to the congregation every sabbath. "Every sabbath he shall set it in order before the LORD **continually**, being taken from the children of Israel by an **everlasting** covenant."[65] Here is an important link between the word "continually" and the word "everlasting." The Hebrew word for "continually" is—you guessed it—tâmîyd. However, the word here translated "everlasting" is 'ôlâm. The bread is set in order continually or perpetually, for an everlasting covenant. The eternal nature of the bread is parallel to the everlasting covenant.

---

[59] Exodus 25:30

[60] See Exodus 35:3.

[61] E. G. White, *Patriarchs and Prophets* (1890), p. 408.4.

[62] Exodus 16:22-23

[63] 1 Chronicles 9:31-32 "And Mattithiah, one of the Levites, who was the firstborn of Shallum the Korahite, had the set office over the things that were made in the pans. And other of their brethren, of the sons of the Kohathites, were over the showbread, to prepare it every sabbath." See also Leviticus 24:8.

[64] Matthew 12:3-6

[65] Leviticus 24:8

The bread, of course, represents the Word, which is eternal, and who "was made flesh and dwelt among us."[66] His eternal nature is represented by the perpetual bread, and is parallel to the everlasting covenant. In fact, the bread also represents the everlasting covenant. What is this everlasting covenant? "Wherefore the children of Israel shall keep the sabbath, to observe the sabbath throughout their generations, for a **perpetual** covenant. It is a sign between me and the children of Israel **for ever**: for in six days the LORD made heaven and earth, and on the seventh day he rested, and was refreshed."[67] The "perpetual covenant" here are the identical words, in Hebrew, as "everlasting covenant" in Leviticus 24:8, above. It is the very same covenant. The sabbath is the "perpetual covenant." "The daily" bread was set in order continually every sabbath.

The little horn power is given an appointed time against the sabbath of the fourth commandment, "**by reason of transgression**," which is the breaking of God's law.[68]

Daniel 8:13 Then I heard one saint speaking, and another saint said unto that certain saint which spake, How long shall be the vision concerning the daily [sacrifice], and the transgression of desolation, to give both the sanctuary and the host to be trodden under foot?

The question asked is then: How long will be the vision concerning the daily (or the sabbath), and the "**transgression of desolation**," to give both the sanctuary and the appointed time (the sabbath) to be trodden down by the papal power?

What is the "**transgression of desolation**"? "Whosoever committeth sin transgresseth also the law: for sin is the transgression of the law."[69] A transgression that causes desolation would be a sin which God punishes with desolation. For what sin, in particular, did God warn of desolation? "As long as it lieth **desolate** it shall rest; because it did not rest in your sabbaths, when ye dwelt upon it.... If they shall

---

[66] John 1:14

[67] Exodus 31:16, 17

[68] 1 John 3:4

[69] *Ibid.*

confess their **iniquity**, and the **iniquity of their fathers**, with their **trespass** which they **trespassed** against me.... Then will I **remember my covenant** ... and I will remember the land. The land also shall be left of them, and shall enjoy her **sabbaths**, while she lieth **desolate** without them: and they shall accept of the punishment of their iniquity: because, even because they despised my judgments, and because their soul abhorred my statutes."[70]

Of all transgressions of the law, the transgression of the sabbath of the fourth commandment—God's perpetual covenant—brought desolation upon the land. Therefore, "transgression of desolation" is specifically the transgression of the fourth commandment. The papacy would take away the perpetual covenant—the seventh-day sabbath—in order to cause the sin of breaking the sabbath.

But God has said, "Remember the sabbath day, to keep it holy. "Six days shalt thou labour, and do all thy work: But the seventh day is the sabbath of the LORD thy God: in it thou shalt not do any work, thou, nor thy son, nor thy daughter, thy manservant, nor thy maidservant, nor thy cattle, nor thy stranger that is within thy gates: For in six days the LORD made heaven and earth, the sea, and all that in them is, and rested the seventh day: wherefore the LORD blessed the sabbath day, and hallowed it."[71]

This is exactly what Daniel 7:25 predicted of the little horn power: "he shall speak great words against the most High, and shall wear out the saints of the most High, and think to change times and laws."

The question is asked, in effect: How long shall be the vision concerning the seventh-day sabbath, and the sin of violating the Sabbath, which causes desolation, to give both the heavenly sanctuary, and the time that God appointed to meet with his people, to be trodden under foot by the papacy?

---

[70] Leviticus 26:35, 40, 42-43
This was fulfilled many times especially in the Babylonian captivity. Nehemiah 13:15-18 "In those days saw I in Judah some treading wine presses on the sabbath, and bringing in sheaves, and lading asses; as also wine, grapes, and figs, and all manner of burdens, which they brought into Jerusalem on the sabbath day.... There dwelt men of Tyre also therein, which brought fish, and all manner of ware, and sold on the sabbath ... in Jerusalem. Then I contended with the nobles of Judah, and said unto them, What evil thing is this that ye do, and profane the sabbath day? **Did not your fathers thus**, and did not our **God bring all this evil upon us**, and upon this city? yet ye bring more **wrath** upon Israel by **profaning** the sabbath."

[71] Exodus 20:8-11

Daniel 8:14 And he said unto me, Unto two thousand and three hundred days; then shall the sanctuary be cleansed.

In answer to the question, Gabriel replies, **"Unto two thousand and three hundred days; then shall the sanctuary be cleansed."**

In the sanctuary services God outlined a yearly cycle of feasts which comprised the Jewish ceremonial year.[72] This symbolic calendar shadowed an outline of the plan of salvation. The year began in the spring with the first symbolic feast being the Passover.

The Passover was commemorative of the exodus from Egypt, when the destroying angel passed over the houses of the Israelites on

---

[72] When Jesus died, the curtain separating the holy place from the most holy place in the temple was torn from top to bottom (Matthew 27:51) indicating that Jesus – the reality of these symbols – had arrived, and that the ceremonies were ended and our attention was to be on the reality rather than the symbols. The Bible predicted this change. An Old Testament prophecy begins to unlock the mystery: Hosea 2:11 "I will also cause all her mirth to cease, her feast days, her new moons, and her sabbaths, and all her solemn feasts." Here the Bible explicitly foretells a time when God would cause Israel's feast days, her new moons, and her sabbaths to cease. The New Testament records the fulfillment of this prophecy: Colossians 2:14-17 "Blotting out the handwriting of ordinances that was against us, which was contrary to us, and took it out of the way, nailing it to his cross;

"Let no man therefore judge you in meat, or in drink, or in respect of an holyday, or of the new moon, or of the sabbath days:

"Which are a shadow of things to come; but the body is of Christ."

Notice that the same components (feast/holydays, new moons, and sabbaths/solemn feasts) are mentioned in the identical order in both passages. Paul, in Colossians, is quoting from Hosea. Paul repeats Colossians 2:14 in Ephesian 2:15: "Having abolished in his flesh the enmity, even the law of commandments contained in ordinances; for to make in himself of twain one new man, so making peace." Here the Bible speaks of a law that has been done away with. Some assume that this is the Ten Commandments, but a careful study of Scriptures indicates that it is the ceremonial law that was abolished at the death of Jesus.

Jesus Himself said, "Think not that I am come to destroy the law, or the prophets: I am not come to destroy, but to fulfill. For verily I say unto you, Till heaven and earth pass, one jot or one tittle shall in no wise pass from the law, till all be fulfilled." Matthew 5:17, 18. Thus, the sabbath days of Colossians 2:16 are ceremonial sabbaths, not the weekly sabbath (because the weekly sabbath is part of the Ten Commandments). The Scripture teaches two different laws. The Bible says clearly that the Ten Commandments were written on stone with the finger of God and put inside the ark. "And I will write on the tables the words that were in the first tables which thou brakest, and thou shalt put them in the ark..." Deuteronomy 10:1-5. The Bible also specifies that Moses wrote words in a book, which was placed in the side of the ark to be there as a witness against the people. "When Moses had made an end of writing the words of this law in a book, until they were finished, That Moses commanded the Levites... saying, take this book of the law, and put it in the side of the ark of the covenant of the LORD your God, that it may be there for a witness against thee." Deuteronomy 31:24-26. This is almost identical wording to the phrase in Colossians 2:14, "handwriting of ordinances that was against us." The Bible tells us that there are sabbaths besides the weekly sabbath of the Lord from the Ten Commandments: "These are the feasts of the LORD, which ye shall proclaim to be holy convocations, to offer an offering made by fire unto the LORD, a burnt offering, and a meat offering, a sacrifice, and drink offerings, every thing upon his day: **Beside the sabbaths of the LORD**, and beside your gifts, and beside all your vows, and beside all your freewill offerings, which ye give unto the LORD." Leviticus 23:37,38.

It is clear that the Bible says that Christ did away with a law. The Bible calls the law which Christ did away with, the "handwriting of" or "the commandments contained in" ordinances. It also defines these laws as "shadows of things to come." This means that it was the ceremonial laws of types and shadows that were nailed to the cross. Not the Ten Commandments, not the entire five books of Moses, not the health laws, not the principles that expanded and enlarged on the moral law (i.e. the prohibition of a man lying with a beast or another man is clearly an expansion of the commandment to not commit adultery); but the ceremonial laws of types and shadows.

So, from the death of Jesus the focus changed from keeping these ceremonies, to understanding their heavenly reality. Despite the fact that these ceremonies have been done away with, they still portray glorious truths that affect our reality today, and guide us in the correct understanding of the plan of salvation.

whose doors he found the blood of the lamb. The Passover also pointed forward to Jesus who would be sacrificed for our sins as that Passover lamb. "For even Christ our Passover is sacrificed for us."[73] Jesus was crucified on Friday afternoon, on the very day of Passover at the very time when the Passover lamb was to be killed.

The Feast of Unleavened Bread was next on the calendar—the seven days immediately following Passover. All leaven (representing sin—1 Corinthians 5:8) was to be removed from their dwelling places during this time. Any bread eaten was to be made without leaven. The second day of the Feast of Unleavened Bread was the day of the wavesheaf offering—an offering of grain waved before the Lord. This pointed forward to Christ's resurrection as the first-fruits of the dead, and was the guarantee of the harvest of resurrected righteous at the end of the world. "But now is Christ risen from the dead, and become the firstfruits of them that slept. But every man in his own order: Christ the firstfruits; afterward they that are Christ's at his coming."[74] Jesus rose from the grave, on Sunday morning, at the very time when the wavesheaf would have been waved.

Pentecost was fifty days from the wavesheaf offering and pointed forward to Jesus' anointing as our high priest in the heavenly sanctuary. "We have such an high priest, who is set on the right hand of the throne of the Majesty in the heavens; A minister of the sanctuary, and of the true tabernacle, which the Lord pitched, and not man."[75] Jesus said "Nevertheless I tell you the truth; It is expedient for you that I go away: for if I go not away, the Comforter will not come unto you; but if I depart, I will send him unto you."[76] Jesus must be anointed in heaven in order that the Holy Spirit could come to the earth. Oil represents the Holy Spirit and as Jesus was anointed with the Spirit in heaven, as our high priest, some of that oil fell on the waiting disciples on earth.[77] The outpouring of the Holy Spirit on the day of Pentecost, occurred exactly fifty days from the

---

[73] 1 Corinthians 5:7

[74] 1 Corinthians 15:20, 23

[75] Hebrews 8:1, 2

[76] John 16:7

[77] Acts 2:1-4

resurrection of Jesus.[78] Thus concluded the spring festivals which pointed to the first coming of Jesus.

The fall festivals pointed to the events relating to his second coming. The first of the fall feasts, on the first day of the seventh month, was the feast of Trumpets.

The trumpets were to sound announcing the day of judgment, which was to occur ten days later.[79]

"The day of atonement, on the tenth day of the seventh month, was also called the day of judgment.[80] This was the day when all the confessed sins were cleansed from the sanctuary. On the day of atonement (and only once a year on that day) lots would be cast for two goats, one the Lord's goat, and the other the scapegoat. Then the high priest would sacrifice the Lord's goat, taking the blood of the sacrifice into the most holy place to cleanse the sanctuary of sin. The sins were then transferred to the high priest who would take them out of the sanctuary and place them on the head of the scapegoat, then to be led by a fit man into the wilderness to die. Jesus is represented as our high priest, cleansing the heavenly sanctuary of all confessed sins, and placing the responsibility, and thus the punishment for them, on the head of Satan, who has tempted God's people to commit these sins. Those whose sins have not been confessed, and thus placed in the heavenly sanctuary to ultimately be blotted out forever, will themselves bear the penalty for their sins. This cleansing of the sanctuary demonstrates the grievous nature of our sins, even the record of which has contaminated the very throne room of the universe. This cleansing must occur before Jesus returns for his people. 'For Christ is not entered into the holy places made with hands, which are the figures of the true; but into heaven itself, now to appear in the presence of God for us: Nor yet that he should offer himself often, as the high priest entereth into the holy place every year with blood of others; For then must he often have suffered since

---

[78] The giving of the law at Sinai was also fifty days from the wavesheaf offering, on the day of Pentecost.

[79] The final feast of the symbolic calendar was the Feast of Tabernacles. This is symbolic of the second coming of Christ when we will dwell, or tabernacle, with God.
See comments on Revelation 21:3.

[80] Atonement and Trumpets were solemn holy days, or ceremonial sabbaths, in which no work was to be done. The others were all joyous festivals or feasts and were not ceremonial sabbaths.

the foundation of the world: **but now once in the end of the world hath he appeared to put away sin by the sacrifice of himself**. And as it is appointed unto men once to die, but after this the judgment: So Christ was once offered to bear the sins of many; and unto them that look for him shall he appear the second time without sin unto salvation.'[81]"[82]

This investigative judgment, "in the end of the world," prior to the second coming, decides every case; for when Jesus comes, his rewards are with him. "And, behold, I come quickly; and my reward is with me, to give every man according as his work shall be."[83]

Just as God promised, "Surely the Lord GOD will do nothing, but he revealeth his secret unto his servants the prophets,"[84] he revealed to the prophet Daniel, exactly when the anti-typical day of atonement would occur: "**Unto two thousand and three hundred days; then shall the sanctuary be cleansed**."

In symbolic Bible prophecy a day stands for a year,[85] therefore 2,300 prophetic days is 2,300 literal years. It would be 2,300 years before the sanctuary and the sabbath would be restored to their rightful place in the minds of God's people.

At the end of this chapter, Daniel is so overwhelmed by this time period,[86] that he fainted, and admitted that no one understood the vision. Therefore, the interpretation for this 2,300-year time period must wait until Gabriel returns to explain the meaning of the vision, at the end of chapter nine.

Daniel 8:15 And it came to pass, when I, even I Daniel, had seen the vision, and sought for the meaning, then, behold, there stood before me as the appearance of a man.

---

[81] Hebrews 9:24-28

[82] Martin Klein, *Thou Hast Magnified Thy Word Above All Thy Name* (2016), p. 236-237.

[83] Revelation 22:13

[84] Amos 3:7

[85] See Numbers 14:34; Ezekiel 4:6

[86] The fact that Daniel faints because of the length of time gives additional evidence that this period is not literal time. Just under six and a half years would be nothing to faint about.

Daniel 8:16 And I heard a man's voice between the banks of Ulai, which called, and said, Gabriel, make this man to understand the vision.

It is the angel Gabriel who is commanded to give Daniel an understanding of what he had seen. This will be especially significant in Daniel 9.

Daniel 8:17 So he came near where I stood: and when he came, I was afraid, and fell upon my face: but he said unto me, Understand, O son of man: for at the time of the end shall be the vision.

The glory of Gabriel is so surpassing that Daniel falls on his face in fear. Daniel is told that this vision is for the **"time of the end."**[87] Therefore, it would not be widely understood before that time.

Daniel 8:18 Now as he was speaking with me, I was in a deep sleep on my face toward the ground: but he touched me, and set me upright.

Daniel is still in vision, with his face on the ground. Gabriel comes near to strengthen him, and assist him to stand.

Daniel 8:19 And he said, Behold, I will make thee know what shall be in the last end of the indignation: for at the time appointed the end shall be.

The angel tells Daniel that what he will show him will occur in the **"last end of the indignation"** of the little horn power against God. There is a specific time appointed for the papacy to rule, and when that time is accomplished, the time of the end shall begin.[88]

Gabriel now begins the interpretation of the vision.

---

[87] This also shows that the little horn cannot be Antiochus Epiphanies; otherwise the end of the vision would be fulfilled more than two millennia ago, during the Grecian Empire.

[88] This will be covered more fully in Daniel 11.

Daniel 8:20 The ram which thou sawest having two horns are the kings of Media and Persia.

This verse, it seems, is impossible to misunderstand, as is the next.

Daniel 8:21 And the rough goat is the king of Grecia: and the great horn that is between his eyes is the first king.

The rough goat is the kingdom of Greece, though the word king is used. This is evident from the second phrase: **"and the great horn that is between his eyes is the first king."** The first king of the Greek Empire was Alexander the Great.

This prophecy has proven accurate with explicit detail, telling us even the very names of the kingdoms which would come, centuries before their advancement as world empires.

Daniel 8:22 Now that being broken, whereas four stood up for it, four kingdoms shall stand up out of the nation, but not in his power.

When Alexander the Great died, contenders fought continuously until within twenty-two years there were only four generals remaining. His kingdom was divided between Cassander who took Macedonia and Greece to the west; Lysimachus who ruled west in Thrace and Bithynia; Seleucus who took Syria in the north and all the region east to the Indus River; and Ptolemy who ruled toward the south in Egypt, Arabia, Libya, and some provinces of Palestine.[89]

Daniel 8:23 And in the latter time of their kingdom, when the transgressors are come to the full, a king of fierce countenance, and understanding dark sentences, shall stand up.

In the latter time of their kingdom, that is during the four divisions of the Grecian Empire, when the transgressors are come to the full, this fierce and wicked king, or the little horn power, would arise. This king of fierce countenance who understands dark sentences, is the iron

---

[89] Alonzo T. Jones, *Great Empires of Prophecy, from Babylon to the Fall of Rome,* (1898), p. 199.

monarchy of Rome which turned into the dreadful papal system that ruled for 1,260 years.

Daniel 8:24 And his power shall be mighty, but not by his own power: and he shall destroy wonderfully, and shall prosper, and practice, and shall destroy the mighty and the holy people.

This power would be mighty, but **"not by his own power."** In Revelation 13 the Scriptures declare that "the dragon" or Satan gave the beast "his power, and his seat, and great authority."[90]

He **"shall destroy the mighty and the holy people."** Both pagan and papal Rome destroyed God's faithful people. Pagan Rome in their conquest destroyed nations and mighty people, but also destroyed many of the holy people of God in their persecution of the Christians. What pagan Rome did however, pales in comparison to the terrible bloodshed of the Inquisition and the horrors of the centuries of persecution perpetrated by papal Rome against the holy people of God.

Daniel 8:25 And through his policy also he shall cause craft to prosper in his hand; and he shall magnify himself in his heart, and by peace shall destroy many: he shall also stand up against the Prince of princes; but he shall be broken without hand.

"For seven centuries the Greeks had called Rome the home of forgeries. Whenever they tried talking with Rome, the Popes brought out forged documents... which the Greeks, naturally, had never seen.
"Gregory went way beyond the Donation of Constantine, he had a whole school of forgers right under his nose, turning out document after document, with the papal seal of approval, to cater for his every need.
"Pope Gregory (and, later, Urban II) might require justification for some action against a prince or bishop. Very well, these prelates literally produced the appropriate document. No need for research; it was all done on the premises.

---

[90] Revelation 13:2

"Many earlier documents were touched up to make them say the opposite of what they said originally. Some of these earlier documents were themselves forgeries.... This instant method of inventing history was marvelously successful, especially as the forgeries were at once inserted into canon law.... Thus was accomplished the quietest and longest lasting of all revolutions: it was all done on paper."[91]

Both pagan and papal Rome magnified themselves. The Roman emperor was called Pontifex Maximus and was considered a god—son of the sun god. The pope inherited the name Pontifex Maximus or Pontiff from the Roman emperor and claims the position Vicar of the Son of God or God on earth.[92]

Pagan Rome stood up against the Prince of princes—Jesus Christ—and crucified him on a tree. Papal Rome stood up against the Prince of princes and usurped Christ's authority, titles, and sanctuary. Everything that Jesus has accomplished in behalf of our salvation has been obscured by this power.[93]

"But, he shall be broken without hand." This is the same promise outlined in Daniel 2, when it was first revealed that this succession of kingdoms was to be terminated by a stone which "was cut out without hands, which smote the image upon his feet that were of iron and clay, and brake them to pieces."[94] "And in the days of these kings shall the God of heaven set up a kingdom, which shall never be destroyed: and the kingdom shall not be left to other people, but it shall break in pieces and consume all these kingdoms, and it shall stand for ever."[95]

Daniel 8:26 And the vision of the evening and the morning which was told is true: wherefore shut thou up the vision; for it shall be for many days.

---

[91] Peter DeRosa, *Vicars of Christ: the Dark Side of the Papacy* (New York: Crown Publishers, 1988), p. 59.

[92] See comments on Daniel 7:25.

[93] See comments on Daniel 8:10-12.

[94] Daniel 2:34

[95] Daniel 2:44

Gabriel assures Daniel that the vision is true. Yet he titled it "**the vision of the evening and morning**." To what does this refer? In Daniel 8:14 it said, "Unto two thousand and three hundred days; then shall the sanctuary be cleansed." In the Hebrew the word for days in this passage is actually two words: ערב 'ereb—evening, and בקר bôqer—morning. Translated literally it would read evening and morning. The angel tells Daniel that the "**vision of the evening and the morning**," or the vision of the 2,300 years is true. The angel calling it the vision of the evening and the morning highlights the time prophecy as the most important part of the vision.

The words were to be shut up; the vision would not be understood until far into the future.

Daniel 8:27 And I Daniel fainted, and was sick certain days; afterward I rose up, and did the king's business; and I was astonished at the vision, but none understood it.

So astonished was Daniel, and so overwhelmed by the scope of the 2,300-year time period and the attack upon God's people and sanctuary, that he became sick. If Daniel thought this period of time was literal days, he would not have been overwhelmed by just over six literal years. Therefore, it is clear that he understood the 2,300 days to represent 2,300 years, causing him to faint. None understood the vision, not even Daniel. The angel's explanation of the vision was interrupted by Daniel fainting. The elderly prophet waited, possibly fifteen years, before Gabriel returned to give the final explanation.

Daniel 9

SUMMARY:
Daniel the prophet is fasting and praying for wisdom to understand the vision of chapter 8. Even as a prophet of God, he turns to other of God's prophets to try to understand, and he reads where the prophet Jeremiah spoke of seventy years of captivity as punishment for the Jewish nation. Being almost at the end of those seventy years, Daniel cannot understand the relation of the 2,300 years (of Daniel 8:14), hoping they are not an extension of the seventy. He prays for forgiveness of his sins and the sins of his nation. Suddenly, during his prayer, the angel Gabriel returns to give him understanding of the previous vision. The angel gives the beginning point for the vision and then explains in detail the first part of the time period—seventy weeks (490 years). This is one of the most astonishing of all Bible prophecies pinpointing the very year of the Messiah's anointing and the year of his death. The time prophecy also identifies the year of the beginning of the investigative judgment when "the judgment was set, and the books were opened."[1]

Daniel 9:1 In the first year of Darius the son of Ahasuerus, of the seed of the Medes, which was made king over the realm of the Chaldeans;

Daniel 9:2 In the first year of his reign I Daniel understood by books the number of the years, whereof the word of the LORD came to Jeremiah the prophet, that he would accomplish seventy years in the desolations of Jerusalem.

Darius the Mede becomes the first king of the Medo-Persian Empire at age sixty-two.[2] The Babylonian Empire had fallen to the kingdom of the Medo-Persians, exactly as Daniel's visions had predicted. Daniel was now at the palace in Shushan serving the Medo-Persian Empire.

---

[1] Daniel 7:10

[2] Daniel 5:31

During the first year, as Darius was organizing his government, he set over the realm "an hundred and twenty princes,"[3] and "over these three presidents."[4] It was then that "Daniel was preferred above the presidents and princes, because an excellent spirit was in him; and the king thought to set him over the whole realm."[5] As a result the princes conspired against Daniel throwing him in the lions den. Satan was seeking to destroy Daniel before he could receive the things God desired to reveal to him in this vision.

"Through another vision further light was thrown upon the events of the future; and it was at the close of this vision that Daniel heard 'one saint speaking, and another saint said unto that certain saint which spake, How long shall be the vision?' Daniel 8:13. The answer that was given, 'Unto two thousand and three hundred days; then shall the sanctuary be cleansed' (verse 14), filled him with perplexity. Earnestly he sought for the meaning of the vision. He could not understand the relation sustained by the seventy years' captivity, as foretold through Jeremiah, to the twenty-three hundred years that in vision he heard the heavenly visitant declare should elapse before the cleansing of God's sanctuary. The angel Gabriel gave him a partial interpretation; yet when the prophet heard the words, 'The vision... shall be for many days,' he fainted away. 'I Daniel fainted,' he records of his experience, 'and was sick certain days; afterward I rose up, and did the king's business; and I was astonished at the vision, but none understood it.' Verses 26, 27.
"Still burdened in behalf of Israel, Daniel studied anew the prophecies of Jeremiah. They were very plain—so plain that he understood by these testimonies recorded in books **'the number of the years, whereof the word of the Lord came to Jeremiah the prophet, that He would accomplish seventy years in the desolations of Jerusalem**.' Daniel 9:2."[6]

Jeremiah had predicted the period of captivity Judah would suffer for disregarding the instructions of God, "And this whole land shall be a desolation, and an astonishment; and these nations shall serve the king of Babylon seventy years. And it shall come to pass, when

---

[3] Daniel 6:1

[4] Daniel 6:2

[5] Daniel 6:3

[6] E. G. White, *Prophets and Kings,* (1917), p. 554.1-2.

seventy years are accomplished, that I will punish the king of Babylon, and that nation, saith the LORD, for their iniquity, and the land of the Chaldeans, and will make it perpetual desolations."[7] "The year that Cyrus succeeded Darius the Mede to the throne of Medo-Persia marked the completion of seventy years since the first company of Hebrews had been carried captive to Babylon by Nebuchadnezzar. Daniel, who was familiar with the prophecies of Jeremiah and Isaiah regarding the duration of the captivity, and with the prophecies of Isaiah regarding the restoration by decree of Cyrus, was still living, and was occupying a position of leading responsibility in the Medo-Persian court. His faith in these prophecies led him to plead with God in behalf of his people."[8]

The prophecy of Jeremiah had been partially fulfilled; the king of Babylon had been punished and Babylon was desolate. Yet, Daniel was looking with hope to the rest of Jeremiah's prophecy: "For thus saith the LORD, That after seventy years be accomplished at Babylon I will visit you, and perform my good word toward you, in causing you to return to this place."[9]

When Daniel saw the desolation of Babylon, he believed that God was about to send the captives back to their own land. But he had been given a vision showing the transgression of desolation over a period of 2,300 years and was likely wondering if the Lord had prolonged their punishment, because of their iniquity. This is the reason he was so overwhelmed by the time period revealed. But he finally is satisfied that he understands Jeremiah's prophecy. God had given his word that they would be in captivity for 70 years, and Daniel knew the time was almost up, so he clings to the promise. The great prophet Daniel had to study the other prophet's writings earnestly before God gave him greater revelation.

"And now, when the time came for the temple in Jerusalem to be rebuilt, God moved upon Cyrus as his agent to discern the prophecies concerning himself, and to grant the Jewish people their liberty. Furthermore, Cyrus furnished them the necessary resources for rebuilding the temple of the Lord."[10]

---

[7] Jeremiah 25:11-12

[8] E. G. White, *The Review and Herald*, March 28, 1907 par. 5.

[9] Jeremiah 29:10

[10] E. G. White, *The Review and Herald*, March 28, 1907 par. 5.

Daniel 9:3 And I set my face unto the Lord God, to seek by prayer and supplications, with fasting, and sackcloth, and ashes:

Now that Babylon was in ruins Daniel began with great earnestness to seek God in prayer about this matter. "With faith founded on the sure word of prophecy, Daniel pleaded with the Lord for the speedy fulfillment of these promises. He pleaded for the honor of God to be preserved. In his petition he identified himself fully with those who had fallen short of the divine purpose, confessing their sins as his own."[11]

Daniel 9:4 And I prayed unto the LORD my God, and made my confession, and said, O Lord, the great and dreadful God, keeping the covenant and mercy to them that love him, and to them that keep his commandments;

Daniel records, "**I prayed...and made my confession**." Even though in Daniel 6 the princes could find no fault in Daniel, he still identified himself with his people making confession of his sins and the sins of his people.

Daniel 9:5 We have sinned, and have committed iniquity, and have done wickedly, and have rebelled, even by departing from thy precepts and from thy judgments:

Daniel 9:6 Neither have we hearkened unto thy servants the prophets, which spake in thy name to our kings, our princes, and our fathers, and to all the people of the land.

Daniel does not separate himself from his people even though he may not have participated directly in their sins, he still laments their iniquity. He does not say: well, they are the ones who are sinning; it was because of their sin that I was taken captive; I am a prophet; I am holy and good; or I have been following your word. Instead he says, "**we have sinned**." Daniel is confessing the sins of his people as if they were his own. It would be well for us, if when we see evils and iniquities among God's people, rather than acting like we are so

---

[11] E. G. White, *Prophets and Kings* (1917), p. 554.3.

holy and those people are so evil, that we would do as Daniel did and confess our sins and the sins of our people.

Daniel 9:7 O Lord, righteousness belongeth unto thee, but unto us confusion of faces, as at this day; to the men of Judah, and to the inhabitants of Jerusalem, and unto all Israel, that are near, and that are far off, through all the countries whither thou hast driven them, because of their trespass that they have trespassed against thee.

Daniel 9:8 O Lord, to us belongeth confusion of face, to our kings, to our princes, and to our fathers, because we have sinned against thee.

"Behold, the LORD's hand is not shortened, that it cannot save; neither his ear heavy, that it cannot hear: But your iniquities have separated between you and your God, and your sins have hid his face from you, that he will not hear."[12]

To us today belongs "**confusion of face**," because we have also sinned against God. We have been influenced by the customs of Babylon among which we are captive. "All have sinned, and come short of the glory of God;"[13] "As it is written, There is none righteous, no, not one.... They are all gone out of the way, they are together become unprofitable; there is none that doeth good, no, not one.... Destruction and misery are in their ways: And the way of peace have they not known:"[14]

Daniel 9:9 To the Lord our God belong mercies and forgivenesses, though we have rebelled against him;

No matter how much we may try, we cannot forgive ourselves and neither can any other man on earth, except one, "the man Christ Jesus; Who gave himself a ransom for all...."[15] Babylonian pop-

---

[12] Isaiah 59:1-2

[13] Romans 3:23

[14] Romans 3:10-17

[15] 1 Timothy 2:5-6

psychology insists that we must forgive ourselves, but forgiveness belongs to the Lord. We cannot forgive ourselves any more than a priest can forgive us. God will forgive even "though we have rebelled against him." "Who is a God like unto thee, that pardoneth iniquity, and passeth by the transgression of the remnant of his heritage? he retaineth not his anger for ever, because he delighteth in mercy."[16]

Daniel 9:10 Neither have we obeyed the voice of the LORD our God, to walk in his laws, which he set before us by his servants the prophets.

Daniel confesses that Israel had not obeyed God's voice nor followed his commandments. This was the reason desolation had come upon them; they were in captivity because they had rebelled against the commandments of God.

Daniel 9:11 Yea, all Israel have transgressed thy law, even by departing, that they might not obey thy voice; therefore the curse is poured upon us, and the oath that is written in the law of Moses the servant of God, because we have sinned against him.

Daniel 9:12 And he hath confirmed his words, which he spake against us, and against our judges that judged us, by bringing upon us a great evil: for under the whole heaven hath not been done as hath been done upon Jerusalem.

Daniel 9:13 As it is written in the law of Moses, all this evil is come upon us: yet made we not our prayer before the LORD our God, that we might turn from our iniquities, and understand thy truth.

The Lord had told his people through Moses, "But it shall come to pass, if thou wilt not hearken unto the voice of the LORD thy God, to observe to do all his commandments and his statutes which I command thee this day; that all these curses shall come upon thee, and overtake thee.... The LORD shall bring thee, and thy king which thou shalt set over thee, unto a nation which neither thou nor thy

---

[16] Micah 7:18

fathers have known; and there shalt thou serve other gods, wood and stone.... Thou shalt beget sons and daughters, but thou shalt not enjoy them; for they shall go into captivity.... Moreover all these curses shall come upon thee, and shall pursue thee, and overtake thee, till thou be destroyed; because thou hearkenedst not unto the voice of the LORD thy God, to keep his commandments and his statutes which he commanded thee: The LORD shall bring a nation against thee from far, from the end of the earth, as swift as the eagle flieth; a nation whose tongue thou shalt not understand; A nation of fierce countenance, which shall not regard the person of the old, nor show favour to the young.... And he shall besiege thee in all thy gates, until thy high and fenced walls come down, wherein thou trustedst, throughout all thy land: and he shall besiege thee in all thy gates throughout all thy land, which the LORD thy God hath given thee.... If thou wilt not observe to do all the words of this law that are written in this book, that thou mayest fear this glorious and fearful name, THE LORD THY GOD;"[17]

King Solomon, after building the temple in Jerusalem, gathered the people together for its dedication, and kneeling down, pleaded with the Lord to bless them, asking that if calamity came upon them because of their sin that God would hear from heaven any who should repent and pray toward God's temple. At the end of his prayer he included the captives, "If they sin against thee, (for there is no man which sinneth not,) and thou be angry with them, and deliver them over before their enemies, and they carry them away captives unto a land far off or near; Yet if they bethink themselves in the land whither they are carried captive, and turn and pray unto thee in the land of their captivity, saying, We have sinned, we have done amiss, and have dealt wickedly; If they return to thee with all their heart and with all their soul in the land of their captivity, whither they have carried them captives, and pray toward their land, which thou gavest unto their fathers, and toward the city which thou hast chosen, and toward the house which I have built for thy name: Then hear thou from the heavens, even from thy dwelling place, their prayer and their supplications, and maintain their cause, and forgive thy people which have sinned against thee."[18]

---

[17] Deuteronomy 28:15, 36, 41, 45, 49-50, 52, 58

[18] 2 Chronicles 6:36-39

Knowing these promises, Daniel confesses, "**yet made we not our prayer before the LORD our God, that we might turn from our iniquities, and understand thy truth.**" Daniel understood that the only way the people could be restored to God's favor, is by repentance and reformation, through an understanding of truth. "And ye shall know the truth, and the truth shall make you free.... If the Son therefore shall make you free, ye shall be free indeed."[19]

Daniel 9:14 Therefore hath the LORD watched upon the evil, and brought it upon us: for the LORD our God is righteous in all his works which he doeth: for we obeyed not his voice.

Daniel 9:15 And now, O Lord our God, that hast brought thy people forth out of the land of Egypt with a mighty hand, and hast gotten thee renown, as at this day; we have sinned, we have done wickedly.

Daniel quotes directly from Solomon's prayer "Yet if they bethink themselves in the land whither they are carried captive, and turn and pray unto thee in the land of their captivity, saying, **We have sinned, we have done amiss, and have dealt wickedly**... Then hear thou from the heavens, even from thy dwelling place, their prayer and their supplications, and maintain their cause, and forgive thy people which have sinned against thee."[20]

Daniel 9:16 O Lord, according to all thy righteousness, I beseech thee, let thine anger and thy fury be turned away from thy city Jerusalem, thy holy mountain: because for our sins, and for the iniquities of our fathers, Jerusalem and thy people are become a reproach to all that are about us.

Jeremiah prophesied that a king of Israel, a son of David, was soon to come, who would be called the Lord Our Righteousness. "Behold, the days come, saith the LORD, that I will raise unto David a righteous Branch, and a King shall reign and prosper, and shall execute judgment and justice in the earth. In his days Judah shall be

---

[19] John 8:32, 36

[20] 2 Chronicles 6:36; emphasis supplied.

saved, and Israel shall dwell safely: and this is his name whereby he shall be called, THE LORD OUR RIGHTEOUSNESS."[21]

Daniel 9:17 Now therefore, O our God, hear the prayer of thy servant, and his supplications, and cause thy face to shine upon thy sanctuary that is desolate, for the Lord's sake.

"Turn us again, O LORD God of hosts, cause **thy face to shine**; and we shall be saved."[22] "O send out thy light and thy truth: let them lead me; let them bring me unto thy holy hill, and to thy tabernacles."[23] "The LORD bless thee, and keep thee The LORD make his face shine upon thee, and be gracious unto thee: The LORD lift up his countenance upon thee, and give thee peace. And they shall put my name upon the children of Israel; and I will bless them"[24]

Daniel 9:18 O my God, incline thine ear, and hear; open thine eyes, and behold our desolations, and the city which is called by thy name: for we do not present our supplications before thee for our righteousnesses, but for thy great mercies.

Daniel understood that the reason desolations had come on Jerusalem was because of their sins. Jeremiah the prophet records this very clearly, "So that the LORD could no longer bear, because of the evil of your doings, and because of the abominations which ye have committed; therefore is your land a desolation, and an astonishment, and a curse, without an inhabitant, as at this day."[25]

How often do we plead with the Lord as did Daniel when we see desolations and iniquity in our church, home, and own lives? Do we turn to the Lord and repent? Do we plead with him to hear, or do we just continue to forsake the laws and commandments of God?

---

[21] Jeremiah 23:5-6

[22] Psalms 80:19

[23] Psalm 43:3

[24] Numbers 6:24-27

[25] Jeremiah 44:22

We do not plead with the Lord because we are righteous, for "all our righteousnesses are as filthy rags;" but we plead with God for his great mercy. "For we have not an high priest which cannot be touched with the feeling of our infirmities; but was in all points tempted like as we are, yet without sin. Let us therefore come boldly unto the throne of grace, that we may obtain mercy, and find grace to help in time of need."[26]

Daniel 9:19 O Lord, hear; O Lord, forgive; O Lord, hearken and do; defer not, for thine own sake, O my God: for thy city and thy people are called by thy name.

Daniel pleads, "**O Lord, hear; O Lord, forgive**;" for thy city and people are "**called by thy name**." Daniel is claiming the promise God gave to Solomon in response to his prayer of dedication. "And the LORD appeared to Solomon by night, and said unto him, I have heard thy prayer, and have chosen this place to myself for an house of sacrifice. If I shut up heaven that there be no rain, or if I command the locusts to devour the land, or if I send pestilence among my people; If my people, which are **called by my name**, shall humble themselves, and pray, and seek my face, and turn from their wicked ways; then will I hear from heaven, and will forgive their sin, and will heal their land."[27] God says to us, "If we confess our sins, he is faithful and just to forgive us our sins, and to cleanse us from all unrighteousness."[28]

Daniel 9:20 And whiles I was speaking, and praying, and confessing my sin and the sin of my people Israel, and presenting my supplication before the LORD my God for the holy mountain of my God;

"The prophet Daniel was an example of true sanctification. His long life was filled up with noble service for his Master. He was a man 'greatly beloved' (Daniel 10:11) of Heaven. Yet instead of claiming to be pure and holy, this honored prophet identified himself with the

---

[26] Hebrews 4:15-16

[27] 2 Chronicles 7:12-14

[28] 1 John 1:9

really sinful of Israel as he pleaded before God in behalf of his people: 'We do not present our supplications before Thee for our righteousness, but for Thy great mercies.' 'We have sinned, we have done wickedly.' He declares: '**I was speaking, and praying, and confessing my sin and the sin of my people.**'"[29]

"No one who claims holiness is really holy. Those who are registered as holy in the books of Heaven are not aware of the fact, and are the last ones to boast of their own goodness. None of the prophets and apostles ever professed holiness, not even Daniel, Paul, or John. The righteous never make such a claim. The more nearly they resemble Christ, the more they lament their unlikeness to him; for their consciences are sensitive, and they regard sin more as God regards it. They have exalted views of God and of the great plan of salvation; and their hearts, humbled under a sense of their own unworthiness, are alive to the honor of being accounted members of the royal family, sons and daughters of the King Eternal."[30]

Daniel 9:21 Yea, whiles I was speaking in prayer, even the man Gabriel, whom I had seen in the vision at the beginning, being caused to fly swiftly, touched me about the time of the evening oblation.

While Daniel is still praying, God fulfilled his promise: "If my people, which are called by my name, shall humble themselves, and pray, and seek my face, and turn from their wicked ways; then **will I hear from heaven,** and **will forgive their sin**, and will heal their land."[31] Daniel makes the point that it is Gabriel, whom he had seen in the vision at the beginning, who arrives and touches him at the time of the evening sacrifice. "**The vision at the beginning**" can refer only to the vision of Daniel 8, because Gabriel is not mentioned by name in any of the other visions of the book of Daniel. Daniel is pointing out that this is the same angel from the vision during which he fainted.

---

[29] E. G. White, *The Great Controversy* (1911), p. 470.3.

[30] E. G. White, "Sanctification—The True and the False," *Signs of the Times,* February 26, 1885, p. 129.

[31] 2 Chronicles 7:14

Daniel 9:22 And he informed me, and talked with me, and said, O Daniel, I am now come forth to give thee skill and understanding.

Gabriel comes to give Daniel skill and understanding of that which he did not understand—namely the vision of Daniel 8. The angel himself confirms this:

Daniel 9:23 At the beginning of thy supplications the commandment came forth, and I am come to show thee; for thou art greatly beloved: therefore understand the matter, and consider the vision.

It was at the beginning of Daniel's prayer that the command was given to Gabriel, in fulfillment of the command in chapter eight, "make this man to understand the vision."[32] The Lord declares, "before they call, I will answer; and while they are yet speaking, I will hear."[33]

Daniel was reminded by the heavenly messenger: "thou art greatly beloved." "The LORD hath appeared of old unto me, saying, Yea, I have loved thee with an everlasting love: therefore with lovingkindness have I drawn thee."[34] The whole universe was riveted on the message about to be invested with Daniel. No greater revelation had ever been entrusted to mortals.

Gabriel himself states his commission to make Daniel understand the matter, and instructs Daniel to consider the vision. Gabriel focuses Daniel's attention on the vision of "evenings and the mornings." Daniel had been so overwhelmed by the 2,300 years of Daniel 8:14 that he fainted before the angel could fulfill his commission to make Daniel understand the vision. Gabriel now declares that he has come to give him understanding of that vision.

This is also made clear by the Hebrew words Daniel uses to speak of the vision. In Daniel 8 when speaking of the vision in general, Daniel

---

[32] Daniel 8:16

[33] Isaiah 65:24

[34] Jeremiah 31:3

uses the Hebrew word חזון châzôn.[35] But when Daniel gets to the part
of the vision that speaks of the 2,300 days, he changes the word for
"vision" from חזון châzôn to the Hebrew word מראה mar'eh.[36]
At the end of the vision of Daniel 8, Daniel says that he "was
astonished at the vision,"—מראה mar'eh—"but none understood it."[37]
The part of the vision that he did not understand was not the vision
as a whole—the חזון châzôn—but the part about the 2,300 days—the
מראה mar'eh.

Daniel 9 uses the same pattern. In verse 21 Daniel records: "whiles I
was speaking in prayer, even the man Gabriel, whom I had seen in
the vision at the beginning..."—vision, that is חזון châzôn, the general
part of the vision of Daniel 8. But in verse 23 when Gabriel said,
"therefore understand the matter, and consider the vision,"[38]
consider, not the חזון châzôn, but the מראה mar'eh or that part which
you did not understand—the 2,300 days.

Most teachers understand that when they want to explain something
that is very complicated to their students, it is best to give their
students a preview of the big picture. Then the instructor breaks
things down into individual parts, explaining piece by piece until the
students understand how the pieces fit in the whole. This is exactly
what the angel does for Daniel. Having already given Daniel a
preview of the whole, in chapter eight, and having directed Daniel's
attention to what he has already revealed, Gabriel begins breaking
down the larger time period into more understandable parts,
explaining them one piece at a time.

*Daniel 9:24 Seventy weeks are determined upon thy people and
upon thy holy city, to finish the transgression, and to make an
end of sins, and to make reconciliation for iniquity, and to bring
in everlasting righteousness, and to seal up the vision and
prophecy, and to anoint the most Holy.*

Gabriel begins to interpret the 2,300 years of Daniel 8:14 by
explaining its first segment, **"seventy weeks are determined."**

[35] See Daniel 8:1-2, 13, 15, 17, 26b.

[36] See Daniel 8:16, 26a, 27.

[37] Daniel 8:27

[38] Daniel 9:23

Determined—חָתַךְ châthak—can also be translated "cut off." Seventy weeks are cut off from the 2,300 years for the probation of Daniel's people, the Jewish nation, and the city of Jerusalem. During this time period several things would be accomplished: finish the transgression, make an end of sin, make reconciliation for iniquity, bring in everlasting righteousness, seal up the vision and the prophecy, and to anoint the most Holy.

Since there are seven days in a week, seventy weeks would be seventy times seven which is 490 days.[39] Applying the same prophetic principle which has been used in Daniel 7 and 8, where a day stands for a year,[40] seventy prophetic weeks represents 490 literal years. Gabriel declared that 490 years were cut off, or set aside from the 2,300 years for the Jewish nation, during which period God would accomplish six things.

1. "To finish the transgression"
Isaiah prophesied of the coming Messiah:
Isaiah 53:1 Who hath believed our report? and to whom is the arm of the LORD revealed?
53:2 For he shall grow up before him as a tender plant, and as a root out of a dry ground: he hath no form nor comeliness; and when we shall see him, there is no beauty that we should desire him.
53:3 He is despised and rejected of men; a man of sorrows, and acquainted with grief: and we hid as it were our faces from him; he was despised, and we esteemed him not.
53:4 Surely he hath borne our griefs, and carried our sorrows: yet we did esteem him stricken, smitten of God, and afflicted.
53:5 But **he was wounded for our transgressions**, **he was bruised for our iniquities**: the chastisement of our peace was upon him; and **with his stripes we are healed**.
53:6 All we like sheep have gone astray; we have turned every one to his own way; and **the LORD hath laid on him the iniquity of us all**.
53:7 He was oppressed, and he was afflicted, yet he opened not his mouth: **he is brought as a lamb to the slaughter**, and as a sheep before her shearers is dumb, so he openeth not his mouth.

---

[39] Jesus alludes to this time period when Peter asked him "Lord, how oft shall my brother sin against me, and I forgive him? till seven times? Jesus saith unto him, I say not unto thee, Until seven times: but, Until seventy times seven." Matthew 18:21-22

[40] See Numbers 14:34; Ezekiel 4:6.

53:8 He was taken from prison and from judgment: and who shall declare his generation? for he was cut off out of the land of the living: **for the transgression of my people was he stricken**.

53:9 And he made his grave with the wicked, and with the rich in his death; because he had done no violence, neither was any deceit in his mouth.

53:10 Yet it pleased the LORD to bruise him; he hath put him to grief: when thou shalt make his soul an offering for sin, he shall see his seed, he shall prolong his days, and the pleasure of the LORD shall prosper in his hand.

53:11 He shall see of the travail of his soul, and shall be satisfied: by his knowledge shall my righteous servant justify many; for **he shall bear their iniquities**.

53:12 Therefore will I divide him a portion with the great, and he shall divide the spoil with the strong; because he hath poured out his soul unto death: and he was numbered with the transgressors; and **he bare the sin of many, and made intercession for the transgressors**.

2. "**To make an end of sin**"

"In that day there shall be a fountain opened to the house of David and to the inhabitants of Jerusalem for sin and for uncleanness."[41] "Who is a God like unto thee, that pardoneth iniquity, and passeth by the transgression of the remnant of his heritage? he retaineth not his anger for ever, because he delighteth in mercy. He will turn again, he will have compassion upon us; **he will subdue our iniquities**; and thou wilt cast all their sins into the depths of the sea."[42]

Of the Messiah it is written, "thou shalt call his name JESUS: for he shall save his people from their sins."[43] "And ye know that he was manifested to take away our sins; and in him is no sin."[44] "Grace be to you and peace from God the Father, and from our Lord Jesus Christ, Who gave himself for our sins, that he might deliver us from this present evil world, according to the will of God and our Father:

---

[41] Zechariah 13:1

[42] Micah 7:18-19

[43] Matthew 1:21

[44] 1 John 3:5

To whom be glory for ever and ever. Amen."[45] Christ was made "to be sin for us, who knew no sin; that we might be made the righteousness of God in him."[46] Therefore, when John the Baptist saw Jesus he cried, "Behold the Lamb of God, which **taketh away the sin of the world.**"[47]

3. "To make reconciliation for iniquity"

"But God commendeth his love toward us, in that, while we were yet sinners, Christ died for us. Much more then, being now justified by his blood, we shall be saved from wrath through him. For **if, when we were enemies, we were reconciled to God** by the death of his Son, **much more, being reconciled, we shall be saved by his life.**"[48] According to this Scripture, Christ reconciled the entire world to himself, while we were yet his enemies. Therefore, God has already reconciled, by his death, those that are still his enemies. This was accomplished for the whole world for verse 19 says, "that God was in Christ, **reconciling the world** unto himself, **not imputing their trespasses** unto them..."[49] He "gave himself for our sins;"[50] he paid for the sins of the whole world, with his life, while we were his enemies. The sacrifice of Jesus paid the penalty of your sins before you even knew who he was. This means that whether you are an atheist, agnostic, New Ager, or hippie, a Buddhist, Hindu, Jew, Muslim, Catholic, or Christian, a man, woman, or child, Christ accomplished something for you, whether you like it, know it, believe it, accept it, or not. This is because "as by the offence of one {Adam} judgment came upon all men to condemnation; even so by the righteousness of one {Jesus Christ} the free gift came upon **all men** unto justification of life;"[51]

There are two aspects of justification. The first—justification of life— was gifted to all men without their choice, placing them in a reconciled relationship with God in which he does not impute their

---

[45] Galatians 1:3-5

[46] 2 Corinthians 5:21

[47] John 1:29

[48] Romans 5:8-10

[49] 2 Corinthians 5:19

[50] Galatians 1:4

[51] Romans 5:18

sins unto them. Justification of life offers a second chance—an opportunity to choose the sovereignty of God for oneself rather than the dominion of Satan; a choice which would be otherwise impossible because of the inheritance from Adam of a sinful nature which naturally gravitates to sin. This is the reason why the wicked have not yet been sentenced to death, which is the "wages of sin."[52] Justification of life was provided by Christ's death.

The second aspect of justification is justification by faith, which comes only to those who believe in the atoning sacrifice of his death, and accept, by faith, his righteous life in place of their life of iniquity. "For if, when we were enemies, we were reconciled to God by the death of his Son, much more, being reconciled, we shall be saved by his life."[53] If the sinner refuses to accept the gracious and infinite provision offered, their sins will eventually be imputed back to them, "and they were judged every man according to their works."[54]

4. "To bring in everlasting righteousness"
The Scriptures declare that God's "righteousness is an everlasting righteousness..."[55] "The righteousness of thy testimonies is everlasting: give me understanding, and I shall live."[56]

Zechariah saw in vision "Joshua the high priest standing before the angel of the LORD, and Satan standing at his right hand to resist him. And the LORD said unto Satan, The LORD rebuke thee, O Satan; even the LORD that hath chosen Jerusalem rebuke thee: is not this a brand plucked out of the fire? Now Joshua was clothed with filthy garments, and stood before the angel. And he answered and spake unto those that stood before him, saying, Take away the filthy garments from him. And unto him he said, Behold, I have caused thine iniquity to pass from thee, and I will clothe thee with change of raiment."[57]

---

[52] Romans 6:23 For the wages of sin is death; but the gift of God is eternal life through Jesus Christ our Lord."

[53] Romans 5:10

[54] Revelation 20:13

[55] Psalm 119:142

[56] Psalm 119:144

[57] Zechariah 3:1-4

After Jesus takes away our sin he then clothes us with his righteousness. Then we "will greatly rejoice in the LORD" because he has clothed us "with the garments of salvation" and covered us "with the robe of righteousness."[58] "My righteousness is near; my salvation is gone forth, and mine arms shall judge the people; the isles shall wait upon me, and on mine arm shall they trust. Lift up your eyes to the heavens, and look upon the earth beneath: for the heavens shall vanish away like smoke, and the earth shall wax old like a garment, and they that dwell therein shall die in like manner: but my salvation shall be for ever, and my righteousness shall not be abolished. Hearken unto me, ye that know righteousness, the people in whose heart is my law; fear ye not the reproach of men, neither be ye afraid of their revilings. For the moth shall eat them up like a garment, and the worm shall eat them like wool: but my righteousness shall be for ever, and my salvation from generation to generation."[59]

5. "To seal up the vision and the prophecy"

The word here in the Hebrew for "seal up" is חתם châtham, and is used only four times in the book of Daniel: twice in this verse ("make an end" and "seal up"), and twice in Daniel 12 when Daniel is told to seal up the book.[60]

If Christ had not come at the time specified in this prophecy, the whole book of Daniel would be a fraud. Even if Christ had come, yet failed in one point of making a perfect righteousness or dying a perfect death, the rest of the prophecies in the book of Daniel would be of no use; the prophecies of Daniel could not have been unsealed in the future.[61] Christ came and prevailed over the prince of darkness, and that fact, sealed up the vision and prophecy. The death of Christ, nearly five centuries from the beginning of the 2,300 years, was the seal of authenticity of the events to occur at its close.

---

[58] Isaiah 61:10

[59] Isaiah 51:5-8

[60] Daniel 12:4, 9 "But thou, O Daniel, shut up the words, and **seal** the book, even to the time of the end.... And he said, Go thy way, Daniel: for the words are closed up and **sealed** till the time of the end."

[61] The unsealing of the book of Daniel is unveiled in Revelation.

6. "To anoint the most Holy"

"According to the prophecy, this period was to reach to the Messiah, the Anointed One... Jesus at His baptism received the anointing of the Holy Spirit and soon afterward began His ministry. Then the message was proclaimed, 'The time is fulfilled.'"[62]

When does the seventy-week time period begin?

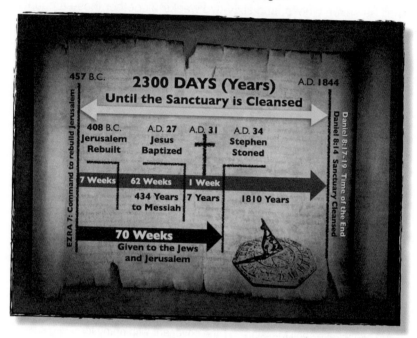

---

[62] E. G. White, *The Desire of Ages* (1898), p. 233.1.

Daniel 9:25 Know therefore and understand, that from the going forth of the commandment to restore and to build Jerusalem unto the Messiah the Prince shall be seven weeks, and threescore and two weeks: the street shall be built again, and the wall, even in troublous times.

From the command to restore and rebuild Jerusalem to the Messiah shall be seven weeks, and sixty-two weeks. Together these amount to sixty-nine of the seventy weeks. Gabriel divided them to show that something occurs during the seven weeks, after which there are sixty-two more weeks unto Messiah the Prince.

These verses are arranged in the literary structure of a Hebrew parallelism. This parallel structure looks like this for these verses:

PARALLEL NATURE OF DANIEL 9:25-27	
1ST HALF	2ND HALF
Daniel 9:25 "from the going forth of the commandment…unto the Messiah the Prince shall be seven weeks, and threescore and two weeks:"	
Daniel 9:25 "seven weeks…"	Daniel 9:25 "the street shall be built again, and the wall, even in troublous times."
Daniel 9:26 "after threescore and two weeks shall Messiah be cut off, but not for himself…"	Daniel 9:27 "he shall confirm the covenant with many for one week: and in the midst of the week he shall cause the sacrifice and the oblation to cease…"
Daniel 9:26 "and the people of the prince that shall come shall destroy the city and the sanctuary; and the end thereof shall be with a flood, and unto the end of the war desolations are determined."	Daniel 9:27 "and for the overspreading of abominations he shall make it desolate, even until the consummation, and that determined shall be poured upon the desolate."

Therefore, the seven weeks refers to the restoration of Jerusalem and the sixty-two weeks apply to the coming of the Messiah.

"In the seventh chapter of Ezra the decree is found. Verses 12-26. In its completest form it was issued by Artaxerxes, king of Persia, 457 B.C. But in Ezra 6:14 the house of the Lord at Jerusalem is said to have been built 'according to the commandment 'decree,' [margin] of Cyrus, and Darius, and Artaxerxes king of Persia.' These three kings, in originating, reaffirming, and completing the decree, brought it to the perfection required by the prophecy to mark the beginning of the 2,300 years. Taking 457 B.C., the time when the decree was completed, as the date of the commandment, every specification of the prophecy concerning the seventy weeks was seen to have been fulfilled."[63] The final command to restore and build Jerusalem, given by Artaxerxes Longimanus, satisfied every specification foretold. The earlier commands gave provision for the rebuilding of the temple, but lacked the command of restoration of the street and the wall. Exactly as the Bible prophesied, from the command to restore and rebuild Jerusalem in the autumn of 457 B.C., seven weeks or 49 years were required for the completion of the street and the wall in 408 B.C.

After the seven weeks there would be sixty-two weeks, representing 434 years, unto Messiah the Prince. Adding 434 years to 408 B.C. brings us to the autumn of A.D. 27, when the Messiah would be anointed to public ministry. The word "Messiah" means "anointed one." Just as prophesied, at the baptism of Christ by John in A.D. 27, "God **anointed** Jesus of Nazareth with the Holy Ghost and with power"[64] for his earthly ministry. Jesus said of himself, "The Spirit of the Lord is upon me, because **he hath anointed me** to preach the gospel to the poor; he hath sent me to heal the brokenhearted, to preach deliverance to the captives, and recovering of sight to the blind, to set at liberty them that are bruised, To preach the **acceptable year of the Lord.**"[65] Jesus began his public ministry on earth "preaching the gospel of the kingdom of God, And saying, **The time is fulfilled**, and the kingdom of God is at hand: repent ye, and believe the gospel."[66] Six centuries after this prophecy was given it was fulfilled exactly as predicted, providing the ultimate evidence that

---

[63] E. G. White, *The Great Controversy*, (1911), p. 326.3.

[64] Acts 10:38

[65] Luke 4:18-19

[66] Mark 1:14-15

Jesus Christ was who he claimed to be—the Son of God, the Lord of heaven.

Not only was Christ to be Messiah, but also "**the Prince**." After the outpouring of the Holy Spirit, when the disciples were asked why they were preaching Christ, they answered and said, "The God of our fathers raised up Jesus, whom ye slew and hanged on a tree. Him hath God exalted with his right hand to be a Prince and a Saviour, for to give repentance to Israel, and forgiveness of sins."[67]

Daniel 9:26 And after threescore and two weeks shall Messiah be cut off, but not for himself: and the people of the prince that shall come shall destroy the city and the sanctuary; and the end thereof shall be with a flood, and unto the end of the war desolations are determined.

Messiah was to be cut off sometime after his anointing at the end of the sixty-two weeks. Isaiah prophesied concerning him, "But he was wounded for our transgressions, he was bruised for our iniquities: the chastisement of our peace was upon him; and with his stripes we are healed... and the LORD hath laid on him the iniquity of us all.... He was taken from prison and from judgment: and who shall declare his generation? for **he was cut off** out of the land of the living: for the transgression of my people was he stricken."[68] Messiah would die, not for himself, but for "the transgression of my people."

Prophecies from the Mikra[69] were fulfilled one after another as Jesus was taken to the cross: "The kings of the earth set themselves, and the rulers take counsel together, against the LORD, and against his anointed." Psalm 2:2[70]; "Yea, mine own familiar friend, in whom I trusted, which did eat of my bread, hath lifted up his heel against me." Psalm 41:9[71]; "And the LORD said unto me, Cast it unto the potter: a goodly price that I was prised at of them. And I took the thirty pieces of silver, and cast them to the potter in the house of the

---

[67] Acts 5:29-31

[68] Isaiah 53:5-8

[69] The Mikra is also called the Tanakh, which is the Old Testament.

[70] Fulfillment: Matthew 26:59, Acts 4:27-31.

[71] Fulfillment: John 13:26.

LORD." Zechariah 11:13[72]; "He was oppressed, and he was afflicted, yet he opened not his mouth: he is brought as a lamb to the slaughter, and as a sheep before her shearers is dumb, so he openeth not his mouth." Isaiah 53:7[73]; "I gave my back to the smiters, and my cheeks to them that plucked off the hair: I hid not my face from shame and spitting." Isaiah 50:6[74]; "For dogs have compassed me: the assembly of the wicked have enclosed me: they pierced my hands and my feet. I may tell all my bones: they look and stare upon me. They part my garments among them, and cast lots upon my vesture." Psalm 22:16-18[75]; "And one shall say unto him, What are these wounds in thine hands? Then he shall answer, Those with which I was wounded in the house of my friends." Zechariah 13:6[76]; "They gave me also gall for my meat; and in my thirst they gave me vinegar to drink." Psalm 69:21[77]; "And I will pour upon the house of David, and upon the inhabitants of Jerusalem, the spirit of grace and of supplications: and they shall look upon me whom they have pierced..." Zechariah 12:10.[78]

Peter, speaking to the Jews after Pentecost said, "Therefore let all the house of Israel know assuredly, that God hath made that same Jesus, whom ye have crucified, both Lord and Christ."[79]

The prophecy specifies that after the Messiah was cut off **"the people of the prince that shall come shall destroy the city and the sanctuary...."**[80] "Rejoice greatly, O daughter of Zion; shout, O daughter of Jerusalem: behold, thy King cometh unto thee: he is just, and having salvation; lowly, and riding upon an ass, and upon a colt the foal of an ass." Zechariah 9:9. One of the last times Christ viewed the temple before he was crucified, as he stood on the Mount of Olives, "he wept in agonizing sobs, his form swayed as a tree

---

[72] Fulfillment: Matthew 27:3-8.

[73] Fulfillment: Matthew 27:12

[74] Fulfillment: Matthew 27:26, 26:65-68.

[75] Fulfillment: John 20:24-28, John 19:23-24.

[76] Fulfillment: Acts 2:22-24.

[77] Fulfillment: Matthew 27:34.

[78] Fulfillment: John 19:34.

[79] Acts 2:36

[80] This is covered in more detail in verse 27.

before the tempest... He saw the retribution that would fall upon Jerusalem, and exclaimed: 'O Jerusalem, Jerusalem, thou that killest the prophets, and stonest them which are sent unto thee, how often would I have gathered thy children together, even as a hen gathereth her chickens under her wings, and ye would not! Behold, your house is left unto you desolate....'

"Jesus hears the tramp of the besieging army. He sees the temple in ruins. He sees famine and distress in the city. His prophetic eye sees Calvary, the hill upon which he shall be lifted up, planted with crosses as thick as the forest trees. He sees the very ones nailed thereon who clamored for his condemnation, and who cried out under their Satanic delusion, "His blood be on us and on our children." The retribution that has fallen upon them is most terrible; for they are left to the mercy of the leader they have chosen, and Satan and his confederacy of evil angels wreak their spite upon the human family.

"All this Jesus sees as the result of their refusal to accept his offers of mercy. Thus they have worked their own present and eternal ruin, and as a nation divorced themselves from God."[81]

So far, the angel has explained 69 weeks or 483 years. But there were a total of 70 weeks or 490 years in this portion, cut off from the 2,300 years. One week remains.

Daniel 9:27 And he shall confirm the covenant with many for one week: and in the midst of the week he shall cause the sacrifice and the oblation to cease, and for the overspreading of abominations he shall make it desolate, even until the consummation, and that determined shall be poured upon the desolate.

"**And he shall confirm**," is referring to the Messiah, from the previous verse, who would "be cut off, but not for himself." Jesus, the prince of life, would "**confirm the covenant**," for the last of the seventy weeks. "For Moses truly said unto the fathers, A prophet shall the Lord your God raise up unto you of your brethren, like unto me... Ye are the children of the prophets, and of **the covenant which God made with our fathers**, saying unto Abraham, And **in thy seed shall all the kindreds of the earth be blessed**. Unto you

---

[81] E. G. White, *The Signs of the Times*, February 27, 1896 par. 10-13.

first **God, having raised up his Son Jesus, sent him to bless you, in turning away every one of you from his iniquities.**[82] The blessing of the covenant promise was that the Messiah would turn away every one who would from his sins.

"**One week**" is seven days, with each day representing one year,[83] for a total of seven years. "**The midst of the week**," is the middle of seven, or three and a half years. Exactly as predicted more than five centuries earlier, the Messiah confirmed the covenant by dying on a cross three and a half years into the seventieth week. On the very day the Passover lamb was slain,[84] in the spring of A.D. 31, the death of Christ caused the "**sacrifice and oblation to cease**." Despite the denial of the priests and rulers of Jesus as the Messiah, the sacrifices were suspended indefinitely. "When the loud cry, 'It is finished,' came from the lips of Christ, the priests were officiating in the temple. It was the hour of the evening sacrifice. The lamb representing Christ had been brought to be slain. Clothed in his significant and beautiful dress, the priest stood with lifted knife, as did Abraham when he was about to slay his son. With intense interest the people were looking on. But the earth trembled and quaked; for the Father himself drew near. With a rending noise the inner veil of the temple is torn from top to bottom by an unseen hand, throwing open to the gaze of the multitude a place once filled with the presence of God. In this place the Shekinah had dwelt. Here God had manifested His glory above the mercy seat. No one but the high priest ever lifted the veil separating this apartment from the rest of the temple. He entered in once a year to make an atonement for the sins of the people. But lo, this veil is rent in twain. The most holy place of the earthly sanctuary is no longer sacred.

"All is terror and confusion. The priest is about to slay the victim; but the knife drops from his nerveless hand, and the lamb escapes. Type has met antitype in the death of God's Son. The great sacrifice has been made. The way into the holiest is laid open. A new and living way is prepared for all. No longer need sinful, sorrowing humanity await the coming of the high priest. Henceforth the Saviour was to officiate as priest and advocate in the heaven of heavens. It was as if a living voice had spoken to the worshipers: There is now an end to all sacrifices and offerings for sin. The Son of God is come according

---

[82] Acts 3:22-26

[83] Ezekiel 4:6; Numbers 14:34

[84] 1 Corinthians 5:7

to His word, 'Lo, I come (in the volume of the Book it is written of Me,) to do Thy will, O God.' 'By His own blood' He entereth 'in once into the holy place, having obtained eternal redemption for us.' Hebrews 10:7; 9:12."[85]

The Messiah was to confirm the covenant for one week, or seven years. Christ's public ministry lasted only three and a half years, from his baptism in the fall of A.D. 27 to his crucifixion in the spring of A.D. 31, in the midst of the seventieth week. Even though the Jewish nation rejected the messiah, Jesus confirmed the last half of the week by sending his eye-witness disciples only to the Jews for three and a half years, from the spring of A.D. 31 to the fall of A.D. 34[86] "Jesus...commanded them, saying, Go not into the way of the Gentiles, and into any city of the Samaritans enter ye not: But go rather to the lost sheep of the house of Israel."[87]

In the year A.D. 34[88] Stephen was stoned by the Jewish Sanhedrin,[89] with Saul participating in his death. This signaled the complete rejection of the Messiah by the Jewish nation, both in person, and in the form of his disciples. The kingdom of God was taken from them and given to a nation bringing forth fruit.[90] Shortly after this, Saul travelled to Damascus to persecute the Christian's and met the risen Jesus on the road. This dramatic experience led to his conversion, a name change to Paul, and a new destiny to become the Apostle to the Gentiles. The Jewish nation sealed their probation. "The seventy weeks, or 490 years, especially allotted to the Jews, ended, as we have seen, in A.D. 34. At that time, through the action of the Jewish Sanhedrin, the nation sealed its rejection of the gospel by the martyrdom of Stephen and the persecution of the followers of Christ.

---

[85] E. G. White, *The Desire of Ages* (1898), p. 756.5-757.1.

[86] Therefore, from the command to restore and rebuild Jerusalem in the fall of 457 B.C. to the fall of A.D. 34 was exactly 490 years, or seventy prophetic weeks.

[87] Matthew 10:5-6

[88] While at Corinth, Paul stood before Gallio for the gospel of Christ. From an inscription at Corinth, we know that Gallio's one-year proconsulship occurred in A.D. 51. Paul's conversion was just after the stoning of Stephen in A.D. 34. After his conversion, Paul did not go to Jerusalem for three years (Galatians 1:18). Subsequently, his second visit to Jerusalem was fourteen years later (Galatians 2:1). Thus, seventeen years before Paul's trial before Gallio in A.D. 51 brings us to the year of the stoning of Stephan is A.D. 34. Therefore, archeology confirms the validity of the seventy-week prophecy of Daniel.

[89] See E. G. White, *The Acts of the Apostles* (1911), p. 99.1-101.1.

[90] Matthew 21:43

Then the message of salvation, no longer restricted to the chosen people, was given to the world. The disciples, forced by persecution to flee from Jerusalem, 'went everywhere preaching the word.' 'Philip went down to the city of Samaria, and preached Christ unto them.' Peter, divinely guided, opened the gospel to the centurion of Caesarea, the God-fearing Cornelius; and the ardent Paul, won to the faith of Christ, was commissioned to carry the glad tidings 'far hence unto the Gentiles.' Acts 8:4, 5; 22:21."

"When Caiaphas rent his garment, his act was significant of the place that the Jewish nation as a nation would thereafter occupy toward God. The once favored people of God were separating themselves from Him, and were fast becoming a people disowned by Jehovah. When Christ upon the cross cried out, 'It is finished' (John 19:30), and the veil of the temple was rent in twain, the Holy Watcher declared that the Jewish people had rejected Him who was the antitype of all their types, the substance of all their shadows. Israel was divorced from God. Well might Caiaphas then rend his official robes, which signified that he claimed to be a representative of the great High Priest; for no longer had they any meaning for him or for the people. Well might the high priest rend his robes in horror for himself and for the nation."[91]

The rejection of Christ and his disciples sealed the fate of the chosen city and nation. Even though the probation of the nation was sealed, mercy still lingered. For nearly forty years the terrible sentence of doom to fall on Jerusalem and Judea was delayed.

Finally, in A.D. 66, the tread of the Roman armies, under the command of Cestius, was heard. "**The overspreading of abominations**" was about to "**make it desolate**." Even then, a way of escape was provided for those who would obey the words of Christ, "When ye therefore shall see the abomination of desolation,[92] spoken of by Daniel the prophet, stand in the holy place, (whoso readeth, let him understand:) Then let them which be in Judaea flee into the mountains: Let him which is on the housetop not come down to take any thing out of his house: Neither let him which is in the field return back to take his clothes. And woe unto them that are with

---

[91] E. G. White, *The Desire of Ages* (1898), p. 709.4.

[92] Luke states, in his parallel passage, "And when ye shall see Jerusalem compassed with armies, then know that the desolation thereof is nigh." Luke 21:20

child, and to them that give suck in those days! But pray ye that your flight be not in the winter, neither on the sabbath day."[93]

"When the idolatrous standards of the Romans should be set up in the holy ground, which extended some furlongs outside the city walls, then the followers of Christ were to find safety in flight. When the warning sign should be seen, those who would escape must make no delay."[94]

"Not one Christian perished in the destruction of Jerusalem. Christ had given His disciples warning, and all who believed His words watched for the promised sign. 'When ye shall see Jerusalem compassed with armies,' said Jesus, 'then know that the desolation thereof is nigh. Then let them which are in Judea flee to the mountains; and let them which are in the midst of it depart out.' Luke 21:20, 21. After the Romans under Cestius had surrounded the city, they unexpectedly abandoned the siege when everything seemed favorable for an immediate attack. The besieged, despairing of successful resistance, were on the point of surrender, when the Roman general withdrew his forces without the least apparent reason. But God's merciful providence was directing events for the good of His own people. The promised sign had been given to the waiting Christians, and now an opportunity was offered for all who would, to obey the Saviour's warning. Events were so overruled that neither Jews nor Romans should hinder the flight of the Christians. Upon the retreat of Cestius, the Jews, sallying from Jerusalem, pursued after his retiring army; and while both forces were thus fully engaged, the Christians had an opportunity to leave the city. At this time the country also had been cleared of enemies who might have endeavored to intercept them. At the time of the siege, the Jews were assembled at Jerusalem to keep the Feast of Tabernacles, and thus the Christians throughout the land were able to make their escape unmolested. Without delay they fled to a place of safety—the city of Pella, in the land of Perea, beyond Jordan."[95]

The reason for the urgency for the Christians to leave immediately on the withdrawal of the first siege, was that if they had been

---

[93] Matthew 24:15-20

[94] E.G. White, *The Great Controversy* (1911), p. 25.4.

[95] E.G. White, *The Great Controversy* (1911), p. 30.2.

discovered escaping by the returning triumphant Jewish army, they would have been executed as traitors. The final destruction of Jerusalem did not occur for three and a half more years, in A.D. 70, when the Roman armies returned under the command of Titus.

THE 2,300 YEAR PROPHECY OF DANIEL 8:14:

Gabriel's revelation to Daniel of the seventy-week period, or 490 years, was all that was needed to understand the 2,300 years of Daniel 8:14, for it provided the start date for the entire period. Therefore, "from the going forth of the commandment to restore and to build Jerusalem," unto the commencement of the cleansing of the heavenly sanctuary[96] would be 2,300 years. The death of Christ in A.D. 31 sealed up the vision; therefore, it not only confirmed the validity of the 457 B.C. command to restore both the city ("the street... and the wall"[97]) and the temple, as the commencement of the prophetic period; but also verified with absolute certainty the termination of the 2,300 years reaching to A.D. 1844.[98]

"According to Scripture, Jesus began the process of cleansing the heavenly sanctuary in 1844. He wanted us to understand the reason for the seeming delay of his return, and know what he was accomplishing on our behalf that we might follow him by faith into the most holy place. 'Let us therefore come boldly unto the throne of grace, that we may obtain mercy, and find grace to help in time of need.'[99]

"Not only do the symbols of the sanctuary services point to Jesus, they also point to the truths of the process of salvation that are the steps to Christ, still today.

"When one of the Israelites committed a sin, they were to bring a lamb without blemish from their flock. This first step in the plan of

---

[96] See comments for Daniel 8:14.

[97] Daniel 9:25

[98] Note that when calculating dates across the B.C./A.D. transition, numbers on the B.C. side (the left of the number line) are negative numbers (457 B.C. being denoted as -457). Therefore, adding -457 + 2,300 is the same as: 2,300 - 457 = 1,843.
Since the B.C./A.D number line has no zero year (unlike a standard number line, A.D. 1 immediately follows 1 B.C.), one year must be added to the resulting number. The formula would then be: 2,300 - 457 = 1,843 +1 = A.D. 1844

[99] Hebrews 4:16

salvation was an admission of guilt and an acknowledgment of the need of a savior, which was to be found only in the 'Lamb of God which taketh away the sin of the world.'[100]

"That lamb was brought to the door of the tabernacle, which represents Jesus. To Jesus we must come even to plead the merits of his sacrifice.

"The sinner, in repentance, was then to confess his sin on the head of the lamb and with his own hand take its life. This was to impress on the mind of the sinner the terrible nature of sin, and that it was his own sin that took the innocent life of the Savior. The lamb was then burnt on the altar of burnt offering demonstrating that the sin was consumed and cleansed by the sacrifice of Christ. Yet, some of the blood of that lamb was taken by the priest (which represents Christ) into the holy place (heaven itself) and sprinkled on the veil between the holy and most holy places. This indicated that, though the sinner was justified, the record of their sin was not yet erased.

"Next, came the public consecration of baptism, where the priest (Jesus) having become sin for us[101] washes the stain of sin away by baptism. Baptism, symbolized by the laver, represents death to sin, burial of the old nature, and resurrection to new life. Jesus did this on our behalf, though he had no sin of his own, and asks us to follow his example.

"As we arise from the waters of baptism, a new creature, we are then to live in the very atmosphere of heaven. We enter, by faith, the holy place not made with hands. Here the spirit of Christ in the form of the Holy Spirit (the candlestick, oil, and light) guides us as we search the Scriptures (the bread of life, or showbread) and as we offer our prayers and petitions at the altar of incense where Christ's righteousness makes them acceptable before the throne of God.

"As we breath the atmosphere of heaven, God brings us into conformity to his character, of which his law is a transcript.[102] His power enables us to gain the victory and keep his holy law while the mercy seat shields us from its condemnation. At the second coming, we will see Jesus face to face with no veil between.[103]

---

[100] John 1:29

[101] 2 Corinthians 5:21

[102] E. G. White, *Christ's Object Lessons* (Nampa, ID: Pacific Press, 1900), p. 305.3.

[103] 1 Corinthians 13:12

"In 1844, Jesus, as our high priest entered the most holy place in the heavenly sanctuary to begin the final process of eradicating even the record of sin. As each name is brought for consideration, one of two things will occur, either the record of their sins will be forever erased, or their name will be erased from the book of life."[104]

Every sin committed in the congregation, through the year, was transferred symbolically to the most holy place. When the sinner confessed on the head of the lamb, he was then to kill the lamb with his own hands, indicating that it was his individual sin that caused the death of Jesus. The officiating priest—who also represented Christ—transferred the sin to the most holy by sprinkling some of the blood of each lamb on the veil between the holy and the most holy place. The sins accumulated in the most holy place for the whole year, until the day of the cleansing of the sanctuary—the day of atonement.

"The day of atonement, on the tenth day of the seventh month, was also called the day of judgment.[105] On the day of atonement (and only once a year on that day) lots would be cast for two goats, one the Lord's goat, and the other the scapegoat. Then the high priest would sacrifice the Lord's goat, taking the blood of the sacrifice into the most holy place to cleanse the sanctuary of sin. The sins were then transferred to the high priest who would take them out of the sanctuary and place them on the head of the scapegoat, then to be led by a fit man into the wilderness to die. Jesus is represented as our high priest, cleansing the heavenly sanctuary of all confessed sins, and placing the responsibility, and thus the punishment, for them on the head of Satan, who has tempted God's people to commit these sins. Those whose sins have not been confessed, and thus placed in the heavenly sanctuary to ultimately be blotted out forever, will themselves bear the penalty for their sins. This cleansing of the sanctuary demonstrates the grievous nature of our sins, even the record of which has contaminated the very throne room of the universe. This cleansing must occur before Jesus returns for his people. 'For Christ is not entered into the holy places made with hands, which are the figures of the true; but into heaven itself, now to appear in the presence of God for us: Nor yet that he should offer

---

[104] Martin Klein, *Thou Hast Magnified Thy Word Above All Thy Name* (2016), p. 254-256.

[105] Atonement and Trumpets were solemn holy days, or ceremonial sabbaths, in which no work was to be done. The others were all joyous festivals or feasts.

himself often, as the high priest entereth into the holy place every year with blood of others; For then must he often have suffered since the foundation of the world: but now once in the end of the world hath he appeared to put away sin by the sacrifice of himself. And as it is appointed unto men once to die, but after this the judgment: So Christ was once offered to bear the sins of many; and unto them that look for him shall he appear the second time without sin unto salvation.'[106]

"This investigative judgment, in the end of the world, prior to the second coming, is necessary since every case will have been decided, for when Jesus comes, his rewards are with him. 'And, behold, I come quickly; and my reward is with me, to give every man according as his work shall be.[107]'"[108]

As the prophetic period of the 2,300 years was drawing to a close, God began opening to the understanding of sincere students of prophecy the meaning of the prophecies of Daniel. Simultaneously around the world there was an awakening to these prophetic truths, and many began to proclaim them publicly. William Miller was the most prominent in America. "Endeavoring to lay aside all preconceived opinions, and dispensing with commentaries, he compared scripture with scripture by the aid of the marginal references and the concordance. He pursued his study in a regular and methodical manner; beginning with Genesis, and reading verse by verse, he proceeded no faster than the meaning of the several passages so unfolded as to leave him free from all embarrassment.

---

[106] Hebrews 9:24-28

[107] Revelation 22:12

[108] Martin Klein, *Thou Hast Magnified Thy Word Above All Thy Name* (2016), p. 250-251.

When he found anything obscure, it was his custom to compare it with every other text which seemed to have any reference to the matter under consideration. Every word was permitted to have its proper bearing upon the subject of the text, and if his view of it harmonized with every collateral passage, it ceased to be a difficulty. Thus whenever he met with a passage hard to be understood he found an explanation in some other portion of the Scriptures. As he studied with earnest prayer for divine enlightenment, that which had before appeared dark to his understanding was made clear. He experienced the truth of the psalmist's words: 'The entrance of Thy words giveth light; it giveth understanding unto the simple.' Psalm 119:130.

"With intense interest he studied the books of Daniel and the Revelation, employing the same principles of interpretation as in the other scriptures, and found, to his great joy, that the prophetic symbols could be understood. He saw that the prophecies, so far as they had been fulfilled, had been fulfilled literally; that all the various figures, metaphors, parables, similitudes, etc., were either explained in their immediate connection, or the terms in which they were expressed were defined in other scriptures, and when thus explained, were to be literally understood. 'I was thus satisfied,' he says, 'that the Bible is a system of revealed truths, so clearly and simply given that the wayfaring man, though a fool, need not err therein.'... Link after link of the chain of truth rewarded his efforts, as step by step he traced down the great lines of prophecy. Angels of heaven were guiding his mind and opening the Scriptures to his understanding."[109]

"Furthermore, all the signs of the times and the condition of the world corresponded to the prophetic description of the last days. He was forced to the conclusion, from the study of Scripture alone, that the period allotted for the continuance of the earth in its present state was about to close.

"'Another kind of evidence that vitally affected my mind,' he says, 'was the chronology of the Scriptures.... I found that predicted events, which had been fulfilled in the past, often occurred within a given time. The one hundred and twenty years to the flood (Genesis 6:3); the seven days that were to precede it, with forty days of predicted rain (Genesis 7:4); the four hundred years of the sojourn of Abraham's seed (Genesis 15:13); the three days of the butler's and

[109] E.G. White, *The Great Controversy* (1911), p. 320.1-302.2

baker's dreams (Genesis 40:12-20); the seven years of Pharaoh's (Genesis 41:28-54); the forty years in the wilderness (Numbers 14:34); the three and a half years of famine (1 Kings 17:1) [see Luke 4:25;]... the seventy years' captivity (Jeremiah 25:11); Nebuchadnezzar's seven times (Daniel 4:13-16); and the seven weeks, threescore and two weeks, and the one week, making seventy weeks, determined upon the Jews (Daniel 9:24-27),—the events limited by these times were all once only a matter of prophecy, and were fulfilled in accordance with the predictions.' "When, therefore, he found, in his study of the Bible, various chronological periods that, according to his understanding of them, extended to the second coming of Christ, he could not but regard them as the 'times before appointed,' which God had revealed unto His servants. 'The secret things,' says Moses, 'belong unto the Lord our God: but those things which are revealed belong unto us and to our children forever;' and the Lord declares by the prophet Amos, that He 'will do nothing, but He revealeth His secret unto His servants the prophets.'"[110]

"The prophecy which seemed most clearly to reveal the time of the second advent was that of Daniel 8:14: 'Unto two thousand and three hundred days; then shall the sanctuary be cleansed.' Following his rule of making Scripture its own interpreter, Miller learned that a day in symbolic prophecy represents a year (Numbers 14:34; Ezekiel 4:6); he saw that the period of 2,300 prophetic days, or literal years, would extend far beyond the close of the Jewish dispensation, hence it could not refer to the sanctuary of that dispensation. Miller accepted the generally received view that in the Christian age the earth is the sanctuary, and he therefore understood that the cleansing of the sanctuary foretold in Daniel 8:14 represented the purification of the earth by fire at the second coming of Christ."[111]

"He had devoted two years to the study of the Bible, when, in 1818, he reached the solemn conviction that in about twenty-five years Christ would appear for the redemption of His people. 'I need not speak,' says Miller, 'of the joy that filled my heart in view of the delightful prospect, nor of the ardent longings of my soul for a participation in the joys of the redeemed. The Bible was now to me a

---

[110] E.G. White, *The Great Controversy* (1911), p. 323.2.

[111] *Ibid.*, p. 324.3.

new book. It was indeed a feast of reason; all that was dark, mystical, or obscure to me in its teachings, had been dissipated from my mind before the clear light that now dawned from its sacred pages; and, oh, how bright and glorious the truth appeared! All the contradictions and inconsistencies I had before found in the word were gone; and although there were many portions of which I was not satisfied I had a full understanding, yet so much light had emanated from it to the illumination of my before darkened mind, that I felt a delight in studying the Scripture which I had not before supposed could be derived from its teachings.'"[112]

Dr. Joseph Wolff, a converted son of a Jewish Rabbi, began preaching in 1821, three years after Miller arrived at his conclusions, that Christ would come near the middle of the nineteenth century. Becoming known as the missionary to the world, Wolff travelled to Egypt, Abyssinia, Palestine, Syria, Persia, Bokhara, Yemen and India. He preached in the United States and even preached before all the members of Congress in the Congress Hall. Robert Winter preached the message in England. In South America, a Spanish Jesuit named Lacunza discovered the truths of the Bible, and published his conclusions of Christ's soon return under the pen-name Rabbi Ben-Israel, in the eighteenth century. His book made its way to England and being translated into English helped to stir interest in the prophecies of the soon coming of Jesus. In Germany a Lutheran minister named Bengel came to the conclusion that Jesus was to come on a date very near to the date that Miller preached. His writings spread through Christendom. Gaussen preached the message in Geneva. The same message was preached in Scandinavia. In America, William Miller was joined by prominent preachers such as Josiah Litch.

"In nearly every town there were scores, in some, hundreds, converted as a result of his preaching. In many places Protestant churches of nearly all denominations were thrown open to him, and the invitations to labor usually came from the ministers of the several congregations. It was his invariable rule not to labor in any place to which he had not been invited, yet he soon found himself unable to comply with half the requests that poured in upon him. Many who did not accept his views as to the exact time of the second advent were convinced of the certainty and nearness of Christ's coming and their

---

[112] E.G. White, *The Great Controversy* (1911), p. 329.2.

need of preparation. In some of the large cities his work produced a marked impression. Liquor dealers abandoned the traffic and turned their shops into meeting rooms; gambling dens were broken up; infidels, deists, Universalists, and even the most abandoned profligates were reformed, some of whom had not entered a house of worship for years. Prayer meetings were established by the various denominations, in different quarters, at almost every hour, businessmen assembling at midday for prayer and praise. There was no extravagant excitement, but an almost universal solemnity on the minds of the people. His work, like that of the early Reformers, tended rather to convince the understanding and arouse the conscience than merely to excite the emotions."[113]

"In 1833, two years after Miller began to present in public the evidences of Christ's soon coming, the last of the signs appeared which were promised by the Saviour as tokens of His second advent. Said Jesus: 'The stars shall fall from heaven.' Matthew 24:29.... This prophecy received a striking and impressive fulfillment in the great meteoric shower of November 13, 1833. That was the most extensive and wonderful display of falling stars which has ever been recorded."[114]

These events effected the greatest religious awakening the world had experienced since the days of the apostles. "Of all the great religious movements since the days of the apostles, none have been more free from human imperfection and the wiles of Satan than was that of the autumn of 1844. Even now, after the lapse of many years, all who shared in that movement and who have stood firm upon the platform of truth still feel the holy influence of that blessed work and bear witness that it was of God."[115]

"Like the first disciples, William Miller and his associates did not, themselves, fully comprehend the import of the message which they bore. Errors that had been long established in the church prevented them from arriving at a correct interpretation of an important point in the prophecy. Therefore, though they proclaimed the message which

---

[113] E.G. White, *The Great Controversy* (1911), p. 331.3.

[114] *Ibid.*, p. 333.1.

[115] *Ibid.*, p. 401.3.

God had committed to them to be given to the world, yet through a misapprehension of its meaning they suffered disappointment."[116]

"What despair and anguish wrung the hearts of those disciples during the days while their Lord was sleeping in the tomb!
"Christ had come at the exact time and in the manner foretold by prophecy. The testimony of Scripture had been fulfilled in every detail of His ministry. He had preached the message of salvation, and 'His word was with power.' The hearts of His hearers had witnessed that it was of Heaven. The word and the Spirit of God attested the divine commission of His Son."[117]

"The announcement which had been made by the disciples in the name of the Lord was in every particular correct, and the events to which it pointed were even then taking place. 'The time is fulfilled, the kingdom of God is at hand,' had been their message. At the expiration of 'the time'—the sixty-nine weeks of Daniel 9, which were to extend to the Messiah, 'the Anointed One'—Christ had received the anointing of the Spirit after His baptism by John in Jordan. And the 'kingdom of God' which they had declared to be at hand was established by the death of Christ. This kingdom was not, as they had been taught to believe, an earthly empire."[118] This misunderstanding caused the disciples a great disappointment when Jesus died, and this same misunderstanding caused the same great disappointment when Jesus entered the most holy place in heaven.

"With bated breath the Adventists, no less than fifty thousand and probably nearer one hundred thousand scattered largely across the northeastern portion of North America, arose to greet the eventful day, Tuesday, October 22, 1844.
"Some sought vantage points where they could peer into the clear heavens, hoping to catch a first glimpse of the coming of their returning Lord. When would Jesus come? The morning hours slowly passed and noon came, then mid-afternoon; finally darkness settled upon the earth. But it was still October 22, and it would be till midnight. At last that hour came, but Jesus did not come. The disappointment was almost beyond description. In later years some

---

[116] E.G. White, *The Great Controversy* (1911), p. 351.2.

[117] *Ibid.*, p. 346.1.

[118] *Ibid.*, p. 346.4.

wrote of the experience. Hiram Edson gave a vivid account of how they looked for the coming of the Lord "until the clock tolled twelve at midnight. Then our disappointment became a certainty." Of his experience in the depths of sorrow he wrote: "Our fondest hopes and expectations were blasted, and such a spirit of weeping came over us as I never experienced before. It seemed that the loss of all earthly friends could have been no comparison. We wept and wept, till the day dawn.

"I mused in my own heart, saying, 'My advent experience has been the richest and brightest of all my Christian experience. If this had proved a failure, what was the rest of my Christian experience worth? Has the Bible proved a failure? Is there no God, no heaven, no golden home city, no Paradise? Is all this but a cunningly devised fable? Is there no reality to our fondest hope and expectation of these things?' And thus we had something to grieve and weep over, if all our fondest hopes were lost. And as I said, we wept, till the day dawn."[119]

"The scripture which above all others had been both the foundation and the central pillar of the advent faith was the declaration: 'Unto two thousand and three hundred days; then shall the sanctuary be cleansed.' Daniel 8:14. These had been familiar words to all believers in the Lord's soon coming. By the lips of thousands was this prophecy repeated as the watchword of their faith. All felt that upon the events therein foretold depended their brightest expectations and most cherished hopes. These prophetic days had been shown to terminate in the autumn of 1844. In common with the rest of the Christian world, Adventists then held that the earth, or some portion of it, was the sanctuary. They understood that the cleansing of the sanctuary was the purification of the earth by the fires of the last great day, and that this would take place at the second advent. Hence the conclusion that Christ would return to the earth in 1844."[120]

"In their investigation they learned that there is no Scripture evidence sustaining the popular view that the earth is the sanctuary; but they found in the Bible a full explanation of the subject of the sanctuary, its nature, location, and services; the testimony of the sacred writers

---

[119] Arthur L. White, *Ellen G. White*: The Early Years, Vol. 1 p. 53.2-5.

[120] E. G. White, *The Great Controversy* (1911), p. 409.1.

being so clear and ample as to place the matter beyond all question. The apostle Paul, in the Epistle to the Hebrews, says: 'Then verily the first covenant had also ordinances of divine service, and a worldly sanctuary. For there was a tabernacle made; the first, wherein was the candlestick, and the table, and the shewbread; which is called the sanctuary. And after the second veil, the tabernacle which is called the holiest of all; which had the golden censer, and the ark of the covenant overlaid round about with gold, wherein was the golden pot that had manna, and Aaron's rod that budded, and the tables of the covenant; and over it the cherubims of glory shadowing the mercy seat.' Hebrews 9:1-5."[121]

"Thus those who were studying the subject found indisputable proof of the existence of a sanctuary in heaven. Moses made the earthly sanctuary after a pattern which was shown him. Paul teaches that that pattern was the true sanctuary which is in heaven. And John testifies that he saw it in heaven.

"In the temple in heaven, the dwelling place of God, His throne is established in righteousness and judgment. In the most holy place is His law, the great rule of right by which all mankind are tested. The ark that enshrines the tables of the law is covered with the mercy seat, before which Christ pleads His blood in the sinner's behalf. Thus is represented the union of justice and mercy in the plan of human redemption. This union infinite wisdom alone could devise and infinite power accomplish; it is a union that fills all heaven with wonder and adoration. The cherubim of the earthly sanctuary, looking reverently down upon the mercy seat, represent the interest with which the heavenly host contemplate the work of redemption. This is the mystery of mercy into which angels desire to look—that God can be just while He justifies the repenting sinner and renews His intercourse with the fallen race; that Christ could stoop to raise unnumbered multitudes from the abyss of ruin and clothe them with the spotless garments of His own righteousness to unite with angels who have never fallen and to dwell forever in the presence of God."[122]

---

[121] E. G. White, *The Great Controversy* (1911), p. 411.1.

[122] *Ibid.*, p. 415.1-2.

Their study led them to realize that the Scriptures themselves had foretold of their disappointment.[123] John the Revelator was given a vision of the book of Daniel open in the hand of a mighty angel, which John is told to eat. As John internalizes the message of the book of Daniel, it is sweet in his mouth and bitter in his belly. The messages of the prophetic periods of Daniel were indeed sweet in the mouth of the Advent believers, yet when it got to their belly it was a bitter disappointment. "And I took the little book out of the angel's hand, and ate it up; and it was in my mouth sweet as honey: and as soon as I had eaten it, my belly was bitter. And he said unto me, Thou must prophesy again before many peoples, and nations, and tongues, and kings. And there was given me a reed like unto a rod: and the angel stood, saying, Rise, and measure the temple of God, and the altar, and them that worship therein."[124] The answer to their disappointment was to be found in the temple of God.

"Clearer light came with the investigation of the sanctuary question. They now saw that they were correct in believing that the end of the 2,300 days in 1844 marked an important crisis. But while it was true that that door of hope and mercy by which men had for eighteen hundred years found access to God, was closed, another door was opened, and forgiveness of sins was offered to men through the intercession of Christ in the most holy. One part of His ministration had closed, only to give place to another. There was still an 'open door' to the heavenly sanctuary, where Christ was ministering in the sinner's behalf.

"Now was seen the application of those words of Christ in the Revelation, addressed to the church at this very time: 'These things saith He that is holy, He that is true, He that hath the key of David, He that openeth, and no man shutteth; and shutteth, and no man openeth; I know thy works: behold, I have set before thee an open door, and no man can shut it.' Revelation 3:7, 8.

"It is those who by faith follow Jesus in the great work of the atonement who receive the benefits of His mediation in their behalf, while those who reject the light which brings to view this work of ministration are not benefited thereby. The Jews who rejected the light given at Christ's first advent, and refused to believe on Him as the Saviour of the world, could not receive pardon through Him.

---

[123] See comments on Revelation 10.

[124] Revelation 10:10-11:1

When Jesus at His ascension entered by His own blood into the heavenly sanctuary to shed upon His disciples the blessings of His mediation, the Jews were left in total darkness to continue their useless sacrifices and offerings. The ministration of types and shadows had ceased. That door by which men had formerly found access to God was no longer open. The Jews had refused to seek Him in the only way whereby He could then be found, through the ministration in the sanctuary in heaven. Therefore they found no communion with God. To them the door was shut. They had no knowledge of Christ as the true sacrifice and the only mediator before God; hence they could not receive the benefits of His mediation.

"The condition of the unbelieving Jews illustrates the condition of the careless and unbelieving among professed Christians, who are willingly ignorant of the work of our merciful High Priest. In the typical service, when the high priest entered the most holy place, all Israel were required to gather about the sanctuary and in the most solemn manner humble their souls before God, that they might receive the pardon of their sins and not be cut off from the congregation. How much more essential in this antitypical Day of Atonement that we understand the work of our High Priest and know what duties are required of us.

"Men cannot with impunity reject the warning which God in mercy sends them. A message was sent from heaven to the world in Noah's day, and their salvation depended upon the manner in which they treated that message. Because they rejected the warning, the Spirit of God was withdrawn from the sinful race, and they perished in the waters of the Flood. In the time of Abraham, mercy ceased to plead with the guilty inhabitants of Sodom, and all but Lot with his wife and two daughters were consumed by the fire sent down from heaven. "So in the days of Christ. The Son of God declared to the unbelieving Jews of that generation: 'Your house is left unto you desolate.' Matthew 23:38. Looking down to the last days, the same Infinite Power declares, concerning those who 'received not the love of the truth, that they might be saved': 'For this cause God shall send them strong delusion, that they should believe a lie: that they all might be damned who believed not the truth, but had pleasure in unrighteousness.' 2 Thessalonians 2:10-12. As they reject the teachings of His word, God withdraws His Spirit and leaves them to the deceptions which they love.

"But Christ still intercedes in man's behalf, and light will be given to those who seek it. Though this was not at first understood by

Adventists, it was afterward made plain as the Scriptures which define their true position began to open before them.

"The passing of the time in 1844 was followed by a period of great trial to those who still held the advent faith. Their only relief, so far as ascertaining their true position was concerned, was the light which directed their minds to the sanctuary above. Some renounced their faith in their former reckoning of the prophetic periods and ascribed to human or satanic agencies the powerful influence of the Holy Spirit which had attended the advent movement. Another class firmly held that the Lord had led them in their past experience; and as they waited and watched and prayed to know the will of God they saw that their great High Priest had entered upon another work of ministration, and, following Him by faith, they were led to see also the closing work of the church. They had a clearer understanding of the first and second angels' messages, and were prepared to receive and give to the world the solemn warning of the third angel of Revelation 14."[125]

"Those who by faith followed their great High Priest as He entered upon His ministry in the most holy place, beheld the ark of His testament. As they had studied the subject of the sanctuary they had come to understand the Saviour's change of ministration, and they saw that He was now officiating before the ark of God, pleading His blood in behalf of sinners."[126]

---

[125] E. G. White, *The Great Controversy* (1911), p. 429.2-431.3.

[126] *Ibid.*, p. 433.1.

Daniel 10

SUMMARY:

Daniel 10 gives us an unusual glimpse into the realm of unseen realities. The angel Gabriel tells Daniel that his struggle against the prince of Persia was so great, that he was obliged to call for help from Michael the prince. Daniel also outlines some of the physical manifestations he experienced while being in vision, which serve as a springboard for identifying the Biblical marks of a true prophet. God assures us that at the end of time He will pour out His "spirit upon all flesh; and your sons and your daughters shall prophesy, your old men shall dream dreams, your young men shall see visions."[1] We are also admonished to "Despise not prophesyings,"[2] yet warned of false prophets.[3] Has God given the gift of the Spirit of Prophecy in these last days? How would one determine, from the Bible, the difference between the true and the false? Daniel 10 offers some amazing identifying marks of the true gift of prophecy. A true prophet, for example, does not breathe while in vision; a sign of the power of God that would be rather difficult to counterfeit.

Daniel 10:1 In the third year of Cyrus king of Persia a thing was revealed unto Daniel, whose name was called Belteshazzar; and the thing was true, but the time appointed was long: and he understood the thing, and had understanding of the vision.

Daniel 10 introduces another vision distinct from the vision of Daniel 7 or the visions of chapter eight and nine, which extends through Daniel 11 and 12—all three chapters comprising one continuous revelation.

The vision takes place in the third year of Cyrus, the king of Persia. Cyrus was the general who conquered Babylon, but his uncle, Darius the Mede, reigned as the first king of the empire. After a short reign of about two years Darius died and Cyrus succeeded to the throne.

---

[1] Joel 2:28

[2] 1 Thessalonians 5:10

[3] Matthew 7:15

Daniel 10:2 In those days I Daniel was mourning three full weeks.

Daniel 10:3 I ate no pleasant bread, neither came flesh nor wine in my mouth, neither did I anoint myself at all, till three whole weeks were fulfilled.

Daniel 10:4 And in the four and twentieth day of the first month, as I was by the side of the great river, which is Hiddekel;

Daniel 10:5 Then I lifted up mine eyes, and looked, and behold a certain man clothed in linen, whose loins were girded with fine gold of Uphaz:

Daniel 10:6 His body also was like the beryl, and his face as the appearance of lightning, and his eyes as lamps of fire, and his arms and his feet like in colour to polished brass, and the voice of his words like the voice of a multitude.

As with the vision of Daniel 9, Daniel is seeking God in prayer as the vision occurs.

The man clothed in linen and girded with the gold of Uphaz is Jesus Christ himself,[4] personally appearing to Daniel, as he did to John the Revelator centuries later. "And in the midst of the seven candlesticks one like unto the Son of man, clothed with a garment down to the foot, and girt about the paps with a golden girdle. His head and his hairs were white like wool, as white as snow; and his eyes were as a flame of fire; And his feet like unto fine brass, as if they burned in a furnace; and his voice as the sound of many waters."[5]

Daniel 10:7 And I Daniel alone saw the vision: for the men that were with me saw not the vision; but a great quaking fell upon them, so that they fled to hide themselves.

When Jesus appeared to Paul on the road to Damascus "the men which journeyed with him stood speechless, hearing a voice, but

---

[4] See E. G. White, *The Sanctified Life*, p. 49.2.

[5] Revelation 1:13-15

seeing no man."[6] In the same manner, when Daniel saw this vision, others were present who were afraid of the manifestation of God's power, yet did not see what Daniel saw.

Daniel 10:8 *Therefore I was left alone, and saw this great vision, and there remained no strength in me: for my comeliness was turned in me into corruption, and I retained no strength.*

Daniel gives us an unusual glimpse into the personal and physical manifestations that he experienced during vision. He describes losing strength at the beginning of the vision. Throughout this chapter we shall see more details of how God reveals himself when he speaks to a prophet in vision.

Daniel 10:9 *Yet heard I the voice of his words: and when I heard the voice of his words, then was I in a deep sleep on my face, and my face toward the ground.*

As a result of losing strength, Daniel had fallen gently to the ground on his face. Daniel was in a deep sleep, no longer conscious of his physical surroundings, yet hearing the voice and seeing the vision, and perceiving the physical manifestations of God's power.

Daniel 10:10 *And, behold, an hand touched me, which set me upon my knees and upon the palms of my hands.*

Wrapped in the panoply of heaven, the angel Gabriel[7] stoops to strengthen Daniel, lifting him to his hands and knees, and speaking words of infinite love:

---

[6] Acts 9:7

[7] "Gabriel then appeared to the prophet, and thus addressed him; 'O Daniel, a man greatly beloved, understand the words that I speak unto thee, and stand upright; for unto thee am I now sent. And when he had spoken this word unto me, I stood trembling. Then said he unto me, Fear not, Daniel; for from the first day that thou didst set thine heart to understand, and to chasten thyself before thy God, thy words were heard, and I am come for thy words.'"
E. G. White, *Review and Herald*, February 8, 1881 par. 30.

Daniel 10:11 And he said unto me, O Daniel, a man greatly beloved, understand the words that I speak unto thee, and stand upright: for unto thee am I now sent. And when he had spoken this word unto me, I stood trembling.

The angel strengthens Daniel so that, from his hands and knees he rises, then stands trembling.

Daniel 10:12 Then said he unto me, Fear not, Daniel: for from the first day that thou didst set thine heart to understand, and to chasten thyself before thy God, thy words were heard, and I am come for thy words.

Daniel 10:13 But the prince of the kingdom of Persia withstood me one and twenty days: but, lo, Michael, one of the chief princes, came to help me; and I remained there with the kings of Persia.

Three weeks earlier,[8] Daniel had begun to earnestly seek God in prayer for understanding, and from the very day Daniel began his supplications Gabriel was on his way to answer the prayer, but was detained by a mighty struggle with the forces of evil. "While Satan was striving to influence the highest powers in the kingdom of Medo-Persia to show disfavor to God's people, angels worked in behalf of the exiles. The controversy was one in which all heaven was interested. Through the prophet Daniel we are given a glimpse of this mighty struggle between the forces of good and the forces of evil. For three weeks Gabriel wrestled with the powers of darkness, seeking to counteract the influences at work on the mind of Cyrus; and before the contest closed, Christ Himself came to Gabriel's aid."[9] "The angel Gabriel was sent to affect the heart of the Persian king. The monarch had resisted the impressions of the Spirit of God during the three weeks while Daniel was fasting and praying, but Heaven's Prince, the archangel, Michael, was sent to turn the heart of the stubborn king to take some decided action to answer the prayer of Daniel."[10]

---

[8] Daniel 10:2

[9] E. G. White, *Prophets and Kings* (1917), p. 571.2.

[10] E. G. White, *The Review and Herald*, February 8, 1881 par. 31.

For three weeks the struggle between Satan and Gabriel rages for the mind and heart of Cyrus. Finally, Gabriel is obliged to request assistance. Gabriel, who stands "in the presence of God,"[11] the highest created being in the Universe, "who stands next in honor to the Son of God,"[12] needed help. What is the glory and majesty of One who could help Gabriel? Who is this **"Michael, one of the chief princes**?" The Hebrew word for "one," אחד'echâd, is often translated "first." Thus, Michael is the first of the chief princes, as we shall see.

At the end of this vision, in Daniel 12:1 we are informed that at the end of time, "shall Michael stand up, the great prince which standeth for the children of thy people." Michael is the great prince which stands for the people of God. Who is this prince above all princes?

"Yet Michael the archangel, when contending with the devil he disputed about the body of Moses, durst not bring against him a railing accusation, but said, The Lord rebuke thee."[13] Not only is Michael the prince of princes, but he is the archangel who, at the end of a fight with the devil over the body of Moses, the patriarch ends up resurrected from the grave and transported to heaven.[14] Who is this archangel that has power over the grave?

"For the Lord himself shall descend from heaven with a shout, with the voice of the archangel, and with the trump of God: and the dead in Christ shall rise first."[15] It is the "the Lord himself" descending with the shout of the archangel, whose voice awakes the dead. Michael is Jesus Christ, the prince of princes who stands for his people and who is the "resurrection, and the life."[16] The Son of God is the only one powerful enough to come to the aid of the mighty Gabriel.

---

[11] Luke 1:19

[12] E. G. White, *The Desire of Ages* (1898), p. 99.1.

[13] Jude 1:9

[14] This is why Moses appears to strengthen Jesus on the mount of transfiguration.
"And after six days Jesus taketh Peter, James, and John his brother, and bringeth them up into an high mountain apart, And was transfigured before them: and his face did shine as the sun, and his raiment was white as the light. And, behold, there appeared unto them Moses and Elias talking with him."
Matthew 17:1-3

[15] 1 Thessalonians 4:16

[16] John 11:25

The word angel in Hebrew— מַלְאָךְmal'âk—simply means messenger, and is a word that may be applied to the angels of heaven, but also to men, or to God himself. This is most clearly seen in the book of Malachi:[17] "Behold, I will send my messenger [mal'âk—John the Baptist], and he shall prepare the way before me: and the Lord, whom ye seek, shall suddenly come to his temple, even the messenger [mal'âk—Jesus Christ] of the covenant, whom ye delight in: behold, he shall come, saith the LORD of hosts."[18]

John the baptist was the messenger to prepare the way for the Lord, "In those days came John the Baptist, preaching in the wilderness of Judaea, And saying, Repent ye: for the kingdom of heaven is at hand. For this is he that was spoken of by the prophet Esaias, saying, The voice of one crying in the wilderness, Prepare ye the way of the Lord, make his paths straight."[19] John the baptist's message was prophesied by Isaiah, and by Malachi, who called him an "angel." In the very same prophecy, the Lord—the messenger of the covenant—is also called an angel. This does not require, nor does it mean, that Jesus is a created being. Jesus is the Creator: "All things were made by him; and without him was not any thing made that was made."[20] The word angel is frequently used in Scripture to refer to God. The word archangel[21] simply means the messenger above all messengers, which title applies only to Jesus Christ.

Just before the Exodus "the angel of the LORD appeared unto {Moses} in a flame of fire out of the midst of a bush: and he looked, and, behold, the bush burned with fire, and the bush was not consumed."[22] The angel (mal'âk) appeared to Moses in a burning bush; "And when **the LORD** saw that he turned aside to see, **God called unto him out of the midst of the bush.**"[23] God was the

---

[17] Even Malachi's own name derives from the word for angel—mal'âk, or messenger.

[18] Malachi 3:1

[19] Matthew 3:1-3

[20] John 1:3

[21] Some confuse the word "archangel" with the covering cherubs on the ark of the covenant. The word "arch" means above, and does not refer to the "ark." Gabriel is one of the covering cherubs, as was Lucifer before his fall from heaven (see Ezekiel 28:12-19). But, Christ is the One who is covered for he is the angel above all angels, including the two covering cherubs.

[22] Exodus 3:2

[23] Exodus 3:4

angel in the bush. A few verses later when Moses asks what name to use for God, "God said unto Moses, I AM THAT I AM: and he said, Thus shalt thou say unto the children of Israel, I AM hath sent me unto you." In the New Testament, when Jesus said to the Pharisees, "Your father Abraham rejoiced to see my day: and he saw it, and was glad. Then said the Jews unto him, Thou art not yet fifty years old, and hast thou seen Abraham? Jesus said unto them, Verily, verily, I say unto you, Before Abraham was, **I am**. Then took they up stones to cast at him: but Jesus hid himself, and went out of the temple, going through the midst of them, and so passed by."[24] The Jews understood exactly the meaning of Jesus. Jesus was claiming to be God. Jesus was the angel of the burning bush.

In Judges 2:1, the Bible tells us, "And **an angel** of the LORD came up from Gilgal to Bochim, and said, I made you to go up out of Egypt, and have brought you unto the land which I sware unto your fathers; and I said, I will never break my covenant with you."

What angel promised to bring the Israelites out of Egypt and delivered to them the everlasting covenant, the ten commandments[25]? "I am the LORD thy God, which have brought thee out of the land of Egypt, out of the house of bondage."[26] Jesus was the saviour from the bondage of Egypt; Jesus was the law-giver at Sinai—the angel of the covenant.

Daniel 10:14 Now I am come to make thee understand what shall befall thy people in the latter days: for yet the vision is for many days.

Gabriel is now able to fulfill his commission to make Daniel understand, to reveal more details of the events of the future.

Daniel 10:15 And when he had spoken such words unto me, I set my face toward the ground, and I became dumb.

---

[24] John 8:56-59

[25] "...And he wrote upon the tables the words of the covenant, the ten commandments." Exodus 34:28

[26] Exodus 20:2

Daniel is struck dumb; at first, completely unable to speak.

Daniel 10:16 Behold, one like the similitude of the sons of men touched my lips. Then I opened my mouth and I spake, and I said to him that stood before me, O my lord, by the vision my sorrows are turned upon me, and I have retained no strength.

Jesus himself, once more assists Gabriel and touches the lips of the prophet. Daniel is healed and at once is able to speak. He expresses his weakness and questions how he is able to speak:

Daniel 10:17 For how can the servant of this my Lord talk with this my Lord? For as for me straight way, there remained no strength in me, neither is there breath left in me.

Once Christ touches Daniel's lips he wonders aloud how he can speak to Jesus when he has no strength and is not breathing. Daniel describes for us how the power of God sustains the prophet's life without breath during vision.

When "the LORD God formed man of the dust of the ground, and breathed into his nostrils the breath of life... man became a living soul." That same Creator God, Jesus Christ,[27] who has the power, by his breath, to make a living being from a lump of clay, also has the power to sustain the life of the prophet in vision though he does not breathe. This is a physical manifestation that would be very difficult for a false prophet to counterfeit.

"Surely the Lord GOD will do nothing, but he revealeth his secret unto his servants the prophets."[28] God ordained that he would communicate his will, directly through special revelation, to faulty and frail human beings of his own choosing, called prophets. These individuals were commissioned by God himself to bear messages of divine revelation to the rest of humankind.

---

[27] "All things were made by him; and without him was not any thing made that was made." John 1:3

[28] Amos 3:7

The prophet did not sign up, or volunteer, or even train for the position. Their commission and message did not come from their will or decision, but by the will of God almighty: "For the prophecy came not in old time by the will of man: but holy men of God spake as they were moved by the Holy Ghost."[29] The power of the Holy Spirit moved upon these consecrated human servants of God, to give an infallible divine message. The writers of Scripture were human; the author was divine. This was the same miraculous combination of human and divine as the divine Son of God becoming a man. Not only did God choose his messengers, but God chose the method of delivery for the message. God said, "Hear now my words: If there be a prophet among you, I the LORD will make myself known unto him in a vision, and will speak unto him in a dream."[30]

When Christ ascended he gave the gifts of the Spirit, "Wherefore he saith, When he ascended up on high, he led captivity captive, and **gave gifts unto men**... And he gave some, apostles; and **some, prophets**; and some, evangelists; and some, pastors and teachers; For the perfecting of the saints, for the work of the ministry, for the edifying of the body of Christ: Till we all come in the unity of the faith, and of the knowledge of the Son of God, unto a perfect man, unto the measure of the stature of the fulness of Christ."

One of the gifts of the Spirit is that some would be prophets, and these gifts, we are told, would be poured out on the body of Christ until we all come "unto the measure of the stature of the fulness of Christ." It is true that the Scriptures were written by prophets of God under the inspiration of the Holy Spirit, but it is also true that those same Scriptures testify that God will continue to bestow the gift of prophecy, at his will, until he comes the second time. "And it shall come to pass afterward, that I will pour out my spirit upon all flesh; and your sons and your daughters shall prophesy, your old men shall dream dreams, your young men shall see visions."[31] Though the prophets were the writers of Scripture, their work was not confined to the writing of the Holy Oracles. The Bible itself records many true prophets, both men and women, who never contributed a word to

---

[29] 2 Peter 1:21

[30] Numbers 12:6

[31] Joel 2:28

Scripture: Gad,[32] Nathan,[33] Huldah,[34] and Deborah[35] are examples in the Old Testament. John the Baptist, whom Jesus said was the greatest prophet,[36] never wrote a word of Scripture. New Testament examples include Simeon, Anna, Agabus, Barnabus, and Phillip's four daughters. In fact, we are commanded of God, "Despise not prophesyings. Prove all things; hold fast that which is good."[37] The very fact that the Bible warns against false prophets, implies that there are true. If there were never again to be another prophet after the completion of the canon of Scripture, God would have told us in the Bible never to listen to another prophet. Instead he says, "Beloved, believe not every spirit, but try the spirits whether they are of God: because many false prophets are gone out into the world." We are to try the spirits, whether they are of God. That means some prophets will not be false. And, just as with Israel of old, to reject a true prophetic message from the Lord would be at the peril of our souls.

Believing in God is only the foundation; if we would prosper, we must believe his prophets. "...Believe in the LORD your God, so shall ye be established; believe his prophets, so shall ye prosper."[38] Yet, the father of lies has created corrupt prophetic messengers, called false prophets. Jesus himself warned us that all the way to the end of time these deceivers would arise. "For there shall arise false Christs, and false prophets, and shall show great signs and wonders; insomuch that, if it were possible, they shall deceive the very elect."[39]

If God has given a genuine prophetic message through divinely chosen messengers, but has warned us to beware of the deceptions of false Christs and false prophets, surely, he has provided the means for discerning the difference.

---

[32] 1 Samuel 22:5

[33] 2 Samuel 7:2

[34] 2 Kings 22:14

[35] Judges 4:4

[36] Luke 7:28

[37] 1 Thessalonians 5:20, 21

[38] 2 Chronicles 20:20

[39] Matthew 24:24

There are at least eight Biblical marks of a true prophet:

1. **A true prophet's message must be in harmony with the word of God and the law of God:** "To the law and to the testimony: if they speak not according to this word, it is because there is no light in them."[40] "Her gates are sunk into the ground; he hath destroyed and broken her bars: her king and her princes are among the Gentiles: the law is no more; her prophets also find no vision from the LORD."[41]

2. **A true prophet will have dreams and visions:** "And he said, Hear now my words: If there be a prophet among you, the LORD will make myself known unto him in a vision, and will speak unto him in a dream."[42]

3. **A true prophet's predictions must come true:** "When a prophet speaketh in the name of the LORD, if the thing follow not, nor come to pass, that is the thing which the LORD hath not spoken, but the prophet hath spoken it presumptuously: thou shalt not be afraid of him."[43]

4. **A true prophet edifies God's people:** "But he that prophesieth speaketh unto men to edification, and exhortation, and comfort. He that speaketh in an unknown tongue edifieth himself; but he that prophesieth edifieth the church."[44]

5. **A true prophet exalts Christ as the Son of God:** "Whosoever shall confess that Jesus is the Son of God, God dwelleth in him, and he in God."[45] "And beginning at Moses and all the prophets, he expounded unto them in all the scriptures the things concerning himself."[46]

6. **A true prophet speaks with authority:** "For he taught them as one having authority, and not as the scribes."[47]

---

[40] Isaiah 8:20

[41] Lamentations 2:9

[42] Numbers 12:6

[43] Deuteronomy 18:22

[44] 1 Corinthians 14:3, 4

[45] 1 John 4:15

[46] Luke 24:27
This verse refers to Jesus himself first turning to the writings of the prophets to prove his divinity and messiahship, before he appealed to the evidence of his resurrection.

[47] Matthew 7:29
This verse refers to Jesus teaching with authority, but it also applies to his prophets, as the Bible refers to Jesus as a prophet. See Deuteronomy 18:15.

7. **A true prophet will bear good fruit:** "Wherefore by their fruits ye shall know them."[48]

8. **A true prophet will exhibit certain physical signs when in vision:**

   a.   The prophet's eyes are open during the vision: "He hath said, which heard the words of God, which saw the vision of the Almighty, falling into a trance, but having his eyes open:"[49]

   b.   A true prophet first falls down and has no strength, then is strengthened, but has no breath (even when speaking) while in vision: "And I Daniel alone saw the vision: for the men that were with me saw not the vision; but a great quaking fell upon them, so that they fled to hide themselves. Therefore I was left alone, and saw this great vision, and there remained no strength in me: for my comeliness was turned in me into corruption, and I retained no strength. Yet heard I the voice of his words: and when I heard the voice of his words, then was I in a deep sleep on my face, and my face toward the ground. And, behold, an hand touched me, which set me upon my knees and upon the palms of my hands.... And when he had spoken this word unto me, I stood trembling... And, behold, one like the similitude of the sons of men touched my lips: then I opened my mouth, and spake, and said unto him that stood before me, O my lord, by the vision my sorrows are turned upon me, and I have retained no strength. For how can the servant of this my lord talk with this my lord? for as for me, straightway there remained no strength in me, neither is there breath left in me."[50] As the all-powerful Creator of the universe, if God chooses to sustain the life of his prophets without breath as unmistakable evidence of the divine origin of the message— evidence that cannot be counterfeited by Satan—divinity has that prerogative.

Just as promised, God has sent a prophetic message of vital importance in these last days. Just as the prophetic period of the 2,300 years of Daniel 8:14 was closing, in December of 1844, Ellen

---

[48] Matthew 7:20

[49] Numbers 24:4

[50] Daniel 10:7-18

G. Harmon (later White),[51] at age 17, had her first vision. Do the messages she received fulfill the Biblical criteria for the prophetic gift?

1. Did she exalt the word and law of God?

"The Holy Scriptures are to be accepted as an authoritative, infallible revelation of His will. They are the standard of character, the revealer of doctrines, and the test of experience."[52] "Brethren, cling to your Bible, as it reads, and stop your criticisms in regard to its validity, and obey the Word, and not one of you will be lost."[53]

"The Bible, and the Bible alone, is to be our creed, the sole bond of union; …God's Word is infallible…. lift up the banner on which is inscribed, The Bible our rule of faith and discipline."[54]

"The Lord designs to warn you, to reprove, to counsel, through the testimonies given, and to impress your minds with the importance of the truth of His word. The written testimonies are not to give new light, but to impress vividly upon the heart the truths of inspiration already revealed. Man's duty to God and to his fellow man has been distinctly specified in God's word, yet but few of you are obedient to

---

[51] On August 30, 1846 Ellen Harmon was united in marriage to James White, becoming Ellen G. White.

[52] E. G. White, *The Great Controversy* (1911), p. vii.1.

[53] E. G. White, *Selected Messages* (Washington D.C.: Review & Herald Publishing Association, 1958), Vol. 1, p. 18.

[54] *Ibid.*, p. 416.

the light given. Additional truth is not brought out; but God has through the Testimonies simplified the great truths already given and in His own chosen way brought them before the people to awaken and impress the mind with them, that all may be left without excuse."[55]

"Then present to them the prophecies; show them the purity and binding claims of the law of God. Not one jot or tittle of this law is to lose its force, but hold its binding claims upon every soul to the end of time."[56]

2. Did she receive vision and dreams?
Over the course of 70 years she received over 2000 visions[57] ranging in length from less than a minute to over four hours.

3. Did her predictions come true?
"Ellen White's Civil War visions were perhaps the most stunning of her many predictions.... Her first Civil War vision, lasting twenty minutes, occurred during an afternoon church service in Parkville, Michigan... on January 12, 1861."[58]

"The Parkville vision occurred three months before the guns fired on Fort Sumter, April 12, 1861. At that time many people believed that there would be no war, but should war begin, it would be short and the North would win in a brief fight."[59]

"In mid-February 1861 Thomas R. R. Cobb, Georgia secessionist and committee member preparing the Confederate constitution, wrote: 'The almost universal belief here [Montgomery] is that we shall not have war.'
"Two days before his Inaugural Address of March 4, 1861, Lincoln declared in Philadelphia: 'I have felt all the while justified in

---

[55] E. G. White, *Testimonies to the Church*, Vol. 5 (1889) p. 665.

[56] E. G. White, *Manuscript Releases*, Vol. 15 (1990) p. 351.

[57] Ellen G. White Estate, *Advent Pioneers Biographical Sketches and Pictures*, p. 22.5.

[58] Herbert Edgar Douglass, *Dramatic Prophecies of Ellen White* (Nampa, ID: Pacific Press, 2007), p. 13.

[59] Herbert Edgar Douglass, *Messenger of the Lord* (Nampa, ID: Pacific Press, 1998), p. 159.

concluding that the crisis, the panic, the anxiety of the country at this time is artificial.' Cited in *Harper's Weekly*, March 2, 1861, p. 135"[60]

At the close of the vision, she stood and related to the congregation what she had seen. "Her words made a lasting impression (as reported by J. N. Loughborough, an eye-witness): 'Men are making light of the secession ordinance that has been passed by South Carolina [Dec. 20, 1860]. They have little idea of the trouble that is coming on our land. No one in this house has even dreamed of the trouble that is coming. I have just been shown in vision that a number of States are going to join South Carolina in this secession, and a terrible war will be the result. In the vision I saw large armies raised by both the North and the South. I was shown the battle raging.'"[61] "There is not a person in this house who has even dreamed of the trouble that is coming upon this land. People are making sport of the secession ordinance of South Carolina, but I have just been shown that a large number of states are going to join that state, and there will be a most terrible war.

"In this vision I have seen large armies of both sides gathered on the field of battle. I heard the booming of the cannon, and saw the dead and dying on every hand. Then I saw them rushing up engaged in hand-to-hand fighting [bayoneting one another].

"'Then I saw the field after battle, all covered with the dead and dying. Then I was carried to prisons, and saw the sufferings of those in want, who were wasting away. Then I was taken to the homes of those who had lost husbands, sons, or brothers in the war. I saw their distress and anguish.' Then, surveying her audience, Ellen slowly added a foreboding note: 'There are those in this house who will lose sons in that war.'"[62] Two men in the congregation, Judge Osborne, and Mr. Shellhouse looked at Elder Loughborough and shook their heads, disbelieving what Ellen White had predicted. One year later they again sat together in the same church as Elder Loughborough preached about the gift of prophecy, using the civil war vision as an example. Tears streamed down the faces of both men. One had lost his only son, the other had lost a son on a different battlefield, with a second son in a Southern prison. The local

---

[60] Herbert Edgar Douglass, *Messenger of the Lord* (1998), p. 167.

[61] *Ibid.*, p. 158.

[62] Roger W. Coon, *The Great Visions of Ellen G. White* (Washington D.C.: Review and Herald Publishing Association), p. 80.

elder stated he could probably count ten families from their congregation who had lost sons in the war.

From the things she was shown in vision, Ellen White predicted the San Francisco earthquake of April 18, 1906;[63] both World Wars;[64] and the events of 9/11 in New York City.[65]

In 1903, from things shown her in vision she stated, "In the world gigantic monopolies will be formed. Men will bind themselves together in unions that will wrap them in the folds of the enemy. A few men will combine to grasp all the means to be obtained in certain lines of business. Trades unions will be formed, and those who refuse to join these unions will be marked men."[66] How could she possibly have predicted this over 110 years ago, without divine enlightenment? On February 20, 2014, CNBC (itself a mega-merger) published an article titled "Why 2014 could be the year of the mega-merger." Following are a list of some recent mega-merger monopolies that have been formed:[67]
Delta and Northwest 2008.
Continental and United 2010-2012.
Microsoft – Hotmail, Skype, NBC, 157 others.
VW and Porsche 2012, plus Audi, Seat, Bugatti, Bentley.
Facebook and WhatsApp 2014 - $16.5 billion 5th largest tech deal ever.
Comcast and Time Warner Cable 2014 - $69.3 billion.
Forest Laboratories and Actavis - $25 billion.
Chrysler and Fiat 2014 - $3.6 billion.
Nest Labs and Google - $3.2 billion.

Against the prevailing opinions of her time, in a day when physicians were prescribing smoking for lung disease, Ellen White predicted, in 1864, "Tobacco is a poison of the most deceitful and **malignant** kind, having an exciting, then a paralyzing influence upon the nerves of

---

[63] E. G. White, *Evangelism* (1946), p. 403.4;
E. G. White, *Life Sketches* (1915), p. 407-409.

[64] E. G. White, *Testimonies for the Church*, Vol. 1 (1871), p. 268.

[65] E. G. White, *Testimonies for the Church*, Vol. 9 (1909), p. 11-14;
E. G. White, *Manuscript Releases*, Vol. 11 (1990), p. 361.1.

[66] E. G. White, *Manuscript Releases*, Vol. 4 (1990), p. 75.1.

[67] Patti Domm, "Why 2014 could be the year of the megamerger" February 20, 2014, http://www.cnbc.com/id/101432520, retrieved January 18, 2017.

the body. It is all the more dangerous because its effects upon the system are so slow, and at first scarcely perceivable. Multitudes have fallen victims to its poisonous influence."[68]

It was not until 1957 (almost 100 years later) that a committee of scientists appointed by the American Cancer Society and the American Heart Association concluded that smoking was a causative factor in lung cancer.

4. Did she edify the church?
"Ellen White received messages for individuals and groups that covered a broad array of subjects. Men and women received admonition, encouragement, and reproof regarding their personal lives and their Christian influence. Individuals and groups received insights, caution, and direction in general ideas, including education, health, administrative policy, evangelistic and publishing principles, and church finance."[69]

"Her messages to the church were far-reaching. On one hand, she covered the whole range of the salvation story; on the other, she dealt with civil government, the home, and questions of race relations, health, and education. The striking point is that all this instruction was creative: whenever followed faithfully, schools and hospitals, publishing houses and ministerial institutes, temperance and welfare societies sprang up worldwide. Even more striking is that this woman, without a church office and without formal training in any one of the many areas of her profound instruction, was the leading inspiration in molding all these various interests into a united organization."[70]

"Every test which can be brought to bear upon such manifestations, proves these genuine. The evidence which supports them, internal and external, is conclusive. They agree with the word of God, and with themselves. They are given, unless those best qualified to judge are invariably deceived, when the Spirit of God is especially present. They are free from the disgusting contortions and grimaces which attend the counterfeit manifestations of Spiritualism. Calm, dignified,

---

[68] E. G. White, *Spiritual Gifts*, Vol. 4, (1864) p. 128.

[69] Herbert Edgar Douglass, *Messenger of the Lord* (1998), p. 138.

[70] *Ibid.*, p. 183.

impressive, they commend themselves to every beholder, as the very opposite of that which is false or fanatical....

"Further, their fruit is such as to show that the source from which they spring is the opposite of evil.

"They tend to the purest morality. They discountenance every vice, and exhort to the practice of every virtue. They point out the perils through which we are to pass to the kingdom. They reveal the devices of Satan. They warn us against his snares. They have nipped in the bud scheme after scheme of fanaticism which the enemy has tried to foist into our midst. They have exposed hidden iniquity, brought to light concealed wrongs, and laid bare the evil motives of the false-hearted. They have warded off dangers from the cause of truth upon every hand. They have aroused and re-aroused us to greater consecration to God, moved zealous efforts for holiness of heart, and greater diligence in the cause and service of our Master.

"They lead us to Christ. Like the Bible, they set him forth as the only hope and only Saviour of mankind. They portray before us in living characters his holy life and his godly example, and with irresistible appeals they urge us to follow in his steps.

"They lead us to the Bible. They set forth that book as the inspired and unalterable word of God. They exhort us to take that word as the man of our counsel, and the rule of our faith and practice. And with a compelling power, they entreat us to study long and diligently its pages, and become familiar with its teaching, for it is to judge us in the last day.

"They have brought comfort and consolation to many hearts. They have strengthened the weak, encouraged the feeble, raised up the despondent. They have brought order out of confusion, made crooked places straight, and thrown light on what was dark and obscure. And no person, with an unprejudiced mind, can read their stirring appeals for a pure and lofty morality, their exaltation of God and the Saviour, their denunciations of every evil, and their exhortations to everything that is holy and of good report, without being compelled to say, 'These are not the words of him that hath a devil.'"[71]

---

[71] Uriah Smith, *The Visions of Mrs. E. G. White* (Battle Creek, MI: Seventh-day Adventist Publishing Association, 1868), p. 5.2-7.2.

5. Did she exalt Christ as the Son of God and our Savior?

"The world's Redeemer was treated as we deserve to be treated, in order that we might be treated as he deserved to be treated. He came to our world and took our sins upon his own divine soul, that we might receive his imputed righteousness. He was condemned for our sins, in which he had no share, that we might be justified by his righteousness, in which we had no share. The world's Redeemer gave himself for us. Who was he?—The Majesty of heaven, pouring out his blood upon the altar of justice for the sins of guilty man. We should know our relationship to Christ and his relationship to us."[72]

6. Did she speak with authority?

"I am instructed to say to those who endeavor to tear down the foundation that has made us Seventh-day Adventists: We are God's commandment-keeping people. For the past fifty years every phase of heresy has been brought to bear upon us, to becloud our minds regarding the teaching of the Word—especially concerning the ministration of Christ in the heavenly sanctuary, and the message of heaven for these last days, as given by the angels of the fourteenth chapter of Revelation. Messages of every order and kind have been urged upon Seventh-day Adventists, to take the place of the truth which, point by point, has been sought out by prayerful study and testified to by the miracle-working power of the Lord. But the waymarks which have made us what we are, are to be preserved, and they will be preserved, as God has signified through His word and the testimonies of His Spirit. He calls upon us to hold firmly with the grip of faith, to the fundamental principles that are based upon unquestionable authority."[73]

7. Did she bear good fruit?

Everywhere she went she raised up churches, hospitals, and universities. Her messages on health have impacted the entire world and saved millions of lives.

On June 6, 1863, in Otsego, Michigan, Ellen White had her famous health vision, revealing the true principles of health. On the basis of the information she received in this vision she helped to found a sanitarium (or health retreat) called the Western Health Reform Institute. During its first ten years, from 1866 to 1876, the Institute

---

[72] E. G. White, *The Review and Herald*, March 21, 1893 par. 6.

[73] E. G. White, *Manuscript Releases*, Vol. 4 (1990), p. 246.1.

served two thousand patients. Of these, ten died: an average of one a year. So unusual was this record that the new institution was soon projected to national prominence. This record was set during the ten years before Koch and Pasteur first demonstrated (in 1876) that the anthrax microbe produced the disease anthrax.

Despite their meager funds, Ellen and her husband James White helped to finance a young student through medical school named

John Harvey Kellogg, eventually of Kellogg's cornflakes fame. Using the principles of health that God showed Ellen White, Kellogg built up

the Institute (renamed Battle Creek Sanitarium) so that by 1885, it had become the largest institution, in the world, of its kind.[74]

Even though most Seventh-day Adventists do not fully avail themselves of the scientific heritage that God has entrusted them through the gift of prophecy, they have still become famous for better health and greater longevity than the rest of the world.

---

[74] In 1926 it had a service staff of eighteen hundred and in 1927, accommodations for over fifteen hundred patients. Its giant furnaces and boilers burned fifty-five tons of coal a day. By 1938 the Sanitarium facilities included thirty-two buildings on 27.5 acres of land and a dining room for eight hundred guests. The sanitarium attracted the attention of many famous guests and patients. President William Howard Taft was patient number 100,000. President Warren G. Harding was also a patient. Other notable guests and patients included:

Industrialists: Henry Ford; James Buick; Harvey Firestone; John D. Rockefeller, Jr.; Alfred du Pont; Edgar Welch, grape juice producer; A. E. McKinstry, president of International Harvester; E. H. Little, president of Colgate-Palmolive Company; and General David Sarnoff, president of Radio Corporation of America.

Businessmen: J. C. Penney; Montgomery Ward; R. H. and A.H. Kress; and S. S. Kresge.

Writers, editors, and publishers: Dr. Morris Fishbein, editor of Journal of the American Medical Association; George Bernard Shaw, Dale Carnegie, author of How to Win Friends and Influence People;

Sportsmen: Bill Tilden, tennis champion; Gene Sarazen, golfer; Johnny Weissmuller, champion swimmer.

Politicians: W. A. Julian, treasurer of the United States; George W. Wickersham, attorney general; William Jennings Bryan, secretary of state; Frank Knox, secretary of the navy; James J. Davis, secretary of labor; plus, governors, congressmen, and senators.

Scientists: Ivan Pavlov, Nobel prize-winning Russian physiologist; Sir Frederick Grant Banting, discoverer of insulin and also a Nobel prize winner; Drs. Charles and William Mayo of the Mayo Clinic; Dr. William M. Scholl, manufacturer of foot appliances and remedies.

Inventor Thomas Edison; explorer Admiral Richard Byrd; oil men Harry F. Sinclair and L. E. Phillips.

Educator Booker T. Washington; Red Cross founder Clara Barton; evangelist Billy Sunday; pilot Amelia Earhart.

Amelia Earhart took Kellogg for an airplane ride over Battle Creek. Admiral Byrd counseled with Kellogg about diet before making his two major expeditions to explore the North and South Poles. Johnny Weissmuller, Olympic champion swimmer, after following a vegetarian diet prescribed by Kellogg, broke his previous record, swimming 300 meters in 3 minutes, 33.6 seconds, a record he had tried to break for several years. Weissmuller had broken fifty-four world records.

Unfortunately, Kellogg did not follow all the advice given to him from God, through the prophetic gift, including to not make the Sanitariums so large. Twice, God's warning hand touched the huge Sanitarium, and twice it burned to the ground. These warnings were tempered with the mercy that not a single person died in either fire. God also sent warnings and reproofs regarding the spiritualism that Kellogg eventually embraced, causing him to apostatize completely from the truths he once believed.

Dan Buettner in his *National Geographic* cover article states, "From 1976 to 1988 the National Institutes of Health funded a study of 34,000 California Adventists to see whether their health-oriented lifestyle affected their life expectancy and risk of heart disease and cancer. The study found that the Adventists' habit of consuming beans, soy milk, tomatoes, and other fruits lowered their risk of developing certain cancers. It also suggested that eating whole wheat bread, drinking five glasses of water a day, and, most surprisingly, consuming four servings of nuts a week reduced their risk of heart disease. And it found that not eating red meat had been helpful to avoid both cancer and heart disease.

"In the end the study reached a stunning conclusion, says Gary Fraser of Loma Linda University: The average Adventist lived four to ten years longer than the average Californian. That makes the Adventists one of the nation's most convincing cultures of longevity."[75]

One of the most notable nutrition researchers in the world, Dr. T. Colin Campbell, director of the famous China Study, the largest nutritional study ever conducted, in an interview with Don Mackintosh on February 24, 2005, said, "I am not aware of anyone who was more on point than Ellen White. Given her background she was truly an amazing woman. I am convinced that almost 100% of her statements are now substantially supported by the scientific evidence that has been developed in the last two to three decades. What I have come to realize, to even deeply worry about, is why it is that this message of Ellen and others has been so mislaid on shelves out of sight. It is now abundantly clear to me that now is the time to bring this forward in whatever way that each of us are able to do."[76] The scientific evidence is only now catching up, in the last two to three decades, with the things she wrote a hundred and fifty years ago.

8. Did she exhibit the physical signs?
She received many of her visions in public often in front of hundreds of witnesses. "In passing into vision, she gives three enrapturing shouts of 'Glory!' which echo and re-echo, the second, and

---

[75] Dan Buettner, "The Secrets of Long Life," *National Geographic Magazine*, November, 2005.

[76] *What's the Connection* directed by Jim Doss, with Don Mackintosh (Three Angel's Media Ministry, 2005), Disk 1, 00:09:55-00:11:30.

especially the third, fainter but more thrilling than the first, the voice resembling that of one quite a distance from you, and just going out of hearing. For about four or five seconds she seems to drop down like a person in a swoon, or one having lost his strength; she then seems to be instantly filled with superhuman strength, sometimes rising at once to her feet and walking about the room.

"There are frequent movements of the hands and arms, pointing to the right or left as her head turns. All these movements are made in a most graceful manner. In whatever position the hand or arm may be placed, it is impossible for anyone to move it. Her eyes are always open, but she does not wink; her head is raised, and she is looking upward, not with a vacant stare, but with a pleasant expression, only differing from the normal in that she appears to be looking intently at some distant object."[77]

Nellie Starr, an eyewitness of the June 12, 1868 vision gives the account as follows:

"She walked back and forth and talked to us, and as she walked, she fell right down. She fell down gently. She went down as if an angel's hands were under her....

"Sister White lay perfectly quiet and unconscious....

"Her eyes were open, with a pleasant expression on her face. Nothing unnatural or unusual.

"Brother White said to these large men, 'Take her hands apart. You have two hands to her one. Just pull her hands apart.' So they tried. They pulled and pulled till some of us got anxious that they would hurt her.

"Brother White said, 'Don't be anxious; she is safe in God's keeping, and you can pull until you are perfectly satisfied.' They said, 'We are satisfied now. We don't need to pull anymore.'

"He said, 'Take up one finger at a time.' That was impossible. They could not do so much as move a finger. It seemed like a block of granite....

"Brother White said to these men, 'Now hold her.' I think they thought they could. They grasped her by the wrists, but they could not retard the motion. It looked like any child could hold her, but she went on just the same.

"Elder White said, 'Now we are satisfied with that. Now we must see if her eyelids will close.' There was a large Rochester [kerosene]

---

[77] Arthur L. White, *Ellen G. White: The Early Years*, Vol. 1 (Hagerstown, MD: Review and Herald Publishing Association, 1985), p. 122.5.

lamp close by on the stand. He removed the shade and put this light right in front of her eyes. We thought she would move her eyes to protect them. She didn't. She was perfectly unconscious.

"'Now,' Brother White said, 'we must see if there is any breath in her body.' There didn't seem to be any. Everything looked all right, only there was no breath. Brother White said, 'Now we will send out and get a mirror, and we will test it.' So someone went to the next door and got a mirror, and it was held close to her face, but no moisture gathered. So there was no breathing."[78]

David H. Lamson of Hillsdale, MI was present on June 26, 1854, when a medical examination was conducted of Mrs. White's physical condition while in vision: "Two physicians came in, an old man and a young man. Brother White was anxious that they should examine Sister White closely, which they did. A looking glass was brought, and one of them held it over her mouth while she talked; but very soon they gave this up, and said, 'She doesn't breathe.' Then they closely examined her sides as she spoke, to find some evidence of deep breathing, but they did not find it.

"As they closed this part of the examination, she arose to her feet, still in vision, holding a Bible high up, turning from passage to passage, quoting correctly, although the eyes were looking upward and away from the Book."[79]

Mrs. Drusilla Lamson, wife of David Lamson's cousin was also present and gave the following testimony. "I remember the meeting when the trial was made, namely, to test what Brother White had frequently said, that Sister White did not breathe while in vision, but I cannot recall the name of the doctor who was present.... It must have been Dr. Fleming, as he was the doctor called sometimes for counsel. He is, however, now dead. I can say this much, that the test was made, and no sign of breath was visible on the looking glass."

David Seeley, of Fayette, Iowa, wrote, "This is to certify that I have read the above testimonials of David Lamson and Mrs. Drusilla Lamson, concerning the physician's statement when examining Mrs. E. G. White while she was in vision, June 26, 1854.

---

[78] Arthur L. White, *Ellen G. White*: The Progressive Years, Vol. 2 (1985), p. 233-234.

[79] Arthur L. White, *Ellen G. White*: The Early Years, Vol. 1 (1985), p. 302.

"I was present at that meeting, and witnessed the examination. I agree with what is stated by Brother and Sister Lamson, and would say further that it was Doctor Fleming and another younger physician who made the examination. After Mrs. White rose to her feet, as they have stated, quoting the texts of Scripture, Doctor Fleming called for a lighted candle. He held this candle as near her lips as possible without burning, and in direct line with her breath in case she breathed. There was not the slightest flicker of the blaze. The doctor then said, with emphasis, 'That settles it forever; there is no breath in her body.'"[80]

Paul Harvey, in his noontime ABC radio-broadcast of September 27, 1997, reported: "Women have been honored on American postage stamps for more than 100 years, starting with one woman who was not an American, Queen Isabella, in 1893. Since then, 86 women have been honored, ranging from Martha Washington to Marilyn Monroe. Also many women authors like Louisa May Alcott, Emily Dickinson, Willa Cather, and Rachel Carson.
"But I can name an American woman author who has never been honored thus, though her writings have been translated into 148 languages. More than Marx or Tolstoy, more than Agatha Christie, more than William Shakespeare. Only now is the world coming to appreciate her recommended prescription for optimum spiritual and physical health: Ellen White. Ellen White! You don't know her? Get to know her."

"Ellen White is thought to be the third [and possibly the second] most translated author in history and the most translated American author, male or female. So far as we know, she wrote and published more books, and in more languages, which circulate to a greater extent than the written works of any other woman in history. By the close of her seventy-year[s of prophetic] ministry, her literary productions totaled approximately 100,000 pages, or the equivalent of 25 million words, including letters, diaries, periodical articles, pamphlets, and books"[81]

"Where there is no vision, the people perish."[82]

---

[80] Arthur L. White, *Ellen G. White*: The Early Years, Vol. 1, (1985) p. 303.

[81] Herbert E. Douglass, *Messenger of the Lord* (1998), p. 108, 121.

[82] Proverbs 29:18

Daniel 10:18 Then there came again and touched me one like the appearance of a man, and he strengthened me,

"My grace is sufficient for thee: for my strength is made perfect in weakness."[83]

Daniel 10:19 And said, O man greatly beloved, fear not: peace be unto thee, be strong, yea, be strong. And when he had spoken unto me, I was strengthened, and said, Let my lord speak; for thou hast strengthened me.

"For God so loved the world, that he gave his only begotten Son, that whosoever believeth in him should not perish, but have everlasting life."[84] When the Lord of life and glory strengthens you; you will be strengthened.

Daniel 10:20 Then said he, Knowest thou wherefore I come unto thee? and now will I return to fight with the prince of Persia: and when I am gone forth, lo, the prince of Grecia shall come.

Gabriel, who is still present, speaks again assuring Daniel that when he is finished delivering his message he will continue his work of guiding the destinies of nations through the reign of Persia until the Greek Empire replaces the Persian, and beyond.

Daniel 10:21 But I will show thee that which is noted in the scripture of truth: and there is none that holdeth with me in these things, but Michael your prince.

Gabriel confesses that there is none in the universe powerful enough, except Jesus "**your prince**," who is able to hold with him the destinies of nations.

---

[83] 2 Corinthians 12:9

[84] John 3:16

Daniel 4b

SUMMARY:
Many of the story chapters of the Book of Daniel also have prophetic implications.[1] This is particularly the case with Daniel 4, to the extent that it will be covered here in an extra chapter. Daniel 4 uses the phrase "seven times" to outline the literal punishment period of seven years that Nebuchadnezzar would spend eating grass with the beasts of the field. Does this chapter contain deeper layers of prophetic meaning? Does modern Israel play a role in the last days? Why so many denominations? Does God have one end-time remnant church that he has preserved, still following the religion of the early disciples? What church would Jesus attend if he were on this earth now? Daniel 4b explores these questions, and more. The significance of this passage is only properly understood in the light of the prophetic passages of Daniel chapters seven, eight, nine and ten.

In Daniel 4 Nebuchadnezzar had a dream that made him afraid and greatly troubled. In the dream, he saw "a tree in the midst of the earth, and the height thereof was great. The tree grew, and was strong, and the height thereof reached unto heaven, and the sight thereof to the end of all the earth: The leaves thereof were fair, and the fruit thereof much, and in it was meat for all: the beasts of the field had shadow under it, and the fowls of the heaven dwelt in the boughs thereof, and all flesh was fed of it."[2]

Daniel 4:13 I saw in the visions of my head upon my bed, and, behold, a watcher and an holy one came down from heaven;

---

[1] For example, the story of Nebuchadnezzar's image and the fiery furnace is a great children's story, but it parallels the prophetic events outlined in Revelation 13 in an amazing way. Both chapters deal with Babylon; the former literal Babylon, and the latter symbolic Babylon; both describe an image, a law requiring worship, a death penalty for disobedience, and the number 666.

[2] Daniel 4:10-12

Daniel 4:14 He cried aloud, and said thus, Hew down the tree, and cut off his branches, shake off his leaves, and scatter his fruit: let the beasts get away from under it, and the fowls from his branches:

Daniel 4:15 Nevertheless leave the stump of his roots in the earth, even with a band of iron and brass, in the tender grass of the field; and let it be wet with the dew of heaven, and let his portion be with the beasts in the grass of the earth:

Nebuchadnezzar was represented by the tree. It was decreed that the tree was to be cut down. As punishment for his pride and wickedness the king was to be wet with dew and eat grass with the beasts for a period of time. Yet the stump and the roots would be kept safe with "**a band of iron and brass.**"

Daniel 4:16 Let his heart be changed from man's, and let a beast's heart be given unto him: and let seven times pass over him.

God decreed that seven times, or seven years, must pass over Nebuchadnezzar while he had the heart of a beast. He would lose his reasoning and live with the beasts of the field, eating grass as they do. This was to be his punishment until Nebuchadnezzar humbled himself before God admitting that the God of Heaven was the arbiter of all destinies.

"**Seven times pass over him**." Verse 23 repeats the punishment length a second time, "till seven times pass over him."

A third time the punishment period is stated in verse 25, "seven times shall pass over thee."

Verse 32, for the fourth time says, "and seven times shall pass over thee."

The punishment period of "seven times" is mentioned four different times in this chapter. Any time God mentions things multiple times, the repetition is highlighting the importance.

Daniel 4:34 And at the end of the days I Nebuchadnezzar lifted up mine eyes unto heaven, and mine understanding returned unto me, and I blessed the most High, and I praised and honoured him that liveth for ever, whose dominion is an everlasting dominion, and his kingdom is from generation to generation:

Nebuchadnezzar testifies that his understanding returned at the end of the punishment period—a "man's heart was given"[3] him.

Daniel 4:36 At the same time my reason returned unto me; and for the glory of my kingdom, mine honour and brightness returned unto me; and my counsellors and my lords sought unto me; and I was established in my kingdom, and excellent majesty was added unto me.

The king's majesty returns with his reason. God fulfilled his promise to Nebuchadnezzar that the kingdom would be kept secure until he knew that "the heaven's do rule."

Daniel 4:37 Now I Nebuchadnezzar praise and extol and honour the King of heaven, all whose works are truth, and his ways judgment: and those that walk in pride he is able to abase.

As a result of this experience Nebuchadnezzar gives praise and honor to the God of heaven. The king admits that his pride was humbled.

In summary:
- The punishment length—"seven times"—is repeated four times
- Iron and brass are mentioned
- Nebuchadnezzar's pride is broken—by being among the beasts
- His understanding returns
- Majesty returns to Nebuchadnezzar
- The King of heaven receives praise and honor
- Nebuchadnezzar becomes a servant of God

---

[3] Daniel 7:4

There is a fascinating Bible chapter in a very unexpected location that contains parallels to this passage found no where else in Scripture.

Leviticus 26:18 And if ye will not yet for all this hearken unto me, then I will punish you **seven times** more for your sins.

Leviticus 26:19 And I will **break the pride of your power**; and I will make your heaven as **iron**, and your earth as **brass**:

Leviticus 26:21 And if ye walk contrary unto me, and will not hearken unto me; I will bring **seven times** more plagues upon you according to your sins.

Leviticus 26:22 I will also **send wild beasts among you**, which shall rob you of your children, and destroy your cattle, and make you few in number; and your high ways shall be desolate.

Leviticus 26:24 Then will I also walk contrary unto you, and will punish you yet **seven times** for your sins.

Leviticus 26:27 And if ye will not for all this hearken unto me, but walk contrary unto me;

Leviticus 26:28 Then I will walk contrary unto you also in fury; and I, even I, will chastise you **seven times** for your sins.

Leviticus 26:29 And **ye shall eat the flesh of your sons, and the flesh of your daughters shall ye eat.**

Leviticus 26:31 And **I will make your cities waste, and bring your sanctuaries unto desolation**, and I will not smell the savour of your sweet odours.

Leviticus 26:33 And I will **scatter you among the heathen**, and will draw out a sword after you: and your land shall be desolate, and your cities waste.

Leviticus 26:34 Then shall **the land enjoy her sabbaths, as long as it lieth desolate**, and ye be in your enemies' land; even **then shall the land rest, and enjoy her sabbaths**.

Leviticus 26:35 As long **as it lieth desolate it shall rest; because it did not rest in your sabbaths**, when ye dwelt upon it.

Leviticus 26:41 And that I also have walked contrary unto them, and have brought them into the land of their enemies; if then their uncircumcised hearts be humbled, and **they then accept of the punishment of their iniquity**:

Leviticus 26:44 And yet for all that, when they be in the land of their enemies, **I will not cast them away, neither will I abhor them, to destroy them utterly, and to break my covenant with them: for I am the LORD their God.**

Leviticus 26:45 But **I will for their sakes remember the covenant** of their ancestors, whom I brought forth out of the land of Egypt in the sight of the heathen, **that I might be their God**: I am the LORD.

Leviticus 26 outlines the blessings that will follow if Israel is obedient and the inevitable curses if they are disobedient. We are considering only the punishment portion. Just as in Daniel 4, the punishment period—"seven times"—is repeated four times. Just as in Daniel 4, the purpose of the punishment is to "**break the pride of your power**." Just as in Daniel 4, iron and brass are mentioned. Just as in Daniel 4, the punishment included exile among the beasts. In symbolic Bible prophecy beasts represent heathen nations. Verse 22 says, "I will also send wild beasts among you," and verse 33 says, "I will scatter you among the heathen." Israel was to be among the beasts, which represented heathen nations. Their understanding would return,[4] when they accept the punishment, just as Nebuchadnezzar in Daniel 4. Just as in Daniel 4, the glory is given to God, as a merciful, covenant-keeping God. Just as Nebuchadnezzar, in Daniel 4, Israel becomes a servant of God—"**that I might be their God.**" Daniel 4 and Leviticus 26 are clearly and dramatically linked, showing us that God intends for them to explain each other.

God reminds Israel that the reason for this punishment is because they did not keep the sabbath; therefore, the land would be desolate and rest. The breaking of the seventh-day sabbath was directly tied to the desolation of Jerusalem. Understanding the reason for the chastisement is necessary to accept their punishments, therefore part of the return of their understanding is a return to an understanding of the Bible sabbath. The return of their understanding would include an insight into the covenant God wanted to make with them: "But this shall be the covenant that I will make with the house of Israel; After those days, saith the LORD, I will put my law in their inward parts, and write it in their hearts; and will be their God, and they shall be my people."[5]

Among other things, Leviticus 26 includes a clear and direct prophecy of the destruction of Jerusalem in A.D 70. Verse 31 refers to their cities and the sanctuaries being brought to desolation. Jesus

---

[4] Leviticus 26:41 "they then accept of the punishment of their iniquity." In order to accept their punishment, they must understand it, therefore their understanding returns at the end of the punishment.

[5] Jeremiah 31:33

used the same language when unveiling the siege of Jerusalem to his disciples: "and his disciples came to him for to show him the buildings of the temple. And Jesus said unto them, See ye not all these things? verily I say unto you, **There shall not be left here one stone upon another, that shall not be thrown down**.... When ye therefore shall see the **abomination of desolation**, spoken of by Daniel the prophet, stand in the holy place, (whoso readeth, let him understand)."[6] Jesus refers to the city and the sanctuary being destroyed and brought to desolation.

Another passage found in Deuteronomy 28, is directly parallel to Leviticus 26, and uses the same imagery of iron and brass: "And thy heaven that is over thy head shall be **brass**, and the earth that is under thee shall be **iron**."[7] Additionally, like Leviticus 26, Deuteronomy 28 prophesies that there would be a siege so severe that the inhabitants would eat their children. Quoting from Deuteronomy 28, the spirit of prophecy directly applies the passage to the destruction of Jerusalem: "The utter wasting of the land and the horrible suffering of the people during the siege of Jerusalem under Titus centuries later, were vividly portrayed: 'He shall eat the fruit of thy cattle, and the fruit of thy land, until thou be destroyed.... And he shall **besiege** thee in all thy gates, **until thy high and fenced walls come down**, wherein thou trustedst, throughout all thy land.... **Thou shalt eat the fruit of thine own body, the flesh of thy sons and of thy daughters**, which the Lord thy God hath given thee, in the **siege**, and in the straitness, wherewith thine enemies shall distress thee.' 'The tender and delicate woman among you, which would not adventure to set the sole of her foot upon the ground for delicateness and tenderness, her eye shall be evil toward the husband of her bosom,... and toward her children which she shall bear: for **she shall eat them** for want of all things secretly in the **siege** and straitness, wherewith thine enemy shall distress thee in thy gates.'"[8] Leviticus 26 and Deuteronomy 28 are describing the same event—the desolation of Jerusalem by the Roman armies in A.D. 70. Therefore, whatever punishment God decreed in Leviticus 26 must encompass the destruction of Jerusalem.

---

[6] Matthew 24:1-2, 15

[7] Deuteronomy 28:23

[8] E. G. White, *Patriarchs and Prophets* (1890), p. 467.2.

In summary:
- The punishment length—"seven times"—is repeated four times
- The time period must encompass the destruction of Jerusalem
- Iron and brass is mentioned
- Israel's pride is broken—by being among the "beasts"
- Israel's understanding returns
- Majesty is given to Christ
- The King of Heaven receives praise & honor
- Israel becomes a servant of God

Perhaps you are wondering, what about these seven times? Seven times are seven years, as we saw from Daniel 4. Yet we have no Biblical record of Israel being punished for seven literal years. Seven years might be an appropriate period of time to punish the king of a pagan nation. If one individual is punished for seven years, would the same amount of time be appropriate to punish an entire nation that has gone into apostasy for centuries? In Daniel 7, 8 and 9 we discovered that in symbolic, prophetic passages of the Bible a day represents a year. If this principle was applied to the "seven times" of Leviticus 26, how many years would be delineated? The Biblical year, outlined at the time of the flood is 360 days long.[9] Seven years therefore would be 2,520 days, which would represent 2,520 years.

The evidence from Leviticus 26 itself indicates that any time period intended must be more than seven literal years since the prophecy encompasses the destruction of Jerusalem in A.D. 70.

At the time that God was giving this instruction, Israel was a united nation. After the glory of Solomon's reign, his son, Rehoboam, took the throne of Israel. His people requested relief from some of the

---

[9] Until the time of the flood, according to Scripture, there were 360 days in a year. Counting 150 days from the seventeenth day of the second month to the seventeenth day of the seventh month, makes each month 30 days in length. Therefore, a year before the flood was 360 days long. Apparently the violence of the flood actually altered the earth's course around the sun.

Genesis 7:11 "In the six hundredth year of Noah's life, **in the second month, the seventeenth day of the month**, the same day were all the fountains of the great deep broken up, and the windows of heaven were opened."

Genesis 7:24 "And the waters prevailed upon the earth **an hundred and fifty days**."

Genesis 8:3 "And the waters returned from off the earth continually: and after the **end of the hundred and fifty days** the waters were abated.

Genesis 8:4 And the ark rested **in the seventh month, on the seventeenth day of the month**, upon the mountains of Ararat.

oppressive measures of his father. Instead of reigning with mercy, he answered, "My father made your yoke heavy, and I will add to your yoke: my father also chastised you with whips, but I will chastise you with scorpions." As a result, ten tribes of Israel rebelled becoming the northern kingdom of Israel. Only Judah and Benjamin remained with Rehoboam, becoming the southern kingdom of Judah. God still considered both kingdoms to be his people, but from that time on he dealt with the apostasy of each one separately. The initial punishment was that they would be scattered among the beasts. A beast in Bible prophecy represents a kingdom.[10] Therefore the initial punishment was captivity by a heathen nation, or the loss of national sovereignty. Scripture records the year in which the punishment of Leviticus 26 went into effect for both Israel, and then Judah. Israel descended into apostasy first.

"In the twelfth year of Ahaz king of Judah began Hoshea... to reign in Samaria.... And he did that which was evil in the sight of the LORD.... Against him came up Shalmaneser king of Assyria; and Hoshea became his servant, and gave him presents. And the king of Assyria found conspiracy in Hoshea:... therefore the king of Assyria shut him up, and bound him in prison. Then the king of Assyria came up throughout all the land, and went up to Samaria, and besieged it three years."[11] Israel first lost national sovereignty to Assyria, the country that would become the Babylonian empire, in the year 723 B.C. Counting 2,520 years from 723 B.C. we arrive at the year A.D.

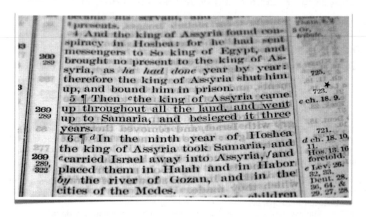

---

[10] See Daniel 7:17.

[11] 2 Kings 17:1-5

1798. The year 1798 has some of the greatest prophetic significance of any time period in Scripture.[12]

Judah sank into the degradation of apostasy somewhat slower. Scripture records the first loss of national sovereignty thus, "So Manasseh made Judah and the inhabitants of Jerusalem to err, and to do worse than the heathen, whom the LORD had destroyed before the children of Israel. And the LORD spake to Manasseh, and to his people: but they would not hearken. Wherefore the LORD brought upon them the captains of the host of the king of Assyria, which took Manasseh among the thorns, and bound him with fetters, and carried him to Babylon."[13]

God deals justly; as soon as the wickedness of his people exceeded divine forbearance, the same punishment that came upon Israel fell upon Judah. The crown of Judah is lost to Assyria, the country that would become the Babylonian empire, in the year 677 B.C. Counting 2,520 years from 677 B.C. we arrive at the year A.D. 1844!

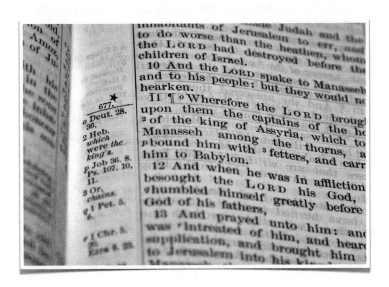

Counting the number of years specified in the punishment from the first loss of the crown, or national sovereignty, of both Israel and Judah and arriving in the years 1798 and 1844, respectively, is beyond the possibility of coincidence. Divine providence and foreknowledge must have thus decreed.

The question then naturally arises—how were Israel and Judah punished, respectively, until 1798 and 1844?

The answer was revealed by God to his servants, the prophets: "'Thus saith the Lord God; Remove the diadem, and take off the crown:... exalt him that is low, and abase him that is high. I will overturn, overturn, overturn, it: and it shall be no more, until he come whose right it is; and I will give it him.'[14] The crown removed from Israel passed successively to the kingdoms of Babylon, Medo-Persia, Greece, and Rome. God says, 'It shall be no more, until he come whose right it is; and I will give it him.'"[15]

The reason that Babylon, Medo-Persia, Greece, and Rome were the four empires to rule the world, is that they successively held the crown of Israel. The God of heaven had decreed that his people would lose their crown to heathen nations for a specified period of time. The Roman Empire consisted of both the pagan and papal aspects of Rome.

God decreed that when Rome lost Israel's crown, it would no longer be an earthly crown, but instead would be given to the true heir of the throne of Israel, to "him whose right it is,"—the son of David, Jesus Christ. In 1798 Rome lost Israel's crown,[16] exactly as the Bible predicted.

In 1844 Jesus entered the throne room of the universe before the Father, to begin the process that would lead to the restoration of the crown of David to the kingdom of Israel. "I saw in the night visions, and, behold, one like the **Son of man** {son of David} came with the clouds of heaven, and came to the Ancient of days, and they brought

---

[14] Ezekiel 21:26-27

[15] E. G. White, *The Review and Herald*, November 23, 1905 par. 4-5.

[16] Therefore, when the papacy asserts world dominance, just before the second coming of Jesus, by implementing, through the second beast of Revelation 13, a law that opposes the law of God, they will be committing an act of high treason against the King of the Universe.

him near before him. And **there was given him dominion, and glory, and a kingdom**, that all people, nations, and languages, should serve him: his dominion is an everlasting dominion, which shall not pass away, and his kingdom that which shall not be destroyed."[17]

"I was shown the disappointment of the disciples as they came to the sepulcher and found not the body of Jesus. Mary said, 'They have taken away my Lord, and I know not where they have laid Him.' Angels told the sorrowing disciples that their Lord had risen, and would go before them into Galilee.

"In like manner I saw that Jesus regarded with the deepest compassion the disappointed ones who had waited for His coming; and He sent His angels to direct their minds that they might follow Him where He was. He showed them that this earth is not the sanctuary, but that **He must enter the most holy place of the heavenly sanctuary** to make an atonement for His people **and to receive the kingdom** from His Father, and that He would then return to the earth and take them to dwell with Him forever."[18]

In 1844 Jesus began the restoration of the kingdom of Israel—not the country of Israel in the Middle East, but spiritual Israel. Christ began the process of making Jerusalem the capital of his kingdom[19]—not the city in the Middle East, but the New Jerusalem in heaven. "That which God purposed to do for the world through Israel, the chosen nation, He will finally accomplish through His church on earth today. He has 'let out His vineyard unto other husbandmen,' even to His covenant-keeping people, who faithfully 'render Him the fruits in their seasons.' Never has the Lord been without true

---

[17] Daniel 7:13-14

[18] E. G. White, *Early Writings* (1892), p. 244.1-2.

[19] "I saw that **while Jesus was in the most holy place He would be married to the New Jerusalem**; and after His work should be accomplished in the holiest, He would descend to the earth in **kingly power** and take to Himself the precious ones who had patiently waited His return. "I was shown what did take place in heaven at the close of the prophetic periods in 1844. As Jesus ended His ministration in the holy place and closed the door of that apartment, a great darkness settled upon those who had heard and rejected the message of His coming, and they lost sight of Him. **Jesus then clothed Himself with precious garments.** Around the bottom of His robe was a bell and a pomegranate, a bell and a pomegranate. A breastplate of curious work was suspended from His shoulders. As He moved, this glittered like diamonds, magnifying letters which looked like names written or engraved upon the breastplate. **Upon His head was something which had the appearance of a crown.** When fully attired, He was surrounded by angels, and in a flaming chariot He passed within the second veil."
E. G. White, *Early Writings* (1892), p. 251.1-2.

representatives on this earth who have made His interests their own. These witnesses for God are numbered among the **spiritual Israel**, and to them will be fulfilled all the covenant promises made by Jehovah to His ancient people."[20]

At the end of the 2,520 years of punishment God re-established the nation of Israel—not the country in the Middle East, but spiritual Israel. In 1798 Rome lost Israel's crown (which event began the time of the end), and in 1844 as spiritual Israel was reinstated, the sabbath was restored to their understanding, the temple was re-established (the door into the heavenly most holy was opened),[21] and the crowned prince stepped into the throne room of spiritual Israel, to receive a kingdom that shall never be destroyed. Thus, when papal Rome claims their temporal power to be restored in 1929 and they once more begin to assume the authority of the crown they lost in 1798, they commit high treason against the government of God.

The advent pioneers[22] that were preaching the message of the soon coming of Jesus, leading up to 1844, and for several years after the great disappointment understood and presented the 2,520-year prophecy. William Miller stated, "Israel began to be carried away in the days of Hoshea, 722 B.C., and from that time to 1798 after Christ, is exactly 2,520 years, or the seven prophetic years. How remarkable, that when the seven years ended, God began to deliver his church from her bondage, which for ages had been made subject to the kings of the earth. In 1798 the church came out of the wilderness, and began to be delivered from her captivity. But the completion of her slavery to the kingdoms of the earth, is reserved for another period. Beginning in 677 B.C., seven prophetic years, or 2,520 common years, would end in A.D. 1843.[23] Therefore, beginning at the captivity of Manasseh and the final dispersion of the

---

[20] E. G. White, *Prophets and Kings* (1917), p. 713.1.

[21] Psalms 77:13 "Thy way, O God, is in the sanctuary: who is so great a God as our God?"

[22] This included William Miller (1842); Joseph Bates (1847); Apollo Hale (1843); Josiah Litch (1843), Joshua V. Himes (1840-1845); S. S. Snow (1844); and James White (1850).

[23] Later they realized that the command to restore and rebuild Jerusalem, which was the beginning of the 2,300 years, went forth in the fall of 457 B.C., which meant that the whole year of 457 could not be counted. Therefore, the termination of the 2,300 years could not occur before the autumn of 1844. This repositioning of the dates was the fulfillment of the prophecy of Habakuk 2:3, "For the vision is yet for an appointed time, but at the end it shall speak, and not lie: though it tarry, wait for it; because it will surely come, it will not tarry."

ten tribes of Israel, where God has fixed the time for the dispersion of the people of God and the scattering of the holy people, until the year 1843, will be the end of the seven years, when the acceptable year of the LORD will commence."[24]

Not until the mid 1850's did some start questioning the validity of the 2,520 years (beginning with Hiram Edson), since none seemed to see an event fulfilling the termination of Israel's punishment in 1798 and 1844.

Their eyes had been drawn heavenward for the fulfillment of the 2,300[25] year prophecy, but then glanced earthward for the explanation of the "seven times." Their minds were captivated by Christ's position as our mediating high priest, but overlooked the importance of his reception of the crown of Israel, and his supreme authority in the judgment as the king of the universe—the sovereign of Israel. As the crown prince he stands for the children of his people.[26] Not only has the defense of your case, in the supreme court of the universe, been assumed by a faithful high priest, but by the one who is to be crowned the King of All Creation.

---

[24] William Miller, *A Lecture on the Typical Sabbaths and Great Jubilee* (Boston: Joshua V. Himes, 1842), p. 18.1.

[25] The 2,520 years provides the second witness, to the 2,300 years, for the prophetic significance of 1844, "that in the mouth of two or three witnesses every word may be established." Matthew 18:16.

[26] Daniel 12:1

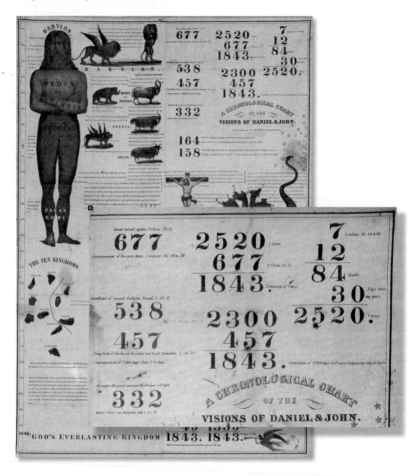

The seventy weeks of Daniel 9 outlines a probationary period of time "cut off" for the Jewish nation. Even after the Jews as a nation rejected Christ as the Messiah, the kingdom of heaven extended to the Jews through the disciples for another three and a half years. "These twelve Jesus sent forth, and commanded them, saying, Go not into the way of the Gentiles, and into any city of the Samaritans enter ye not: But go rather to the lost sheep of the house of Israel. And as ye go, preach, saying, The kingdom of heaven is at hand."[27] "Then by the stoning of Stephen the Jews finally sealed their rejection of the gospel; the disciples who were scattered abroad by persecution 'went everywhere preaching the word' (Acts 8:4); and shortly after, Saul the persecutor was converted, and became Paul, the apostle to the Gentiles."[28]

Today Christians are looking to the Middle East to see what will happen with the earthly nation of Israel, not realizing that the Bible has declared that, as a nation, they are no longer God's chosen people. "Jesus saith unto them, Did ye never read in the scriptures, The stone which the builders rejected, the same is become the head of the corner: this is the Lord's doing, and it is marvellous in our eyes? Therefore say I unto you, The kingdom of God shall be taken from you, and given to a nation bringing forth the fruits thereof."[29]

"And if ye be Christ's, then are ye Abraham's seed, and heirs according to the promise."[30] "For he is not a Jew, which is one outwardly; neither is that circumcision, which is outward in the flesh: But he is a Jew, which is one inwardly; and circumcision is that of the heart, in the spirit, and not in the letter; whose praise is not of men, but of God."[31] "Not as though the word of God hath taken none effect. For they are not all Israel, which are of Israel: Neither, because they are the seed of Abraham, are they all children: but, In Isaac shall thy seed be called. That is, They which are the children of the flesh, these are not the children of God: but the children of the promise are counted for the seed."[32]

---

[27] Matthew 10:5-7

[28] E. G. White, *The Desire of Ages* (1898), p. 233.3.

[29] Matthew 21:42-43

[30] Galatians 3:29

[31] Romans 2:28-29

[32] Romans 9:6-8

According to Scripture, Israel is no longer composed of the children of the flesh, or physical descendants of Abraham, but constituted rather by children of the promise. Isaac was the child of promise. All who believe in the promise of salvation through Jesus Christ may be numbered with spiritual Israel. "Neither is there salvation in any other: for there is none other name under heaven given among men, whereby we must be saved."[33]

Many Christians claiming the name of Jesus will be lost: "Not every one that saith unto me, Lord, Lord, shall enter into the kingdom of heaven; but he that doeth the will of my Father which is in heaven. Many will say to me in that day, Lord, Lord, have we not prophesied in thy name? and in thy name have cast out devils? and in thy name done many wonderful works? And then will I profess unto them, I never knew you: depart from me, ye that work iniquity."[34]

"For though the people of Israel be as the sand of the sea, yet a remnant of them shall return. The consumption decreed shall overflow with righteousness."[35] Only a remnant of Israel will return to Jerusalem—that heavenly city "for wide is the gate, and broad is the way, that leadeth to destruction, and many there be which go in thereat: Because strait is the gate, and narrow is the way, which leadeth unto life, and few there be that find it."[36]

Paul speaks of the remnant of Israel, quoting from Isaiah, "Esaias also crieth concerning Israel, Though the number of the children of Israel be as the sand of the sea, a remnant shall be saved:"[37] Under the inspiration of the Holy Spirit, Paul interprets Isaiah's remnant that shall return, as a remnant that "shall be saved." There will be many physical descendants of Abraham, and many who claim to be members of spiritual Israel, claiming the name of Jesus, but only a remnant will be saved. Zephaniah says the same thing in different words: "The remnant of Israel shall not do iniquity, nor speak lies; neither shall a deceitful tongue be found in their mouth: for they shall

---

[33] Acts 4:12

[34] Matthew 7:21-23

[35] Isaiah 10:22

[36] Matthew 7:13-14

[37] Romans 9:27

feed and lie down, and none shall make them afraid."[38] The characteristic of the remnant of Israel is that they follow the will of God. By his grace and through his power they keep his commandments.

Paul, recounting the story of Elijah when all the children of Israel were following after Baal, and Elijah thought he might be the only one left following the commands of God, states, "But what saith the answer of God unto him? I have **reserved** to myself seven thousand men, who have not bowed the knee to the image of Baal. Even so then at this present time also there is a **remnant** according to the election of grace."[39] Though it was a small number, God had preserved a remnant—more than Elijah expected—who refused to break the second commandment.[40] "For whosoever shall keep the whole law, and yet offend in one point, he is guilty of all."[41]

When a seamstress shops for cloth at a fabric store, the fabric store has a section that is called the remnant section. Those remnants are segments of the original bolts of cloth that are now not big enough to make a full piece of clothing but may be just what is needed to finish a garment that needs a little more of the original fabric. What is the characteristic of that remnant cloth? It is identical to the original.

God has a remnant church that follows the pattern of the original exactly. "And as many as walk according to this rule, peace be on them, and mercy, and upon the Israel of God."[42] God has a remnant church on this earth—the Israel of God—who follow the commands of their king.

---

[38] Zephaniah 3:13

[39] Romans 11:4-5

[40] Exodus 20:4-5

[41] James 2:10

[42] Galatians 6:16

It is estimated that there are over 30,000 denominations claiming the name of Christ.[43] This is called Babylon—confusion.[44] The Bible says, "There is one body, and one Spirit, even as ye are called in one hope of your calling; One Lord, one faith, one baptism."[45] It is not Biblical to have all different kinds of baptisms. The Bible says nothing about sprinkling for baptism. Biblical Baptism is always by immersion. "And John also was baptizing in Aenon near to Salim, because there was **much water** there: and they came, and were baptized."[46] "And it came to pass in those days, that Jesus came from Nazareth of Galilee, and was baptized of John in Jordan. And straightway **coming up out of the water**, he saw the heavens opened, and the Spirit like a dove descending upon him."[47] In the same way, there is one body and one faith. What does God's remnant church—spiritual Israel—look like today? "And the dragon was wroth with the woman,[48] and went to make war with **the remnant of her seed**, which keep the commandments of God, and have the testimony of Jesus Christ."[49] The remnant church of God at the end of time, according to Scripture, have two characteristics:
1. They keep the commandments of God and,
2. they have the testimony of Jesus Christ.

The New Testament, decades after the resurrection of Jesus, informs us that the first characteristic of Christ's end-time remnant church is keeping the commandments. Yet the majority of preachers today assert that commandment keeping is unnecessary, or

---

[43] Matthew 15:8-9 "This people draweth nigh unto me with their mouth, and honoureth me with their lips; but their heart is far from me. But in vain they do worship me, teaching for doctrines the commandments of men."

[44] There have been true followers of God in every single denomination, through all ages, even those who have never heard the name of Jesus, who lived up to all the truth that they had that will be saved, for, "the times of this ignorance God winked at; but now commandeth all men every where to repent." Acts 17:30

"None will be condemned for not heeding light and knowledge that they never had, and they could not obtain. But many refuse to obey the truth that is presented to them by Christ's ambassadors, because they wish to conform to the world's standard; and the truth that has reached their understanding, the light that has shone in the soul, will condemn them in the Judgment." E. G. White, The Review and Herald, November 25, 1884 par. 27.

[45] Ephesians 4:4-5

[46] John 3:23

[47] Mark 1:9-10

[48] A woman in Bible prophecy represents a church. See comments on Revelation 12:1.

[49] Revelation 12:17

impossible. The remnant church of Bible prophecy, will keep all ten of the commandments, including the fourth command to keep holy the seventh-day sabbath. "The word of God through His prophet to those who should yield themselves to Him and observe His law was that they should thenceforth be numbered among spiritual Israel—His church on earth."[50] If you want to find God's church on earth, this one characteristic rules out 99.9% of all faiths, religions, and Christian denominations. There are only a handful that keep the sabbath of the Creator. "And on the seventh day God ended his work which he had made; and he rested on the seventh day from all his work which he had made. And God blessed the seventh day, and sanctified it: because that in it he had rested from all his work which God created and made."[51]

None will be saved by keeping the commandments, for we are saved by grace, by the blood of Jesus, through faith. "Knowing that a man is not justified by the works of the law, but by the faith of Jesus Christ, even we have believed in Jesus Christ, that we might be justified by the faith of Christ, and not by the works of the law: for by the works of the law shall no flesh be justified."[52] "Do we then make void the law through faith? God forbid: yea, we establish the law."[53] "And hereby we do know that we know him, if we keep his commandments. He that saith, I know him, and keepeth not his commandments, is a liar, and the truth is not in him. But whoso keepeth his word, in him verily is the love of God perfected: hereby know we that we are in him."[54] "If ye love me, keep my commandments."[55]

"The keeping of all the commandments of God is sanctification. Proving yourselves obedient children to God's word is sanctification. The word of God is to be our guide, not the opinions or ideas of men. Let those who would be truly sanctified search the word of God with patience, with prayer, and with humble contrition of soul. Let them

---

[50] E. G. White, *Prophets and Kings* (1917), p. 371.3.

[51] Genesis 2:2-3

[52] Galatians 2:16

[53] Romans 3:31

[54] 1 John 2:3-5

[55] John 14:15

remember that Jesus prayed. 'Sanctify them through thy truth: thy word is truth.'"[56]

The second characteristic of spiritual Israel—God's end-time remnant people—is that they have the testimony of Jesus. What is the testimony of Jesus? There is no need for speculation, because the Bible defines the term explicitly: "And I fell at his feet to worship him. And he said unto me, See thou do it not: I am thy fellowservant, and of thy brethren that have the **testimony of Jesus**: worship God: for **the testimony of Jesus is the spirit of prophecy**."[57] The remnant of Israel will keep the commandments of God and have in their midst the gift of prophecy. There is only one sabbath-keeping church in the world that even claims to have the gift of prophecy[58]— the Seventh-day Adventist Church. These two characteristics are enough to identify spiritual Israel—the remnant church of Bible prophecy. However, there is still more evidence.

Some think Peter is the foundation of the church of God. Jesus said to Peter, "And I say also unto thee, That thou art Peter, and upon this rock I will build my church; and the gates of hell shall not prevail against it."[59] The Catholic church uses this verse to say that Peter was the first pope upon whom the church of God is built. The name "Peter" means pebble, little stone, or little pebble. Jesus was actually using a play on words. Jesus says to Peter that he is a little pebble, but upon this rock—Jesus is pointing to himself—upon the rock of ages I will build my church, and the gates of hell will not prevail against it. To prove this, we need only read down to verse 23, "But he turned, and said unto Peter, Get thee behind me, Satan: thou art an offence unto me: for thou savourest not the things that be of God, but those that be of men."[60] Jesus does not found the Christian on the little pebble whom he rebukes as Satan, "For other foundation can no man lay than that is laid, which is Jesus Christ."[61] Jesus is the

---

[56] E. G. White, *The Review and Herald*, March 25, 1902 par. 8.

[57] Revelation 19:10

[58] For for information on the spirit of prophecy see comments on Daniel 10:17.

[59] Matthew 16:18

[60] Matthew 16:23

[61] 1 Corinthians 3:11

stone that the builders rejected.[62] Jesus is the rock. On the foundation of the rock of Jesus Christ alone, God's remnant church would take the everlasting gospel to the whole world: "And this gospel of the kingdom shall be preached in all the world for a witness unto all nations; and then shall the end come."[63] As of 2015, of the 237 nations recognized by the United Nations, the Seventh-day Adventist church has an established work in 215 of them. No other Protestant denomination comes anywhere close to having an official work in this many countries.

"I saw another angel fly in the midst of heaven, having **the everlasting gospel** to preach unto them that dwell on the earth, and to every nation, and kindred, and tongue, and people, Saying with a loud voice..."[64] Revelation defines the everlasting gospel message as messages coming from three angels consisting of four main points:
1. "The hour of his judgment is come"[65]
2. worship the Creator ("him that made..."),
3. "Babylon is fallen,"
4. and do not receive the mark of the beast.

There is only one church in the world that teaches the clear Bible doctrine of the investigative judgment in the heavenly sanctuary beginning at a set hour at the end of time. There are only a handful of organized churches that recognize the Creator by worshipping on the day he made holy as a commemoration of his creative power.[66] There is only one denomination who still identifies Babylon and preaches the message that it has fallen.[67] There is only one denomination in the world that identifies Biblically what the mark of the beast is, and how to avoid its reception.[68] These three angel's messages will lead to a world-wide proclamation for any of God's people still in Babylon to separate from her communion: "Come out

---

[62] Luke 20:17

[63] Matthew 24:14

[64] Revelation 14:6-7

[65] Revelation 14:7

[66] Genesis 2:2-3

[67] There are still many true Protestants in many different denominations who protest the corruptions and deceptions of Rome, but their denominations as a whole, no longer accept the Scripture's definitions of the beasts of Bible prophecy.

[68] See comments on Revelation 13 and 14.

of her, my people, that ye be not partakers of her sins, and that ye receive not of her plagues."

In summary, the remnant—the Israel of God, whom God raised up when he reestablished the kingdom of Israel (spiritual Israel) in 1844, will have the following characteristics:

1. Like the original apostolic church, every doctrine would be based on Scripture alone.
2. Like the original apostolic church, spiritual Israel keeps all of God's commandments, including the seventh-day sabbath.
3. Like the original apostolic church, spiritual Israel has the testimony of Jesus—the spirit of prophecy.
4. Like the original apostolic church, spiritual Israel is built on the faith of Jesus.
5. Like the original apostolic church, spiritual Israel carries the everlasting gospel (consisting of four parts) to all the world:
   a. "The hour of his judgment is come"
   b. worship the Creator ("him that made..."),
   c. "Babylon is fallen,"
   d. and do not receive the mark of the beast.

During the dark ages, every single truth of the sanctuary service was obscured by the traditions of the papal church: The truth of the altar of burnt offering, that our sins are forgiven by the sacrifice of Christ was replaced with the doctrine of salvation by works and the Eucharist.

The rite of baptism, represented by the laver, for those of an age who could understand its meaning, was modified into infant sprinkling[69]—once again creating a doctrine that salvation could be

---

[69] The Catholic doctrine of infant baptism sprang out of their doctrine of "original sin." This false doctrine claims that every decedent of Adam is directly guilty of Adam's sin. Thus, they claim that the newborn baby is guilty of Adam's original sin unless baptized. This is directly contrary to Scripture which states: "The soul that sinneth, it shall die. The son shall not bear the iniquity of the father, neither shall the father bear the iniquity of the son: the righteousness of the righteous shall be upon him, and the wickedness of the wicked shall be upon him." Ezekiel 18:20. A child is not guilty of sin, until they sin. When they come to the age of accountability, if they reject the provisions for forgiveness, they will be condemned for their sins alone.

Biblically, each descendent of Adam has inherited a sinful nature with its propensity to sin and the inability to overcome the bent toward evil without the direct intervention of God. "God has not left us to battle with evil in our own finite strength. Whatever may be our inherited or cultivated tendencies to wrong, we can overcome through the power that He is ready to impart." E. G. White, *Temperance*, p. 112.1.

achieved by our own deeds, or by the performance of a ritual, rather than placing our faith in the saving power of Jesus.

The Bible, represented by the showbread, was taken from the people and in its place was substituted the traditions of men and the authority of the priest.

In place of the fire of the Holy Spirit, or light of the candlestick to guide the conscience, the fires of the Inquisition determined what most could believe.

Rather than going to Jesus for the forgiveness of sins, and having the smoke of his incense cover us with his righteousness, the sinner was directed for forgiveness to a fellow sinner in the form of the priest.

And, just as prophesied in Scripture, this same power thought "to change times and laws,"[70] even modifying the very law of God, and substituting the commandments of men.[71]

During the Protestant reformation, each of these sanctuary truths were returned, step by step, to prominence in the minds of God's people. Martin Luther recovered the truth of the altar of burnt offering, that we are saved by grace through faith alone in the death of Jesus. John Smyth rediscovered the Bible truth of baptism by immersion, following our Savior's example. Wycliffe, Tyndale, Erasmus, Luther and others restored to the people the bread of life— the word of God. John Calvin resurrected the Bible doctrine that we can bring our prayers "boldly unto the throne of grace, that we may obtain mercy, and find grace to help in time of need;"[72] rather than going through a priest, "there is one God, and one mediator between God and men, the man Christ Jesus."[73] John Wesley rekindled interest in the work and person of the Holy Spirit.

The final sanctuary truths to be reignited were the existence of the true tabernacle in heaven, and the eternal nature of God's law as the

---

[70] Daniel 7:25

[71] See comments on Daniel 7.

[72] Hebrews 4:16

[73] 1 Timothy 2:5

foundation of his throne. This revealed the binding claims of the Sabbath as the signature of authorship of the lawgiver[74] and soon return of the judge of all the earth. These truths were brought to view by William Miller, Ellen White, and others, in the great American reformation—the advent awakening—during the ten years leading up to 1844.

God raised up each step of additional light, but in each case, the people who accepted the truths their leaders discovered began to follow the human instrument rather than the divine originator of the message. Rather than accepting any further light, the followers of Luther became Lutherans, the followers of Calvin became Calvinists (Presbyterians), the followers of John Wesley became Methodist, the followers of John Smyth became Baptists; hence the innumerable sects of the Christian faith today. God was seeking to restore the entire sanctuary message of salvation. Only the advent awakening of 1844 brought to light the complete message of salvation, restoring spiritual Israel—the Seventh-day Adventist remnant church of Bible prophecy.

"It is the unity of Christ's followers that convinces the world that God has indeed sent his Son to die for sinners.... Christ declares, 'There shall be one fold, and one shepherd.' He came to our world to live the life that was to be the pattern for all his children. He came to reveal the love that was to bind them heart to heart. And he made unity the badge of their discipleship."[75]

"We cannot surrender the truth in order to accomplish this union; for the very means by which it is to be gained is sanctification through the truth. Human wisdom would change all this, thinking this basis of union too narrow. Men would effect a union through conformity to popular opinions, through a compromise with the world. But truth is God's basis for the unity of his people."[76]

---

[74] "All who keep the seventh day signify by this act that they are worshipers of Jehovah. Thus the Sabbath is the sign of man's allegiance to God as long as there are any upon the earth to serve Him. The fourth commandment is the only one of all the ten in which are found both the name and the title of the Lawgiver. It is the only one that shows by whose authority the law is given. Thus it contains the seal of God, affixed to His law as evidence of its authenticity and binding force." E. G. White, *Patriarchs and Prophets* (1890), p. 307.2.

[75] E. G. White, *The Review and Herald*, July 21, 1903 par. 10.

[76] E. G. White, *Gospel Workers* (1892), p. 391.2.

Daniel 11

SUMMARY:
The eleventh chapter of Daniel is the culmination of detail in the
prophetic chapters of Daniel. Each prophetic chapter gives the same
basic outline of four world empires, then climaxes with the second
coming of Jesus Christ. Each prophetic chapter gives greater and
greater detail than the preceding one and, in each case, this
additional detail brings us closer, by date, to the second coming.
Chapter eleven follows the same pattern and gives the greatest
detail of all, outlining events that flow down to the very days in which
we live. Chapter eleven differs from the preceding prophetic chapters
by delivering, from the angel, a verbal description of the events
rather than Daniel receiving a symbolic representation of events.
Like chapters eight and nine, chapters eleven and twelve are
linked—with chapter twelve answering the unanswered questions of
chapter eleven (as chapter nine answers the unanswered questions
of chapter eight). Daniel 11 is considered by many Bible students,
scholars, and casual readers alike, to be one of the most difficult
chapters in the Bible. Indeed, on initial observation, it seems to be
full of confusing language and terms, and poses several enigmatic
sections that seem to be out of order, or defy explanation. However,
with careful comparison, with consistent application of the
terminology, and with a knowledge of a few simple Hebrew literary
structures, the chapter becomes clear, consistent, and beautiful
evidence for the divine origin of Scripture, for the power and
foreknowledge of God, for his loving kindness and mercy in revealing
these things through his servants the prophets, and for the nearness
of his soon coming. This chapter identifies such historical figures as:
Alexander the Great, Seleucus, Ptolemy, Berenice, Laodice,
Cassander, Lysimachus, Julius Caesar, Cleopatra, Augustus, and
Tiberius. It even identifies that the Messiah would be born during the
reign of Augustus, and die during the reign of Tiberius.

The vision of chapter eleven actually begins in chapter ten. The
setting is the river Hiddekel in the third year of Cyrus king of Persia.
Initially, Daniel sees a man clothed in linen having the same

description as Jesus in Revelation 1. Then Gabriel strengthens him and begins the prophetic revelation. First the angel relates that Daniel's prayer was heard from the very first day, but that he had been delayed by his struggles with the prince of Persia, who had withstood him twenty-one days (10:12-13), before being helped by Michael himself. Gabriel then clarifies for Daniel that he is revealing what will happen to the people of God in the end of time (latter days), and that the vision is concerning things yet far in the future (10:14).

Gabriel also assures Daniel that once he leaves him, he will return to his post of duty with Persia and will cause the kingdom of Greece to take its place (10:20). Even though the vision is concerning the distant future, and even though Daniel has already been given several visions predicting the four world empires, for reference, Gabriel begins by outlining in some detail the remaining three world empires (Babylon having already passed away).

"As we near the close of this world's history, the prophecies recorded by Daniel demand our special attention, as they relate to the very time in which we are living. With them should be linked the teachings of the last book of the New Testament Scriptures. Satan has led many to believe that the prophetic portions of the writings of Daniel and of John the revelator cannot be understood. But the promise is plain that special blessing will accompany the study of these prophecies. 'The wise shall understand' (verse 10), was spoken of the visions of Daniel that were to be unsealed in the latter days; and of the revelation that Christ gave to His servant John for the guidance of God's people all through the centuries, the promise is, 'Blessed is he that readeth, and they that hear the words of this prophecy, and keep those things which are written therein.' Revelation 1:3."[1]

Daniel 11:1 Also I in the first year of Darius the Mede, even I, stood to confirm and to strengthen him.

---

[1] E. G. White, *Prophet and Kings* (1917), p. 547.2.

Alluding to his struggles with Cyrus,[2] Gabriel indicates that it was he who had confirmed Darius the Mede some two years before.[3] Darius the Mede was the first king of the Medo-Persian Empire. His reign is already history, as chapter ten indicates that his nephew Cyrus the Great is now the monarch of the empire. Daniel had found great favor with Darius the Mede and had been advanced to be president of the presidents, which set the stage for his sentence to and subsequent rescue from the lion's den.

Daniel 11:2 And now will I show thee the truth. Behold, there shall stand up yet three kings in Persia; and the fourth shall be far richer than they all: and by his strength through his riches he shall stir up all against the realm of Grecia.

Cyrus the Great, nephew of Darius the Mede, became the second king of Medo-Persia. His reign was followed by that of his son, Cambyses. Following Cambyses was an unscrupulous impostor called the false Smerdis (called Artaxerxes in Ezra 4:7, also Guamata), who in turn was replaced by Darius Hystaspes (Darius I or Darius the Great). The richest of the Medo-Persian Kings was Xerxes the Great (the Ahasuerus of the book of Esther and Son of Darius Hystaspes). Xerxes the Great was succeeded by Artaxerxes I Longimanus. Then, "...Artaxerxes Longimanus came to the throne of Medo-Persia. The name of this king is connected with sacred history by a series of remarkable providences. It was during his reign that Ezra and Nehemiah lived and labored. He is the one who in 457 B.C. issued the third and final decree for the restoration of Jerusalem."[4]

As Artaxerxes Longimanus was the son of Xerxes or Ahasuerus, it is possible, perhaps even likely, that his mother was Queen Esther. This may explain, in part, his willingness to order the restoration of Jerusalem.

Since Daniel's vision is given during the reign of Cyrus (Daniel 10:1), **"yet three kings in Persia,"** would be: Cambyses, false Smerdis, and Darius Hystaspes. The fourth rich one is Xerxes. Indeed, history

---

[2] Daniel 10:20

[3] E. G. White, *Prophets and Kings* (1917), p. 556.4.

[4] *Ibid.*, p. 607.1.

confirms that Xerxes organized a massive campaign to overthrow Greece, and although he achieved several victories, including the battle of Thermopylae, he lost at the battle of Salamis and was defeated by the Greeks at Mycale. Although these battles did not mark the end of the Medo-Persian Empire, nor the beginning of the Greek Empire under Alexander the Great, and although Xerxes was succeeded by other Medo-Persian rulers, his exploits did initiate the receding of the Persian Empire, and the advancement of Greece.

Daniel 11:3 And a mighty king shall stand up, that shall rule with great dominion, and do according to his will.

Just as prophesied, Alexander the Great (356–323 B.C.) arose and assumed world dominion.

Daniel 11:4 And when he shall stand up, his kingdom shall be broken, and shall be divided toward the four winds of heaven; and not to his posterity, nor according to his dominion which he ruled: for his kingdom shall be plucked up, even for others beside those.

Hardly had Alexander scaled the summit of world dominance when he died suddenly at 32 years of age. Since Alexander had no obvious and legitimate heir (his son Alexander IV was born after his death, and his other son was by a concubine and not a wife) his kingdom was eventually divided among his four generals, Cassander, Lysimachus, Seleucus and Ptolemy, toward the four points of the compass.

Daniel 11:5 And the king of the south shall be strong, and one of his princes; and he shall be strong above him, and have dominion; his dominion shall be a great dominion.

The largest portions of the empire, in the northeast and south (of Palestine) were taken by Seleucus and Ptolemy respectively, and the smaller western portions by Cassander (Macedonia), Lysimachus (Thrace). Verses five through fifteen focus on the two strongest divisions of the Greek Empire, and their struggles against each other, for the supremacy. These two divisions are also the ones that had the most to do with God's people during this period. Seleucus took the northeastern division corresponding to Syria. Ptolemy took the southern portion controlling Egypt. Palestine is in between. After being driven from Babylon, Seleucus I Nicator became one of Ptolemy's generals ("princes"), before regaining his territories in Mesopotamia, and later becoming stronger ("**he shall be strong above him**") than Ptolemy.

Eventually, Lysimachus conquered Cassander and Seleucus killed Lysimachus in battle, leaving only two divisions of Greece— Seleucus, the king of the north; and Ptolemy, the king of the south.

Daniel 11:6 And in the end of years they shall join themselves together; for the king's daughter of the south shall come to the king of the north to make an agreement: but she shall not retain the power of the arm; neither shall he stand, nor his arm: but she shall be given up, and they that brought her, and he that begat her,[5] and he that strengthened her in these times.

Later, to bring peace to the two kingdoms, Antiochus II Theos, grandson of Seleucus I married Berenice, a daughter of the Egyptian king, Ptolemy II Philadelphus. Berenice displaced the previous wife, Laodice. After having a son by Berenice, Antiochus reconciled with Laodice,[6] who then took out her jealous revenge by murdering Antiochus II, then Berenice and her infant son. Laodice then installed her son Seleucus II Callinicus on the throne. That Laodice was connected to the death of Berenice's father Ptolemy II, shortly before in Egypt, seems to be indicated here. This is likely, since part of the marriage agreement with Ptolemy II, in exchange for his daughter Berenice, was that her offspring would be heir to the throne of the Seleucid empire.

Daniel 11:7 But out of a branch of her roots shall one stand up in his estate, which shall come with an army, and shall enter into the fortress of the king of the north, and shall deal against them, and shall prevail:

---

[5] The margin of the 1611 King James Version states "whom she brought forth" for "**he that begat her.**"

[6] The city of Laodicea was founded by Antiochus II for his wife Laodice.

Ptolemy III Euergetes, son of Ptolemy II Philadelphus "and a brother of Berenice, a shoot from her roots, advanced into the territory of Antiochus with a large army,"[7] in revenge for his sister's murder. Ptolemy III seems to have been completely successful in this invasion of Syria. Ptolemy III also succeeded in tracking down and killing Laodice.

Daniel 11:8 And shall also carry captives into Egypt their gods, with their princes, and with their precious vessels of silver and of gold; and he shall continue more years than the king of the north.

Ptolemy III carried captives back to Egypt with the recovered temple gods and great treasure.

Daniel 11:9 So the king of the south shall come into his kingdom, and shall return into his own land.

Ptolemy III had to return suddenly to Egypt because of a sedition that arose there, else he probably would have completely taken over the Seleucid empire.

Daniel 11:10 But his sons shall be stirred up, and shall assemble a multitude of great forces: and one shall certainly come, and overflow, and pass through: then shall he return, and be stirred up, even to his fortress.

The king of the north, Seleucus II, had two sons, Seleucus III Ceraunus Soter, who was murdered after a short reign, and Antiochus III the Great. These two set about to conquer Palestine from the rival, Ptolemy IV Philopator.

Daniel 11:11 And the king of the south shall be moved with choler, and shall come forth and fight with him, even with the king of the north: and he shall set forth a great multitude; but the multitude shall be given into his hand.

---

[7] S. N. Haskell, *The Story of Daniel the Prophet* (Battle Creek, MI: Review and Herald Publishing Company, 1901), p. 195.1

"As soon as the spring of 217 B.C. opened, Ptolemy [IV] Philopator with an army of seventy-five thousand men and seventy-three elephants marched out of Egypt to do battle with Antiochus [III] wherever they might meet. Antiochus was also early in the field with seventy-eight thousand men and one hundred and two elephants. The battle was fought at Gaza [the battle of Raphia]. Antiochus was defeated with a loss of ten thousand killed and four thousand taken prisoners; upon which he abandoned all his late conquests, and with the remains of his army returned to his capital. "[8]

Daniel 11:12 And when he hath taken away the multitude, his heart shall be lifted up; and he shall cast down many ten thousands: but he shall not be strengthened by it.

Ptolemy IV did not finish conquering Syria after his victory at Raphia and during the years 212–204 B.C., Antiochus III systematically recovered his eastern territories as far as the border of India.

Ptolemy IV's death was concealed for some time; then a son, aged four or five, succeeded him as Ptolemy V Epiphanes.

Daniel 11:13 For the king of the north shall return, and shall set forth a multitude greater than the former, and shall certainly come after certain years with a great army and with much riches.

"Seeing that the kingdom and the dominions of Egypt had thus fallen to an infant, Antiochus the Great [III] and Philip king of Macedon formed a league to take the whole realm and divide it between them,"[9] invading Palestine in 201 B.C.

Daniel 11:14 And in those times there shall many stand up against the king of the south: also the robbers of thy people shall exalt themselves to establish the vision; but they shall fall.

---

[8] A. T. Jones, *The Great Empires of Bible Prophecy: from Babylon to the Fall of Rome*, (Battle Creek, MI: Review and Herald Publishing Company, 1898) p. 211.4.

[9] *Ibid.*, p. 215.1.

Antiochus IV (Epiphanes) ruled from 175 to 164/163 B.C. "A zealot in paganism, [he] bitterly and scornfully detested the Jewish religion, and resolved to root it out. His general Apollonius, had orders to massacre the people in the observance of their rites, to abolish the Temple service and the Sabbath, to destroy the sacred books, and introduce idol worship. The altar on Mount Moriah was especially desecrated, and afterward dedicated to Jupiter. A herd of swine were driven into the Temple, and there sacrificed.... The outrage in the Temple was the consummation of a series of humiliations and crimes; for in addition to the desecration of the Jewish religion, Antiochus had taken Jerusalem with a great army, had entered into the Temple..., and had taken away to his capital the golden candlesticks, the altar of incense, the table of shew bread, and the various vessels and censers and crowns which were used in the service of God.... Jerusalem was sacked and burned, woman and children were carried away as captives, and a great fortress was erected on an eminence that overlooked the Temple and the city.... The plundered inhabitants fled from Jerusalem, which became the habitation of strangers, with all its glory gone."[10]

Daniel 11:15 So the king of the north shall come, and cast up a mount, and take the most fenced cities: and the arms of the south shall not withstand, neither his chosen people, neither shall there be any strength to withstand.

Verse 14 appears to be parenthetical remarks with this verse continuing the narrative begun in verse 13. Gaza fell to Antiochus III in 201 B.C., after a sustained siege.

Daniel 11:16 But he that cometh against him shall do according to his own will, and none shall stand before him: and he shall stand in the glorious land, which by his hand shall be consumed.

Suddenly, after eleven verses of reference to the king of the North and the king of the South, all mention of them evaporates before a new power—a king that "**shall do according to his own will.**" Just as outlined in the preceding prophetic chapters of Daniel, the Greek

---

[10] John Lord, LL.D., *Beacon Lights of History*, (New York: Fords, Howard, and Hulbert, 1888), First Series, p. 442-43.

Empire is succeeded by the iron monarchy of Rome. The general Pompey conquered Palestine, and Rome began to make itself felt as a world power.

Daniel 11:17 He shall also set his face to enter with the strength of his whole kingdom, and upright ones with him; thus shall he do: and he shall give him the daughter of women, corrupting her: but she shall not stand on his side, neither be for him.

Cleopatra, the daughter of Ptolemy XI, and queen of Egypt, was eighteen years old when Julius Caesar invaded Egypt. Three years later, she became his mistress when she had herself carried into his presence, rolled up in a carpet, on the shoulder of Apollodorus the Sicilian. Cleopatra may have been involved in the subsequent assassination of Julius Caesar, which this verse seems to imply.

Daniel 11:18 After this shall he turn his face unto the isles, and shall take many: but a prince for his own behalf shall cause the reproach offered by him to cease; without his own reproach he shall cause it to turn upon him.

War in other parts of the empire drew Julius Caesar from Egypt. The party of Pompey was soon defeated on the coastlands of Africa. In Syria and Asia Minor, Caesar was successful against Pharnaces, king of the Cimmerian Bosporus.

Daniel 11:19 Then he shall turn his face toward the fort of his own land: but he shall stumble and fall, and not be found.

Julius Caesar was assassinated in Rome in 44 B.C. After his assassination, Cleopatra turned her seductions toward Mark Antony, the rival of Caesar's heir, Octavian. Octavian (who later became Caesar Augustus), defeated the combined armies of Cleopatra and Antony at the battle of Actium in 31 B.C. At the height of battle Cleopatra fled with her fleet, causing Antony to follow in rescue. Apparently, according to Plutarch, fearing his wrath for causing the defeat, Cleopatra locked herself in her mausoleum with two handmaids, and sent Mark Antony a message that she was dead— perhaps to make him feel bad for being angry. Instead, on hearing this, he stabbed himself in the stomach. However, the bleeding stopped, and as he pled for someone to finish him off, he got the message that Cleopatra was alive. She would not unlock the door, however, but the three women dragged him up and through the window with ropes. This nearly finished him off, and Cleopatra raved and cried, tearing off her clothes to cover him. He told her to calm down, drank a glass of wine and died, at which point Cleopatra killed herself with the bite from an Egyptian cobra.

Daniel 11:20 Then shall stand up in his estate a raiser of taxes in the glory of the kingdom: but within few days he shall be destroyed, neither in anger, nor in battle.

"And it came to pass in those days, that there went out a decree from Caesar Augustus, that all the world should be taxed."[11] Augustus established the foundations of the Empire during a reign of more than 40 years, and died peacefully in his bed in A.D. 14, at age 76.

Daniel 11:21 And in his estate shall stand up a vile person, to whom they shall not give the honour of the kingdom: but he shall come in peaceably, and obtain the kingdom by flatteries.

Tiberius Caesar succeeded Augustus peacefully, but was neither liked nor honored.

Daniel 11:22 And with the arms of a flood shall they be overflown from before him, and shall be broken; yea, also the prince of the covenant.

Tiberius was one of Rome's greatest generals leading many successful military campaigns, especially in Germania. Tiberius was emperor for 22 years, but, was eventually broken. Someone else was also broken: it was during the reign of Tiberius Caesar that Jesus Christ, the **"prince of the covenant,"** was crucified on a Roman cross, in A.D. 31.

---

[11] Luke 2:1

Daniel 11:23 And after the league made with him he shall work deceitfully: for he shall come up, and shall become strong with a small people.

It is true that pagan Rome continued for several hundred years after Christ, so some see verses 23-30 as applying to that history. However, there is abundant contextual evidence that these verses do not concern themselves with the pagan Roman history after Christ's death, but rather introduce the next world power—papal Rome. Indeed, a league was made between the Roman Emperors' and the Bishop of Rome. More and more power was transferred to the Bishop from the Emperor as papal Rome came up and became **"strong with a small people;"** language very similar to Daniel 7's "little horn" "whose look was more stout than his fellows."

Daniel 11:24 He shall enter peaceably even upon the fattest places of the province; and he shall do that which his fathers have not done, nor his fathers' fathers; he shall scatter among them the prey, and spoil, and riches: yea, and he shall forecast his devices against the strong holds, even for a time.

The phrase **"He shall enter peaceably even upon the fattest places of the province,"** is parallel to the phrase, "by peace shall destroy many," from the description of the papacy in Daniel 8:25. A second linguistic link to the papacy is provided in the phrase **"he shall do that which his fathers have not done, nor his fathers' fathers,"** which is directly parallel to the statement in verse 37, "Neither shall he regard the God of his fathers." The papacy is clearly the power delineated in verse 37. How does the papacy regard not the God of his fathers, or do that which his fathers have not done? The papacy claims an unbroken lineage of popes beginning with Peter, the disciple of Jesus. Therefore, they claim the apostles as their fathers—but they do not the works of the apostles, nor do they worship as the apostles worshipped. Instead they venerate Mary, and bow to graven images. The removal of the second commandment from Catholic catechisms,[12] is an irrefutable admission that the Catholic veneration of images is a violation of the law of God. Rather than being conformed to the command of God, they modify God's word. "Thus have ye made the commandment of

---

[12] See comments on Daniel 7:25 and Revelation 14:10.

God of none effect by your tradition. Ye hypocrites, well did Esaias prophesy of you, saying, This people draweth nigh unto me with their mouth, and honoureth me with their lips; but their heart is far from me. But in vain they do worship me, teaching for doctrines the commandments of men."[13]

In occult circles Isis represents Satan. Isis is the supreme deity of sun worship, often being depicted with the solar disk above her head with cow horns on either side, and baby Horus in her lap. Isis was transferred directly into the pagan Roman religion, and from there "baptized" into Catholicism with a name change to Mary.

"Some scholars believe that Isis worship in late Roman times was an influence behind Catholic development of the cult of the Blessed Virgin Mary. Evidence suggests that this allowed the Catholic Church to absorb a huge number of converts who had formerly believed in Isis, and would not have converted unless Catholicism offered them an 'Isis-like' female focus for their faith. Iconographically the similarities between the seated Isis holding or suckling the child Horus (Harpocrates) and the seated Mary and the baby Jesus are apparent."[14] Helena Blavatsky, mother of modern occultism, describes the relabeling of pagan deities with Bible names, to become objects of Catholic veneration, "'Olympus was restored but the divinities passed under other names.... Views of the trinity in accordance with the Egyptian traditions were established. Not only was the adoration of Isis under a new name restored, but even her image, standing on the crescent moon, reappeared. The well-known effigy of that goddess with the infant Horus in her arms has descended to our days, in the beautiful artistic creations of the Madonna and child.'" "'Immaculate is our Lady Isis,' is the legend around an engraving of Serapis and Isis... the very terms applied afterwards to that personage (the Virgin Mary) who succeeded to her form, titles, symbols, rites, and ceremonies. Thus, her devotees carried into the new priesthood the former badges of their profession, the obligation to celibacy, the tonsure, and the surplice.... The Black Virgins, so highly reverenced in certain French cathedrals proved, when at last critically examined, basalt figures of Isis!'"[15]

---

[13] Matthew 15:6-9

[14] http://en.wikipedia.org/wiki/Isis#Parallels_in_Catholicism_and_Orthodoxy retrieved June, 2007.

[15] H. P. Blavatsky, *Isis Unveiled*, Vol. 2—Theology (New York: J. W. Bouton, 1877), p. 49, 95.

In Catholicism, Mary is placed as an intercessor between the sinner and Jesus. This is certainly not the religion of the disciples of Jesus, whom the Catholic religion claims as their fathers. Diana, the goddess of the Ephesians, was another name for Isis.[16] The apostle Paul nearly got killed because, in the words of the idol manufacturers, he "persuaded and turned away much people, saying that they be no gods, which are made with hands: So that not only this our craft is in danger to be set at nought; but also that the temple of the great goddess Diana should be despised, and her magnificence should be destroyed, whom all Asia and the world worshippeth."[17] Paul was, in essence, preaching against the veneration of Mary. The papacy has indeed done "that which his fathers have not done, nor his fathers' fathers," "Neither shall he regard the God of his fathers." Peter did not pray to Mary. "Now the Spirit speaketh expressly, that in the latter times some shall depart from the faith, giving heed to seducing spirits, and doctrines of devils."[18]

The papal power who would become strong with a small people while implementing a new religion, and "by peace destroy many,"[19] would only be able to "'**forecast his devices**" for a predetermined period of time (Daniel 7:25).

Daniel 11:25 And he shall stir up his power and his courage against the king of the south with a great army; and the king of the south shall be stirred up to battle with a very great and

---

[16] Apuleius was a Latin prose writer (c. A.D. 124 – c. 170) who wrote the only Latin novel to have survived in its entirety, *Metamorphoses*. In this obscene, pagan and occult work he identifies Isis both as Diana, and the queen of heaven (the Catholic title given to Mary), as well as using the language of Lucifer in Isaiah 14:13, "I will ascend into heaven, I will exalt my throne above the stars of God: I will sit also upon the mount of the congregation, in the sides of the north: I will ascend above the heights of the clouds; I will be like the most High."
Speaking of Isis, Apuleius states, "I, who am nature, the parent of all things, the mistress of all elements,..., the supreme among the Divinities, the queen of departed spirits, the first of the celestials, and the uniform manifestation of the Gods and Goddesses; who govern by my nod the luminous heights of heaven...: whose one sole divinity the whole orb of the earth venerates under a manifold form... and under a variety of appellations [names]. Hence the Phrygians call me Pessinutica, the mother of the Gods... the Cyprians, Venus; the... Cretans, **Diana**... the Eleusinians, the ancient Goddess Ceres. Some call me Juno.... The Egyptians... call me by my true name, **Queen Isis**."
Apuleius *Metamorphoses*, 11.2.

[17] Acts 19:26-27

[18] 1 Timothy 4:1

[19] Daniel 8:25

mighty army; but he shall not stand: for they shall forecast devices against him.

Daniel 11:26 Yea, they that feed of the portion of his meat shall destroy him, and his army shall overflow: and many shall fall down slain.

Without mention since verse fifteen, the king of the South suddenly reappears in verse 25. Previously, we understood the king of the South to be Egypt (or the division of the Greek empire controlling Egypt). Its disappearance was caused by the subsumption of all remaining divisions of Greece by the Roman Empire. Maintaining a consistent interpretation of terms would require this instance of the king of the South to be closely related to Egypt. Indeed, in 1095 the papacy began the Crusades against the Muslims who were ruled by the Caliph of Egypt. Huge armies were amassed on both sides, but the Muslim forces fell to the power of the papal armies, with large losses of life. The defeat of the Caliph's armies was apparently a result of treachery by his own soldiers, as seen from verse 26.

Daniel 11:27a And both these kings' hearts shall be to do mischief, and they shall speak lies at one table; but it shall not prosper:

Is it possible that a deceptive alliance was executed between the Muslims and the papists that has set the stage for the current situation in the Middle East? Indeed, in almost all Muslims countries today, Christianity is banned on pain of death, yet throughout the region, Muslim mosques and Catholic cathedrals sit on the same corner, sometimes even being physically connected. How is it that in countries where Christianity is banned, a Catholic cathedral crowns almost every ancient holy site? How is it that in almost any Muslim country you may attend the market on Friday (the Muslim holy day), but the market is completely closed on Sunday? Perhaps such a secret alliance could explain the following picture of Pope Francis kissing Mahmud Abbas, leader of the Palestinians, while Israeli president Shimon Peres looks on. The Muslim world bows to the power of the papacy and is therefore one of the many fronts to distract while the papacy regains world supremacy. "And let it be remembered, it is the boast of Rome that she never changes. The principles of Gregory VII and Innocent III are still the principles of the

Roman Catholic Church. And had she but the power, she would put them in practice with as much vigor now as in past centuries. Protestants little know what they are doing when they propose to accept the aid of Rome in the work of Sunday exaltation. While they are bent upon the accomplishment of their purpose, Rome is aiming to re-establish her power, to recover her lost supremacy. Let the principle once be established in the United States that the church may employ or control the power of the state; that religious observances may be enforced by secular laws; in short, that the authority of church and state is to dominate the conscience, and the triumph of Rome in this country is assured.

"God's word has given warning of the impending danger; let this be unheeded, and the Protestant world will learn what the purposes of Rome really are, only when it is too late to escape the snare. She is silently growing into power. Her doctrines are exerting their influence in legislative halls, in the churches, and in the hearts of men. She is piling up her lofty and massive structures in the secret recesses of which her former persecutions will be repeated. Stealthily and unsuspectedly she is strengthening her forces to further her own ends when the time shall come for her to strike. All that she desires is vantage ground, and this is already being given her. We shall soon see and shall feel what the purpose of the Roman element is. Whoever shall believe and obey the word of God will thereby incur reproach and persecution."[20]

---

[20] E. G. White, *The Great Controversy* (1911), p. 581.1-2.

Daniel 11:27b ...for yet the end shall be at the time appointed[1a].
Daniel 11:28 Then shall he return[2a] into his land with great
riches; and his heart shall be against the holy covenant[3a]; and
he shall do exploits[4a], and return to his own land.
Daniel 11:29 At the time appointed[1b] he shall return[2b], and come
toward the south; but it shall not be as the former, or as the
latter.
Daniel 11:30 For the ships of Chittim shall come against him:
therefore he shall be grieved, and return, and have indignation
against the holy covenant[3b]: so shall he do; he shall even
return, and have intelligence with them that forsake the holy
covenant.
Daniel 11:31 And arms shall stand on his part, and they shall
pollute the sanctuary of strength, and shall take away the daily
[sacrifice], and they shall place the abomination that maketh
desolate.
Daniel 11:32 And such as do wickedly against the covenant
shall he corrupt by flatteries: but the people that do know their
God shall be strong, and do exploits[4b].

Verses 27b-32 are a parenthetical statement demarcated by a
simple Hebrew literary structure called a parallelism, in which the
same concept is given in two parallel halves, with the first half stating
the information in one way and the second half repeating it in
another way, with greater detail. Sometimes a parallelism is given
with the parallel thoughts using different phrases, which interpret
each other (such as Revelation 12:1-6 and 12:7-17). At other times
marker words are used that repeat in each half of the parallelism.
These verses have four parallel marker phrases.

First half (a)		Second half (b)	
1. time appointed	11:27b	1. time appointed	11:29
2. return	11:28	2. return	11:29
3. holy covenant	11:28	3. holy covenant	11:30
4. do exploits	11:28	4. do exploits	11:32

There are a number of phrases in this passage that, when defined by
Scripture, allow the whole passage to be clearly and simply
understood:

The "**time appointed**" refers to the termination, in 1798,[21] of the 1,260-year period allotted to papal supremacy, which also commences the "time of the end." In other words, the "time appointed" is from A.D. 538-1798 and the time of the end is from 1798 until the end of time.[22] Notice that in verse 27 "the time appointed" is yet in the future.

The culmination of the "time appointed," in 1798, corresponds directly to the deadly wound of the sea beast of Revelation 13.[23] The prophesied healing of that wound, is synonymous with the "**return into his land**" of Daniel 11:28, 29. Indeed history shows that the papacy returned to his land with the restoration of political power. On February 12, 1929, almost as if speaking prophetic words, the San Francisco Chronicle published a front-page article entitled, "Heal Wound Of Many Years." The article reported that on the prior day, February 11, Mussolini, dictator of Italy, signed a concordant with the Vatican granting them back their political power and lands. From where did the "**great riches**" come, with which he returned to his land? Within months of the popes return to his land, the economies of the world were devastated by the Great Depression.

The "**holy covenant**" is the ten commandments: "And he declared unto you **his covenant**, which he commanded you to perform, even **ten commandments**; and he wrote them upon two tables of stone."[24] But his covenant is especially the portion of the commandments that identifies the Law-giver: "Blessed is the man that doeth this, and the son of man that layeth hold on it; that **keepeth the sabbath** from polluting it, and keepeth his hand from doing any evil. Also the sons of the stranger, that join themselves to

---

[21] Just as the Bible predicted, the papacy gained its political power in A.D. 538 with Justinian's recovery of Rome from the Ostrogoths for the papacy. Precisely 1,260 years later, on February 15, 1798, Napoleon's general Berthier took Pope Pius VI captive (who died in exile), bringing an end to the papacy's status as a nation. At this time, they lost most of their lands and buildings. Later, on September 20, 1870, the last of the papal states were lost, when Italian troops seized the city of Rome again leaving the pope a virtual prisoner.

The wound was delivered to the head of the beast. A beast in Bible prophecy is a political power. Therefore, it was the monarchy of the papacy that was wounded, not the ecclesiastical power. It was the state of the papacy that received "as it were," a deadly wound; the church continued to function during this time; popes continued to be elected; functioning as prime bishop, but not as head of the Vatican State. The words of Scriptures were fulfilled exactly.

[22] See E. G. White, *The Great Controversy* (1911), p. 355.1-356.2.

[23] Revelation 13:3

[24] Deuteronomy 4:13; Exodus 34:28

the LORD, to serve him, and to love the name of the LORD, to be his servants, every one that **keepeth the sabbath** from polluting it, and taketh hold of **my covenant**."[25]

The "**exploits**" in verse 28 refer to the exploits of the papacy to undo all the reformation has done, to reestablish their lost supremacy, and manipulate the world's last superpower to cause the earth to "make an image to the beast."[26] In a unique twist, the first half of the parallelism reveals the papacy doing exploits, but in the second half of the parallelism, it is God's people doing the exploits—the loud cry of Revelation 14 and 18:4 goes to all the world. So, this parallelism gives a brief parenthetical outline of history from 1798 to the second coming. Daniel 12:7 gives an almost identical outline: "...it shall be for a time, times, and an half [terminating in 1798]; and when he shall have accomplished to scatter the power of the holy people [the Loud Cry—the Gospel goes to all the world], all these things shall be finished [the second coming of Jesus]." Jesus quotes the last part of Daniel 12:7 giving a similar outline: "And this gospel of the kingdom shall be preached in all the world for a witness unto all nations; and then shall the end come."[27]

Ships in Bible prophecy indicate military and economic power.[28] The "**ships of Chittim**" is often footnoted to be the "ships of the west" or "ships of Cyprus" (which is west from Palestine). During the time outlined by this parenthetical statement (from 1798 to the second coming), what military and economic power is rising in the west promoting principles that "**come against**" the papacy? This can be nothing other than the United States of America. But, is there more Biblical evidence for this? Many commentators say Chittim is Cyprus—can this be ruled out? Pioneer authors suggested everything from Rome, to Africa, Carthage, Italy, the Huns, Hungary, Cyprus and "ships of the west." Scripture reveals evidence which rules out each of these suggestions: "...the company of the Ashurites have made thy benches of ivory, brought out of the isles of Chittim."[29] First, according to this verse, Chittim must have more than one island, since "isles" (plural), are indicated. This, rules out

---

[25] Isaiah 56:2,6

[26] See comments on Revelation 13, especially13:14.

[27] Matthew 24:14

[28] Ezekiel 27:9,27

[29] Ezekiel 27:6

Cyprus, because it is but one island. It also rules out Rome, Carthage, Huns/Hungary, as they are not/have not islands. Africa might seem to fit the ivory part, but is not known for any significant islands, except Madagascar—which has no ivory. How does Ezekiel's description relate to America? America has a place famous for its islands—over 300 islands—the Aleutian Chain in Alaska. Alaska also has ivory—walrus ivory, and also large numbers of frozen wooly mammoths. Even secular scientists[30] admit that live mammoths were still present in Alaska as recent as 1650 B.C. The United States of America[31] was the only power rising into prominence in the west during the period specified, with many islands having ivory. Indeed, it was the principles of civil and religious liberty, republicanism and Protestantism that grieved the papacy. Revelation 12 prophesies that the land of America would provide a temporary escape in which the pure woman (God's church) would find refuge.[32]

In the phrase **"the daily [sacrifice],"** the word sacrifice is supplied. The King James Bible indicates words supplied by the translators by either italics or a different font, or in most recent editions, square brackets. There are many places where this occurs, most of which require the supplied word for the sense to be correct in English. Many times, in fact, when a supplied word is added, it is demanded by the original language. In this case the supplied word does not belong, as the word that Daniel used for daily—tâmîyd—is in the form of a noun. Adding the word "sacrifice" after a noun "daily" would force the noun to become an adjective. This does injustice to the word form the prophet chose to use. "Then I saw in relation to the 'daily' (Daniel 8:12) that the word 'sacrifice' was supplied by man's wisdom, and does not belong to the text."[33] This word תמיד tâmîyd means "continual, perpetual, always, ever, and ever more." "The daily" therefore could be called "the perpetual."[34]

---

30 Secular scientists usually greatly expand estimates of historical timeframes.

31 We clearly see America in the book of Revelation (Rev. 13:11-17); should we not expect to see America in the book of Daniel?
"The books of Daniel and the Revelation are one. One is a prophecy, the other a revelation; one a book sealed, the other a book opened."
E. G. White, *Manuscript Releases*, Vol. 1, p. 99.3.

32 See comments on Revelation 12:6, 13:11.

33 E. G. White, *Early Writings* (1892), p. 74.2.

34 See comments on Daniel 8:12 for a more complete treatment of "the daily."

"Wherefore the children of Israel shall keep the sabbath, to observe the sabbath throughout their generations, for **a perpetual covenant**. It is a sign between me and the children of Israel for ever: for in six days the LORD made heaven and earth, and on the seventh day he rested, and was refreshed."[35] **"The Sabbath** is a token between God and His people. It is a holy day, given by the Creator to us as a day upon which to rest, and reflect upon sacred things. God designed it to be observed through every age as **a perpetual covenant....**"[36] **"It is not enough to worship God on the Sabbath.** The religious services held on that day should be of an uplifting character. Those who preach the truth should be able to present it with power because they live it **in the daily life**. The church **members should carry the influence of the correct observance of the Sabbath through every day of the week**, in all their business relations and in all their home relations."[37] Thus, "the daily" correctly describes true Sabbath keeping.

Jesus personally defines the "abomination of desolation" for us. In Matthew 24 the disciples pointed Jesus to the beauty of the temple, and in response Jesus told them that the time was not far distant when not one stone would be left upon another. In their shock and amazement, the disciples, imagining that the destruction of Jerusalem must be the end of the world, asked Jesus two questions:
1. "When shall these things be?" (the destruction of Jerusalem) and,
2. "what shall be the sign of thy coming, and of the end of the world?"[38]
Jesus responds by giving a blended prophecy of the two events. "His words were not then fully understood; but their meaning was to be unfolded as His people should need the instruction therein given. The prophecy which He uttered was twofold in its meaning; while foreshadowing [1] the destruction of Jerusalem, it prefigured also [2] the terrors of the last great day."[39] To explain himself Jesus refers to "the abomination of desolation, spoken of by Daniel the prophet."[40] Daniel speaks of the abomination of desolation in three places,

---

[35] Exodus 31:16-17

[36] E. G. White, *The Review and Herald,* October 28, 1902 par. 8.

[37] E.G. White, *Letter 66*, 1900, pp. 1, 2.

[38] Matthew 24:3

[39] E. G. White, *The Great Controversy* (1911), p. 25.3.

[40] Matthew 24:15

Daniel 9:27, 11:31 and 12:11. The first reference is clearly to the destruction of Jerusalem. The last two clearly cannot refer to the destruction of Jerusalem. Therefore, there must be a second abomination of desolation spoken of by Daniel the prophet. To what then, do they refer? Luke gives us the exact definition of the first abomination of desolation: "And when ye shall see Jerusalem compassed with armies, then know that the desolation thereof is nigh."[41] Rather than using the phrase "abomination of desolation," as Matthew does, Luke interprets the abomination as Jerusalem being compassed with armies. The armies standing "in the holy place," as Matthew says is not describing the armies inside the holy place of the temple for once that occurred there was no opportunity for anyone to flee. Instead the phrase is a reference to the holy ground which extended outside the city walls. In the days of Nehemiah, the Jews were being tempted to buy things on the sabbath from the pagan merchants who set up shop just outside the city wall. Nehemiah informed the merchants that if they did not leave, he would have them arrested, and then he designated an area some distance outside the city walls as holy ground into which no Gentile was allowed. This provision was to protect the sanctity of the sabbath. "When the idolatrous standards of the Romans should be set up in the holy ground, **which extended some furlongs outside the city walls**, then the followers of Christ were to find safety in flight. When the warning sign should be seen, those who would escape must make no delay. Throughout the land of Judea, as well as in Jerusalem itself, the signal for flight must be immediately obeyed. He who chanced to be upon the housetop must not go down into his house, even to save his most valued treasures. Those who were working in the fields or vineyards must not take time to return for the outer garment laid aside while they should be toiling in the heat of the day. They must not hesitate a moment, lest they be involved in the general destruction."[42] The abomination of desolation was the idolatrous standards or flags, exalting the worship of the sun god, being placed in the holy ground in opposition to the sabbath of the Lord.

Ezekiel 8 gives us a very good clue as to the nature of the second abomination of desolation. After being shown progressively greater abominations, Ezekiel is shown the culmination of abominations in

---

[41] Luke 21:20

[42] E. G. White, *The Great Controversy* (1911), p. 25.4.

Ezekiel 8:16. Here, about 25 men, in the house of God, are worshiping the rising sun in the east. To do this they must turn their backs towards the temple, thus turning their backs on the law of God. They are worshipping the sun, instead of the Creator of the fourth commandment who made the sun. The same scenario will be brought to play in the end of time when men will be required to worship the sun god, on Sunday, in place of the Creator on the sabbath. For this reason, immediately after mentioning the abomination of desolation (Matthew 24:15) Jesus emphasizes the importance of sabbath keeping in Matthew 24:20 when he says "pray that your flight be not in the winter neither on the sabbath day." The spirit of prophecy crystallizes the two separate events that are the abomination of desolation. "**As the siege of Jerusalem** by the Roman armies was the signal for flight to the Judean Christians, **so the assumption of power on the part of our nation** in the decree enforcing the papal Sabbath will be a warning to us."[43] Therefore both the Bible and the spirit of prophecy define the abomination of desolation as two events: 1. the first siege of Jerusalem and 2. a decree enforcing the papal sabbath at the end of time.[44]

"**The people that do know their God shall be strong, and do exploits.**" How do we know that we know our God? "And hereby we do know that we know him, if we keep his commandments."[45] The exploits of the people of God are to turn others to righteousness: "And they that understand among the people shall instruct many,"[46] "And they that be wise shall shine as the brightness of the firmament; and they that turn many to righteousness as the stars for ever and ever."[47] "I was pointed down to the time when the third angel's message was closing. The power of God had rested upon His people; they had accomplished their work and were prepared for the trying hour before them. They had received the latter rain, or refreshing from the presence of the Lord, and the living testimony had been revived. The last great warning had sounded everywhere,

---

[43] E. G. White, *Testimonies*, Vol. 5 (1883), p. 464.

[44] See Revelation 13 on the mark of the beast.

[45] 1John 2:3

[46] Daniel 11:33

[47] Daniel 12:3

and it had stirred up and enraged the inhabitants of the earth who would not receive the message."[48]

Having defined each phrase in verses 27b-32, whose meaning is not immediately apparent, inserting those definitions into the passages, yields the following paragraph:

11:27b ...in the future, the papacy's political power will come to an end in 1798.
11:28 After this, the papacy shall return into his land with great riches in 1929; and then his heart shall be against the holy Law of God; and he shall persecute, the remnant, which keep the commandments of God, and have the testimony of Jesus.
11:29 After 1798 he shall return in 1929 and come toward the south; but it shall not be as the former, or as the latter.
11:30 For the military and economic power of America shall come up against him: therefore, he shall be grieved, and as he returns, he shall have indignation against the holy sabbath: so shall he do; he shall even return, and have intelligence with apostate Protestantism who has forsaken the holy sabbath.
11:31 And the military and economic might of America shall stand on the side of the papacy, and America and the papacy together shall pollute the sanctuary, and shall take away the sabbath, and they shall place the decree enforcing the papal sabbath.
11:32 And such apostate Protestants as do wickedly against the sabbath shall the papacy corrupt by flatteries: but the people that keep the commandments shall be strong, and give the loud cry.

Recognizing this parallelism clears up all difficulties relating to the chronological order of this chapter.

Daniel 11:33 And they that understand among the people shall instruct many: yet they shall fall by the sword, and by flame, by captivity, and by spoil, many days.

Once the parenthetical statement (verses 27b-32) gives us a preview from 1798 to just before the second coming, the subsequent verses continue chronologically from where we left off in verse 27a, prior to 1798 (this will become evident in the subsequent verses). God's

---

[48] E. G. White, *Early Writings* (1892), p. 279.1.

people certainly instructed many during the terrible persecutions of the dark ages. Many of them fell by the sword, by flame, and imprisonment during the "days" allotted to the papal supremacy from A.D. 538-1798.

Daniel 11:34 Now when they shall fall, they shall be holpen with a little help: but many shall cleave to them with flatteries.

During the persecution of the dark ages God's people would be helped with a little help. Jesus alludes to this verse in the New Testament: "For then shall be great tribulation, such as was not since the beginning of the world to this time, no, nor ever shall be. And except those days should be shortened, there should no flesh be saved: but for the elect's sake those days shall be shortened."[49] God's people were helped with a little help by the shortening of the days of persecution in the dark ages. Indeed, as a result of the Protestant reformation, the persecution had almost completely ceased twenty-five years before the wounding of the papacy in 1798. "The 1260 days, or years, terminated in 1798. A quarter of a century earlier, persecution had almost wholly ceased."[50] Therefore, the date for the cessation of persecution was 1773.[51]

"Following this persecution, according to the words of Christ, the sun was to be darkened. On the 19th of May, 1780, this prophecy was fulfilled."[52] That the tribulation Jesus speaks of here is the persecution of the dark ages is clear from the later verses and from

---

[49] Matthew 24:21,22

[50] E. G. White, *The Great Controversy* (1911), p. 306.1.

[51] This was the very year the Jesuit order, who was running the papal engine of persecution, was banned by the pope. "France and Spain elected Pope Clement XIV upon his pledge that he would dissolve the Order. **He issued his bull July 21, 1773, directing that, for the welfare of the church and the good of mankind, the institution of Loyola [Jesuit Order, or Society of Jesus] should be abolished.'** —Historical Studies, Id.
"For these reasons we believe that the abolition of the Order of Jesuits is the event, and July 21, 1773, is the date, when 'the tribulation of those days' ended.
"NOTE.—The Jesuits were restored in 1814, by Pope Pius VII.; but not to their persecuting power. In the different countries of Europe since that time the Order has been expelled and restored several times, and even by the Papacy once. But Pius IX., after his return from Gaeta in 1849, gave them its entire confidence till the day of his death, and **in his Vatican decrees is seen the crowning triumph of Jesuit Ultramontanism."**
A. T. Jones, "The End of the Tribulation of Those Days," *Signs of the Times*, August 12, 1886, p. 487.13.

[52] E. G. White, *The Great Controversy* (1911), p. 306.1.

history. "**Immediately after the tribulation of those days** shall the sun be darkened, and the moon shall not give her light, and the stars shall fall from heaven, and the powers of the heavens shall be shaken."[53] Seven years from the end of the persecution the great dark day[54] occurred, exactly as Jesus predicted.

Jesus further stated, "the stars shall fall from heaven,"[55] and John in the Revelation declared, as he beheld in vision the scenes that heralded the day of God: "And the stars of heaven fell unto the earth, even as a fig tree casteth her untimely figs, when she is shaken of a mighty wind."[56] "This prophecy received a striking and impressive fulfillment in the great meteoric shower of November 13, 1833. That was the most extensive and wonderful display of falling stars[57] which has ever been recorded."[58]

Daniel 11:35 And some of them of understanding shall fall, to try them, and to purge, and to make them white, even to the time of the end: because it is yet for a time appointed.

As the reformation gained more and more light from Scripture, they were purged and sanctified with these truths up through the beginning of the time of the end (1798). At the time of this verse, this **"time of the end"** is yet in the future—**"it is yet for a time appointed."** God's people continued to seal their faith with their blood, enduring the purifying of affliction until the time was shortened and the persecution ended in 1773.[59]

Daniel 11:36 And the king shall do according to his will; and he shall exalt himself, and magnify himself above every god, and shall speak marvellous things against the God of gods, and

---

[53] Matthew 24:29

[54] For more details of the fulfillment of this prophecy see comments on Revelation 6:12-13.

[55] Matthew 24:29

[56] Revelation 6:13

[57] For more details of the fulfillment of this prophecy see comments on Revelation 6:12-13.

[58] E. G. White, *The Great Controversy* (1911), p. 333.1.

[59] Three years later the United States Declaration of Independence was signed.

shall prosper till the indignation be accomplished: for that that is determined shall be done.

The pope did **"according to his will"**—it seemed that the whole world, kings and princes alike, bowed to his power. He exalted himself even above the God of heaven, and **"spoke marvelous things against the God of gods."**[60] In *Ferrari's Ecclesiastical Dictionary* (originally in Latin) under the heading Papa (Pope) we find the following: "The Pope is of so great dignity that he is not a man, but as it were God, and the Vicar of God. The Pope is called 'Most Holy' because he is rightfully presumed to be such. The Pope alone is deservedly called 'Most Holy' because he alone is the Vicar of Christ, who is the fountain and source and fullness of all holiness. He is likewise the divine Monarch, and Supreme Emperor, and King of Kings. Hence the Pope is crowned with a triple crown, as king of heaven and of earth and of the lower regions. Moreover, the superiority, and the power of the Roman Pontiff, but by no means pertain only to heavenly things, to earthly things, and to things under the earth, but are even over angels, of whom he is greater. So that if it were possible that angels might err in faith, or might think contrary to the faith, they could be judged and excommunicated by the Pope. The Pope is as is it were God on earth, sole sovereign of the faithful of Christ, chief King of Kings, having plentitude of power."[61]

He would prosper until the time for his reign, decreed by God, ended; and the wound, which was determined, was inflicted.[62]

Daniel 11:37 Neither shall he regard the God of his fathers, nor the desire of women, nor regard any god: for he shall magnify himself above all.

The papacy claims that Peter was the first of an unbroken succession of popes. Therefore, they claim the disciples of Jesus as their fathers, but they do not regard the God of those they claim as their fathers, for he commanded, "Thou shalt not make unto thee any graven image, or any likeness of any thing that is in heaven above,

---

[60] See comments on Daniel 7:25; and 8:24,25.

[61] http://biblelight.net/1827r.gif Retrieved: 01-31-2016.

[62] Revelation 13:3

or that is in the earth beneath, or that is in the water under the earth: Thou shalt not bow down thyself to them, nor serve them."[63] Regarding not **"the desire of women"** refers to the supposed celibacy of the priests. This doctrine of devils has brought untold woe, suffering, and sexual depravity, and is explicitly forbidden in Scripture.[64]

Daniel 11:38 But in his estate shall he honour the God of forces: and a god whom his fathers knew not shall he honour with gold, and silver, and with precious stones, and pleasant things.

Instead of regarding the Creator God, the papacy honors Mary, **"a god whom his fathers knew not."** As noted in verse 24, in paganism and occultism Mary (Isis) represents Satan, who could aptly be called a god of forces. Mary is honored with gold, silver, precious stones and pleasant things.

Daniel 11:39 Thus shall he do in the most strong holds with a strange god, whom he shall acknowledge and increase with glory: and he shall cause them to rule over many, and shall divide the land for gain.

He increases the glory of this **"strange god"**—Mary—in many lands and uses it as a tool to rule and profit. Graven images of Mary are found all over the world, in every culture, and on every continent.

Daniel 11:40 And at the time of the end shall the king of the south push at him: and the king of the north shall come against

---

[63] Exodus 20:4-5

[64] Romans 1:27 "And likewise also the men, leaving the natural use of the woman, burned in their lust one toward another; men with men working that which is unseemly, and receiving in themselves that recompense of their error which was meet."
1 Corinthians 7:3 "Let the husband render unto the wife due benevolence: and likewise also the wife unto the husband. The wife hath not power of her own body, but the husband; and likewise also the husband hath not power of his own body, but the wife. Defraud ye not one the other, except [it be] with consent for a time, that ye may give yourselves to fasting and prayer; and come together again, that Satan tempt you not for your incontinency."
1 Corinthians 9:5 "Have we not power to lead about a sister, a wife, as well as other apostles, and as the brethren of the Lord, and Cephas?"
Cephas (or Peter), whom the papacy claims as the first pope, had a wife!
See also Matthew 8:14.

him like a whirlwind, with chariots, and with horsemen, and with many ships; and he shall enter into the countries, and shall overflow and pass over.

The phrase **"at the time of the end,"** indicates that we have finally come to the events surrounding the year 1798. As the 1,260 years of papal supremacy came to a close just prior to 1798, the king of the south pushed at the papacy. The king of the south applied to Egypt throughout the chapter. Once again, the king of the south applies to Egypt—this time spiritual Egypt. Speaking of the two witnesses, Revelation 11 says, "And their dead bodies shall lie in the street of the great city, which spiritually is called Sodom and Egypt, where also our Lord was crucified."[65] Clearly, Jesus was not crucified in Sodom or Egypt, so this language is symbolic. "'The great city' in whose streets the witnesses are slain, and where their dead bodies lie, is 'spiritually' Egypt. Of all nations presented in Bible history, Egypt most boldly denied the existence of the living God and resisted His commands. No monarch ever ventured upon more open and highhanded rebellion against the authority of Heaven than did the king of Egypt. When the message was brought him by Moses, in the name of the Lord, Pharaoh proudly answered: 'Who is Jehovah, that I should hearken unto His voice to let Israel go? I know not Jehovah, and moreover I will not let Israel go....' This is atheism, and the nation represented by Egypt would give voice to a similar denial of the claims of the living God and would manifest a like spirit of unbelief and defiance. 'The great city' is also compared, 'spiritually,' to Sodom. The corruption of Sodom in breaking the law of God was especially manifested in licentiousness. And this sin was also to be a pre-eminent characteristic of the nation that should fulfill the specifications of this scripture.

"According to the words of the prophet, then, a little before the year 1798 some power of satanic origin and character would rise to make war upon the Bible. And in the land where the testimony of God's two witnesses should thus be silenced, there would be manifest the atheism of the Pharaoh and the licentiousness of Sodom.

This prophecy has received a most exact and striking fulfillment in the history of France."[66]

---

[65] Revelation 11:8

[66] E. G. White, *The Great Controversy* (1911), p. 269.

Egypt, in this verse, specifies the atheism of France. How does atheism push at the papacy, during the French Revolution? "All too well the people had learned the lessons of cruelty and torture which Rome had so diligently taught. A day of retribution at last had come. It was not now the disciples of Jesus that were thrust into dungeons and dragged to the stake. Long ago these had perished or been driven into exile. Unsparing Rome now felt the deadly power of those whom she had trained to delight in deeds of blood. 'The example of persecution which the clergy of France had exhibited for so many ages, was now retorted upon them with signal vigor. The scaffolds ran red with the blood of the priests. The galleys and the prisons, once crowded with Huguenots, were now filled with their persecutors. Chained to the bench and toiling at the oar, the Roman Catholic clergy experienced all those woes which their church had so freely inflicted on the gentle heretics.'"[67]

But, it is not only the king of the South that comes against the papacy—the king of the North[68] also comes against him like a whirlwind. In 1798 Napoleon's general Berthier captured the Pope, delivering the deadly wound.[69]

The semi-colon at the end of "**many ships**," completes that thought similar to a period, with the next phrase "**and he shall enter into the countries, and shall overflow and pass over**" referring to the papacy's resurgence to power, with the healing of the deadly wound (in 1929), rather than Napoleon's continued exploits.

Daniel 11:41 He shall enter also into the glorious land, and many countries shall be overthrown: but these shall escape out of his hand, even Edom, and Moab, and the chief of the children of Ammon.

---

[67] E. G. White, *The Great Controversy* (1911), p. 283.2.

[68] Some see the king of the north of verse 40 as referring to the papacy. However, the papacy has been described throughout many verses as "he" or "him" with no mention of the king of the North (even though the king of the north and the king of the south are mentioned in almost every verse when they are present in verses 5-15). Consistent with the "he" and "him" referring to the papacy in verses 23 through 39, verse 40 again calls the papacy "him" when it says the king of the South comes against "him." It makes no sense for the papacy to be the king of the North, in verse 40, for then the papacy would be coming against itself.

[69] See comments on Daniel 7:25 and Revelation 13:3 for more details.

The papacy enters even Palestine and overthrows many. Edom literally refers to Esau and his descendants. Esau once had the birthright but rejected it. Moab was the son of Lot and his eldest daughter; a child of incest and fornication. It was the eldest daughter of Lot who suggested to the younger the harlotry of getting their father drunk and impregnating themselves by him. Ammon was the son of Lot and his youngest daughter. The Ammonites were particularly notorious for their occult practice of sacrificing children to their god Moloch. So here, Edom represents apostate Protestantism, who had the birthright, but rejected it; Moab represents the Roman power, Babylon the great, the mother of Harlots; and Ammon represents spiritualism and the occult. These three powers correspond directly to the unclean spirits like frogs that come out of the mouth of the dragon, and out of the mouth of the beast, and out of the mouth of the false prophet.[70] In this verse it is the apostate Protestant, the Roman Catholic, and the spiritualistic countries that escape the overt power of the papacy.

Daniel 11:42 He shall stretch forth his hand also upon the countries: and the land of Egypt shall not escape.

Another category of country does not escape the overt power of the papacy—the atheistic countries. *Time Magazine*, Feb. 24, 1992, demonstrates how the papacy overtly warred against atheism (spiritual Egypt).

"Only President Ronald Reagan and Pope John Paul II were present in the Vatican Library on Monday, June 7, 1982. It was the first time the two had met, and they talked for 50 minutes…. In that meeting, Reagan and the Pope agreed to undertake a clandestine campaign to hasten

---

[70] Revelation 16:13

the dissolution of the communist empire....' This was one of the great secret alliances of all time....' One of his earliest goals as President, Reagan says, was to recognize the Vatican as a state 'and make them an ally.... in their first meeting, the Holy Father and the President committed themselves and the institutions of the church and America to such a goal. And from that day, the focus was to bring it about in Poland.' Step by reluctant step, the Soviets and the communist government of Poland bowed to the moral, economic and political pressure imposed by the Pope and the President."[71]

Daniel 11:43 But he shall have power over the treasures of gold and of silver, and over all the precious things of Egypt: and the Libyans and the Ethiopians shall be at his steps.

This text tells us who controls the riches of Egypt or the atheistic countries that did not escape overt papal power. Most European countries had colonized quite a few African countries by the end of the 19th century. Italy, with its capital at Rome (the steps of the papacy) had only colonized one African country—Libya, and that only by 1912. Ethiopia, by contrast, was the only African country to remain independent and uncolonized—that is until after the healing of the deadly wound in 1929. Up to this time Ethiopia had been the birthplace and bastion of Biblical Christianity in Africa, keeping for centuries the sabbath of the Bible and the apostles. Indeed, its name could come from the old Egyptian words: Et (truth), Op (high), Bia (Land);—Land of Higher Truth. But, just as the Bible predicted, as the papacy rose back into political power, Ethiopia (and the bordering territories of Eritrea and part of Somalia) came under the power of the papacy. These countries have since suffered more than their share of misery—punishment for their long resistance of papal dogmas. How quickly we forget history.

Daniel 11:44 But tidings out of the east and out of the north shall trouble him: therefore he shall go forth with great fury to destroy, and utterly to make away many.

---

[71] Carl Bernstein, "The Holy Alliance," June 24, 2001, *Time Magazine*. http://content.time.com/time/magazine/article/0,9171,159069,00.html

"On one occasion, when in New York City, I was in the night season called upon to behold buildings rising story after story toward heaven. These buildings were warranted to be fireproof, and they were erected to glorify the owners and builders. Higher and still higher these buildings rose, and in them the most costly material was used. Those to whom these buildings belonged were not asking themselves: 'How can we best glorify God?' The Lord was not in their thoughts.

"The scene that next passed before me was an alarm of fire. Men looked at the lofty and supposedly fire-proof buildings and said: 'They are perfectly safe.' But these buildings were consumed as if made of pitch. The fire engines could do nothing to stay the destruction. The firemen were unable to operate the engines.

"But who reads the warnings given by the fast-fulfilling signs of the times? What impression is made upon worldlings? What change is seen in their attitude? No more than was seen in the attitude of the inhabitants of the Noachian world. Absorbed in worldly business and pleasure, the antediluvians 'knew not until the Flood came, and took them all away.' Matthew 24:39. They had heaven-sent warnings, but they refused to listen. And today the world, utterly regardless of the warning voice of God, is hurrying on to eternal ruin."[72]

Apparently, the happenings of 9/11 were our heaven-sent warning. The very next sentence is even more amazing: **"The world is stirred with the spirit of war. The prophecy of the eleventh chapter of Daniel has nearly reached its complete fulfillment.** Soon the scenes of trouble spoken of in the prophecies will take place."[73]

Could it be that the happenings of 9/11 were the kick-off for the fulfillment of the last few verses of Daniel 11? Could it be that the terrorists from the east, are the **"tidings out of the east"** that troubles him? The parenthetical statement (verses 27b-32) already pre-warned us that America and the papacy would be working together by this point. Indeed, America and the papacy have been going forth with great fury to destroy many (and destroy many liberties) since 9/11. On September 16, 2001, on the south lawn of the White House, President George W. Bush stated, "This **crusade,**

---

[72] E. G. White, *Testimonies to the Church*, Vol. 9 (1909), p. 12.1-14.2.

[73] *Ibid.*

this war on terrorism is going to take a while."[74] Crusades are religious wars fought on behalf of the papacy.

Daniel 11:45 And he shall plant the tabernacles of his palace between the seas in the glorious holy mountain; yet he shall come to his end, and none shall help him.

In an interview with Professor Milford Melton, Catholic priest, Father Hethlon, said the following ominous words, "The Roman state and church wink at the claims of the United States Government of heretics, for it is expedient for the purposes of Rome that this Protestant nation go on in their blind confidence of security while Catholics prepare for the great conflict.... At that time, Catholics will rise up and the Pope of Rome will plant his palace here."[75] A tabernacle is a house of worship; a palace is a house of state. One of the final acts of the papal power will be to initiate a church-state coalition[76] in the United States of America—"**between the seas in the glorious holy mountain**." But, God will bring him to his end and none shall rescue him. "Therefore shall her plagues come in one day, death, and mourning, and famine; and she shall be utterly burned with fire: for strong is the Lord God who judgeth her."[77]

Indeed, we have a song that describes the glorious (majestic) mountain "between the seas," that we call the United States of America.

> O beautiful for spacious skies,
> For amber waves of grain,
> For **purple mountain majesties**
> Above the fruited plain!
> America! America!
> God shed His grace on thee,
> And crown thy good with brotherhood
> **From sea to shining sea!**[78]

---

[74] https://georgewbush-whitehouse.archives.gov/news/releases/2001/09/20010916-2.html, retrieved 1-30-2017.

[75] P. D. Stuart, *Codeword Barbêlôn*, Vol. 2 (London: Lux Verbi Books, 2009), p. 466.

[76] This church-state coalition is referred to as an image to the beast, in Revelation 13.

[77] Revelation18:8

[78] Katharine Lee Bates, 1904.

Daniel 12

SUMMARY:
Daniel 12 outlines the events surrounding the close of probation.
The great time of trouble, the special resurrection, and the sealing up
of the book of Daniel are delineated. This chapter contains two
additional cryptic time prophecies: the 1,290 and 1,335-day periods.
The taking away of the daily [sacrifice], and the setting up of the
abomination of desolation are pivotal events already mentioned in
other chapters of Daniel, coming to climax in Daniel 12. The vision of
chapter twelve is a continuation of the vision of the previous chapter.

***Daniel 12:1 And at that time shall Michael stand up, the great
prince which standeth for the children of thy people: and there
shall be a time of trouble, such as never was since there was a
nation even to that same time: and at that time thy people shall
be delivered, every one that shall be found written in the book.***

"At that time," refers back to the events of the previous verse: "he
shall plant the tabernacles of his palace between the seas in the
glorious holy mountain; yet he shall come to his end, and none shall
help him." Just after the judgments of God fall on the papacy,[1] **"shall
Michael stand up."**

Michael is **"the great prince which standeth"** for the people of
God.[2] Jude identifies Michael as the archangel.[3] The identity of the
archangel is revealed in 1 Thessalonians 4:16: "For the Lord himself
shall descend from heaven with a shout, with the voice of the
archangel, and with the trump of God: and the dead in Christ shall
rise first:" It is the Lord who has the voice of the archangel—
therefore the Lord is the archangel. Michael is simply another name

---

[1] See also comments on Revelation 17, 18.

[2] See comments on Daniel 10:13.

[3] See Jude 1:9. The archangel is not one of the two covering cherub over the Ark of the Covenant
—that is A-R-K. The word "arch-angel"—A-R-C-H—means angel above all angels.

for Jesus.[4] The name Michael, actually means who is what God is or who is like God. Jesus is the one victorious against Satan over the body of Moses[5]—the resurrection and the life—and Jesus was victorious over Satan in the war in heaven.[6]

When Michael stands up **"a time of trouble,"** is initiated, **"such as never was since there was a nation even to that same time"**. This is the great time of Jacob's trouble prophesied by Jeremiah: "Alas! for that day is great, so that none is like it: it is even the time of Jacob's trouble; but he shall be saved out of it."[7] Both prophets identify this time of trouble as the worst there has ever been. This does not predict persecution that is worse than ever witnessed, for Jesus, referring to the persecution of the Dark Ages (immediately preceding the falling of the stars), pronounces it the worst tribulation (or persecution) that shall ever be.[8] Instead, the time of Jacob's trouble is worse because God's judgments will be poured out, yet, **"at that time thy people shall be delivered, every one that shall be found written in the book"**. The fact that this is the worst time of trouble ever seen, yet God's people are all delivered indicates that

---

[4] Some may think that calling Jesus an angel implies that he is a created being. This is certainly not the case. In Scripture the title "angel" does not apply exclusively to created beings. The word "angel" simply means "messenger." Jesus is certainly the messenger above all messengers. There are many times in the Bible where God is portrayed as appearing as an angel. We find one of the most notable in Exodus 3:2. "And the angel {mal'ak} of the LORD appeared unto him {Moses} in a flame of fire out of the midst of a bush: and he looked, and, behold, the bush burned with fire, and the bush was not consumed." In this passage the angel of the Lord appears in the bush out of the flame of fire. Exodus 3:4 says, "And when the LORD saw that he turned aside to see, God called unto him out of the midst of the bush, and said, Moses, Moses. And he said, Here am I. And he said, Draw not nigh hither: put off thy shoes from off thy feet, for the place whereon thou standest is holy ground." God called to him out of the midst of the bush. So in the one verse, it says it is the angel of the Lord who is in the midst of the bush, and in subsequent verses, it says it is the Lord who calls out of the bush. This makes the Lord the angel.

We find another example of this in the book of Malachi: "Behold, I will send my messenger, and he shall prepare the way before me:" The word for "messenger" in the original language is מלאך mal'âk. "Mal'âk" is the same word that is translated "angel," in Exodus 3:2. We can see clearly that an angel is a messenger, for it says, "I will send my messenger." The verse continues on, "and the Lord, whom ye seek, shall suddenly come to his temple, even the messenger of the covenant, whom ye delight in: behold, he shall come, saith the LORD of hosts." Again, the word for messenger is mal'âk. Here you have two messengers: the Lord's messenger (mal'ak) who is to prepare the way of the Lord, and the Lord himself, the messenger (mal'ak) of the covenant. The Lord is called an angel. The first messenger refers to John the Baptist, the second to Jesus Christ himself.

[5] Jude 1:9

[6] Revelation 12:7-9

[7] Jeremiah 30:7

[8] See Matthew 24:21-29.

the door of mercy has been shut. The standing up of Michael signals the close of probation. At the commencement of the judgment, the language of Daniel 7 refers to all being seated: "thrones were [placed]," "the Ancient of days did sit," and "the judgment was set." Even today we use the phrase "to sit in judgment." The significance of Michael standing is that it indicates the conclusion of the investigative judgment. When the investigative judgment closes, probation for the inhabitants of the earth ceases, for the heavenly sanctuary has been completely cleansed of all confessed sins, after which there is no longer provision for further forgiveness. The record of the sins of all whose names are **"found written in the book,"** have been erased by the blood of Jesus. Responsibility for those sins will be placed on the head of Satan. The wicked have had their sins imputed back on themselves, to be judged according to their deeds: "For the Son of man shall come in the glory of his Father with his angels; and then he shall reward every man according to his works."[9]

"God would not have heard the prayer of Jacob, and mercifully saved his life, if he had not previously repented of his wrongs in obtaining the blessing by fraud.
"The righteous, like Jacob, will manifest unyielding faith and earnest determination, which will take no denial. They will feel their unworthiness but will have no concealed wrongs to reveal. If they had sins, unconfessed and unrepented of, to appear then before them, while tortured with fear and anguish, with a lively sense of all their unworthiness, they would be overwhelmed. Despair would cut off their earnest faith, and they could not have confidence to plead with God thus earnestly for deliverance, and their precious moments would be spent in confessing hidden sins, and bewailing their hopeless condition.
"Those professed believers who come up to the time of trouble unprepared, will, in their despair, confess their sins before all in words of burning anguish, while the wicked exult over their distress. The case of all such is hopeless. When Christ stands up, and leaves the most holy place, then the time of trouble commences, and the case of every soul is decided, and there will be no atoning blood to cleanse from sin and pollution. As Jesus leaves the most holy, he speaks in tones of decision and kingly authority: 'He that is unjust, let him be unjust still; and he which is filthy, let him be filthy still; and he

---

[9] Matthew 16:27

that is righteous, let him be righteous still; and he that is holy, let him be holy still. And behold, I come quickly; and my reward is with me, to give every man according as his work shall be.'

"Those who have delayed a preparation for the day of God, cannot obtain it in the time of trouble, or at any future period. The righteous will not cease their earnest, agonizing cries for deliverance. They cannot bring to mind any particular sins; but in their whole life they can see but little good. Their sins had gone beforehand to judgment, and pardon had been written. Their sins had been borne away into the land of forgetfulness, and they could not bring them to remembrance. Certain destruction threatens them, and, like Jacob, they will not suffer their faith to grow weak because their prayers are not immediately answered. Though suffering the pangs of hunger, they will not cease their intercessions. They lay hold of the strength of God, as Jacob laid hold of the angel; and the language of their soul is, 'I will not let thee go except thou bless me.' The saints at length prevail, like Jacob, and are gloriously delivered by the voice of God."[10]

"Before His crucifixion the Saviour explained to His disciples that He was to be put to death and to rise again from the tomb, and angels were present to impress His words on minds and hearts. But the disciples were looking for temporal deliverance from the Roman yoke, and they could not tolerate the thought that He in whom all their hopes centered should suffer an ignominious death. The words which they needed to remember were banished from their minds; and when the time of trial came, it found them unprepared. The death of Jesus as fully destroyed their hopes as if He had not forewarned them. So in the prophecies the future is opened before us as plainly as it was opened to the disciples by the words of Christ. **The events connected with the close of probation and the work of preparation for the time of trouble, are clearly presented. But multitudes have no more understanding of these important truths than if they had never been revealed.** Satan watches to catch away every impression that would make them wise unto salvation, and the time of trouble will find them unready."[11]

---

[10] E. G. White, *The Spirit of Prophecy*, Vol. 1 (Battle Creek, MI: Steam Press, 1870), p. 122.3-123.3.

[11] E. G. White, *The Great Controversy* (1911), p. 594.1.

Daniel 12:2 And many of them that sleep in the dust of the earth shall awake, some to everlasting life, and some to shame and everlasting contempt.

The second coming has not yet occurred, nevertheless, there are some that are resurrected "**to everlasting life, and some to shame and everlasting contempt**." This is not the general resurrection when "the Lord himself shall descend from heaven with a shout, with the voice of the archangel, and with the trump of God: and the dead in Christ shall rise first,"[12] rather it is a special resurrection just prior to the coming of Jesus, for the purpose of allowing this group of people to observe the entire event of the second coming. Those righteous who died without knowing the truth of the doctrine of the second coming would presumably be quite terrified by such an event. They wait in their graves for the voice of Christ to be greeted first in the air. But, those who have always looked for his coming and have understood the truth of the sabbath will be resurrected in this special resurrection, to see the whole event take place. These will join the righteous living when "we which are alive and remain shall be caught up together with them in the clouds, to meet the Lord in the air: and so shall we ever be with the Lord."[13]

Also raised in the special resurrection will be those who were especially wicked, so they might see the glory of Christ coming with the clouds of heaven. The apostle John describes the same event: "And shall come forth; they that have done good, unto the resurrection of life; and they that have done evil, unto the resurrection of damnation."[14] Jesus, at his trial by the Sanhedrin, assured the high priest that he would be present: "the high priest answered and said unto him, I adjure thee by the living God, that thou tell us whether thou be the Christ, the Son of God. Jesus saith unto him, Thou hast said: nevertheless I say unto you, Hereafter shall ye see the Son of man sitting on the right hand of power, and coming in the clouds of heaven."[15] The soldiers that nailed Christ to the cross will be part of this special resurrection. "Behold, he cometh with clouds; and every eye shall see him, and they also which

---

[12] 1 Thessalonians 4:16

[13] 1 Thessalonians 4:17-18

[14] John 5:29

[15] Matthew 26:63-64

pierced him: and all kindreds of the earth shall wail because of him. Even so, Amen."[16]

Notice how the special resurrection and the general are outlined in chronological order by the spirit of prophecy,[17] with the special resurrection and its purpose being described prior to the occurrence of the general resurrection:

"It was at midnight that God chose to deliver His people. As the wicked were mocking around them, suddenly the sun appeared, shining in his strength, and the moon stood still. The wicked looked upon the scene with amazement, while the saints beheld with solemn joy the tokens of their deliverance. Signs and wonders followed in quick succession. Everything seemed turned out of its natural course. The streams ceased to flow. Dark, heavy clouds came up and clashed against each other. But there was one clear place of settled glory, whence came the voice of God like many waters, shaking the heavens and the earth. **There was a mighty earthquake. The graves were opened, and those who had died in faith under the third angel's message, keeping the Sabbath, came forth from their dusty beds**, glorified, to hear the covenant of peace that God was to make with those who had kept His law...." "**Soon appeared the great white cloud, upon which sat the Son of man**. When it first appeared in the distance, this cloud looked very small. The angel said that it was the sign of the Son of man. As it drew nearer the earth, we could behold the excellent glory and majesty of Jesus as He rode forth to conquer. A retinue of holy angels, with bright, glittering crowns upon their heads, escorted Him on His way. No language can describe the glory of the scene. The living cloud of majesty and unsurpassed glory came still nearer, and we could clearly behold the lovely person of Jesus. He did not wear a crown of thorns, but a crown of glory rested upon His holy brow. Upon His vesture and thigh was a name written, King of kings, and Lord of lords. His countenance was as bright as the noonday sun, His eyes were as a flame of fire, and His feet had the appearance of fine brass. His voice sounded like many musical instruments. The earth trembled before Him, the heavens departed as a scroll when it is rolled together, and every mountain and island were moved out of their places.... Those who a short time before would have destroyed

---

[16] Revelation 1:7

[17] For more information on the spirit of prophecy, see the comments on Daniel 10:17.

God's faithful children from the earth, now witnessed the glory of God which rested upon them. And amid all their terror they heard the voices of the saints in joyful strains, saying, 'Lo, this is our God; we have waited for Him, and He will save us.'

"**The earth mightily shook as the voice of the Son of God called forth the sleeping saints**. They responded to the call and came forth clothed with glorious immortality, crying, 'Victory, victory, over death and the grave! O death, where is thy sting? O grave, where is thy victory?' **Then the living saints and the risen ones raised their voices in a long, transporting shout of victory**. Those bodies that had gone down into the grave bearing the marks of disease and death came up in immortal health and vigor. The living saints are changed in a moment, in the twinkling of an eye, and caught up with the risen ones, and together they meet their Lord in the air. Oh, what a glorious meeting! Friends whom death had separated were united, never more to part."[18]

Daniel 12:3 And they that be wise shall shine as the brightness of the firmament; and they that turn many to righteousness as the stars for ever and ever.

We have the privilege of participating in the salvation of souls for a moment, that we might have the honor and glory of the stars for all eternity. Those who have "known the holy scriptures, which are able to make thee wise unto salvation through faith which is in Christ Jesus,"[19] **"shall shine as the brightness of the firmament."** But, those will be lost that "received not the love of the truth, that they might be saved...." They shall be sent a "strong delusion, that they should believe a lie: That they all might be damned who believed not the truth, but had pleasure in unrighteousness."[20]

Daniel 12:4 But thou, O Daniel, shut up the words, and seal the book, even to the time of the end: many shall run to and fro, and knowledge shall be increased.

---

[18] E. G. White, *Early Writings* (1892), p. 285.1.

[19] 2 Timothy 3:15

[20] 2 Thessalonians 2:10-12

The prophecy of Daniel was to be sealed until "**the time of the end**," which began in 1798,[21] when many would "**run to and fro**" ("a Hebrew expression for observing and thinking upon the time")[22] and "**knowledge shall be increased**." This is not particularly knowledge leading to modern inventions, but knowledge about the word of God, knowledge about prophecy—specifically knowledge about the book of Daniel.

"The book of Daniel is unsealed in the revelation to John, and carries us forward to the last scenes of this earth's history."[23]

Daniel 12: 5 Then I Daniel looked, and, behold, there stood other two, the one on this side of the bank of the river, and the other on that side of the bank of the river.

Daniel 12:6 And one said to the man clothed in linen, which was upon the waters of the river, How long shall it be to the end of these wonders?

Daniel sees three heavenly beings: Christ clothed in linen, standing on the water; with an angel on either bank of the river. When the high priest entered the most holy place on the day of atonement, he first wore the embroidered coat, the linen turban on his head, and carried upon his heart the ephod and breastplate, with its twelve stones, one for each tribe of Israel. "And they shall be upon Aaron's heart, when he goeth in before the LORD: and Aaron shall bear the judgment of the children of Israel upon his heart before the LORD continually."[24] After the atonement had been made and the intercession completed the high priest removed the robes of judgment and put on the

---

[21] See comments on Daniel 11:27-40.

[22] E. G. White, *The Great Controversy* (1911), p. 359.2.

[23] E. G. White, *Testimonies to Minister and Gospel Workers* (1923), p. 115.3.

[24] Exodus 28:30

garments of vengeance to send forth the scapegoat.[25] "For he put on righteousness as a breastplate, and an helmet of salvation upon his head; and he put on the garments of vengeance for clothing, and was clad with zeal as a cloak. According to their deeds, accordingly he will repay, fury to his adversaries, recompense to his enemies; to the islands he will repay recompense."[26] Ezekiel portrays Christ executing vengeance, clothed in linen with a writer's inkhorn at his side. "He cried also in mine ears with a loud voice, saying, Cause them that have charge over the city to draw near, even every man with his destroying weapon in his hand.... And he called to the man clothed with linen, which had the writer's inkhorn by his side; and the Lord said unto him, Go through the midst of the city, through the midst of Jerusalem, and set a mark upon the foreheads of the men that sigh and that cry for all the abominations that be done in the midst thereof. And to the others he said in mine hearing, Go ye after him through the city, and smite: let not your eye spare, neither have ye pity: slay utterly old and young, both maids, and little children, and women: but come not near any man upon whom is the mark; and begin at My sanctuary. Then they began at the ancient men which were before the house."[27]

"When Jesus rises up in the most holy place, lays off His mediatorial robes, and clothes Himself with the garments of vengeance, the mandate will go forth: 'He that is unjust, let him be unjust still: . . . and he that is righteous, let him be righteous still: and he that is holy, let him be holy still. And, behold, I come quickly; and My reward is with Me, to give every man according as his work shall be.' Revelation 22:11, 12."[28]

---

[25] Leviticus 16:2-4, 10 "And the LORD said unto Moses, Speak unto Aaron thy brother, that he come not at all times into the holy place within the veil before the mercy seat, which is upon the ark; that he die not: for I will appear in the cloud upon the mercy seat. Thus shall Aaron come into the holy place: with a young bullock for a sin offering, and a ram for a burnt offering. He shall put on the holy linen coat, and he shall have the linen breeches upon his flesh, and shall be girded with a linen girdle, and with the linen mitre shall he be attired: these are holy garments; therefore shall he wash his flesh in water, and so put them on....
"But the goat, on which the lot fell to be the scapegoat, shall be presented alive before the LORD, to make an atonement with him, and to let him go for a scapegoat into the wilderness."

[26] Isaiah 59:17-18

[27] Ezekiel 9:1-6

[28] E. G. White, *Testimonies to the Church*, Vol. 8. p. 315.1.

Christ's standing position indicates the completion of the investigative judgment and the close of probation, just as in verse one. His garments are a portent of destruction for the wicked; a portrait of deliverance for the saints.

The view that Daniel beholds consists of further sanctuary imagery, for there is "a pure river of water of life, clear as crystal, proceeding out of the throne of God and of the Lamb"[29]—which throne is the ark of the covenant in the most holy. The river proceeds from the throne of God and on either side of the river is a covering cherub. Therefore, the man in linen, above the water and between the cherubs is in the position of the throne of the universe. Christ is thus revealing the final moments before the judgments of God are poured out in the form of the seven last plagues.

"The question, '**How long shall it be to the end of these wonders?**' undoubtedly has reference to all that has previously been mentioned including the standing up of Michael, the time of trouble, the deliverance of God's people, and the special and antecedent resurrection of verse 2."[30] Therefore, the question asks how long will it be until the great time of trouble, when God's people are delivered, and how long until probation closes, and Michael stands up.

Daniel uses the third-party reference "and one said," to refer to himself; similar to the gospel writer, Mark.[31] "Twice Daniel inquired, How long shall it be to the end of time?"[32]

Daniel 12:7 And I heard the man clothed in linen, which was upon the waters of the river, when he held up his right hand and his left hand unto heaven, and sware by him that liveth for ever that it shall be for a time, times, and an half; and when he shall have accomplished to scatter the power of the holy people, all these things shall be finished.

---

[29] Revelation 22:1

[30] Uriah Smith, *Daniel and the Revelation*, (1897) p. 338.4

[31] Mark 14:51-52

[32] E. G. White, *Testimonies to Ministers and Gospel Workers* (1923), p. 114.6.

Jesus himself replies to Daniel's question, and with a most solemn oath, "because he could swear by no greater, he sware by himself."[33] His reply outlines the time frame for the entire context of Daniel twelve, which is from the time of the end to the end of time. The reply lists three events: first, the 1,260 years (**"time, times, and an half"**[34]) will come to an end in 1798; second, God will **"scatter the power of"** his people; third, the end shall come.

Speaking to his disciples, in Matthew, Jesus refers them to the prophet Daniel, "When ye therefore shall see the abomination of desolation, spoken of by Daniel the prophet, stand in the holy place, (whoso readeth, let him understand)."[35] In the verse immediately prior to Christ's reference to the book of Daniel, Jesus quotes Daniel 12:7: "And this gospel of the kingdom shall be preached in all the world for a witness unto all nations; and then shall the end come" — **"when he shall have accomplished to scatter the power of the holy people, all these things shall be finished."** The gospel being preached in all the world is the scattering of the power of the holy people—the loud cry. The man in linen speaking in Daniel 12:7 is Jesus. The One speaking in Matthew 24:14 is Jesus. Therefore, Jesus, in infinite condescension is quoting himself in Matthew, yet he refers us to the prophet Daniel.

Daniel 12:8 And I heard, but I understood not: then said I, O my Lord, what shall be the end of these things?

Daniel heard the words of Christ, but could not understand their meaning. Thus, he twice asked the question "how long?"

Daniel 12:9 And he said, Go thy way, Daniel: for the words are closed up and sealed till the time of the end.

Jesus initially replies, don't worry Daniel, **"the words are closed up and sealed till the time of the end."** Then Christ proceeds to tell Daniel additional detail.[36]

---

[33] Hebrews 6:13

[34] For the explanation of this time prophecy, see comments on Daniel 7:25.

[35] Matthew 24:15

[36] John 16:12 "I have yet many things to say unto you, but ye cannot bear them now."

Daniel 12:10 Many shall be purified, and made white, and tried; but the wicked shall do wickedly: and none of the wicked shall understand; but the wise shall understand.

"Many shall be purified, and made white, and tried," is the process of sanctification. This statement is the pronouncement of the close of probation that Michael declares when he stands up. "He that is unjust, let him be unjust still: and he which is filthy, let him be filthy still: and he that is righteous, let him be righteous still: and he that is holy, let him be holy still."[37]

Daniel 12:11 And from the time that the daily [sacrifice] shall be taken away, and the abomination that maketh desolate set up, there shall be a thousand two hundred and ninety days.

In the King James Version either italics or brackets around words indicate those words that were supplied by the translators. There are many places where this occurs, most of which need the supplied word for the sense to be correct in English. Many times, in fact, when a supplied word is added, it is demanded by the original language. In one language a single word might actually require two words to express in English. For example, in English the phrase "let us go," uses three words whereas in Spanish only one word "vamos" supplies the same meaning. That said, the word "sacrifice" in this verse is one place where the supplied word does not belong.[38] It can be seen why they put the word "sacrifice" there, since most of the other places where the original word for "daily" is used in the Old Testament, it is associated with the word sacrifice. However, in this particular passage the words for **"the daily"** are התמיד ha tâmîyd. In most of the other passages where this word is used in Scripture, outside the book of Daniel, only the word תמיד tâmîyd is used, not התמיד ha tâmîyd. In a few passages the words התמיד ha tâmîyd are used,[39] but in these instances there is a noun following, making התמיד ha tâmîyd into a adjective. Daniel only uses the words התמיד ha tâmîyd, and in every place he uses it as a proper noun—"the daily."

---

[37] Revelation 22:11

[38] "Then I saw in relation to the 'daily' (Daniel 8:12) that the word 'sacrifice' was supplied by man's wisdom, and does not belong to the text."
E. G. White, *Early Writings* (1892), p. 74.2.

[39] See Numbers 4:7, 16; 28:10, 15, 23, 24, 31; 29:6, 11, 16, 19, 22, 25, 28, 31, 34, 38.

Because Daniel uses "the daily" as a noun, adding the noun "sacrifice," turns "the daily" into an adjective, violating Daniel's usage.

Why is this understanding important? There are two main interpretations for the phrase "the daily" in Daniel. The first view is that "the daily" represents pagan Romanism which must be taken out of the way in order for this little horn power to arise. The second view is that "the daily" refers to Jesus' continual ministry in the heavenly sanctuary. These two views are clearly quite opposite to each other.

As always, allowing the Bible to interpret itself is the only safe course. Considering the definition of this word, gives us some clues as to which view might be right, or wrong. The meaning of the word תמיד tâmîyd is: continual, perpetual, always, ever, and ever more. "The daily" therefore could be called "the perpetual" or "the continual."

Does the phrase "the perpetual" or "the continual" apply to pagan Romanism? No. Praise the Lord that pagan Romanism was not continual or perpetual. The Bible says in many places that pagan Romanism would be superseded by another power.[40] The pagan Roman Empire disintegrated in A.D. 476, therefore one cannot apply the meaning of this word—"the perpetual"—to pagan Romanism.

On the other hand, does the meaning of "the daily" or "the perpetual" fit Christ's ministry in the heavenly sanctuary? The fact is, the Bible tells us that Jesus' ministry in the heavenly sanctuary is not perpetual. It will not go on forever. There will be a point at which he will finish that ministration in the heavenly sanctuary, praise the Lord, for that ministry must come to an end for sin to be eradicated. "For Christ is not entered into the holy places made with hands, which are the figures of the true; but into heaven itself, now to appear in the presence of God for us: Nor yet that he should offer himself often, as the high priest entereth into the holy place every year with blood of others; For then must he often have suffered since the foundation of the world: but now once in the end of the world hath he appeared to put away sin by the sacrifice of himself. And as it is appointed unto men once to die, but after this the judgment: So

---

[40] See Daniel 2:40-41; 7:17-18;

Christ was once offered to bear the sins of many; and unto them that look for him shall he appear the second time **without sin unto salvation**."[41] When Christ appears the second time it will be without sin. The heavenly sanctuary will be cleansed of even the record of sin, and sin will be no more. Christ's intercession in the heavenly sanctuary will cease at the close of probation, when every case is decided, therefore Christ's ministry also cannot be called "the perpetual."[42]

What then does "the daily" mean? The Bible defines its own meaning. The sanctuary provides the answers. "And upon the table of showbread they shall spread a cloth of blue, and put thereon the dishes, and the spoons, and the bowls, and covers to cover withal: and the **continual** bread shall be thereon:"[43] Upon the table of showbread was placed the "continual bread." The Hebrew word translated continual is tâmîyd—the perpetual bread. "And thou shalt set upon the table showbread before me **alway**."[44] The Hebrew word translated "alway" is tâmîyd. "During the sojourn in the wilderness the kindling of fires upon the seventh day had been strictly prohibited.[45] The prohibition was not to extend to the land of Canaan, where the severity of the climate would often render fires a necessity; but in the wilderness, fire was not needed for warmth."[46] This would preclude the baking of bread on the sabbath. In fact, the Israelites were specifically instructed to accomplish any food preparation, even of the manna that God provided by miracle, on Friday before the sabbath began.[47] However, the bread which was placed upon the table of showbread was baked fresh once a week, on the sabbath.[48] This is the reason why Jesus said, "Have ye not read what David did, when he was an hungred, and they that were

---

[41] Hebrews 9:24-28

[42] This is covered in more depth in Daniel 8:14

[43] Numbers 4:7

[44] Exodus 25:30

[45] Exodus 35:3

[46] E. G. White, *Patriarchs and Prophets* (1890), p. 408.4.

[47] Exodus 16:22-23

[48] "And Mattithiah, one of the Levites, who was the firstborn of Shallum the Korahite, had the set office over the things that were made in the pans. And other of their brethren, of the sons of the Kohathites, were over the showbread, to prepare it every sabbath." 1 Chronicles 9:31-32
See also Leviticus 24:8.

with him; How he entered into the house of God, and did eat the showbread, which was not lawful for him to eat, neither for them which were with him, but only for the priests? Or have ye not read in the law, how that on the sabbath days the priests in the temple profane the sabbath, and are blameless? But I say unto you, That in this place is one greater than the temple."[49] Christ, the bread of life, was David's salvation. The priests profaned the sabbath by baking bread on that day, yet they were blameless because that bread represented the fresh serving of the bread of life that was to be given to the congregation every sabbath. "Every sabbath he shall set it in order before the LORD **continually**, being taken from the children of Israel by an **everlasting** covenant."[50] Here is an important link between the word "continually" and the word "everlasting." The Hebrew word for "continually" is—you guessed it—tâmîyd. However, the word translated "everlasting" is 'ôlâm. The bread is set in order continually or perpetually, for an everlasting covenant. The eternal nature of the bread is parallel to the everlasting covenant. The bread, of course, represents the Word of God, which is eternal, and "who was made flesh and dwelt among us."[51] His eternal nature is represented by the perpetual bread which also represents the everlasting covenant. What is this everlasting covenant? "Wherefore the children of Israel shall keep the sabbath, to **observe the sabbath throughout their generations, for a perpetual covenant**. It is a sign between me and the children of Israel **for ever**: for in six days the LORD made heaven and earth, and on the seventh day he rested, and was refreshed."[52] The "perpetual covenant" here, is identical, in Hebrew, to "everlasting covenant" in Leviticus 24:8, above. It is the very same covenant. The sabbath is the "perpetual covenant"—"the daily" bread which was set in order continually every sabbath.

"Wherefore the children of Israel shall keep the sabbath, to observe the sabbath throughout their generations, for **a perpetual covenant**. It is a sign between me and the children of Israel for ever: for in six days the LORD made heaven and earth, and on the seventh day he

---

[49] Matthew 12:3-6

[50] Leviticus 24:8

[51] John 1:14

[52] Exodus 31:16, 17

rested, and was refreshed."[53] **"The Sabbath** is a token between God and His people. It is a holy day, given by the Creator to us as a day upon which to rest, and reflect upon sacred things. God designed it to be observed through every age as **a perpetual covenant**...."[54] **"It is not enough to worship God on the Sabbath.** The religious services held on that day should be of an uplifting character. Those who preach the truth should be able to present it with power because they live it **in the daily life**. The church **members should carry the influence of the correct observance of the Sabbath through every day of the week**, in all their business relations and in all their home relations."[55]

Jesus personally defines **"the abomination that maketh desolate"** for us. In Matthew 24 the disciples pointed Jesus to the beauty of the temple, and in response Jesus told them that the time was not far distant when not one stone would be left upon another. In their shock and amazement, the disciples, imagining that the destruction of Jerusalem must be the end of the world, asked Jesus two questions:
1. "When shall these things be?" (the destruction of Jerusalem) and,
2. "what shall be the sign of thy coming, and of the end of the world?"[56]
Jesus responded by giving a blended prophecy of the two events. "His words were not then fully understood; but their meaning was to be unfolded as His people should need the instruction therein given. The prophecy which He uttered was twofold in its meaning; while foreshadowing [1] the destruction of Jerusalem, it prefigured also [2] the terrors of the last great day."[57] To explain himself Jesus refers to "the abomination of desolation, spoken of by Daniel the prophet."[58] Daniel speaks of the abomination of desolation in three places, Daniel 9:27, 11:31 and 12:11. The first reference is clearly to the destruction of Jerusalem. The last two are clearly not referring to the destruction of Jerusalem. Therefore, there must be a second abomination of desolation spoken of by Daniel the prophet. To what

---

[53] Exodus 31:16-17

[54] E. G. White, *The Review and Herald,* October 28, 1902 par. 8.

[55] E.G. White, *Letter 66,* 1900, pp. 1, 2.

[56] Matthew 24:3

[57] E. G. White, *The Great Controversy* (1911), p. 25.3.

[58] Matthew 24:15

then, do they refer? Luke gives us the exact definition of the first abomination of desolation: "And when ye shall see Jerusalem compassed with armies, then know that the desolation thereof is nigh."[59] Rather than using the phrase "abomination of desolation," as Matthew does, he interprets the abomination as Jerusalem being compassed with armies. The armies standing "in the holy place," as Matthew says is not describing the armies inside the holy place of the temple, for once that occurred there was no opportunity for anyone to flee. Instead, the phrase is a reference to the holy ground which extended outside the city walls. In the days of Nehemiah, the Jews were being tempted to buy things on the sabbath from the pagan merchants who set up shop just outside the city wall. Nehemiah informed the merchants that if they did not leave, he would have them arrested, and then he designated an area some distance outside the city as holy ground into which no gentile was allowed. This provision was to protect the sanctity of the sabbath. "When the idolatrous standards of the Romans should be set up in the holy ground, which extended some furlongs outside the city walls, then the followers of Christ were to find safety in flight. When the warning sign should be seen, those who would escape must make no delay. Throughout the land of Judea, as well as in Jerusalem itself, the signal for flight must be immediately obeyed. He who chanced to be upon the housetop must not go down into his house, even to save his most valued treasures. Those who were working in the fields or vineyards must not take time to return for the outer garment laid aside while they should be toiling in the heat of the day. They must not hesitate a moment, lest they be involved in the general destruction."[60] The abomination was the idolatrous standards or flags, exalting the worship of the sun god, being placed in the holy ground in opposition to the sabbath of the Lord.

Ezekiel 8 gives us a very good clue as to the nature of the second abomination of desolation. After being shown progressively greater abominations, Ezekiel is shown the culmination of abominations in Ezekiel 8:16. Here are twenty-five men, in the house of God, worshipping the rising sun in the east. To do this they must turn their backs towards the temple, thus turning their backs on the law of God. They are worshipping the sun, instead of the Creator of the fourth commandment who made the sun. The same scenario will be

---

[59] Luke 21:20

[60] E. G. White, *The Great Controversy* (1911), p. 25.4.

brought into play in the end of time when men will be required to honor the sun god, by worshipping on Sunday, instead of worshipping the Creator on the sabbath. For this reason, immediately after mentioning the abomination of desolation (Matthew 24:15) Jesus emphasizes the importance of keeping the sabbath in Matthew 24:20 when he says "pray that your flight be not in the winter neither on the Sabbath day." The spirit of prophecy crystallizes the two separated events that are the abomination of desolation. "**As the siege of Jerusalem** by the Roman armies was the signal for flight to the Judean Christians, **so the assumption of power on the part of our nation** in the decree enforcing the papal Sabbath will be a warning to us."[61] Therefore the Bible and the spirit of prophecy define the abomination of desolation as two events: 1. the first siege of Jerusalem and, 2. an American[62] decree enforcing the papal sabbath at the end of time.

Therefore, Daniel 12:11 informs us that from the time the Bible sabbath is taken away, by the Sunday law being set up, there shall be a thousand two hundred and ninety days.

Daniel 12:12 Blessed is he that waiteth, and cometh to the thousand three hundred and five and thirty days.

The starting point for both time periods are the same with the 1,335 days extending forty-five days beyond the 1,290 days, and a blessing being pronounced on those that make it to the termination of the longer period. The period defined at the beginning of the chapter that would need a special blessing—specifically the blessing of being delivered—is the great time of Jacob's trouble. Therefore, the period of time from the end of the 1,290 days to the conclusion of the 1,335 days is the period of Jacob's trouble during which the death penalty, prophesied in Revelation 13, is in place.

After the implementation of the Sunday laws, at the beginning of the 1,290 days, God's people are filled with the Holy Spirit from the

---

[61] E. G. White, *Testimonies*, Vol. 5 (1889), p. 464.

[62] "The decree enforcing the worship of this day is to go forth to all the world.
As America, the land of religious liberty, shall unite with the papacy in forcing the conscience and compelling men to honor the false sabbath, the people of every country on the globe will be led to follow her example."
E. G. White, *Last Day Events*, p. 134.5-135.1.

outpouring of the latter rain, which causes the message to swell to a loud cry. This is the last warning for our planet. "In a special sense Seventh-day Adventists have been set in the world as watchmen and light-bearers. To them has been entrusted the last warning for a perishing world. On them is shining wonderful light from the word of God. They have been given a work of the most solemn import,—the proclamation of the first, second, and third angels' messages. There is no other work of so great importance. They are to allow nothing else to absorb their attention.

"The most solemn truths ever entrusted to mortals have been given us to proclaim to the world. The proclamation of these truths is to be our work. The world is to be warned, and God's people are to be true to the trust committed to them...."[63] Those honest hearted individuals who are God's people, yet still in Babylon, escape before it is too late. Warning plagues fall to wake up any that will heed the warning. Once the people of God have been sealed, probation closes and the seven last plagues begin to fall.

"I saw that the four angels would hold the four winds until Jesus' work was done in the sanctuary, and then will come the seven last plagues."[64]

"These plagues enraged the wicked against the righteous; they thought that we had brought the judgments of God upon them, and that if they could rid the earth of us, the plagues would then be stayed. A decree went forth to slay the saints, which caused them to cry day and night for deliverance. **This was the time of Jacob's trouble.** Then all the saints cried out with anguish of spirit, and were delivered by the voice of God. The 144,000 triumphed. Their faces were lighted up with the glory of God"[65] The death decree against the saints, triggered by the seven last plagues, begins the time of Jacob's trouble, "such as never was since there was a nation."[66] A special blessing is pronounced for **"he that waiteth, and cometh to the... end of the days"**. The saints are "left alone to wrestle with a man until the breaking of the day." [67] For forty-five days they cling

---

[63] E. G. White, *Early Writings* (1882), p. 119.3-120.1.

[64] *Ibid.*, p. 36.1-2.

[65] *Ibid.*, p. 36.2.

[66] Daniel 12:1

[67] Genesis 32:24-30

with superhuman strength, as did Jacob, to the merits of their divine Saviour. "Jacob's experience during that night of wrestling and anguish represents the trial through which the people of God must pass just before Christ's second coming. The prophet Jeremiah, in holy vision looking down to this time, said, 'We have heard a voice of trembling, of fear, and not of peace.... All faces are turned into paleness. Alas! for that day is great, so that none is like it: it is even the time of Jacob's trouble; but he shall be saved out of it.' Jeremiah 30:5-7."[68]

The question that should naturally come to any student of prophecy, is whether these time periods should be prophetic days (each day representing a year), or literal days, and if literal what precedent would there be for switching from the prophetic time of the other periods in Daniel to literal time?

First, there is Biblical precedent for switching from literal-time prophecies to prophetic-time prophecies in the book of Daniel itself. The prophet Daniel was studying the prophetic writings of Jeremiah,[69] which gave a time period in literal time. "For thus saith the LORD, That after seventy years be accomplished at Babylon I will visit you, and perform my good word toward you, in causing you to return to this place."[70] God had revealed to Jeremiah a time period, expressed in literal time, and shortly afterwards revealed several time periods to Daniel expressed in prophetic/symbolic time using the day for a year principle. Why would the prophecies of Daniel be expressed in symbolic time when Jeremiah had been given a time prophecy in literal time; and how are we able to know the difference?

The time period of Jeremiah is stated in the natural way of expressing time—seventy years; and the passage in which the time prophecy occurs uses non-symbolic language. Therefore, the time prophecy of Jeremiah is literal time and non-symbolic. The time prophecies of Daniel 7, 8, and 9 are stated in an unusual way for expressing time—"time and times and the dividing of time," "two thousand and three hundred evening mornings," and "seventy

---

[68] E. G. White, *Patriarchs and Prophets* (1890), *p.* 201.1.

[69] Daniel 9:2

[70] Jeremiah 29:10

weeks;" and the passages in which these time prophecies occur are highly symbolic. Therefore, these time prophesies of Daniel outline prophetic/symbolic time using the day for a year principle. The time period of Daniel 12:7—"time, times, and an half"—is a reiteration of the period already delineated in Daniel 7, and therefore should be understood to refer to the same 1,260 year period of papal supremacy. However, the final time periods of Daniel 12—the 1,290 days, and the 1,335 days, are not only stated in a natural way of expressing literal time, but also occur within a passage that is highly non-symbolic. "The language of the Bible should be explained according to its obvious meaning, unless a symbol or figure is employed."[71]

Second, there is additional evidence from the Hebrew word יוֹם yôm used for "**days**" in Daniel 12:11-13. This word is the same word used in Daniel 1 when Daniel asks for pulse and water for ten days and is the word used throughout the book of Daniel for literal days. Further, the word yôm is not used for any of the other time periods in Daniel. "It is also a fact that every time the writers of the Old Testament used the word yôm (day) or yämîm (days), with an ordinal or cardinal number, the meaning is always literal."[72] Therefore, to interpret the 1,290 days and the 1,335 days as prophetic/symbolic time, using the day for a year principle, would be to make them the only exception in all of Scripture, which is a questionable method of interpreting the Bible.

Third, the context of Daniel 12 is the great time of trouble, the close of probation and the special resurrection; all events immediately preceding the second coming. The sanctuary imagery of Jesus with an angel on either side of the river while he answers Daniel's questions about the end of time depicts Christ in the most holy place. This indicates that the revelation Jesus gives Daniel about the future, in chapter 12, must occur after he enters the most holy in 1844. Therefore, the context of the Scripture passage itself demands a

---

[71] E. G. White, *The Great Controversy* (1911), p. 598.3.

[72] Samuel Nunez, Ph.D., *Las Profecías Apocalípticas de Daniel*, 2 Vols. (Mexico, D.F.: Datacolor Impresores, 2006), 2:192.

future application of the time periods, and a future application demands that the time periods be literal.[73]

Fourth, the spirit of prophecy unequivocally places these time periods in the future: "In the Scriptures are presented truths that relate especially to our own time. To the period just prior to the appearing of the Son of man, the prophecies of Scripture point, and here their warnings and threatenings **pre-eminently apply**. **The prophetic periods of Daniel, extending to the very eve of the great consummation, throw a flood of light upon events then to transpire**. The book of Revelation is also replete with warning and instruction for the last generation. The beloved John, under the inspiration of the Holy Spirit, portrays the fearful and thrilling scenes connected with the close of earth's history, and presents the duties and dangers of God's people. **None need remain in ignorance, none need be unprepared for the coming of the day of God**."[74]

---

[73] Some object to a literal/future 1,290/1,335-days by asserting that it would predict the day of Christ's second coming, which practice the spirit of prophecy warns against, and which day the Bible says "no man knoweth." First, a literal/future view of the 1,290/1,335-days cannot predict the day of the coming of Jesus, because the 1,335 culminates in the special resurrection and not the second coming. The scripture gives no hint how much time elapses between the special resurrection and the second coming. Second, the Bible does not say we will never know the year of his coming, it says: "Watch therefore: for ye know not what **hour** your Lord doth come." Matthew 24:42 "And this know, that if the goodman of the house had known what hour the thief would come, he would have watched, and not have suffered his house to be broken through. Be ye therefore ready also: for the Son of man cometh at an **hour** when ye think not." Luke 12:39-40 "But of that **day and hour** knoweth no man, no, not the angels of heaven, but my Father only." Matthew 24:36

Some argue that the Bible says Christ will come as a thief in the night, implying that we simply cannot know anything about the imminence of Christ's coming. Reading the entire verse this assertion is based on gives a very different picture: "But of the **times and the seasons**, brethren, ye have no need that I write unto you. For yourselves know perfectly that the day of the Lord so cometh as a thief in the night. **But ye, brethren, are not in darkness, that that day should overtake you as a thief**. Ye are all the children of light, and the children of the day: we are not of the night, nor of darkness. Therefore, let us not sleep, as do others; but let us watch and be sober." 1 Thessalonians 5:1-2; 4-6 If the Lord's coming overtakes us as a thief in the night, we are on the wrong side. Indeed, all the Scripture passages that speak of the Lord's coming being as a thief, speak only of the day and the hour.

"Remember therefore how thou hast received and heard, and hold fast, and repent. If therefore thou shalt not watch, I will come on thee as a thief, and thou shalt not know what **hour** I will come upon thee." Revelation 3:3

The closer we are to the second coming; the more accurate will be our perception of its nearness. The spirit of prophecy tells us that there will come a time when even the day and the hour will be known: "The voice of God is heard from heaven, declaring the day and hour of Jesus' coming, and delivering the everlasting covenant to His people. Like peals of loudest thunder His words roll through the earth. The Israel of God stand listening, with their eyes fixed upward. Their countenances are lighted up with His glory, and shine as did the face of Moses when he came down from Sinai. The wicked cannot look upon them."

E. G. White, *The Great Controversy*, p. 640.2.

[74] E. G. White, *The Review and Herald*, September 25, 1883 par. 6.

The only prophetic periods in the book of Daniel that can possibly extend to the "very eve of the great consummation" are the 1,290 and 1,335 days, and this only if they are future, literal time periods.

"**The light** that Daniel received direct from God was **given especially for these last days**. The visions he saw by the banks of the **Ulai and the Hiddekel**, the great rivers of Shinar, are now in process of fulfillment, and **all the events foretold will soon have come to pass**."[75]

"The people of God need to study what characters they must form in order to pass through the test and proving of the last days. Many are living in spiritual weakness and backsliding. They know not what they believe. **Let us read and study the twelfth chapter of Daniel. It is a warning that we shall all need to understand before the time of the end**."[76] The first sentence of this statement refers to the characters that must be formed by God's people "to pass through the test and proving of the last days." This is an allusion to Daniel 12:10 which speaks of sanctification and the close of probation. After admonishing us to read and study Daniel 12, the words of Jesus to Daniel from verse nine are quoted: "It is a warning that we shall all need to understand before **the time of the end**." The only part of the chapter that can possibly be a warning for the time of the end is the last five verses. This passage was written in 1903, nearly sixty years after the investigative judgment began in 1844. We "**shall need to**" understand the warning of Daniel 12 in the future from 1903, implying that the warning was not yet understood in 1903 and would require reading and study to come to the correct understanding before the time of the end. This statement cannot possibly be referring to the traditional interpretation of these time periods which takes the 1,290 and the 1,335 days to be prophetic day-for-a-year and places them in the past ending in 1798 and 1843 respectively.

"There are many at the present day thus clinging to the customs and traditions of their fathers. When the Lord sends them additional light, they refuse to accept it, because, not having been granted to their fathers, it was not received by them. We are not placed where our fathers were; consequently our duties and responsibilities are not the same as theirs. We shall not be approved of God in looking to the

---

[75] E.G. White, *Manuscript Releases*, Vol. 16 (1990), p. 334.2.

[76] E.G. White, *Manuscript Releases*, Vol. 15 (1990), p. 228.2.

example of our fathers to determine our duty instead of searching the word of truth for ourselves. Our responsibility is greater than was that of our ancestors. We are accountable for the light which they received, and which was handed down as an inheritance for us, and we are accountable also for the additional light which is now shining upon us from the word of God."[77]

Since the 1,290 and the 1,335 days commence with the removal of "the daily," and the setting up of the "abomination of desolation," the meaning of "the daily" is central to understanding the two time periods, yet, it has been a source of controversy among Seventh-day Adventists from Ellen White's lifetime until today. Two views developed, the first, which became known as the "old view," interpreted "the daily" as pagan Romanism, and the second, which became known as the "new view" regarded the "the daily" as referring to Christ's ministration in the heavenly sanctuary. The controversy between the two views became quite heated, and those subscribing to the "old view" claimed they had the support of the spirit of prophecy, citing a statement from *Early Writings:* "I have seen that the 1843 chart was directed by the hand of the Lord, and that it should not be altered; that the figures were as He wanted them; that His hand was over and hid a mistake in some of the figures, so that none could see it, until His hand was removed. Then I saw in relation to the 'daily' (Daniel 8:12) that the word 'sacrifice' was supplied by man's wisdom, and does not belong to the text, and that the Lord gave the correct view of it to those who gave the judgment hour cry. When union existed, before 1844, nearly all were united on the correct view of the 'daily'; but in the confusion since 1844, other views have been embraced, and darkness and confusion have followed."[78] At first glance this statement would seem to settle the question in favor of the "old view." However, the statement was actually being taken out of context, even in Ellen White's day. When the statement was written, there was no controversy over the meaning of "the daily;" rather the controversy regarding "the daily" was over whether or not the supplied word [sacrifice] belonged in the text. Her *Early Writings* statement was settling the fact that "the word 'sacrifice' was supplied by man's wisdom, and does not belong to the text," not making a statement regarding the meaning of the phrase "the daily." When the statement was written there were some who

---

[77] E.G. White, *The Great Controversy* (1911), p. 164.1

[78] E.G. White, *Early Writings*, p. 74.1-2.

were apparently using the supplied word [sacrifice] to claim that it was necessary to go to old Jerusalem—not unlike popular movements today. Just a couple sentences later Ellen White states, "Then I was pointed to some who are in the great error of believing that it is their duty to go to Old Jerusalem, and think they have a work to do there before the Lord comes. Such a view is calculated to take the mind and interest from the present work of the Lord, under the message of the third angel; for those who think that they are yet to go to Jerusalem will have their minds there, and their means will be withheld from the cause of present truth to get themselves and others there."[79]

"Ellen White had made no mention of the daily in *The Great Controversy*, her volume dealing with prophecy. Her only use of the term is found in *Early Writings*, pages 74, 75, where she reports a vision given to her on September 23, 1850, and this in connection with the subject of time setting.

"*The Review and Herald* of April 4, 1907, carried an article from the pen of pioneer worker J. N. Loughborough, entitled 'The Thirteen Hundred and Thirty-five Days,' which, while not making reference to it as such, upheld the old view. As the months passed, *Review* editor W. W. Prescott found it difficult to refrain from introducing the new view of the daily, which to him carried great light. He was aware that while still in Australia, Ellen White had received a letter from L. R. Conradi, leader of the church's work in Europe, stating that he could not harmonize his views on the question with Smith's and that if she had any light on the subject, he would appreciate receiving it. If she had no light, he intended to publish his view—the new view. The fact that Ellen White did not reply to Conradi's letter left the impression that she had no light on the point.

"The matter simmered, Daniells unwilling to make it an issue since he had his hands more than full in the reorganization of the work of the church and the struggle with Battle Creek problems. The matter was discussed now and again at General Conference Committee meetings, with both viewpoints being considered, but no conclusion was reached...

"As careful students took time to examine all the evidence, many were led to accept the new view—A. G. Daniells and W. C. White

---

[79] E.G. White, *Early Writings*, p. 75.2.

[son of Ellen White and father of Arthur White] among them—and polarization began to develop."[80]

Ellen White herself then "referred to her own relation to the matter and the fact that God had given no special revelation on it, declaring: **'I have had no special light on the point presented** for discussion, and I do not see the need of this discussion.'"[81]

"The advocates of the old view maintained that the wording of this statement [the *Early Writings* statement] placed Heaven's endorsement on the view of the daily held by Miller and eventually repeated by Uriah Smith. The new-view advocates held that the statement must be taken in its context—the context of time setting. Ellen White's repeated statements that 'I have no light on the point' (Letter 226, 1908) and 'I am unable to define clearly the points that are questioned' (Letter 250, 1908), and her inability to make a definite statement when the question was urged upon her, seemed to give support to their conclusion. They were confident also that the messages given through Ellen White would not conflict with the clearly established events of history."[82]

"At one point... Elder Daniells, accompanied by W.C. White and C.C. Crisler, eager to get from Ellen White herself just what the meaning was of her *Early Writings* statement, went to her and laid the matter before her. Daniells took with him *Early Writings* and the 1843 chart. He sat down close to Ellen White and plied her with questions. His report of this interview was confirmed by W. C. White:
'I first read to Sister White the statement given above in *Early Writings*. Then I placed before her our prophetic chart used by our ministers in expounding the prophecies of Daniel and Revelation. I called her attention to the picture of the sanctuary and also to the 2,300-year period as they appeared on the chart.
'I then asked if she could recall what was shown her regarding this subject.
'As I recall her answer, she began by telling how some of the leaders who had been in the 1844 movement endeavored to find new dates for the termination of the 2,300-year period. This endeavor was to fix

---

[80] Arthur L. White, *The Later Elmshaven Years 1905-1915*, Vol. 6, p. 247.3-248.1.

[81] *Ibid.*, p. 249.5.

[82] *Ibid.*, p. 252.3.

new dates for the coming of the Lord. This was causing confusion among those who had been in the Advent Movement.

'In this confusion the Lord revealed to her, she said, that the view that had been held and presented regarding the dates was correct, and that there must never be another time set, nor another time message.

'I then asked her to tell what had been revealed to her about the rest of the 'daily'—the Prince, the host, the taking away of the 'daily,' and the casting down of the sanctuary.

She replied that these features were not placed before her in vision as the time part was. She would not be led out to make an explanation of those points of the prophecy.'"[83]

"Ellen White watched with growing anxiety and distress the time-consuming controversy between leading brethren on an unimportant point and one on which she repeatedly said she had received no light. On July 31, 1910, she could restrain herself no longer. She took her pen and wrote:

'I have words to speak to my brethren east and west, north and south. I request that my writings shall not be used as the leading argument to settle questions over which there is now so much controversy. **I entreat of Elders Haskell, Loughborough, Smith, and others of our leading brethren, that they make no reference to my writings to sustain their views of the 'daily.'**

'It has been presented to me that this is not a subject of vital importance. I am instructed that our brethren are making a mistake in magnifying the importance of the difference in the views that are held. **I cannot consent that any of my writings shall be taken as settling this matter. The true meaning of the 'daily' is not to be made a test question.**

'**I now ask that my ministering brethren shall not make use of my writings in their arguments regarding this question; for I have had no instruction on the point under discussion**, and I see no need for the controversy. Regarding this matter under present conditions, silence is eloquence.'"[84] Therefore, those who use the *Early Writings* statement to support the claim that "the daily" is pagan Romanism directly contradict the spirit of prophecy's own testimony. The individuals named were supporters of the "old view," who were using the *Early Writings* statement. It is therefore abundantly clear

---

[83] Arthur L. White, *Ellen G. White: The Later Elmshaven Years 1905-1915*, Vol. 6 p. 256.2-8.

[84] Arthur L. White, *Ellen G. White: The Later Elmshaven Years 1905-1915*, Vol. 6 p. 257.5-258.1.

that Ellen White did not intend for the statement to define the meaning of "the daily," otherwise she would be contradicting her statement that she had no light on the subject. Notice that she said "under present conditions, silence is eloquence," implying that there would come a time when the subject would again be an important point of discussion. Indeed, we are given instruction that this is the case: "**Let us read and study the twelfth chapter of Daniel. It is a warning that we shall all need to understand before the time of the end.**"[85]

Daniel 12:13 But go thou thy way till the end be: for thou shalt rest, and stand in thy lot at the end of the days.

Jesus promised Daniel that he would sleep in the grave, and be resurrected at the end of the days.[86]

"Honored by men with the responsibilities of state and with the secrets of kingdoms bearing universal sway, Daniel was honored by God as His ambassador, and was given many revelations of the mysteries of ages to come. His wonderful prophecies, as recorded by him in chapters 7 to 12 of the book bearing his name, were not fully understood even by the prophet himself; but **before his life labors closed, he was given the blessed assurance that 'at the end of the days'—in the closing period of this world's history—he would again be permitted to stand in his lot and place.**"[87] Before Daniel died he was assured that he would be resurrected "at the end of the days." These days, therefore, can only be in the future, for Daniel was not resurrected in 1843, rather he will rise at the end of the 1,335 days, "in the closing period of this world's history."

"The things revealed to Daniel were afterward complemented by the revelation made to John on the Isle of Patmos. These two books should be carefully studied. Twice Daniel inquired, How long shall it be to the **end of time**?

---

[85] E.G. White, *Manuscript Releases*, Vol. 15 (1990), p. 228.2.

[86] While it is true that the spirit of prophecy alludes to this verse metaphorically to say that the message of Daniel stands in its lot or has stood in its lot in the past, she also refers to the verse in a very literal way to indicate Daniel's resurrection, in the future, at the end of the days.

[87] E.G. White, *Prophets and Kings* (1917), p. 547.1.

"'And I heard, but I understood not: then said I, O my Lord, what shall be the end of these things? And He said, Go thy way, Daniel: for the words are closed up and sealed till the time of the end. Many shall be purified, and made white, and tried; but the wicked shall do wickedly: and none of the wicked shall understand; but the wise shall understand. And from the time that the daily sacrifice shall be taken away, and the abomination that maketh desolate set up, there shall be a thousand two hundred and ninety days. Blessed is he that waiteth, and cometh to the thousand three hundred and five and thirty days. But go thou thy way till the end be: for thou shalt rest, and stand in thy lot at the end of the days.'

"It was the Lion of the tribe of Judah who unsealed the book and gave to John the revelation of what should be in these last days.

"Daniel stood in his lot to bear his testimony which was sealed until the time of the end, when the first angel's message should be proclaimed to our world. These matters are of infinite importance in these last days; but while 'many shall be purified, and made white, and tried,' 'the wicked shall do wickedly: and none of the wicked shall understand.' How true this is! Sin is the transgression of the law of God; and those who will not accept the light in regard to the law of God will not understand the proclamation of the first, second, and third angel's messages. The book of Daniel is unsealed in the revelation to John, and **carries us forward to the last scenes of this earth's history**.

"Will our brethren bear in mind that **we are living amid the perils of the last days**? Read Revelation in connection with Daniel. Teach these things."[88]

This passage interprets what Daniel meant by his questions: "How long shall it be to the end of time?" Ellen White interprets the questions to refer to the end of time, or the second coming of Jesus, not the beginning of the time of the end (1798). The book of Daniel also "carries us forward to the last scenes of this earth's history." For this to be the case, it must carry us beyond 1844.

One final statement from the spirit of prophecy often used to deny the possibility of a future/literal interpretation of the 1,290 and 1,335 days must be considered—the statement about time setting and no prophetic time after 1844. A portion of this quote is as follows:

"...After this period of time, reaching from 1842 to 1844, there can be

---

88 E.G. White, *Testimonies to Ministers and Gospel Workers* (1923), p. 114.6-115.4.

no **definite** tracing of the prophetic time. The longest reckoning reaches to the autumn of 1844." Taken alone, this statement seems to rule out a future understanding of the days of Daniel 12. However, a careful look at the context of her statement and of the careful wording she uses in virtually all such statements reveals the consistency of her God-given messages. Before we look at the context, notice her use of the word "definite." She uses this word to qualify the word time. Here is the rather lengthy context of the above statement: "After these seven thunders uttered their voices, the instruction comes to John as to Daniel in regard to the little book: 'Seal up those things which the seven thunders uttered.' **These relate to future events which will be disclosed in their order. Daniel shall stand in his lot at the end of the days**. John sees the little book unsealed. Then Daniel's prophecies have their proper place in the first, second, and third angels' messages to be given to the world. The unsealing of the little book was the message in relation to time.

"The books of Daniel and the Revelation are one. One is a prophecy, the other a revelation; one a book sealed, the other a book opened. John heard the mysteries which the thunders uttered, but he was commanded not to write them.

"The special light given to John which was expressed in the seven thunders was a delineation of events which would transpire under the first and second angels' messages. It was not best for the people to know these things, for their faith must necessarily be tested. In the order of God most wonderful and advanced truths would be proclaimed. The first and second angels' messages were to be proclaimed, **but no further light was to be revealed before these messages had done their specific work**. This is represented by the Angel standing with one foot on the sea, proclaiming with a most solemn oath that time should be no longer.

"**This time**, which the angel declares with a solemn oath, **is not the end of this world's history, neither of probationary time, but of prophetic time, which should precede the advent of our Lord. That is, the people will not have another message upon definite time.** After this period of time, reaching from 1842 to 1844, there can be no **definite** tracing of the **prophetic time**. The longest reckoning reaches to the autumn of 1844."[89]

In the very passage that seems, at first glance, to rule out future/ literal time periods in Daniel 12, she again refers first to future events

---

[89] E.G. White, *Manuscript Releases*, Vol. 19 (1990), p. 320.1-321.1.

that will be disclosed in their order, and then to Daniel standing in his lot, in the future ("shall stand"), at the end of the days. She continues by saying that no further light would be shed on these prophecies until the earlier messages did their work. Finally, she states that the time that the angel said would be no longer, was the prophetic time that terminated on a specific date, in 1844.

Even a cursory overview, of the context of the 87 times the phrase "definite time" is used in the spirit of prophecy; shows that it means specific date. Most often it refers to October 22, 1844. As highlighted earlier,[90] a literal 1,290/1,335-days cannot give a specific date, or definite time, for the second coming, even after the implementation of Sunday laws. The spirit of prophecy does not say that there will not be another message based upon time, but that we will not have one based upon **definite time**. In each similar statement, she carefully qualifies the word time with the word "definite."

What is the purpose of this message, which cannot tell us a specific date? Jesus gives us this message so that in the darkest hour we will have hope to carry on just a little while longer.

"Let us read and study the twelfth chapter of Daniel. It is a warning that we shall all need to understand before the time of the end. There are ministers claiming to believe the truth who are not sanctified through the truth. Unless a change comes in their lives, they will say, 'My Lord delayeth His coming.'"[91] "A great work will be done in a short time. **A message will** soon be given by God's appointment that **will swell into a loud cry. Then Daniel will stand in his lot**, to give his testimony."[92]

"He that testifieth these things saith, surely I come quickly. Amen. Even so, come, Lord Jesus."[93]

---

[90] See footnote 73.

[91] E.G. White, *Manuscript Releases*, Vol. 15 (1990), p. 228.2.

[92] E. G. White, *Manuscript Releases*, Vol. 21 (1990), p. 437.3.

[93] Revelation 22:20

The Revelation of Jesus Christ

Revelation 1

SUMMARY:
Revelation 1 begins with the introduction of the book. A blessing is pronounced on those who read and hear the words of the Revelation; the setting of John's exile is described; and the stated purpose of the message is given. The vision occurs on the lonely prison island of Patmos, on the Lord's day. John is informed that he will be given messages to send to the seven churches of Asia. Then John sees a most impressive vision of Jesus Christ in the midst of seven golden candlesticks, which causes John to fall at his feet as dead. After John is strengthened, he is instructed that the seven golden candlesticks represent the seven churches, and that the seven stars are the angels of the seven churches.

If one wanted to learn first-hand information about a character of history, what better place to start than their autobiography, if such a book were available? This would likely be the place where the most information about the person would be revealed. If one wanted to learn first-hand information about Jesus Christ, what better place to start than the autobiography titled: The Revelation of Jesus Christ? If you love Jesus, and long to learn about him and speak of him, would this not be a primary resource? If you are not sure you can love him because you have heard bad things about God, or even if you hate God or do not acknowledge his existence, perhaps you will see his deep love for you for the first time, unveiled in the Revelation of Jesus Christ.

If you had a loved one held hostage in foreign territory, and you were working on a plan for their rescue, any communication you had with them would endeavor to make them aware of your plan (so they would be ready) without revealing it to their captors. This would reveal your deep love—that you would risk so much to save them.

Revelation is a cryptic message to show us where we came from and why we are now locked in a world full of suffering and death. It shows us how we can leave this hostage prison and go to a new home where sin and sorrow will be forever banished.

Revelation is God's rescue plan to liberate the human race from the pain and sorrow of sin. It shows us how the rescue mission will be executed, so that we are ready when the deliverer arrives to liberate the hostages. It tells us the secret plans of our captor. Is it any wonder our captor would want to discourage us from reading the book that is sure to free us from his bondage?

God's infinite love for the human race necessitates this disclosure of top-secret, inside-information, that we might be unafraid during fearful times.

Many believe that the book of Revelation is a hidden book; a closed book; something that you should not study, or could never understand. Others say we should not focus on it too much; we need to just talk about Jesus, because all these beasts and future disasters are scary. If people refuse the warnings Christ has given of the imminence of his coming, then they do not "love his appearing;"[1] they do not really want him to return.

Most Bibles have a supplied heading at the beginning of the book of Revelation that reads: "The Revelation of Saint John the Divine." However, the beginning of the first verse, states, "**The Revelation of Jesus Christ**." So, this book is a revelation about Jesus; a revelation of the heart of God. Not only does this book reveal Jesus Christ and his love for us, but it is a message about the future. Your future!

Revelation 1:1 The Revelation of Jesus Christ, which God gave unto him, to show unto his servants things which must shortly come to pass; and he sent and signified it by his angel unto his servant John:

The stated purpose of the book of Revelation is to show God's servants what is to occur in the near future. Above all it is a message that reveals the character of Christ, as his hand draws back the veil of time exposing the mysteries of the ages.

Verse one informs us that the Father gave the Revelation to Jesus who "**sent and signified it by his angel unto his servant John**." This is rather interesting legal language which outlines multiple

---

[1] 2 Timothy 4:8

witnesses and a notarized, authenticated document. "Signified" comes from the same root from which we get the word signature. Why would God open the book that reveals his love for us, in such a formal and legal way? God wants us to know that it is genuine, and can be trusted. The angel that signifies this book for Jesus is Gabriel, the highest created being in the courts of glory. "Of Gabriel the Saviour speaks in the Revelation, saying that '**He sent and signified it by His angel unto His servant John**.'"[2]

God the Father delivers the message to Jesus, who sends it to his angel. Gabriel notarizes it, and delivers it to the servant of Jesus— John. Then John, also, becomes a witness to its authenticity—for in verse two, the Bible tells us:

Revelation 1:2 Who bare record of the word of God and of the testimony of Jesus Christ, and of all the things that he saw.

John bares record of the things he saw, becoming a witness of the message of Revelation. Thus, we have four separate beings involved in the delivery of a message that is authenticated—notarized, from the hand of God.

Further, God gives a special blessing to each individual that will read or hear the words of this book;

Revelation 1:3 Blessed is he that readeth, and they that hear the words of this prophecy, and keep those things which are written therein: for the time is at hand.

Along with the blessing for reading and hearing, there is also the blessing for those who do the things that are written in the book; with a reminder that time is short. These things are to occur in rapid succession. This message has particular significance to each generation since the words were penned, but especially to us in these last days of earth's history. Yet how many understand this message of infinite importance?

---

[2] E. G. White, *The Desire of Ages* (1898), p. 99.1.

"Let us give more time to the study of the Bible. We do not understand the Word as we should. The book of Revelation opens with an injunction to us to understand the instruction that it contains. 'Blessed is he that readeth, and they that hear the words of this prophecy,' God declares, 'and keep those things which are written therein; for the time is at hand.' When we as a people understand what this book means to us, there will be seen among us a great revival. We do not understand fully the lessons that it teaches, notwithstanding the injunction given us to search and study it."[3]

Revelation 1:4 John to the seven churches, which are in Asia: Grace be unto you, and peace, from him which is and which was, and which is to come; and from the seven spirits, which are before his throne.

As one of the witnesses giving the message of the book of Revelation, John greets us. He tells us that he is writing this message specifically to the seven churches of Asia.

Notice how he introduces seven churches and seven spirits in this verse. The Book of Revelation contains many numbers. In particular, the number seven features very prominently. In fact, there are seven churches, seven spirits, seven candlesticks, seven stars, seven seals, seven horns, seven eyes, seven angels, seven trumpets, seven thunders, 7,000 men slain, seven heads, seven crowns, seven last plagues, seven golden vials, seven mountains, seven kings; the book of life is mentioned seven times, the bottomless pit is mentioned seven times, the word blessed is used seven times, and the lamb receives seven blessings.

Such a usage of the number seven in Scripture, is unique to this book alone. Seven is a number that indicates completion. The seventh-day was the completion of creation. The book of Revelation is the completion of the Bible, but also communicates the completion of the plan of salvation; the completion of everything that God purposed to accomplish in the restoration of Eden. In Genesis, Eden is lost. In Revelation, Eden is restored.

---

[3] E. G. White, *Manuscript Releases*, Vol. 4 (1990), p. 287.1.

John continues writing, and not only does he greet us, but he transmits to us a greeting coming directly from Jesus Christ.

Revelation 1:5 And from Jesus Christ who is the faithful witness, and the first begotten of the dead, and the prince of the kings of the earth. Unto him that loved us, and washed us from our sins in his own blood.

This is the continuation of the greeting. John transmits directly to us the greeting of Christ. We are reminded, again in legal language, that he is the faithful witness to the truth of this message. The Majesty of the universe is trying in every way possible to convince us of the importance and veracity of this message. Yet, he condescends to ask John (and us) to be his witnesses.[4]

Jesus is the prince of the kings of the earth who "**loved us and washed us from our sins in his own blood**." God risked the entire universe to become a man and pour out his own blood on the cross of Calvary, to rescue those whom he calls his friends.[5] "Wherefore Jesus also, that he might sanctify the people with his own blood, suffered without the gate."[6] "And without controversy great is the mystery of godliness: **God was manifest in the flesh**, justified in the Spirit, seen of angels, preached unto the Gentiles, believed on in the world, received up into glory."[7]

God did this while we were his enemies: "For if, when we were enemies, we were reconciled to God by the death of his Son, much more, being reconciled, we shall be saved by his life."[8] Therefore, the sacrifice of Jesus paid the penalty of our sins before we even knew who he was—while we were his enemy. This means that whether one is an atheist, Muslim, Buddhist, Hindu, Jew, New Ager, hippie,

---

[4] Acts 1:8 "But ye shall receive power, after that the Holy Ghost is come upon you: and ye shall be witnesses unto me both in Jerusalem, and in all Judaea, and in Samaria, and unto the uttermost part of the earth."

[5] John 15:15 "Henceforth I call you not servants; for the servant knoweth not what his lord doeth: but I have called you friends; for all things that I have heard of my Father I have made known unto you."

[6] Hebrews 13:12

[7] 1 Timothy 3:16

[8] Romans 5:10

Catholic, agnostic, Christian; man, woman, or child; Christ accomplished something for each, whether we like it, know it, believe it, accept it, or not.

Christ made provision for the whole world. "To wit, that God was in Christ, **reconciling the world unto himself**, **not imputing their trespasses unto them**; and hath committed unto us the word of reconciliation."[9] "Therefore as by the offence of one judgment came upon all men to condemnation; even so by the righteousness of one the free gift came upon **all men** unto justification of life."[10]

His death already freed us from the condemnation of our sin, and gives us an opportunity for a second probation. The Bible calls this **justification of life**. We were not executed the moment we were guilty of death. "For the wages of sin is death; but the gift of God is eternal life through Jesus Christ our Lord."[11]

Justification of life is not enough to save us, however. He values our freedom of choice more than he values our salvation! He will not save us against our will. Therefore, to be saved, you must accept his life and righteousness in place of yours; you must accept the infinite sacrifice of his death on your behalf. "For if, when we were enemies, we were reconciled to God by the death of his Son, much more, being reconciled, we shall be saved by his life."[12] This is called **justification by faith**.

If we never accept his life for ours, then those sins, which he already paid for, will eventually be imputed back to us. "Blessed is the man to whom the Lord will not impute sin."[13]

Our neighbors called us one night asking if we could help find their lost dog. To make a long story short, I found the dog. They were so grateful, that they sent us a $400 money order. My wife felt bad accepting their money, when we would have been willing to help find the dog without any payment. So she said, "Well, let's just not cash

---

[9] 2 Corinthians 5:19

[10] Romans 5:18

[11] Romans 6:23

[12] Romans 5:10

[13] Romans 4:8; Matthew 18:23-35

it," and was about to shred it, when I said "Wait! It is a money order, not a check!" You see, our neighbors, anticipating that we might be reluctant to cash a check, paid the bank to give us a money order. They had already spent the money whether we accepted it, or not— whether we cashed, or shredded it.

God wrote a money order for you—with his own blood—to purchase your salvation. Why not trust him and cash it? If you shred it, he still spent it. He spent it all for you. Scripture says, he "loved us, and washed us from our sins in his own blood!" "For God so loved the world, that he gave his only begotten Son, that whosoever believeth in him should not perish, but have everlasting life."[14] It is this Son of God, that spilled his blood for you, who will be judging you.[15] He proposes to substitute his life in place of yours, so that in the judgment he sees only his perfect righteousness in place of your sinfulness.

There are many people today who have in their hands an un-cashed money order of infinite value, and they are about to shred it. Won't you accept it?

"The world's Redeemer was treated as we deserve to be treated, in order that we might be treated as he deserved to be treated. He came to our world and took our sins upon his own divine soul, that we might receive his imputed righteousness. He was condemned for our sins, in which he had no share, that we might be justified by his righteousness, in which we had no share. The world's Redeemer gave himself for us. Who was he?—The Majesty of heaven, pouring out his blood upon the altar of justice for the sins of guilty man. We should know our relationship to Christ and his relationship to us."[16]

Revelation is a message about salvation; a message of love from the heart of an infinite God who spent everything—even his very blood— to purchase our salvation.

---

[14] John 3:16

[15] John 5:22-23 "For the Father judgeth no man, but hath committed all judgment unto the Son: That all men should honour the Son, even as they honour the Father. He that honoureth not the Son honoureth not the Father which hath sent him."

[16] E. G. White, *Review and Herald, March 21, 1893,* par. 6.

Verse five also refers to Jesus as "**the first begotten of the dead**." Certainly, Jesus was not the first person ever to be raised from the dead. The Bible testifies of earlier resurrections: the prophet Elisha raised a boy from the dead;[17] Jesus raised several people before he himself was resurrected.[18] Therefore, "**the first begotten of the dead**" cannot mean that Jesus was the first person to be raised from the dead. In other places, the Bible calls him "the only begotten son." John 3:16, is one of the verses that uses this term. Perhaps you have heard this most famous verse in the Bible: "For God so loved the world, that he gave his only begotten Son that whosoever believeth in him should not perish, but have everlasting life."

Some will claim that this means that Jesus was begotten as a human when he was conceived in Mary; or maybe at his birth. Let us allow the Bible to interpret itself. Jesus was born in Bethlehem, and a prophecy in Micah tells us how long Jesus has existed. "But thou Bethlehem Ephratah, though thou be little among the thousands of Judah, yet out of thee shall come forth unto me that is to be ruler in Israel; whose goings forth have been from old, **from everlasting**."[19] The king of Israel to be born in Bethlehem has existed from all eternity.

Some claim that just as Seth was begotten of Adam,[20] so Jesus was begotten of God; that Jesus had some kind of a cosmic birth or was created by God the father, just as Adam procreated Seth. However, the word begotten, in Scripture, does not demand the connotation of human procreation. "I beseech thee for my son, Onesimus, whom I have begotten in my bonds."[21] Paul, writing a letter to Philemon, calls Onesimus his son, whom he has begotten. Onesimus was a slave who ran away from Philemon, and Paul is writing a letter to Philemon to help smooth the way for Onesimus to return. Onesimus is not Paul's procreated son, but he uses the term begotten, because Onesimus was born-again as a Christian as a result of Paul's labors.

---

[17] 2 Kings 4:8-37

[18] John 11:1-45; Matthew 9:23-26; Luke 7:12-16

[19] Micah 5:2
Some versions, instead of "everlasting," say "days of old," "ancients days," or something similar. For an in-depth study of this issue see Martin Klein, *Thou Hast Magnified Thy Word Above All Thy Name.*

[20] Genesis 5:4

[21] Philemon 1:10

Thus, the word begotten does not demand that it have some element of procreation.

The Bible tells us that Jesus has been in existence with the Father from all eternity.[22] He did not have some point of creation or some period of cosmic birth, but the Bible gives us testimony of his eternity. The New Testament also testifies to Christ's eternal nature: "That which was from the beginning, which we have heard, which we have seen with our eyes, which we have looked upon, and our hands have handled, of the Word of life; (For the life was manifested, and we have seen it, and bear witness, and show unto you **that eternal life, which was with the Father**, and was manifested unto us;)"[23]

Yet, we must still explore the question of what the Bible means by Jesus being begotten, to discover when it occurred. The Bible says in Psalms 2:7, "I will declare the decree. The Lord hath said unto me, thou art my son, **this day have I begotten thee**." Thus, Scripture specifies a day on which God the Father begat God the Son.

The obvious question is, on what day was he begotten? We find the answer in Acts 13:33-34 "God hath fulfilled the same unto us their children, in that **he hath raised up Jesus again. As it is also written in the second Psalms, thou art my son, this day I have begotten thee**. And **as concerning that he raised him up from the dead**, now no more to return to corruption, he said on this wise, I give you the sure mercies of David." The day on which Jesus was begotten was the day of the resurrection. The context of these verses is speaking of the resurrection, and Luke quotes the verse in the second Psalms specifying the day that Jesus was begotten. So, Christ was not begotten in some cosmic birth millions of years ago. Jesus was not begotten when he was created by God—for he is not a created being, but is instead the Creator.[24] Jesus was not begotten at his conception in the womb of Mary. Jesus was not begotten at his birth as Mary's son; but Jesus was begotten on the day he rose from the tomb. This is the reason he is called "**the first begotten of the dead**."

---

[22] See *Selected Messages*, Vol. 1 (1958), p. 247.2-248.3.

[23] 1 John 1:1, 2

[24] John 1:1-3, 14

Why does Scripture call him the "**first**" begotten of the dead when he was not the first one to be resurrected? The answer to that question follows: "The Word was made flesh and dwelt among us, and we beheld his glory, the glory of **the only begotten of the Father** full of grace and truth."[25] Here Christ is called the "**only begotten of the Father**." In the same passage, the Bible tells us: "In the beginning was the Word, and the Word was with God, and the Word was God. The same was in the beginning with God. All things were made by him; and without him was not any thing made that was made."[26]

How many things, according to the Bible, were made without Jesus? The answer is—nothing. Nothing was made without him. That means that the Bible is telling us that Jesus is the Creator of everything. He gave life to all living. For this reason, Jesus cannot be a created being. It is also the reason why Jesus is called "**the first begotten of the dead**," because Jesus is the first thing the Father gave life to, when he raised him from the tomb. The Bible tells us that it was God the Father that raised Jesus from the dead: "Paul, an apostle, (not of men, neither by man, but by Jesus Christ, and God the Father, who raised him from the dead;)"[27]

Thus, Jesus is called the only begotten, the first begotten of the dead, and the only begotten of the Father. This explains why his resurrection day was the day he was begotten, because on that day he became the first begotten of the Father, from the dead.

Revelation 1:6 And hath made us kings[28] and priests unto God and his Father; to him be glory and dominion forever and ever. Amen.

Here is additional evidence for the divinity of Jesus. Notice the wording carefully: "**he hath made us kings and priests unto God and his Father**." This means that God has a Father, which means that the Bible is calling Jesus God.

---

[25] John 1:14

[26] John 1:1-3

[27] Galatians 1:1

[28] As a side note, in Proverbs 31:4, the Bible tells us "it is not for kings to drink wine, nor for princes strong drink." If God has made us kings and priests, then it would not be a stretch to say that God expects that we abstain from fermented beverages. See also the story of the Rechabites in Jeremiah 35.

We are also told in this verse that "**he hath made us kings and priests**." What an amazing thought. We have been so degraded, so sinful, so rebellious. God could have saved us and told us, you can scrub the streets—just be happy to be a janitor on these golden streets. But, instead of giving us the most menial position in his kingdom, he exalts us as kings and priests unto God and his Father. Amazing love. Amazing grace.

Revelation 1:7 Behold, he cometh with clouds; and every eye shall see him, and they also which pierced him; and all kindreds of the earth shall wail because of him. Even so, Amen.

In verse seven we see one of the primary themes of the book of Revelation—the message that he is coming back soon. This is a promise from a loving God intent on reuniting his family. His return to earth is the culmination of salvation. If it were not for this promise, being a Christian would be in vain.[29]

Here we are also told some details of the manner in which Jesus will come. He comes "**with clouds; and every eye shall see him**." This includes those that pierced him; which means those individuals will be resurrected to behold this event.[30] Matthew also tells us that the second coming of Jesus will not be a secret: "For as the lightning cometh out of the east and shineth even unto the west, so shall also the coming of the Son of Man be."[31]

There is a popular theory in Christianity that the second coming of Jesus will be a secret. It is popular on bumper stickers and dramatic in Christian movies, but it does not come from Scripture. The Bible tells us in this verse that every eye will see him. The second coming will not be a secret event. The resurrection takes place while the nations of the earth are wailing in anguish for "men loved darkness

---

[29] 1 Corinthians 15:19-23 "If in this life only we have hope in Christ, we are of all men most miserable. But now is Christ risen from the dead, and become the firstfruits of them that slept. For since by man came death, by man came also the resurrection of the dead. For as in Adam all die, even so in Christ shall all be made alive. But every man in his own order: Christ the firstfruits; afterward they that are Christ's at his coming."

[30] Daniel 12:2 "And many of them that sleep in the dust of the earth shall awake, some to everlasting life, and some to shame and everlasting contempt."

[31] Matthew 24:17

rather than light, because their deeds were evil. For every one that doeth evil hateth the light, neither cometh to the light, lest his deeds should be reproved."[32] "Behold, he cometh with clouds; and every eye shall see him, and they also which pierced him: and all kindreds of the earth shall wail because of him. Even so, Amen."[33] "Behold, I show you a mystery; We shall not all sleep, but we shall all be changed, In a moment, in the twinkling of an eye, at the last trump: for the trumpet shall sound, and the dead shall be raised incorruptible, and we shall be changed."[34] Imagine the terror and sorrow that will be felt by those who knew the truths of Scripture, and rejected them. They realize that they have lost out on all eternity and that judgment is pronounced against them. God is a God of love; but a God of love must also be a God of justice. He will respect the choice of those who refuse his provision for rescue.

Yet the Bible tells us of another group who cry, "Lo, this is our God, we have waited for him, and he will save us."[35] May we be among those that exclaim, "Henceforth there is laid up for me a crown of righteousness, which the Lord, the righteous judge, shall give me at that day: and not to me only, but unto all them also that love his appearing."[36] "Abide in him; that, when he shall appear, we may have confidence, and not be ashamed before him at his coming."[37]

Revelation 1:8 I am Alpha and Omega, the beginning and the ending, sayeth the Lord, which is, and which was, and which is to come, the Almighty.

Alpha and Omega refers to the first and last letters of the Greek[38] alphabet—the beginning and the ending. That this expression refers to Jesus is clear from the phrase **"which is and which was and which is to come."** The one **"which is and which was and which is to come"** is also the **"the Almighty"** God of the universe.

---

[32] John 3:19-20

[33] Revelation 1:7

[34] 1 Corinthians 15:51-52

[35] Isaiah 25:9

[36] 2 Timothy 4:8

[37] 1 John 2:28

[38] The original language of the New Testament was Greek.

Therefore, the divinity of Christ is once more clearly established. Jesus is exalted above every name that is named. "Let this mind be in you, which was also in Christ Jesus: Who, being in the form of God, thought it not robbery to be equal with God: But made himself of no reputation, and took upon him the form of a servant, and was made in the likeness of men: And being found in fashion as a man, he humbled himself, and became obedient unto death, even the death of the cross. Wherefore God also hath highly exalted him, and given him a name which is above every name: That at the name of Jesus every knee should bow, of things in heaven, and things in earth, and things under the earth; And that every tongue should confess that Jesus Christ is Lord, to the glory of God the Father."[39]

To further demonstrate the divinity of Christ, the title "**Alpha and Omega, the beginning and the ending,**" is synonymous with the phrase in Revelation 1:11, "Alpha and Omega, the first and the last." Comparing these titles to a passage in the Old Testament shows how these terms describe the one true God, the only God, the Lord of all eternity. "Thus saith the Lord, the God, the King of Israel, and his Redeemer, the Lord of hosts; I am the first, and I am the last; and besides me there is no God."[40] This is the one and only God, and he declares himself to be the first and the last. Notice also, he is presented co-equal with Jesus, because it says that he is the Lord, the King of Israel, and it says that he has a Redeemer, who is the Lord of hosts. Both the individuality and yet the complete unity of the Godhead are here portrayed.

Notice another parallel statement in Revelation 2:8 "And unto the angel of the church in Smyrna write, these things saith the first and the last, {the same expression used in Isaiah} which was dead, and is alive." Jesus was the only one who God the Father resurrected from the tomb. This can only be describing Jesus, for he was "dead and is alive." Therefore, the person who is the first and the last is Jesus, and yet in Isaiah we are told that the first and the last is the only God. This is the mystery of godliness that "God was manifest in the flesh."[41] Jesus is both fully God, and fully human. To some this may seem difficult to understand. However, if we could fully understand everything there is to understand about God, he would

---

[39] Philippians 2:5-11

[40] Isaiah 44:6

[41] 1 Timothy 3:16

not be God. The very fact that we cannot understand everything about him is additional evidence of his divinity.

Revelation 1:9 I John, who also am your brother, and companion in tribulation, and in the kingdom and patience of Jesus Christ, was in the isle that is called Patmos for the word of God and for the testimony of Jesus Christ.

John was exiled on the prison island of Patmos for his faith. So it was, that the aged prophet, banished to this lonely place at almost one hundred years of age,[42] was transported in vision to the courts of heaven where Jesus gave him the incredible message of the book of Revelation. God came very close to the beloved apostle before his life work closed.

Revelation 1:10 I was in the Spirit on the Lord's day and heard behind me a great voice, as of a trumpet,

John began to see the vision of the Lord, on the Lord's day. Scripture defines what day is the Lord's day: "And he said unto them, The sabbath was made for man, and not man for the sabbath. Therefore, the Son of man is Lord also of the sabbath."[43] The Bible tells us clearly that Jesus is the Lord of the sabbath. The Lord's day is the sabbath. There is no other day in Scripture of which Jesus is said to be the Lord. The ten commandments tell us which day is the sabbath: "Remember the sabbath day, to keep it holy. Six days shalt thou labour, and do all thy work: But **the seventh day is the sabbath of the LORD thy God**."[44]

Many today, when they hear the term "the Lord's day," assume that it refers to Sunday. However, it was more than two hundred years after the death of the apostle John before anyone ever used the term "the Lord's day" to refer to Sunday. Prior to his professed conversion to

---

[42] "In his old age John revealed the life of Christ in his life. He lived to be nearly one hundred years old, and over and over again he repeated the story of the crucified and risen Saviour."
E. G. White, *The Seventh-day Adventist Bible Commentary*, Vol. 7 (Washington, D.C.: Review and Herald Publishing Association, 1955), p 947.9.

[43] Mark 2:27-28

[44] Exodus 20:8-10

Christianity, the pagan Roman emperor, Constantine, implemented a
law requiring the veneration of the day of the sun—to enforce the
worship of the pagan sun god. Therefore, the bishop Eusebius,
"special friend and flatterer of Constantine"[45] attempted the first
theological reasoning for Sunday sacredness, while Pope Sylvester
I, first applied the term "Lord's day" to Sunday. John the Revelator
and the other apostles knew no such designation.[46]

***Revelation 1:11 Saying, I am Alpha and Omega, the first and the
last: and, What thou seest, write in a book, and send it unto the
seven churches which are in Asia; unto Ephesus, and unto
Smyrna, and unto Pergamos, and unto Thyatira, and unto
Sardis, and unto Philadelphia, and unto Laodicea.***

John recorded the things he saw in these visions to be shared with
all Christianity, and these words have blessed and excited people of
all ages since.

The names of the seven churches are mentioned in the order in
which a mail currier would deliver a letter from Patmos, through the
ancient mail service, Cursus publicus. These seven churches were
literal congregations established in Asia during the lifetime of the
apostles. God is addressing his letter to these churches, therefore,
the messages had applicability to their local time and place. But
more broadly, they have applicability to God's church through all
ages, to the very end of time. This is clear from the fact that there
were many other Christian churches, not just in Asia, to which this
letter would be applicable. Therefore, it makes sense to see that the
seven are also symbolic of the Christian church as a whole.

"The names of the seven churches are symbolic of the church in
different periods of the Christian Era. The number seven indicates
completeness, and is symbolic of the fact that the messages extend
to the end of time, while the symbols used reveal the condition of the
church at different periods in the history of the world."[47]

---

[45] E. G. White, *The Great Controversy* (1911), p. 574.2.

[46] More evidence for this is given in the comments on Daniel chapter seven.

[47] E. G. White, *Acts of the Apostles* (1911), p. 585.3

Revelation 1:12 And I turned to see the voice that spake with me. And being turned, I saw seven golden candlesticks;

John is conveyed in vision into the holy place of the heavenly sanctuary where he sees the seven golden candlesticks on its south side.

Revelation 1:13 And in the midst of the seven candlesticks one like unto the Son of man, clothed with a garment down to the foot, and girt about the paps with a golden girdle.

This is none other than Jesus himself standing among the seven candlesticks. Not only the divinity of Christ is emphasized in Revelation, but also his humanity. **"The Son of man"** indicates his relationship to us, being born into the human family as a descendant of King David.[48] "The LORD hath sworn in truth unto David; he will not turn from it; Of the fruit of thy body will I set upon thy throne."[49] "Of the increase of his government and peace there shall be no end, upon the throne of David, and upon his kingdom, to order it, and to establish it with judgment and with justice from henceforth even for ever. The zeal of the LORD of hosts will perform this."[50]

Revelation 1:14 His head and his hairs were white like wool, as white as snow; and his eyes were as a flame of fire;

The appearance of Christ to John, in the New Testament, was the same as his appearance to Daniel in the Old: "His body also was like the beryl, and his face as the appearance of lightning, and his eyes as lamps of fire, and his arms and his feet like in colour to polished brass, and the voice of his words like the voice of a multitude."[51]

---

[48] Matthew 25:31-32 "When the **Son of man** shall come in his glory, and all the holy angels with him, then shall he sit upon the throne of his glory: And before him shall be gathered all nations: and he shall separate them one from another, as a shepherd divideth his sheep from the goats."

Matthew 15:22 "And, behold, a woman of Canaan came out of the same coasts, and cried unto him, saying, Have mercy on me, O Lord, **thou son of David**; my daughter is grievously vexed with a devil."

[49] Psalms 132:11

[50] Isaiah 9:7

[51] Daniel 10:6

The hair of Jesus appeared to John as the hair of the father (the ancient of days) appeared to Daniel: "I beheld till the thrones were cast down, and the Ancient of days did sit, whose garment was white as snow, and the hair of his head like the pure wool: his throne was like the fiery flame, and his wheels as burning fire."[52]

Revelation 1:15 and his feet like unto fine brass, as if they burned in a furnace; and his voice as the sound of many waters.

The sound of the voice of Jesus is described here with the same language used by the prophet Ezekiel: "And, behold, the glory of the God of Israel came from the way of the east: and **his voice was like a noise of many waters**: and the earth shined with his glory."[53]

Revelation 1:16 And he had in his right hand seven stars: and out of his mouth went a sharp two-edged sword: and his countenance was as the sun shineth in his strength.

The seven stars are the angels of the seven churches,[54] commissioned to guide and protect God's people.

Allowing the Bible to interpret itself, Scripture tells us exactly what the sword represents. "And take the helmet of salvation, and the sword of the spirit, which is the word of God:"[55] The sword represents the word of God, which explains why it is coming out of the mouth of Jesus. "For the word of God is quick and powerful and sharper than any two-edged sword, piercing even to the dividing asunder of soul and spirit, of the joints and marrow, and is a discerner of the thoughts and intents of the heart."[56] The word of God is that sharp two-edged sword proceeding out of the mouth of Jesus. Since it is the word of God that is coming from the mouth of Jesus and since the word of God is the sword, this is evidence for the divinity of Christ.

---

[52] Daniel 7:9

[53] Ezekiel 43:2

[54] Revelation 1:20

[55] Ephesians 6:17

[56] Hebrews 4:12

As John sees this, he is terrified, and records:

Revelation 1:17 And when I saw him, I fell at his feet as dead. And he laid his right hand upon me, saying unto me, fear not; I am the first and the last:

This is Jesus that John is seeing in vision; the same Jesus that walked with him on this earth. This is the same Jesus that sat with him in the boat on the Sea of Galilee; the same Jesus he leaned against at supper, yet as he sees him in his glorified state, he is so terrified that he falls down. John was called the beloved disciple, and Jesus reaches down, puts his right hand on him, and says, do not be afraid, I am the first and the last. This Jesus says to us today—do not be afraid.

Revelation 1:18 I am he that liveth, and was dead; and behold, I am alive forevermore, Amen; and have the keys of hell and of death.

Jesus comforts John by telling him: I am the same one that was raised from the tomb. When you came, and you looked at the empty tomb, and you later saw me, I am the same person. I am the one who was dead, and I am alive forever more, and I "**have the keys of hell and of death**." Jesus is "the resurrection and the life."[57]

Let us examine more deeply the symbolism of the keys. The Bible explains what keys represent in Isaiah 22:22 "And the key of the house of David will I lay upon his shoulder; so he shall open, and none shall shut; he shall shut, and none shall open." What allows him to shut and open?[58] The key, of course. We compare this verse with Isaiah 9:6 "For unto us a child is born, unto us a son is given: and the government shall be upon his shoulder: and his name shall be called Wonderful, Counsellor, The mighty God The everlasting Father, The Prince of Peace." Here the government is upon his shoulder, and in Revelation 1:18, the key is on his shoulder; therefore, the key represents government. Jesus is given the

---

[57] John 11:25

[58] The opening and closing of doors in the heavenly sanctuary reveals Christ's duties in Revelation chapters three and four.

government; he is given the authority, the kingship, the right to open what none can shut and shut what none can open.

Notice that in Isaiah 9:6 Jesus is called all the same names as God the Father, demonstrating his unity with the Father, as well as affirming his divinity once again.

Revelation 1:19 Write the things which thou hast seen, and the things which are, and the things which shall be hereafter.

God is telling John, write this down for those to read who come in the future; show them the things which are present and the things which will come to pass.

Revelation 1 serves as an introduction to the book. This introduction tells us that this book will reveal things in the future, as well as present events. Notice it does not particularly say anything about things in the past. Revelation does not dwell much on events prior to John's life, except to use some of the symbols that let us know that the books of Daniel and Revelation are very closely connected and should be used to explain one another.[59]

Revelation 1:20 The mystery of the seven stars which thou sawest in my right hand, and the seven golden candlesticks. The seven stars are the angels of the seven churches: and the seven candlesticks which thou sawest are the seven churches.

Jesus explains the mystery of the seven stars as the angels that watch over and have specific jurisdiction to protect his churches. The seven candlesticks represent those seven churches.

In Revelation chapters two and three, these seven churches are each given an individual message that delineates very explicitly the history of God's church and its condition during each period of church history. These messages are detailed enough so as to enable us to identify the very time periods outlined, when they are compared with history.

---

[59] "The books of Daniel and the Revelation are one. One is a prophecy, the other a revelation; one a book sealed, the other a book opened..."
E. G. White, *Manuscript Releases*, Vol. 1 (1990), p. 99.3.

"When the books of Daniel and Revelation are better understood, believers will have an entirely different religious experience. They will be given such **glimpses of the open gates of heaven** that heart and mind will be impressed with the character that all must develop in order to realize the blessedness which is to be the reward of the pure in heart. The Lord will bless all who will seek humbly and meekly to understand that which is revealed in the Revelation. This book contains so much that is large with immortality and full of glory that all who read and search it earnestly receive the blessing to those 'that hear the words of this prophecy, and keep those things which are written therein.' One thing will certainly be understood from the study of Revelation—that the connection between God and His people is close and decided.

"Let us give more time to the study of the Bible. We do not understand the Word as we should. The book of Revelation opens with an injunction to us to understand the instruction that it contains.... When we... understand what this book means to us, there will be seen among us a great revival."[60] Amen.

---

[60] E. G. White, *The Faith I Live By* (1958), p. 345.3-4.

Revelation 2

SUMMARY:
Revelation chapters two and three are the continuation of chapter one and describe the specific messages given to each of the seven churches: unto Ephesus, and unto Smyrna, and unto Pergamos, and unto Thyatira, and unto Sardis, and unto Philadelphia, and unto Laodicea. Each church but one, receives a commendation, and five of the seven receive a reproof. Besides being messages to these literal churches, "the symbols used reveal the condition of the church at different periods in the history of the world."[1] The angel of each of the seven churches was to receive a message from God by the pen of the aged apostle John. Chapter two begins with the message for the angel of the first church.

Revelation 2:1 Unto the angel of the church of Ephesus write; These things saith he that holdeth the seven stars in his right hand, who walketh in the midst of the seven golden candlesticks;

"The seven stars are the angels of the seven churches: and the seven candlesticks which thou sawest are the seven churches."[2]

Revelation 1 gave a description of the attributes of Christ. In the message to each church he reminds them of one or two of his attributes that are particularly suited for their conditions to guide and encourage them through their trials. To this church he is the one who holds the seven stars and walks in the midst of the churches. It was during the period of the church of Ephesus—during the apostolic period—that Jesus physically walked among the churches. But, it was also this church that had to transition to being without his physical presence and had to be reminded that he still held in his hand the angels sent to protect and guide each church. He was still in control and exercising the most tender care over his church even though now in heaven.

---

[1] E. G. White, *Acts of the Apostles* (1911), p. 585.3.

[2] Revelation 1:20

Revelation 1 also revealed that "The names of the seven churches are symbolic of the church in different periods of the Christian Era. The number seven indicates completeness, and is symbolic of the fact that the messages extend to the end of time, while the symbols used reveal the condition of the church at different periods in the history of the world."[3] As we look at the symbols given and compare them with history, we can deduce what interval defines each church period, from apostolic times to the second coming of Jesus.

Revelation 2:2 I know thy works, and thy labour, and thy patience, and how thou canst not bear them which are evil: and thou hast tried them which say they are apostles, and are not, and hast found them liars:

Outlined here is the very first church, the apostolic church, in place when Jesus left the earth. Among the challenges that they would face were people claiming to be apostles yet having a different message; a message that was tried and found wanting. The true followers of God found them to be liars, and would not tolerate this evil in the church; for this a special commendation is given. The church of Ephesus protected the doctrine of the Church, and did not allow false doctrine to creep in. This period of relative purity only lasted while the apostles were still living. By the time John died, around A.D. 100, the purity of the church began to slip.

Revelation 2:3 And hast borne, and hast patience, and for my name's sake hast laboured, and hast not fainted.

"The apostles built upon a sure foundation, even the Rock of Ages. To this foundation they brought the stones that they quarried from the world. Not without hindrance did the builders labor. Their work was made exceedingly difficult by the opposition of the enemies of Christ. They had to contend against the bigotry, prejudice, and hatred of those who were building upon a false foundation. Many who wrought as builders of the church could be likened to the builders of the wall in Nehemiah's day, of whom it is written: 'They which builded on the wall, and they that bare burdens, with those

---

3 E. G. White, *Acts of the Apostles* (1911), p. 585.3.

that laded, everyone with one of his hands wrought in the work, and with the other hand held a weapon.' Nehemiah 4:17.

"Kings and governors, priests and rulers, sought to destroy the temple of God. But in the face of imprisonment, torture, and death, faithful men carried the work forward; and the structure grew, beautiful and symmetrical. At times the workmen were almost blinded by the mists of superstition that settled around them. At times they were almost overpowered by the violence of their opponents. But with unfaltering faith and unfailing courage they pressed on with the work.

"One after another the foremost of the builders fell by the hand of the enemy. Stephen was stoned; James was slain by the sword; Paul was beheaded; Peter was crucified; John was exiled. Yet the church grew. New workers took the place of those who fell, and stone after stone was added to the building. Thus slowly ascended the temple of the church of God."[4]

"John was cast into a caldron of boiling oil; but the Lord preserved the life of His faithful servant, even as He preserved the three Hebrews in the fiery furnace. As the words were spoken, Thus perish all who believe in that deceiver, Jesus Christ of Nazareth, John declared, My Master patiently submitted to all that Satan and his angels could devise to humiliate and torture Him. He gave His life to save the world. I am honored in being permitted to suffer for His sake. I am a weak, sinful man. Christ was holy, harmless, undefiled. He did no sin, neither was guile found in His mouth.

"These words had their influence, and John was removed from the caldron by the very men who had cast him in.

"Again the hand of persecution fell heavily upon the apostle. By the emperor's decree John was banished to the Isle of Patmos, condemned 'for the word of God, and for the testimony of Jesus Christ.' Revelation 1:9. Here, his enemies thought, his influence would no longer be felt, and he must finally die of hardship and distress.

"Patmos, a barren, rocky island in the Aegean Sea, had been chosen by the Roman government as a place of banishment for criminals; but to the servant of God this gloomy abode became the gate of heaven."[5]

---

[4] E. G. White, *Acts of the Apostles* (1911), p. 596.3-597.2.

[5] *Ibid.,* p. 570.1-570.3.

Revelation 2:4 Nevertheless I have somewhat against thee, because thou hast left thy first love.

After marriage there is usually a honeymoon period where everything is wonderful, fabulous, and lovely. But after some time, stress and selfishness often cause the honeymoon period to wane. Habits not noticed before begin to irritate. Original courtesies wane. For some people that honeymoon period might last a couple of weeks, and for others a few years. It takes devotion and effort to make the honeymoon period last for an entire life. But God is telling them here that early on they were excited about their relationship with the Lord. It was that first love experience, and it was a sort of honeymoon experience with the Lord, but now they have settled back and become complacent. Maybe the Christians were no longer treating each other very nicely. Perhaps they were not so excited about sharing the gospel anymore. Jesus is telling this first church that they have lost their first love. They need to go back to the state they were in when they were very enthusiastic and full of zeal for the gospel. Perhaps they forgot that Jesus still walks among his churches.

So, the apostolic church covers the period from the time that Jesus commissioned his disciples in A.D. 31, until about A.D. 100. John was the last apostle to die, and he wrote the book of Revelation about A.D. 96. Thus, Ephesus is the apostolic church; the period where the apostles themselves labored earnestly.

Revelation 2:5 Remember therefore from whence thou art fallen, and repent, and do the first works; or else I will come unto thee quickly, and will remove thy candlestick out of his place, except thou repent.

Go back to that first date. Go back to that honeymoon stage when you were excited about the gospel. This is a serious indictment; a serious warning and reproof to return to that first love experience with the Lord. The steps for relationship renewal are given:
1. Recognize that you fell
2. Remember from where you fell
3. Repent and reverse your course
4. Revive the first works

Revelation 2:6 But this thou hast, that thou hatest the deeds of the Nicolaitanes, which I also hate.

God says he really hates what the Nicolaitanes do, and he knows that this early church also could not bear their deeds. Who are the Nicolaitanes?

"The Nicolaitanes, referred to in verse six, are said by Mosheim to have been a branch of the Gnostics, a sect living in Asia, who denied the divinity of Christ, and 'boasted of their being able to restore to mankind the knowledge of the true and Supreme Being.' Their belief concerning the creation of the world conflicted with the writings of Moses, and led to a denial of the divine authority of the Old Testament. Still other beliefs, contrary to the teachings of Christ, the result of a mixture of Greek and Oriental philosophy, led to practices which the church of Christ could not tolerate."[6]

"The doctrine is now largely taught that the gospel of Christ has made the law of God of no effect; that by 'believing' we are released from the necessity of being doers of the Word. But this is the doctrine of the Nicolaitans, which Christ so unsparingly condemned."[7]

According to Iraneus the Nicolaitanes were known for leading lives of unrestrained indulgence.[8] There was profligacy, including sexual indulgence, indulgence of appetite, and indulgence of luxury. Essentially, they were lazy, depraved gluttons.[9] The Nicolaitanes

---

[6] S.N. Haskell, *The Story of the Seer of Patmos* (Nashville, TN: Southern Publishing Association, 1905), p. 46.2.

[7] E. G. White, *Signs of the Times*, February 25, 1897 par. 6

[8] Iranaeus, *Against Heresies*, Book 1, ch. XXVI.

[9] God says that He hates the doctrine of the Nicolaitanes; and we have today, in modern times, a deity called St. Nicholas. He is omnipotent, omnipresent (he can give gifts individually to a billion children all in one night?), knows what you are thinking and keeps track of your good and bad deeds. Everyone knows this is the other name for Santa Claus. Whether or not this is historically connected with the Nicolaitanes, it is interesting that they have a similar name. Nicholas— Nicolaitanes. Basically, St. Nicholas epitomizes a life of unrestrained indulgence. He is passing out all kinds of gifts, and people eat all the candy he brings at Christmas time. Christmas has the highest rate of heart attacks and strokes of any day on the calendar. It is a very dangerous day, because people pig-out on Christmas day. They lead lives, at least for that day, of unrestrained indulgence. And, of course, mommy has a fling with Santa. (Adults sanitize the song, I suppose, by believing that Santa is daddy, but what message is given to the kids by such a song?)
So, this would qualify as a doctrine of the Nicolaitanes. We have pagan aspects coming into something that is supposedly Christian— 'Christ' 'mas. These are things that God says he hates, and we should avoid these kinds of worldly pagan aspects in our lives as Christians. Celebration of Christ's birth does not require, nor does it have anything to do with "St. Nic!"

were a branch of the Gnostics, incorporating elements of pagan mysticism into Christianity. They had the idea that Christianity, or encountering God, was some kind of a mystical experience. They taught all kinds of different types of mystical prayers.

Gnosticism is mystical, philosophical theology that is based on occultism and spiritualism. It has many different components and is rather hard to define because it tends to be loosely organized, and is somewhat of a chameleon in character. It changes its nature, but it includes things like monasticism. "Historian Will Durant defines Gnosticism as 'the quest of godlike knowledge (gnosis or illumination) through mystic means.'"[10] We actually see components of this very same doctrine, this doctrine of the Nicolaitanes, which God said he hates, coming into Christianity today, in a massive way, under the guise of "spiritual formation."

Mystical experiences; with occult activities; spiritualistic ways of "talking to God," and "communicating with angels," are being practiced by professed Christians today under the name of "spiritual disciplines." These "disciplines" are nothing more than methods of self-hypnosis in which an individual becomes highly susceptible to demonic possession. Once such an experience is achieved, it is almost impossible to convince a person that they have not had some intimate experience with God. But God says he hates it, and explicitly condemns such practices. Paul admonishes, "I marvel that ye are so soon removed from him that called you into the grace of Christ unto another gospel: Which is not another; but there be some that trouble you, and would pervert the gospel of Christ. But though we, or an angel from heaven, preach any other gospel unto you than that which we have preached unto you, let him be accursed."[11]

Revelation 2:7 He that hath an ear, let him hear what the Spirit saith unto the churches; To him that overcometh will I give to eat of the tree of life, which is in the midst of the paradise of God.

The closing admonition to each of the seven churches is to hear what the Spirit says to the churches. But, for the first three churches,

---

[10] Thomas Holland, Th.D., *Crowned with Glory: The Bible from Ancient Text to Authorized Version* (San Jose: Writers Club Press, 2000), p. 21.

[11] Galatians 1:6-8

to this admonition is added a specific message from the Spirit. These three messages parallel three other messages that come later in the book of Revelation: the three angel's messages of Revelation 14. The first message from the Spirit is that overcomers will eat from the tree of life in paradise. As Jesus is the Creator and source of all life, this promise is a call, like the first angel's message to worship the Creator.[12]

To each church God gives a promise to those who overcome. The first church is given the promise to eat of the tree of life, which is in the midst of the paradise of God. There is overcoming to be done—overcoming of appetites and passions. God promises us that he wants to save us **from** our sins; not **in** our sins, and so he wants to give us victory. He wants us to be able to overcome by his grace and by his power. It is not popular to speak of overcoming. Pop theology says that you do not need to do anything. Scripture says we must overcome. It is true that the power for overcoming comes from God,[13] but we must overcome, nonetheless. The overcoming is in surrender to his will and his power.

Revelation 2:8 And unto the angel of the church in Smyrna write; These things saith the first and the last, which was dead, and is alive;

The introduction to the second church identifies the first and the last. Multiple times Revelation speaks about the Alpha and Omega, the beginning and the ending, the first and the last. The first and the last **"was dead, and is alive."** Jesus died on the cross, and was resurrected for us, therefore we know with certainty that the first and the last is Jesus himself. This is the attribute of Christ from chapter one[14] which he rehearses to this church. Though they will be tried, cast into prison and killed (verse 10), Jesus reminds them that he was dead and is alive—he has the "the keys of hell and of death."[15]

---

[12] Revelation 14:6

[13] John 15:5 "I am the vine, ye are the branches: He that abideth in me, and I in him, the same bringeth forth much fruit: for without me ye can do nothing."

[14] Revelation 1:17-18

[15] Revelation 1:18

Revelation 2:9 I know thy works, and tribulation, and poverty, (but thou art rich) and I know the blasphemy of them which say they are Jews, and are not, but are the synagogue of Satan.

Just because someone is a Jew, just because they claim direct lineage to Abraham, does not mean that they are Jews. Some say they are Jews, but are not—they are of the synagogue of Satan. Thus, in the Christian era, it is not lineage from Abraham that defines a Jew. In the New Testament, a Jew is a spiritual Israelite[16]—one who is actually following what God says. These who are claiming to be Jews while committing blasphemy, may be Jews by lineage, but Scripture attests that they are from the synagogue of Satan.

Revelation 2:10 Fear none of those things which thou shalt suffer: behold, the devil shall cast some of you into prison, that ye may be tried; and ye shall have tribulation ten days: be thou faithful unto death, and I will give thee a crown of life.

This church period was to be characterized by severe persecution under the Roman emperor Diocletian. Specifically, tribulation that would last for ten days. In prophetic, symbolic, Bible prophecy a day equals a year,[17] so ten days represents ten years. Therefore, this church period may be called the persecuted church, extending from A.D. 100, with the death of the last Apostle and the end of the Apostolic church period, to A.D. 313. The severe ten years of persecution from A.D. 303 to 313, prophesied here, is the primary feature of this church.

This is one of only two churches that does not receive a reproof; it has only a commendation. "Prosperity multiplies a mass of professors. Adversity purges them out of the church."[18] Unfortunately, it often takes persecution for God's church to be purified.

---

[16] The subject of spiritual Israel is covered in more detail in Daniel 4b. Paul has a lot to say on this subject as well, particularly in Romans 2:28-29; 9:6-8.

[17] See Ezekiel 4:6 and Numbers 14:34.

[18] E. G. White, *Last Day Events* (1992), p. 173.5.

Revelation 2:11 He that hath an ear, let him hear what the Spirit saith unto the churches; He that overcometh shall not be hurt of the second death.

The second specific message from the Spirit promises that those who overcome will not be hurt by the second death,[19] which is the punishment prepared for the devil and his angels.[20] This is the death that you do not want to experience. Through the infinite provision made by Jesus on the cross, none need experience this death. Only those who reject the payment already made for their sins will experience the death that is eternal. This message parallels the second angel's message of Revelation 14, which announces the fall of Babylon. The Spirit is calling his people to be overcomers that they "be not partakers of her sins, and that ye receive not of her plagues."[21] Those that refuse to come out of Babylon will suffer the second death.

The promises given to each church are not exclusively for that church, but God personalizes his message and promises; with something special for each church—something that would be particularly meaningful to their circumstance. In a time when persecution is severe, when people are being killed for their faith, being promised that they will not be hurt by the second death would be a very comforting promise. The Bible speaks, in other places, about these two deaths and their corresponding resurrections. "And shall come forth; they that have done good, unto the resurrection of life; and they that have done evil, unto the resurrection of damnation."[22] Clearly there are two resurrections being portrayed in Scripture: "Blessed and holy is he that hath part in the first resurrection: on such the second death hath no power...."[23]

The first death is followed by the first resurrection. The second resurrection is followed by the second death. We do not want to be part of the second death, even if we must face the first death. God

---

[19] The Bible teaching regarding the second death, will be revealed more fully in Revelation 20 and 21.

[20] Matthew 25:41

[21] Revelation 18:4

[22] John 5:29

[23] Revelation 20:6

resurrects the righteous from the first death in the first resurrection, but the wicked are raised in the second resurrection to die the second death.[24]

Revelation 2:12 And to the angel of the church in Pergamos write; These things saith he which hath the sharp sword with two edges;

The message to the angel of the third church is introduced by Jesus, highlighting one of the attributes from his description in chapter one—the sharp sword from his mouth.[25] At the very time when deceptions threaten his church, Jesus reminds them of the power of his Word—"the sword of the Spirit."[26] "For the word of God is quick, and powerful, and sharper than any twoedged sword, piercing even to the dividing asunder of soul and spirit, and of the joints and marrow, and is a discerner of the thoughts and intents of the heart."[27]

Revelation 2:13 I know thy works and where thou dwellest, even where Satan's seat is: and thou holdest fast my name, and hast not denied my faith, even in those days wherein Antipas was my faithful martyr, who was slain among you, where Satan dwelleth.

"The grand original Babylonian system... after the death of Belshazzar, and the expulsion of the Chaldean priesthood from Babylon by the Medo-Persian kings, was at Pergamos, where afterward was one of the seven churches of Asia. There, in consequence, for many centuries was 'Satan's seat' (Rev. 2:13). There, under favor of the deified kings of Pergamos, was his favorite abode, there was the worship of Æsculapius, under the form of the serpent, celebrated with frantic orgies and excesses, that elsewhere were kept under some measure of restraint. At first, the Roman Pontiff had no immediate connection with Pergamos and the hierarchy there; yet, in course of time, the pontificate of Rome and the pontificate of Pergamos came to be identified. Pergamos itself

---

[24] See comments on Revelation 20.

[25] Revelation 1:13-17

[26] Ephesians 6:17

[27] Hebrews 4:12

became part and parcel of the Roman Empire, when Attalus III., the last of its kings, at his death, left by will all his dominions to the Roman people, 133 B.C. For some time after the kingdom of Pergamos was merged in the Roman dominions, there was no one who could set himself openly and advisedly to lay claim to all the dignity inherent in the old title of the kings of Pergamos. The original powers even of the Roman pontiffs seem to have been by that time abridged, but when Julius Caesar, who had previously been elected Pontifex Maximus, became also, as emperor, the supreme civil ruler of the Romans, then, as head of the Roman state and head of the Roman religion, all the powers and functions of the true legitimate Babylonian pontiff were supremely vested in him, and he found himself in a position to assert these powers... Then, on certain occasions, in the exercise of his high pontifical office, he appeared of course in all the pomp of the Babylonian costume, as Belshazzar himself might have done, in robes of scarlet, with the crosier of Nimrod in his hand, wearing the miter of Dagon, and bearing the keys of Janus and Cybele."[28]

Pergamos was a city given to occult idolatry. It was the home of the Asclepeion—the healing temple. Snakes were considered sacred and used in healing rituals and allowed to crawl through the sleeping quarters of the guests.[29] The library at Pergamos was rivaled only by the library at Alexandria, Egypt. There was an acropolis and a temple of Zeus. Later Pergamos became famous for the Pergamon Altar, covered with idol carvings of Olympian gods, dedicated to Zeus, father of the gods.[30] Zeus is the equivalent of Marduk in Babylon, Baal in Canaan, Adad in Assyria, and Jupiter in Rome. Pergamos stood then as the capitol of the religion of Babylon, which was afterward transferred to the city of Rome,[31] the inheritor of all the idolatry of Babylon, Persia, Canaan, Greece and Assyria. It is Rome which has led the world to incorporate paganism and idolatry into Christianity. Even the statue of "Peter" at St. Peter's Basilica is an idol of Jupiter[32] moved from the Pantheon.

---

[28] Alexander Hislop, *The Two Babylons*, Fifth ed. (London: S. W. Partridge and Co., 1873), p. 392-395.

[29] http://en.wikipedia.org/wiki/Asclepeion retrieved 1-22-2017

[30] https://en.wikipedia.org/wiki/Pergamon_Altar retrieved 1-22-2017

[31] S.N. Haskell, *The Story of the Seer of Patmos* (1905), p. 53.2.

[32] Alexander Hislop, *The Two Babylons* (1873), p. 338.

It was during this church period that Christianity was exalted by the pagan emperor Constantine at the imperial city of Rome.

God understood that they would face many deceptions and persecutions, yet there were martyrs who stood faithful. This was a period of time when great compromise, with massive amounts of false doctrine, infiltrated the church. During this time the papal system was rising to prominence in Rome (yet without its political power, at this point). Jesus portrays this as the very seat of Satan.

There is no evidence of a specific historical person named Antipas. The word literally means anti or against, pas—father. Anti-father. This is clearly a metaphorical reference to all those people who were opposed to the setting up of the bishop of Rome as the head of all churches—anti-father. They were against the idea of a pope; of someone being considered the spiritual father. They were willing to die for this Bible doctrine.

Matthew 23:9 says, "And call no man your father upon the earth: for one is your Father, which is in heaven." This does not mean you cannot call your own biological father by that name. It is referring to the practice of making a human being your spiritual guide or mentor. Our heavenly father is the only one to whom we should turn as our master and guide. We may not call a human our spiritual master, mentor, guide, or our father on this earth. In Latin, the pope's name is papa, which literally means father. Catholic priests and popes are called father in direct opposition to Scripture.

Revelation 2:14 But I have a few things against thee, because thou hast there them that hold the doctrine of Balaam, who taught Balac to cast a stumblingblock before the children of Israel, to eat things sacrificed unto idols, and to commit fornication.

The time period framed by the church of Pergamos was a dark period in church history when idolatry—spiritual adultery—threatened the church. Idols and images were introduced into the worship service. "The nominal conversion of Constantine, in the early part of the fourth century, caused great rejoicing; and the world, cloaked with a form of righteousness, walked into the church. Now the work of corruption rapidly progressed. Paganism, while appearing to be vanquished, became the conqueror. Her spirit controlled the church. Her doctrines, ceremonies, and superstitions were incorporated into the faith and worship of the professed followers of Christ."[33]

God calls this the doctrine of Balaam, because Balaam introduced this style of worship to the ancient Israelites. Balaam was requested to go and curse Israel for Balak, the king of the Moabites. Because he had been a prophet of the Lord, God would not allow his voice to utter such a curse against Israel. He tried several times, though God warned him otherwise.[34] Yet he coveted the money that was offered.[35]

Eventually, since he could not pronounce anything other than a blessing, he went back to the king and said, Listen, I can't curse them, but I'll tell you what you can do if you want to overcome them. This is what you do: you get some pretty women, you get a more exciting worship service, and get the music and the drums going. Introduce this exciting pagan worship style, with some images and idols, and invite the children of Israel to come to the program. They'll think your worship service is very exciting, and as they see the contrast, they'll begin to view their own as boring. As a result, they will fall into fornication with the pretty women, and God's blessing will be removed; then you can overcome them.

Balac followed Balaam's instructions, and it worked like a charm. Exactly as he had hoped, God removed his protection when the children of Israel went after pagan idolatry, and they were overcome as a result. This should be a warning to us today to avoid the allurement of worship styles conditioned by the surrounding culture. Pergamos was foremost in allowing the doctrine of Balaam to bring these pagan philosophies into the church.[36]

---

[33] E. G. White, *The Great Controversy* (1911), p. 49.2.

[34] See Numbers 22-24.

[35] Jude 1:11; 2 Peter 2:15-16

[36] "There are many in the world today whose character is represented by that of Balaam. They have a correct knowledge of most of the doctrines of religion, but with these are mingled superstitions and heresies. Satan has a knowledge of the truth, and so do many who are his servants. Excellent words may proceed from their lips; they may claim to possess great faith, and to enjoy much of the divine blessing; but their hearts are destitute of the grace of God. They are not followers of Christ, and do not those things that please him. The only safety for any, at the present day as well as in ancient times, is to seek diligently to know the will of God, and then be ready to obey that will." E. G. White, *Signs of the Times*, November 25, 1880 par. 24.

Revelation 2:15 So hast thou also them that hold the doctrine of the Nicolaitanes, which thing I hate.

Like the church at Ephesus, Pergamos was being infiltrated by spiritual formation, by "Christian mysticism," illluminism, monasticism, and various "spiritual disciplines"—the doctrine of the Nicolaitanes.[37]

We could call this church the self-elevated church. Pergamon means elevation or exaltation.[38] They became puffed up with the idea that Christianity was being accepted by society in general, and promoted by the government. After Constantine's baptism, Christianity was legalized. This was right after the terrible persecution during the period of the church of Smyrna. As persecution relaxed and Christianity became prominent, false doctrines and deceptions came flooding in.

The church at Pergamos represents the period of church history from A.D. 313, with the end of the persecution under Diocletian, to A.D. 538,—the beginning of the 1,260 years of papal political power.[39]

Revelation 2:16 Repent; or else I will come unto thee quickly, and will fight against them with the sword of my mouth.

Revelation 2:17 He that hath an ear, let him hear what the Spirit saith unto the churches; To him that overcometh will I give to eat of the hidden manna, and will give him a white stone, and in the stone a new name written, which no man knoweth saving he that receiveth it.

The third specific message from the Spirit gives a special promise; a token of God's love—the hidden manna and a white stone. The manna is the bread of heaven.[40] "He that eateth my flesh, and drinketh my blood, dwelleth in me, and I in him. This is that bread which came down from heaven: not as your fathers did eat manna,

---

[37] See Revelation 2:6

[38] S.N. Haskell, *The Story of the Seer of Patmos* (1905), p. 53.2.

[39] See Daniel 7.

[40] Psalms 78:24; John 6:31

and are dead: he that eateth of this bread shall live for ever."[41] The white stone with the new name represents the crown of life, given to those clothed in the white righteousness of Jesus Christ.[42] Just as the "mystery of iniquity,"[43] was rising to prominence[44] the Spirit reminds this church that eternal life is the reward for those that overcome. This message from the Spirit parallels the third angel's message of Revelation 14, which warns not to receive the mark of the beast. None will be able to resist this mark without overcoming Satan and his temptations. "And they overcame him by the blood of the Lamb, and by the word of their testimony; and they loved not their lives unto the death."[45] Jesus has given himself as the pledge and power for our victory over sin.

Revelation 2:18 And unto the angel of the church in Thyatira write; These things saith the Son of God, who hath his eyes like unto a flame of fire, and his feet are like fine brass;

This fourth church of the Dark Ages, is the very church that Christ reminds us of his characteristic of **"eyes like unto a flame of fire, and his feet are like fine brass**." When the darkness is the deepest, Jesus says, "I will instruct thee and teach thee in the way which thou shalt go: I will guide thee with mine eye,"[46] for "The light of the body is the eye." Jesus is the light to illuminate the dark path this church must tread—a path whose every hardship the feet of Christ have walked before.

Revelation 2:19 I know thy works, and charity, and service, and faith, and thy patience, and thy works; and the last to be more than the first.

---

[41] John 6:56, 58

[42] "He promises to give to his people the privilege of eating of the tree of life, and the hidden manna. He holds forth the crown of life, the white stone with the new name written therein." E. G. White, *Review and Herald*, December 17, 1889 par. 3.

[43] 2 Thessalonians 2:7

[44] Though the papacy had not yet received political power until the end of this church period—in A.D. 538—the Bishop of Rome was gaining great ascendency in the fourth and fifth centuries.

[45] Revelation 12:11

[46] Psalms 32:8

God knew that these people would have a very difficult path to tread. He knew they had much work to do and would suffer many things, for his church was now entering the period of the Dark Ages. The church of the Dark Ages would face persecution, darkness, and spiritual declension. But God knew that many of his faithful people would cling to the words of life rather than the traditions of men.

Notice this verse mentions their works twice. "**I know thy works, thy charity, service, faith, patience, and thy works**..." God also knew that many sincere Christians would pass through this period of time during which they believed that their works would give them merit with God. Yet he gently reminds them that the last works are more than the first. It was at the end of this church period, which extended from A.D. 538 to 1521, that the truth of salvation by faith in Jesus began to be opened to God's church—the knowledge that the works of Jesus are the only works that can give us merit. "By a recent decretal an indulgence had been promised by the pope to all who should ascend upon their knees 'Pilate's staircase,' said to have been descended by our Saviour on leaving the Roman judgment hall and to have been miraculously conveyed from Jerusalem to Rome. Luther was one day devoutly climbing these steps, when suddenly a voice like thunder seemed to say to him: 'The just shall live by faith.' Romans 1:17. He sprang to his feet and hastened from the place in shame and horror. That text never lost its power upon his soul. From that time he saw more clearly than ever before the fallacy of trusting to human works for salvation, and the necessity of constant faith in the merits of Christ. His eyes had been opened, and were never again to be closed, to the delusions of the papacy. When he turned his face from Rome he had turned away also in heart, and from that time the separation grew wider, until he severed all connection with the papal church."[47]

Revelation 2:20 Notwithstanding I have a few things against thee, because thou sufferest that woman Jezebel, which calleth herself a prophetess, to teach and to seduce my servants to commit fornication, and to eat things sacrificed unto idols.

This church has a reproof. God's true church has allowed a harlot woman named Jezebel to seduce them. Clearly this does not refer to

---

[47] E. G. White, *The Great Controversy* (1911), p. 125.1.

the literal Jezebel. The story of King Ahab and Queen Jezebel, comes from the Old Testament, and occurred almost a thousand years earlier, so this must be a symbolic Jezebel. Notice that she is teaching and seducing God's servants to commit fornication, and eat things sacrificed to idols. This is symbolic of spiritual adultery and idolatry—the teaching of false doctrines.

Jezebel has the same identity as the woman portrayed in Revelation 17:1, 2. The Bible says, "And there came one of the seven angels which had the seven vials, and talked with me, saying unto me, Come hither; I will show unto thee the judgment of the great whore that sitteth upon many waters: With whom the kings of the earth have committed fornication, and the inhabitants of the earth have been made drunk with the wine of her fornication."

In both passages a woman is seducing into fornication. Spiritual fornication is an illicit relationship with a god other than the true God.[48] Wine, in Scripture, is a representation of false doctrine,[49] and so this has to do with adultery, idolatry, and false doctrine.

Revelation 2:21 And I gave her space to repent of her fornication; and she repented not.

In Bible prophecy, a woman represents a church.[50] A pure woman represents God's true church, and an impure woman Satan's apostate church. This harlot woman, Jezebel, actually claims to be God's church on earth. Because of her claim God even gives her an opportunity to repent. He sends messages of warning, even to this harlot church, but she does not repent. However, God's true church of Thyatira would remain faithful despite this tremendous pressure from Jezebel for idolatry, adultery, and false doctrines.

---

[48] 2 Corinthians 11:2 "For I am jealous over you with godly jealousy: for I have espoused you to one husband, that I may present you as a chaste virgin to Christ."

[49] In Revelation 14:8 the Bible connects the wine with the fornication, "And there followed another angel, saying, Babylon is fallen, is fallen, that great city, because she made all nations drink of the wine of the wrath of her fornication."
If the fornication is a illegitimate relationship with a false god, then false doctrine is necessary to seduce people into false worship.

[50] Jeremiah 6:2 "I have likened the daughter of Zion to a comely and delicate woman."
Zion is God's church.
Isaiah 51:16 "...and say unto Zion, Thou art my people."

Revelation 2:22 Behold, I will cast her into a bed, and them that commit adultery with her into great tribulation, except they repent of their deeds.

God promises Jezebel special retribution. Revelation 18 details the punishments that he will bring on her.

Revelation 2:23 And I will kill her children with death; and all the churches shall know that I am he which searcheth the reins and hearts: and I will give unto every one of you according to your works.

This woman is also represented as having children just as the harlot of Revelation 17. It was at the end of the Dark Ages that this apostate church first began to have daughters (churches coming out of her). As people turned to Scripture as their guide, they saw problems in the papal church and this led to the Protestant Reformation which created many new church organizations that came out of Catholicism. Yet as each new denomination formed, on the basis of discoveries of Bible truth, they would go no further than their founder. Each reformer uncovered additional light, but their followers would not accept any truth their leader did not discover. This is one reason for so many different denominations today. Each of these churches, over time, began to lose that first love, and began to apostatize, going back to the pagan doctrines they had once renounced. For this, God proclaims that he would not only punish the harlot church but that he would also punish her apostate children.

Thyatira therefore, can aptly be called the church of the Dark Ages, from A.D. 538 with the beginning of the papal political supremacy, to about A.D. 1521 and the full establishment of the Protestant Reformation. In 1521 Martin Luther stood before the Diet of Worms.[51] At this assembly "The papacy had sustained a defeat which would be felt among all nations and in all ages."[52] Shortly before this, Martin Luther had nailed his 95 theses to the door of the Church of Wittenberg. Over 100 years earlier, the Reformation started small, but not until the time of Martin Luther did the

---

[51] This does not refer to the food of a burrowing invertebrate. This was a National assembly held in the city of Worms, Germany, in which the council condemned the teachings of Luther.

[52] E. G. White, *Spirit of Prophecy,* Vol. 4 (1884), p. 135.2.

movement really gain power. In 1529 at the Diet of Spires, the princes stood for the Protestant faith, rejecting the Catholic mandates.[53] Thus we see a new church period commencing in the early 1500's with the establishment of the Protestant Reformation.

Revelation 2:24 But unto you I say, and unto the rest in Thyatira, as many as have not this doctrine, and which have not known the depths of Satan, as they speak; I will put upon you none other burden.

God knew what this church was going to face: such corruption that could only be called the depths of Satan. Yet, God would still have a small remnant of faithful people, who would not join with the harlot church, or know the depths of Satan, on whom He would put no further burden.

Revelation 2:25 But that which ye have already hold fast till I come.

Just hold on a little bit longer. You are in a tough position; God understands.

Revelation 2:26 And he that overcometh, and keepeth my works unto the end, to him will I give power over the nations:

This promise is especially meaningful for the church of the dark ages, for that apostate woman Jezebel tried to use civil and political power to accomplish her ends, to punish heretics, and to force the consciences of men. She used a combination of church and state to gain power over the nations. God says, That's not my way; that's not my doctrine. That doctrine is the depths of Satan. "My kingdom is not of this world: if my kingdom were of this world, then would my

---

[53] "One of the noblest testimonies ever uttered for the Reformation was the Protest offered by the Christian princes of Germany at the Diet of Spires. The courage, faith, and firmness of these men of God, gained for succeeding ages liberty of thought and of conscience. Their Protest gave to the reformed church the name of Protestant; its principles are the very essence of Protestantism." "Well has that day been pronounced 'the greatest day of the Reformation, and one of the most glorious in the history of Christianity and of the world.'"
E. G. White, *Spirit of Prophecy,* Vol. 4 (1884), p. 156.1, 166.1.

servants fight... but now is my kingdom not from hence."[54] Those who follow God will one day be given power over the nations. The power that others have illegitimately grasped and wielded, God will finally commit to his people.

Revelation 2:27 *And he shall rule them with a rod of iron; as the vessels of a potter shall they be broken to shivers: even as I received of my Father.*

The authority for judgment will be given to the people of God. "Do ye not know that the saints shall judge the world? and if the world shall be judged by you, are ye unworthy to judge the smallest matters?"[55] Judgment is how they have power over nations—it does not mean that they will have some servants that they can knock on the head with a rod of iron throughout ceaseless ages of eternity. The rod of iron represents judgment and justice. As we will discover in Revelation 20, the Lord includes the righteous in the process of executing judgment on the wicked.

Jesus is also portrayed as ruling with a rod of iron in Revelation 12:5. This church period is portrayed as ruling with a rod of iron because they will help him to execute the final punishment on the apostate religions of the earth. God will allow them to participate in bringing that justice that they probably so longed for, during those terrible days of darkness in the Middle Ages.

Revelation 2:28 *And I will give him the morning star.*

As with the other promises, this amazing promise is not exclusive to this church, but is particularly meaningful to them. Without guessing or speculating, we allow the Bible to define the morning star: "I Jesus have sent mine angel to testify unto you these things in the churches. **I am** the root and the offspring of David, and **the bright and morning star**."[56]

---

[54] John 18:36

[55] 1 Corinthians 6:2

[56] Revelation 22:16

Jesus himself is the morning star.[57] He promises this church that when the darkness seems the deepest, he has given them himself. The prophetic messages give the assurance that dawn approaches. "We have also a more sure word of prophecy; whereunto ye do well that ye take heed, as unto a light that shineth in a dark place, until the day dawn, and the day star arise in your hearts."[58] Amazing promise.

Revelation 2:29 He that hath an ear, let him hear what the Spirit saith unto the churches.

Though the Spirit gives no further specific messages to the seven churches, Jesus reminds each remaining church to hear what the Spirit has already revealed. Christ is pleading with his church—with you—for he knows that they (and you) might be hearing, but not listening. Jesus wants to give you spiritual discernment, that you may hear and understand his message to his churches in the book of Revelation. Amen.

---

[57] Satan aspired to be in the position of Jesus in heaven. Isaiah 14:12-14 describes what happened: "How art thou fallen from heaven, O Lucifer, son of the morning! how art thou cut down to the ground, which didst weaken the nations! For thou hast said in thine heart, I will ascend into heaven, I will exalt my throne above the stars of God: I will sit also upon the mount of the congregation, in the sides of the north: I will ascend above the heights of the clouds; I will be like the most High."

In the earthly tabernacle, which is the pattern of the temple in heaven (see Hebrew 9:23-24), the only piece of furniture on the north side, is the table of showbread. This represents the throne of Jesus. Jesus said, "I am the bread of life."

Satan was not content to be a son of the morning, a son of God, a son of Jesus. He wanted to be equal with Jesus. He wanted to claim equality with, or even superiority to Jesus. So he wanted the place that Jesus had. He aspired to the throne of Christ on the sides of the north. He wanted to grasp the titles of Jesus.

Today Satan still tries to usurp the title "morning star." He did not want to be a son of the morning, he wanted to be a brother of Jesus. Not satisfied with being a son of Jesus, he wanted to be above Jesus. Many modern versions (see the NIV, for example), not only leave out the only reference to Lucifer in the Bible, but also call him the "morning star" rather than "son of the morning." Satan is surely pleased with this, because this is what he tried to accomplish in Heaven in the first place.

To learn more about this issue, see Martin Klein, *Thou Hast Magnified Thy Word Above All Thy Name*. This book demonstrates how God preserved the Bible, yet how Scripture itself reveals that Satan would attempt to corrupt the very Words of God; how he managed to corrupt some manuscripts; and how to know which manuscripts are correct; which version you might want to follow; and which translations are the accurate, true word of God.

[58] 2 Peter 1:19

Revelation 3

SUMMARY:
The angel of each of the seven churches was to receive a message from God by the pen of the aged apostle John. Revelation chapters two and three are the continuation of chapter one and describe the messages given to each of the seven churches: unto Ephesus, and unto Smyrna, and unto Pergamos, and unto Thyatira, and unto Sardis, and unto Philadelphia, and unto Laodicea.

Each church but one receives a commendation, and five receive a reproof. Besides being messages to literal churches, these messages also give profound insight regarding, and counsel to the periods of history that each church represents, from apostolic times until the second coming of Jesus.

The third chapter of Revelation resumes with the messages to the last three of the seven churches.

Revelation 3:1 And unto the angel of the church in Sardis write, these things saith he that hath the seven Spirits of God and the seven stars. I know thy works, that thou hast a name that thou livest, and art dead.

"There were seven lamps of fire burning before the throne, which are the **seven Spirits of God**."[1] The seven lamps are the seven Spirits, and the seven eyes of the lamb who had been slain also symbolize the seven Spirits of God.[2] We see the connection to both symbols, since "his eyes were as a flame of fire."[3]

The seven stars are the angels of the seven churches. Not since Apostolic times was the presence of Christ more apparent than during the period of the church of the Reformation, so Jesus reminds

---

[1] Revelation 4:5

[2] Revelation 5:6 "And I beheld, and, lo, in the midst of the throne and of the four beasts, and in the midst of the elders, stood a Lamb as it had been slain, having seven horns and seven eyes, which are the seven Spirits of God sent forth into all the earth."

[3] Revelation 1:14; 2:18; 19:12

them that it is he who holds the destiny of his church in his hands; that his eyes guide their course and illuminate their duty.[4]

The church at Sardis has a name—a reputation—for being alive, but Christ indicts them for, in fact, being dead. Apparently, they were alive initially, but imperceptibly began to die spiritually. They claimed to be Christian, but their works showed otherwise.

Revelation 3:2 Be watchful, and strengthen the things which remain, that are ready to die: for I have not found thy works perfect before God.

Only a small remnant—the things which remain—persist, just barely alive. This was a church that began with much zeal, rediscovering many forgotten Bible truths as they came out of the superstitions of the dark ages. Yet, they did not accept all the truth that God wanted them to receive. For this reason, their works were not complete before God; and they were ready to die. Many of the errors they rejected in their early days, they began to embrace again, as they forgot their history. This describes precisely the condition of the church of the reformation between A.D. 1521 and 1798 (when the papacy lost its political supremacy).[5]

The church of the reformation had great light and privileges. They began to break the chains of darkness and superstition of the Dark Ages, yet they did not continue in the full light of the gospel. They did not accept all the light of Scripture that was shining on their pathway. Ironically, this church, which was rooted in the discovery of the Bible truth of righteousness by faith, is indicted for imperfect works. "But wilt thou know, O vain man, that faith without works is dead?"[6]

Revelation 3:3 Remember therefore how thou hast received and heard, and hold fast, and repent. If therefore thou shalt not watch, I will come on thee as a thief, and thou shalt not know what hour I will come upon thee.

---

[4] Revelation 1:16, 20

[5] See Daniel 7.

[6] James 2:20

"A warning is given of a time when errors would come in as a thief to steal away the faith of God's people, when they must watch diligently and be constantly guarded against the delusions of the enemy.
"In Sardis many had been converted through the preaching of the apostles. The truth had been received as a bright and shining light. But some had forgotten the wonderful manner in which they had received the truth, and Jesus found it necessary to send reproof.
"One after another of the old standardbearers had fallen, and some had become wearied of the oft-repeated truths. They desired a new phase of doctrine, more pleasing to many minds. They thought they needed a wonderful change, and in their spiritual blindness did not discern that their sophistries would uproot all the experiences of the past.
"But the Lord Jesus could see the end from the beginning. Through John He sent them the warning, 'Remember therefore how thou hast received and heard, and hold fast, and repent. If therefore thou shalt not watch, I will come on thee as a thief.'"[7]

Christ comes as a thief only to those who are not watching. "For yourselves know perfectly that the day of the Lord so cometh as a thief in the night. For when they shall say, Peace and safety; then sudden destruction cometh upon them, as travail upon a woman with child; and they shall not escape. But ye, brethren, are not in darkness, that that day should overtake you as a thief. Ye are all the children of light, and the children of the day: we are not of the night, nor of darkness. Therefore let us not sleep, as do others; but let us watch and be sober."[8]

Revelation 3:4 Thou hast a few names even in Sardis which have not defiled their garments; and they shall walk with me in white: for they are worthy.

Despite the grand and glorious potential of the church of the Reformation, this sad testimony declares that only a few did not defile their garments; only a few were clothed in the righteousness of Christ. So it is today. Living in a time of great light, we must accept every ray of truth God sends us and walk in that light.

---

[7] E. G. White, *The Seventh-day Adventist Bible Commentary*, Vol. 7 (1955), p 958.5-8.

[8] 1 Thessalonians 5:2-6

"Many refuse to obey the truth through fear that they will lose their standing in the world. They allow the inconveniences in the pathway of truth to prevent them from following the Saviour. They do not realize that to reject truth means to lose eternal life."[9]

Revelation 3:5 He that overcometh, the same shall be clothed in white raiment; and I will not blot out his name out of the book of life, but I will confess his name before my Father, and before his angels.

The church of the Reformation, especially Martin Luther, championed the Bible doctrine of righteousness by faith—that we are saved by grace through faith. This promise is full of meaning to those who belonged to this period of church history—to those who desired to be clothed in white raiment, and have the assurance that their names were not blotted out of the book of life. This promise is also for us today.

Revelation 3:6 He that hath an ear, let him hear what the Spirit saith unto the churches.

"But the natural man receiveth not the things of the Spirit of God: for they are foolishness unto him: neither can he know them, because they are spiritually discerned."[10]

Revelation 3:7 And to the angel of the church in Philadelphia write; These things saith he that is holy, he that is true, he that hath the key of David, he that openeth, and no man shutteth; and shutteth, and no man openeth;

The angel of the church of Philadelphia is presented with a message of an open door in the heavenly sanctuary.[11] "Our Redeemer has opened the way so that the most sinful, the most needy, the most oppressed and despised, may find access to the Father. All may

---

[9] E. G. White, *The Review and Herald*, November 13, 1900 par. 21.

[10] 1 Corinthians 2:14

[11] See comments on Daniel 8 and 9.

have a home in the mansions which Jesus has gone to prepare."[12] "Let us therefore come boldly unto the throne of grace, that we may obtain mercy, and find grace to help in time of need."[13]

"After this I looked, and, behold, a door was opened in heaven: and the first voice which I heard was as it were of a trumpet talking with me; which said, Come up hither, and I will show thee things which must be hereafter. And immediately I was in the spirit; and, behold, a throne was set in heaven, and one sat on the throne."[14] "And the temple of God was opened in heaven, and there was seen in his temple the ark of his testament."[15] "The open door in heaven reveals the temple of God, in the most holy place of which is the ark, and in this ark is the law of ten commandments written with the finger of God on tables of stone."[16]

The name Philadelphia means brotherly love. This is the church spanning the period between 1798 and 1844; the time just prior to the commencement of the heavenly judgment.[17] In prophetic portrayal God placed before this church an open door. To the church of brotherly love was granted the potential to understand the new phase of ministration Christ was about to commence. Though there was remarkable love and unity evidenced during this church period, as the soon coming of Jesus was proclaimed around the world, they failed of fully comprehending the divine message.

Moses was told to make a sanctuary in the desert for God to dwell in, which was to be constructed after the pattern that God showed him in the mount.[18] Paul tells us that this pattern was to serve as an example and shadow of things in heaven.[19] Each piece of furniture, each color, and each material was significant of a part of the plan of salvation. The mercy seat of the ark of the covenant, in that earthly

---

[12] E. G. White, *Desire of Ages* (1898), p. 113.2.

[13] Hebrews 4:16

[14] Revelation 4:1-2

[15] Revelation 11:19

[16] E. G. White, *The Present Truth*, November 3, 1885 par. 3.

[17] See Daniel 7, 8 and 9.

[18] Exodus 25:40

[19] Hebrews 8:5

tabernacle, represented God's throne in heaven.[20] "Mercy and truth preserve the king, and his throne is upholden by mercy."[21] God's throne is called the mercy seat, because his throne is upheld by mercy. Beneath the mercy seat are the Ten Commandments[22] which give us a knowledge of sin.[23] As with each sanctuary symbol, the mercy seat represents Jesus. "Being justified freely by his grace through the redemption that is in Christ Jesus: Whom God hath set forth to be a **propitiation** through faith in his blood, to declare his righteousness for the remission of sins that are past, through the forbearance of God."[24] Jesus is set forth as a propitiation. The Greek word for propitiation is hilastērion, which means an atoning victim, or specifically the lid of the ark, or mercy seat. It is Jesus himself that shields the sinner from the condemnation of the law. We are condemned by the law as sinners, because we have violated its precepts, and therefore deserve to die.[25] But, Jesus shields us from the condemnation of the law by his mercy, thus the mercy seat covers the law. That is how his throne is upheld by mercy. It is called the mercy **seat**, because it is a throne.

In the wilderness tabernacle, once a year on the day of atonement, the high priest alone would enter the most holy place to cleanse the sanctuary of the sins accumulated there through the year.[26] Jesus, the true high priest to whom all the sanctuary services pointed,[27] wanted this church to understand that the door into the most holy place in heaven was to be opened, which no man could shut, "For Christ is not entered into the holy places made with hands, which are the figures of the true; but into heaven itself, now to appear in the presence of God for us."[28] In preparation for the ministry in the most holy place, its door was opened and another would be shut that none

---

[20] Exodus 25:18-22; Isaiah 37:16

[21] Proverbs 20:28

[22] Exodus 40:20; Deuteronomy 10:1-5

[23] Romans 3:20

[24] Romans 3:24-25

[25] Romans 6:23

[26] Exodus 30:10; Hebrews 9:7

[27] Hebrews 2:17; 4:14; 8:1

[28] Hebrews 9:24

could open. Christ would shut the door into the holy place as he opened and entered the door into the most holy.[29]

Jesus Christ is portrayed as having the key to this door. Isaiah refers to the same event, door, and key as John sees in Revelation: "And the key of the house of David will I lay upon his shoulder; so he shall open, and none shall shut; and he shall shut, and none shall open."[30] This key gives the power and authority to open the door into the most holy place—the throne room of the universe. Notice that the key is on his shoulder. What does the key represent? "For unto us a child is born, unto us a son is given: and the government shall be upon his shoulder: and his name shall be called Wonderful, Counsellor, The mighty God, The everlasting Father, The Prince of Peace."[31] The key of David represents the government. Jesus possesses the master key to the government of the universe.

Revelation 3:8 I know thy works: behold, I have set before thee an open door, and no man can shut it: for thou hast a little strength, and hast kept my word, and hast not denied my name.

The church of Philadelphia would pass through the great disappointment of believing that Jesus was coming when they mistook that open door for his second coming. They believed that the termination of the 2,300-year prophecy of Daniel 8 would climax in the coming of Jesus.[32] Because of this Jesus is very tender and understanding toward them. Philadelphia began to demonstrate the brotherly love present in the apostolic church. They came together to preach the word of God, to study and know the prophecies of Scripture. They were serious about being ready for the second coming of Jesus, which they believed was very soon. Yet, they were destined to be disappointed. God says, I know, you have little strength, but you have kept my faith. This church is the second of only two churches that has no reproof—only a commendation.

---

[29] See E. G. White, *Early Writings*, p. 42.1. Also, see diagram of the sanctuary layout, *Glimpses of the Open Gates of Heaven*, p. 206.

[30] Isaiah 22:22

[31] Isaiah 9:6

[32] See the chapters on Daniel 8, 9 and Revelation 10.

"Of all the great religious movements since the days of the apostles, none have been more free from human imperfection and the wiles of Satan than was that of the autumn of 1844. Even now, after the lapse of many years, all who shared in that movement and who have stood firm upon the platform of truth still feel the holy influence of that blessed work and bear witness that it was of God."[33]

Revelation 3:9 Behold, I will make them of the synagogue of Satan, which say they are Jews, and are not, but do lie. Behold, I will make them come and worship before thy feet, and to know that I loved thee.

After experiencing the overwhelming embarrassment and agonizing ridicule of the great disappointment, the church of Philadelphia was promised something very meaningful. Those claiming to be spiritual Jews who were, in fact, of the synagogue of Satan, would one day bow before their feet, admitting that these saints were loved and honored of Christ. The fulfillment of this prophecy is to be literal for these individuals will be resurrected in the special resurrection.[34] The wicked will bow down at the feet of the saints [35] and admit that God loved them, as Christ descends in glory.

Revelation 3:10 Because thou hast kept the word of my patience, I also will keep thee from the hour of temptation, which shall come upon all the world, to try them that dwell upon the earth.

Jesus promises the Philadelphian church that they will be kept from the hour of temptation. Because they endured the severe trial of the great disappointment, Jesus promises to hide them from the final trial in earth's history. They will simply sleep in the grave until the special

---

[33] E. G. White, *The Great Controversy* (1911), p. 401.3.

[34] See comments on Daniel 12:2.

[35] "Then kings and nobles, the mighty man, and the poor man, and the mean man, alike, cry there most bitterly. They who in the days of their prosperity despised Christ and the humble ones who followed in His footsteps, men who would not humble their dignity to bow to Christ, who hated His despised cross, are now prostrate in the mire of the earth.
"Their greatness has all at once left them, and they do not hesitate to bow to the earth at the feet of the saints."
E. G. White, *Testimonies,* Vol. 2 (1871), p. 41.3.

resurrection.[36] As they longed patiently for the coming of Jesus, they are promised that they will see him come in the clouds of heaven, without suffering the time of trouble and sorrow preceding his coming.

Revelation 3:11 Behold, I come quickly: hold that fast which thou hast, that no man take thy crown.

The One about to be crowned monarch of the universe concerns himself that his children do not lose their crowns.

Revelation 3:12 Him that overcometh will I make a pillar in the temple of my God, and he shall go no more out: and I will write upon him the name of my God, and the name of the city of my God, which is new Jerusalem, which cometh down out of heaven from my God: and I will write upon him my new name.

The discovery of the Bible truth of the existence and purpose of the heavenly sanctuary explained the disappointment experienced by the Philadelphian believers.[37] When they began to understand that in 1844 Christ commenced the judgment in the most holy place, the temple became very meaningful to them. Jesus promises to make them a part of that temple.

Revelation 3:13 He that hath an ear, let him hear what the Spirit saith unto the churches.

For the fourth time Christ directs the attention of his people to the message the Spirit is sending to the churches. To each of the first three churches, the Spirit sent a specific message. These three messages corresponded to the three angel's messages of Revelation 14. The last four churches are each given a reminder to hear the Spirit's message.

---

[36] See comments on Daniel 12:2.

[37] Revelation 10 discloses that the misunderstanding leading to the great disappointment was actually revealed by God through prophecy before it happened.

Revelation 3:14 And unto the angel of the church of the Laodiceans write; These things saith the Amen, the faithful and true witness, the beginning of the creation of God;

Jesus begins the final message to the last of the seven churches by reminding us of his attribute (from chapter 1) as **"the Amen, the faithful witness,"**[38] and as the originator of all creation.[39] This language parallels the first angel's message of Revelation 14:6; in "the hour of his judgment {which} is come,"[40] Jesus will be **"the faithful and true witness."** As the originator of all creation, Christ alone is worthy of adoration: "worship him that made heaven, and earth, and the sea, and the fountains of waters."[41]

Laodicea means the judging of the people. It is the church that is living during the time of the investigative judgment now presiding in the heavenly sanctuary above.[42] The Laodicean church is participating in the great antitypical day of atonement in which Jesus is cleansing that heavenly sanctuary from all sin. As soon as he is finished with that process, he will return to take us home.

Laodicea is a church that is self deceived, faulty and failing, to whom Christ gives multiple reproofs. "Enfeebled and defective as it may appear, the church is the one object upon which God bestows in a special sense His supreme regard. It is the theater of His grace, in which He delights to reveal His power to transform hearts."[43] Laodicea represents the final church on earth; therefore, there will not be a "coming out" of this church into some other organization.[44]

---

[38] Revelation 1:5

[39] John 1:1-3, 14

[40] Revelation 14:6

[41] *Ibid.*

[42] The judgment must occur prior to the second coming because Jesus says, "And, behold, I come quickly; and my reward is with me, to give every man according as his work shall be." Revelation 22:12
The rewards cannot be given without first having reached a decision regarding eligibility of the reward.

[43] E. G. White, *The Acts of the Apostles* (1911), p. 12.1.

[44] "You will take passages in the Testimonies that speak of the close of probation, of the shaking among God's people, and you will talk of a coming out from this people of a purer, holier people that will arise. Now all this pleases the enemy.... Should many accept the views you advance, and talk and act upon them, we would see one of the greatest fanatical excitements that has ever been witnessed among Seventh-day Adventists. This is what Satan wants."
E. G. White, *Last Day Events* (1992), p. 51.1.

Revelation 3:15 I know thy works, that thou art neither cold nor hot: I would thou wert cold or hot.

For Laodicea, Jesus begins with reproof and there is no commendation.

Revelation 3:16 So then because thou art lukewarm, and neither cold nor hot, I will spue thee out of my mouth.

The lukewarm condition of his church during this period is so sickening to him that he is about to spit them out of his mouth.

The city of Laodicea was supplied with water from a hot springs that came from the nearby Hierapolis. By the time the hot water got to Laodicea it had cooled making the city famous for its lukewarm water.

Revelation 3:17 Because thou sayest, I am rich, and increased with goods, and have need of nothing; and knowest not that thou art wretched, and miserable, and poor, and blind, and naked:

Laodicea was a very wealthy town, famous for their banking system. Certain medicinal products[45] must have contributed to their wealth. When the city was destroyed by an earthquake in A.D. 60 Laodicea, in their self-sufficiency, refused the imperial aid for rebuilding, rather paying for it themselves.

In the last days, the church of the judgment, extending from 1844 to the second coming of Jesus, has indeed become rich and increased with goods. Not only is this church wealthy in worldly goods (material things that absorb our attention and keep us away from our commitment to God); but also rich in spiritual goods and knowledge. We have increased knowledge, much of which we do not apply to our lives. God has given us vast resources. To this final church has been entrusted the messages of the Testimony of Jesus—the spirit

---

[45] See Revelation 3:18.

of prophecy.[46] This privileged wealth of inspired council has been granted to no previous generation. Increased with these amazing blessings, the privileges are ignored or treated with Laodicean apathy. In reality our condition is most pitiful; we are wretched, miserable, poor, blind, and naked, because we have not actually heeded the messages we have been given. We have not taken Christ's righteousness instead of our own. We think we are good enough.

Revelation 3:18 I counsel thee to buy of me gold tried in the fire, that thou mayest be rich; and white raiment, that thou mayest be clothed, and that the shame of thy nakedness do not appear; and anoint thine eyes with eyesalve, that thou mayest see.

The city of Laodicea, was apparently famous for their pharmaceuticals, especially eyesalve. The people of Laodicea would have identified with these symbols. They had eyesalve but God declares their desperate need of spiritual eyesalve. They had treasures of gold but God says, You think you're rich, but you're really poor. His invitation is, **"buy of me."** How can one buy gold and be rich when he is really poor? How will one buy raiment to cover nakedness, when ignorant of their lack of clothes? How can one anoint his own eyes with eyesalve, when he cannot see? The Bible gives the answer in Isaiah 55:1, "Ho, every one that thirsteth, come ye to the waters, and he that hath no money; come ye, buy, and eat; yea, come, buy wine and milk without money and without price." God tells us that we must buy, but we do not buy with money. We must buy it with our lives. We must offer ourselves a living sacrifice unto God. We must die to self. It is only then that Jesus Christ can give to us what we have purchased. It is only then that we can receive his perfect righteousness, his perfect wealth and riches, and his perfect eyesalve.

Then we can no longer say I have what it takes; I have the righteousness, but rather we say, I'm laying everything that I have on the altar so that Christ can give me his righteousness. "But what do we give up, when we give all? A sin-polluted heart, for Jesus to

---

[46] See comments on Daniel 10.

purify, to cleanse by His own blood, and to save by His matchless love. And yet men think it hard to give up all!"[47]

"Heaven will be cheap enough, if we obtain it through suffering. We must deny self all along the way, die to self daily, let Jesus alone appear, and keep His glory continually in view."[48] "God will not be trifled with; Christ accepts no divided service. He asks for all. It will not do to withhold anything. He has purchased you with an infinite price, and He requires that all you have shall be yielded to Him a willing offering. If you are fully consecrated to Him in heart and life, faith will take the place of doubts, and confidence the place of distrust and unbelief."[49]

Revelation 19:8 tells us of the fine white linen with which Christ wants to clothe us, "And to her was granted that she should be arrayed in fine linen, clean and white: for the fine linen is the righteousness of saints." It is their righteousness, because it was given to them; and they are now the owners. But from where did it come? Only from Jesus. It has become their own because they accepted his gift without money, without price.

"The gold that Jesus would have us buy of him is gold tried in the fire; it is the gold of faith and love, that has no defiling substance mingled with it. The white raiment is the righteousness of Christ, the wedding garment which Christ alone can give. The eyesalve is the true spiritual discernment that is so wanting among us, for spiritual things must be spiritually discerned."[50]

Revelation 3:19 As many as I love, I rebuke and chasten: be zealous therefore, and repent.

God is giving a rebuke, but this is a sign of his love. It is those he loves that he rebukes and chastens. He wants us to repent of our Laodicean condition in which we think we are good enough.

---

[47] E. G. White, *Steps to Christ* (Boise, ID: Pacific Press Publishing Association, 1892), p. 46.1.

[48] E. G. White, *The Faith I Live By* (1958), p. 359.4.

[49] E. G. White, *Testimonies for the Church,* Vol. 4 (1881), p. 214.1.

[50] E. G. White, *Review and Herald, April 1, 1890* par. 10.

"It is by grace that the sinner is saved, being justified freely by the blood of Christ. But Christ did not die to save the sinner in his sins. The whole world is condemned as guilty before God, for they are transgressors of his holy law; and they will certainly perish unless they repent, turn from their disobedience, and through faith in Christ claim the merits of his precious blood. The sin of Adam and Eve lost holy Eden for themselves and their posterity, and those who continue to live in the transgression of God's law will never regain the lost paradise. But through the grace of Christ man may render acceptable obedience, and gain a home in the beautiful Eden restored."[51]

Revelation 3:20 Behold, I stand at the door, and knock: if any man hear my voice, and open the door, I will come in to him, and will sup with him, and he with me.

This is the church that realizes that Jesus began interceding in that heavenly most holy with its open door. Christ would enter the throne room of the universe on our behalf. Christ was to receive all power in heaven and earth,[52] the key of David—the access to the door of the government of heaven—and yet, he politely stands at the door of our heart and knocks, hoping to gain entrance. He will not force his presence unwanted. Will you open your heart to him today? As you read these words will you allow the words that he has given, the message that he has sent to these churches to convert your heart? He has the master key to the universe, and is soon returning with the authority of the King of Israel, the government of all creation upon his shoulders. Will you let him have the government of your heart? Will you give him the key to the door of your life? Will you submit your will and your way to him, and allow him to come in? Consider his desire. The Creator of the universe wants to come in and have supper with you; he yearns for fellowship and communion with you. The King of the Universe desires an audience—a meal with you. This is how much he loves you. He is asking you, pleading with you—please, I would like to come in. But, he will not enter without your invitation.

---

[51] E. G. White, *The Signs of the Times*, July 29, 1886 par. 3.

[52] Matthew 28:18

Revelation 3:21 To him that overcometh will I grant to sit with me in my throne, even as I also overcame, and am set down with my Father in his throne.

What amazing grace. God could rescue us from our sin and tell us to just be happy that we are saved. He could remind us of all the trouble we have caused him and what he has had to go through in order to get us to heaven, and assigned us the lowest position; instead he will elevate us to the heights to which Satan illegitimately aspired—to sit with him on his throne.[53] What incomprehensible love!

Scripture brings to view here two thrones in heaven: the throne of Jesus, and the throne of the Father. "I grant to sit with me in my throne, even as I also overcame, and am sat down with my father in his throne." These two thrones represent aspects of the plan of salvation, and were symbolized in miniature, in the wilderness sanctuary. They are represented by the table of showbread and the ark of the covenant. Jesus said, "I am the bread of life."[54] The table of showbread represents the throne of Jesus. The throne of the Father is represented by the mercy seat, on the ark of the covenant, inside the tabernacle's most holy place.

"Beautiful for situation, the joy of the whole earth, is mount Zion, on the sides of the north, the city of the great King."[55] There is a mountain in heaven, and it is on the north side of the sanctuary. In the tabernacle in the wilderness, only one piece of furniture was on the north side—the table of showbread—representing the throne of Jesus in the heavenly sanctuary. Notice what the Bible says in Isaiah 14:12, 13, "How art thou fallen from heaven, O Lucifer, son of the morning! how art thou cut down to the ground, which didst weaken the nations! For thou hast said in thine heart, I will ascend into heaven, I will exalt my throne above the stars of God: I will sit also

---

[53] "The world's Redeemer was treated as we deserve to be treated, **in order that we might be treated as he deserved to be treated**. He came to our world and took our sins upon his own divine soul, that we might receive his imputed righteousness. He was condemned for our sins, in which he had no share, that we might be justified by his righteousness, in which we had no share. The world's Redeemer gave himself for us. Who was he?—The Majesty of heaven, pouring out his blood upon the altar of justice for the sins of guilty man. We should know our relationship to Christ and his relationship to us."
E. G. White, *Review and Herald*, March 21, 1893 par. 6.

[54] John 6:35

[55] Psalms 48:2

upon the mount of the congregation, in the sides of the north." Satan wanted to sit on the sides of the north. He aspired to the throne of Jesus, or Mount Zion.

Those who overcome will be given the honor that Lucifer tried to take by force. How may we overcome? "And they overcame him by the blood of the Lamb, and by the word of their testimony; and they loved not their lives unto the death."[56] Without the blood of the lamb covering us, we cannot overcome; without a testimony of the Lord's power in our lives, we cannot gain the victory. We must first be covered with the blood of the Lamb. Then, when we discover the change that blood makes in our lives, we will bear testimony of the power of the blood of the Lamb by the experience of his grace in our lives.

Revelation 3:22 He that hath an ear, let him hear what the Spirit saith unto the churches.

The final plea Christ gives in the message to his churches is: please listen. "I call heaven and earth to record this day against you, that I have set before you life and death, blessing and cursing: therefore choose life that thou mayest live, thou and thy seed."[57] Amen.

---

[56] Revelation 12:11

[57] Deuteronomy 30:19

Revelation 4

SUMMARY:
Revelation 4 and 5 open before us glimpses of the throne room of heaven, with its emerald rainbow-encircled throne, the twenty-four elders, the four living creatures—each with six wings (the first like a lion, the second like a calf, the third like a man, and the fourth like an eagle), a book sealed with seven seals, and a sacrificial lamb who has earned the right to open the seals. The reader is drawn into the scene with the realization that a solemn yet beautiful work is being accomplished in this throne room: one that affects our lives today and for eternity. The atmosphere is one of tremendous splendor, celestial music, intercession and praise.

"Then Jesus rose up and shut the door of the holy place, and **opened the door** into the most holy, and passed within the second veil, where He now stands by the ark, and where the faith of Israel now reaches."[1]

Revelation 4:1 After this I looked, and, behold, a door was opened in heaven: and the first voice which I heard was as it were of a trumpet talking with me; which said, Come up hither, and I will show thee things which must be hereafter.

After seeing the vision of chapters one through three which was set in the holy place, in the midst of the seven golden candlesticks, John sees a door opened.

"I will show thee things which must be hereafter." John wrote the book of Revelation about the year A.D. 96 (65 years after the

---

[1] E. G. White, *Early Writings* (1882), p. 42.1.

ascension of Christ). Jesus emphasizes to John that the things he will reveal in this vision are to occur in the future from John's day.[2]

Christ himself is the primary figure in this chapter, being referred to three times—in the first verse, in the last verse, and in the midst of the chapter. First, the voice "**as it were of a trumpet**," refers to Jesus as identified in Revelation 1:10-11. Second, Revelation 4:8, saying "Lord God Almighty, which was, and is, **and is to come**," refers to Jesus and his promise to return the second time, as established in Revelation 1:8. Third, Revelation 4:11 (the last verse of the chapter) refers to Jesus, saying "Thou art worthy, O Lord, to receive glory and honour and power: **for thou hast created all things**." John 1:1-3, 14 tells us that Jesus is the Creator, therefore, Jesus is present throughout Revelation chapter four.

Revelation 4:2 And immediately I was in the spirit; and, behold, a throne was set in heaven, and one sat on the throne.

The door in heaven that John sees opens into the very throne room of the universe. There he sees the throne of the Almighty. As John was already transported in vision into the first compartment, or holy place in chapters 1-3, the open door through which he now sees a throne, can only be the door into the most holy.[3] The cherubim guarded mercy seat[4] on top of the ark of the covenant represents the throne of God the father.[5]

---

[2] "Again, as the Holy Spirit rested upon the prophet, he sees a door opened in heaven, and hears a voice calling him to look upon the things which shall be hereafter. And he says, 'Behold, a throne was set in heaven, and one sat on the throne. And he that sat was to look upon like a jasper and a sardine stone.' Ministering angels were around about Him, waiting and eager to do His will, while the rainbow of God's promise, which was a token of His covenant with Noah, was seen by John encircling the throne on high—a pledge of God's mercy to every repentant, believing soul. It is an everlasting testimony that 'God so loved the world, that he gave his only begotten Son, that whosoever believeth in him should not perish, but have everlasting life.' It declares to the whole world that God will never forget His people in their struggle with evil."
E. G. White, *Christ Triumphant* (1999), p. 314.5.

[3] The only other door he could have seen from his location in the holy place would be the door to the outer court, through which he would not see a throne.

[4] It is called the mercy seat because it is the throne where the mercy of God resides. This is also the reason we find the rainbow of mercy to be above this throne, as we shall see in the next verse.

[5] See comments on Daniel 9 for a discussion of how the tabernacle services in the wilderness, represented heavenly realities.

"In the temple in heaven, the dwelling place of God, His throne is established in righteousness and judgment. In the most holy place is His law, the great rule of right by which all mankind are tested. The ark that enshrines the tables of the law is covered with the mercy seat, before which Christ pleads His blood in the sinner's behalf. Thus is represented the union of justice and mercy in the plan of human redemption."[6]

Revelation 4:3 And he that sat was to look upon like a jasper and a sardine stone: and there was a rainbow round about the throne, in sight like unto an emerald.

As John looks into the most holy place, viewing the very throne of the universe, he sees God the Father[7] seated, with the rainbow of mercy above his head. "Jesus is seated with His Father on the throne, high and lifted up, and all who come to God through Him will find access into the **inner** sanctuary. The view of the glory of God in His excellent majesty prepares the heart to humility; and the very work done for Isaiah will be done for all who humble themselves and acknowledge their sins; for **the bow of promise is above the throne.**"[8] And, "upon the **sapphire throne**, was the Eternal One; and **round about the throne a rainbow**, the emblem of divine mercy."[9]

Ezekiel also saw the glorious sapphire throne encircled by a rainbow.[10] Moses and the seventy elders saw the sapphire foundation of God's throne.[11] Sapphire is a clear, deep, sky-blue in color. Blue represents God's law—his ten commandments; for the children of Israel were required to wear a "ribband of blue"[12] on the

---

6 E. G. White, *Amazing Grace* (1973), p. 69.2.

7 "The **Ancient of Days** is God the Father.... It is He, the source of all being, and the fountain of all law, that is to preside in the judgment. And holy angels as ministers and witnesses, in number '**ten thousand times ten thousand, and thousands of thousands,**' {Rev. 5:11} attend this great tribunal."
E. G. White, *The Great Controversy* (1911), p. 479.2.

8 E. G. White, "God's Word to Israel, Ancient and Modern," *The Bible Echo,* September 9, 1895 par. 13.

9 E. G. White, *Education* (1903), p. 177.3.

10 Ezekiel 1:26-28; 10:1

11 Exodus 24:9-10

12 Numbers 15:38

fringes of their garments to remind them to obey God's law. God's law is the foundation of his throne and government, and it resides directly beneath the mercy seat, in the most holy place. Therefore, the sapphire throne is the mercy seat on the ark of the covenant, before which Christ is interceding since the anti-typical day of atonement began in 1844.[13]

"In heaven the semblance of a rainbow encircles the throne and overarches the head of Christ.... The revelator declares, 'Behold, a throne was set in heaven, and one sat on the throne... There was a rainbow round about the throne, in sight like unto an emerald.' Revelation 4:2, 3. When man by his great wickedness invites the divine judgments, the Saviour, **interceding** with the Father in his behalf, points to the bow in the clouds, to the rainbow around the throne and **above His own head**, as a token of the **mercy** of God toward the repentant sinner."[14]

"By faith let us look upon the rainbow round about the throne, the **cloud of sins confessed behind it**. The rainbow of promise is an assurance to every humble, contrite, believing soul, that his life is one with Christ, and that Christ is one with God. The wrath of God will not fall upon one soul that seeks refuge in Him. God Himself has declared, 'When I see the blood, I will pass over you.' 'The bow shall be in the cloud; and I will look upon it, that I may remember the everlasting covenant.'"[15]

Revelation 4:4 And round about the throne were four and twenty seats: and upon the seats I saw four and twenty elders sitting, clothed in white raiment; and they had on their heads crowns of gold.

Twenty-four seats or thrones (thronos in Greek) have been set up for the twenty-four elders. The thrones help us to discover the identity of the elders. Crowns represent victory.[16]

---

[13] See comments on Daniel 8 & 9.

[14] E. G. White, *Patriarchs and Prophets* (1890), p. 107.1.

[15] E. G. White, *Testimonies to Ministers* (1923), p. 157.2.

[16] See E. G. White, *Last Day Events* (1992), p. 282.4.

"I saw the Father rise from the throne, and in a flaming Chariot go into the Holy of Holies, within the veil, and did sit. There I saw thrones that I had never seen before."[17] These thrones are also mentioned in the book of Daniel. In Daniel 7:9, the Bible says, "And I beheld till the thrones were cast down." The Aramaic word translated "cast down" is one word, and can mean placed or set rather than overturned as some might assume. David declares that in the house of God "there are **set thrones** of judgment, the thrones of the house of David."[18] "'I beheld,' says the prophet Daniel, '**till thrones were placed**, and One that was Ancient of Days did sit: His raiment was white as snow, and the hair of His head like pure wool; His throne was fiery flames, and the wheels thereof burning fire.'"[19] From this we see that it is not just the throne of God brought to view, but thrones—plural—being set or placed. These thrones are evidently for the twenty-four elders. "These four and twenty elders... are supposed to be assistants of Christ in his mediatorial work in the sanctuary on high: and when the judgment scene described in Dan. 7:9 commenced in the most holy place, their seats, or thrones, would be set, or placed, there, according to the testimony of that passage."[20]

"Thus was presented to the prophet's vision the opening of the investigative Judgment. The coming of Christ here described is not his second coming to the earth. He comes to the Ancient of days in Heaven to receive dominion, and glory, and a kingdom, which will be given him at the close of his mediatorial work. It is this coming, and not his second advent to the earth, that was foretold in prophecy to take place at the termination of the 2,300 days, in 1844. Attended by a cloud of heavenly angels, our great High Priest enters the holy of holies, and there appears in the presence of God to engage in the last acts of his ministration in behalf of man,—to perform the work of investigative Judgment, and to make an atonement for all who are shown to be entitled to its benefits."[21]

---

[17] E. G. White, "To the Little Remnant Scattered Abroad," *Broadside 1*, April 6, 1846 par. 7.

[18] Psalms 122:5

[19] E. G. White, *The Great Controversy* (1911), p. 479.1.

[20] Uriah Smith, *Daniel and the Revelation*, (1897), p. 416.2.

[21] E. G. White, *Spirit of Prophecy,* Vol. 4 (1884), p. 307.1-2.

Daniel 7 portrays the identical scene as Revelation 4 & 5.[22] The parallels between the judgment scene of Daniel 7 and the throne room scene of Revelation 4 and 5 demonstrate that God intended for these chapters to interpret one another. No other passage in Scripture parallels the judgment of Daniel 7 in such a manner. No other scene in Revelation portrays the investigative judgment described in Daniel 7, 8, and 9.

Daniel 7		Revelation 4 & 5	
verse 9	"I beheld till **thrones were placed**"	verse 4:2, 4	"**a throne was set** in heaven" "And round about the throne were **four and twenty thrones**"
verse 9	"the **Ancient of days did sit**"	verse 4:2	"and **one sat on the throne**"
verse 9, 10	"his throne was like the **fiery flame**..." "A **fiery stream** issued and came forth from before him"	verse 4:5	"And out of the throne **proceeded lightnings** and thunderings"
verse 13	"one like the **Son of man** came"	verse 5:5	"behold, the Lion of the tribe of Juda, **the Root of David**, hath prevailed"

---

[22] The spirit of prophecy makes a clear link between the judgment scene of Daniel 7 and the throne room scene of Revelation 4 & 5 in *The Great Controversy*:
"The **Ancient of Days** {Daniel 7:9} is God the Father.... It is He, the source of all being, and the fountain of all law, that is to **preside in the judgment**. And holy angels as ministers and witnesses, in number 'ten thousand times ten thousand, and thousands of thousands,' {Rev. 5:11} attend this great **tribunal**." E. G. White, *The Great Controversy* (1911), p. 479.2.
The expression "Ancient of Days" is quoted from Daniel 7; a phrase that in all of Scripture is found only in that chapter. Then, instead of quoting "thousand thousands ministered unto him, and ten thousand times ten thousand stood before him" from the same chapter, reference is made to "the number of them was ten thousand times ten thousand, and thousands of thousands" which wording occurs only in Revelation 5:11.

Daniel 7		Revelation 4 & 5	
verse 13	"they brought him **near before him**"	verse 5:6	"**in the midst of the throne** and of the four beasts, and in the midst of the elders, stood a Lamb as it had been slain"
verse 10	"**thousand thousands** ministered unto him, and **ten thousand times ten thousand** stood before him"	verse 5:11	"the number of them was **ten thousand times ten thousand, and thousands of thousands**"
verse 14	"And there was given him **dominion**, and **glory**, and a **kingdom**, that all people, nations, and languages, should **serve him**: his **dominion** is an **everlasting dominion**, which **shall not pass away**"	verse 4:11; 5:13	"Thou art worthy, O Lord, to receive **glory** and honour and **power**:" "Blessing, and honour, and **glory**, and **power**, be unto him that sitteth upon the **throne**, and unto the Lamb **for ever and ever**."
verse 22	"the time came that the **saints possessed the kingdom**."	verse 5:10	"and **we shall reign on the earth**."

The identity of the twenty-four elders is revealed in Revelation 5:9: "And they sung a new song, saying, Thou art worthy to take the book, and to open the seals thereof: for thou wast slain, and **hast redeemed us to God by thy blood out of every kindred, and tongue, and people, and nation;**"

In strains of melody the twenty-four elders tell us that they have been redeemed by the blood of the lamb. They are therefore humans like us, who have walked the pathway of suffering, who have known the malignity of sin, who have met temptations and gained the victory by the power of Christ. They are represented here as the jury in the court of heaven. Not only did Jesus, our divine advocate,[23] become human to understand our infirmities, but God has provided a jury of our peers. On earth, we consider it very important that the jury is composed of people who are our peers; not people who are above us or below us or from a completely different walk of life, but people who would be understanding of our situation. God is doing the same thing. His sense of justice is where we derive our sense of justice— when we actually follow it.

The Bible says, the twenty-four elders are redeemed by the blood of Jesus from every kindred, tongue, people and nation. Although Scripture is very clear that the righteous dead are sleeping in their graves,[24] waiting for the second coming when Jesus will resurrect them, it testifies that there are some individuals who have already been taken to heaven. The first to be translated, without seeing death, was Enoch, "By faith Enoch was translated that he should not see death; and was not found, because God had translated him..."[25]

Another person who was taken to heaven without seeing death was Elijah, as recorded in 2 Kings 2:11: "And it came to pass, as they still went on, and talked, that, behold, there appeared a chariot of fire, and horses of fire, and parted them both asunder; and Elijah went up by a whirlwind into heaven."

---

[23] John 5:22 "For the Father judgeth no man, but hath committed all judgment unto the Son." Hebrews 4:14-15 "Seeing then that we have a great high priest, that is passed into the heavens, Jesus the Son of God, let us hold fast our profession.
For we have not an high priest which cannot be touched with the feeling of our infirmities; but was in all points tempted like as we are, yet without sin."

[24] See comments on Revelation 20:10.

[25] Hebrews 11:5

One more individual, named in Scripture, who was taken to heaven, was Moses. However, Moses was resurrected shortly after his death to arrive at the heavenly Canaan. He would not have died, except that he made one last mistake on the borders of the promised land. The Bible tells us in Jude 1:9, "Yet Michael the archangel, when contending with the devil he disputed about the body of Moses, durst not bring against him a railing accusation, but said, The Lord rebuke thee."

The Bible gives us the identity of Michael. We saw in Daniel chapter 10 and 12 that Michael is Jesus. The name Michael means one who is what God is. Jude informs us that Michael is the archangel. In 1 Thessalonians 4:16, it says that the archangel has the voice of the Lord. So, if the Lord has the voice of the archangel, and Michael is the archangel, that makes Michael the Lord. This is not to say that Jesus is therefore a created being. The Bible is very clear that Jesus is not a created being. He is God. But the Bible in many places calls God an angel. The word angel simply means messenger, and Jesus was certainly a messenger. Applying the word angel to Jesus does not demand that He be a created being any more that calling him a prophet[26] demands that he be a created being.

Some misunderstand the word archangel to refer to the covering cherubim on the ark of the covenant. However, that word is ark of the covenant—A-R-K. Archangel is A-R-C-H. Therefore, Jesus is not one of the covering cherubs, such as is Gabriel,[27] and as was Lucifer.[28] The word archangel literally means angel above all angels. Jesus would certainly be the messenger above all messengers. The archangel is the Lord himself.

Clearly, Jesus would win in a contest with Satan over the body of Moses, because Scripture testifies that Jesus is "the resurrection and the life."[29] Thus we know that Moses was taken to heaven after he

---

[26] Deuteronomy 18:15; Acts 3:20-26; Matthew 13:54-57; Luke 13:33

[27] Luke 1:19

[28] Ezekiel 28:16

[29] John 11:25

was resurrected, before his body saw corruption.[30] When Jesus was on the Mount of Transfiguration, Moses and Elijah came to minister to him. God made sure to inform us in his word that he took these two to heaven, so we would not think they were spirits of the dead.

Perhaps then, Moses, Enoch, and Elijah are numbered among these twenty-four elders. We know someone who is not a part of this group of twenty-four elders. "Men and brethren, let me freely speak unto you of the patriarch David, that he is both dead and buried, and his sepulchre is with us unto this day. **For David is not ascended into the heavens**: but he saith himself, The Lord said unto my Lord, Sit thou on my right hand, Until I make thy foes thy footstool."[31]

Scripture reveals one additional group of people who were resurrected, "And the graves were opened; and many bodies of the saints which slept arose, And came out of the graves after his resurrection, and went into the holy city, and appeared unto many."[32] The Bible does not tell us how many were resurrected when Jesus came out of his tomb. It simply says "**many**" bodies of the saints arose, at the same time as Jesus, and appeared to many people in the city.

The Old Testament prophesied that some would rise from the dead with Christ. "Thy dead men shall live, together with my dead body shall they arise. Awake and sing, ye that dwell in dust: for thy dew is as the dew of herbs, and the earth shall cast out the dead."[33]

"...those who came forth from the grave at Christ's resurrection were raised to everlasting life. They ascended with Him as trophies of His victory over death and the grave. These, said Christ, are no longer the captives of Satan; I have redeemed them. I have brought them

---

[30] "Had Moses remained steadfast, the Lord would have brought him to the promised land, and would then have translated him to Heaven without his seeing death.
"As it was, Moses passed through death, but the Son of God came down from Heaven and resurrected him before his body had seen corruption. Though Satan contended with Michael for the body of Moses, and claimed it as his rightful prey, he could not prevail against the Son of God, and Moses, with a resurrected and glorified body, was borne to the courts of Heaven, and was now one of the honored two, commissioned by the Father to wait upon his Son."
E. G. White, *Spirit of Prophecy*, Vol. 2 (1877), p. 329.2-330.1.

[31] Acts 2:29, 34-35

[32] Matthew 27:52-53

[33] Isaiah 26:19

from the grave as the first fruits of My power, to be with Me where I am, nevermore to see death or experience sorrow."[34]

At least 21 were in this group,[35] since there are twenty-four elders, and 21 more were needed to complete the 24, counting the three already named. These are the only clues that the Scripture gives us. One thing is certain—that these individuals were redeemed from the earth among men—regarding this, the Bible is very explicit.[36]

Revelation 4:5 And out of the throne proceeded lightnings and thunderings and voices: and there were seven lamps of fire burning before the throne, which are the seven Spirits of God.

Lightning, thunder and voices are referred to together five times in Scripture—four in Revelation and once at Mt. Sinai.[37] Each time these words are used in conjunction they are associated with the throne room in the most holy.[38]

John also reminds us of the seven lamps of fire burning in the holy place, before the throne of God, now visible from inside the most holy, through its open door. The seven lamps of fire are used to represent the Spirit of God.

---

[34] E. G. White, *The Desire of Ages* (1898), p. 786.2.

[35] There may have been more: "As Christ arose, He brought from the grave **a multitude of captives**. The earthquake at His death had rent open their graves, and when He arose, they came forth with Him. They were those who had been co-laborers with God, and who at the cost of their lives had borne testimony to the truth. Now they were to be witnesses for Him who had raised them from the dead."
E. G. White, *The Desire of Ages* (1898), p. 786.1.

"Those favored, resurrected saints came forth glorified. **They were a few chosen and holy ones who had lived in every age from creation, even down to the days of Christ**. And while the chief priests and Pharisees were seeking to cover up the resurrection of Christ, God chose to bring up a company from their graves to testify that Jesus had risen, and to declare his glory.
"Those who were resurrected were of different stature and form. I was informed that the inhabitants of earth had been degenerating, losing their strength and comeliness. Satan has the power of disease and death, and in every age the curse has been more visible, and the power of Satan more plainly seen."
E. G. White, Spiritual Gifts, Vol. 1 (1858), p. 69.1-2.

[36] Revelation 5:9

[37] Revelation 4:5; 8:5; 11:19; 16:18; Exodus 16:18

[38] When these words are used in Exodus, they describe the delivery of the law on Mt. Sinai. In the sanctuary, the law resides in the most holy place.

Revelation 4:6 And before the throne there was a sea of glass like unto crystal: and in the midst of the throne, and round about the throne, were four beasts full of eyes before and behind.

In front of the throne is a "sea of glass mingled with fire,"[39] **"like unto crystal."** This crystal sea is the same as the sea of glass mingled with fire of Revelation 15:2. The river of life courses from the throne of God in the most holy, flowing eastward through the holy place (on the south side of the altar of incense[40]), forming this sea. Apparently, the river of life continues flowing out of the sea of glass mingled with fire, cascading down to the city below,[41] nourishing the New Jerusalem, forming another sea of glass outside the city gates.[42]

Around the throne are four beasts full of eyes before and behind. The eyes represent the omniscience of God—his ability to see all things. The lamb is also full of eyes, evincing the divinity of Christ.[43] The beasts are intimately connected with the process of judgment and justice, as they are represented as being around and in the very midst of the throne.

---

[39] Revelation 15:2

[40] Ezekiel 47:1

[41] The temple and throne are above the city. See Isaiah 6:1.
"Now Christ again appears to the view of His enemies. Far above the city, upon a foundation of burnished gold, is a throne, high and lifted up. Upon this throne sits the Son of God, and around Him are the subjects of His kingdom. The power and majesty of Christ no language can describe, no pen portray. The glory of the Eternal Father is enshrouding His Son. The brightness of His presence fills the City of God, and flows out beyond the gates, flooding the whole earth with its radiance."
E.G. White, *Darkness Before Dawn*, p. 54.2.

[42] **"Angels were all about us as we marched over the sea of glass to the gate of the city. Jesus raised His mighty, glorious arm, laid hold of the pearly gate, swung it back on its glittering hinges,** and said to us: 'You have washed your robes in My blood, stood stiffly for My truth, enter in.' We all marched in and felt we had a perfect right there.
"Within the city we saw the tree of life and the throne of God. Out of the throne came a pure river of water, and on either side of the river was the tree of life. On one side of the river was a trunk of a tree, and a trunk on the other side of the river, both of pure, transparent gold. At first I thought I saw two trees; I looked again, and saw that they were united at the top in one tree. So it was the tree of life on either side of the river of life. Its branches bowed to the place where we stood; and the fruit was glorious, which looked like gold mixed with silver."
E.G. White, *Testimonies for the Church*, Vol. 1 (1868), p. 60.3-61.1.

[43] Revelation 5:6

Revelation 4:7 And the first beast was like a lion, and the second beast like a calf, and the third beast had a face as a man, and the fourth beast was like a flying eagle.

John describes the four beasts as a lion, a calf, one having the face of a man, and the last appearing like an eagle. It is possible that there are actual heavenly beings, cherubs, or seraphs, or some other order of being, that appeared to John similar to a calf, a man, a flying eagle, and a lion. John, not knowing quite how to describe them, used the closest things with which he was familiar in his description.

However, they are presented to John in vision with these characteristics for a specific reason, for the attributes are also symbolic. As we consider the symbolic nature of their traits, we notice some interesting features.

Revelation 4:8 And the four beasts had each of them six wings about him; and they were full of eyes within: and they rest not day and night, saying, Holy, holy, holy, Lord God Almighty, which was, and is, and is to come.

The four creatures are seraphs, an order of angelic being, which were also glimpsed by the prophets Isaiah and Ezekiel.[44] The beasts are giving glory and honor to God Almighty, which was and is and is to come. Jesus is the one who promised to come back to take us home. Jesus was, Jesus is, and Jesus is to come. This can only be a reference to Christ himself,[45] who is here described as "**Lord God Almighty.**" The unity of the Godhead is here emphasized for Christ is described in terms synonymous with the Father.[46] This is the second of three references to the presence of Jesus in the throne-room scene of Revelation 4. The four beasts are pointing us to Jesus. They direct our attention to Christ in a very special and specific way, saying constantly: "**Holy, holy, holy, Lord God Almighty, which was, and is, and is to come.**"

---

[44] Isaiah 6:1-3; Ezekiel 1:5-25

[45] Revelation 1:8

[46] Other passages in Scripture emphasize the individual personality of the members of the Godhead. See Matthew 3:16, 17; Matthew 28:19; 1 John 5:7; Romans 8:26,27, 1 Corinthians 2:10, etc.

Revelation 4:9 And when those beasts give glory and honour and thanks to him that sat on the throne, who liveth for ever and ever,

The four beasts (along with the twenty-four elders) present the prayers of the saints before Christ, represented by odours from their golden vials.[47] These prayers are apparently entered as evidence in the investigative judgment. Therefore, the beasts are participating in the legal proceedings. Christ said, "He that rejecteth me, and receiveth not my words, hath one that judgeth him: the word that I have spoken, the same shall judge him in the last day." The words Christ spoke while on earth, in human form, are the words which will judge in the last day. It appears that the four beasts are actually representative of the four eye-witness accounts of the life of Jesus while on this earth. The four gospels present four different testimonies of the words that Jesus spoke on this earth—the words Christ said would judge us in the last day.

Considering the attributes of each one of the four accounts of Jesus' life, we find that the gospel of Matthew emphasizes the royal dignity of Jesus—his kingly aspects. This brings to mind the description of Jesus as the "lion of the tribe of Juda."[48] Matthew also records the royal lineage of Christ.

Mark, on the other hand, portrays Jesus as a patient toiler, like a beast of burden. The ox just patiently plods along, faithfully performing his humble work. The ox, of course, was also used in sanctuary services as one of the symbols to represent Christ.

Luke, the physician, is interested in the physical nature of Jesus, and he portrays Jesus as a man. Luke depicts Jesus as tired; he refers to his thirst—his hunger. He emphasizes the human aspects of Jesus, to show how Jesus must have felt to walk in our footsteps as a human being. Luke records the genetic lineage of Jesus.

The language that John uses to describe Jesus in his gospel, soars to the heights of heaven on wings like eagles. He uses incredible poetic language that transports you into heaven with his descriptions of the divinity of Christ. "In the beginning was the Word, and the

---

[47] Revelation 5:8

[48] Revelation 5:5

Word was with God, and the Word was God. The same was in the beginning with God. All things were made by him; and without him was not any thing made that was made. In him was life; and the life was the light of men. And the light shineth in darkness; and the darkness comprehended it not."[49]

In the judgment, Jesus is pleading the evidence of his life on our behalf—the life that he lived on this earth as the royal son of David, as the patient toiler, as a man with all the weaknesses of humanity, as the divine son of God. All of this has been recorded and presented in these four gospels—entered as the standard of judgment in the heavenly courtroom. Christ presents his life in place of ours.[50] His words shall be the judge.

Revelation 4:10 The four and twenty elders fall down before him that sat on the throne, and worship him that liveth for ever and ever, and cast their crowns before the throne, saying,

Crowns have been bestowed on these representatives of the human race to signify their royal inheritance as family of the one to be crowned as king of the universe.

Revelation 4:11 Thou art worthy, O Lord, to receive glory and honour and power: for thou hast created all things, and for thy pleasure they are and were created.

The twenty-four elders cast their golden crowns of victory on the ground before the throne and in rapturous melody give all the praise, glory, and honor to Jesus Christ their creator and redeemer; praise for all he has done for the salvation of their souls, and for the process of righteous judgment he is executing to save as many humans as possible, to join their celestial anthem.

"Let us therefore come boldly unto the throne of grace, that we may obtain mercy, and find grace to help in time of need."[51] Amen.

---

[49] John 1:1-5

[50] Romans 5:10 "For if, when we were enemies, we were reconciled to God by the death of his Son, much more, being reconciled, we shall be saved by his life."

[51] Hebrews 4:16

Revelation 5

SUMMARY:
Revelation chapters 4 and 5 give a glimpse of the heavenly throne room, with the emerald rainbow encircled throne, twenty-four elders, four living creatures—each with six wings (the first like a lion, the second like a calf, the third like a man, and the fourth like an eagle). A book sealed with seven seals is presented to the sacrificial lamb who has earned the right to open the seven seals.

"The fifth chapter of Revelation needs to be closely studied. **It is of great importance to those who shall act a part in the work of God for these last days.** There are some who are deceived. They do not realize what is coming on the earth."1

Revelation 5:1 And I saw in the right hand of him that sat on the throne a book written within and on the backside, sealed with seven seals.

Let us discover what book is held in the hand of the Father, by allowing the Bible to interpret itself. Here in Revelation 5 we see a book sealed, which is unsealed in Revelation 6. Later, in Revelation 10 we find a book that is open. The prophet Ezekiel also saw a vision of a book written on both sides, the description of which allows us to identify the book of Revelation 5 as the same book portrayed in Revelation 10. Ezekiel describes his view of the book thus: **"eat that I give thee.** And when I looked, behold, **an hand was sent unto me; and, lo, a roll of a book was therein**; And **he spread it before me**; and **it was written within and without**: and there was written therein lamentations, and mourning, and woe. Moreover he said unto me, Son of man, **eat that thou findest; eat this roll**, and go speak unto the house of Israel. So I opened my mouth, and **he caused me to eat that roll**. And he said unto me, Son of man, **cause thy belly to eat**, and fill thy bowels with this roll that I give thee. **Then did I eat it; and it was in my mouth as honey for sweetness... and I went in bitterness..."2**

---

1 E. G. White, *Testimonies for the Church*, Vol. 9 (1909), p. 267.1.

2 Ezekiel 2:8-3:3, 14

Ezekiel sees a vision of a roll of an open book; in a hand; which he is told to eat; which is sweet in his mouth but subsequently causes bitterness. This book is specified to be written within and without (inside and out). Ezekiel is clearly describing the same book as John saw in Revelation 10.

Revelation 10 describes a little open book; in a hand; which John is told to eat; which is sweet in his mouth and bitter in his belly. This book is **not** specified to be written within and without (this does not mean that it is not written on both sides, simply that it is not here specified). However, the book in Revelation 5 **is** "written within and on the backside." Since Ezekiel specifies that the book that will be sweet in the mouth and bitter in the belly is the book that is "written within and without[3]" therefore, the book of Revelation 10 that will make the mouth sweet and belly bitter is the same book as the book of Revelation 5 that is "written within and on the backside."

The book of Revelation 10 is the book of Daniel, therefore the book of Revelation 5, according to Ezekiel, must also be the book of Daniel. "In the Revelation the Lion of the tribe of Judah[4] has opened to the students of prophecy the book of Daniel, and thus is Daniel standing in his place."[5]

Revelation 5:2 And I saw a strong angel proclaiming with a loud voice, Who is worthy to open the book, and to loose the seals thereof?

The Bible speaks elsewhere of a sealed book that will be unsealed. Isaiah is told in vision that the things he was seeing would be like a

---

[3] The Testimony of Jesus uses Ezekiel's phrase "written within and without" rather than the Revelation 5 phrase "written within and on the backside," when describing the book from Revelation 5, providing a deliberate link between the two passages.

"'And I saw in the right hand of Him that sat on the throne a book written within and on the backside, sealed with seven seals. And I saw a strong angel proclaiming with a loud voice, Who is worthy to open the book, and to loose the seals thereof? And no man in heaven, nor in earth, neither under the earth, was able to open the book, neither to look thereon' (Revelation 5:1-3).

There in His open hand lay the book, the roll of the history of God's providences, the prophetic history of nations and the church... This roll **was written within and without.**"
E. G. White, *Manuscript Releases*, Vol. 9 (1990), p. 7.1-4.

[4] The familiar phrase "Lion of the tribe of Juda," is only found once in Scripture—in Revelation 5:5. Therefore the opened book, specified here by the spirit of prophecy to be the book of Daniel, must be the book presented to the lamb in Revelation 5.

[5] E. G. White, *Selected Messages*, Vol. 2 (1958), p. 109.1.

sealed book,[6] which was to be in the future, which would only be understood "in that day." The book which Isaiah predicted to come, was to be the book of Daniel,[7] the vision whose words "is become unto you as the words of a book that is sealed."[8] The book of Daniel was to cause the meek to "increase their joy in the LORD" for it would reveal the first advent of the Messiah, by date. That book would also cause "the poor among men" to "rejoice in the Holy One of Israel, For the terrible one is brought to nought, and the scorner is consumed, and all that watch for iniquity are cut off," because it would reveal the second coming of the Messiah, the great investigative judgment to immediately precede his coming, and the judgments to be visited on "the terrible one," just prior to Messiah's coming.

The book of Daniel states unequivocally that it is indeed the book to be sealed until "that day:" "But thou, O Daniel, shut up the words, and seal the book, even to the time of the end: many shall run to and fro, and knowledge shall be increased."[9] Daniel's book would not be fully comprehended, until that time of history which would be called the "time of the end," when many would "run to and fro" ("a Hebrew expression for observing and thinking upon the time").[10] At the time of the end "knowledge shall be increased"[11]—not particularly knowledge leading to modern inventions, but knowledge about the word of God, knowledge about prophecy—specifically knowledge about the book of Daniel.

In Revelation, John sees into the future, to the time of the end, when Daniel's book would be unsealed. "The book of Daniel is unsealed in

---

[6] Isaiah 29:11-24

[7] "[Quoted Isaiah 29:9-14] **How verily have these words been fulfilled by the Jewish nation,** and by every nation that has followed the same course, turning away from the truth unto fables! The Lord Jesus was the foundation of the whole Jewish economy. Its imposing rites were of divine appointment. They were designed to make the worship of God impressive, and **to teach the people that at the time appointed One would come to whom these ceremonies pointed**. E. G. White, "The Jews Require a Sign," *The Signs of the Times*, November 3, 1898 par. 8-9. The book of Daniel is the book that reveals the time appointed for the coming of the One to whom the ceremonies pointed.

[8] Isaiah 29:11

[9] Daniel 12:4

[10] E. G. White, *The Great Controversy* (1911), p. 359.2.

[11] Daniel 12:4

411

the revelation to John, and carries us forward to the last scenes of this earth's history."[12]

Revelation 5:3 And no man in heaven, nor in earth, neither under the earth, was able to open the book, neither to look thereon.

Initially, no one in the universe was found who is worthy to open the book.

Revelation 5:4 And I wept much, because no man was found worthy to open and to read the book, neither to look thereon.

John is clearly disturbed by the fact that this book is sealed and people are unable to see inside. The book that is in the right hand of him that sits on the throne is apparently to be entered as part of the evidence in the investigative judgment, and it is a book that is sealed with seven seals.

All through the ages, people have attempted to understand the prophecies of Daniel, yet they seemed shrouded in mystery—closed, and sealed. Some of the early prophecies in Daniel people understood, but the prophecies in the later chapters of Daniel dealing with time, that carry us far into the future, were not understood by most for years; for centuries; even for millennia. "The books of Daniel and the Revelation are one. One is a prophecy, the other a revelation; one a book sealed, the other a book opened..."[13]
"There in His open hand lay the book, the roll of the history of God's providences, the **prophetic history of nations and the church.** Herein was contained the divine utterances, His authority, His commandments, His laws, the whole **symbolic** counsel of the Eternal, and the history of all ruling powers in the nations. **In symbolic language** was contained in that roll the influence of every nation, tongue, and people from the beginning of earth's history to its close....

---

[12] E. G. White, *Testimonies to Ministers and Gospel Workers* (1923), p. 115.3.

[13] E. G. White, *Manuscript Releases*, Vol. 1 (1990), p. 99.3.

"Revelation is a sealed book, but it is also an opened book. It records marvelous events that are to take place in the last days of this earth's history. The teachings of this book are definite, not mystical and unintelligible. **In it the same line of prophecy is taken up as in Daniel. Some prophecies God has repeated, thus showing that importance must be given to them. The Lord does not repeat things that are of no great consequence.**"14

The book of Daniel, in combination with Revelation outlines, in symbolic language, "the prophetic history of nations and the church." It contains the destiny of all nations in the last great conflict between Christ and his people and Satan—it contains your destiny.

Revelation 5:5 And one of the elders saith unto me, Weep not: behold, the Lion of the tribe of Juda, the Root of David, hath prevailed to open the book, and to loose the seven seals thereof.

The familiar phrase "**Lion of the tribe of Juda,**" is found only once in Scripture—here in Revelation 5:5. "In the Revelation the **Lion of the tribe of Judah** has opened to the students of prophecy the book of Daniel, and thus is Daniel standing in his place."15

The only one able to open this book must have prevailed. Jesus, the Lion of the tribe of Juda, the Root of David, has prevailed. Before this book could be unsealed, Jesus must have gained the victory at the cross—that is when He prevailed against Satan and his kingdom. The book of Daniel could never be unsealed unless Jesus prevailed. It contains prophesies that foretell exactly when the Messiah would be baptized; precisely when the Messiah would be crucified. These predictions were made by Daniel hundreds of years before the Messiah came. If Jesus had not prevailed at the cross, these prophecies would have been completely false. In order for this book to be demonstrated true, in order for it to be an accurate revelation of God's love, Jesus had to prevail at the cross. Therefore, the book could not be opened any time before he came to this earth and lived, died, and was resurrected. Before the book can be unsealed, Christ

---

14 E. G. White, *Manuscript Releases,* Vol. 9 (1990), p. 7.3-5.

15 E. G. White, *Selected Messages*, Vol. 2 (1958), p. 109.1.

must also enter the heavenly most holy at the end of the 2,300 years of Daniel 8:14.

Not only is the coming of the Messiah outlined in Daniel more specifically than any other book of Scripture, and the date for the cleansing of the heavenly sanctuary revealed, but the history and destiny of nations are contained in this book. The Omnipotent hand, that decreed the destinies of nations, would not be all powerful if Jesus had not prevailed. Jesus has prevailed on your behalf; therefore, your destiny is contained in the book of Daniel, and unsealed in the Revelation of Jesus Christ. If you reject the revelation of his character in you, your fate is certain. When Jesus Christ is revealed in you, your destiny is sure.

Revelation 5:6 And I beheld, and, lo, in the midst of the throne and of the four beasts, and in the midst of the elders, stood a Lamb as it had been slain, having seven horns and seven eyes, which are the seven Spirits of God sent forth into all the earth.

Jesus is portrayed here as a Lamb. John 1:29 says, "The next day John seeth Jesus coming unto him, and saith, Behold the Lamb of God, which taketh away the sin of the world." John the Baptist, without having met Jesus before,[16] recognized him as the Lamb of God who was to take away the sins of the world. The Baptist was announcing the fulfillment of the prophecy in Daniel that the Messiah would come to be slain.[17] He was saying the same thing that John the revelator writes decades later when he says, "I beheld...a Lamb as it had been slain."

The Lamb standing before the throne is the only one able to fulfill the prophecies of the book of Daniel, and therefore the only one able to unseal, or reveal, these prophecies to our understanding.

Revelation 5:7 And he came and took the book out of the right hand of him that sat upon the throne.

---

[16] E. G. White, *The Desire of Ages* (1898), p. 109.2.

[17] Daniel 9:26

Revelation 5:8 And when he had taken the book, the four beasts and four and twenty elders fell down before the Lamb, having every one of them harps, and golden vials full of odours, which are the prayers of saints.

The twenty-four elders are seen, offering the prayers of the saints as evidence in the investigative process.

Many have the idea that the smoke arising from the altar of incense represents the prayers of the saints. A careful reading of the evidence reveals otherwise. Revelation 8:4 says, "And the smoke of the incense, which came **with** the prayers of the saints, ascended up before God out of the angel's hand." The prayers are with the smoke; therefore, they cannot be the smoke. The smoke represents the righteousness of Jesus, which makes our prayers acceptable before his throne—giving them a sweet odor. The odors in the golden vials, are the prayers of the saints,[18] mingled with the smoke of Christ's righteousness. The twenty-four elders, holding golden vials full of the prayers of the saints, are in a sense, representative[19] of the saints themselves, because they are offering this evidence in behalf of the saints who are not physically present. This judgment is certainly not a hostile environment to humans.

Revelation 5:9 And they sung a new song, saying, Thou art worthy to take the book, and to open the seals thereof: for thou wast slain, and hast redeemed us to God by thy blood out of every kindred, and tongue, and people, and nation;

In strains of melody the twenty-four elders tell us that they have been redeemed by the blood of the lamb. They are therefore humans like us, who have walked the pathway of suffering, who have known the malignity of sin, who have met temptations and gained the victory by the power of Christ. They are represented here as the jury in the

---

[18] 2 Corinthians 2:15 "For we are unto God a sweet savour of Christ, in them that are saved, and in them that perish:

[19] "It was as a representative of those who shall be thus translated that Elijah, near the close of Christ's earthly ministry, was permitted to stand with Moses by the side of the Saviour on the mount of transfiguration.... they saw Moses, representing those who will be raised from the dead at the time of the second advent; and there also stood Elijah, representing those who at the close of earth's history will be changed from mortal to immortal and be translated to heaven without seeing death."
E.G. White, *Heaven* (2003), p. 102.3.

court of heaven. Not only did Jesus, our divine advocate,[20] become human to understand our infirmities, but God has provided a jury of our peers. On earth, we consider it very important that the jury is composed of people who are our peers; not people who are above us or below us or from a completely different walk of life, but people who would be understanding of our situation. God is doing the same thing. His sense of justice is where we derive our sense of justice—when we actually follow it.[21]

The twenty-four elders are redeemed by the blood of the Lamb "out of every kindred, and tongue, and people, and nation."

Revelation 5:10 And hast made us unto our God kings and priests: and we shall reign on the earth.

The redeemed are looking forward to the time when God's kingdom will be set up on the earth.[22] They will take part in the government of God in the new earth. "For the earth shall be filled with the knowledge of the glory of the LORD, as the waters cover the sea."[23]

Revelation 5:11 And I beheld, and I heard the voice of many angels round about the throne and the beasts and the elders: and the number of them was ten thousand times ten thousand, and thousands of thousands;[24]

---

[20] John 5:22 "For the Father judgeth no man, but hath committed all judgment unto the Son." Hebrews 4:14-15 "Seeing then that we have a great high priest, that is passed into the heavens, Jesus the Son of God, let us hold fast our profession. For we have not an high priest which cannot be touched with the feeling of our infirmities; but was in all points tempted like as we are, yet without sin."

[21] See comments on Revelation 4:4 for more information about the twenty-four elders.

[22] When this event occurs, is the subject of Revelation 20 and 21.

[23] Habakkuk 2:14

[24] "The **Ancient of Days** is God the Father.... It is He, the source of all being, and the fountain of all law, that is to preside in the judgment. And holy angels as ministers and witnesses, in number 'ten thousand times ten thousand, and thousands of thousands,' {Rev. 5:11} attend this great tribunal." E. G. White, *The Great Controversy* (1911), p. 479.2.
Here the Testimony of Jesus links the phrase "Ancient of Days" (which occurs only in the investigative judgment scene of Daniel 7), with the phrase '**ten thousand times ten thousand, and thousands of thousands**" from Revelation 5:11, rather than quoting the very similar "thousand thousands ministered unto him, and ten thousand times ten thousand stood before him" from Daniel 7, which could have been more easily done. This demonstrates unequivocally the link between the investigative judgment of Daniel 7 and the scenes of Revelation 4 and 5.

These angelic beings, at least 100 million in number, are gathered about the throne of God. A throne room[25] large enough to accommodate 100 million, possibly 600 million[26] heavenly beings, is almost inconceivably vast.

Revelation 5:12 Saying with a loud voice, Worthy is the Lamb that was slain to receive power, and riches, and wisdom, and strength, and honour, and glory, and blessing.

Seven things are offered in worship to the Lamb: power, riches, wisdom, strength, honor, glory, and blessing. In Revelation 1 we saw how this book is unique in Scripture for its use of the number seven, which represents perfection and completeness.

Revelation 5:13 And every creature which is in heaven, and on the earth, and under the earth, and such as are in the sea, and all that are in them, heard I saying, Blessing, and honour, and glory, and power, be unto him that sitteth upon the throne, and unto the Lamb for ever and ever.

John sees the whole universe admitting that God is just and Christ is supreme. The ministration of Jesus in the most holy place, as our high priest, will climax in his coronation as the king of the universe, the establishment of his eternal kingdom, and the rescue of his people from the earth. John is transported in this prophetic view to the culmination of the plan of salvation.

Revelation 5:14 And the four beasts said, Amen. And the four and twenty elders fell down and worshipped him that liveth for ever and ever.

Amen.

---

[25] How big is the most holy place? To discover the answer to this question, see comments on Revelation 21. In that chapter we explore Scriptural evidence for the actual dimensions, not only of the New Jerusalem, but also of the temple, including the most holy place.

[26] See Revelation 9:16

Revelation 6

SUMMARY:
Revelation 6 describes what happens when each of the seals from Revelation 5 are opened. With the opening of the first seal there appears a white horse, the rider of which has a bow and a crown. When the second seal is opened a red horse appears with the rider having a sword who takes peace from the earth. The third seal reveals a rider on a black horse with a pair of balances in his hand. As the fourth seal is opened a pale horse appears, the name of its rider is death with hell following after. When the fifth seal is opened, the souls beneath the altar cry for justice. The opening of the sixth seal causes a great earthquake; and the sun became black as sackcloth of hair, and the moon became as blood; and the stars of heaven fell unto the earth. The opening of the seventh seal does not occur until chapter eight.

Revelation 6:1 And I saw when the Lamb opened one of the seals, and I heard, as it were the noise of thunder, one of the four beasts saying, Come and see.

Revelation 6:2 And I saw, and behold a white horse: and he that sat on him had a bow; and a crown was given unto him: and he went forth conquering, and to conquer.

Two white horses are depicted in Revelation, the first here and the second in Revelation 19. Though they are both white horses, there are some significant differences between them. Let us consider the second white horse: "And I saw heaven opened, and behold a white horse; and he that sat upon him was called Faithful and True, and in righteousness he doth judge and make war. His eyes were as a flame of fire, and on his head were many crowns; and he had a name written, that no man knew, but he himself. And he was clothed with a vesture dipped in blood: and his name is called The word of God. And the armies which were in heaven followed him upon white horses, clothed in fine linen, white and clean. And out of his mouth goeth a sharp sword, that with it he should smite the nations: and he shall rule them with a rod of iron: and he treadeth the winepress of the fierceness and wrath of Almighty God. And he hath on his vesture and on his thigh a name written, KING OF KINGS, AND LORD OF LORDS."[1]

The description of the rider on the white horse in Revelation 19 gives at least twelve identifying marks. Every one of them clearly represents the rider as Jesus. This is not so of the rider and white horse in Revelation 6. There are no eyes like fire. There is no name written on the garment. The weapon is not the same. In Revelation 19, the rider has a sword coming out of his mouth, which is the word of God, identifying the rider as Jesus. In Revelation 6 the rider has a bow, rather than a sword. The rider in Revelation 19 has many crowns on his head. The rider in Revelation 6 is given a crown,— almost as if it is on loan. There are more significant differences than there are similarities. The only similarity is that the horses are both white. In verse four we will explore the identity of the white horse of Revelation 6.

Revelation 6:3 And when he had opened the second seal, I heard the second beast say, Come and see.

Revelation 6:4 And there went out another horse that was red: and power was given to him that sat thereon to take peace from the earth, and that they should kill one another: and there was given unto him a great sword.

The prophet Zechariah saw a vision of white and red horses that reveals the meaning of the horses of Revelation 6. "Upon the four and twentieth day of the eleventh month, which is the month Sebat, in the second year of Darius, came the word of the LORD unto Zechariah, the son of Berechiah, the son of Iddo the prophet, saying, I saw by night, and behold a man riding upon a red horse, and he stood among the myrtle trees that were in the bottom; and behind him were there red horses, speckled, and white."[2]

In Zechariah's vision we see red horses and white horses, as in Revelation 6. Zechariah's vision occured during the second year of the reign of Darius, of the Medo-Persian Empire.

---

1 Revelation 19:11-16

2 Zechariah 1:7-8

At first glance, verse 8 might seem to refer to three categories of horses—red horses, speckled horses, and white horses. However, in Hebrew, the word used for speckled can also be translated red.[3] Therefore the word appears to designate a second group of red horses rather than a third category of speckled animals.[4] Notice that the red horses come first and the white horses are behind. The order is significant. The Bible clearly identifies what these horses represent. "Then said I, O my lord, what are these? And the angel that talked with me said unto me, I will show thee what these be. And the man that stood among the myrtle trees answered and said, These are they whom the LORD hath sent to walk to and fro through the earth. And they answered the angel of the LORD that stood among the myrtle trees, and said, We have walked to and fro through the earth, and, behold, all the earth sitteth still, and is at rest."[5] A beast in Bible prophecy represents a kingdom or empire. The horses represent the kingdoms in control of the earth. They have the ability to walk to and fro as they please. They say, we have everything under control, we are at ease; everything is at rest.

The historical context of Zechariah's vision is that the Jews had been taken captive, and the prophet Jeremiah had prophesied that Judah would be in captivity for 70 years. Judah has been punished now for 70 years, and the predicted time period has come to an end. In vision, Zechariah hears an angel ask the question, "how long wilt thou not have mercy on Jerusalem and on the cities of Judah, against which thou hast had indignation these threescore and ten years?"[6] The reply comes in verses 13-15: "And the LORD answered the angel that talked with me with good words and comfortable words. So the angel that communed with me said unto me, Cry thou, saying, Thus saith the LORD of hosts; I am jealous for Jerusalem and for Zion with a great jealousy. And **I am very sore displeased with the heathen that are at ease: for I was but a little displeased, and they helped forward the affliction.**"

---

[3] Brown-Driver-Briggs' Hebrew Definitions (e-Sword) defines it as: sorrel, reddish, tawny, bay. Strong's Hebrew and Greek Dictionary (e-Sword) defines it as: bright red (as piercing to the sight), that is, bay: - speckled.

[4] Additional evidence for this conclusion will follow.

[5] Zechariah 1:9, 11

[6] Zechariah 1:12

The horses represent the heathen that are at ease, that say that the earth is still, with everything at rest—the heathen that "helped forward the affliction."[7] There were only two kingdoms or world empires that forwarded the affliction of God's people during the 70 years of captivity. Those two heathen nations were Babylon and Medo-Persia. God says that these are the heathen that are at ease, who say that the earth is still, with everything fine under their control. Therefore, the horses represent the kingdoms of Babylon and Medo-Persia.

Zechariah 1:16 continues, "Therefore thus saith the LORD; I am returned to Jerusalem with mercies: my house shall be built in it, saith the LORD of hosts, and a line shall be stretched forth upon Jerusalem." What heathen nation ended the 70 years of captivity by giving a decree to allow Jerusalem to be rebuilt—for a line to be stretched forth upon Jerusalem? It was the combined empire of the Medes and the Persians, the very powers portrayed as two groups of red horses. The red horses representing Medo-Persia are in the front, while the white horses representing Babylon are behind, indicating that Medo-Persia was current and Babylon was historical.[8]

The Bible's definition of red and white horses in Zechariah reveal the meaning of the same symbols when they appear in Revelation. The white horse has a rider with a bow who is given a crown and goes forth conquering and to conquer. Daniel chapter four outlines the astonishing story of the conversion[9] of the founder and supreme

---

[7] Zechariah 1:15

[8] There is Biblical precedent for a reversed order of kingdoms reaching into history. Recalling Daniel 7, four beasts represented four chronological world empires: a lion, a bear, a leopard, and a terrible beast. When Daniel received the vision, he was physically present in the kingdom of Babylon. Therefore, he saw Babylon represented first as the lion, Medo-Persia pictured next as the bear, Greece represented third as the leopard, and Rome portrayed last as the terrible beast. Aspects of those same world powers appear in a composite beast in Revelation 13:1, 2: "And I... saw a beast rise up out of the sea, having seven heads and ten horns.... And the beast which I saw was like unto a leopard, and his feet were as the feet of a bear, and his mouth as the mouth of a lion...." The political power represented by this beast combines aspects of all four preceding pagan empires of Daniel 7. However, in this depiction the components are mentioned in the exact reverse order as they were portrayed in Daniel 7. When John sees the vision of Revelation 13, he is physically located in the kingdom of Rome. From this vantage point, John is looking back on history. Therefore, he sees first Rome, then Greece, later Medo-Persia, and finally Babylon. The components are portrayed in the reverse order, just as the horses in Zechariah 1.

[9] "King Nebuchadnezzar, before whom Daniel so often honored the name of God, was finally thoroughly converted, and learned to 'praise and extol and honour the King of heaven.'" E. G. White, *Review and Herald, January 11, 1906*, par. 10.

monarch of the most powerful and magnificent empire "the like of which our world has never since beheld"[10]—Nebuchadnezzar. Nebuchadnezzar is portrayed by God as representing the entire Babylonian empire: "Thou art this head of gold."[11] Nebuchadnezzar is the only ruler in Scripture that is called a "king of kings" by God himself.[12] The Lord gives Nebuchadnezzar that title through both the prophets Daniel and Ezekiel.[13] Nebuchadnezzar humbled himself before the monarch of the universe, and was saved by faith in the righteousness of Jesus Christ, who revealed himself personally to Nebuchadnezzar.[14] The love of heaven knew no bounds, as Christ stooped to save even a proud pagan king and through him to distribute, by letter, the gospel to the entire planet: "Nebuchadnezzar the king, unto all people, nations, and languages, that dwell in all the earth; Peace be multiplied unto you. I thought it good to show the signs and wonders that the high God hath wrought toward me. How great are his signs! and how mighty are his wonders! his kingdom is an everlasting kingdom, and his dominion is from generation to generation."[15] The purpose of God for the Jewish nation was to carry the message of salvation to the entire planet. God intended for the Jewish nation to be the world's superpower.[16] Because of their apostasy, God's purpose for his chosen people had to be accomplished through the empire of Babylon. Through the influence of God's faithful servant Daniel and his three friends, the king of Babylon went forth conquering and to conquer, gaining victory in the ultimate battle with self, and becoming a citizen of heaven. This is the message of righteousness by faith. Doubtless, untold millions in the Babylonian empire came to a saving knowlege of God through this monarch's witness.

---

[10] E. G. White, *Prophets and Kings* (1917), p. 548.1.
See also E. G. White, "The Prophetic Word," *Bible Training School*, December 1, 1912 par. 4.

[11] Daniel 2:38

[12] Artaxerxes calls himself a "king of kings," Ezra 7:12.

[13] Ezekiel 26:7; Daniel 2:37

[14] Daniel 3:25

[15] Daniel 4:1-3

[16] "As the numbers of Israel increased, they were to enlarge their borders until their kingdom should embrace the world. But ancient Israel did not fulfill God's purpose."
E. G. White, *Prophets and Kings* (1917), p. 19.1.

Nebuchadnezzar, by the decree of God, was one of the monarchs to wear the crown of David, which Jesus would eventually receive: "The crown removed from Israel passed successively to the kingdoms of Babylon, Medo-Persia, Greece, and Rome. God says, 'It shall be no more, until He come whose right it is; and I will give it Him.'"[17] Thus Nebuchadnezzar and his kingdom are represented by a rider on a white horse, clothed in the righteousness of Jesus Christ, going "forth conquering and to conquer."[18]

The red horse has a rider that is given a sword with which to take peace from the earth and cause that they should kill one another. Medo-Persia conquered by sword the earth's first world empire. Babylon had given to the world unprecedented peace and prosperity; any kingdom that did not resist Babylon was given unusual peace and autonomy. With the conquests of Media and Persia, that peace and wealth took flight from the earth, to return no more.

Revelation 6:5 And when he had opened the third seal, I heard the third beast say, Come and see. And I beheld, and lo a black horse; and he that sat on him had a pair of balances in his hand.

If the white horse represents Babylon, and the red horse Medo-Persia, then the third black horse must be Greece. Do the characteristics portrayed by this third horse and rider fit the kingdom of Greece?

The rider of the black horse carries a pair of balances in his hand. Balances represent justice or a legal system—a system of weighing the evidence to arrive at the correct verdict.[19] The system of law that Greece set up is the basis of the legal systems around the world

---

[17] E. G. White, *Education* (1903), p. 179.2-3.
See also commentary on Daniel 4b for more on the successive transfer of Israel's crown.

[18] "God desired his people to obey him because they realized that obedience would make them men and women of understanding. He drew the willing and obedient to him with cords of love. He desired his people to go forth conquering and to conquer. It was their privilege to reveal in their lives the character of their leader."
E. G. White, "The Lord's Vineyard," *Review and Herald*, July 10, 1900 par. 15.

[19] See Daniel 5:26-27.
"But the Word of God plainly states that in the Judgment the scales will be balanced accurately, and the decisions will be based on the evidence adduced."
E. G. White, *Selected Messages*, Vol. 3 (1980), p. 147.3.

today. Thus, the rider carrying a pair of balances would well represent the kingdom of Greece.

Revelation 6:6 And I heard a voice in the midst of the four beasts say, A measure of wheat for a penny, and three measures of barley for a penny; and see thou hurt not the oil and the wine.

Under Greek jurisdiction God's people had relative economic well-being. They were able to buy and sell, and live fairly comfortably. They had been allowed, by the Medo-Persian empire, to return to Jerusalem by this time, so they had some degree of autonomy in Palestine. There were a few notable times of persecution of the Jews during the reign of Greece, but primarily it was a time of prosperity. Therefore, food is represented as inexpensive: "**A measure of wheat for a penny and three measures of barley for a penny.**"

Let us contrast this situation to the scenario that happened later in history under the reign of Rome. Speaking of the siege of Jerusalem in A.D. 70, we are told: "Terrible were the calamities that fell upon Jerusalem when the siege was resumed by Titus. The city was invested at the time of the Passover, when millions of Jews were assembled within its walls. Their stores of provision, which if carefully preserved would have supplied the inhabitants for years, had previously been destroyed through the jealousy and revenge of the contending factions, and now all the horrors of starvation were experienced. A measure of wheat was sold for a talent. So fierce were the pangs of hunger that men would gnaw the leather of their belts and sandals and the covering of their shields."[20]

In the terrible famine caused by the siege a measure of wheat was sold for a talent. This is presumably referring to a silver talent, not a gold talent, since at this time, people dealt mostly with silver money. Today a talent of silver is worth almost $5,300—for one measure of wheat. A measure of wheat is about enough wheat to feed one person of average appetite, for one day. The food for a day would be over $5,000. Yet in the time of Greece, a measure of wheat was sold for a penny or about $0.44 for us today. Compare the economics of buying one day's food supply for $0.44, in the time of Greece, versus

---

[20] E. G. White, *The Great Controversy* (1911), p. 31.2.

one day's food supply for over $5,000 during the Roman siege of Jerusalem.

Revelation 6:7 And when he had opened the fourth seal, I heard the voice of the fourth beast say, Come and see.

Revelation 6:8 And I looked, and behold a pale horse: and his name that sat on him was Death, and Hell followed with him. And power was given unto them over the fourth part of the earth, to kill with sword, and with hunger, and with death, and with the beasts of the earth.

These are fit symbols for the empire of Rome—a pale horse whose rider was death, representing pagan Rome, followed by hell, depicting papal Rome. Death ruled the world with iron, breaking and subduing all things.[21] It was typical for Rome to kill with the sword, with hunger, with death, and with the beasts of the earth. Did the

---

[21] Daniel 2:40

killing stop with pagan Rome? No. During the Dark Ages, the papacy killed, on the most conservative estimates, as many as 200 million martyrs.[22] How did they kill? They killed with the sword, with hunger, with death, and with the beasts of the earth, just as pagan Rome had before them.

"From the rise and fall of nations as made plain in the books of Daniel and the Revelation, we need to learn how worthless is mere outward and worldly glory. Babylon, with all its power and magnificence, the like of which our world has never since beheld, — power and magnificence which to the people of that day seemed so stable and enduring,—how completely has it passed away! As 'the flower of the grass,' it has perished. James 1:10. So perished the Medo-Persian kingdom, and the kingdoms of Grecia and Rome. And so perishes all that has not God for its foundation. Only that which is bound up with His purpose, and expresses His character, can endure. His principles are the only steadfast things our world knows."[23]

Revelation 6:9 And when he had opened the fifth seal, I saw under the altar the souls of them that were slain for the word of God, and for the testimony which they held:

As the fifth seal is opened God represents, in vision to John, the souls of all those who have been slain by the hell that followed death. This is a representation of the millions of martyrs slain during the Dark Ages.

Revelation 6:10 And they cried with a loud voice, saying, How long, O Lord, holy and true, dost thou not judge and avenge our blood on them that dwell on the earth?

Some will try to use this verse as evidence that when you die, your soul goes to heaven. This position does not make sense, for the language cannot be taken literally without the souls in heaven being literally stuck underneath an altar. This scenario would not be paradise. Instead, this is symbolic language. Metaphorically, their

---

[22] See comments on Daniel 7:25.

[23] E. G. White, *Prophets and Kings* (1917), p. 548.1.

blood is crying for justice. How long will you not judge and avenge our blood?

There is another example of blood crying metaphorically in Genesis 4:9, 10, when the Bible says, "And the LORD said unto Cain, Where is Abel thy brother? And he said, I know not: Am I my brother's keeper? And he said, What hast thou done? the voice of thy brother's blood crieth unto me from the ground." This statement does not mean that the blood was actually making a literal sound. Clearly this is metaphoric language meaning that the blood is crying to God for justice. The blood was evidence of the crime that Cain had committed. In the same manner, the blood of the martyrs is symbolically being represented as being under the altar, because their lives were sacrificed. Their blood symbolically cries for justice.

Additionally, in sanctuary symbolism, the altar of sacrifice is in the outer court, which represents the earth. This is evident from Revelation 11:2 which says, "But the court which is without the temple leave out, and measure it not; for it is given unto the Gentiles: and the holy city shall they tread under foot forty and two months." Therefore, the souls crying out for justice rest in the earth, on which altar their blood was shed.

Revelation 6:11 And white robes were given unto every one of them; and it was said unto them, that they should rest yet for a little season, until their fellowservants also and their brethren, that should be killed as they were, should be fulfilled.

This verse provides additional evidence for the symbolic application made in verse 10. The souls of them that were slain for the word of God and the testimony which they held, are told to rest. Notice the passage in John 11:11-14, when Jesus resurrected Lazarus from the dead: "These things said he: and after that he saith unto them, Our friend Lazarus sleepeth; but I go, that I may awake him out of sleep. Then said his disciples, Lord, if he sleep, he shall do well. Howbeit Jesus spake of his death: but they thought that he had spoken of taking of rest in sleep. Then said Jesus unto them plainly, Lazarus is dead."

Scripture portrays Lazarus as sleeping or resting in the grave when he was dead. When Jesus called him out of the tomb, Jesus did not say, "Lazarus, come down," he said, "Lazarus, come forth." When Lazarus came forth from the tomb, he did not have any stories about being in heaven. He was completely unconscious. He had been dead four days—already decomposing. If, as soon as Lazarus died, his spirit or soul went straight to the bliss of Paradise, where he was enjoying the presence of God and of the angels; it would have been a dirty trick for Jesus to call him back down to his body to experience more misery and another death on this earth. This would make no sense whatsoever. The Bible presents no such idea. We willl look at this subject in greater detail in future chapters of Revelation.

Daniel 12:13 is another example where the Bible portrays someone sleeping in the grave as resting. "But go thou thy way till the end be: for thou shalt rest, and stand in thy lot at the end of the days." Daniel was promised that at the end of the specified period of time, he would be resurrected; in the meantime, he was to rest, or sleep in the grave. The Bible refers to death as a sleep. The souls under the altar were likewise told to rest. They are not alive or disembodied souls; they are not conscious entities stuck beneath an altar. They are resting in the grave and their blood is symbolically crying for justice. We are assured that they had obtained the robe of Christ's righteousness.

Revelation 6:12 And I beheld when he had opened the sixth seal, and, lo, there was a great earthquake; and the sun became black as sackcloth of hair, and the moon became as blood;

Revelation 6:13 And the stars of heaven fell unto the earth, even as a fig tree casteth her untimely figs, when she is shaken of a mighty wind.

Four specific and consecutive events are represented that commence as the sixth seal is opened: first, a great earthquake; second, the sun was to become black; third, the moon would look like blood; and fourth, the stars would fall to the earth.

Matthew speaks of the same events, "Immediately after the tribulation of those days shall the sun be darkened, and the moon shall not give her light, and the stars shall fall from heaven, and the powers of the heavens shall be shaken:"[24] Exactly as the Bible predicted, these events immediately followed the persecution of the dark ages.[25] Just after the time when all those millions of martyrs were being killed for their faith in Christ, the signs that would testify of the imminence of the judgment hour and the second coming, would take place. These signs took place in the exact order the Bible outlined, and at the very time specified by this prophecy.

The first event occured on November 1, 1755, as the persecution was ending and the papal power was losing its hold on Europe to the Reformation. A great earthquake, centered in Lisbon, Portugal, shook the world. This was the greatest earthquake, as far as casualties, that the earth had ever seen. The second event occured, just a few years after, on May 19, 1780—the sun was darkened in the famous great dark day. The third event happened the same night—the moon rose blood-red. The fourth event occured just over fifty years later—the stars fell from heaven in the greatest meteoric shower ever recorded, on November 13, 1833.

We will consider some historical accounts of these things that have been mostly forgotten in the dust of history.

The GREAT EARTHQUAKE

"These signs were witnessed before the opening of the nineteenth century. In fulfillment of this prophecy there occurred, in the year 1755, the most terrible earthquake that has ever been recorded. "Though commonly known as the earthquake of Lisbon, it extended to the greater part of Europe, Africa, and America. It was felt in Greenland, in the West Indies, in the island of Madeira, in Norway and Sweden, Great Britain and Ireland. It pervaded an extent of not less than four million square miles. In Africa the shock was almost as severe as in Europe. A great part of Algiers was destroyed; and a short distance from Morocco, a village containing eight or ten thousand inhabitants was swallowed up. A vast wave swept over the

---

[24] Matthew 24:29

[25] "The 1260 days, or years, terminated in 1798. A quarter of a century earlier, persecution had almost wholly ceased. Following this persecution, according to the words of Christ, the sun was to be darkened. On the 19th of May, 1780, this prophecy was fulfilled."
E. G. White, *The Great Controversy* (1911), 306.1.

coast of Spain and Africa engulfing cities and causing great destruction.

"It was in Spain and Portugal that the shock manifested its extreme violence. At Cadiz the inflowing wave was said to be sixty feet high. Mountains, 'some of the largest in Portugal, were impetuously shaken, as it were, from their very foundations, and some of them opened at their summits, which were split and rent in a wonderful manner, huge masses of them being thrown down into the adjacent valleys. Flames are related to have issued from these mountains.' - Sir Charles Lyell, *Principles of Geology*, page 495.

"At Lisbon 'a sound of thunder was heard underground, and immediately afterwards a violent shock threw down the greater part of that city. In the course of about six minutes sixty thousand persons perished. The sea first retired, and laid the bar dry; it then rolled in, rising fifty feet or more above its ordinary level.'"[26]

Even today the Lisbon earthquake is considered one of history's deadliest earthquakes and is estimated to be the 17th strongest earthquake ever, by magnitude.

SUN AS BLACK AS SACKCLOTH

"'Almost if not altogether alone as the most mysterious and as yet unexplained phenomenon of its kind, . . . stands the dark day of May 19, 1780,—a most unaccountable darkening of the whole visible heavens and atmosphere in New England.' That the darkness was not due to an eclipse is evident from the fact that the moon was then nearly full. It was not caused by clouds, or the thickness of the atmosphere, for in some localities where the darkness extended, the sky was so clear that the stars could be seen. Concerning the inability of science to assign a satisfactory cause for this manifestation, Herschel the astronomer declares: 'The dark day in North America was one of those wonderful phenomena of nature which philosophy is at a loss to explain.'

"'The extent of the darkness was also very remarkable. It was observed at the most easterly regions of New England; westward, to the farthest part of Connecticut, and at Albany, N.Y.; to the southward, it was observed all along the sea coast; and to the north, as far as the American settlements extended. It probably far

---

[26] E. G. White, *The Great Controversy* (1911), p. 304.2-305.1.

exceeded those boundaries, but the exact limits were never positively known. With regard to its duration, it continued in the neighborhood of Boston for at least fourteen or fifteen hours.'

"'The morning was clear and pleasant, but about eight o'clock there was observed an uncommon appearance in the sun. There were no clouds, but the air was thick, having a smoky appearance, and the sun shone with a pale, yellowish hue, but kept growing darker and darker, until it was hid from sight.' There was 'midnight darkness at noonday.'

"'The occurrence brought intense alarm and distress to multitudes of minds, as well as dismay to the whole brute creation, the fowls fleeing bewildered to their roosts, and the birds to their nests, and the cattle returning to their stalls.' Frogs and night hawks began their notes. The cocks crew as at daybreak. Farmers were forced to leave their work in the fields. Business was generally suspended, and candles were lighted in the dwellings. 'The Legislature of Connecticut was in session at Hartford, but being unable to transact business adjourned. Everything bore the appearance and gloom of night.'"[27]

Interestingly enough, even some famous poets have written poems about this great dark day. The poet Whittier penned the following verse:

"'Twas on a May-day of the far old year
Seventeen hundred eighty, that there fell
Over the bloom and sweet life of the spring,
Over the fresh earth, and the heaven of noon,
A horror of great darkness.
Men prayed, and women wept; all ears grew sharp
To hear the doom-blast of the trumpet shatter
The black sky."[28]

When people saw these dramatic signs happen, they thought it was the end of the world and the coming of the Lord.

---

[27] E. G. White, *The Great Controversy* (1888), p. 306.1-307.2.

[28] *Ibid.*, p. 308.1.

MOON TURNS TO BLOOD

"The intense darkness of the day (May 19, 1780) was succeeded, an hour or two before evening, by a partially clear sky, and the sun appeared, though it was still obscured by the black, heavy mist. But 'this interval was followed by a return of the obscuration with greater density, that rendered the first half of the night hideously dark beyond all former experience of the probable million of people who saw it. From soon after sunset until midnight, no ray of light from moon or star penetrated the vault above. It was pronounced 'the blackness of darkness!" Said an eye-witness of the scene: 'I could not help conceiving, at the time, that if every luminous body in the universe had been shrouded in impenetrable darkness, or struck out of existence, the darkness could not have been more complete.' Though the moon that night rose to the full, 'it had not the least effect to dispel the death-like shadows.' After midnight the darkness disappeared, and the moon, when first visible, had the appearance of blood."[29]

THE FALLING OF THE STARS

The night of November 13, 1833 was the falling of the stars. "This prophecy received a striking and impressive fulfillment in the great meteoric shower of November 13, 1833. That was the most extensive and wonderful display of falling stars which has ever been recorded; 'the whole firmament, over all the United States, being then, for hours, in fiery commotion. No celestial phenomenon has ever occurred in this country, since its first settlement, which was viewed with such intense admiration by one class in the community, or such dread and alarm by another.' 'Its sublimity and awful beauty still linger in many minds.... Never did rain fall much thicker than the meteors fell toward the earth; east, west, north, and south, it was the same. In a word, the whole heavens seemed in motion.... The display, as described in Professor Silliman's journal, was seen all over North America.... From two o'clock until broad daylight, the sky being perfectly serene and cloudless, an incessant play of dazzlingly brilliant luminosities was kept up in the whole heavens.'
"'No language indeed can come up to the splendor of that magnificent display; no one who did not witness it can form an

---

[29] E. G. White, *The Great Controversy* (1888), p. 306.1-307.3.

adequate conception of its glory. It seemed as if the whole starry heavens had congregated at one point near the zenith, and were simultaneously shooting forth, with the velocity of lightning, to every part of the horizon; and yet they were not exhausted—thousands swiftly followed in the track of thousands, as if created for the occasion.' 'A more correct picture of a fig-tree casting its figs when blown by a mighty wind, it is not possible to behold.'"[30]

These eye witness accounts, using Biblical language in their descriptions, tell us of the most amazing fulfillments of these Bible prophecies occuring in the exact order and in the precise manner as foretold almost 2,000 years before they occured.

Revelation 6:14 And the heaven departed as a scroll when it is rolled together; and every mountain and island were moved out of their places.

Revelation 6:15 And the kings of the earth, and the great men, and the rich men, and the chief captains, and the mighty men, and every bondman, and every free man, hid themselves in the dens and in the rocks of the mountains;

Revelation 6:16 And said to the mountains and rocks, Fall on us, and hide us from the face of him that sitteth on the throne, and from the wrath of the Lamb:

The very next event portrayed in this passage, after the great earthquake, the dark day, the moon turning to blood, and the falling of the stars, is the second coming of Jesus.[31]

Revelation 6:17 For the great day of his wrath is come; and who shall be able to stand?

This is the question that we all must ask ourselves today. When the great day of his wrath comes, will I be able to stand?

---

[30] E. G. White, *The Great Controversy* (1888), p. 332.4-333.1.

[31] There are additional events to occur between verses 12-13 and 14-16, which will be covered in the parenthetical statement of Revelation 7.

434

In Psalm 24:3-5, David both asks and answers the same question, "Who shall ascend into the hill of the LORD? or who shall stand in his holy place? He that hath clean hands, and a pure heart; who hath not lifted up his soul unto vanity, nor sworn deceitfully. He shall receive the blessing from the LORD, and righteousness from the God of his salvation."

Only those who have clean hands and a pure heart will be able to stand in that day. The only way we may have a pure heart is through Christ, for "we are all as an unclean thing, and all our righteousnesses are as filthy rags."[32] But God made Christ to be "sin for us," so "that we might be made the righteousness of God in him."[33] If we try to stand in our own power, we will not be able to stand. Thus, we must stand in the power, strength and righteousness of God Almighty. Ask God to fill you with his power, to give you his strength and righteousness to be able to stand in that great day. The events unveiled in the book of Revelation tell us that that day is fast approaching. Through the acceptance of Christ's righteousness, we may be ready! Praise God. Amen.

---

[32] Isaiah 64:6

[33] 2 Corinthians 5:21

Revelation 7

SUMMARY:
The seventh chapter of Revelation introduces us to 144,000 servants of God who are to be sealed with the seal of God, at the very end of time, just prior to the second coming of Jesus.

Revelation 7:1 And after these things I saw four angels standing on the four corners of the earth, holding the four winds of the earth, that the wind should not blow on the earth, nor on the sea, nor on any tree.

Winds in Bible prophecy represent strife and trouble,[1] so these angels are holding back the strife and trouble from blowing on the earth until specific things can be accomplished. Revelation 7 is a parenthetical statement, most of which, falls chronologically between verse 13 and 14 of the previous chapter. Revelation 6:13 "And the stars of heaven fell unto the earth, even as a fig tree casteth her untimely figs, **when she is shaken of a mighty wind**." Notice that when the fig tree is shaken it casts her **untimely** figs. In other words, the figs are not yet ripe, but the wind blows which causes some figs to fall before they are ripe. Something must be done, for the fruit is not ready for harvest. For this reason, God sends a message to the four angels to hold back the winds of strife a little longer. Revelation 6:14 portrays the second coming of Jesus. In between these two verses, after the stars fall and before the Lord comes, God delays his coming, because his people are not yet ready. The four angels are portrayed as holding back the winds of strife, holding back the trouble that is to come upon the earth, until a certain work is accomplished. The work that must be accomplished is the sealing of the 144,000.

The release of the four winds signals the close of probation, which can occur only after God's people have been sealed. "I saw that the four angels would hold the four winds until Jesus' work was done in the sanctuary, and then will come the seven last plagues."[2]

---

[1] Daniel 7:2-3; Jeremiah 25:31-33

[2] E. G. White, *Early Writings* (1882), p. 36.2.

Revelation 7:2 And I saw another angel ascending from the east, having the seal of the living God: and he cried with a loud voice to the four angels, to whom it was given to hurt the earth and the sea,

Revelation 7:3 Saying, Hurt not the earth, neither the sea, nor the trees, till we have sealed the servants of our God in their foreheads.

"I saw four angels who had a work to do on the earth, and were on their way to accomplish it. Jesus was clothed with priestly garments. He gazed in pity on the remnant, then raised His hands, and with a voice of deep pity cried, *'My blood, Father, My blood, My blood, My blood!'* Then I saw an exceeding bright light come from God, who sat upon the great white throne, and was shed all about Jesus. Then I saw an angel with a commission from Jesus, swiftly flying to the four angels who had a work to do on the earth, and waving something up and down in his hand, and crying with a loud voice, *'Hold! Hold! Hold! Hold!* until the servants of God are sealed in their foreheads.'"[3]

These four angels were about to initiate the final plagues to fall on the earth. They had been given power from God to restrain the winds of strife and destruction, but now they had orders to let them go. As the four angels were releasing the winds, Christ, in his mercy, seeing that his remnant people were not ready for probation to close, pleads his blood with the Father. The Father agrees and the message is quickly sent to hold the winds once more until the servants of God are sealed with the seal of the living God.

As God's servants were unready to be sealed, the coming of Jesus was delayed. Scripture testifies that we have the privilege to hasten the coming of Jesus.[4] Therefore we also have the capacity of delaying it, by being unready.

God's people were not ready. The servants of God must be sealed in their foreheads, before the earth is hurt. Revelation 14 also brings to view the sealing: "And I looked, and, lo, a Lamb stood on the mount

---

[3] E. G. White, *Early Writings* (1882), p. 38.1.

[4] 2 Peter 3:11-12 "What manner of persons ought ye to be in all holy conversation and godliness, Looking for and hasting unto the coming of the day of God."

Sion, and with him an hundred forty and four thousand, having his Father's name written in their foreheads."[5]

Revelation 7 specifies that they are to be sealed in their foreheads. Revelation 14 tells us that the Father's name is to be written on their foreheads. This shows that the seal is the Father's name.

What constitutes the Father's name? Exodus 33:18, 19 tells part of the story of Moses going up the mountain to receive the Ten Commandments. While on the mountain Moses asks God to show him his glory: "And he said, 'I beseech thee, show me thy glory.' And he said, 'I will make all my goodness pass before thee, and I will proclaim the name of the LORD before thee; and will be gracious to whom I will be gracious, and will show mercy on whom I will show mercy.'" In response to Moses asking to see the glory of God, Moses is shown his goodness and God proclaims his name. Therefore, God's name is his goodness or the attributes of his character.

Exodus 34:6, 7, continues the story. "And the LORD passed by before him, and proclaimed, 'The LORD, The LORD God, merciful and gracious, longsuffering, and abundant in goodness and truth, Keeping mercy for thousands, forgiving iniquity and transgression and sin, and that will by no means clear the guilty; visiting the iniquity of the fathers upon the children, and upon the children's children, unto the third and to the fourth generation.'"

God's glory, his mercy, his graciousness, his long-suffering (or patience) and his abundance of goodness and truth are the attributes of God's character and constitute his name. In English we use such expressions for representing character. When we say that a certain person blackened our name, we mean that they defamed our character. In a similar manner God informs us that his name is his character.

From this we understand that his seal is not a visible mark; not some kind of a stamp or branding that all of a sudden appears on our foreheads, but it is the settling into the truth in our minds.[6] It is the

---

[5] Revelation 14:1

[6] "Just as soon as the people of God are sealed in their foreheads—it is not any seal or mark that can be seen, but a settling into the truth, both intellectually and spiritually, so they cannot be moved—just as soon as God's people are sealed and prepared for the shaking, it will come." E. G. White, *Last Day Events* (1992), p. 219.4.

reproduction of the character of God in our thoughts as revealed in our actions.

God's character has the same attributes as his law. Let us compare the attributes of God's character with those of his law:

God is:	The law is:
Holy - Leviticus 11:44	Holy - Romans 7:12
Truth - Deuteronomy 32:4	Truth - Psalms 119:142
Righteous - Ezra 9:15	Righteous - Deuteronomy 4:8
Just - Deuteronomy 32:4	Just - Romans 7:12
Good - Psalms 52:1	Good - Romans 7:12
Love - 1 John 4:8	Love - Romans 13:8, 10
Liberty - Isaiah 61:1	Liberty - James 2:12
Peace - Romans 15:33	Peace - Psalms 119:165

"Great peace have they which love thy law: and nothing shall offend them."[7] Each of the characteristics of God portrayed in the Bible are also applied to his law, which shows us that his law is a transcript of his character. Therefore, if his character is stamped in our foreheads, impressed upon our hearts and revealed in our lives, that means his law will be placed there also. "Bind up the testimony, **seal the law** among my disciples."[8] When God puts his name in our forehead, it means he puts his character there. Since his law is a transcript of that character, he therefore wants to put his law in our minds and write it in our hearts.[9] "He that hath received his testimony hath set to his seal that God is true."[10] We must receive the testimony of God. That testimony is his law, which is the seal that God is true.

God used the symbol of circumcision in the Old Testament to represent this. Paul, speaking of Abraham, tells us, "And he received the **sign of circumcision**, a **seal of the righteousness** of the faith which he had yet being uncircumcised: that he might be the father of all them that believe, though they be not circumcised; that righteousness might be imputed unto them also:"[11] In order for

---

[7] Psalm 119:165

[8] Isaiah 8:16

[9] Jeremiah 31:33

[10] John 3:33

[11] Romans 4:11

righteousness to be imputed unto them, God was going to give them a seal of righteousness. The seal of righteousness that God wanted to give them was symbolized by circumcision in the Old Testament. Eventually the Jewish nation lost sight of the meaning of circumcision, viewing it rather as a means of earning salvation. They performed the ceremony without a change of heart. God said that this was not what he had in mind. "For he is not a Jew, which is one outwardly; neither is that circumcision, which is outward in the flesh: But he is a Jew, which is one inwardly; and circumcision is that of the heart, in the spirit, and not in the letter; whose praise is not of men, but of God."[12] God never meant, in the Old Testament, for circumcision to be an outward symbol that could be done to earn salvation. What he intended was to actually change their hearts. He wanted to stamp his character in their minds, and impress his law in their hearts. He wanted to transform them into his likeness. Notice what the Old Testament Scriptures say regarding this: "Circumcise therefore the foreskin of your heart, and be no more stiffnecked."[13] Even in the Old Testament God wanted the change to affect their heart and mind. He wanted their character to be transformed into his likeness. This is why he wanted to put his law in their hearts and in their minds.

Revelation 9:4 says that certain punishments will be visited only on those who do not have the seal of God. "And it was commanded them that they should not hurt the grass of the earth, neither any green thing, neither any tree; but only those men which have not the seal of God in their foreheads." Some of the events that are coming upon the earth will affect only those who have not allowed God to transform their lives, their characters, and their minds, into the likeness of his character; to conform their motives, their actions, and their wills to the requirements of his law.

Ezekiel portrays a very similar picture, describing a sealing and what it constitutes: "And the LORD said unto him, Go through the midst of the city, through the midst of Jerusalem, and set a mark upon the foreheads of the men that sigh and that cry for all the abominations that be done in the midst thereof."[14] God will place his sign, mark, or

---

[12] Romans 2:28, 29

[13] Deuteronomy 10:16

[14] Ezekiel 9:4

seal, in the foreheads of those who are sighing and crying for the abominations that are done in his church. We will never feel the need to sigh and cry for the abominations that are done in God's church unless we have allowed God to transform our thoughts into his thoughts—to remake us with his divine character.

"Mark this point with care: Those who receive the pure mark of truth, wrought in them by the power of the Holy Ghost, represented by a mark by the man in linen, are those 'that sigh and that cry for all the abominations that be done' in the church.
"The class who do not feel grieved over their own spiritual declension, nor mourn over the sins of others, will be left without the seal of God....
"Not all who profess to keep the Sabbath will be sealed. There are many even among those who teach the truth to others who will not receive the seal of God in their foreheads. They had the light of truth, they knew their Master's will, they understood every point of our faith, but they had not corresponding works."[15]

Jesus said of the Pharisees, "Woe unto you, scribes and Pharisees, hypocrites! for ye are like unto whited sepulchers, which indeed appear beautiful outward, but are within full of dead men's bones, and of all uncleanness. Even so ye also outwardly appear righteous unto men, but within ye are full of hypocrisy and iniquity."[16] The Pharisees appeared to be righteous on the outside, but did they really keep God's law? Jesus said, "For I say unto you, That except your righteousness shall exceed the righteousness of the scribes and Pharisees, ye shall in no case enter into the kingdom of heaven."[17] And to the Pharisees he said, "none of you keepeth the law."[18] The unbelieving Jews never attained to the righteous requirements of the law, because they refused the only One who could make them righteous before God. The Bible says, "They being ignorant of God's righteousness, and going about to establish their own righteousness, have not submitted themselves unto the righteousness of God."[19]

---

[15] E. G. White, *Maranatha* (1976), p. 240.2-4.

[16] Matthew 23:27-28

[17] Matthew 5:20

[18] John 7:19

[19] Romans 10:3

Because our natures are fallen, we cannot make ourselves righteous. We cannot meet the righteous requirements of the law of God in human strength alone. Every action we do will be tainted with sin. We must give ourselves to Christ; we must be crucified with Christ. We cannot seek to establish our own righteousness, like the Jews did; the only thing we can do is to by faith surrender ourselves to the righteousness of God. It is then that Christ's character stands in the place of our character; his life becomes our own; and as a result we are like him in mind, in character and life.

"Jesus said, Be perfect as your Father is perfect. If you are the children of God you are partakers of His nature, and you cannot but be like Him. Every child lives by the life of his father. If you are God's children, begotten by His Spirit, you live by the life of God. In Christ dwells 'all the fullness of the Godhead bodily' (Colossians 2:9); and the life of Jesus is made manifest 'in our mortal flesh' (2 Corinthians 4:11). That life in you will produce the same character and manifest the same works as it did in Him. Thus you will be in harmony with every precept of His law; for 'the law of the Lord is perfect, restoring the soul.' Psalm 19:7, margin. Through love 'the righteousness of the law' will be 'fulfilled in us, who walk not after the flesh, but after the Spirit.' Romans 8:4." [20]

"We should study more earnestly the character of our Saviour. We should imitate the lovely Pattern that God has given us. We should dwell upon the matchless charms of Jesus until there will be nothing satisfying in this perishing world. We should desire to reflect his image in kindness, in courtesy, in gentleness, and love, then 'when he shall appear, we shall be like him; for we shall see him as he is. And every man that hath this hope in him purifieth himself, even as he is pure.' In a little while every one who is a child of God will have his seal placed upon him. O that it may be placed upon our foreheads! Who can endure the thought of being passed by when the angel goes forth to seal the servants of God in their foreheads?"[21]

When, by looking into the face of Jesus Christ, we are changed into the same image, by the working of the Spirit of God upon the soul,

---

[20] E. G. White, *Thoughts from the Mount of Blessings* (1896), p. 77.3.

[21] E. G. White, *Review & Herald,* May 28, 1889, par. 8.

443

then the same Spirit will affix there the seal of the living God[22]—the eternal impress of his own image.

Revelation 7:4 And I heard the number of them which were sealed—and they were sealed 144,000 of all the tribes of the children of Israel.

There will be 144,000 sealed of the tribes of Israel. This refers to spiritual Israel.[23]

"The language of the Bible should be explained according to its obvious meaning, unless a symbol or figure is employed."[24] Therefore the number of individuals that comprise this group are exactly 144,000, just as the Bible states. "Soon we heard the voice of God like many waters, which gave us the day and hour of Jesus' coming. The **living saints, 144,000 in number**, knew and understood the voice, while the wicked thought it was thunder and an earthquake."[25]

The 144,000 are the righteous who are still alive to see the Lord coming in the clouds of heaven. This may seem like a very few, but it is many more than Noah had in the ark. Noah had eight—the 144,000 constitute 18,000 times more. Lest you despair, these are not the only people who will be saved. Revelation 7:9 speaks of a "great multitude, which no man could number," in addition to the 144,000. The 144,000 are people—all in one generation—who actually allow themselves to be so imbued with the Spirit of God, so covered with his righteousness, so filled with his power, that they stand faultless before his throne, through an experience that none have gone through before. By the power of God, they stand without an intercessor in the heavenly sanctuary—and therefore with no provision for any additional sins—enduring the time of Jacob's trouble. God's purpose through this group is to give one final, ultimate demonstration that his people can overcome sin by dependence upon the power of God, just as Christ overcame.

---

[22] Ephesians 4:30

[23] See Daniel 4b for more detail on spiritual Israel.

[24] E. G. White, *The Great Controversy* (1911), p. 598.3.

[25] E. G. White, *Early Writings* (1882), p. 14.1.

"They sing 'a new song' before the throne, a song which no man can learn save the hundred and forty and four thousand. It is the song of Moses and the Lamb—a song of deliverance. None but the hundred and forty-four thousand can learn that song, for it is the song of their experience—an experience such as no other company has ever had. 'These are they which follow the Lamb whithersoever He goeth.' These, having been translated from the earth, from among the living, are counted as 'the first fruits unto God and to the Lamb' (Revelation 15:2, 3; 14:1-5.) 'These are they which came out of great tribulation'; they have passed through the time of trouble such as never was since there was a nation; they have endured the anguish of the time of Jacob's trouble; they have stood without an intercessor through the final outpouring of God's judgments."[26]

God intends to demonstrate to the entire universe that it is possible for us, as his people, to keep his law, through his power, just as Jesus was able to keep the law, through the power and strength of his Father. Although they have sinned in the past, they have been covered by Christ's robe of righteousness; and stand faultless before his throne. Jesus cannot close things off until this group is no longer sinning, because any sin that might be committed from the time that Jesus stops his intercession in the heavenly sanctuary, until his arrival on this earth, would have no more provision for forgiveness. "When the character of Christ shall be perfectly reproduced in His people, then He will come to claim them as His own."[27]

Some suppose that the purpose of the 144,000 is to deliver the loud cry. The individuals that will compose the 144,000 would certainly have participated in giving the loud cry (many others will participate in giving that final message[28]), but the loud cry occurs before the sealing of the 144,000.[29] Therefore the 144,000 do not yet exist, as a group, at the time of the loud cry. The loud cry is part of what fits them to be in that group, rather than the other way around. The

---

[26] E. G. White, *Last Day Events* (1992), p. 268.4.

[27] E. G. White, *Christ's Object Lessons* (1900), p. 69.1.

[28] There may be many of God's people who take part in at least a portion of the loud cry, who will not be a part of the 144,000. Perhaps they give their lives for the sake of the gospel. Perhaps they die in the judgments that come on the earth, or perhaps, the Lord allows them to go to sleep because he knows that they would not be able to make it through the last final hours of earth's history.

[29] See E. G. White, *The Great Controversy* (1911), p. 613.2. The third angel's message is the same as the "loud cry."

mission of this special group is to stand through the final judgments without an intercessor. The 144,000 will be those who are translated without seeing death as Enoch and Elijah.

Revelation 7:5 Of the tribe of Juda were sealed twelve thousand. Of the tribe of Reuben were sealed twelve thousand. Of the tribe of Gad were sealed twelve thousand.

Revelation 7:6 Of the tribe of Aser were sealed twelve thousand. Of the tribe of Nephthalim were sealed twelve thousand. Of the tribe of Manasses were sealed twelve thousand.

Revelation 7:7 Of the tribe of Simeon were sealed twelve thousand. Of the tribe of Levi were sealed twelve thousand. Of the tribe of Issachar were sealed twelve thousand.

Revelation 7:8 Of the tribe of Zabulon were sealed twelve thousand. Of the tribe of Joseph were sealed twelve thousand. Of the tribe of Benjamin were sealed twelve thousand.

This specification of the twelve tribes is further evidence that this passage refers to spiritual Israel, by the fact that today you could not find 12,000 people from each one of the literal tribes of Israel, as most of them no longer exist.

Revelation 7:9 After this I beheld, and, lo, a great multitude, which no man could number, of all nations, and kindreds, and people, and tongues, stood before the throne, and before the Lamb, clothed with white robes, and palms in their hands;

Note well that it is not only the 144,000 in heaven—those that do not see death—but also a great multitude of the redeemed, that no man could number. We can trust God with knowing whether or not we can be among that 144,000, or whether he might lay us to rest, knowing that it would be too much for us to pass through that time of trouble. However, "Let us strive with all the power that God has given us to be among the hundred and forty-four thousand."[30]

---

[30] See E. G. White, *Review & Herald,* March 9, 1905 par. 4.

Revelation 7:10 And cried with a loud voice, saying, Salvation to our God which sitteth upon the throne, and unto the Lamb.

Revelation 7:11 And all the angels stood round about the throne, and about the elders and the four beasts, and fell before the throne on their faces, and worshipped God,

Revelation 7:12 Saying, Amen: Blessing, and glory, and wisdom, and thanksgiving, and honour, and power, and might, be unto our God for ever and ever. Amen.

Seven things are mentioned which the four creatures and the elders give to God in worship: blessing, glory, wisdom, thanksgiving, honor, power, and might.

Revelation 7:13 And one of the elders answered, saying unto me, What are these which are arrayed in white robes? and whence came they?

Revelation 7:14 And I said unto him, Sir, thou knowest. And he said to me, These are they which came out of great tribulation, and have washed their robes, and made them white in the blood of the Lamb.

The righteousness of God's people comes from the fact that they have washed away their sins in the blood of the Lamb. This is the message of the whole Bible and this is the message of Revelation: Jesus, the Lamb, died for our sins, that he might give us the gift of eternal life.

Revelation 7:15 Therefore are they before the throne of God, and serve him day and night in his temple: and he that sitteth on the throne shall dwell among them.

Revelation 7:16 They shall hunger no more, neither thirst any more; neither shall the sun light on them, nor any heat.

Revelation 7:17 For the Lamb which is in the midst of the throne shall feed them, and shall lead them unto living fountains of waters: and God shall wipe away all tears from their eyes.

The message of the Book of Revelation is the restoration of the sinner to the throne room of God, restoration to a face-to-face relationship with the king of the universe, where God will dwell with us, and be our God, and we shall be his people. "For now we see through a glass, darkly; but then face to face..."[31] God longs to put an end to sin and suffering, and that is the Revelation of Jesus Christ. Amen.

---

[31] 1 Corinthians 13:12

Revelation 8

SUMMARY:
The eighth chapter of Revelation introduces seven trumpets which span both chapters eight and nine. The sounding of the seven trumpets announce successive disasters to afflict the planet.

Additionally, in Revelation 6 the seven seals were being opened, yet the seventh seal was missing. Chapter seven contained the parenthetical statement describing the sealing of the 144,000, then the seventh seal finally appears here in Revelation 8:1.

Revelation 8:1 And when he had opened the seventh seal, there was silence in heaven about the space of half an hour.

When the seventh seal is opened, heaven is strangely silent for a half hour. Using symbolic prophetic time in which a day represents a year,[1] we could say that an hour is 1/24 of a day and therefore represents 1/24 of a year. If we divide a Biblical year which is 360 days by 24, we find that an hour would represent 15 days. Therefore, a half hour of silence would be seven and a half days in length. "The length of this period of silence, if we consider it prophetic time, would be about seven days."[2] What could possibly cause silence in heaven for any period of time? The Bible tells us in Revelation 4:8 that the seraphim "rest not day and night, saying, Holy, holy, holy, Lord God Almighty, which was, and is, and is to come." So, there is always praise ascending to God in heaven. This would clearly make a sound, therefore the only thing that could cause silence in heaven is for heaven to be empty.[3] Everyone in heaven is on their way to this earth to rescue human beings! None of the beings who live there would miss it for anything. This is the event of all ages; the moment heaven has been longing for since sin entered the universe. Imagine

---

[1] Ezekiel 4:6; Numbers 14:34; See also Daniel 7-8.

[2] Uriah Smith, *Daniel and the Revelation* (Nashville, TN: Southern Publishing Association, 1897), p. 476.1.

[3] "Jesus is coming... in the glory of the Father, and with all the retinue of holy angels with Him, to escort Him on His way to earth. **All heaven will be emptied of the angels**." E. G. White, *Sons and Daughters of God* (1955), p. 360.2.

heaven entirely empty. They are all on their way to get us! This shows how intensely interested all of heaven is in our salvation. Before Jesus opens to us the great last scenes of earth's history and the deceptions of Satan, he gives us the assurance that the entire universe is deeply interested in our complete salvation from sin.

Seven and a half days of silence in heaven implies half a day for the angels and the retinue of heavenly beings that attend Jesus to approach this earth—at which time we are taken up into the clouds—and seven days for return travel to heaven. What an amazing journey that will be.

"We all entered the cloud together, and were seven days ascending to the sea of glass, when Jesus brought the crowns, and with His own right hand placed them on our heads. He gave us harps of gold and palms of victory."[4]

Revelation 8:2 And I saw the seven angels which stood before God; and to them were given seven trumpets.

After the vision of the seven seals, John beholds seven angels who are presented with seven trumpets, and another angel ministering with the golden censer.

Revelation 8:3 And another angel came and stood at the altar, having a golden censer; and there was given unto him much incense, that he should offer it with the prayers of all saints upon the golden altar which was before the throne.

The golden altar is before the veil that separates the holy from the most holy place. On the other side of the veil is the ark of the covenant, or mercy seat, representing the throne of God. This angel is carrying a golden censer for which much incense is given him, to burn in the censer, and on the golden altar.

---

[4] E. G. White, *Early Writings* (1882), p. 16.2.

If we review the earthly sanctuary and its services in the wilderness,[5] we recognize this as sanctuary language for in the sanctuary service there was just one day per year when someone would take a golden censer and also have much incense. Every day of the year, except one, the priest would offer a pinch of incense on that golden altar. But, on that exceptional day, called the Day of Atonement,[6] the high priest, with his hands full of incense to burn on the altar and in the golden censer, would enter the most holy place to cleanse it from sin.[7] This would create so much smoke as to partially obscure the ark of the covenant "that he die not."[8]

Therefore this angel, having the golden censer and much incense, is the high priest, which Scripture says is Jesus himself.[9] Jesus is portrayed here as about to go into the most holy place to begin the process of cleansing the heavenly sanctuary on the anti-typical Day of Atonement.[10] In Daniel 10, 12 and Revelation 4 we have discussed several different instances where the Bible calls Jesus, or God, an angel. This does not imply that Jesus is a created being. Jesus is fully divine. However, the word angel does not demand that it be limited to a created being; rather it simply means messenger.

---

[5] See Daniel 9 for more detail on the sanctuary and its services.

[6] See Daniel 8 and 9 for more detail about the day of atonement.

[7] Hebrews 9:23 "It was therefore necessary that the patterns of things in the heavens should be purified with these; but the heavenly things themselves with better sacrifices than these.
"For Christ is not entered into the holy places made with hands, which are the figures of the true; but into heaven itself, now to appear in the presence of God for us."

[8] Leviticus 16:11-14 "and Aaron the high priest shall bring the bullock of the sin offering, which is for himself, and shall make an atonement for himself, and for his house, and shall kill the bullock of the sin offering, which is for himself. And he shall take a censer full of burning coals of fire from off the altar before the Lord, and his hands full of sweet incense beaten small, and bring it within the veil."

[9] Hebrews 4:14-15 "Seeing then that we have a great high priest, that is passed into the heavens, Jesus the Son of God, let us hold fast our profession.
"For we have not an high priest which cannot be touched with the feeling of our infirmities; but was in all points tempted like as we are, yet without sin."

[10] The anti-typical day of atonement, as we saw in Daniel 8 and 9, began in 1844. Thus Jesus is pictured here in Revelation 8:3 as just about to begin that process.
"Let those who would meet the divine standard, search the Scriptures for themselves.... **Let them behold him as their Advocate, standing within the veil, having in his hand the golden censer, from which the holy incense of the merits of his righteousness ascends to God in behalf of those who pray to him.** Could they thus behold him, they would feel an assurance that they have a powerful, influential Advocate in the heavenly courts, and that their suit is gained at the throne of God. What an experience may be attained at the footstool of mercy, which is the only place of sure refuge!"
E. G. White, "Wise or Foolish, Which?," *Youth Instructor*, January 16, 1896 par. 4.

Jesus was certainly a messenger; this is why he is called the archangel, or messenger above all messengers.

Revelation 8:4 And the smoke of the incense, which came with the prayers of the saints, ascended up before God out of the angel's hand.

The smoke is ascending with the prayers of the saints; therefore, the smoke is not the prayers of the saints. The prayers of the saints are indeed there, but the smoke is ascending with those prayers. The prayers of the saints, in Revelation 5:8, are represented by sweet odors in golden vials, but the smoke itself represents something infinitely greater[11]: "Could they look into the censer of the angel that stands at the golden altar before the rainbow-encircled throne, they would see that the merit of Jesus must be mingled with our prayers and efforts, or they are as worthless as was the offering of Cain. Could we see all the activity of human instrumentality as it appears before God, we would see that only the work accomplished by much prayer, which is sanctified by the merit of Christ, will stand the test of judgment.[12]" The smoke of the incense is the righteousness or merit of Christ, which must be mingled with our prayers in order to make them acceptable before the throne of God. This is a solemn thought. Prayers that are not mingled with his righteousness are as worthless as the offering of Cain. We need to make sure that we ask God to make our prayers acceptable in his sight, by his righteousness, before the throne of God.

Revelation 8:5 And the angel took the censer, and filled it with fire of the altar, and cast it into the earth: and there were voices, and thunderings, and lightnings, and an earthquake.

Whereas in verse three we read of Jesus about to enter the most holy, with the golden censer and his hands full of incense, indicating the beginning of the process of cleansing the heavenly sanctuary,

---

[11] "The golden censer is waved, and **the incense, the representation of the purity and righteousness of Christ**, ascends, bearing the prayers of every soul that receives and believes on Christ to the altar which is before the throne of God."
E. G. White, *Manuscript Releases,* Vol. 12 (1990), p. 415.3.

[12] E. G. White, *Christian Service* (1923), p. 263.2.

this verse is portraying the closing scenes of that cleansing. Jesus has finished his ministration in the heavenly most holy, the smoke has covered the mercy seat, and now he is about to exit. This verse is a picture of the censer being thrown to the earth, **"and there were voices, and thunderings, and lightnings, and an earthquake,"** indicating the close of the investigative judgment. "I saw angels hurrying to and fro in heaven. An angel with a writer's inkhorn by his side returned from the earth and reported to Jesus that his work was done, and the saints were numbered and sealed. Then I saw Jesus, who had been ministering before the ark containing the ten commandments, throw down the censer. He raised His hands, and with a loud voice said, 'It is done.' And all the angelic host laid off their crowns as Jesus made the solemn declaration, 'He that is unjust, let him be unjust still: and he which is filthy, let him be filthy still: and he that is righteous, let him be righteous still: and he that is holy, let him be holy still.'"[13]

At the declaration that everyone who is holy will remain holy and everyone who is unholy, will remain such, "the destiny of all will have been decided for life or death."[14] This pronouncement is not an arbitrary decree on God's part—every person on the planet has made their final decision for or against God, and there is no point in the great controversy continuing any longer. Therefore, Jesus can say, "it is done." This act and pronouncement signals the close of probation.

Revelation 8:2-5 is therefore a summary of the investigative judgment, or anti-typical day of atonement, from its commencement in 1844, to its conclusion at the close of probation. This summary provides the context for the sounding of the seven trumpets.

Revelation 8:6 And the seven angels which had the seven trumpets prepared themselves to sound.

---

[13] E. G. White, *Early Writings* (1882), p. 279.2.

[14] "When the work of the investigative judgment closes, the destiny of all will have been decided for life or death. Probation is ended a short time before the appearing of the Lord in the clouds of heaven."
E. G. White, *The Great Controversy* (1911), p. 490.2.

Trumpets in Scripture are frequently used as a means of delivering a message of warning, or to announce a coming king.[15] The Feast of Trumpets came ten days before the Day of Atonement, warning of the coming judgment.

The trumpets of Revelation 8 announce the imminent termination of the investigative judgment, the impending judgments of the seven last plagues, and the soon return of the King of Glory. "The time of God's destructive judgments is the time of mercy for those who have had no opportunity to learn what is truth. Tenderly will the Lord look upon them. His heart of mercy is touched; His hand is still stretched out to save, while the door is closed to those who would not enter."[16] "Those who choose to remain disloyal must be visited in mercy with judgments, in order that, if possible, they may be aroused to a realization of the sinfulness of their course."[17]

Scripture places the primary application of the seven trumpets in the future, as evidenced by the text of Revelation 8 and 9 itself:[18] first, the introduction of the trumpets immediately follows the summary of the investigative judgment, which provides the context for their

---

[15] See Ezekiel 33:2-6, Numbers 10:9, Joshua 6, Judges 7, 2 Chronicles 13:12, 1 Kings 1:39, 2 Kings 9:13, 2 Kings 11, etc.

[16] E. G. White, *Testimonies for the Church*, Vol. 9 (1909), p. 97.2.

[17] *Ibid.*, p. 93.3.

[18] The trumpets are also considered to have had an historical application, in which the wording is taken to be symbolic. The symbols predicted events that happened in the past from our day. Although the spirit of prophecy does not define what each one of the trumpets symbolized historically, the sixth is mentioned as a dramatic fulfillment of prophecy—see E. G. White, *The Great Controversy* (1911), p. 334.4-335.1.

A brief outline of the historical fulfillment of the seven trumpets are as follows:
1. The invasion of Alaric, king of the Goths, AD 410.
2. The invasion of Attila the Hun, AD 447.
3. The sack of Rome by Genseric, king of the Vandals, AD 455.
4. The final conquest of Rome, by Odoacer, king of the Heruli, who assumed the title of King of Italy, AD 476.
5. Chosroes (the fallen star) and Mohammed (the smoke from the bottomless pit). The 150 days represented 150 years: 'The first assault of Othman upon the Eastern Empire took place on the 27th day of July, 1299. Commencing the five months' torment from this event, they would end 150 years later, in 1449. As we inquire for the events which mark the termination of that period, we are brought to the sounding of the next trumpet.' Uriah Smith, *The Biblical Institute*, p. 264.1.
6. The reign and fall of the Turks on August 11, 1840.
Source Book for Bible Students, p. 499.5-518.1.

sounding;[19] second, the fifth trumpet falls only upon "those men which have not the seal of God in their foreheads,"[20] (the placement of the seal of God in the foreheads of his people is an event yet future); third, the sixth trumpet is the release of the four angels holding the four winds,[21] which, according to Revelation 7:4 cannot be executed until the 144,000 are sealed. Taking this passage as it reads demands a future primary application. "In the Scriptures are presented truths that relate especially to our own time. To the period just prior to the appearing of the Son of man, the prophecies of Scripture point, and here their warnings and threatenings **pre-eminently** apply."[22]

The Testimony of Jesus explicitly places the sounding of the trumpets in the future: "Solemn events before us are yet to transpire. Trumpet after trumpet is to be sounded. Vial[23] after vial poured out one after another upon the inhabitants of the Earth."[24] In a description of a ride in a horse-drawn carriage through a terrific hailstorm, in which the hailstones were as big around as a hen's egg, but not as long, Ellen White's mind turned to the judgments of the last day: "I thought of the day when the judgment of God would be poured out upon the world, when blackness and horrible darkness would clothe the heavens as sackcloth of hair.... My imagination anticipated what it must be in that period when the Lord's mighty voice shall give commission to His angels, '**Go your ways, and pour out the vials of the wrath of God upon the earth**' (Revelation 16:1).... Terrible are the judgments of God revealed. **The seven angels stood before God to receive their commission. To them were given seven trumpets.** The Lord was going forth to punish the inhabitants of the earth for their iniquity, and the earth was to disclose her blood and no more cover her slain.... When the plagues of God shall come upon the earth, hail will fall upon the wicked about

---

[19] This does not mean that all seven trumpets occur chronologically following the final pronouncement of destinies at the casting down of the censer in verse 5. The trumpets themselves define when probation closes, as will be seen in subsequent verses.

[20] Revelation 9:4

[21] Revelation 9:13-14

[22] E. G. White, "The Bible a Means of Both Mental and Moral Culture," *The Review and Herald*, September 25, 1883 par. 6.

[23] The vials are the seven last plagues. See Revelation 16.

[24] E. G. White, *Last Day Events* (1992), p. 238.

the weight of a talent."[25] Again the seven trumpets are associated with the seven vials as future, end-time, judgments.

Revelation 8:7 The first angel sounded, and there followed hail and fire mingled with blood, and they were cast upon the earth: and the third part of trees was burnt up, and all green grass was burnt up.

The first four trumpets are warning plagues while probation still lingers. God provides one last opportunity for sinners to repent and be saved from the seven last plagues. The first four trumpets are separated from the last three in that the last three are called woes, indicating that they are much worse than the first four. The first four are limited in scope, affecting just one third of the earth, showing that they are still tempered with mercy. Regardless, they are the worst disasters ever witnessed this side of the flood. During the sound of the first trumpet, hail and fire mingled with blood[26] are cast upon the earth. The resulting fires destroy a third of the world's trees and all the green grass. "The language of the Bible should be explained according to its obvious meaning, unless a symbol or figure is employed,"[27] "If men would but take the Bible as it reads, if there were no false teachers to mislead and confuse their minds, a work would be accomplished that would make angels glad and that would bring into the fold of Christ thousands upon thousands who are now wandering in error."[28]

"Last Friday morning, just before I awoke, a very impressive scene was presented before me. I seemed to awake from sleep but was not in my home. From the windows I could behold a terrible

---

[25] A talent weighs more than 60 pounds.
E. G. White, *Manuscript Releases*, Vol. 15 (1990), p. 219.1.

[26] Scripture frequently uses metaphoric language when describing literal events, for example: Acts 2:20 states, "The sun shall be turned into darkness, and the moon into blood." This was fulfilled on May 19, 1780, when the sun was darkened and the moon unexplainably turned blood red. Taking the language literally does not necessitate an over-literalization of the metaphor—such as insisting that the moon would be converted into a blob of biological blood, rather than turning blood red in color. In the same way, the fire mingled with blood in verse seven is fire mixed with brimstone that is blood-red in color, rather than biological blood. Also, when the sea becomes blood in verse eight, it becomes the color of blood.

[27] E. G. White, *The Great Controversy* (1911), p. 598.3.

[28] *Ibid.*

conflagration. Great balls of fire were falling upon houses, and from these balls fiery arrows were flying in every direction. It was impossible to check the fires that were kindled, and many places were being destroyed. The terror of the people was indescribable. After a time I awoke and found myself at home."[29]

"When I was at Nashville, I had been speaking to the people, and in the night season in a dream, there was an immense ball of fire that came right from heaven and settled in Nashville. There were flames going out like arrows from that ball; houses were being consumed; houses were tottering and falling. Some of our people were standing there. 'It is just as we expected,' they said, 'we expected this.' Others were wringing their hands in agony and crying unto God for mercy. 'You knew it,' said they, 'you knew that this was coming, and never said a word to warn us!' They seemed as though they would almost tear them to pieces, to think they had never told them or given them any warning at all.... A few nights ago I was awakened with this, 'They know not the time of their visitation.' Why don't they know it? Because nobody is there to tell them"[30]

The raining of balls of fire from heaven in the future would not be without precedent for God's punishment of wickedness—Sodom and Gomorrah were destroyed by fire and brimstone: "As the sun rose for the last time upon the cities of the plain, the people thought to begin another day of godless riot. All were eagerly planning their business or their pleasure, and the messenger of God was derided for his fears and his warnings. Suddenly as a peal of thunder from an unclouded sky fell balls of fire on the doomed capital."[31]

Small meteorites would certainly fit the descriptions of "balls of fire" and **"fire mingled with blood"** being cast on the earth.

Revelation 8:8 And the second angel sounded, and as it were a great mountain burning with fire was cast into the sea: and the third part of the sea became blood;

[29] E. G. White, *Last Day Events* (1992), p. 24.3.

[30] E. G. White, *Manuscript 188, 1905*, par. 13.

[31] E. G. White, "The Blessed Hope," *The Review and Herald*, November 13, 1913 par. 6.

An asteroid (or meteoroid for smaller pieces) is a chunk of rock, nickel, or iron debris orbiting the sun which, if it collided with Earth, would burn with fire from the friction of falling through our atmosphere. An asteroid becomes a meteor if it enters our atmosphere, which we then call a "shooting star." A meteorite is a meteor that survives passage through our atmosphere to impact the planet. Scientists, studying these celestial bodies through computer analysis, have projected models of what could happen to our planet if it were struck with an asteroid or large meteorite. "Projecting what would happen if an asteroid struck Earth has occupied a number of researchers since 1980.... Computer scenarios tracking the short- and long-term events associated with such a calamity recall Biblical tales of fire, flood and famine. One version... considers the slamming of a six-mile-wide meteorite into the ocean. The energy of the impact—equivalent to the explosion of five billion atomic bombs— would transform cool, blue Earth into a flaming crucible. When the smoke cleared, a transmuted planet would emerge: a hobbled and barren world, reeling toward some new destiny."[32]

"'Earth runs its course about the sun in a swarm of asteroids,' says astronomer Donald Yeomans of NASA's Jet Propulsion Laboratory in Pasadena, Calif. 'Sooner or later, our planet will be struck by one of them.'"[33]

"Diving toward the ocean at 55,000 miles per hour—seventy times the speed of sound—the massive object [an asteroid/meteorite six miles across] would blast the air aside, heating the surrounding atmosphere to about 50,000 degrees Fahrenheit. Air molecules, stripped of their electrons by the extreme temperature, would cloak the meteorite in a blazing envelope of visible, ultraviolet, and infrared radiation. Out of this incandescence, a reddish brown smog would materialize: Ionized oxygen and nitrogen would react to form acrid-smelling nitrogen oxide compounds—the progenitors of acid rain. All of this would happen in a fraction of a second."[34]

As the second angel sounds a great mountain is thrown into the sea, causing it to become blood-red.

---

[32] Time Life Education, *Comets, Asteroids and Meteorites*, p. 121.

[33] Sharon Begley, "The Science of Doom, *Newsweek*, November 23, 1992, pp. 56, 57. http://www.newsweek.com/science-doom-196978, retrieved 11-19-16.

[34] Time Life Education, *Comets, Asteroids and Meteorites*, p. 125.

According to *National Geographic* an asteroid impact would cause a red tide: "The splash of the extraterrestrial impact," would "bring up anoxic water from depth." "The seas would have looked like the aftermath of a global red tide—dead animals floating everywhere."[35] As a result, most of the world's fish would perish. Speaking of a six-mile asteroid thought to have hit the planet in the past: "As much as 90 percent of the world's forests must have burned." "The fireball must have had a radius of several thousand kilometers. Winds of hundreds of kilometers an hour would have swept the planet for hours, drying trees like a giant hair dryer. Two-thousand-degree rock vapor would have spread rapidly. It would have condensed to white-hot grains that could have started additional fires. In addition, lightning discharges like those in a volcanic eruption could have ignited windswept fires on all landmasses."[36]

"When the monster made contact with the ocean bed, 100 million megatons of energy would be released, eventually shaking the entire planet... In the passage of only three minutes, an expanding fireball of steam and molten ejecta would level any city within a distance of 1,200 miles and scour the terrain down to bedrock."[37]

The Bible does not tell us the size of the mountain that God will throw into the sea. If the assessment of these scientists is correct, then the asteroid of the second trumpet will be significantly smaller than six miles in diameter, as its effect is limited to one third of the planet.

Revelation 8:9 And the third part of the creatures which were in the sea, and had life, died; and the third part of the ships were destroyed.

Scientists say that if an asteroid or comet six miles in diameter "hit in the Gulf of Mexico, it would have created a wave three miles high. Nine hundred miles away, the mammoth wall of water would still be

[35] Rick Gore, "Extinctions," *National Geographic*, June 1989, p. 681.

[36] Rick Gore, "Extinctions," *National Geographic*, June 1989, p. 673.

[37] Time Life Education, *Comets, Asteroids and Meteorites*, p. 127.

1,500 feet high. Such an asteroid landing in the Gulf of Mexico would cause floods in Kansas City."[38]

Speaking of an asteroid only about a quarter mile in diameter, Time Life's *Comets, Asteroids and Meteorites*, states, "Its collision with Earth would have been catastrophic, if not apocalyptic. At sea it might have raised tsunamis hundreds of feet high that would have obliterated the coastal areas they washed over."[39]

These events are to occur on earth as God's final, merciful effort to waken the world to the fact that there is a God in heaven and his mercy has almost reached its limit. Perhaps yet a few more will avail themselves of his sacrifice before it is too late.

Revelation 8:10 And the third angel sounded, and there fell a great star from heaven, burning as it were a lamp, and it fell upon the third part of the rivers, and upon the fountains of waters;

Revelation 8:11 And the name of the star is called Wormwood: and the third part of the waters became wormwood; and many men died of the waters, because they were made bitter.

This star falls from heaven, and affects a third part of the fresh water. We have just seen in the previous trumpet the destruction of a third of the saltwater habitats, and now this plague affects the drinking water.

The star is called Wormwood, which means bitter. Such an impact as described under the second trumpet would eventually cause the very conditions the Bible describes for the third trumpet. "From the globe-girdling miasma, a deadly rain would begin to fall: The cloud's burden of vapor would gradually condense out, mixing with nitric oxide to form precipitation as corrosive as battery acid. The toxic rainfall would defoliate any remaining land plants, acidify lakes, and leach normally insoluble, highly poisonous metals from soils and

---

[38] Sharon Begley, "The Science of Doom, *Newsweek*, November 23, 1992, pp. 60. http://www.newsweek.com/science-doom-196978, retrieved 11-19-16.

[39] Time Life Education, *Comets, Asteroids and Meteorites*, p. 52.

rocks, depositing them in streams, ponds, and rivers, where they would sicken or kill much of the surviving aquatic life."[40]

Revelation 8:12 And the fourth angel sounded, and the third part of the sun was smitten, and the third part of the moon, and the third part of the stars; so as the third part of them was darkened, and the day shone not for a third part of it, and the night likewise.

Smoke from the fires of the first trumpets would certainly contribute to the fulfillment of the fourth trumpet. An asteroid or meteorite impact would also create the conditions described for the sounding of the fourth trumpet. "Trillions of tons of microfine rock particles and condensed vapor droplets thrown up by the asteroid impact would soar spaceward, reaching stratospheric heights within seconds.... Soot from the fires mixed with nitrogen oxide smog produced by the initial and subsequent shock waves would combine with the rapidly spreading dust to form a shroud seventeen miles thick. It would envelop the entire planet within twenty-four hours... the surface of the earth would be locked away in a blackness thirty times more inky than the darkest moonless night."[41]

Verse seven informed us that a third of the trees of the world are to burn. Can you imagine what would happen if a third of the trees on the planet burned? What kind of habitat destruction would that be? What would that mean to the world's food supplies? What would that do to the atmosphere from the smoke? The third part of the day would certainly be darkened as a result of this smoke. These plagues are falling on the planet in God's last attempt to try to turn anyone yet wavering to a knowledge of him.

Revelation 8:13 And I beheld, and heard an angel flying through the midst of heaven, saying with a loud voice, Woe, woe, woe, to the inhabiters of the earth by reason of the other voices of the trumpet of the three angels, which are yet to sound!

---

[40] Time Life Education, *Comets, Asteroids and Meteorites*, p. 133.

[41] Time Life Education, *Comets, Asteroids and Meteorites*, p. 131.

This is a very solemn pronouncement. The first four trumpets were mingled with mercy to wake people up, but woe, woe, woe to the inhabiters of the earth for the next three trumpets yet to come. Amen.

Revelation 9

SUMMARY:
The seven trumpets span both Revelation 8 and 9. The ninth chapter of Revelation brings to view the fifth and sixth trumpets, which are the first and second woes.

Revelation 9:1 And the fifth angel sounded, and I saw a star fall from heaven unto the earth: and to him was given the key of the bottomless pit.

"The language of the Bible should be explained according to its obvious meaning, unless a symbol or figure is employed."[1]

When the fifth angel sounds, Scripture employs the figure of a star, falling from heaven, to describe an intelligent being. That this star is an intelligent being is evident from the fact that he is "**given the key of the bottomless pit.**" Angels are at times referred to as stars.[2] In fact, Revelation 9:11 demonstrates that this star is an angel by calling him "the angel of the bottomless pit." As with all Biblical symbolism, the identity of this angel, and what is represented by the key to the bottomless pit, is revealed in Scripture.

Jesus said, "I beheld Satan as lightning fall from heaven."[3] Christ represents the fall of Lucifer, at his expulsion from the courts of paradise, as lightning falling from heaven. Therefore, the star falling from heaven to earth is Satan himself. In fact, the angel of the bottomless pit is given the Hebrew name Abaddon, and the Greek name Apollyon[4]—both names meaning the destroyer.

---

[1] E. G. White, *The Great Controversy* (1911), p. 598.3.

[2] This is evident in the parallel passage in Revelation 12:4, and 12:9.

[3] Luke 10:18

[4] Revelation 9:11

Additional evidence for this star representing Satan is found in the meaning of the bottomless pit:[5] Revelation 20 predicts a time when Satan will be restricted to the bottomless pit for one thousand years. "That the expression 'bottomless pit' represents the earth in a state of confusion and darkness is evident from other scriptures."[6] Another example of the bottomless pit being associated with Satan occurs in Revelation 11:7 when Satan, through "the beast that ascendeth out of the bottomless pit," makes war on God's two witnesses. "Here is brought to view a new manifestation of satanic power."[7]

Before Satan is confined to the bottomless pit during the millennium, Revelation 9 is revealing that Satan will be given the key to the bottomless pit, designating that he and his angels will be temporarily released from the restrictions under which God has placed them in relation to human beings. Rather than describing a physical place, the bottomless pit is symbolic of the restrictions God has placed on Satan's ability to coerce, and on his freedom to appear unveiled to human beings. This is the first woe. "Woe to the inhabiters of the earth and of the sea! for the devil is come down unto you, having great wrath, because he knoweth that he hath but a short time."[8]

Revelation 9:2 And he opened the bottomless pit; and there arose a smoke out of the pit, as the smoke of a great furnace; and the sun and the air were darkened by reason of the smoke of the pit.

Revelation 9:3 And there came out of the smoke locusts upon the earth: and unto them was given power, as the scorpions of the earth have power.

Revelation 9:4 And it was commanded them that they should not hurt the grass of the earth, neither any green thing, neither

---

[5] Although speaking of a different subject (mesmerism), the following statement helps us to define the bottomless pit. Mesmerism is defined as being "from the devil, from the bottomless pit." Therefore, the two terms are synonymous. From "the bottomless pit" is the same as having Satanic origin.
"The Lord had shown me in vision that mesmerism was from the devil, from the bottomless pit."
E. G. White, *Early Writings* (1882), p. 21.2.

[6] E. G. White, *The Great Controversy* (1911), p. 658.3.

[7] *Ibid.*, p.268.3.

[8] Revelation 12:12

any tree; but only those men which have not the seal of God in their foreheads.

Verse four shows clearly that by the fifth trumpet the people of God have been sealed. All but those sealed with the seal of God will have the mark of the beast.[9] Satan and his angels will be unable to torment those who have the seal of God. They will be able to torment only those who have consciously chosen Satan as their leader—those with the mark of the beast. "When God's restraining hand is removed, the destroyer begins his work. Then in our cities the greatest calamities will come."[10]

Revelation 9:5 And to them it was given that they should not kill them, but that they should be tormented five months: and their torment was as the torment of a scorpion, when he striketh a man.

Satan will be given permission (the key) to unleash his demons on planet earth in a way that has never before occurred. Christ himself tells us that these scorpion-like creatures (see also verse 10), ascending from the bottomless pit, are in fact demons. When Jesus sent forth the seventy disciples to spread the gospel, they returned rejoicing, saying, "Lord, even the devils are subject unto us through thy name. And he said unto them, I beheld Satan as lightning fall from heaven. Behold, I give unto you power to tread on serpents and scorpions, and over all the power of the enemy: and nothing shall by any means hurt you. Notwithstanding in this rejoice not, that the spirits are subject unto you; but rather rejoice, because your names are written in heaven."[11] By saying that he gave the disciples power to tread on serpents and scorpions, Jesus was not telling them to handle poisonous snakes in their worship services, as some churches do today; nor was he telling them they could never be stung by the tail of a stinging arachnid; rather he was giving them power over the enemy—Satan and his angels. Thus, Jesus himself refers to Satan's angels as scorpions and to Satan as the serpent.[12]

---

[9] Revelation 13:8, 16

[10] E. G. White, *Last Day Events* (1992), p. 111.1.

[11] Luke 10:17-20

[12] Revelation 12:9

This passage reveals the period of time during which demons will be able to interact freely on a visible, audible, and tangible basis with men—at least with those men who do not have the seal of God. Though the destinies of all intelligent beings on earth have been fixed with the implementation of the mark of the beast and the seal of God, the process of the close of probation is not finished until it is shown that none will change their position. God must demonstrate to the universe that the proclamation of final destinies was not an arbitrary decision on his part, but rather the result of each individual's free choice. God values our freedom more than he values our salvation. He will not resort to coercion. The trumpets accomplish two things:

1. Demonstrate that the final pronouncement of destinies was not arbitrary and,
2. Allow the universe to see fully the style of government of the being that the wicked have voted to be their god.

"Study Revelation in connection with Daniel, for history will be repeated…. We, with all our religious advantages, ought to know far more today than we do know."[13]

Revelation 9:6 And in those days shall men seek death, and shall not find it; and shall desire to die, and death shall flee from them.

God does not yet allow the demons to bring further destruction on the planet, or to kill people—only to torment them.

Revelation 9:7 And the shapes of the locusts were like unto horses prepared unto battle; and on their heads were as it were crowns like gold, and their faces were as the faces of men.

Apparently, John was having difficulty describing what these creatures looked like, since he had never before seen an undisguised demon. John describes them here as looking something like horses with crowns of gold on their heads and faces like the faces of men.

---

[13] E. G. White, *Maranatha* (1976), p. 30.5.

Revelation 9:8 And they had hair as the hair of women, and their teeth were as the teeth of lions.

Revelation 9:9 And they had breastplates, as it were breastplates of iron; and the sound of their wings was as the sound of chariots of many horses running to battle.

Revelation 9:10 And they had tails like unto scorpions, and there were stings in their tails: and their power was to hurt men five months.

For a period of five months, Satan and his angels are able to torment those who do not have the seal of God. This period occurs after God's people have been sealed and immediately prior to the final close of probation.[14]

Revelation 9:11 And they had a king over them, which is the angel of the bottomless pit, whose name in the Hebrew tongue is Abaddon, but in the Greek tongue hath his name Apollyon.

The creatures with tails like scorpions have a king over them who is the angel of the bottomless pit. This verse specifies that the star who is given the key to the bottomless pit is, in fact, an angel. This angel has two names both meaning the destroyer. Clearly these terms are specifically applicable to Satan, and reveal the identity of the angel of the bottomless pit. Therefore, the beings he releases, over which he is king, are fallen angels, who will physically appear to human beings who do not have the seal of God, and torment them.

Revelation 9:12 One woe is past; and, behold, there come two woes more hereafter.

What follows will be even worse.

---

[14] "Reference to our published works will show our belief that the living righteous will receive the seal of God prior to the close of probation...."
E. G. White, *Selected Messages*, Book 1 (1958), p. 66.2.

Revelation 9:13 And the sixth angel sounded, and I heard a voice from the four horns of the golden altar which is before God,

Revelation 9:14 Saying to the sixth angel which had the trumpet, Loose the four angels which are bound in the great river Euphrates.

Revelation 9:15 And the four angels were loosed, which were prepared for an hour, and a day, and a month, and a year, for to slay the third part of men.

Six beings are involved in the implementation of the sixth trumpet: first, the angel sounding the sixth trumpet, second the one whose voice gives the order for four additional angels to be loosed. These six correspond directly to Ezekiel's vision of five men with slaughter weapons, with a sixth who is clothed in linen with a writer's inkhorn by his side.[15] In Ezekiel nine, a mark is placed on those that sigh and cry for the abominations done in God's church—these only are safe from the destruction about to begin. When the slaughter commences, it begins at God's sanctuary. Those professing Christianity, who do not have the seal of God will be the first to fall.

"Who are standing in the counsel of God at this time? Is it those who virtually excuse wrongs among the professed people of God, and murmur in their hearts, if not openly, against those who would reprove sin? Is it those who take their stand against them, and sympathize with those who commit wrong? No, indeed! These, unless they repent, and leave the work of Satan in oppressing those who have the burden of the work, and holding up the hands of sinners in Zion, will never receive the mark of God's sealing approval. They will fall in the general destruction of all the wicked, represented by the five men bearing slaughter weapons. Mark this point with care: Those who receive the pure mark of truth, wrought in them by the power of the Holy Ghost, represented by a mark by the man in linen, are those 'that sigh and cry for all the abominations that are done' in the church. Their love for purity and the honor and glory of God is such, and they have so clear a view of the exceeding

---

[15] See Ezekiel chapter nine.

sinfulness of sin, that they are represented as being in an agony, even sighing and crying. Read Ezekiel, chapter nine."[16]

"While Jesus had been standing between God and guilty man, a restraint was upon the people; but when He stepped out from between man and the Father, the restraint was removed and Satan had entire control of the finally impenitent."[17]

The sixth trumpet is the final close of probation which will signal the wrath of God in the initiation of the seven last plagues. This is evident by the release of the four angels in verse 15. These are the same four angels that are holding the winds of strife in Revelation 7. The winds of destruction cannot be released until God's people are sealed in their foreheads. "I saw that the four angels would hold the four winds until Jesus' work was done in the sanctuary, and then will come the seven last plagues."[18]

By the Euphrates river is represented the waters (or nations[19]) that nourish Babylon. End-time Babylon is nourished by the entire world.[20] These angels are bound there until earth's last warning message can be given, for any of God's people remaining in Babylon to come out and escape the coming judgments.[21] When the four winds are released, it is clear that probation has closed, for all who would heed the call to come out of Babylon are now safe. The plagues will fall especially on Babylon. One third of the wicked are to be slain.

The release of these winds signals the beginning of the seven last plagues—the wrath of God against sin, un-mixed with mercy.[22] It also signals the final restriction lifted from Satan and his hosts. The restriction placed on the demonic forces that they could not kill, but only torment, is now removed and they are able to kill vast numbers of human beings. The destruction continues for just over thirteen

---

[16] E. G. White, "The Laodicean Church," *The Review and Herald*, September 23, 1873 par. 5.

[17] E. G. White, *Early Writings* (1882), p. 280.2.

[18] *Ibid.*, p. 36.1-2.

[19] Revelation 17:15

[20] See Revelation 17.

[21] Revelation 18:2-4

[22] See Revelation chapter 16.

months (verse 15). This time period is the duration of the seven last plagues.

"These plagues enraged the wicked against the righteous; they thought that we had brought the judgments of God upon them, and that if they could rid the earth of us, the plagues would then be stayed. A decree went forth to slay the saints, which caused them to cry day and night for deliverance. This was the time of Jacob's trouble. Then all the saints cried out with anguish of spirit, and were delivered by the voice of God. The 144,000 triumphed. Their faces were lighted up with the glory of God"[23] The death decree against the saints, triggered by the seven last plagues, begins the time of Jacob's trouble, "such as never was since there was a nation."[24] A special blessing is pronounced for "he that waiteth, and cometh to the... end of the days." The saints are "left alone to wrestle with a man until the breaking of the day." [25] For forty-five days[26] they cling with superhuman strength, as did Jacob, to the merits of their divine Saviour. "Jacob's experience during that night of wrestling and anguish represents the trial through which the people of God must pass just before Christ's second coming. The prophet Jeremiah, in holy vision looking down to this time, said, 'We have heard a voice of trembling, of fear, and not of peace.... All faces are turned into paleness. Alas! for that day is great, so that none is like it: it is even the time of Jacob's trouble; but he shall be saved out of it.' Jeremiah 30:5-7."[27]

Revelation 9:16 And the number of the army of the horsemen were two hundred thousand thousand: and I heard the number of them.

Two hundred thousand thousand is 200 million. This vast host is Satan's army. Perhaps this is the number of angels that fell with Satan from heaven—one third of the total.[28]

---

[23] E. G. White, *Early Writings* (1882), p. 36.2.

[24] Daniel 12:1

[25] Genesis 32:24-30

[26] See comments on Daniel chapter twelve.

[27] E. G. White, *Patriarchs and Prophets* (1890), p. 201.1.

[28] Revelation 12:4, 9

Revelation 9:17 And thus I saw the horses in the vision, and them that sat on them, having breastplates of fire, and of jacinth, and brimstone: and the heads of the horses were as the heads of lions; and out of their mouths issued fire and smoke and brimstone.

Apparently, these beings have a very strange and striking appearance with rather frightening capabilities. Would this not be completely terrifying if God had not pre-warned us of the terrible things coming on the earth, and assured us of his protection?

Revelation 9:18 By these three was the third part of men killed, by the fire, and by the smoke, and by the brimstone, which issued out of their mouths.

Revelation 9:19 For their power is in their mouth, and in their tails: for their tails were like unto serpents, and had heads, and with them they do hurt.

The four angels holding the winds of strife are God's angels, and when Christ releases them, Satan is able to do all the things that he has wanted to do to humans. When every intelligent being on planet earth has made their final decision, and they say, we want only to be led by Satan, we do not want to have the seal of God, we desire Satan as our god and leader; God will give them what they want. God will allow the wicked to experience the full reality of Satan's kingdom. Some may think that this is harsh, but in reality, it demonstrates God's loving mercy even toward the wicked. God honors their power to choose another leader. God wants everyone to have an opportunity to see how Satan first tempts people, then leads them into sin, then ensnares them in his deceptions, but once he actually gains control, he destroys his own kingdom and kills his own subjects.

The two competing kingdoms in this great controversy are finally completely contrasted. Jesus gave everything, poured out all of heaven, sacrificed his own life, to offer eternal life to all. Once God allows Satan full and open control of the wicked (the devils church and his faithful subjects who worship him), he begins to torture and annihilate them. They served him, and this is their reward. God allows the universe to see the unrestrained consequences of Satan's reign of terror. This is that ultimate picture, demonstrating to the whole universe how far Satan will take his antagonism and fury towards human beings and their Creator. Even if they are serving him; even if they love, worship and obey him; he tortures and kills them! Why do people insist on serving this kingdom?

Revelation 9:20 And the rest of the men which were not killed by these plagues yet repented not of the works of their hands, that they should not worship devils, and idols of gold, and silver, and brass, and stone, and of wood: which neither can see, nor hear, nor walk:

Even when tormented and killed by Satan and his angels, the wicked refuse to repent. They still love to do the things that their leader has tempted them to do. They still want to worship demons, even after they see what demons do to them. Before the entire universe is demonstrated the ultimate anger of Satan, the ultimate point to which he will take his kingdom if allowed unrestricted access to his subjects. What astonishing hatred contrasted with the amazing love of God.

Revelation 9:21 Neither repented they of their murders, nor of their sorceries, nor of their fornication, nor of their thefts.

None of the things that they have done to violate God's law cause them to repent. They are of their father, the devil. They like to torture people, and they can understand, apparently, why demons like to torture them too.

God is showing us a picture of how horrendous Satan's kingdom really is. He is giving us a glimpse of the glory of his kingdom in contrast to Satan's. Jesus is painting the picture in the starkest way he possibly can to give us all the information we need to make our decision. Will you purpose in your heart to be on the side of God?

You might feel at some point that you must violate God's law to avoid pain and suffering, or deprivation. But, before you do that, remember that the word of God has revealed to us what will happen to those who make that decision to be on Satan's side. In the long run, Satan's followers will not avoid pain and suffering. If you have no other motivation than to avoid pain and suffering, you should choose to be on God's side. Of course, that reason alone will not be a good enough motivation, for God wants to have a loving relationship with you.

How then do we escape? "'Man shall not live by bread alone, but by every word of God.' Often the follower of Christ is brought where he cannot serve God and carry forward his worldly enterprises. Perhaps it appears that obedience to some plain requirement of God will cut off his means of support. Satan would make him believe that he must sacrifice his conscientious convictions. But the only thing in our world upon which we can rely is the word of God. 'Seek ye first the kingdom of God, and His righteousness; and all these things shall be added unto you.' Matthew 6:33. Even in this life it is not for our good to depart from the will of our Father in heaven. When we learn the power of His word, we shall not follow the suggestions of Satan in order to obtain food or to save our lives. Our only questions will be, What is God's command? and what His promise? Knowing these, we shall obey the one, and trust the other."[29]

God is painting this picture for us so that we may choose this day whom we will serve.[30] What God has for us is so much better than being under Satan's rule. It is only by "the blood of the Lamb"[31] and the word of God that we can overcome today and escape tomorrow what is coming upon this earth. "For a day in thy courts is better than a thousand. I had rather be a doorkeeper in the house of my God, than to dwell in the tents of wickedness. For the LORD God is a sun and shield: the LORD will give grace and glory: no good thing will he withhold from them that walk uprightly. O LORD of hosts, blessed is the man that trusteth in thee."[32]

The goal of heaven is for the salvation of every soul, but God will not violate your power of choice. Choose to serve the Lord, because he alone is the way, the truth, and the life; and Satan has terrible things planned for his followers. Amen.

---

[29] E. G. White, *The Desire or Ages* (1898), p. 121.2.

[30] Joshua 24:15

[31] Revelation 12:11

[32] Psalm 84:10-12

SIMILARITIES BETWEEN THE SEVEN TRUMPETS AND THE SEVEN LAST PLAGUES:

Seven Trumpets	Seven Vials
1. Hail, blood, fire—1/3 of trees and all grass burnt up.	1. Sores on those with the mark of the beast.
2. Mountain of fire cast in sea—1/3 of sea turns blood; 1/3 of sea life dies; 1/3 ships destroyed.	2. Sea turns to blood—everything in the sea dies.
3. Star falls on 1/3 of rivers & springs: many men die because of resulting bitter water	3. Rivers & springs turn to blood.
4. 1/3 of sun, moon, stars darkened to 1/3 of the day.	4. Sun scorches men with fire.
5. Star falls from heaven: given key to bottomless pit; unlocks it and smoke/locusts come out and torment men (only those who don't have the seal of God) for 5 months.	5. The kingdom of the beast is full of darkness gnawed tongues for their pains and their sores.
6. Four angels are loosed and slay 1/3 of men; along with 200 million horsemen. Three types of fire.	6. Euphrates dried up—battle of Armageddon; spirits of devils go out to deceive. Three spirits like frogs that will be destroyed by fire.
7. Kingdom becomes Christ's; temple of God was opened and there were lightnings and voices and thunderings, and an earthquake, and great hail.	7. Voice from the temple. "it is done!" Voices, and thunders, and lightnings: and greatest earthquake ever and hail.

Chronology of Trumpets and Vials		
1st Trumpet		1st Vial
2nd Trumpet		2nd Vial
3rd Trumpet		3rd Vial
4th Trumpet		4th Vial
5th Trumpet		5th Vial
6th Trumpet		6th Vial
7th Trumpet		7th Vial

Revelation 10

SUMMARY:
In Revelation 10 John sees an angel standing with one foot on the earth, and one on the sea, having a little book open in his hand. John hears seven thunders, and is told to eat the little book which would be sweet as honey in his mouth, but would make his belly bitter. Finally, he is told that he must prophecy again.

Revelation 10:1 And I saw another mighty angel come down from heaven, clothed with a cloud: and a rainbow was upon his head, and his face was as it were the sun, and his feet as pillars of fire:

Clearly, this mighty being is none other than Christ himself. Comparing this description with other passages of Scripture demonstrates that this is Jesus: "And in the midst of the seven candlesticks one like unto the Son of man, clothed with a garment down to the foot.... **And his feet like unto fine brass, as if they burned in a furnace**.... and **his countenance was as the sun shineth in his strength**."[1] Matthew, speaking of Jesus on the Mount of Transfiguration, says that Jesus "was transfigured before them: and his face did shine as the sun, and his raiment was white as the light."[2]

This passage is one of the most obvious examples in Scripture where Christ is called an angel.[3] This does not imply that Jesus is a created being. The word angel simply means messenger in the Bible, and Jesus is the ultimate messenger.

Revelation 10:2 And he had in his hand a little book open: and he set his right foot upon the sea, and his left foot on the earth,

---

[1] Revelation 1:13-16

[2] Matthew 17:2

[3] See also Revelation 8:3.

"The mighty angel who instructed John was no less a personage than Jesus Christ. Setting His right foot on the sea, and His left upon the dry land, shows the part which He is acting in the closing scenes of the great controversy with Satan. This position denotes His supreme power and authority over the whole earth....

"The angel's position, with one foot on the sea, the other on the land, signifies the wide extent of the proclamation of the message. It will cross the broad waters and be proclaimed in other countries, even to all the world."[4]

Jesus has in his hand a little book open. What is this book? There is only one book in Scripture which the writer is directed by God to seal up.[5] At the end of the book of Daniel,[6] God tells the aged prophet to shut up the words and seal the book, for it was not to be opened or fully understood until the time of the end. Then knowledge would be increased in regard to the prophecies contained in the book of Daniel. In Revelation 5:9 the Bible says, "And they sung a new song, saying, **Thou art worthy to take the book, and to open the seals thereof**...." The sealed book of Daniel is introduced in Revelation, still in its sealed state, but about to be unsealed. Jesus was the only one worthy to unseal the book of Daniel. The first coming of Jesus was prophesied in the book of Daniel, with highly specific details about his life—when he would die, when he would be baptized, what would be his purpose in coming, and the timing of the investigative judgment during which he would enter the most holy place as our high priest to intercede before the throne of God. All these events were prophesied in the book of Daniel long before Jesus actually came and fulfilled them, therefore, in order for the book to be accurate and properly understood, Christ must fulfill the predicted events. All that was prophesied about him in the book of Daniel, he has fulfilled exactly.

To summarize: in Daniel 12, the book of Daniel is sealed until the time of the end; in Revelation 5, the sealed book appears in a sealed condition, but about to be unsealed. Revelation 5 and 6 show the process of the book being unsealed, and finally, in Revelation 10, the book now appears fully open.

---

[4] E. G. White, *The Seventh-day Adventist Bible Commentary,* Vol. 7 (1955), p. 971.

[5] See Daniel 12:4. The sealed book that Isaiah refers to is the book of Daniel. See Revelation 5:2.

[6] Daniel 12:4 "But thou, O Daniel, shut up the words, and seal the book, even to the time of the end: many shall run to and fro, and knowledge shall be increased."

"The things revealed to Daniel were afterward complemented by the revelation made to John on the Isle of Patmos. These two books should be carefully studied....

"'And He said, Go thy way, Daniel: for the words are closed up and sealed till the time of the end'.... It was the Lion of the tribe of Judah who unsealed the book and gave to John the revelation of what should be in these last days.... These matters are of infinite importance in these last days.... **The book of Daniel is unsealed in the revelation to John**, and carries us forward to the last scenes of this earth's history.

"Will our brethren bear in mind that we are living amid the perils of the last days? Read Revelation in connection with Daniel."[7]

The book of Daniel is now open; unsealed by the hands of Jesus, for all who would to understand.

Revelation 10:3 And cried with a loud voice, as when a lion roareth: and when he had cried, seven thunders uttered their voices.

This verse links us to the opening of the book in Revelation 5, for the "Lion of the tribe of Juda, the Root of David, hath prevailed to open the book, and to loose the seven seals thereof,"[8] and the lion here utters his voice.

Revelation 10:4 And when the seven thunders had uttered their voices, I was about to write: and I heard a voice from heaven saying unto me, Seal up those things which the seven thunders uttered, and write them not.

The book of Revelation is not a sealed book, for its very title—the Revelation of Jesus Christ—tells us it cannot be sealed: it declares itself an open book, a revelation. But there is one part of the vision of Revelation that was sealed and therefore not recorded in the book. The declarations of the seven thunders were sealed. Scripture does not tell us what they are or what they mean, but apparently, they

---

[7] E. G. White, *Testimonies to Ministers and Gospel Workers* (1923), p. 114.6-115.4.

[8] Revelation 5:5

were things that were critical for John to know as he wrote the rest of the book of Revelation, that would become clear to God's people when the time was right.

"After these seven thunders uttered their voices, the injunction comes to John as to Daniel in regard to the little book: 'Seal up those things which the seven thunders uttered' (Revelation 10:4). **These relate to future events which will be disclosed in their order. Daniel shall stand in his lot at the end of the days.** John sees the little book unsealed. Then Daniel's prophecies have their proper place in the first, second, and third angels' messages to be given to the world. **The unsealing of the little book was the message in relation to time.**[9]

"The books of Daniel and the Revelation are one. One is a prophecy, the other a revelation; one a book sealed, the other a book opened. John heard the mysteries which the thunders uttered, but he was commanded not to write them. **The special light given to John which was expressed in the seven thunders was a delineation of events which would transpire under the first and second angels' messages. It was not best for the people to know these things, for their faith must necessarily be tested.** In the order of God, most wonderful and advanced truths would be proclaimed. The first and second angels' messages were to be proclaimed, **but no further light was to be revealed before these messages had done their specific work.** This is represented by the angel standing with one foot on the sea, proclaiming with a most solemn oath that time should be no longer."[10]

Revelation 10:5 And the angel which I saw stand upon the sea and upon the earth lifted up his hand to heaven,

Revelation 10:6 And sware by him that liveth for ever and ever, who created heaven, and the things that therein are, and the earth, and the things that therein are, and the sea, and the things which are therein, that there should be time no longer:

---

[9] There are seven messages in Daniel relating to time. The full understanding of these time messages was hid during the proclamation of the first and second angels' messages, for the faith of the people must be tested. Additional light regarding these time prophecies would be revealed only once these messages had done their work, which would open the way for most wonderful and advanced truths to be proclaimed.

[10] E. G. White, *Manuscript Releases*, Vol. 1 (1990), p. 99.2-3.

There is a distinct parallel between this passage and Daniel 12. Daniel is told to "shut up the words, and seal the book, even to the time of the end."[11] In Daniel 12:6-7, Daniel sees a "man clothed in linen, which was upon the waters of the river.... hold "up his right hand and his left hand unto heaven, and **sware by him that liveth for ever** that it shall be for a time, times, and an half." In Revelation 10 John sees the angel clothed with a cloud, holding the little book, place "**his right foot upon the sea, and his left foot on the earth**," and lift "**his hand to heaven, And sware by him that liveth for ever and ever, who created**" all things, "**that there should be time no longer**." "Sware by him that liveth for ever" is identical language.

These two passages contain, respectively, the announcements of the termination of the 1,260 year prophecy in 1798 and the conclusion of the 2,300-year prophecy, in 1844.[12] "This time, which the Angel declares with a solemn oath, is not the end of this world's history, neither of probationary time, but of **prophetic time**, which would precede the advent of our Lord. That is, the people will not have another message upon **definite time**."[13]

Jesus is the angel holding the little book, and therefore the one who swears by him that liveth forever and ever, who created all things. In John 1, the Bible says Jesus "was the Word...and the Word was God." The apostle John then proceeds to tell us that "all things were made by him; and without him was not any thing made that was made." Jesus created everything. Here Christ is his own witness[14] for he is swearing by the Creator, and he is the Creator. "When God made promise to Abraham, because he could swear by no greater, he sware by himself."[15] When God makes a promise to us he can swear by no one greater than himself, for he lives forever and his promises are sure.

---

[11] Daniel 12:4

[12] The "time, times, and an half," is 1,260 years—see Daniel chapter 7. See Daniel 8 and 9 for a full explanation of the 2,300-year prophecy.

[13] E. G. White, *Christ Triumphant* (1999), p. 344.5.

[14] Revelation 1:5

[15] Hebrews 6:13

Revelation 10:7 But in the days of the voice of the seventh angel, when he shall begin to sound, the mystery of God should be finished, as he hath declared to his servants the prophets.

This verse clarifies that the termination of time referred to in the previous verse is not the end of earth's history, for it reminds us that the mystery of God would not be finished until the seventh angel sounds, which does not occur until Revelation 11:15. The mystery of God is that the monarch of the universe assumed human flesh in order that we might be saved: "great is the mystery of godliness: God was manifest in the flesh."[16] We are also told that the mystery of God is "Christ in you, the hope of glory."[17] Our only hope of glory, or salvation, is Christ in us. Jesus said, "Abide in me, and I in you."[18] For "whosoever abideth in him sinneth not."[19] How are we to abide in Christ and he in us? He said "my words abide in you,"[20] for it is by the precious promises of the word of God, that we may be "partakers of the divine nature."[21] God intends to manifest his likeness—his character—in us. "When the character of Christ shall be perfectly reproduced in His people, then He will come to claim them as His own."[22] The process of salvation is almost complete, but he is reminding us that it is yet in the future. When the seventh angel begins to sound, then the mystery of God will be finished, the process of salvation complete—"Christ in you, the hope of glory."[23]

Revelation 10:8 And the voice which I heard from heaven spake unto me again, and said, Go and take the little book which is open in the hand of the angel which standeth upon the sea and upon the earth.

---

[16] 1 Timothy 3:16

[17] Colossians 1:27

[18] John 15:4

[19] 1 John 3:6

[20] John 15:7

[21] 2 Peter 1:4

[22] E. G. White, *Christ's Object Lessons* (1900), p. 69.1.

[23] Colossians 1:27

Revelation 10:9 And I went unto the angel, and said unto him, Give me the little book. And he said unto me, Take it, and eat it up; and it shall make thy belly bitter, but it shall be in thy mouth sweet as honey.[24]

The discovery that the book, open in the hand of the angel, is the book of Daniel gives us clues as to what is happening when John eats the book and finds it in his mouth as sweet as honey, but bitter in his belly. As history neared the "time of the end" [25] all around the world, students of Scripture began studying the book of Daniel. As God opened these prophecies to their understanding, they discovered a time period revealed in Daniel 8:14, "Unto two thousand and three hundred days; then shall the sanctuary be cleansed." This led to the realization that 2,300 prophetic days must represent 2,300 literal years which would terminate in the year 1844.[26] Many of these students of the Bible assumed that the cleansing of the sanctuary referred to the cleansing of the earth by fire at the second coming of Jesus. Therefore, they came to the conclusion that the coming of Christ would occur in the year 1844.[27] As a result, they began to preach the message of the soon coming of Jesus. This message was indeed as sweet as honey in their mouth. But as it got to their belly, it became a bitter disappointment. Jesus did not return in 1844, as expected. But, God left this prophetic utterance to assure them that he had decreed the events they experienced, and that he had not forsaken them.[28] Just as the disciples of Jesus misunderstood the prophetic utterances of the Saviour, and as a result experienced a bitter disappointment at his death, so these faithful ones misunderstood and experienced a great disappointment. Christ intended for the attention of the entire world

---

[24] Ezekiel 2:8-10 through Ezekiel 3:1-3 contains an account of the same events. See comments on Revelation 5:1 regarding the parallel vision of Ezekiel.

[25] Daniel 12:4

[26] See Daniel 8 and 9.

[27] An initial mistake in the starting point brought the 2,300 years to A.D. 1,843. Once this mistake was rectified, the period ended in A.D. 1844. See Daniel 9.

[28] "'And the angel which I saw stand upon the sea and upon the earth lifted up his hand to heaven, and sware by him that liveth for ever and ever, who created heaven, and the things that therein are, and the earth, and the things that therein are, and the sea, and the things which are therein, that there should be time no longer' (Revelation 10:5, 6). This message announces the end of the prophetic periods. The disappointment of those who expected to see our Lord in 1844 was indeed bitter to those who had so ardently looked for His appearing. It was in the Lord's order that this disappointment should come, and that hearts should be revealed."
E. G. White, *Selected Messages*, Vol. 2 (1958), p. 108.1.

to be directed to his soon return, so their focus might be drawn to the commencement of his intercession in the most holy on behalf of his people, that they might know the reason for his long delay in returning to the earth to claim his people as his own.

Revelation 10:10 And I took the little book out of the angel's hand, and ate it up; and it was in my mouth sweet as honey: and as soon as I had eaten it, my belly was bitter.

This sweet message was the result of partaking of the bread of life contained in the book of Daniel. One of the amazing things about this message is that there was a simultaneous worldwide proclamation. People all over the world with little or no contact with each other began preaching the identical message, simultaneously.[29] God's hand was guiding these events, in fulfillment of his Word. One of the most prominent individuals to begin preaching the message that Jesus was coming in 1844, was an American-born farmer named William Miller (1782-1849), who became a Baptist preacher.

A remarkable reformation was wrought in America with the preaching of the message of the soon coming of Christ. "Of all the great religious movements since the days of the apostles, none have been more free from human imperfection and the wiles of Satan than was that of the autumn of 1844. Even now, after the lapse of many years, all who shared in that movement and who have stood firm upon the platform of truth still feel the holy influence of that blessed work and bear witness that it was of God."[30] But, as with the first coming of

---

[29] Dr. Joseph Wolff, a converted son of a Jewish Rabbi, began preaching in 1821, three years after Miller arrived at his conclusions, that Christ would come near the middle of the nineteenth century. Becoming known as the missionary to the world, Wolff travelled to Egypt, Abyssinia, Palestine, Syria, Persia, Bokhara, Yemen and India. He preached in the United States and even preached before all the members of Congress in the Congress Hall. Robert Winter preached the message in England. In South America, a Spanish Jesuit named Lacunza discovered the truths of the Bible, and published his conclusions of Christ's soon return under the pen-name Rabbi Ben-Israel, in the eighteenth century. However, his book made its way to England and being translated into English helped to stir interest in the prophecies of the soon coming of Jesus. In Germany a Lutheran minister named Bengel came to the conclusion that Jesus was to come on a date very near to the date that Miller preached. His writings spread through Christendom. Gaussen preached the message in Geneva. The same message was preached in Scandinavia. In America, William Miller was joined by prominent preachers such as Josiah Litch. Even Martin Luther three centuries earlier, understood the 2,300-year prophecy, for he declared: "I persuade myself verily, that the day of Judgment will not be absent full three hundred years. God will not, cannot, suffer this wicked world much longer." E. G. White, *The Great Controversy* (1888), p. 303.1.

[30] E. G. White, *The Great Controversy* (1911), p. 401.3.

Christ, Jesus was not yet coming to set up his earthly kingdom, rather he was dealing with the problem of sin.

Scripture had foretold their disappointment. God had everything in his hand, "declaring the end from the beginning, and from ancient times the things that are not yet done."[31] It was according to his will and his purposes, even though they did not understand everything at the time. God wanted us to know, with certainty, that the prophetic time period they preached was true. Only the event was mistaken. Jesus gave confirmation in the book of Revelation, showing that he knew of this disappointment before it occurred.

In the earthly sanctuary, which is a pattern of the heavenly; on the Day of Atonement the priest made a special sacrifice to cleanse the sanctuary of the sins that had accumulated during that year. All the sins confessed throughout the year were symbolically transferred into that sanctuary. The sins were recorded there until the time of the cleansing of the sanctuary, or the day of Atonement, which the Israelites called the day of judgment. During this solemn service the congregation was searching their hearts and confessing sins. On the day of judgment all confessed sins were blotted out, cleansing the sanctuary from even their record. The earthly sanctuary was a prophecy of the process of the plan of salvation. Paul describes the cleansing of the heavenly sanctuary to which the earthly services pointed: "Now of the things which we have spoken this is the sum: We have such an high priest, who is set on the right hand of the throne of the Majesty in the heavens; A minister of the sanctuary, and of the true tabernacle, which the Lord pitched, and not man."[32] "For when Moses had spoken every precept to all the people according to the law, he took the blood of calves and of goats.... It was therefore necessary that the patterns of things in the heavens[33] should be purified with these; but the heavenly things themselves with better sacrifices than these. For Christ is not entered into the holy places made with hands, which are the figures of the true; but into heaven itself, now to appear in the presence of God for us: Nor yet that he should offer himself often, as the high priest entereth into the {most} holy place every year with blood of others; For then must

---

[31] Isaiah 46:10

[32] Hebrew 8:1-2

[33] The earthly tabernacle was patterned after the heavenly sanctuary.

he often have suffered since the foundation of the world: but now once in the end of the world hath he appeared to put away sin by the sacrifice of himself. And as it is appointed unto men once to die, but after this the judgment: So Christ was once offered to bear the sins of many; and unto them that look for him shall he appear the second time without sin unto salvation."[34]

Once, in the end of the world (beginning in 1844), Christ must appear to put away sin by his sacrifice. It was appointed for him once to die, but, before he could return to the earth, he must intercede, in the judgment, with the merits of his sacrifice for the removal of even the record of every confessed sin that has been transferred to the heavenly sanctuary. Then when he appears the second time it is without sin unto salvation.

Because the anti-typical day of Atonement has been in process since 1844, it is imperative for us to make sure that our sins are confessed—that they have been transferred to that heavenly most holy place so that when Jesus finishes cleansing the sanctuary, our sins will be erased forever. This is what makes the judgment good news.[35]

Revelation 10:11 And he said unto me, Thou must prophesy again before many peoples, and nations, and tongues, and kings.

Along with the prophecy that they would be disappointed, was an announcement that God's people would have to preach the message of his soon coming once more. They must **"prophesy again."**

Sometimes when we read our Bibles we read just a chapter and when we reach the end of the chapter, we stop. This is a fine way to remember where we left off reading. But when studying carefully we cannot just assume that the chapter is all there is to the story. Sometimes you can find the answer to some mystery by reading a little farther—by looking at the context, looking at the chapters on either side, or even going to other books of the Bible to compare similar language. This passage is a good example of this principle.

---

[34] Hebrews 9:19, 23-28

[35] See Daniel chapters 8 and 9.

This chapter contains the prophecy of the great disappointment and the declaration that the prophecy must be given again. The very next verse, which happens to be in the next chapter, gives the explanation of the great disappointment, when Jesus did not return in 1844. It tells us where they were to look to understand why they were disappointed and what they misunderstood. Thus, Revelation 11:1 will conclude our study of Revelation chapter 10.

Revelation 11:1 And there was given me a reed like unto a rod: and the angel stood, saying, Rise, and measure the temple of God, and the altar, and them that worship therein.

The answer to their terrible disappointment and misunderstanding; the answer to what really happened in 1844, was to be found in the temple of heaven. Jesus is revealing to us that he would move into the most holy place of the heavenly sanctuary to begin a most important work in the finalization of the process of salvation—the cleansing of the sanctuary. In that work he wants us to know exactly where he is and what he is doing. Therefore, he gives us this glimpse of the open gates of heaven, that we can follow him there by faith.

The vast majority of the Christian world has no explanation for why it has taken Jesus over 2,000 years to return the second time as promised. Why would he leave us on this earth for that long? If we do not understand the message of the work that Christ is doing on our behalf, to fully wipe out sin forever, then it makes no sense why he has not yet returned. Once we comprehend this message, we can see that Jesus wants us to understand at every step where he is in the ministration process and what he is accomplishing. "Surely the Lord GOD will do nothing, but he revealeth his secret unto his servants the prophets."[36]

We must be certain that our sins are confessed—transferred to that heavenly sanctuary—so that in this judgment which has been in session since 1844, our sins may be wiped away forever. This is exciting news. Amen.

---

[36] Amos 3:7

Revelation 11

SUMMARY:

Revelation 11 presents a prophecy of two witnesses—the two olive trees, or two candlesticks which stand before the God of the earth. These two witnesses prophesy for three and a half days, are killed, and then resurrected. The first verse of Revelation 11 contains the answer to the great disappointment of 1844—the prophetic message from Revelation 10 that was sweet in the mouth and bitter in the belly.

Revelation 11:1 And there was given me a reed like unto a rod: and the angel stood, saying, Rise, and measure the temple of God, and the altar, and them that worship therein.

Jesus reveals to John that the answer to their disappointment is to be found by looking to the temple in heaven. This is a clear reference to the temple that is in heaven for the simple reason that at the time John is receiving this vision, the temple in Jerusalem had been destroyed for over 20 years and there was no temple on the earth.

Revelation 11:2 But the court which is without the temple leave out, and measure it not; for it is given unto the Gentiles: and the holy city shall they tread under foot forty and two months.

The sanctuary service contains multiple layers of symbolism. One of the things symbolized by the sanctuary service is that the outer court represents the earth, which is shown by this verse. The angel informs us not to look to earth for the answer to the sweet message which turns to a bitter disappointment. We are told that the answer will not be found in the outer court. The furniture that is in the outer court symbolized what Jesus did while on the earth: the altar of sacrifice, representing Christ's death on the cross; and the laver, initially representing his baptism, then foreshadowing his death burial and resurrection to new life. The furniture that is contained within the holy and most holy places of the temple represent heaven, and the aspects of Jesus' ministry in the courts above.[1] Therefore, these verses are telling us: do not look to the earth; leave out the court; measure the heavenly temple, and you will understand this mystery.

The holy city in heaven cannot be trodden under foot by Gentiles, therefore this refers to spiritual Israel, still exiled to this earth. In Hebrews 12:22-23 the Bible says, "But ye are come unto mount Sion, and unto the city of the living God, the heavenly Jerusalem, and to an innumerable company of angels, to the general assembly and church of the firstborn, which are written in heaven, and to God the Judge of all, and to the spirits of just men made perfect." The New Jerusalem, the city of God, is his church. Before his earthly church is joined with the heavenly church, it is to be purified on earth. Revelation also calls the New Jerusalem the bride of Christ. "And I John saw the holy city, new Jerusalem, coming down from God out of heaven, prepared as a bride adorned for her husband." In Revelation 12, we will see again how God represents his church as a woman—a woman that must flee into the wilderness.

Therefore, **"the holy city"** in Revelation 11:2 refers to God's church; persecuted for 1,260 years in the outer court of the earth. This is the same as Christ's church being given into the hands of the little horn power of Daniel 7 that arises out of the fourth beast and speaks "great words against the most High, and shall wear out the saints of the most High, and think to change times and laws: and they shall be given into his hand until a time and times and the dividing of time."[2]

Scripture is revealing that some power would tread down Christ's church for 1,260 years. The events of history exactly match the prediction of Scripture. In A.D. 538, the papacy gained its political power after uprooting the last of the three tribes prophesied in Daniel

---

[1] "Every heavenly intelligence is interested in the assemblies of the saints who on earth meet to worship God. In the **inner court of heaven** they listen to the testimony of the witnesses for Christ in the **outer court on earth**..."
E. G. White, *Counsels for the Church* (1991), 240.5.

[2] Daniel 7:25
Time is one year. Times being plural is two years (for, if it were any more than two, the number intended would have to be specified). The dividing of times is half a year. When we add these up, they total 3 1/2 years. A Biblical year contains 360 days (see the story of the flood in Genesis 6-8). Three and a half years multiplied by 360 days in a year is a total of 1,260 days. Forty-two months (of thirty days each) also equals 1,260 days. This time prophecy is mentioned seven different times in Scripture: twice in Daniel and five times in Revelation. The 42 months in Revelation 11:2 is the first mentioned in Revelation. In symbolic Biblical prophecy, one day is equal to one year (see Numbers 14:34 and Ezekiel 4:6). Thus 1,260 days represents 1,260 prophetic years.

7:8, 20, 24. Exactly 1,260 years later, in 1798, Napoleon's General Berthier took the pope captive, apparently ending the political power of the papacy. This prophecy is repeated in Revelation 12 and 13 with additional details.

Many Christians through history understood this time prophecy. Every Protestant reformer understood and preached about the 1,260 years of persecution. This prophecy was so explicit, that in 1689, Drue Cressener, vicar of the Church of England, pronounced "For if the first time of the beast was at Justinian's recovery of the city of Rome, then must not it end till a little before the year 1800."[3] Cressener knew 109 years before it came to pass when this prophecy was to be fulfilled.

Revelation 11:3 And I will give power unto my two witnesses, and they shall prophesy a thousand two hundred and threescore days, clothed in sackcloth.

Here for the second time, the 1,260-year time prophecy is mentioned in Revelation. In this instance, the prophetic period is given as, "a thousand two hundred and three score days." A score is 20, therefore three score is 60. A thousand two hundred and threescore days is 1,260 years. God's two witnesses, or messengers, would prophesy for 1,260 years clothed in sackcloth. Obviously, these two witnesses, are not literal people, because no literal person lives for 1,260 years. Who then are these two witnesses?

Revelation 11:4 These are the two olive trees, and the two candlesticks standing before the God of the earth.

The two witnesses are also called two olive trees and two candlesticks and are portrayed as "**standing before the God of the earth.**" Allowing the Bible to interpret itself, we discover the identity of these two witnesses. The prophet Zechariah records, "And said unto me, What seest thou? And I said, I have looked, and behold a candlestick all of gold, with a bowl upon the top of it, and his seven lamps thereon, and seven pipes to the seven lamps, which are upon the top thereof: and **two olive trees** by it, one upon the right side of

---

[3] Drue Cressener, D.D., *The Judgments of God upon the Roman Catholick Church* (1689), p. 312.

the bowl, and the other upon the left side thereof. So I answered and spake to the angel that talked with me, saying, What are these, my lord?"[4] Zechariah sees in vision the very symbols seen by John— candlesticks and two olive trees, and inquires about the meaning: "Then the angel that talked with me answered and said unto me, Knowest thou not what these be? And I said, No, my lord. Then he answered and spake unto me, saying, **This is the word of the LORD** unto Zerubbabel, saying, Not by might, nor by power, but by my spirit, saith the LORD of hosts."[5] The angel gives the answer. The olive trees and the candlesticks represent the Word of the Lord. Continuing in Zechariah 4:12-14, the Bible says, "And I answered again, and said unto him, What be these two olive branches which through the two golden pipes empty the golden oil out of themselves? And he answered me and said, Knowest thou not what these be? And I said, No, my lord. Then said he, These are the two anointed ones, that stand by the Lord of the whole earth." Zechariah records directly parallel language to that used in Revelation 11. The two olive trees are the two anointed ones or two witnesses that stand by the Lord of the whole earth.

Exodus 25:31-34 describes the candlestick that was used in the sanctuary that Moses made in the wilderness. "And thou shalt make a candlestick of pure gold: of beaten work shall the candlestick be made: his shaft, and his branches, his bowls, his knops, and his flowers, shall be of the same. And six branches shall come out of the sides of it; three branches of the candlestick out of the one side, and three branches of the candlestick out of the other side. Three bowls made like unto almonds, with a knop and a flower in one branch; and three bowls made like almonds in the other branch, with a knop and a flower: so in the six branches that come out of the candlestick. And in the candlestick shall be four bowls made like unto almonds, with their knops and their flowers."

The bowls are shaped like almonds; the almond being the fruit, the bud leading to the flower, and the flower giving rise to the fruit. Three items: bud, flower, and fruit, are repeated three times in each of the six branches. This means that there are nine different items on one branch. If we add up the three branches on one side we find there

---

[4] Zechariah 4:2-4

[5] Zechariah 4:5-6

are twenty-seven items on one side of the candlestick; with twenty-seven items on the other side. In the candlestick (the main stalk in the center), there are four bowls like almonds with their knops and flowers. Therefore, there are four sets of three items, or 12 items, on the middle stalk. If you add 12 with 27 from the other side of the candlestick, you have 39 items. There are 39 books in the Old Testament and 27 books in the New Testament. Scripture says in Psalms 119:105, "Thy word is a lamp unto my feet, and a light unto my path." Therefore, the candlestick represents the Bible. This is a prophecy of precisely what would constitute the canon of Scripture, thousands of years before it was completed. The two witnesses which are also called the two candlesticks, are therefore the Old and New Testament, which must witness for God clothed in sackcloth during the 1,260 years of papal suppression. During this period, the Bible was hidden from the people, forbidden by the papal church.

Revelation 11:5 And if any man will hurt them, fire proceedeth out of their mouth, and devoureth their enemies: and if any man will hurt them, he must in this manner be killed.

During the dark ages, people were burned at the stake for owning a Bible, and the Bibles were also committed to the flames. However, this verse now tells us, if any man hurts the two witnesses, fire proceeds out of their mouths and devours their enemies. When people burned the Bible during the dark ages, the Bible did not burn them. But, God's Word testifies that anyone who goes against it, or hurts it, will one day be burned. God's Word specifies that fire will consume anyone who has violated that Word, and rejected the infinite provisions for their salvation. Those burning the Scriptures during the dark ages will one day regret their actions.

Revelation 11:6 These have power to shut heaven, that it rain not in the days of their prophecy: and have power over waters to turn them to blood, and to smite the earth with all plagues, as often as they will.

God's word is that which proceeds from his mouth, of which we have record in the Bible. It was God's word that turned water to blood in Egypt, and God's word will once more do the same thing. "He that rejecteth me, and receiveth not my words, hath one that judgeth him:

the word that I have spoken, the same shall judge him in the last day."[6] It was God's word which stopped the rain in the days of Elijah. Elijah prophesied that it would not rain for three and a half years. Here God's word was to be hidden away from the people for a prophetic three and a half years—a drought for the word of God.

Revelation 11:7 And when they shall have finished their testimony, the beast that ascendeth out of the bottomless pit shall make war against them, and shall overcome them, and kill them.

Could someone kill God's word; his two witnesses—the Old and New Testament? The next verse outlines who, when, and where.

Revelation 11:8 And their dead bodies shall lie in the street of the great city, which spiritually is called Sodom and Egypt, where also our Lord was crucified.

This city symbolizes a nation overcome by an ideology, rather than specifying a literal place, for the text refers to the place as spiritually **"called Sodom and Egypt."** It is a city that is called both Sodom and Egypt, and a literal city would not be called by the name of a city and a country. The city is where Jesus was crucified, yet Jesus was not crucified in Sodom or Egypt and could not be literally crucified in two places at once. Therefore, the language of the passage is symbolic and encodes a message that we need to understand.

"It had been Rome's[7] policy, under a profession of reverence for the Bible, to keep it locked up in an unknown tongue and hidden away from the people. Under her rule the witnesses prophesied 'clothed in sackcloth.' But another power[8]—the beast from the bottomless pit— was to arise to make open, avowed war upon the word of God. "'The great city' in whose streets the witnesses are slain, and where their dead bodies lie, is 'spiritually' Egypt. Of all nations presented in Bible history, Egypt most boldly denied the existence of the living

---

[6] John 12:48

[7] Papal Rome—the Roman Catholic Church.

[8] The words "another power," indicate a political power (beast) distinct from, yet connected to the Papacy, that would be even more Satanic than before ("from the bottomless pit").

God and resisted His commands. No monarch ever ventured upon more open and highhanded rebellion against the authority of Heaven than did the king of Egypt. When the message was brought him by Moses, in the name of the Lord, Pharaoh proudly answered: 'Who is Jehovah, that I should hearken unto His voice to let Israel go? I know not Jehovah, and moreover I will not let Israel go.' [Exodus 5:2] This is atheism, and the nation represented by Egypt would give voice to a similar denial of the claims of the living God and would manifest a like spirit of unbelief and defiance. 'The great city' is also compared, 'spiritually,' to Sodom. The corruption of Sodom in breaking the law of God was especially manifested in licentiousness. And this sin was also to be a pre-eminent characteristic of the nation that should fulfill the specifications of this scripture."

"According to the words of the prophet, then, a little before the year 1798 some power of satanic origin and character would rise to make war upon the Bible. And in the land where the testimony of God's two witnesses should thus be silenced, there would be manifest the atheism of the Pharaoh and the licentiousness of Sodom.

"This prophecy has received a most exact and striking fulfillment in the history of France."[9]

The great city **"which spiritually is called Sodom and Egypt,"** in whose streets God's word is slain represents France. During the French Revolution a law was proclaimed that there was no God and the Bible was outlawed. The people danced in the streets exalting a prostitute, termed the goddess of Reason, as the only divinity. For the first time, a civilized nation, through its official legislative body outlawed the Bible and worship of Deity.[10] In the streets of France some power of satanic origin would make war on the Bible by creating and controlling the French revolution. This power would war against the word of God by inciting atheism and promoting immorality. The Jesuit's work "was most fully developed in France. That country had received the light of the Reformation, but on this ground the Jesuits found excellent material.... the Jesuit teaching... was as subtile a mixture of the good and evil as the devil ever compounded. It was when the two witnesses were escaping from the bondage of the Dark Ages, where they had finished their testimony in sackcloth, that the beast, which ascended out of the bottomless pit,

---

[9] E. G. White, *The Great Controversy* (1911), p. 269.1-4.

[10] Sir Walter Scott, *Life of Napoleon*, Vol. 1 (New York: J & J Harper, 1827), ch. 17.

493

made war against them and overcame them, and killed them."[11] "The destruction of the papal clergy in France wonderfully prepared the way for the triumph of the Jesuits. The clergy stood by their king against the Pope. Professor Ranke observes, speaking of the time of Louis XIV and Innocent XI., 'It has ever been a maxim of the French court to control the papal power by means of the national clergy, and the national clergy by means of the papal power.'"[12] Even the famous British Prime Minister, Sir Winston Churchill, alludes to the political power behind the French Revolution—the beast from the bottomless pit: "From the days of Spartacus (the codename of Jesuit Adam Weishaupt), Weishophf, Karl Marx, Trotski, Belacoon, Rosa Luxenburg, and Ema Goldman, this world conspiracy has been steadily growing. This conspiracy played a definite recognizable role in the tragedy of the French revolution. It has been the mainspring of every subversive movement during the 19th Century."[13] France had been foremost among the nations of Europe in calling for the suppression of the Jesuit order for their part in tumults, disturbances, violence and of disturbing the peace of the church and the nations. "The Pope himself enumerated their weaknesses and faults, and declared that these were so great as to outweigh their manifest and signal services."[14] The French parliament passed a resolution for

---

[11] "The organization of the order of Jesuits, in reality a papacy of the papacy, sent into the world a body of active workers, shrewd, well educated, and armed with a double-faced conscience, which enabled them to penetrate anywhere and assume any role. One of their most efficient methods of procedure was in the schools. They founded new schools in the very shadow of the Protestant institutions, and drew from their patronage; or when this was impossible, they entered Protestant schools under the guise of Protestant teachers. Everywhere they gained the children and the youth. They were more zealous, more ambitious than the Protestants, consequently the succeeding generation surprised the Reformers by turning a large part of Europe back under papal control. Their work **was most fully developed in France. That country had received the light of the Reformation, but on this ground the Jesuits found excellent material.** The universities of France clung to their old methods, and they likewise clung to the subjects taught during the Dark Ages. Under the forms and ceremonies of Mediævalism, papal principles of government lurked, ready to spring into active service at the first opportunity. The renewal of these teachings wrought the same effect in the sixteenth century that the false teachings of the Alexandrian philosophers did in the church of the early Christians.

One cannot condemn **the Jesuit teaching** as wholly evil. It **was as subtile a mixture of the good and evil as the devil have compounded. It was when the two witnesses were escaping from the bondage of the Dark Ages, where they had finished their testimony in sackcloth, that the beast, which ascended out of the bottomless pit, made war against them and overcame them, and killed them."**

S. N. Haskell, *The Story of the Seer of Patmos* (1905), p. 198.2-200.1.

[12] J. V. Himes, "Prof. Gaussen on Papacy" *The Advent Herald*, July 24, 1844, p. 193.16.

[13] Sir Winston Churchill, "Zionism versus Bolshevism," *Illustrated Sunday Herald*, 8 February, 1920, p. 5.

[14] William Walker Rockwell, "The Jesuits as Portrayed by Non-Catholic Historians," *The Harvard Theological Review*, Vol. 7, No. 3 (July, 1914), p. 358.

their suppression in 1762. On July 23, 1773, Pope Clement XIV, signed a Papal decree suppressing the Jesuit order. In just sixteen years (1789), the French Revolution burst upon Europe—punishment of the suppression of the order. Pope Clement XIV was also punished, with death by poisoning. The pope cried out on his deathbed, "Alas! I knew they would poison me, but I did not expect to die in so slow and cruel a manner."[15] The punishing was not over. Nine years after the French Revolution began, and before it was terminated, the Papacy was further punished by the Jesuits for their suppression, with a "deadly wound"—the confiscation of temporal power and Papal properties in 1798.[16]

Revelation 11:9 And they of the people and kindreds and tongues and nations shall see their dead bodies three days and an half, and shall not suffer their dead bodies to be put in graves.

As a day represents a year in symbolic Bible prophecy,[17] God's Word would be dead for three and a half years, without honorable burial. In 1793, the legislative assembly of France outlawed the Bible, a law which continued in force for three and a half years.

Revelation 11:10 And they that dwell upon the earth shall rejoice over them, and make merry, and shall send gifts one to another; because these two prophets tormented them that dwelt on the earth.

During the French Revolution there was great rejoicing at the announcement that there was no God, and no Bible. However, as a result of this law, France descended into such anarchy and chaos that the legislature was shortly forced to rescind their law.

---

[15] P. D. Stuart, *Codeword Barbêlôn*, Vol. 1 (London: Lux Verbi Books, 2006), p. 251.

[16] See comments on Revelation 13:3, and Revelation 17:8.

[17] See comments on Daniel 7:25 and Revelation 11:2.

Revelation 11:11 And after three days and an half the Spirit of life from God entered into them, and they stood upon their feet; and great fear fell upon them which saw them.

"It was in 1793 that the decrees which abolished the Christian religion and set aside the Bible passed the French Assembly. Three years and a half later a resolution rescinding these decrees, thus granting toleration to the Scriptures, was adopted by the same body. The world stood aghast at the enormity of guilt which had resulted from a rejection of the Sacred Oracles, and men recognized the necessity of faith in God and His word as the foundation of virtue and morality."[18] Just as the Bible predicted, God's two witnesses were raised back to life.

Revelation 11:12 And they heard a great voice from heaven saying unto them, Come up hither. And they ascended up to heaven in a cloud; and their enemies beheld them.

Shortly after the French Revolution Bible societies were formed all over the world, and the Bible literally went like wildfire to every corner of the globe. Very few of these missionary societies existed prior to this, but God resurrected his Word, sent it throughout the earth and exalted it to heaven.

Revelation 11:13 And the same hour was there a great earthquake, and the tenth part of the city fell, and in the earthquake were slain of men seven thousand: and the remnant were affrighted, and gave glory to the God of heaven.

Since this passage is highly symbolic in nature, the earthquake is also taken as symbolic.

"When France publicly rejected God and set aside the Bible, wicked men and spirits of darkness exulted in their attainment of the object so long desired—a kingdom free from the restraints of the law of God. Because sentence against an evil work was not speedily executed, therefore the heart of the sons of men was 'fully set in them to do evil.' Ecclesiastes 8:11. But the transgression of a just

---

[18] E. G. White, *The Great Controversy* (1911), p. 287.1.

and righteous law must inevitably result in misery and ruin. Though not visited at once with judgments, the wickedness of men was nevertheless surely working out their doom. Centuries of apostasy and crime had been treasuring up wrath against the day of retribution; and when their iniquity was full, the despisers of God learned too late that it is a fearful thing to have worn out the divine patience. The restraining Spirit of God, which imposes a check upon the cruel power of Satan, was in a great measure removed, and he whose only delight is the wretchedness of men was permitted to work his will. Those who had chosen the service of rebellion were left to reap its fruits until the land was filled with crimes too horrible for pen to trace. From devastated provinces and ruined cities a terrible cry was heard—a cry of bitterest anguish. **France was shaken as if by an earthquake.** Religion, law, social order, the family, the state, and the church—all were smitten down by the impious hand that had been lifted against the law of God. Truly spoke the wise man: 'The wicked shall fall by his own wickedness.' 'Though a sinner do evil a hundred times, and his days be prolonged, yet surely I know that it shall be well with them that fear God, which fear before Him: but it shall not be well with the wicked.' Proverbs 11:5; Ecclesiastes 8:12, 13. 'They hated knowledge, and did not choose the fear of the Lord;' 'therefore shall they eat of the fruit of their own way, and be filled with their own devices.' Proverbs 1:29, 31."[19]

Revelation 11:14 The second woe is past; and, behold, the third woe cometh quickly.

Revelation 10:1 through 11:13 is a parenthetical statement in the middle of the seven trumpets. The first six trumpets come before this parenthetical statement. The last three trumpets are called woes. The first two woes are declared in chapter nine. The third woe is the seventh trumpet, and is outlined here.

Revelation 11:15 And the seventh angel sounded; and there were great voices in heaven, saying, The kingdoms of this world are become the kingdoms of our Lord, and of his Christ; and he shall reign for ever and ever.

---

[19] E. G. White, *The Great Controversy* (1911), p. 286.1.

The seventh trumpet is the proclamation of the second coming of Jesus, and the commencement of his eternal kingdom. "In the days of the voice of the seventh angel, when he shall begin to sound, the mystery of God should be finished, as he hath declared to his servants the prophets."[20] The "mystery of godliness" is that "God was manifest in the flesh,"[21] and in Colossians 1:27 we are told that the mystery of God "is Christ in you, the hope of glory." Our only hope of salvation is having Christ in us. We abide in Christ by his words abiding in us;[22] and it is by the word of God, that we are made "partakers of the divine nature."[23] God intends to manifest his character in us. When the seventh angel begins to sound, the mystery of God is to be finished. The marriage of Christ to his church is spoken of as a "great mystery." Notice the following passage from Ephesians: "Christ also loved the church, and gave himself for it; that he might sanctify and cleanse it with the washing of water by the word, that he might present it to himself a glorious church, not having spot, or wrinkle, or any such thing; but that it should be holy and without blemish.... For we are members of his body, of his flesh, and of his bones. For this cause shall a man leave his father and mother, and shall be joined unto his wife, and they two shall be one flesh. **This is a great mystery**: but I speak concerning Christ and the church."[24] Christ will sanctify and cleanse his church by the washing of water by the Word and present her to himself a glorious church without spot—holy and without blemish; perfectly reflecting his character. This is the mystery of God. When Jesus commenced intercession in the most holy place he began this process. His work will be finished in the days of the sounding of the seventh angel when the cleansing of the sanctuary as foretold by Daniel the prophet is complete.

Jesus spoke of this in his parable of the wedding garment.[25] "The parable of the wedding garment opens before us a lesson of the highest consequence. By the marriage is represented the union of humanity with divinity; the wedding garment represents the character

---

[20] Revelation 10:7

[21] 1 Timothy 3:16

[22] John 15:7

[23] 2 Peter 1:4

[24] Ephesians 5:25-32

[25] Matthew 22:1-14

which all must possess who shall be accounted fit guests for the wedding."[26]

The judgment scene or beginning of the cleansing of the Sanctuary in Daniel 7 refers to Jesus' reception of the kingdom from his Father.[27] In Luke, Jesus tells a parable of a nobleman who goes to a far country to receive a kingdom, and in another place he warns his disciples to be ready when he returns from the wedding to receive them.[28] The marriage, the receiving of a kingdom, and the cleansing of the sanctuary describe the same event.

"I saw the Father rise from the throne, and in a flaming chariot go into the holy of holies within the veil, and sit down. Then Jesus rose up from the throne, and the most of those who were bowed down arose with Him... and we heard His lovely voice saying, 'Wait here; I am going to My Father to **receive the kingdom**; keep your garments spotless, and in a little while I will **return from the wedding** and receive you to Myself.'"[29]

"The coming of Christ as our high priest to the most holy place, for the **cleansing of the sanctuary**, brought to view in Daniel 8:14; the coming of the Son of man to the Ancient of Days, as presented in Daniel 7:13; and the coming of the Lord to His temple, foretold by Malachi, are descriptions of the same event; and this is also represented by the **coming of the bridegroom to the marriage**, described by Christ in the parable of the ten virgins of Matthew 25.

"The proclamation, 'Behold, the Bridegroom cometh,' in the summer of 1844, led thousands to expect the immediate advent of the Lord. At the appointed time the Bridegroom came, not to the earth, as the people expected, but to the Ancient of Days in heaven, to the marriage, the reception of His kingdom. 'They that were ready went in with Him to the marriage: and the door was shut.' They were not to be present in person at the marriage; for it takes place in heaven, while they are upon the earth. The followers of Christ are to 'wait for their Lord, when He will return from the wedding.' Luke 12:36. But they are to understand His work, and to follow Him by faith as He goes in before God. It is in this sense that they are said to go in to the marriage.

---

26 E. G. White, *Christ's Object Lessons* (1900), p. 307.1.

27 Daniel 7:9-10, 13-14

28 Luke 19:11-12; 12:35-36

29 E. G. White, *Early Writings* (1882), p. 55.1.

"In the parable it was those that had oil in their vessels with their lamps that went in to the marriage.... And all who through the testimony of the Scriptures accept the same truths, following Christ by faith as He enters in before God to perform the last work of mediation, and at its close to receive His kingdom—all these are represented as going in to the marriage.

"In the parable of Matthew 22 the same figure of the marriage is introduced, and the investigative judgment is clearly represented as taking place before the marriage. Previous to the wedding the king comes in to see the guests, to see if all are attired in the wedding garment, the spotless robe of character washed and made white in the blood of the Lamb. Matthew 22:11; Revelation 7:14. He who is found wanting is cast out, but all who upon examination are seen to have the wedding garment on are accepted of God and accounted worthy of a share in His kingdom and a seat upon His throne. This work of examination of character, of determining who are prepared for the kingdom of God, is that of the investigative judgment, the closing of work in the sanctuary above.

"When the work of investigation shall be ended, when the cases of those who in all ages have professed to be followers of Christ have been examined and decided, then, and not till then, probation will close, and the door of mercy will be shut. Thus in the one short sentence, 'They that were ready went in with Him to the marriage: and the door was shut,' we are carried down through the Saviour's final ministration, to the time when the great work for man's salvation shall be completed."[30]

In the days when the seventh angel begins to blow his trumpet the mystery of God will be finished. God's people will be perfected; for his character will be manifested in them. His church will be without spot or wrinkle, and he will be able to present her to himself a glorious church, holy and without blemish. It is then that Jesus receives his kingdom.[31] When the last mediatorial work of Christ is finished, probation closes.

---

[30] E. G. White, *The Great Controversy* (1911), p. 426.1-428.2.

[31] "I saw that while Jesus was in the Most Holy place he would be married to the New Jerusalem, and after his work should be accomplished in the Holiest, he would descend to earth in kingly power and take the precious ones to himself who had patiently waited his return." E. G. White, *Spiritual Gifts,* Vol. 1 (1958), p. 157.1.

Revelation 11:16 And the four and twenty elders, which sat before God on their seats, fell upon their faces, and worshipped God,

Revelation 11:17 Saying, We give thee thanks, O Lord God Almighty, which art, and wast, and art to come; because thou hast taken to thee thy great power, and hast reigned.

The one who has promised to come again is Jesus. He receives the praise and worship of the twenty-four elders. They praise him because he has taken this great power to reign. All the kingdoms of the world are to be given to him. The one who died to save you from your sins is to be crowned the supreme monarch of all the universe.

Revelation 11:18 And the nations were angry, and thy wrath is come, and the time of the dead, that they should be judged, and that thou shouldest give reward unto thy servants the prophets, and to the saints, and them that fear thy name, small and great; and shouldest destroy them which destroy the earth.

God's wrath is come: "And I saw another sign in heaven, great and marvelous, seven angels having the seven last plagues; for in them is filled up the wrath of God."[32] The seven last plagues are the wrath of God. They will be covered in more detail in Revelation 16.

The time has come for God to give his servants their reward. When do God's servants receive their reward? In Revelation 22:11-12 Jesus makes a proclamation announcing the close of probation, "He that is unjust, let him be unjust still: and he which is filthy, let him be filthy still: and he that is righteous, let him be righteous still: and he that is holy, let him be holy still. And, behold, I come quickly; and my reward is with me, to give every man according as his work shall be."

"I saw that Jesus would not leave the most holy place until every case was decided either for salvation or destruction, and that the wrath of God could not come until Jesus had finished His work in the most holy place, laid off His priestly attire, and clothed Himself with the garments of vengeance. Then Jesus will step out from between the Father and man, and God will keep silence no longer, but pour

---

[32] Revelation 15:1

out His wrath on those who have rejected His truth. I saw that the anger of the nations, the wrath of God, and the time to judge the dead were separate and distinct, one following the other, also that Michael had not stood up, and that the time of trouble, such as never was, had not yet commenced. The nations are now getting angry, but when our High Priest has finished His work in the sanctuary, He will stand up, put on the garments of vengeance, and then the seven last plagues will be poured out.

"I saw that the four angels would hold the four winds until Jesus' work was done in the sanctuary, and then will come the seven last plagues."[33]

Revelation 11:19 And the temple of God was opened in heaven, and there was seen in his temple the ark of his testament: and there were lightnings, and voices, and thunderings, and an earthquake, and great hail.

Verse nineteen is a summary from the investigative judgment, beginning in 1844 ("the temple of God was opened in heaven"), to the second coming ("lightnings, and voices, and thunderings, and an earthquake, and great hail"). With almost identical language Revelation 16:18-20 says, "And there were voices, and thunders, and lightnings; and there was a great earthquake, such as was not since men were upon the earth, so mighty an earthquake, and so great.... And every island fled away, and the mountains were not found," adding the phrase referring to the islands and mountains disappearing. This statement comes immediately after the pronouncement "it is done." Revelation 6:14 also links the disappearance of the mountains and islands to the second coming, "And the heaven departed as a scroll when it is rolled together; and every mountain and island were moved out of their places."

Revelation 8:2-11:19 contains an inverted parallelism. The inverted parallelism takes us from the events surrounding the close of probation (Revelation 8:2-9:21) back in time to 1844 (Revelation 10), further back to events leading up to 1798 (Revelation 11:3-11:13), then returning to 1844 (Revelation 11:14-18), and finally revisiting the close of probation (verse 19). Recognizing this literary structure

---

[33] E. G. White, *Early Writings* (1882), p. 36.1-2.

helps to understand these events and their order and relation to each other.

There are several places in the book of Revelation which speak of an open or closed door. On the Day of Atonement in the earthly sanctuary when the priest would go into the most holy place, he would close the door of the temple, and open the door into the most holy place. In Revelation 4, we saw a door that opened into that most holy place. As Jesus went into the most holy place to begin his ministry, he first closed the door between the outer court and the holy place—so that as he opened the door into the most holy, one could not see in from the outer court. This symbolized the fact that it was not possible to see directly into the heavenly sanctuary from earth (the outer court) when Jesus entered there in 1844—our minds must enter by faith, not by sight.

"Then Jesus rose up and shut the door of the holy place, and opened the door into the most holy, and passed within the second veil, where **He now stands by the ark, and where the faith of Israel now reaches.**"[34]

"As foretold in the Scriptures, the ministration of Christ in the most holy place began at the termination of the prophetic days in 1844. To this time apply the words of the Revelator, 'The temple of God was opened in Heaven, and there was seen in his temple the ark of his testament.' [Revelation 11:19] The ark of God's testament is in the second apartment of the sanctuary. As Christ entered there, to minister in the sinner's behalf, the inner temple was opened, and the ark of God was brought to view. To those who by faith beheld the Saviour in his work of intercession, God's majesty and power were revealed. As the train of his glory filled the temple, light from the holy of holies was shed upon his waiting people on the earth."[35] Amen.

---

[34] E. G. White, *Early Writings* (1882), p. 42.1.

[35] E. G. White, *Spirit of Prophecy,* Vol. 4 (1884), p. 273.2.

Revelation 12

SUMMARY:
Revelation 12 describes more history of this world in one chapter, than any other in the Bible. Events are revealed from the rebellion of Lucifer in heaven, prior to the creation of this earth, to events immediately preceding the second coming of Christ. The great red dragon called the Devil and Satan tries to devour the pure woman clothed with the sun, and the moon under her feet. The woman flees into the wilderness for 1,260 years.

Revelation 12:1 And there appeared a great wonder in heaven; a woman clothed with the sun, and the moon under her feet, and upon her head a crown of twelve stars:

John's astonishment at what he sees in the vision of Revelation 12 is apparent from the words "**there appeared a great wonder in heaven**." God shows him a pure woman, clothed with the sun, with the moon under her feet, and 12 stars on her head. In Bible prophecy a woman represents a church. Jeremiah 6:2 says, "I have likened the daughter of Zion to a comely and delicate woman." The daughter of Zion is the church of God: "and say unto Zion, Thou art my people."[1] Zion also refers to a mountain located on the north side[2] of the temple in heaven. Isaiah refers to Zion as the mount of the congregation.[3] The daughter of Zion is therefore God's church, represented by a beautiful and pure woman. The Bible uses an impure woman to represent a false or apostate church—as will be apparent from Revelation 17.

The woman is "**clothed with the sun**." "But unto you that fear my name shall the Sun of righteousness arise with healing in his wings."[4] "I will greatly rejoice in the LORD, my soul shall be joyful in my God; for he hath…covered me with the robe of righteousness."[5]

---

[1] Isaiah 51:16

[2] Psalms 48:2

[3] Isaiah 14:12-14

[4] Malachi 4:2

[5] Isaiah 61:10

God's church is clothed with the Sun—the robe of Christ's righteousness.[6] "Who is she that looketh forth as the morning, fair as the moon, clear as the sun, and terrible as an army with banners?"[7] "The Sun of Righteousness has arisen; Christ is waiting to clothe his people with the garments of salvation."[8]

The moon under her feet represents the foundation of the ceremonial laws of types and shadows that reflected the light of the Sun of Righteousness. "It is the closing of one era, the age of types and shadows, which, like the moon, reflect the light of the true. The moon is under the feet of the church, and the glorious sunrising of a new day is ushered in. The paler light of the moon seems dim in that more glorious day. The types and ceremonies of the sanctuary service, which had been a shadow of the real, were passing away; for type met antitype in the Child that was born. Every sacrifice from the Garden of Eden to the cross, shadowed forth the great Sacrifice, and taught the everlasting Gospel. By faith, the sinner confessing his sins over the head of the innocent lamb, saw the real Sacrifice, and the light from Calvary reflected from the sacrifice shone into his heart. This service typified the Gospel in its fullness. This is the foundation upon which the church stands. It is not a stone slipping away, a sliding foundation, but a solid foundation upon which the living church rests. To-day the record of that typical service, emits light to the one who will search it. True, it does not have the full blaze of sunlight like the record of the antitypical offering, but there is a mild and gentle light emitted from it that well repays the searcher after truth."[9]

The crown of twelve stars symbolize the twelve apostles— representatives of the New Testament church. "As in the Old Testament the twelve patriarchs stood as representatives of Israel, so the twelve apostles stand as representatives of the gospel church."[10]

---

[6] See also Revelation 19:8.

[7] Song of Solomon 6:10

[8] E. G. White, The *Review and Herald,* July 2, 1895 par. 5.

[9] S. N. Haskell, *The Story of the Seer of Patmos* (1905), p. 212.3.

[10] E. G. White, *Acts of the Apostles* (1911), p. 19.1.

Revelation 12:2 And she being with child cried, travailing in birth, and pained to be delivered.

God's church is represented as being ready to give birth. From the entrance of sin into the world the promise was given of the seed of the woman who would come to crush the power of the serpent. This woman is represented as being pregnant, having the promised seed in her womb. Genesis 3:15 records this prophecy: "And I will put enmity between thee and the woman, and between thy seed and her seed; it shall bruise thy head, and thou shalt bruise his heel." Immediately after Adam and Eve sinned God came and spoke to them of the curses that sin would bring to the earth. He then pronounced a curse upon the serpent, and issued a promise that he would put enmity between Satan and the woman, between Satan's seed and the woman's seed. God promised that even though our human nature would be deranged by sin, he would place a natural enmity between those that follow God and those that follow Satan. Finally, God promised that the seed of the woman would come and bruise the head of the serpent, and in the process his heel would receive a bruise from the serpent. The vision of Revelation twelve portrays to John the very same promise given to Adam and Eve in Eden.

Genesis 3:16, continues: "Unto the woman he said, I will greatly multiply thy sorrow and thy conception; in sorrow thou shalt bring forth children; and thy desire shall be to thy husband, and he shall rule over thee." In the continuation of his pronouncement, God says that the woman's conception would be multiplied and that she would experience suffering and travail in childbirth. The woman of Revelation 12:2, **"cried, travailing in birth, and pained to be delivered."** It would be a painful process for God's church (which was literal Israel when the Messiah arrived) to receive the seed of the woman, Jesus Christ, as their redeemer from the power of Satan, for they sought political power rather than deliverance from sin.

Revelation 12:3 And there appeared another wonder in heaven; and behold a great red dragon, having seven heads and ten horns, and seven crowns upon his heads.

The dragon represents Satan as we shall see in verse nine.

Revelation 12:4 And his tail drew the third part of the stars of heaven, and did cast them to the earth: and the dragon stood before the woman which was ready to be delivered, for to devour her child as soon as it was born.

The "**third part of the stars**" being cast to the earth will be covered in verse nine.

The dragon's intention was to destroy the seed of the woman as soon as he was born. Truly Satan tried everything he could to destroy Jesus at his birth.[11]

"The line of prophecy in which these symbols are found begins with Revelation 12, with the dragon that sought to destroy Christ at His birth. The dragon is said to be Satan (Revelation 12:9); he it was that moved upon Herod to put the Saviour to death. But the chief agent of Satan in making war upon Christ and His people during the first centuries of the Christian Era was the Roman Empire, in which paganism was the prevailing religion. Thus while the dragon, primarily, represents Satan, it is, in a secondary sense, a symbol of pagan Rome."[12]

"When Jesus came into the world, Satan's power was turned against Him. From the time when He appeared as a babe in Bethlehem, the usurper worked to bring about His destruction. In every possible way he sought to prevent Jesus from developing a perfect childhood, a faultless manhood, a holy ministry, and an unblemished sacrifice. But he was defeated. He could not lead Jesus into sin. He could not discourage Him, or drive Him from a work He had come on earth to do. From the desert to Calvary, the storm of Satan's wrath beat upon Him, but the more mercilessly it fell, the more firmly did the Son of God cling to the hand of His Father, and press on in the bloodstained path. All the efforts of Satan to oppress and overcome Him only brought out in a purer light His spotless character."[13]

---

[11] See Matthew 2.

[12] E. G. White, *The Great Controversy* (1911), p. 438.2.

[13] E. G. White, *The Desire of Ages* (1898), p. 759.4.

Revelation 12:5 And she brought forth a man child, who was to rule all nations with a rod of iron: and her child was caught up unto God, and to his throne.

Here we see clearly that the child of the woman is Jesus, for it is he who is to rule all nations with the rod of iron.[14] Even though this woman is portrayed as giving birth to Jesus, it is not speaking of Mary the mother of Jesus, as some may suggest. This is evident in the following verse. God simply represents Jesus being born of a woman or coming through his established church at the time of his first coming.

Revelation 12:6 And the woman fled into the wilderness, where she hath a place prepared of God, that they should feed her there a thousand two hundred and threescore days.

This prophetic time period is repeated seven different times in Scripture.[15] As outlined in Daniel seven, 1,260 days represents 1,260 years.[16] Therefore this cannot symbolize Mary, the literal mother of Jesus, because Mary did not flee into the wilderness for 1,260 years.[17] Rather it is a symbolic picture of God's church fleeing into the wilderness during this prophetic period of persecution.

"The faith which for centuries was held and taught by the Waldensian Christians was in marked contrast to the false doctrines put forth from Rome. Their religious belief was founded upon the written word of God, the true system of Christianity. But those humble peasants, in their obscure retreats, shut away from the world, and bound to daily toil among their flocks and their vineyards, had not by themselves arrived at the truth in opposition to the dogmas and heresies of the apostate church. Theirs was not a faith newly received. Their religious belief was their inheritance from their fathers. They contended for the faith of the apostolic church, — 'the faith which was once delivered unto the saints.' Jude 3. 'The church in the wilderness,' and not the proud hierarchy enthroned in the

---

[14] See Revelation 19:15; Psalm 2:7-9.

[15] See comments on Daniel 7:25.

[16] Numbers 14:34; Ezekiel 4:6

[17] Revelation 12:14

world's great capital, was the true church of Christ, the guardian of the treasures of truth which God has committed to His people to be given to the world."[18]

Revelation 12:7 And there was war in heaven: Michael and his angels fought against the dragon; and the dragon fought and his angels,

Revelation chapter twelve is divided into two halves, which we will cover in more detail towards the end of the chapter; however, this verse is the beginning of the second half of the chapter. This division forms a Hebrew parallelism, where Scripture states something in one way and then restates it in another way, repeating and enlarging. This verse carries us back to the beginning by saying, "**there was war in heaven**," a parallel statement to "there appeared a great wonder in heaven," from verse one. The curtain of celestial history is drawn back and we glimpse a galactic warfare waged in heaven itself. Normally we do not think of heaven as being a place of warfare, but Scripture testifies that the dragon and his angels battled Michael and his angels in the courts of paradise. War in heaven is certainly a great wonder.

Many today have a misunderstanding of the identity of Michael. As always, we must allow the Bible to be its own interpreter. "Yet Michael the archangel, when contending with the devil he disputed about the body of Moses, durst not bring against him a railing accusation, but said, The Lord rebuke thee."[19] Michael was in a dispute with the devil in heaven; in Jude, Michael contends with the devil again.[20] Jude identifies Michael as the archangel.[21] Paul identifies the archangel: "For the Lord himself shall descend from heaven with a shout, with the voice of the archangel, and with the trump of God: and the dead in Christ shall rise first."[22] It is the Lord

---

[18] E. G. White, *The Great Controversy* (1911), p. 64.2.

[19] Jude 1:9

[20] Jude 1:9 also demonstrates that Moses was raised from the dead, and taken to heaven. This is the reason why Moses appeared to Jesus on the Mount of Transfiguration.

[21] The archangel is not one of the two covering cherubs over the ark of the covenant. The ark of the covenant is spelled A-R-K. The word "arch-angel"—A-R-C-H—means angel above all angels.

[22] 1 Thessalonians 4:16

who has the voice of the archangel, therefore he is the archangel. Michael is another name for Jesus.[23] The name Michael means "who is what God is" or "who is like God." Jesus is the one victorious against Satan over the body of Moses—the resurrection and the life—and Jesus was victorious over Satan in the war in heaven.

Revelation 12:8 And prevailed not; neither was their place found any more in heaven.

Revelation 12:9 And the great dragon was cast out, that old serpent, called the Devil, and Satan, which deceiveth the whole world: he was cast out into the earth, and his angels were cast out with him.

The symbol of the dragon is defined by Scripture as representing Satan. This passage also allows us to understand what the Bible was speaking of when it said, in verse four, that the dragon's "tail drew the third part of the stars of heaven, and did cast them to the earth." In verse four it says the tail of the dragon cast down a third of the stars, and here, it tells us that Satan was cast out with his angels. Because of the parallel nature of the chapter, we can see that the angels who were cast out with Satan are the same as the stars who were cast down from heaven by the tail of the dragon. Thereby we

---

[23] Some may think that calling Jesus an angel implies that he is a created being. This is certainly not the case. In Scripture the title "angel" does not apply exclusively to created beings. The word "angel" simply means "messenger." Jesus is certainly the messenger above all messengers. Frequently in Scripture God is portrayed as an angel. We find one of the most notable in Exodus 3:2. "And the angel {mal'ak} of the LORD appeared unto him {Moses} in a flame of fire out of the midst of a bush: and he looked, and, behold, the bush burned with fire, and the bush was not consumed." In this passage the angel of the Lord appears in the bush out of the flame of fire. Just a few verses later the Bible says, "And when the LORD saw that he turned aside to see, **God called unto him out of the midst of the bush**, and said, Moses, Moses. And he said, Here am I. And he said, Draw not nigh hither: put off thy shoes from off thy feet, for the place whereon thou standest is holy ground."[18] God called to him out of the midst of the bush. So, in the one verse, it says it is the angel of the Lord who is in the midst of the bush, and in subsequent verses, it says it is the Lord who calls out of the bush. This makes the Lord the angel.

We find another example of this in the book of Malachi: "Behold, I will send my messenger, and he shall prepare the way before me:" Malachi 3:1. The word for "messenger" in the original language is מלאך mal'âk. "Mal'âk" is the same word that is translated "angel," in Exodus 3:2. We can see clearly that an angel is a messenger, for it says, "I will send my messenger." The verse continues on, "and the Lord, whom ye seek, shall suddenly come to his temple, even the messenger of the covenant, whom ye delight in: behold, he shall come, saith the LORD of hosts." Again, the word for messenger is mal'âk. Here there are two messengers: the Lord's messenger (mal'ak) who is to prepare the way of the Lord, and the Lord himself, the messenger (mal'ak) of the covenant. The Lord is called an angel. The first messenger refers to John the Baptist, the second to Christ himself.

know that a third of the angels of heaven placed their allegiance on the side of Satan and were expelled with him.

Revelation 12:10 And I heard a loud voice saying in heaven, Now is come salvation, and strength, and the kingdom of our God, and the power of his Christ: for the accuser of our brethren is cast down, which accused them before our God day and night.

Satan is called "**the accuser of our brethren**." Of this Zechariah has written, "And he showed me Joshua the high priest"—representing the people of God—"standing before the angel of the LORD, and Satan standing at his right hand to resist him."[24] Satan stands before God as the accuser of his people. "With masterly power he presents their objectionable features of character as sufficient reason for the withdrawal of Christ's protecting power, thus allowing Satan to discourage and destroy those whom he has caused to sin. But Christ has made atonement for every sinner. We may by faith hear our Advocate saying, 'The Lord rebuke thee, O Satan; even the Lord that hath chosen Jerusalem rebuke thee: is not this a brand plucked out of the burning?'" [25]

"When one who has wandered far in sin seeks to return to God, he will encounter criticism and distrust. There are those who will doubt whether his repentance is genuine, or will whisper, 'He has no stability; I do not believe that he will hold out.' These persons are doing not the work of God but the work of Satan, who is the accuser of the brethren. Through their criticisms the wicked one hopes to discourage that soul, and to drive him still farther from hope and from God. Let the repenting sinner contemplate the rejoicing in heaven over the return of the one that was lost. Let him rest in the love of God and in no case be disheartened by the scorn and suspicion of the Pharisees."[26]

This verse tells us, "**Now is come salvation, and strength, and the kingdom of our God, and the power of his Christ**." This is an

---

[24] Zechariah 3:1

[25] E. G. White, *Sermons and Talks*, Vol. 2 (1994), p. 211.2.

[26] E. G. White, *Christ's Object Lessons* (1900), p. 190.2.

announcement that Jesus, the Messiah, has come; that he is our salvation; that he has tasted "death for every man;"[27] that he has met the devil and won. When Jesus came to this earth he "came into Galilee, preaching the gospel of the kingdom of God, And saying, The time is fulfilled, and the kingdom of God is at hand: repent ye, and believe the gospel."[28]

The power of Christ is in Christ crucified for "we preach Christ crucified, unto the Jews a stumblingblock, and unto the Greeks foolishness; But unto them which are called.... Christ the power of God, and the wisdom of God."[29]

"Could one sin have been found in Christ, had He in one particular yielded to Satan to escape the terrible torture, the enemy of God and man would have triumphed. Christ bowed His head and died, but He held fast His faith and His submission to God. '**And I heard a loud voice saying in heaven, Now is come salvation, and strength, and the kingdom of our God, and the power of His Christ: for the accuser of our brethren is cast down, which accused them before our God day and night.**' Revelation 12:10.

"Satan saw that his disguise was torn away. His administration was laid open before the unfallen angels and before the heavenly universe. He had revealed himself as a murderer. By shedding the blood of the Son of God, he had uprooted himself from the sympathies of the heavenly beings. Henceforth his work was restricted. Whatever attitude he might assume, he could no longer await the angels as they came from the heavenly courts, and before them accuse Christ's brethren of being clothed with the garments of blackness and the defilement of sin. The last link of sympathy between Satan and the heavenly world was broken.

"Yet Satan was not then destroyed. The angels did not even then understand all that was involved in the great controversy. The principles at stake were to be more fully revealed. And for the sake of man, Satan's existence must be continued. Man as well as angels must see the contrast between the Prince of light and the prince of darkness. He must choose whom he will serve."[30]

---

[27] Hebrews 2:9

[28] Mark 1:14-15

[29] 1 Corinthians 1:23-24.

[30] E. G. White, *The Desire of Ages* (1898), p. 761.1-3.

Revelation 12:11 And they overcame him by the blood of the Lamb, and by the word of their testimony; and they loved not their lives unto the death.

It is **"by the blood of the Lamb"** that we overcome Satan. His blood is our only safety in our warfare against the powers of darkness. We also overcome by the **"word of {our} testimony."** If we do not have a testimony of what the Lord has done for us, we cannot overcome Satan. It is when we have an experience with Jesus, when we see him working in our lives, when we know that He has transformed our lives, when He has forgiven our sins and made us a new creation; when we have that testimony to give, we have evidence that we have applied his blood. We must experience the transforming power of the grace provided by his sacrifice. God has provided the power to gain victory over sin and temptation; "there are struggles before us all, but we may be overcomers. We may overcome by the blood of the Lamb and the word of His testimony."[31]

"They loved not their lives unto the death". The gospel of Christ and the truth of Scripture become more precious than life itself to the people of God. Their life is hid in Christ, who died for them.

Revelation 12:12 Therefore rejoice, ye heavens, and ye that dwell in them. Woe to the inhabiters of the earth and of the sea! for the devil is come down unto you, having great wrath, because he knoweth that he hath but a short time.

Even the heavens are rejoicing. Though they know that the earth is in trouble, the angels of heaven are rejoicing that Satan is no longer there to accuse and tempt. Satan comes against the inhabitants of earth with **"great wrath, because he knoweth"** his time is short; therefore he is filled with fury. When Satan sees someone coming to a knowledge of truth; when he sees someone gaining an experience with Jesus that would allow him to have that testimony that would overcome the dragon, the devil becomes angry, and brings all kinds of distractions, discouragement, deceptions, detours, drowsiness, doubt, darkness, disease and disaster to keep this from happening.

---

[31] E. G. White, *The Wisconsin Reporter,* September 15, 1909 par. 10.

Revelation 12:13 And when the dragon saw that he was cast unto the earth, he persecuted the woman which brought forth the man child.

Satan has been seeking to destroy Christ's church since the beginning. When he sees that he is cast down to the earth by Christ's victory over him, he takes out his hatred for Christ on his church.

Revelation 12:14 And to the woman were given two wings of a great eagle, that she might fly into the wilderness, into her place, where she is nourished for a time, and times, and half a time, from the face of the serpent.

God's true church fled to the wilderness to escape the terrible persecution of the serpent. It is the wilderness that protects the woman. In symbolic Bible prophecy, waters represent peoples, nations, multitudes, and tongues.[32] Wilderness, therefore, by contrast, represents the lack of people, nations, multitudes, and tongues—relatively unpopulated places of the world. These are the places that were the strongholds for God's church during those fierce days of persecution.

"Some will ask, Should not we look to the church which for ages has been the favored of kings and nations to find the true church instead of looking to a people who for centuries were never the dominant church, and who many times were obscure? Let the prophet John answer this question: 'The woman [church] fled into the wilderness.' (Revelation 12:6.) In order to recognize the true church, it is imperative that we fix our eyes upon those Christian bodies which have largely been forgotten in the works of history.
Divine revelation teaches that the light which was to shine upon the last generation of men would be a continuation and an enlargement of the light which shone upon the Church in the Wilderness throughout almost thirteen centuries; namely, the 1,260 year period."[33]

---

[32] Revelation 17:15.

[33] B.G. Wilkinson, Ph.D., *Truth Triumphant: The Church in the Wilderness* (1944), p. 10.

Again, we see that the passage cannot be speaking of Mary, because she was not given wings to fly into the wilderness. Rather the passage is highly symbolic, representing the church as the woman taking refuge in the wilderness. Her wings indicate the fact that God carries her there with swiftness where she can be safe for the specified period of time.

As noted in the previous chapter a "time" is a year;[34] "times," therefore, must be two years and half a time is half a year. Three and a half years are therefore specified. One Biblical year is 360 days;[35] two years are 720 days; half a year is 180 days. The sum is 1,260 days, which represent 1,260 years.[36]

God emphasizes the importance of this time prophecy by repeating it seven different times in Scripture,[37] so we do not miss its gravity.

As revealed in Daniel 7 and Revelation 11, the 1,260 years were the period of papal supremacy, the time during which the papacy was given political power from A.D. 538 to 1798. The Bible prophesied that this power would reign during the specified time, while God's church would be shielded, to some degree, from Satanic persecution, by the fortresses of the wilderness.

---

[34] Daniel 4:16.

[35] See the story of the flood in Genesis 6-8.

[36] The prophetic principle of one day representing one year is found in Ezekiel 4:6 and Numbers 14:34. See also comments on Daniel 7:25.

[37] Daniel 7:25: "time, times, and a dividing of time."
Daniel 12:7: "time, times, and an half"
Revelation 11:2: "forty and two months"
Revelation 11:3: "a thousand two hundred and threescore days"
Revelation 12:6: "a thousand two hundred and threescore days"
Revelation 12:14: "time, and times, and half a time"
Revelation 13:5: "forty and two months"

The way in which the Bible presents this time period in so many forms helps us to verify any of the assumptions we might have made. For example, someone might say, Well, you're making an assumption to say a dividing of times is a half a time. No, for in one place it mentions it as a "dividing of time," but in the other place it mentions it as a "half a time." Others might say, You're making the assumption to say that there are 360 days in a year. The fact is that 360 days in a year, times three and a half, comes out to exactly 1,260 days; therefore, we know that we were correct in the conclusion that a Biblical year is 360 days. The time period is also presented as 42 months, which if you multiply by 30 days—in a 360-day year every month has 30 days—it comes to 1,260 days. The various presentations of the same information provide validation, allowing Scripture to interpret itself. The different passages in which these time periods are given were written in three different languages—Aramaic for the first passage, Hebrew for the second, and Greek for the last five—yet it all matches perfectly so that we do not misunderstand or misinterpret.

Revelation chapter 12 follows a literary pattern called a Hebrew parallelism. The first half of the parallelism is comprised of verses 1 through 6. The second half of the parallelism is verses 7 through 14. Verses 15-17 give additional detail not in the first half of the parallelism.

12:1 "wonder in heaven"	12:7 "war in heaven"
12:2 the woman "travailing in birth"	12:8 dragon "prevailed not"
12:3 "great red dragon"	12:9 "the great dragon was cast out"
12:4 "his tail drew the third part of the stars of heaven, and did cast them to the earth"	12:9b "his angels were cast out with him."
12:5 "And she brought forth a man child, who was to rule all nations with a rod of iron" "her child was caught up unto God, and to his throne."	12:10 "Now is come salvation, and strength, and the kingdom of our God, and the power of his Christ" "for the accuser of our brethren is cast down, which accused them before our God day and night."
12:6 "woman fled into the wilderness, where she hath a place prepared of God" "that they should feed her there a thousand two hundred and threescore days."	12:14 "to the woman were given two wings of a great eagle, that she might fly into the wilderness, into her place" "where she is nourished for a time, and times, and half a time"

Revelation 12:15 And the serpent cast out of his mouth water as a flood after the woman, that he might cause her to be carried away of the flood.

As with the rest of the passage, the flood is symbolic. The Bible defines its own symbols: "The waters which thou sawest, where the whore sitteth, are peoples, and multitudes, and nations, and tongues."[38] Waters represent masses of people. Satan would cause a flood of people—the armies of Western civilization—to war against

---

[38] Revelation 17:15

God's church in an attempt to swallow her up, yet God provided help for the woman in the form of the earth.

Revelation 12:16 And the earth helped the woman, and the earth opened her mouth, and swallowed up the flood which the dragon cast out of his mouth.

The earth, being the opposite of water, therefore represent the unpopulated places of the world which would swallow up the nations that came against the woman. The earth allowed God's people to worship freely, protected by God in the solitary places of the world. During the rise and peak of the midnight darkness of papal tyranny in Western Europe, we find that God's church fled into the wilderness, taking the Scriptures with them, thereby spreading the Gospel to the entire planet. The converts to Christianity in China during the middle ages numbered in the millions.[39] A stone monument, discovered in 1625 and erected in A.D. 781, stands in Pei Lin commemorating the arrival of Christianity in China.[40] Tamerlane (c. A.D. 1333-1405) slew Christians by the hundreds of thousands, if not, by the millions.[41] Christianity penetrated to Syria, India, Mongolia, China, Japan, the Philippines, and Africa. The Los Lunas Decalogue stone discovered in 1933, in New Mexico, has an abridged Ten Commandments inscribed in paleo-Hebrew text. The stone's inscription is considered to be from 500-2000 years old. There were the Albigenses and Huguenots of France, and the Waldenses of the Piedmont, who kept the faith alive in Europe. God's faithful people lived in the lonely mountain fastness away from the multitudes of people, and were protected there, yet were driven to carry the gospel further and further to the ends of the earth. Near the end of the 1,260 years, Christians fled from the masses of Europe to the shores of the new lands of America—wilderness lands—to escape religious persecution, and worship God in freedom. The principles of religious liberty in the United States of America were born of a fulfillment of this prophecy.

---

[39] B.G. Wilkinson, Ph.D., *Truth Triumphant: The Church in the Wilderness* (Mountain View, CA: Pacific Press, 1944), p. 290-291.

[40] *Ibid.*, p. 332-334.

[41] *Ibid.*, p. 357.

"In the midst of exile and hardship their love and faith waxed strong. They trusted the Lord's promises, and He did not fail them in time of need. His angels were by their side, to encourage and support them. And when God's hand seemed pointing them across the sea, to a land where they might found for themselves a state, and leave to their children the precious heritage of religious liberty, they went forward, without shrinking, in the path of providence.

"God had permitted trials to come upon His people to prepare them for the accomplishment of His gracious purpose toward them. The church had been brought low, that she might be exalted. God was about to display His power in her behalf, to give to the world another evidence that He will not forsake those who trust in Him. He had overruled events to cause the wrath of Satan and the plots of evil men to advance His glory and to bring His people to a place of security. Persecution and exile were opening the way to freedom."[42]

Revelation 12:17 And the dragon was wroth with the woman, and went to make war with the remnant of her seed, which keep the commandments of God, and have the testimony of Jesus Christ.

After the dark ages, the 1,260 years of papal persecution; after the woman fled into the wilderness; after the dragon poured out his fury on the pure woman; he is once more angry with the remnant (or remainder) of her seed. There is a small remnant of Christ's church still keeping the commandments of God, who have the testimony of Jesus Christ, and this makes the dragon furious.

"Zechariah's vision of Joshua and the Angel applies with peculiar force to the experience of God's people in the closing up of the great day of atonement. The remnant church will be brought into great trial and distress. Those who **"keep the commandments of God"** and the faith of Jesus will feel the ire of the dragon and his hosts. Satan numbers the world as his subjects, he has gained control of the apostate churches; but here is a little company that are resisting his supremacy. If he could blot them from the earth, his triumph would be complete. As he influenced the heathen nations to destroy Israel, so in the near future he will stir up the wicked powers of earth to destroy the people of God. All will be required to render obedience to

---

[42] E. G. White, *The Great Controversy* (1911), p. 291.1-2.

human edicts in violation of the divine law. Those who will be true to God and to duty will be menaced, denounced, and proscribed. They will 'be betrayed both by parents, and brethren, and kinsfolks, and friends.'
"Their only hope is in the mercy of God; their only defense will be prayer."[43]

Scripture provides here two criteria for identifying God's faithful remnant people at the end of time. First, they will "**keep the commandments of God**."[44] Second, they will "**have the testimony of Jesus Christ**." What is the testimony of Jesus Christ? The Bible tells us in Revelation 19:10, "the testimony of Jesus is the spirit of prophecy." God's end-time remnant people, according to Scripture, will posses the gift of the spirit of prophecy.[45] "There is but one church in the world who are... fulfilling the description given of the remnant people, who keep the commandments of God and have faith in Jesus."[46] The Seventh-day Adventist Church is the only organization in the world that meets the specification of this verse as the remnant church of Bible prophecy.[47]

Revelation chapter twelve encompasses momentous events, giving us a sweep of history, from the war in heaven prior to the creation of this world, down to the very end of time when the dragon is angry with the remnant people who are following God's law and his prophets. May you be on the side of God and not on the side of the dragon. Make the stand to be among God's remnant people, who love not their lives unto death, who overcome the dragon by the blood of the Lamb and the word of their testimony, who keep his commandments and have the testimony of Jesus Christ. Amen.

---

[43] E. G. White, *Testimonies for the Church,* Vol. 5 (1889), p. 472.2-3.

[44] The commandments of God are recorded in Exodus 20 and Deuteronomy 5.

[45] For more on the spirit of prophecy, see comments on Daniel 10.

[46] E. G. White, *Last Day Events* (1992), p. 43.3.

[47] See comments on Daniel 4b.

Revelation 13

SUMMARY:

Revelation chapter 13 introduces a beast that rises out of the sea with seven heads and ten horns, a mouth like a lion, feet like a bear, and a body like a leopard. It reigns for forty-two months (1260 days), and appears to receive a deadly wound which is subsequently healed, causing all the world to worship him. Another beast arises out of the earth, with horns like a lamb, which eventually speaks as a dragon. The earth beast creates an image to the sea beast and causes the whole earth to worship the sea beast, via the image, forcing the reception of the mark of the beast. The beast has a cryptic number which is the most famous (or infamous) number in all of Scripture—666.

"The thirteenth chapter of Revelation presents a power that is to be made prominent in these last days. Let all understand that it is Christ, the Captain of the Lord's host, who gave these visions to John. Christ came in person to the lonely isle of Patmos, and showed John the things that must be, things that were of the highest importance to His people... This message is to come to God's people, straight, sharp, and clean from all mixture of human wisdom and tradition."[1]

Revelation 13 parallels the seventh chapter of Daniel. In Daniel 7 were portrayed four beasts representing four world empires. Also outlined were at least ten different identifying marks for the little horn power. In Revelation 13, Jesus provides even more marks of identification for the same power.

Revelation 13:1 And I stood upon the sand of the sea, and saw a beast rise up out of the sea, having seven heads and ten horns, and upon his horns ten crowns, and upon his heads the name of blasphemy.

The sea or water in Bible prophecy represents multitudes, nations, peoples, and tongues.[2] A beast in Bible prophecy represents a

---

[1] E. G. White, *Manuscript Releases*, Vol. 18 (1990), p. 33.2.

[2] Revelation 17:15

kingdom or a political power.[3] This verse is revealing that the specified kingdom or political power would rise up in the midst of the populated places of the earth. It also has the characteristic of having seven heads and ten horns. This characteristic is directly parallel to the characteristics of the dragon outlined in Revelation 12:3.

The heads of the beast have a blasphemous name inscribed on them. The location of this name of blasphemy on the heads is important in verse eighteen, where the Bible unmasks the famous number of the beast—666.

Revelation 13:2 And the beast which I saw was like unto a leopard, and his feet were as the feet of a bear, and his mouth as the mouth of a lion: and the dragon gave him his power, and his seat, and great authority.

Direct parallels to the seventh chapter of Daniel are outlined here. In Daniel 7 there were four world empires represented by four beasts, which arose from the sea. The first beast was like a lion, the second was like a bear, the third like a leopard, and the fourth was a terrible beast.

This leopardlike sea-beast, from Revelation 13, is a composite of the four beasts from Daniel 7, yet the components that make up this beast are mentioned in the exact reverse order from the order given in Daniel 7. Daniel was physically located in the empire of Babylon when he received the vision of Daniel 7. From his position in history, he glimpsed the future empires represented by the lion, the bear, the leopard and the terrible beast—Babylon, Medo-Persia, Greece, and Rome. When John receives his vision he is physically located in the fourth kingdom of Rome. In Revelation 13 he is viewing empires that have passed into history. From his vantage point, he sees Rome in his day, Greece, Medo-Persia, with Babylon being the furthest in the past. This is the reason for mentioning the components of this beast in the reverse from the order of the beasts in Daniel 7.

The leopard-like beast receives its power, seat, and great authority directly from the dragon, or Satan himself.

---

[3] Daniel 7:17, 23

Revelation 13:3 And I saw one of his heads as it were wounded to death; and his deadly wound was healed: and all the world wondered after the beast.

Here Jesus brings to view three stages of the beast's power. First, the stage prior to being wounded, during which time it wields its full political power. Second, the stage during which a seemingly deadly wound is received which curtails this power. Third, the stage when the wound is healed and all the world wonders after the beast. From the progression of the verse, we see that it is as a result of the healing of the wound that the world wonders after the beast. Therefore, the wondering must occur after the healing.

In Daniel 7 we are told that the little horn power would persecute the saints for 1,260 years. "In [Revelation] chapter 13 (verses 1-10) is described another beast, 'like unto a leopard,' to which the dragon gave 'his power, and his seat, and great authority.' This symbol, as most Protestants have believed, represents the papacy, which succeeded to the power and seat and authority once held by the ancient Roman Empire. Of the leopardlike beast it is declared: 'There was given unto him a mouth speaking great things and blasphemies.... And he opened his mouth in blasphemy against God, to blaspheme His name, and His tabernacle, and them that dwell in heaven. And it was given unto him to make war with the saints, and to overcome them: and power was given him over all kindreds, and tongues, and nations.' This prophecy, which is nearly identical with the description of the little horn of Daniel 7, unquestionably points to the papacy."[4]

Just as the Bible predicted, the papacy gained its political power in A.D. 538 with Justinian's recovery of Rome from the Ostrogoths for the papacy. Precisely 1,260 years later, on February 15, 1798, Napoleon's general Berthier took Pope Pius VI captive (who died in exile), bringing an end to the papacy's status as a nation. At this time they lost most of their lands and buildings. Later, on September 20, 1870, the last of the papal states were lost, when Italian troops seized the city of Rome again leaving the pope a virtual prisoner.[5]

---

[4] E. G. White, *The Great Controversy* (1911), p. 439.1.

[5] http://biblelight.net/satan.htm retrieved 1-29-2017

The wound was delivered to the head of the beast. A beast in Bible prophecy is a political power. Therefore, it was the monarchy of the

papacy that was wounded, not the ecclesial presence. It was the state of the papacy that received "**as it were**," a deadly wound; the church continued to function during this time; popes continued to be elected, functioning as prime bishop, but not as head of the Vatican State. The words of Scriptures were fulfilled exactly.

However, Christ also came to the lonely isle of Patmos to reveal to the apostle John that the deadly wound was to be healed. On February 12, 1929, almost as if speaking prophetic words, the San Francisco Chronicle published a front-page article entitled, "Heal Wound Of Many Years."[6] The article reported that on the prior day, February 11, Mussolini, dictator of Italy, signed a concordant with the Vatican granting them back their political power and lands.
Some have advanced the idea that the wound cannot really be healed until the papacy becomes a persecuting power again. This is not consistent with Scripture, for if we allow the Bible to define what the deadly wound was, we recognize that the wounding was the loss

---

[6] http://biblelight.net/wound.htm retrieved 1-29-2017

of their political power and lands in 1798. Therefore, simple logic demands that the healing of that wound must be the restoration of what was lost in the wounding, not the reinstatement of persecution. In fact, persecution had almost wholly ceased over a quarter of a century before 1798, making it impossible for the deadly wound to be the cessation of persecution. "The 1260 days, or years, terminated in 1798. A quarter of a century earlier, persecution had almost wholly ceased."[7] Clearly the events of February 11, 1929, meet the criteria for the healing of the wound—that is, the restoration of what was lost in 1798.

The San Francisco Chronicle was not the only newspaper to mention this event. The same day, Arnaldo Cortesi, writing for the *New York Times* stated: "From 11 o'clock this morning there was another sovereign independent State in the world."[8] The papacy is now "another sovereign independent State." This is very similar language to the San Francisco Chronicle. In other words, its political power had been restored; its deadly wound healed. It is amazing that secular news commentators recognize things that many Christians do not seem to see. As a result of the deadly wound being healed, all the world is now wondering after the beast, just as Scripture predicted.

Revelation 13:4 And they worshipped the dragon which gave power unto the beast: and they worshipped the beast, saying, Who is like unto the beast? who is able to make war with him?

Worship is a primary theme in this and the next chapter with a contrast being made between the worship of the dragon and the worship of the Creator. The dragon (Satan[9]) attempts to force the entire world to worship him, but God accepts worship only as a voluntary choice from a heart filled with love for his mercy. They that dwell on the earth worship the dragon who gave power unto the beast, and they worship the beast. In the closing scenes of earth's

---

[7] E. G. White, *The Great Controversy* (1911), p. 306.1.

[8] Arnaldo Cortesi, "Pope Becomes Ruler Of A State Again," *New York Times*, February 12, 1929, p. 1.

[9] "the great dragon was cast out, that old serpent, called the Devil, and Satan, which deceiveth the whole world: he was cast out into the earth, and his angels were cast out with him." Revelation 12:9

history, the choice must be made between worshipping Christ or worshipping Satan. Recall in Revelation 12:3 that the Bible told us that "there appeared another wonder in heaven; and behold a great red dragon, having seven heads and ten horns, and seven crowns upon his heads." The dragon of Revelation 12 has the same characteristics as the beast in Revelation 13—namely seven heads and ten horns. Somehow the world is going to worship Satan through this beast. How this happens is disclosed in chapter fourteen.

In wondering after the beast, the worldlings and professed Christians say, "**who is like unto this beast? who is able to make war with him?**" This has been dramatically fulfilled in our lifetimes. In an article on August 20, 2015, in the *Huffington Post,* entitled, *Why the Pope Matters,* speaking of the global influence of Pope Francis, it says, "There is no other religious, entertainment or political leader alive today who could garner anywhere near the kind of response inspired by the pope." Who is like unto the beast?

In a documentary film by Newt Gingrich about Pope John Paul II, it is stated, "We all remember that Stalin famously asked at some point during the Second World War, how many divisions has the pope? Well, he got his answer in June '79—more than Stalin could imagine, many more divisions than Stalin could imagine. Perhaps at no time in the 20th century had one man so influenced the nation. The power of the papacy was never more visible, and the Soviets learned this to their dismay, that he could turn their empire inside out."[10] Who is able to make war with him?

Revelation 13:5 And there was given unto him a mouth speaking great things and blasphemies; and power was given unto him to continue forty and two months.

We recognize the time period mentioned here as the same as that in Daniel 7:25—"time and times and the dividing of time." This was the probation allotted for the little horn to exercise its political power. A

---

[10] http://www.ninedaysthatchangedtheworld.com/

Biblical month consists of 30 days;[11] 42 months totals 1,260 days, which symbolizes 1,260 years.[12] This time prophecy is so important that it is mentioned seven different times in Scripture.[13] The common time period fully demonstrates that the sea beast of Revelation 13 represents the same power as the little horn of Daniel 7.

Revelation 13:6 And he opened his mouth in blasphemy against God, to blaspheme his name, and his tabernacle, and them that dwell in heaven.

The theme of blasphemy occurs repeatedly in this chapter, in contrast to the theme of worship. Verse one informed us that the heads of this beast had a blasphemous name on them. Verse 5 says that he has a blasphemous mouth, and verse 6 portrays this mouth speaking blasphemies against God, against those that dwell in heaven and against the tabernacle of God. Not much could be more blasphemous than the following claim by Catholicism:
"The pope is so great dignity that he is not a man, but as it were God, and the vicar of God. The Pope is called 'Most Holy' because he is rightfully presumed to be such. The pope is alone deservedly called 'Most Holy' because he alone is the Vicar of Christ, who is the fountain and source and fullness of all holiness. He is likewise the Divine Monarch, and Supreme Emperor, and King of Kings, hence the Pope is crowned with a triple crown, as king of heaven and of earth and of the lower regions. Moreover, the superiority, and the

---

[11] Genesis 7:11 "In the six hundredth year of Noah's life, **in the second month, the seventeenth day of the month**, the same day were all the fountains of the great deep broken up, and the windows of heaven were opened."
Genesis 7:24 "And the waters prevailed upon the earth **an hundred and fifty days**."
Genesis 8:3 "And the waters returned from off the earth continually: and after the **end of the hundred and fifty days** the waters were abated.
Genesis 8:4 And the ark rested **in the seventh month, on the seventeenth day of the month**, upon the mountains of Ararat.

Until the time of the flood, according to Scripture, there were 360 days in a year. Counting 150 days from the seventeenth day of the second month to the seventeenth day of the seventh month, makes each month 30 days in length.

[12] In symbolic Bible prophecy a day represents a year. See Numbers 14:34 and Ezekiel 4:6.

[13] Daniel 7:25, "time, times, and a dividing of time"
Daniel 12:7, "time, times, and an half"
Revelation, 11:2 "forty-two months"
Revelation, 11:3 "a thousand two hundred and sixty days"
Revelation, 12:6 "a thousand two hundred and sixty days"
Revelation, 12:14 "time, and times, and half a time"
Revelation, 13:5 "forty-two months."

power of the Roman Pontiff, but by no means pertain only to heavenly things, to earthly things, and to things under the earth, but are even over angels, of whom he is greater. So that if it were possible that angels might err in faith, or might think contrary to the faith, they could be judged and excommunicated by the Pope. The pope is as it were God on earth, sole sovereign of the faithful of Christ, chief King of Kings, having plentitude of power."[14]

The claim is even advanced that any holiness that you might have actually comes from the pope. This is ultimate blasphemy. The Pope claims all the titles and prerogatives of God himself. Notice that he speaks blasphemy against God, against those that dwell in heaven (angels), and against God's throne,[15] exactly as specified by this Scripture.

Revelation 13:7 And it was given unto him to make war with the saints, and to overcome them: and power was given him over all kindreds, and tongues, and nations.

This is one of the very predictions that Daniel 7 made of the little horn power;[16] the power represented by this beast would persecute the saints of God. The sad record of history bears witness to the persecutions inflicted on God's saints by the Roman Catholic Church, in the name of Jesus. David Plaisted, in an article entitled *"Estimates of the Number Killed by the Papacy in the Middle Ages and Later,"* demonstrates that the documented murders by the papacy during the Middle Ages could easily be well over 200 million individuals. "They were stoned, they were sawn asunder, were tempted, were slain with the sword: they wandered about in sheepskins and goatskins; being destitute, afflicted, tormented; (Of whom the world was not worthy:) they wandered in deserts, and in mountains, and in dens and caves of the earth."[17]

---

[14] Lucii Ferraris, *Prompta Bibliotheca Canonica, Juridica, Moralis, Theologica, nec non Ascetica, Polemica, Rubristica, Historica,* Editio Quarta, Superiorum Permissu, AC Privilegio (Paris: J. P. Migne, 1858), Latin, Vol. P-R, p. 9-24.

[15] The tabernacle or sanctuary in heaven is God's throne room, therefore claiming the titles "Divine Monarch, and Supreme Emperor, and King of Kings," is speaking blasphemies against God's throne or tabernacle.

[16] Daniel 7:21

[17] Hebrews 11:37-38

There are, however, many sincere Roman Catholic people in that church today who serve God to the best of their ability and to the best of their knowledge, believing they are following the Bible. Scripture is not condemning these sincere people. In fact, Revelation 18 tells us that God is going to make a special effort to call these people out of this power so that they have an opportunity to avoid the plagues that God has reserved for its punishment. Sincere Christians who are in the Roman Catholic Church will hear the truth from God's word calling them out of Babylon.[18]

Revelation 13:8 And all that dwell upon the earth shall worship him, whose names are not written in the book of life of the Lamb slain from the foundation of the world.

This is a very sobering statement for it declares that to have your name written in the book of life, you cannot worship the beast. Conversely, if you worship this power, your name is not written in the book of life. This is a life or death matter at the end of time. Notice again that the issue of worship is the deciding factor. The word for "worship" in the original language of Greek is the word προσκυνέω, proskuneō. Translating it as worship is the best way to translate it, but it also can mean: (according to Thayer's Greek Definitions), "to kiss the hand to (towards) one, in token of reverence." Revelation is providing us with another identifying mark of this power. Who in our world travels around having people kiss his hand?

Rowan Williams, Archbishop of Canterbury, the religious head of the Church of England—supposed to be Protestant from a church in which there were millions of martyrs, many of whom died for the principle of believing that the pope was not God on earth and therefore could not be worshipped—bowed, kissing the hand of Pope John Paul II in 2003. Exactly as Scripture foretold, the whole world will bow in worship—even kissing his hand. Kissing the hand is clearly not the only way to worship, but it is interesting that the word John uses can have that connotation. Other famous pictures from recent news include Nancy Pelosi, 60th Speaker of the U.S. House of Representative, and Hugo Chavez, 64th President of Venezuela,

---

[18] Those individuals in denominations clinging to the doctrines of Rome are also a part of Babylon, and will be called out of her communion.

kissing the hand of Pope Benedict—also Philippine President Duterte kissing the hand of Pope Francis.

How else does the world worship this beast and wonder after him? At the funeral of Pope John Paul II, not one, not two, but three U.S. presidents lined up on their knees, bowing down before a dead pope. Never before in America's history had an American president even attended a papal funeral. Hundreds of world leaders attended John Paul's funeral. It was reported to be the largest such gathering in world history, including four kings, five queens, seventy presidents and prime ministers, fourteen leaders of other religions, with over four million pilgrims arriving in Rome—a city with only three million residents. The funeral likely had the world's largest TV audience for any event, exceeding two billion viewers—fully one third of the entire world's population—a staggering statistic. The Bible told us the whole world would wonder after the beast, and this is exactly what is occurring. This prophecy can be fulfilled by no other power.

Following is an excerpt from an interview of President George Bush, Jr. on Catholic television network EWTN, April 13, 2008. Bush is speaking about abortion and various different political issues at the beginning of this interview, but notice how he ends the interview.

Interviewer: "Do you think it's important, though, to have a pro-life president on the Republican ticket?"
Bush: "I think it's important for people to understand that a culture of life is in our national interest. And that it is also important to understand that the politics of abortion isn't going to change until people's hearts change and fully understand the meaning of life and what it means for a society to value life in all forms, whether it be the life of the unborn or the life of the elderly, whether it be the life of the less fortunate among us or the life of the rich guy. I mean it's a moral touchstone, I think, that will speak to a healthy society in the long run. And I don't know what's going to happen in American politics. I really don't. I do know that in order for a president to be effective, he better bring a set of principles from which he will not deviate, and articulate them as clearly as he can, and then not worry about immediate popularity. Because popularity comes and goes, but what doesn't change are solid principles. And I'm going to remind his Holy Father how important his voice is in making it easier for politicians like me to be able to kind of stand and defend our positions, that are I think very important positions to take."

Interviewer: "Mr. President, final question."

Bush: "Yes, sir."

Interviewer: "You said famously, when you looked into Vladimir Putin's eyes, you saw his soul. When you look into Benedict XVI's eyes, what do you see?"

Bush: "God."

Interviewer: "Good way to end the interview."

Bush: "Thank you, sir."

Interviewer: "Thank you, sir, my pleasure."

When he looks into Benedict XVI's eyes, he sees God? This is blasphemy. This is the same thing that was quoted from *Ferrari's Ecclesiastical Dictionary*. Is it only the Republicans who are following this beast power?

One of the first things that President Obama did after he took office was go and meet with Pope Benedict, to receive the newly-written, white-leather-bound encyclical from the pope. That encyclical was issued on June 29, 2009, entitled, *Caritas In Veritate—In Charity and Truth*, and contained five things for which the pope was calling: "To [1] manage the global economy; to revive economies hit by the crisis; to avoid any deterioration of the present crisis and the greater imbalances that would result; [2] to bring integral and timely disarmament, food [3] security and peace; to guarantee the [4] protection of the environment and to [5] regulate migration: for all this, there is urgent need of a true world political authority, as my predecessor Blessed John XXIII indicated some years ago."[19]

When he speaks of regulating migration, he is not talking about the birds. This is referring to controlling the movements of people. He makes the point that he wants security and peace. Another word for security is safety. The Bible says, "when they shall say, Peace and

---

[19] *CARITAS IN VERITATE – IN CHARITY AND TRUTH:* ENCYCLICAL LETTER OF THE SUPREME PONTIFF BENEDICT XVI, June 29th, the solemnity of the Holy Apostles Peter and Paul, in the year 2009, Chapter 5, Number 67.

safety; then sudden destruction cometh upon them."[20] This is one of the first times that we see world leaders at the very highest levels in their very most public proclamations and official documents all calling for peace and security or peace and safety. The Bible warns us that destruction is just around the corner.

Even more sobering is that President Obama, on September 23, 2009, just a few months after he received this encyclical from the pope, gave his first address to the United Nations. Notice how he too calls for five things, (which he calls four pillars, with the fifth one possibly appearing in veiled language): "Today, let me put forward four pillars that I believe are fundamental to the future that we want for our children: [2.] non-proliferation and disarmament; the promotion of [3.] peace and security; the [4.] preservation of our planet; and a [1.] global economy that [5.] advances opportunity for all people."[21]

Perhaps this opportunity for all people is a veiled reference to number five—regulate migration (this may explain why this world suddenly has a problem with refugee migration). It seems that the president of the United States, the greatest nation on the planet, is now calling for the exact same things that the pope called for, which shows he is taking his orders from the Vatican.

On May 24, 2017, one of the first things President Trump did after taking office, is to meet privately with Pope Francis.

Revelation 13:9 If any man have an ear, let him hear.

God is imploring, Please, won't you hear? Don't you see the things that are occurring in this world? Won't you listen to all the details that I have put in these prophecies to show you exactly where you are in the stream of time, to identify the dangers and the deceptions so that you do not have to experience the plagues that I am about to pour out? God is pleading, **"If any man have an ear, let him hear,"** please won't you hear?

---

[20] 1 Thessalonians 5:3.

[21] REMARKS BY THE PRESIDENT TO THE UNITED NATIONS GENERAL ASSEMBLY, September 23, 2009. http://www.whitehouse.gov/the_press_office/Remarks-by-the-President-to-the-United-Nations-General-Assembly/

Revelation 13:10 He that leadeth into captivity shall go into captivity: he that killeth with the sword must be killed with the sword. Here is the patience and the faith of the saints.

This promise required patience for the saints to cling to through the dark ages when so many were being killed for their faith in Jesus and for adherence to the word of God. But God had given his promise that one day justice would be given, and those killing with the sword would suffer the same fate.

"'Power was given unto him to continue forty and two months.' And, says the prophet, 'I saw one of his heads as it were wounded to death.' And again: 'He that leadeth into captivity shall go into captivity: he that killeth with the sword must be killed with the sword.' The forty and two months are the same as the 'time and times and the dividing of time,' three years and a half, or 1260 days, of Daniel 7—the time during which the papal power was to oppress God's people. This period, as stated in preceding chapters, began with the supremacy of the papacy, A.D. 538, and terminated in 1798. At that time the pope was made captive by the French army, the papal power received its deadly wound, and the prediction was fulfilled, 'He that leadeth into captivity shall go into captivity.'"[22]

Revelation 13:11 And I beheld another beast coming up out of the earth; and he had two horns like a lamb, and he spake as a dragon.

Jesus is revealing that after the first beast from the sea, another power would arrive on the scene of global dominance. This second power would rise to global prominence shortly after the leopard-like beast was taken captive—namely, between the deadly wound of 1798 and its healing in 1929.

The second power does not come up out of the sea but out of the earth. We saw that the sea represents the populated places of the world, and its turbulence represents the strife[23] of nations. The Scriptures do not explicitly define what the earth represents, but we

---

[22] E. G. White, *The Great Controversy* (1911), 439.2.

[23] Daniel 7:2

can infer it by logical comparison. If the sea represents masses of people, then the earth represents the relative absence of masses of people. Coming up out of the earth therefore signifies the peaceable rise of a power, apart from the contentions of nations. "This power, the last that is to wage war against the church and the law of God, was symbolized by a beast with lamblike horns. The beasts preceding it had risen from the sea, but this came up out of the earth, representing the peaceful rise of the nation which is symbolized."[24]

The second beast would rise peaceably to power, out of the earth, in a relatively unpopulated area, around the year 1798. It would have two horns like a lamb, but eventually, would begin to speak as a dragon. Who could fail to recognize the symbol that this beast represents?

"Both the appearance of this beast and the manner of its rise indicate that the nation which it represents is unlike those presented under the preceding symbols. The great kingdoms that have ruled the world were presented to the prophet Daniel as beasts of prey, rising when 'the four winds of the heaven strove upon the great sea.' Daniel 7:2. In Revelation 17 an angel explained that waters represent 'peoples, and multitudes, and nations, and tongues.' Revelation 17:15. Winds are a symbol of strife. The four winds of heaven striving upon the great sea represent the terrible scenes of conquest and revolution by which kingdoms have attained to power. "But the beast with lamblike horns was seen 'coming up out of the earth.' Instead of overthrowing other powers to establish itself, the nation thus represented must arise in territory previously unoccupied and grow up gradually and peacefully. It could not, then, arise among the crowded and struggling nationalities of the Old World—that turbulent sea of 'peoples, and multitudes, and nations, and tongues.' It must be sought in the Western Continent.
"What nation of the New World was in 1798 rising into power, giving promise of strength and greatness, and attracting the attention of the world? The application of the symbol admits of no question. One nation, and only one, meets the specifications of this prophecy; it points unmistakably to the United States of America. Again and again the thought, almost the exact words, of the sacred writer has been unconsciously employed by the orator and the historian in describing the rise and growth of this nation. The beast was seen

[24] E. G. White, *Signs of the Times, November 1,* 1899 par. 4.

'coming up out of the earth;' and, according to the translators, the word here rendered 'coming up' literally signifies 'to grow or spring up as a plant.' And, as we have seen, the nation must arise in territory previously unoccupied. A prominent writer, describing the rise of the United States, speaks of 'the mystery of her coming forth from vacancy,' and says: 'Like a silent seed we grew into empire.'... A European journal in 1850 spoke of the United States as a wonderful empire, which was 'emerging,' and 'amid the silence of the earth daily adding to its power and pride.'... Edward Everett, in an oration on the Pilgrim founders of this nation, said: 'Did they look for a retired spot, inoffensive for its obscurity, and safe in its remoteness, where the little church of Leyden might enjoy the freedom of conscience? Behold the mighty regions over which, in peaceful conquest,... they have borne the banners of the cross!'... "'And he had two horns like a lamb.' The lamblike horns indicate youth, innocence, and gentleness, fitly representing the character of the United States when presented to the prophet as 'coming up' in 1798. Among the Christian exiles who first fled to America and sought an asylum from royal oppression and priestly intolerance were many who determined to establish a government upon the broad foundation of civil and religious liberty. Their views found place in the Declaration of Independence, which sets forth the great truth that 'all men are created equal' and endowed with the inalienable right to 'life, liberty, and the pursuit of happiness.' And the Constitution guarantees to the people the right of self-government, providing that representatives elected by the popular vote shall enact and administer the laws. Freedom of religious faith was also granted, every man being permitted to worship God according to the dictates of his conscience. Republicanism and Protestantism became the fundamental principles of the nation. These principles are the secret of its power and prosperity. The oppressed and downtrodden throughout Christendom have turned to this land with interest and hope. Millions have sought its shores, and the United States has risen to a place among the most powerful nations of the earth."[25]
"The 'two horns like a lamb' well represent the character of the United States Government, as expressed in its two fundamental principles, Republicanism and Protestantism. These principles are the secret of our power and prosperity as a nation. Those who first found an asylum on the shores of America rejoiced that they had reached a country free from the arrogant claims of popery and the

---

[25] E. G. White, *The Great Controversy* (1911), 439.3-441.1.

tyranny of kingly rule. They determined to establish a government upon the broad foundation of civil and religious liberty."[26]

The principles of Republicanism and Protestantism are the secret of its power and prosperity. It should be clear to most Americans that we have been losing some of our power and prosperity lately. Could it be that we have moved away from the secrets of our power and prosperity—Protestantism and Republicanism? This country was supposed to be a Republic. All we hear today is about our country promoting democracy. We were not founded as a democracy (although our government does have some democratic process and principles). Democracy means the majority rules. When in history has the majority ever been right? There are some important principles about having representatives from the people, but Republicanism puts the ruling power in the hands of the people with the constitution as the governing document. This does not mean that by definition every republic is a good nation. It simply means if we have a good constitution, we can have a good republic because in a republic the constitution is what determines the principles of governance. Could it be then that we have been moving away from our Constitution and therefore speaking less and less about the republic and more and more about democracy?

The Bible has uttered the sad words that this Christian nation would eventually speak like a dragon. The lamb represents Christ and the dragon represents Satan. The power represented must be a power that was originally a Christian nation founded on the Christ-like principles of civil and religious freedom. According to Scripture, the United States of America will move away from the Christ-like characteristics of civil and religious liberty and freedom to display the satanic characteristics of persecution and coercion of conscience, going so far as to try to force people—by legislation—to worship in a specified way.

"The lamblike horns and dragon voice of the symbol point to a striking contradiction between the professions and the practice of the nation thus represented. The 'speaking' of the nation is the action of its legislative and judicial authorities. By such action it will give the lie to those liberal and peaceful principles which it has put forth as the foundation of its policy. The prediction that it will speak 'as a dragon'

---

[26] E. G. White, *Signs of the Times, November 1,* 1899 par. 4.

and exercise 'all the power of the first beast' plainly foretells a development of the spirit of intolerance and persecution that was manifested by the nations represented by the dragon and the leopardlike beast."[27]

Revelation 13:12 And he exerciseth all the power of the first beast before him, and causeth the earth and them which dwell therein to worship the first beast, whose deadly wound was healed.

Protestant America will exercise all the power of the papacy. "In 1960, John Kennedy went from Washington down to Texas to assure Protestant preachers that he would not obey the pope. In 2001, George Bush came from Texas up to Washington to assure a group of Catholic bishops that he would."[28]

America causes everyone in the world to worship the papacy? Sadly, according to the Revelation of Jesus, our nation of religious liberty and freedom will become a place of religious intolerance and persecution, even causing the whole world to worship the papal beast.

"And the statement that the beast with two horns 'causeth the earth and them which dwell therein to worship the first beast' indicates that the authority of this nation is to be exercised in enforcing some observance which shall be an act of homage to the papacy."[29]

America will not force everyone to become Roman Catholic. All will be allowed to have whatever religion they choose, as long as homage is paid to the papacy. What symbol or sign of authority does the Catholic Church claim is paying them homage in worship?

In an excerpt from a letter written by Father Enright, a Roman Catholic, of Redemptorist College, Kansas City, Mo., to E. Franke a minister in Maryland, January 11, 1892, he says:

---

[27] E. G. White, *The Great Controversy* (1911), p. 442.1.

[28] Thomas B. Edsall, *Bush Aims to Strengthen Catholic Base; The Washington Post*, April 16, 2001. http://www.washingtonpost.com/archive/politics/2001/04/16/bush-aims-to-strengthen-catholic-base/0088d7ee-9a6d-495d-b725-5b51d79549c3/

[29] E. G. White, *The Great Controversy* (1911), p. 442.1.

"I have repeatedly offered $1,000 to any one who can prove to me from the Bible alone that I am bound to keep Sunday holy. There is no such law in the Bible. It is a law of the holy Catholic Church alone. The Bible says, 'Remember that thou keep holy the Sabbath day.' The Catholic Church says: 'No ! By my divine power I abolish the Sabbath day, and command you to keep holy the first day of the week.' And, lo! the entire civilized world bows down in reverent obedience to the command of the holy Catholic Church. Yours respectfully, T. ENRIGHT, CSS. R."[30]

In a Catholic work entitled *Plain Talk about Protestantism of To-day,* we are told: "The observance of Sunday by Protestants is an homage they pay in spite of themselves to the authority of the [Catholic] Church."[31]

Catholic authors boldly assert that the change of the day of worship from Sabbath to Sunday is the sign of their authority to which the whole world is bowing and giving homage (worship).

Revelation 13:13 And he doeth great wonders, so that he maketh fire come down from heaven on the earth in the sight of men,

Fire represents the Holy Spirit. A beast speaking as the dragon cannot dispense the true gift of the Holy Ghost therefore a false spirit revival is here outlined.

Revelation 13:14 And deceiveth them that dwell on the earth by the means of those miracles which he had power to do in the sight of the beast; saying to them that dwell on the earth, that they should make an image to the beast, which had the wound by a sword, and did live.

America takes the lead in a false holy spirit revival to validate false doctrines not found in the Scriptures. By the miracles and wonders

---

[30] Fr. Enright, CSS. R. to E.E. Franke, January 11, 1892, in "An Adventist Minister on Sunday Laws," *American Sentinel,* June 1, 1893, p. 173

[31] Louis Gaston de Segur, *Plain Talk About Protestants Today,* p. 213; as cited in *American Sentinel,* June 1, 1893.

that Protestant America displays, the people of the earth are deceived into making an image to the papacy.

"But what is the '**image to the beast**'? and how is it to be formed? The image is made by the two-horned beast, and is an image to the beast. It is also called an image of the beast. Then to learn what the image is like and how it is to be formed, we must study the characteristics of the beast itself—the papacy.

"When the early church became corrupted by departing from the simplicity of the gospel and accepting heathen rites and customs, she lost the Spirit and power of God; and in order to control the consciences of the people, she sought the support of the secular power. The result was the papacy, a church that controlled the power of the state and employed it to further her own ends, especially for the punishment of 'heresy.' In order for the United States to form an image of the beast, the religious power must so control the civil government that the authority of the state will also be employed by the church to accomplish her own ends.

"Whenever the church has obtained secular power, she has employed it to punish dissent from her doctrines. Protestant churches that have followed in the steps of Rome by forming alliance with worldly powers have manifested a similar desire to restrict liberty of conscience."[32] "The 'image to the beast' represents that form of apostate Protestantism which will be developed when the Protestant churches shall seek the aid of the civil power for the enforcement of their dogmas...."[33]

By integrating religious and political power (which violates our Constitution), America will establish a system of control that mirrors the power of the papacy in the Dark Ages. Thus, will be set up a system of worship that is ultimately worshipping the dragon or Satan, in violation of the word of God.

On June 18, 2015, Pope Francis released his 183-page encyclical *Praised Be You: On the Care of Our Common Home,* in which he states that we by our "...lifestyle could bring healthy pressure to bear on those who wield political, economic and social power..." and that "Sunday, like the Jewish Sabbath, is meant to be a day which heals

---

[32] E. G. White, *The Great Controversy* (1911), p. 443.1-3.

[33] E. G. White, *Maranatha* (1976), p. 169.3.

our relationships with God, with ourselves, with others and with the world."[34]

The pope is tying together his claim of Sunday sacredness with his call to save the planet from climate change. On the same day the encyclical was released, President Obama proclaimed: "I welcome His Holiness Pope Francis's encyclical, and deeply admire the Pope's decision to make the case—clearly, powerfully, and with the full moral authority of his position—for action on global climate change....

"I believe the United States must be a leader in this effort, which is why I am committed to taking bold actions at home and abroad to cut carbon pollution, to increase clean energy and energy efficiency, to build resilience in vulnerable communities, and to encourage responsible stewardship of our natural resources....

"I look forward to discussing these issues with Pope Francis when he visits the White House in September... it is my hope that all world leaders—and all God's children—will reflect on Pope Francis's call to come together to care for our common home."[35]

"God's word has given warning of the impending danger; let this be unheeded, and the Protestant world will learn what the purposes of Rome really are, only when it is too late to escape the snare. She is silently growing into power. Her doctrines are exerting their influence in legislative halls, in the churches, and in the hearts of men... The dignitaries of church and state will unite to bribe, persuade, or compel all classes to honor the Sunday. The lack of divine authority will be supplied by oppressive enactments. Political corruption is destroying love of justice and regard for truth; and even in free America, rulers and legislators, in order to secure public favor, will yield to the popular demand for a law enforcing Sunday observance."[36]

---

[34] Pope Francis, Encyclical Letter *Laudato si' (Praise Be You) of the Holy Father Francis On the Care for our Common Home,* Section 206, 237.
http://w2.vatican.va/content/francesco/en/encyclicals/documents/papa-francesco_20150524_enciclica-laudato-si.html

[35] *White House Press Release,* June 18, 2015. https://www.whitehouse.gov/the-press-office/2015/06/18/statement-president-pope-francis%E2%80%99s-encyclical

[36] E. G. White, *The Great Controversy* (1911), p. 581.2, 592.3.

Already in 1985 elected officials were speaking with negativity of the separation of church and state; Supreme Court Justice Rehnquist, later Chief Justice (1986-2005) stated: "The 'wall of separation between church and State' is a metaphor based on bad history, a metaphor which has proved useless as a guide to judging. It should be frankly and explicitly abandoned."[37]

You may be thinking; how can this be? Will a Protestant nation really fall for this?

"The wide diversity of belief in the Protestant churches is regarded by many as decisive proof that no effort to secure a forced uniformity can ever be made. But there has been for years, in churches of the Protestant faith, a strong and growing sentiment in favor of a union based upon common points of doctrine. To secure such a union, the discussion of subjects upon which all were not agreed—however important they might be from a Bible standpoint—must necessarily be waived....
"When the leading churches of the United States, uniting upon such points of doctrine as are held by them in common, shall influence the state to enforce their decrees and to sustain their institutions, then Protestant America will have formed an image of the Roman hierarchy, and the infliction of civil penalties upon dissenters will inevitably result."[38]

On August 6, 2015, "Some 170 evangelicals—pastors, religion professors, nonprofit directors and others—sent an open letter to the president 'to offer our support and encouragement for your efforts to overcome the climate challenge....'
"'As Pope Francis made clear in his encyclical this summer,' the president said in his speech, 'taking a stand against climate change is a moral obligation.'
"The Catholic Church would usually condemn blatant politicization of theological documents like Pope Francis' encyclical Laudato Si', but not this time. The United States Conference of Catholic Bishops wrote on Monday to 'welcome this important move by the administration to adopt long-awaited standards to mitigate climate change and safeguard public health.'

---

[37] *Wallace v. Jaffree*, 472 U.S. 38, 106 (Rehnquist, J., dissenting) http://www.belcherfoundation.org/wallace_v_jaffree_dissent.htm

[38] E. G. White, *The Great Controversy* (1911), p. 444.2-445.1.

"…This teaming up of church and state on environmental issues has become common."[39]

We are already hearing the language of the dragon in our country amongst the Protestant churches: "By definition, each and every Sunday is a call to Christian unity since it is on this day that we are called to communion with the Lord, by the Lord. In spite of all of the challenges that have tugged at the threads of Christian unity, the Lord's Day remains the one, **unassailable marker of Christian unity** since it is on this day that all of us, despite our many differences, gather together as believers in Christ.

"There were always differences about days and dates in the Christian world…. Therefore, what better **marker of Christian unity** can we have? Indeed, what stronger case can one make for the significance of **Sunday as a hallmark of Christian unity** than the understanding that Christians throughout the centuries have conceived of this day as a day of new creation, an eighth day set apart from all others… It is a communion of all believers, at all times. Put simply, nothing in the calendar unites us like Sunday…

"Sunday worship is something more than simply what our parents and grandparents did. Sunday worship is even more than what our local faith community has done. Sunday worship is something that *all Christians*, at all times have celebrated. When we gather on Sunday the unity we achieve takes us back in time, across the ages to the earliest believer; it also moves us forward in time to embrace generations not yet born. **In this way, the spiritual unity we have thus achieved possesses an eschatological character**. The unity to which we bear witness and which we embody is a manifestation of the kingdom to which we all aspire.

"In order to fully appreciate **Sunday as a mark** of Christian unity we must expand our definition of unity…. When we assemble in faith on Sundays, we gather not simply with other parishioners in a local place of worship, but with Christians throughout every land and all the ages—and there is no greater evidence of unity than this. In our century, as with its predecessors, challenges large and small threaten Sunday. However, when we stand in faith, as members of a

---

[39] *Nicholas G. Hahn III, The Religion of Climate Change; Lending the power of the pulpit to the cause of environmental politics, Wall Street Journal, August 6, 2015.*
http://www.wsj.com/articles/the-religion-of-climate-change-1438903522

Church beyond all churches, we reclaim Sunday for the God who gave it to us."[40]

"None are condemned until they have had the light and have seen the obligation of the fourth commandment. But when the decree shall go forth enforcing the counterfeit sabbath, and the loud cry of the third angel shall warn men against the worship of the beast and his image, the line will be clearly drawn between the false and the true. Then those who still continue in transgression will receive the mark of the beast.

"When Sunday observance shall be enforced by law, and the world shall be enlightened concerning the obligation of the true Sabbath, then whoever shall transgress the command of God to obey a precept which has no higher authority than that of Rome, will thereby honor popery above God. He is paying homage to Rome, and to the power which enforces the institution ordained by Rome. He is worshiping the beast and his image.

"As men then reject the institution which God has declared to be the sign of His authority, and honor in its stead that which Rome has chosen as the token of her supremacy, they will thereby accept the sign of allegiance to Rome—'the mark of the beast.' And it is not until the issue is thus plainly set before the people, and they are brought to choose between the commandments of God and the commandments of men, that those who continue in transgression will receive 'the mark of the beast.'"[41]

Revelation 13:15 And he had power to give life unto the image of the beast, that the image of the beast should both speak, and cause that as many as would not worship the image of the beast should be killed.

The speaking of a beast (a kingdom or nation) is its legislative declarations. Jesus is unveiling to us that there will come a time when religious intolerance will be so great that this combination of church and state will legislate that anyone who does not worship the image of the beast should be killed—a death penalty for those who

---

[40] Rev. Dr. Demetrios E. Tonias, "Sunday as a Mark of Christian Unity" *The Lord's Day Alliance of the U.S.* April, 2015.
http://www.ldausa.org/lda/sunday-as-a-mark-of-christian-unity/

[41] E. G. White, *Last Day Events* (1992), p. 225.4-226.2.

protest against enforced Sunday worship; for those who would follow the commandments of God rather than the traditions of men. Jesus "answered and said unto them, Why do ye also transgress the commandment of God by your tradition?"[42]

"When our nation [the United States] shall so abjure the principles of its government as to enact a Sunday law, Protestantism will in this act join hands with popery; it will be nothing else than giving life to the tyranny which has long been eagerly watching its opportunity to spring again into active despotism."[43]

Revelation 13:16 And he causeth all, both small and great, rich and poor, free and bond, to receive a mark in their right hand, or in their foreheads:

The seal of God, introduced in Revelation 7, will be covered in greater detail in Revelation 14, but since God's mark is important in our understanding of the mark of the beast, we note here that the seal of God is received only in the forehead. However, the mark of the beast may be received in the forehead or in the right hand.

Throughout this chapter the theme of worship is repeated. The final conflict is an issue of worship—it is not over receiving a chip under the skin—it is a dispute over allegiance to one of two powers—Jesus or Satan, Christ or anti-Christ. Why then, is the seal of God only in the forehead and the mark of the beast in either the forehead or in the hand? The reason is simple: to receive the seal of God, one must make a decision to follow God—this happens in the frontal lobe of the brain; therefore, you receive the seal of God **in** your forehead.

However, there are two ways to receive the mark of the beast. First, one may receive the mark of the beast by making a decision in the mind to follow Satan and the commands of men, over the principles and commands of the word of God. Second, one may receive the mark of the beast by default. In other words, one might say, I don't believe in all this worship stuff; I'm an atheist and I think this is ridiculous; I cannot believe they are trying to legislate religion, and I

---

[42] Matthew 15:3

[43] E. G. White, *Maranatha* (1976), p. 190.5.

do not agree with it, but in order to avoid persecution, or the death penalty, I will just go along with it even though I don't believe it. In this case, you would receive the mark of the beast in the hand, for with your actions you declare who has your allegiance.

Revelation 13:17 And that no man might buy or sell, save he that had the mark, or the name of the beast, or the number of his name.

"He that had the mark" denotes apostate Protestants who pay homage to the authority of the papacy by acknowledging Sunday, thereby receiving her mark of authority, or their mark of unity. These refuse God's call to come out of Babylon.

"He that had the name of the beast" specifies those that bear the name of the papal system; they are the Roman Catholics who refuse God's call to come out of Babylon.[44]

"He that had the number of his name" signifies those who follow the beast through the deceptions of spiritualism. The number 666 has pagan origins connected with sun worship. There is no greater abomination, in God's eyes, than sun worship masquerading as God's true worship.[45] These refuse God's plea to come out of the spiritualism of Babylon.

The three-fold union—Apostate Protestantism, Roman Catholicism, and Spiritualism[46]—encompasses and deceives nearly the entire planet. Economic sanctions are placed on anyone who does not fall into one of these three categories. The mark of the beast will be very easily recognizable as no such thing as economic sanctions for refusing to worship in a prescribed manner has ever before been implemented in this country.

"'Man shall not live by bread alone, but by every word of God.' Often the follower of Christ is brought where he cannot serve God and carry forward his worldly enterprises. Perhaps it appears that

---

[44] Revelation 18:4

[45] See Ezekiel 8

[46] Also symbolized in Revelation 16:13 by three unclean spirits like frogs that come out of the mouth of the dragon, out of the mouth of the beast, and out of the mouth of the false prophet.

obedience to some plain requirement of God will cut off his means of support. Satan would make him believe that he must sacrifice his conscientious convictions. But the only thing in our world upon which we can rely is the word of God. 'Seek ye first the kingdom of God, and His righteousness; and all these things shall be added unto you.' Matthew 6:33. Even in this life it is not for our good to depart from the will of our Father in heaven. When we learn the power of His word, we shall not follow the suggestions of Satan in order to obtain food or to save our lives. Our only questions will be, What is God's command? and what His promise? Knowing these, we shall obey the one, and trust the other.

"In the last great conflict of the controversy with Satan those who are loyal to God will see every earthly support cut off. Because they refuse to break His law in obedience to earthly powers, they will be forbidden to buy or sell. It will finally be decreed that they shall be put to death. See Revelation 13:11-17. But to the obedient is given the promise, 'He shall dwell on high: his place of defense shall be the munitions of rocks: bread shall be given him; his waters shall be sure.' Isaiah 33:16. By this promise the children of God will live. When the earth shall be wasted with famine, they shall be fed. 'They shall not be ashamed in the evil time: and in the days of famine they shall be satisfied.' Psalm 37:19. To that time of distress the prophet Habakkuk looked forward, and his words express the faith of the church: 'Although the fig tree shall not blossom, neither shall fruit be in the vines; the labor of the olive shall fail, and the fields shall yield no meat; the flock shall be cut off from the fold, and there shall be no herd in the stalls: yet I will rejoice in the Lord, I will joy in the God of my salvation.' Habakkuk 3:17, 18."[47]

"The time is not far distant when the test will come to every soul. The mark of the beast will be urged upon us. Those who have step by step yielded to worldly demands and conformed to worldly customs will not find it a hard matter to yield to the powers that be, rather than subject themselves to derision, insult, threatened imprisonment, and death. The contest is between the commandments of God and the commandments of men."[48]

---

[47] E. G. White, *The Desire of Ages* (1898), p. 121.2-3.

[48] E. G. White, *Testimonies for the Church,* Vol. 5 (1889), p. 81.1.

"Every one who is not centered in Christ will fail to stand the test and ordeal of that day. While those who are clothed with Christ's righteousness will stand firm to truth and duty, those who have trusted in their own righteousness will be ranged under the black banner of the prince of darkness. Then it will be seen whether the choice is for Christ or Belial. Those who have been self-distrustful, who have been so circumstanced that they have not dared to face stigma and reproach, will at last openly declare themselves for Christ and his law; while many who have appeared to be flourishing trees, but who have borne no fruit, will go with the multitude to do evil, and will receive the mark of apostasy in the forehead or in the hand."[49]

Revelation 13:18 Here is wisdom. Let him that hath understanding count the number of the beast: for it is the number of a man; and his number is Six hundred threescore and six.

This is probably one of the most famous verses in the entire Bible—the number 666. Six hundred, threescore—a score is twenty, multiplied by three is sixty—and six. Almost everyone on the planet has heard of this number. Many have seen it in rock concerts, in movies, on t-shirts, and tattoos, etc., yet very few people know its Biblical meaning. This is the number of the leopard-like sea beast, which is the papacy—there we must begin our search for the meaning of the number.

First, the Bible says we must have wisdom in order to understand this number, which wisdom comes only from the Holy Spirit.[50] Second, the number of the beast must be counted. In other words, the number itself is not emblazoned in someone's tattoo, or on a T-shirt; rather we must add it up. Lastly, Scripture says that it is the number of a man, therefore this number must be applied to a specific individual.

In a Roman-Catholic document, Ferrari's Ecclesiastical Dictionary, which is written in Latin, under the heading of Papa—the pope—we read: "Ut sicut Beatus Petrus in terries **vicarious Filii Dei** fuit

---

[49] E. G. White, *Review and Herald, November 8,* 1892 par. 7.

[50] Luke 11:13

constitutus, ita et Pontifices ejus successors in terries principatus potestatem umplius..."[51] This document applies an official title to the pope—Vicarius Filii Dei, which means Vicar of the Son of God.

Our Sunday Visitor, a Roman Catholic periodical (still in print), published the following, on April 18, 1915: "What are the letters supposed to be in the Pope's crown, and what do they signify, if anything? The letters inscribed in the Pope's mitre are these: Vicarius Filii Dei, which is the Latin for Vicar of the Son of God...hence the Bishop of Rome, as head of the Church, was given the titile 'Vicar of Christ.'"[52] Here it is plainly stated that the pope has a mitre which contains the name, Vicarius Filii Dei. People can deny that the title existed, or claim it is not official, yet here it is in their own published writings. This quote also mentions another common title for the pope: Vicarius Christi—Vicar of Christ. The two names are synonymous. Even more recently, Vicarius Filii Dei is used twice by Pope Paul VI in his official papal decree of June 28, 1968— Acta Apostolicae Sedis.[53]

In 1943, two young Protestant students, Benjamin Mondics and Robert Correia, wanted to verify that this was an actual title of the pope and so they visited the Catholic University of America.[54] They managed to secure an interview with one of the leading professors, Dr. J. Quasten, and requested that he sign a document stating that Vicarius Filii Dei was indeed a title of the pope. This he did, after which they had it notarized, adding their own signatures as witness to the fact that they had observed him write and sign the document. Dr. Quasten wrote, "The title Vicarius Filii Dei as well as the title Vicarius Christi is very common as the title of the Pope."

Latin is the official language of Rome and the official language of the Catholic Church, from which we derive Roman numerals. Therefore, adding the Roman numeral values for the letters in the title Vicarius Filii Dei yields the sum of 666, just as the Bible prophesied. It is indeed the number of a man, specifically, the number of the pope.

---

[51] http://biblelight.net/1827r.gif

[52] http://biblelight.net/Sources/OSV%20Apr%2018%201915.pdf

[53] Acta Apostolicae Sedis, Commentarium Officiale, Vol. LX (1968), n. 6, pp. 317-319. Libreria Editrice Vaticana. ISBN: 8820960680, 9788820960681.

[54] http://biblelight.net/vicarius-filii-dei-documentation.htm retrieved 12-6-2016.

The Catholic University of America
Washington, D. C.

The title _Vicarius Filii Dei_
as well as the title _Vicarius Christi_
is very common as the title
for the Pope.

J. J. Quasten

DISTRICT OF COLUMBIA)
(SS
CITY OF WASHINGTON)

R. F. Correia and Benjamin Mondics being first duly
sworn on oath depose and say; that on March 5, 1943,
Dr. J. Quasten, S. T. D., professor of Ancient History and
Christian Archaeology, School of Sacred Theology, Catholic University of America, Washington, D. C., wrote the
above statement in our presence and signed the same and
delivered it to us on the above date.

R. F. Correia
Benjamin Mondics

Subscribed and sworn to before me this tenth day of
March, A. D. 1943.

M. Stella Fleisher
Notary Public, District of Columbia
My commission expires Aug. 31, 1947

V	-	5
I	-	1
C	-	100
A	-	0
R	-	0
I	-	I
U	-	5
S	-	0

(V and U are the same letter in Latin)

F	-	0
I	-	1
L	-	50
I	-	1
I	-	1

D	-	500
E	-	0
I	-	1

666

The title is also a blasphemous name meeting the specification that this power would have "upon his heads the name of blasphemy."[55] Here we see it is the head of the papacy, the pope, who places this blasphemous title on his mitre, or head.

What about the other equivalent title, Vicarius Christi? Although the title is synonymous with Vicarius Filii Dei, it is true that this title, if you add the numbers, does not total 666. However, it is an interesting title because vicarius means in place of or against. Therefore, Vicarius Christi literally means anti-Christ—against or in place of Christ. Both titles of the pope specify the identity of this power—the anti-Christ of Bible prophecy.

This clearly may be disturbing to some people, particularly if you happen to be a Roman Catholic, since you have likely never heard anything like this before. Examine the Biblical evidence and see the messages Jesus gives us in love. He does not want you to be deceived. God loves everyone, including those faithful, sincere Roman Catholic believers. He has his true followers in all denominations of the world. Those true followers he will call out of Babylon so that there will "be one fold and one shepherd." John 10:16.

---

[55] Revelation 13:1

Some might assert that perhaps it is only coincidence that this name counts up to 666. Let us see if God leaves us only a little evidence, or if he provides us overwhelming evidence. More than seven other titles that apply to the papacy or the pope,[56] in a total of three different languages (the three languages written on the cross—Hebrew, Greek and Latin), add up to 666. God wanted to provide evidence that was beyond coincidence.

Latin DUX CLERI*—Captain of the Clergy

D	-	500
U	-	5
X	-	10
C	-	100
L	-	50
E	-	0
R	-	0
I	-	1
		666

Latin LUDOVICUS*—Vicar of the Court

L	-	50
U	-	5
D	-	500
O	-	0
V	-	5
I	-	1
C	-	100
U	-	5
S	-	0
		666

---

56 See *Andreas Helwig, *Antichristus Romanus* (Wittenburg: Typis Laurentij Seuberlichs, 1612).
‡ Johannis Gerhardi, SS., *Adnotationes in Apocalypsin* (Germany: Johannis Jacobi Bauhofferi, 1665), p. 119.
§ Alexander Campbell, A Debate on the Roman Catholic Religion (Cincinnati: H. S. Bosworth, 1865), p. 229, 249.
http://biblelight.net/666.htm

Greek LATEINOS*—"the Latin speaking man" (Latin being the papacy's official language—and no other nation, power or church speaks Latin today.)

L	-	30	lambda
A	-	1	alpha
T	-	300	tau
E	-	5	epsilon
I	-	10	iota
N	-	50	nu
O	-	70	omicron
S	-	200	sigma

| | | 666 | |

The ancient Greek ITALIKA EKKLESIA‡ is "Italian Church"

I	-	10	iota
T	-	300	tau
A	-	1	alpha
L	-	30	lambda
I	-	10	iota
K	-	20	kappa
A	-	1	alpha
E	-	5	epsilon
K	-	20	kappa
K	-	20	kappa
L	-	30	lambda
E	-	8	eta
S	-	200	sigma
I	-	10	iota
A	-	1	alpha

| | | 666 | |

The ancient Greek HE LATINE BASILEIA§ is "The Latin Kingdom"

H	-	0	(transliterated)
E	-	8	eta
L	-	30	lambda
A	-	1	alpha
T	-	300	tau
I	-	10	iota
N	-	50	nu
E	-	8	eta
B	-	2	beta
A	-	1	alpha
S	-	200	sigma
I	-	10	iota
L	-	30	lambda
E	-	5	epsilon
I	-	10	iota
A	-	1	alpha

———

666

The Hebrew ROMIITH*‡ means the "Roman Kingdom"

R	-	200	resh
O	-	6	waw (vav)
M	-	40	mem
I	-	10	yod
I	-	10	yod
TH	-	400	taw

———

666

ROMITI, in Hebrew, means the "Roman Man"

R	-	200	resh
O	-	6	waw (vav)
M	-	40	mem
I	-	10	yod
T	-	400	taw
I	-	10	yod

———

666

The number 666 is associated with pagan sun worship, and originated in the ancient mysteries of Babylon. In Revelation 17, a beast with seven heads and ten horns and names of blasphemy (just like this leopard-like beast from chapter thirteen), carries a harlot who has a name in her forehead—"MYSTERY, BABYLON THE GREAT, THE MOTHER OF HARLOTS AND ABOMINATIONS OF THE EARTH."

Who is Babylon? Peter writes to "the church that is at Babylon, elected together with you, saluteth you; and so doth Marcus my son."[57] At the time of Peter there was no apostolic church in Babylon, for the city of ancient Babylon was in ruins and had been for centuries. The Bible predicted that Babylon would be a wasteland, that no one would dwell there, that the beasts of the field would lie there, and that even the shepherds would avoid it[58]; therefore, there could be no church at Babylon. What does Peter mean when he says the church at Babylon? We know from history that in the early Christian church the term Babylon was used as a code word for Rome since persecution was so severe that they veiled their language.

Even the Catholic James Cardinal Gibbons in his book, *Faith of our Fathers* writes: "'Babylon,' from which Peter addresses his first Epistle, is understood by learned annotators, Protestant and Catholic, to refer to Rome."[59]

The Catholic Archbishop Henry Edward Manning, who was at the time Archbishop of Westminster, states the facts in the most stark terms possible:[60] "Now a system like this [Roman Catholicism] is so unlike anything human, it has upon it notes, tokens, marks so altogether supernatural that men now acknowledge it to be either Christ or Antichrist. There is nothing between these extremes. Most true is this alternative. The Catholic church is either the masterpiece of Satan or the kingdom of the Son of God."[61]

---

[57] 1 Peter 5:13

[58] Isaiah 13:19-22 "And Babylon, the glory of kingdoms, the beauty of the Chaldees' excellency, shall be as when God overthrew Sodom and Gomorrah. It shall never be inhabited, neither shall it be dwelt in from generation to generation: neither shall the Arabian pitch tent there; neither shall the shepherds make their fold there. But wild beasts of the desert shall lie there; and their houses shall be full of doleful creatures; and owls shall dwell there, and satyrs shall dance there. And the wild beasts of the islands shall cry in their desolate houses, and dragons in their pleasant palaces: and her time is near to come, and her days shall not be prolonged."

[59] James Cardinal Gibbons, *The Faith of Our Fathers*, p.87.6; 111th printing. ISBN 0-89555-158-6.

[60] The famous Cardinal, John Henry Newman said the same thing: "If the Church be from Christ, even her least acceptable words or deeds *ex cathedra* may be taken on faith: if she be not, even her best are presumptuous, and call for a protest. She is an honoured servant in one case ; an usurper and tyrant in another.... The Church... if not divinely appointed, it is doctrinally the essence of Antichrist."
John Henry Cardinal Newman, *Essays Critical and Historical*, Vol. 2 (London: Longmans, Green, and Co., 1891) p. 172, 173.

[61] Henry Edward Manning, Archbishop of Westminster, *The Fourfold Sovereignty of God*, 1872, p. 171-172. (Archbishop Manning was elevated to Cardinal in 1875.)

God has left us with very little room for doubt. Satan indeed has a masterpiece on this earth—a masterpiece that is leading the whole world into deception.

"Let no man deceive you by any means: for that day {the second coming of Jesus} shall not come, except there come a falling away first, and that man of sin be revealed, the son of perdition; Who opposeth and exalteth himself above all that is called God, or that is worshipped; so that he as God sitteth in the temple of God, showing himself that he is God. Remember ye not, that, when I was yet with you, I told you these things? And now ye know what withholdeth that he might be revealed in his time. For the mystery of iniquity doth already work: only he who now letteth {prevents} will let {prevent}, until he be taken out of the way. And then shall that Wicked be revealed, whom the Lord shall consume with the spirit of his mouth, and shall destroy with the brightness of his coming: Even him, whose coming is after the working of Satan with all power and signs and lying wonders, And with all deceivableness of unrighteousness in them that perish; because they received not the love of the truth, that they might be saved. And for this cause God shall send them strong delusion, that they should believe a lie. That they all might be damned who believed not the truth, but had pleasure in unrighteousness."[62]

God is pleading with you, "If any man have an ear, let him hear." He says "choose you this day whom ye will serve."[63] There are only two choices. Will you be deceived and follow the masterpiece of Satan— the Antichrist, the papacy? Or will you choose to "follow the Lamb whithersoever he goeth?"[64] Do you want to follow God and his Word and be on his side? Do you want to receive the seal of God so that you will not receive the mark of the beast? The Lamb shed his blood to save you. Will you reject all that he has done and follow his archenemy? May you be among those who receive his righteousness, follow him, and stand solely upon his Word. Amen.

---

[62] 2 Thessalonians 2:3-12

[63] Joshua 24:15

[64] Revelation 14:4

Revelation 14

SUMMARY:
Revelation chapter 14 commences with additional information about the 144,000, leading to the famous three angels' messages. The first angel's message is an announcement of the gospel, the commencement of the judgment, and a call to worship the Creator of the universe. The second angel announces the fall of Babylon. Finally, the third angel warns, in most severe terms, not to receive the mark of the beast, nor to worship the beast or his image. The chapter concludes with a partial description of some of the punishments for those who receive the mark of the beast, and culminates in a description of the harvest of the clusters of the vine of the earth.

"The fourteenth chapter of Revelation is a chapter of the deepest interest. This scripture will soon be understood in all its bearings, and the messages given to John the revelator will be repeated with distinct utterance."[1]

Revelation 14:1 And I looked, and, lo, a Lamb stood on the mount Sion, and with him an hundred forty and four thousand, having his Father's name written in their foreheads.

Here we recognize sanctuary language, which all throughout Scripture is a key to understanding Biblical symbols. "Beautiful for situation, the joy of the whole earth, is mount Zion, on the sides of the north, the city of the great King."[2] Mt. Zion is on the sides of the north in the heavenly temple. The sanctuary in the wilderness, which was a shadow of the heavenly,[3] had only one piece of furniture on the north side—the table of showbread.

---

[1] E. G. White, *Review and Herald*, October 13, 1904, par. 2.

[2] Psalm 48:2

[3] Hebrews 8:5; 9:11, 24

Jesus said, "I am the bread of life: he that cometh to me shall never hunger."[4] Scripture also tells us that there are two thrones in heaven,[5] the throne of God the Father and the throne of Jesus.

When Lucifer began to harbor jealousy in his heart, he coveted the position and throne of Christ: "How art thou fallen from heaven, O Lucifer, son of the morning! how art thou cut down to the ground, which didst weaken the nations! For thou hast said in thine heart, I will ascend into heaven, I will exalt my throne above the stars of God: I will sit also upon the mount of the congregation, in the sides of the north: I will ascend above the heights of the clouds; I will be like the most High."[6] Satan coveted the position of Christ and wanted to take his throne, represented by the table of showbread.

In Revelation 14 Jesus, the Lamb of God, is pictured standing on mount Zion, in his very throne room, accompanied by the 144,000. Christ promised, "To him that overcometh will I grant to sit with me in my throne, even as I also overcame, and am set down with my Father in his throne."[7] Not only did Jesus sacrifice his life to save us and to take us to heaven to live eternally, but by this transaction, has made us members of his royal family, and invited us to sit with him on his throne. Amazing is the exaltation of the sons and daughters of God who have been so degraded. "Behold, what manner of love the Father hath bestowed upon us, that we should be called the sons of God."[8]

"While John was shown the last great struggles of the church with earthly powers, he was also permitted to behold the final victory and deliverance of the faithful. He saw the church brought into deadly conflict with the beast and his image, and the worship of that beast enforced on pain of death. But looking beyond the smoke and din of the battle, he beheld a company upon Mount Zion with the Lamb, having, instead of the mark of the beast, the 'Father's name written in their foreheads.' And again he saw 'them that had gotten the victory over the beast, and over his image, and over his mark, and

---

[4] John 6:35

[5] Revelation 3:21

[6] Isaiah 14:12-14

[7] Revelation 3:21

[8] 1 John 3:1

over the number of his name, stand on the sea of glass, having the harps of God' and singing the song of Moses and the Lamb."[9]

In Revelation 13, the entire world wonders after the beast and receives its mark in the forehead or on the hand. But, here is depicted a group of people called the 144,000 who have the seal of God in their forehead; therefore, these have not received the mark of the beast. It is imperative that we identify the seal of God and the mark of the beast and understand how the first may be obtained and the second avoided. This chapter outlines this all-important revelation.

The 144,000 [10] have the **"Father's name written in their foreheads."** Revelation 7 revealed that the final judgment will not fall on the earth "till we have **sealed** the servants of our God in their **foreheads**...."[11] This shows that the 144,000 are sealed in their foreheads. Revelation 14:1 shows that the 144,000 have the name of God in their foreheads. Therefore, the seal of God is the name of God.

When Moses spoke with God, on Mt. Sinai, he made a bold request: "And he said, I beseech thee, show me thy glory. And he said, I will make all my goodness pass before thee, and I will proclaim the name of the LORD before thee; and will be gracious to whom I will be gracious, and will show mercy on whom I will show mercy."[12] When Moses asked to see God's glory, God responded "I will proclaim my goodness and the name of the Lord." God's glory is his

---

[9] E. G. White, *Testimonies for the Church,* Vol. 5 (1889), p. 752.3.

[10] Frequent are the arguments that occur over whether the 144,000 is a literal or a symbolic number. Allowing Scripture to be its own interpreter we see that 144,000 must be a literal number. Why? Simply because there is no Biblical precedence for a number to symbolically represent another number. For example, three never symbolically represents 30 or 300; 100 never represents 1,000 etc. It is true that a day represents a year, but one day represents one year, not five, or thirty. In Bible prophecy a number simply is that number. When we see ten horns on a beast, we take those to be ten kingdoms emanating from that beast (Daniel 7:24); we do not take it to be 75 or 100 kingdoms. Four heads represent four leaders of a divided kingdom (Daniel 7:6; 11:3-4). When Revelation describes seven last plagues, we take that to be seven plagues, not 700. Therefore, it would not make sense, nor is there any mathematical equation for a calculation where one number represents another. The 144,000 are simply and literally 144,000.
"The living saints, **144,000 in number**, knew and understood the voice of God, while the wicked thought it was thunder and an earthquake."
E. G. White, *Early Writings* (1882), p.14.1.

[11] Revelation 7:3-4

[12] Exodus 33:18-19

name, and his name is his goodness. "And the LORD descended in the cloud, and stood with him there, and proclaimed the name of the LORD. And the LORD passed by before him, and proclaimed, The LORD, The LORD God, merciful and gracious, longsuffering, and abundant in goodness and truth, Keeping mercy for thousands, forgiving iniquity and transgression and sin, and that will by no means clear the guilty; visiting the iniquity of the fathers upon the children, and upon the children's children, unto the third and to the fourth generation."[13]

When God proclaimed his name to Moses, he proclaimed his character. God's name is his glory and his glory is his character. Therefore the 144,000 have the character of God written in their foreheads. The character of God has been fully reproduced in the minds and lives of his people.

When the Lord appeared to Moses in the burning bush he said, "**I am the God of thy father, the God of Abraham, the God of Isaac, and the God of Jacob.**"[14] When God told him to go back to Egypt to free the children of Israel, Moses asked, "Behold, when I come unto the children of Israel, and shall say unto them, The God of your fathers hath sent me unto you; and they shall say to me, **What is his name?** what shall I say unto them? And God said unto Moses, **I AM THAT I AM**: and he said, Thus shalt thou say unto the children of Israel, **I AM** hath sent me unto you. And God said moreover unto Moses, Thus shalt thou say unto the children of Israel, The LORD God of your fathers, the God of Abraham, the God of Isaac, and the God of Jacob, hath sent me unto you: **this is my name for ever**, and **this is my memorial** unto all generations."[15] The children of Israel knew that their fathers worshipped God—the God of Abraham, Isaac, and Jacob. But God told Moses to tell them that the God of their fathers is the God whose name is "I AM THAT I AM," and that "this is my name forever, and this is my memorial unto all generations." His name is not simply **I AM**, that is, that he exists, but that he is that which he is.

---

[13] Exodus 34:5-7

[14] Exodus 3:6

[15] Exodus 3:13-15

First, God is Creator of all things in the entire universe. Whatever then that continually points to him as the Creator, as Lord of heaven and earth, is to be his memorial: "And hallow my sabbaths; and they shall be a sign between me and you, that ye may know that **I am the LORD your God**."[16] The sabbath is a sign between us and God that he is the Lord our God; not only that he has existence, but that he is the "LORD your God"—"I AM THAT I AM." "It is a sign between me and the children of Israel for ever: for in six days the LORD made heaven and earth, and on the seventh day he rested, and was refreshed."[17] The sabbath is a sign that he is the Lord our God because "in six days," he "**made** heaven and earth, and on the seventh day he rested;" therefore, the first thing the sabbath signifies is that God is our Creator. It signifies that his name: "I AM THAT I AM" is his memorial to all generations.

Second, God is redeemer to every person that has ever lived on this planet, for he is "the Lamb slain from the foundation of the world."[18] The sabbath memorial also points to the Lord as redeemer. "Moreover also I gave them my sabbaths, to be a sign between me and them, that they might know that **I am the LORD that sanctify them**."[19] To sanctify is to make holy. The process of redemption is for the Lord Jesus to take us—unholy, filthy, and defiled; wash us in his own blood,[20] cover us with his righteousness[21] and makes us faultless before his throne with exceeding joy.[22]

The sabbath, therefore, is God's memorial of his creative and redemptive power and it continually points to his name: I AM THAT I AM–Creator and Redeemer.

Where then shall we find the seal of God? "Bind up the testimony, seal the law among my disciples."[23] The testimony must be bound

---

[16] Ezekiel 20:20

[17] Exodus 31:17

[18] Revelation 13:8

[19] Ezekiel 20:12

[20] Revelation 1:5

[21] Isaiah 61:10; Revelation 19:8

[22] Jude 1:24

[23] Isaiah 8:16

and the law sealed among his disciples. His seal therefore is to be found in the law of God.

Consider the officials of any secular government, or entity, from the President of the United States, to the King of England, to the county clerk. They all have seals. In every case a seal is comprised of three components: First, a seal contains the name of the person in authority. Second, a seal always has the title of the official. Third, a seal contains their territory, or jurisdiction.

The seal for King George VI, would contain his name—George VI; his title—King; and his territory—Great Britain and Dominions. If this was applied to the President of the United States, we have the name—Donald Trump; title—President; territory—the United States of America. Each of the three components—the name, the title, and the territory must be present for a seal to make any sense and to have any true authority. If you go to the city park in Seattle and the sign at the gate posts the park rules, and at the end of the rules it says, "By authority—The King of England," most people probably would get a good laugh, and completely disregard the rules.

God's seal is no different; it must contain those three characteristics—name, title, and territory. It is the very heart of God's law—the fourth commandment—that contains his seal: "Remember the sabbath day, to keep it holy. Six days shalt thou labour, and do all thy work: But the seventh day is the sabbath of the LORD thy God: in it thou shalt not do any work, thou, nor thy son, nor thy daughter, thy manservant, nor thy maidservant, nor thy cattle, nor thy stranger that is within thy gates: For in six days **the LORD made heaven and earth, the sea, and all that in them is**, and rested the seventh day: wherefore the LORD blessed the sabbath day, and hallowed it."[24]

No other commandment contains the three elements of a seal: the name, the title, and the territory. No other commandment gives the name of the Lawgiver. The fourth commandment contains his name—"the Lord;" his Title—Creator ("made"); and his territory—"heaven and earth, the sea, and all that in them is." The three elements of God's seal are indeed found in his law, in the fourth commandment. The seal of God is his seventh-day sabbath.

---

[24] See Exodus 20:8-11 and Deuteronomy 5:12-15.

If you remove the fourth commandment from the law of God, it becomes impossible to know who wrote the law. If it were not for this fourth commandment, you would not know whether it was Buddha, or Vishnu, or Krishna, or the Lord of heaven that gave this law. Buddha instructs his followers to live at peace with people and avoid doing bad things. Buddha could have made a law that said thou shalt not kill. It is the seal of God which gives authority to his law. This is the reason why Satan is so angry at this specific commandment, causing almost the entire world to worship on the first day of the week, Sunday, rather than Saturday, God's seventh-day sabbath. "Those who would have the seal of God in their foreheads must keep the Sabbath of the fourth commandment."[25]

The contest between the mark of the beast and the seal of God is simply a battle in every heart and mind over whose character they will represent—the character of Jesus or Satan; and whose authority they will accept—Christ or Anti-christ. It is a contest over who has your worship—the Creator or the Destroyer.

"Is this the language of your heart? 'I am wholly thine, my Saviour; thou hast paid the ransom for my soul, and all that I am or ever hope to be is thine...' In all you do, let your thought be, 'Is this the way of the Lord? Will this please my Saviour? He gave his life for me; what can I give back to God?' I can only say, 'Of thine own, O Lord, I freely give thee.' Unless the name of God is written in your forehead,—written there because God is the center of your thoughts,—you will not be meet for the inheritance in light. It is your Creator who has poured out to you all heaven in one wondrous gift,—his only begotten Son."[26]

Revelation 14:2 And I heard a voice from heaven, as the voice of many waters, and as the voice of a great thunder: and I heard the voice of harpers harping with their harps:

John hears a resounding, yet reassuring, voice accompanied by celestial music.

---

[25] E. G. White, *Last Day Events*, p. 220.2.

[26] E. G. White, *Review and Herald,* December 23, 1890, par. 5.

Revelation 14:3 And they sung as it were a new song before the throne, and before the four beasts, and the elders: and no man could learn that song but the hundred and forty and four thousand, which were redeemed from the earth.

The 144,000 have gone through a series of trials, experienced things that no one else has experienced, and therefore have this unique song to sing. They have trusted God through the great time of Jacob's trouble. This verse also shows that they have been redeemed from the earth. They are human beings. By God's grace we may be among them.

Revelation 14:4 These are they which were not defiled with women; for they are virgins. These are they which follow the Lamb whithersoever he goeth. These were redeemed from among men, being the firstfruits unto God and to the Lamb.

In Bible prophecy a pure woman represents God's true and pure church,[27] and therefore by contrast, an impure woman represents an apostate church.[28] These 144,000 are not defiled by apostate churches and their false doctrines.

"Let us strive with all the power that God has given us to be among the hundred and forty-four thousand. And let us do all that we can to help others to gain heaven. We are to have an intense interest in Christ Jesus; for he is our Saviour. He came to this world to be tempted in all points as we are, to prove to the universe that in this world of sin human beings can live lives that God will approve."[29]

"We need not wait till we are translated to follow Christ. God's people may do this here below. We shall follow the Lamb of God in the courts above only if we follow him here. Following him in heaven depends on our keeping his commandments now. We are not to follow Christ fitfully or capriciously, only when it is for our advantage. We must choose to follow him. In daily life we must follow his example, as a flock trustfully follows its shepherd. We are to follow

---

[27] Jeremiah 6:2; Isaiah 51:16

[28] Isaiah 1:21 "How is the faithful city {Jerusalem—which was also God's church} become an harlot! it was full of judgment; righteousness lodged in it; but now murderers."

[29] E. G. White, *Review and Herald,* March 9, 1905 par. 4.

him by suffering for his sake, saying, at every step, 'Though he slay me, yet will I trust in him.' His life practise [sic] must be our life practise. And as we thus seek to be like him, and to bring our wills into conformity to his will, we shall reveal him."[30]

The 144,000 are redeemed from among men, being the first fruits unto God and unto the lamb. Scripture calls people "first fruits" in many cases when they are not necessarily the first. Why should that surprise us? Jesus said, "the last shall be first, and the first last."[31] The 144,000 are the last generation of God's people on earth who live through the very final events of this earth's history, but are the first to see Jesus coming in the clouds of heaven.[32] What does being first fruits represent? "Israel was holiness unto the LORD, and the firstfruits of his increase."[33] Israel is represented as being a first fruit, because they were holiness unto the Lord. The 144,000 are the first group of people to stand, by the blood of the lamb, and the power of his grace, without a mediator. They stand by the power of God alone when there is no more provision for the forgiveness of sin—when every sin has been blotted out of the heavenly sanctuary and the investigative judgment has been closed; they stand from the time probation closes until Jesus comes in the clouds of heaven to claim them as his own. By the grace of Christ and through his power, they have so allowed God's character to transform their hearts and their minds, that they have the Father's name written in their foreheads, they are clothed with the robe of Christ's righteousness, they have allowed him to consecrate, to justify, to sanctify their characters to the point where they have gained victory over sin, and are sealed.

Revelation 14:5 And in their mouth was found no guile: for they are without fault before the throne of God.

They are holy before God. They have no lie, no falsehood in their mouths. How can this be? The fact that these individuals were

---

[30] E. G. White, *Review and Herald,* April 12, 1898, par. 19.

[31] Matthew 20:16

[32] Contrary to popular belief, the righteous are not raptured before the tribulation. The Bible says they came out of great tribulation. That means they went through the tribulation. The righteous living go through the terrible, seven last plagues that will be poured out upon the earth. The righteous dead, sleeping in their graves, are resurrected at the second coming of Jesus.

[33] Jeremiah 2:3

redeemed from among men tells us that they needed a redeemer. If they needed a redeemer, that means that they were sinners. The Bible tells us that "all have sinned, and come short of the glory of God."[34] Since this is the case, how can these be without fault before the throne of God?

"For even hereunto were ye called: because Christ also suffered for us, leaving us an example, that ye should follow his steps: Who did no sin, **neither was guile found in his mouth**: Who, when he was reviled, reviled not again; when he suffered, he threatened not; but committed himself to him that judgeth righteously. Who his own self bare our sins in his own body on the tree, that we, being dead to sins, should live unto righteousness: by whose stripes ye were healed."[35]

Christ had no guile in his mouth, and yet he bare our sins in his own body that we might be saved. Christ "gave himself a ransom for all."[36] "That he might redeem us from all iniquity, and purify unto himself a peculiar people."[37] "He will turn again, he will have compassion upon us; he will subdue our iniquities; and thou wilt cast all their sins into the depths of the sea."[38] "For I will be merciful to their unrighteousness, and their sins and their iniquities will I remember no more."[39] "Now unto him that is able to keep you from falling, and to present you faultless before the presence of his glory with exceeding joy, To the only wise God our Saviour, be glory and majesty, dominion and power, both now and for ever. Amen."[40]

The Bible tells us that we have a Saviour, who is able to keep us from falling and to present us faultless before his throne. The only way for us to be saved is by accepting the righteousness of Jesus. If we accept his perfect life, in place of our sinful lives, he makes us faultless.

---

[34] Romans 3:23

[35] 1 Peter 2:21-24

[36] 1 Timothy 2:6

[37] Titus 2:14

[38] Micah 7:19

[39] Hebrews 8:12

[40] Jude 24-25

Revelation 7, speaking of the 144,000 says, "These are they which came out of great tribulation, and have washed their robes, and made them white in the blood of the Lamb. Therefore are they before the throne of God."[41] "And I saw another angel ascending from the east, having the seal of the living God: and he cried with a loud voice to the four angels, to whom it was given to hurt the earth and the sea, Saying, Hurt not the earth, neither the sea, nor the trees, till we have sealed the servants of our God in their foreheads. And I heard the number of them which were sealed: and there were sealed an hundred and forty and four thousand of all the tribes of the children of Israel."[42]

God is holding back the winds of strife until his servants are sealed. Once they are sealed, the winds will begin to blow. This shows that these are people who are living at the very end of time.

From the time the heavenly sanctuary is finally cleansed by Christ from the defilement of every sin, until he arrives on the earth, these people will not sin. No further sin can contaminate heaven. Jesus is no longer ministering on their behalf in the most holy place. Therefore, they must stand faultless, by the power and blood of Jesus, before the throne of God.

"Those who are living upon the earth when the intercession of Christ shall cease in the sanctuary above are to stand in the sight of a holy God without a mediator. Their robes must be spotless, their characters must be purified from sin by the blood of sprinkling. Through the grace of God and their own diligent effort they must be conquerors in the battle with evil. While the investigative judgment is going forward in heaven, while the sins of penitent believers are being removed from the sanctuary, there is to be a special work of purification, of putting away of sin, among God's people upon earth. This work is more clearly presented in the messages of Revelation 14."

---

[41] Revelation 7:14-15

[42] Revelation 7:2-4

Perhaps you are worried when the Bible speaks of the 144,000, thinking that 144,000 is so few.[43] These are not the only people who are saved. Notice that in Revelation 7:9, immediately after describing the 144,000, John writes: "After this I beheld, and, lo, a great multitude, which no man could number, of all nations, and kindreds, and people, and tongues, stood before the throne, and before the Lamb, clothed with white robes, and palms in their hands...."

The 144,000 are simply the final generation that have a specific function to perform—to demonstrate to the entire Universe that a large group of people; in a single generation; when the conditions are the very worst; while the seven last plagues are convulsing the planet; stand, by the power of God, without committing sin, after the investigative judgment has been closed. Many others—a great multitude which no man can number, the Bible says—will be standing on that sea of glass. A great multitude will be saved, but there will be many laid to rest prior to the terrible events that are coming on this world at the very end of time, for God knows that they cannot make it through that period of time. Therefore, if one must face death, either by natural causes, or by persecution before the coming of the Lord, it may be the mercy of God shielding him from that trying hour.

If we are not among this group, we can thank God for his mercy in laying us to rest before this terrible time, so that we might be saved. God is not willing that any should be lost but is longing to bring all to repentance, though not everyone will accept his glorious and gracious provisions.

Revelation 14:6 And I saw another angel fly in the midst of heaven, having the everlasting gospel to preach unto them that dwell on the earth, and to every nation, and kindred, and tongue, and people,

"The angels are represented as flying in the midst of heaven, proclaiming to the world a message of warning, and having a direct bearing upon the people living in the last days of this earth's history.

---

[43] Some might say that 144,000 are so few out of eight billion people on the planet. But there was an estimated one billion people on the earth at the time of the flood, and only eight got on the ark. Eight is a lot less than 144,000, proportionally. 144,000 is 2,250 times more.

No one hears the voice of these angels, for they are a symbol to represent the people of God who are working in harmony with the universe of heaven."[44] God did not commit to angels the spreading of the gospel to the whole world, though he could have—it would have been much more efficient. Instead, as feeble and erring as we are, infinite wisdom saw fit to give us the privilege of working with heavenly agencies for the salvation of men. "And he {Jesus} said unto them, Go ye into all the world, and preach the gospel to every creature."[45] Christ gave us the commission to preach the gospel to every creature—to every nation, tongue, kindred, and people. This angel flying in the midst of heaven proclaiming the gospel is a portrayal of the message that goes forth with power, by the people of God, at the end of time.

Revelation 14:7 Saying with a loud voice, Fear God, and give glory to him; for the hour of his judgment is come: and worship him that made heaven, and earth, and the sea, and the fountains of waters.

The first angel's message is the message of the "**everlasting gospel**" (good news), which contains the following parts:
1. Fear God
2. Give him glory
3. The hour of his judgment is come
4. Worship the Creator (him that made)

1. What does it mean to "**fear God**?"
"The fear of the LORD is the beginning of wisdom: a good understanding have all they that do his commandments: his praise endureth for ever."[46] "The fear of the LORD is to hate evil."[47] The fear of the Lord is to hate evil and to obey the commandments of God. Do we fear man more than God? The gospel "is the power of God unto salvation to every one that believeth;"[48] the power to save us from our evil natures and enable us to obey. "For thou, O God, hast heard

---

[44] E. G. White, *Maranatha* (1976), p. 173.4.

[45] Mark 16:15

[46] Psalm 111:10. See also Proverbs 9:10; 14:26-27; 15:31-33.

[47] Proverbs 8:13

[48] Romans 1:16

my vows: thou hast given me the heritage of those that fear thy name."[49]

"Noah did not mix the soft, pleasing deceptions of Satan with his message. He did not utter the sentiment of many of his day who declared that God was too merciful to do such a terrible work. Many asserted that God would grant the wicked another season of probation; but Noah did not indulge them in the faintest hope that those who neglected the present opportunity, who rejected the present message, would be favored with another opportunity of salvation. God means that men shall not only love him, but that his fear shall be in their hearts. Noah's faith was mingled with fear; for it is written that Noah, being warned of God, moved with fear, prepared an ark for the saving of his house. His faith intensified his fear; for it was no cowardly fear that moved him. He dared not suppress the words of God for fear of men, or withhold his message in dread of the consequences that might result because of the opposition and hate of the wicked and unbelieving about him. He knew the power of God, and realized that God would fulfill his word. His fear of God did not separate him from God, but served to draw him closer to him, and to lead him to pour out his soul in earnest supplication. There were many who at first received Noah's message, but the fear of men was greater than the fear of God, and they turned away from the truth of God to believe a lie. As time passed on, and reproach and ridicule were heaped upon them, their hearts failed them, and they did not bear the test. It is the testing time that will measure professed faith and assurance in God. Courage and integrity cannot be estimated rightly by men until the day of trial puts them to the test."[50]

We are to fear God because the hour of his judgment is come. Ecclesiastes echoes the same refrain: "Let us hear the conclusion of the whole matter: **Fear God, and keep his commandments**: for this is the whole duty of man. **For God shall bring every work into judgment**, with every secret thing, whether it be good, or whether it be evil."[51] Because God will bring every work into judgment, we are to fear God and keep his commandments.

---

[49] Psalms 61:5

[50] E. G. White, *Signs of the Times,* April 18, 1895 par. 9.

[51] Ecclesiastes 12:13-14

2. What does it mean to "**give glory**" to God?
"Whether therefore ye eat, or drink, or whatsoever ye do, **do all to the glory of God**."[52] "Herein is my Father glorified, that ye bear much fruit; so shall ye be my disciples."[53]

When Moses asked to see the glory of God, God showed him his character. God's character is the same as his glory, which is synonymous with his name. Each of the characteristics of God, portrayed in the Bible, are also descriptions of his law.[54] This shows that the commandments of God are a transcript of his character. From this we see that giving glory to God is the same as keeping his commandments and shows that when the 144,000 have the Father's name or his seal written in their foreheads, they have the commandments of God written in their minds and hearts. "But this shall be the covenant that I will make with the house of Israel; After those days, saith the LORD, I will put my law in their inward parts, and write it in their hearts; and will be their God, and they shall be my people."[55]

3. What does "**the hour of his judgment is come**" mean?
This phrase refers to the investigative judgment or the cleansing of the heavenly sanctuary, as described in Daniel 8 and 9.[56] It is part of the everlasting gospel (good news) that the hour of his judgment is come, which requires that the judgment be good news. Have you ever considered the judgment as good news? We all have probably been a little nervous about the judgment at times, perhaps because we wonder if we are ready for the judgment. We are to fear God and keep his commandments because his judgment is at hand, "for God shall bring every work into judgment, with every secret thing, whether it be good, or whether it be evil."[57] This might not seem like good news at first because we know that we "all have sinned, and come short of the glory of God;"[58] and that "there is none righteous, no, not

---

[52] 1 Corinthians 10:31

[53] John 15:8

[54] See comments on Revelation 7:3.

[55] Jeremiah 31:33

[56] See comments on Daniel 8, 9.

[57] Ecclesiastes 12:14

[58] Romans 3:23

one…They are all gone out of the way, they are together become unprofitable; there is none that doeth good, no, not one."[59] "We are all as an unclean thing, and all our righteousnesses are as filthy rags; and we all do fade as a leaf; and our iniquities, like the wind, have taken us away."[60] Even our best goodness is as filthy rags. Therefore, if God brought only our good works into judgment we would not pass the judgment because our goodness is filthy. We know that "the soul that sinneth, it shall die,"[61] "for the wages of sin is death."[62] The question is asked by Job, "How then can man be justified with God? or how can he be clean that is born of a woman?"[63]

"For God so loved the world, that he gave his only begotten Son, that whosoever believeth in him should not perish, but have everlasting life. For God sent not his Son into the world to condemn the world; but that the world through him might be saved."[64] The Bible says that Christ "gave himself for me;"[65] he "gave himself for our sins;"[66] he became my sin, so that I "might be made the righteousness of God in him."[67] "Who is a God like unto thee, that pardoneth iniquity, and passeth by the transgression of the remnant of his heritage? he retaineth not his anger for ever, because he delighteth in mercy. He will turn again, he will have compassion upon us; he will subdue our iniquities; and thou wilt cast all their sins into the depths of the sea."[68]

God has paid for the sins of the whole world,[69] and he is offering you forgiveness for your portion of those sins. All he asks is that you confess the truth—that you have a debt of sin and are in need of his

---

[59] Romans 3:10-12

[60] Isaiah 64:6

[61] Ezekiel 18:20

[62] Romans 6:23

[63] Job 25:4

[64] John 3:16-17

[65] Galatians 2:20

[66] Galatians 1:4

[67] 2 Corinthians 5:21

[68] Micah 7:18-19

[69] 1 John 2:2

forgiveness.[70] "The grace of Christ is freely to justify the sinner without merit or claim on his part. Justification is a full and complete pardon of sin. **The moment a sinner accepts Christ by faith, that moment he is pardoned.** The righteousness of Christ is imputed to him, and he is no more to doubt God's forgiving grace."[71]

You need not fear the judgment for there is no condemnation when you have the righteousness of Christ and are trusting him for holiness. But, if you are trusting in your own strength, claiming your own righteousness, you will never be ready for the judgment, because "if I justify myself, mine own mouth shall condemn me: if I say, I am perfect, it shall also prove me perverse."[72] "Behold, his soul which is lifted up is not upright in him: but the just shall live by his faith."[73] If we are lifted up in pride, we cannot be righteous, but if we live by the faith of Jesus we have nothing to fear in the judgment. Obedience is the result of being righteous. Christ said, "Now ye are clean through the word which I have spoken unto you."[74] "Abide in me, and I in you. As the branch cannot bear fruit of itself, except it abide in the vine; no more can ye, except ye abide in me. I am the vine, ye are the branches: He that abideth in me, and I in him, the same bringeth forth much fruit: for without me ye can do nothing."[75] Trying to be obedient in order to be righteous is like a branch trying to bear fruit in order to connect to the vine. If the branch is connected to the vine, it bears fruit by the power of the vine.[76]

Once we have an abiding relationship with the vine, the judgment becomes good news because Jesus, who gave his life for us, is the judge.[77] Believe it or not, he is also the defense attorney![78]

The process of cleansing that heavenly sanctuary means that the sins committed that have been transferred to the heavenly sanctuary

---

[70] See Romans 5; also, Martin Klein, *The Most Precious Message*, Ch. 2.

[71] E. G. White, *The Faith I Live By* (1958), p. 107.2.

[72] Job 9:20

[73] Habakkuk 2:4

[74] John 15:3

[75] John 15:4-5

[76] See Martin Klein, *The Most Frecious Message,* Ch. 5.

[77] John 5:22

[78] 1 John 2:1

will be blotted out. Having our sins blotted out forever is good news! The only reason why the judgment might not be good news is if your sins have not been confessed ahead of time to be erased by the blood of Christ.

In Psalms 67:3-4 the Bible says: "Let the people praise thee, O God; let all the people praise thee. **O let the nations be glad and sing for joy: for thou shalt judge the people righteously**, and govern the nations upon earth. Selah." God portrays the judgment as something over which everyone should be glad and sing with great joy. This is because God will judge righteously. Have you ever been the recipient of something that was unfair, or wrong? If you have, you can rest in the glad assurance that we have a righteous judge. Every wrong will eventually be made right. Praise the Lord! Judgment is good news.

4. What does it mean to "**worship him that made heaven, and earth, and the sea, and the fountains of waters**"?
In Revelation 13 we saw that the final conflict is a war over worship. The dragon, the sea beast, the earth beast, and the image to the sea beast are all demanding worship. Revelation 14 gives the call to "**worship him that made heaven, and earth, and the sea, and the fountains of waters**." This resounding message from the first angel defies the theory of evolution. God made the world as recorded in the creation account. In fact, the first angel of Revelation 14:7 is referencing, as its authority, nothing less than the Ten Commandments, written with the very finger of God.

"Of the 404 verses found in the book of Revelation, 278 of them are echoes from other stories and prophecies in the Old Testament."[79] Twenty-six books of the Bible are quoted in the book of Revelation. The book of Revelation is not introducing an abundance of new things—although there are some new details there—but rather amplifying the rest of Scripture to paint a more vivid Revelation of Jesus Christ.

The call to "worship him that **made heaven, and earth, and the sea, and** the fountains of waters," is a direct quote from the fourth commandment in Exodus 20:8-11, "Remember the sabbath day, to

---

[79] Doug Batchelor, http://www.amazingfacts.org/media-library/storacle/e/5327/t/back-to-jerusalem/laststatus/mobile/mrtype/mobile/postback1387/1?skinsrc=%5Bg%5Dskins/amazingfacts/af-mobile Retrieved 3-10-2017.

keep it holy. Six days shalt thou labour, and do all thy work: But the seventh day is the sabbath of the LORD thy God: in it thou shalt not do any work, thou, nor thy son, nor thy daughter, thy manservant, nor thy maidservant, nor thy cattle, nor thy stranger that is within thy gates: For in six days the LORD **made heaven and earth, the sea, and** all that in them is, and rested the seventh day: wherefore the LORD blessed the sabbath day, and hallowed it."[80]

Who is the Creator of all things, including the sabbath? "In the beginning was the Word, and the Word was with God, and the Word was God. The same was in the beginning with God. **All things were made by him**; and without him was not any thing made that was made. And the Word was made flesh, and dwelt among us, (and we beheld his glory, the glory as of the only begotten of the Father,) full of grace and truth."[81] It is our Creator and Redeemer who gave us the sabbath, for when the Lord Jesus finished his work of creation and "ended his work which he had made... he rested on the seventh day from all his work which he had made. And God blessed the seventh day, and sanctified it: because that in it he had rested from all his work which God created and made."[82] The sabbath is a memorial of the creative genius, and omnipotent power of Jesus Christ our Saviour, and he desires us to rest with him on his seventh-day sabbath. The first angel's message is a call for our return to the Biblical sabbath.

"When the foundations of the earth were laid, then was also laid the foundation of the Sabbath. I was shown that if the true Sabbath had been kept, there would never have been an infidel or an atheist. The observance of the Sabbath would have preserved the world from idolatry."[83]

Revelation 14:8 And there followed another angel, saying, Babylon is fallen, is fallen, that great city, because she made all nations drink of the wine of the wrath of her fornication.

---

[80] Exodus 20:8-11

[81] John 1:1-3, 14

[82] Genesis 2:2-3

[83] E. G. White, *Christians Experience and Teachings of Ellen G. White* (1922), p. 86.1.

The second angel's message is a cry that Babylon is fallen. This message does not refer to literal Babylon. Isaiah already prophesied, hundreds of years before its fulfillment, and long before John was born: "And Babylon, the glory of kingdoms, the beauty of the Chaldees' excellency, shall be as when God overthrew Sodom and Gomorrah. It shall never be inhabited, neither shall it be dwelt in from generation to generation: neither shall the Arabian pitch tent there; neither shall the shepherds make their fold there."[84] Scripture says that literal Babylon would be so desolate that the shepherds would not even graze their sheep there, and the Arabians would not even pitch their tents there. Photographs from the 1930's show that the city of Babylon was still completely desolate. No Arabians pitched their tents there, no shepherds grazed their sheep there, just the ruins of a city that lay completely forgotten. In 2003 a partial reconstruction was made of Babylon, but to this very day there is nothing but ruins there, just as the Bible predicted.

"A tablet dated 275 BC states that the inhabitants of Babylon were transported to Seleucia, where a palace and a temple (Esagila) were built. With this deportation, Babylon became insignificant as a city...."[85] Over 300 years before John wrote these things, Babylon was completely desolate, in direct fulfillment of Isaiah's prophecy. Therefore, when the message is given that Babylon is fallen, it is not speaking of the ancient city of Babylon, but spiritual Babylon, also brought in to view in Revelation 17. "So he carried me away in the spirit into the wilderness: and I saw a woman sit upon a scarlet coloured beast, full of names of blasphemy, having seven heads and ten horns. And upon her forehead was a name written, MYSTERY, BABYLON THE GREAT, THE MOTHER OF HARLOTS AND ABOMINATIONS OF THE EARTH."[86]

The woman of Revelation 17 represents none other than the Roman Catholic Church.[87] Her name is: Babylon the Great, the Mother of Harlots and Abominations of the Earth.

"Babylon is said to be 'the mother of harlots.' By her daughters must be symbolized **churches that cling to her doctrines and**

---

[84] Isaiah 13:19-20

[85] https://en.wikipedia.org/wiki/Babylon retrieved 9-4-2016.

[86] Revelation 17:3, 5

[87] See comments on Revelation 17.

traditions, and follow her example of sacrificing the truth and the approval of God, in order to form an unlawful alliance with the world. The message of Revelation 14, announcing the fall of Babylon, must apply to religious bodies that were once pure and have become corrupt. Since this message follows the warning of the judgment, it must be given in the last days; therefore it cannot refer to the Roman Church alone, for that church has been in a fallen condition for many centuries."[88]

Babylon not only consists of the Romish power but constitutes all daughter churches who at one time were pure but have now apostatized, by sacrificing God's word and principles for friendship with the world. Rome claims these apostate churches as her own, Joseph Ratzinger (later pope Benedict XVI) asserting, "It must always be clear, when the expression sister Churches is used in this proper sense, that the one, holy, catholic and apostolic Universal Church is not sister but mother of all the particular Churches."[89]

"Furthermore, in the eighteenth chapter of the Revelation, in a message which is yet future, the people of God are called upon to come out of Babylon. According to this scripture, many of God's people must still be in Babylon. And in what religious bodies are the greater part of the followers of Christ now to be found? Without doubt, in the various churches professing the Protestant faith.... 'Thou didst trust in thine own beauty, and playedst the harlot because of thy renown.'"[90]

Babylon now consists of all the fallen churches who are no longer following the word of God but are following the commandments of men. "The following significant paragraph is from the *Watchman and Reflector*, the leading organ of the Baptist denomination:—'Dr. Guthrie, speaking of the exit of the Presbyterian church from Rome, says, 'Three hundred years ago, our church, with an open Bible on her banner, and this motto, Search the Scriptures, on her scroll,

---

[88] E. G. White, *The Great Controversy* (1911), p. 382.3.

[89] Cardinal Joseph Ratzinger, September 4, 2000.
http://www.vatican.va/roman_curia/congregations/cfaith/documents/rc_con_cfaith_doc_20000630_chiese-sorelle_en.html#_ftn8 Retrieved 12-13-2016.

[90] E. G. White, *The Great Controversy* (1888), p. 382.3

marched out from the gates of Rome.' Then he significantly asks, 'Did they come clean out of Babylon?'"[91]

Babylon is fallen because she made all nations drink of the wine of her fornication. The word Babylon is derived from the word Babel, which means confusion. All these churches are imbibing in the intoxicating confusion of the false doctrines of Rome.

"The wine of Babylon is the exalting of the false and spurious sabbath above the Sabbath which the Lord Jehovah hath blessed and sanctified for the use of man, also it is the immortality of the soul. These kindred heresies, and the rejection of the truth, convert the church into Babylon. Kings, merchants, rulers, and religious teachers are all in corrupt harmony."[92] "The fallen denominational churches are Babylon. Babylon has been fostering poisonous doctrines, the wine of error. This wine of error is made up of false doctrines, such as the natural immortality of the soul, the eternal torment of the wicked, the denial of the pre-existence of Christ prior to his birth in Bethlehem, and advocating and exalting the first day of the week above God's holy, sanctified day. These and kindred errors are presented to the world by the various, churches, and thus the Scriptures are fulfilled that say, 'For all nations have drunk of the wine of the wrath of her fornication.' It is a wrath which is created by false doctrines, and when kings and presidents drink this wine of the wrath of her fornication, they are stirred with anger against those who will not come into harmony with the false and Satanic heresies which exalt the false Sabbath, and lead men to trample under foot God's memorial."[93]

Revelation 14:9 And the third angel followed them, saying with a loud voice, If any man worship the beast and his image, and receive his mark in his forehead, or in his hand,

Revelation 14:10 The same shall drink of the wine of the wrath of God, which is poured out without mixture into the cup of his indignation; and he shall be tormented with fire and brimstone

---

[91] *Collection of Facts for the Times, Consisting of Valuable Extracts from Eminent Authors,* 2nd Rev. ed. (Battle Creek, MI: Steam Press, 1875), p. 70.

[92] E. G. White, *Selected Messages,* Book. 2 (1958), p. 68.2.

[93] E. G. White, *Review and Herald,* September 12, 1893 par. 20.

in the presence of the holy angels, and in the presence of the Lamb:

"The most fearful threatening ever addressed to mortals is contained in the third angel's message. That must be a terrible sin which calls down the wrath of God unmingled with mercy. Men are not to be left in darkness concerning this important matter; the warning against this sin is to be given to the world before the visitation of God's judgments, that all may know why they are to be inflicted, and have opportunity to escape them. Prophecy declares that the first angel would make his announcement to 'every nation, and kindred, and tongue, and people.' The warning of the third angel, which forms a part of the same threefold message, is to be no less widespread. It is represented in the prophecy as being proclaimed with a loud voice, by an angel flying in the midst of heaven; and it will command the attention of the world."[94]

This thundering message is to be given to an impenitent world, just before Jesus comes. God is not willing that any should perish. This final call is to be made before he pours out his wrath on those that receive the mark of the beast. God warns us in no uncertain terms not to receive the mark of the beast, for if you do you will suffer the wrath of God, which is poured out without mixture—without dilution—or no longer mixed with mercy. Yet God, in his mercy, is revealing here the critical information necessary to identify the mark of the beast and how it may be avoided. If we are to avoid receiving this mark, it is imperative that we know what it is. Revelation 13 provided the framework for the identification of the mark of the beast. "And he had power to give life unto the image of the beast, that the image of the beast should both speak, and cause that as many as would not worship the image of the beast should be killed."[95]

Protestant America, represented by the lamb-like beast,[96] will give life unto the image of the beast—the system of false worship legislated by the illegitimate union of church and state. A decree is finally passed that any who will not worship the image of the beast should be killed. Worship is the central issue in the reception of the mark of the beast. In Revelation 13, the word worship is repeated

---

[94] E. G. White, *The Great Controversy* (1911), p. 449.2.

[95] Revelation 13:15

[96] See comments on Revelation 13:11-12.

several times revealing Satan's plan to cause the whole world to worship himself. By worshiping the image of the beast, they will worship the beast and by worshiping the beast they will worship the devil. In Revelation 14 the issue of worship is repeated again, with the call given to worship God, the Creator of all things, and a warning being pronounced against worshiping the beast or anything with which it is connected.

The contrast becomes apparent. On the one hand we see Satan and the beast and all he stands for, seeking to kill all who will not follow him; on the other hand, we see our loving Creator, the Lord Jesus who gave his life to save us, inviting us to his side. On the one side Satan is working to deceive the whole world into receiving the mark of the beast; on the other side God is working to enlighten all to choose the seal of God. There are only two sides in this conflict. Every inhabitant of our planet will receive either the mark of the beast or the seal of God. Therefore, the warning against the mark of the beast is also a call to receive the seal of God.

The seal of God or the mark of the beast are not literal or physical marks. They are an issue of allegiance; an issue of worship; an issue of authority. In Daniel 7:25 God warned that the little-horned power "shall speak great words against the most High, and shall wear out the saints of the most High, and **think to change times and laws**." This blasphemous power would think to change God's times and laws. The papacy[97] has indeed changed God's law and especially the part of the law that references time—the holy, seventh-day sabbath.

The mark of the beast is not complicated—it is simply the mark of the papacy's presumed authority. Here is what the Roman Catholic church tells us: "the Church is above the Bible. And this transference of Sabbath observance from Saturday to Sunday is proof positive of that fact."[98]

The Catholic church claims to be above the Bible, and the evidence they advance for this is that they changed the sabbath to Sunday.

---

[97] See comments on Daniel 7.

[98] "Sabbath Observance," *The Catholic Record*, September 1, 1923, p. 4, http://biblelight.net/c-record.htm. Retrieved 02-09-2016.

Therefore, she claims as the mark of her authority, Sunday worship in place of God's command to worship on the seventh-day. Alexander Campbell, in speaking of the change of the sabbath, says: "But some say it was changed from the seventh to the first day. Where? when? and by whom? No man can tell. No; it never was changed, nor could it be, unless creation was to be gone through again; for the *reason assigned must be changed* before the observance or respect to the reason can be changed! It is old wives' fables to talk of the change of the Sabbath from the seventh to the first day. If it be changed, it was that august personage changed it who changes times and laws ex officio. I think his name is Dr. Antichrist."[99]

In a letter, dated February 10, 1920, written and signed by Albert Smith, secretary of Cardinal Gibbons, for the Archdiocese of Baltimore, Maryland, in which he is answering a letter that was sent with the question as to whether it is true that the Catholic church changed the day of worship, he said: "Your letter of January 31st addressed to the Cardinal came in due time. Be sure of it, your Seventh Day Adventist friends are telling you the truth, when they say that it was the Catholic Church which changed the day of worship from the Jewish Sabbath to the Christian Sunday. If protestants would follow the Bible, they should worship God on the Sabbath day. In keeping the Sunday, they are following a law of the Catholic Church. During the first three centuries, practice and tradition had consecrated the Sunday to the worship of God. In the year 300, the Council of Elvira made the law a definite one. I am enclosing a catechism as requested. Very truly yours, Albert Smith."[100]

In a Catholic work entitled *Plain Talk about Protestantism of Today,* it says: "The observance of Sunday by Protestants is an homage they pay in spite of themselves to the authority of the [Catholic] Church."[101]

---

[99] Alexander Campbell, *Christian Baptist,* Vol. 1, p. 44; as cited in *Collection of Facts for the Times.*

[100] Albert Smith, Chancellor of Archdiocese of Baltimore, replying for the cardinal in a letter dated Feb. 10, 1920. http://biblelight.net/Sources/Albert-Smith.gif Retrieved 3-10-2017.

[101] Louis Gaston de Segur, *Plain Talk About Protestantism of Today* (London: Thomas Richardson and Son, 1874), p. 213.

"I have repeatedly offered $1,000 to any one who can prove to me from the Bible alone that I am bound to keep Sunday holy. There is no such law in the Bible. It is a law of the holy Catholic Church alone. The Bible says, 'Remember that thou keep holy the Sabbath day.' The Catholic Church says: 'No ! By my divine power I abolish the Sabbath day, and command you to keep holy the first day of the week.' And, lo! the entire civilized world bows down in reverent obedience to the command of the holy Catholic Church. Yours respectfully, T. ENRIGHT, CSS. R."[102]

The Roman Catholic Church views the near universal reverence of Sunday, as the entire civilized world bowing in obedience to the authority of the Catholic Church! This is how "all that dwell upon the earth shall worship,"[103] the beast except those few whose names are written in the book of life. God is giving a final warning, that when Sunday worship becomes legislated, we cannot, even on the pain of death or economic sanctions, receive the mark of the beast. "When the test comes, it will be clearly shown what the mark of the beast is. It is the keeping of Sunday."[104]

Martin Luther and Melancthon, in the Augsburg Confession, said the following: "They [Roman Catholic church] allege the Sabbath changed into Sunday, the Lord's day, contrary to the Decalogue, as it appears; neither is there any example more boasted of than the changing of the Sabbath day. Great, say they, is the power and authority of the church, since it dispensed with one of the ten commandments."[105]

God revealed in Daniel 7:25, that the papacy would think to change God's times and laws. Have they, in fact, attempted such a brazen and blasphemous act as to mutilate the commandments of God? The following chart compares the ten commandments as recorded in Scripture with the ten commandments as commonly abbreviated in a Roman Catholic catechism. The first thing that is obvious is that there are dramatically fewer words. Secondly, it is the second and fourth commandments which are diminished the most. In fact, the

---

[102] Fr. Enright, CSS. R. to E.E. Franke, January 11, 1892, in "An Adventist Minister on Sunday Laws," *American Sentinel,* June 1, 1893, p. 173.

[103] Revelation 13:8

[104] E. G. White, *Last Day Events* (1992), p. 224.2.

[105] Luther & Melancthon, *Augsburg Confession,* (1530) p. 171.1.

second commandment is completely gone. It forbids bowing to images, which is an accepted Catholic practice. Because the second commandment has been removed, each subsequent commandment is shifted up one number, with the third commandment becoming second, and the fourth commandments becoming the third, etc. Of course, everybody knows that there are Ten Commandments, so the last one is split in two and reversed in its order. Their third (the fourth in the Bible) commandment tells you to keep holy the sabbath, but the portion identifying which day is the sabbath has been removed. There is indeed a clear, concerted, intentional changing of God's laws especially the command that deals with time, just as the Bible predicted. Over and over, Catholic writers boast of this very change.

"Sunday is a Catholic institution, and its claims to observance can be defended only on Catholic principles... from the beginning to the end of scriptures there is not a single passage which warrants the transfer of the weekly public worship from the last day of the week to the first."[106]

"If protestants would follow the Bible, they should worship God on the Sabbath day. In keeping the Sunday, they are following a law of the Catholic Church."[107] "Protestantism, in disregarding the authority of the Roman [Catholic] Church, has no good reason for its Sunday theory and ought logically to keep Saturday as the Sabbath."[108]

"Reason and common sense demand the acceptance of one or the other of these alternatives: either Protestantism and the keeping holy of Saturday. Or Catholicity and the keeping holy of Sunday. Compromise is impossible."[109]

Those readers who are Catholics, I plead with you; God is not attacking you, he is not condemning you; he is giving you a message of love because he wants to save you from Satan's deceptions. You

---

[106] M. Long, "Rampant Sabbaterianism," *Catholic Press,* August 25, 1900, p. 22, biblelight.net/Catholic Press.jpg Retrieved: 01-31-2016.

[107] Albert Smith, Chancellor of Archdiocese of Baltimore, replying for the cardinal in a letter dated February 10, 1920.

[108] John Gilmary Shea, L.L.D., *American Catholic Quarterly Review,* Vol. 8—January, 1883—No. 29 (Philadelphia: Hardy & Mahony, Publishers and Proprietors, 1883), p. 152.

[109] "The Christian Sabbath," *The Catholic Mirror,* December 23, 1893, p. 8-9.

may have grown up all your life not knowing these things. God understands the sincerity of your past worship. He knows your heart and that you have been doing everything to the best of your knowledge and ability. The Bible says, "the times of this ignorance God winked at; but now commandeth all men every where to repent."[110] Once we see what the Bible says and understand the truth, then he calls us to repentance, to fall down on our knees and say, "God, I didn't realize I was breaking one of your laws. Please forgive me. And by your grace and by your strength, help me to follow your word and your law."

The Catholic Church boasts, "Since the Catholic Church, probably influenced by Constantine, made the day Sunday a holiday, it can claim the honor of having granted man a rest from his labors every seven days."[111]

"Perhaps the boldest thing, the most revolutionary change the Church ever did, happened in the first century. The holy day, the Sabbath, was changed from Saturday to Sunday. 'The Day of the Lord' (dies Dominica) was chosen, not from any directions noted in scripture, but from the Church's sense of its own power. The day of the resurrection, the day of Pentecost, fifty days later, came on the first day of the week. So this would be the new Sabbath. **People who think that the Scriptures should be the sole authority, should logically become 7th Day Adventists, and keep Saturday holy.**"[112]

Jesus says, with tears in his eyes, "Ye hypocrites, well did Esaias prophesy of you, saying, This people draweth nigh unto me with their mouth, and honoureth me with their lips; but their heart is far from

---

[110] Acts 17:30

[111] C. S. Mosna, S.C.J., *Storia della Domenica Dalle Origini Fino Agli Inizi del v Secolo [History of Sunday From its Origins to the Early Fifth Century]* (Rome: Libreria Editrice dell'Universita Gregoriana, 1969), p. 366,
http://biblelight.net/Sources.htm Retrieved: 03-13-2016.
Italian: "Avendo la Chiesa influito probabilmente su Costantino per rendere la domenica giorno <<festivo>>, Essa può rivendicarsi l'onore di aver voluto concedere all'uomo una pausa alle sue fatiche ogni sette giorni."

[112] Fr. Leo Broderick, "Pastor's Page," *The Sentinel*, May 21, 1995,
biblelight.net/st-cath.htm Retrieved: 03-13-2016.

10 COMMANDMENTS AS FOUND IN SCRIPTURE	10 COMMANDMENTS AS COMMONLY ABBREVIATED IN A ROMAN CATHOLIC CATECHISM
1. I am the LORD thy God, which have brought thee out of the land of Egypt, out of the house of bondage. Thou shalt have no other gods before me.	1. I am the LORD thy God. Thou shalt have no strange gods before Me.
2. Thou shalt not make unto thee any graven image, or any likeness of any thing that is in heaven above, or that is in the earth beneath, or that is in the water under the earth: Thou shalt not bow down thyself to them, nor serve them: for I the LORD thy God am a jealous God, visiting the iniquity of the fathers upon the children unto the third and fourth generation of them that hate me; And showing mercy unto thousands of them that love me, and keep my commandments.	Removed.
3. Thou shalt not take the name of the LORD thy God in vain; for the LORD will not hold him guiltless that taketh his name in vain.	2. Thou shalt not take the name of the LORD thy God in vain.
4. Remember the sabbath day, to keep it holy. Six days shalt thou labour, and do all thy work: But the seventh day is the sabbath of the LORD thy God: in it thou shalt not do any work, thou, nor thy son, nor thy daughter, thy manservant, nor thy maidservant, nor thy cattle, nor thy stranger that is within thy gates: For in six days the LORD made heaven and earth, the sea, and all that in them is, and rested the seventh day: wherefore the LORD blessed the sabbath day, and hallowed it.	3. Remember to keep holy the Sabbath day.
5. Honour thy father and thy mother: that thy days may be long upon the land which the LORD thy God giveth thee.	4. Honour thy father and thy mother.
6. Thou shalt not kill.	5. Thou shalt not kill.
7. Thou shalt not commit adultery.	6. Thou shalt not commit adultery.
8. Thou shalt not steal.	7. Thou shalt not steal.
9. Thou shalt not bear false witness against thy neighbor.	8. Thou shalt not bear false witness against thy neighbor.
10. Thou shalt not covet thy neighbor's house, thou shalt not covet thy neighbor's wife, nor his manservant, nor his maidservant, nor his ox, nor his ass, nor any thing that is thy neighbor's.	9. Thou shalt not covet thy neighbor's wife.
	10. Thou shalt not covet thy neighbor's goods.

me. But in vain they do worship me, teaching for doctrines the commandments of men."[113]

Friend, do not let your worship be in vain. Jesus loves you. He gave all of heaven and poured out his blood for your sins, to redeem you and save you from the deception and the grasp of Satan. Eve was no match for the sophistries of Satan. A third of the angels, who had never fallen before, who had never seen sin before, followed Satan, because his deceptions were so powerful. Do you think it would be any different today? Do you think the majority of the world would really be following God's way and not Satan's? The Bible tells us otherwise, "Enter ye in at the strait gate: for wide is the gate, and broad is the way, that leadeth to destruction, and many there be which go in thereat: Because strait is the gate, and narrow is the way, which leadeth unto life, and few there be that find it."[114]

Rather than following the commandments of men and receiving the mark of the beast, let us follow God's commandments as recorded in the Bible.

Some people say, that this commandment was just given for the Israelites at Mount Sinai. However, the sabbath was put into effect long before the Jews existed. At the completion of creation, when God had finished creating the world, he gave the sabbath as a gift to man. "Thus the heavens and the earth were finished, and all the host of them. And on the seventh day God ended his work which he had made; and he rested on the seventh day from all his work which he had made. And God blessed the seventh day, and sanctified it: because that in it he had rested from all his work which God created and made."[115]

God made a special day on which he wants to meet with his people. Imagine you made a special day to commemorate your fiancé's birthday, and you told her that you would meet her on her birthday for the special date. She arrives to meet you at the designated place, at the appointed time, and you are not there. She waits, and she waits, and she waits—all day. Finally, she goes home in tears, because you never showed up. The next day, you happen to see her

---

[113] Matthew 15:9

[114] Matthew 7:13-14

[115] Genesis 2:1-3

and notice that she seems to be upset, so you ask her, "What is the matter?" She says, "Well, I waited for you all day yesterday. You said we were going on a special outing for my birthday, and you didn't even show up!" But you tell her, "Why are you upset? What difference does it make anyway? All days of worship are the same. I mean, all birthdays and fiancé dates are the same! I love you every day of the week!" Do you think she would accept this reasoning? No indeed!

Imagine your boss tells you to be at work at such and such a time on Monday morning. You show up on Tuesday. When you ask him what is the matter, he tells you, "I told you to come yesterday." You reply, "Hey boss, what difference does it make? All days are the same! I'm your employee everyday day of the week" Do you think your boss would go for this? Absolutely not! You would likely not have a job.

No one on this planet, in their right mind, would accept such kind of reasoning. Yet we think we can apply that reasoning to God? Your Creator and your redeemer has a special day, each week on which he requests your fellowship. The seventh-day sabbath is that special time in which he wants to meet with us; the special token that God has given; the evidence of your allegiance to the Creator; the sign that he will sanctify us; the seal of obedience; and we are considering coming a day late?

The Bible says, "without me ye can do nothing."[116] Without the help of God, we can do nothing, including avoiding the mark of the beast. So, in this terrible warning is the implied promise of victory. Victory over everything that would keep us from receiving the seal of God; anything that would dishonor God in our bodies or minds. God, in this message of warning, is giving the promise of victory.

"Choose you this day whom ye will serve."[117] And Jesus said, "He that is not with me is against me."[118] "Blessed are they that **do his commandments**, that they may have right to the tree of life, and

---

[116] John 15:5

[117] Joshua 24:15

[118] Luke 11:23

may enter in through the gates into the city."[119] "But wilt thou know, O vain man, that faith without works is dead?"[120]

Some might worry whether their friends, relatives, or ancestors might have already received the mark of the beast. The mark of the beast is received only when worship of the beast or his image is made into mandatory legislation. "Sundaykeeping is not yet the mark of the beast, and will not be until the decree goes forth causing men to worship this idol sabbath. The time will come when this day will be the test, but that time has not come yet."[121]

"There are many who have never had the light. They are deceived by their teachers, and they have not received the mark of the beast. The Lord is working with them; He has not left them to their own ways. Until they shall be convicted of the truth and trample upon the evidence given to enlighten them, the Lord will not withdraw His grace from them.
"God is going to bring around a condition of things where the good men and the men in authority will have an opportunity to know what is truth indeed. And because a people will not bow the knee to the image, and receive the mark of the beast in the hand or the forehead, but will stand to the truth because it is truth, there will be oppression, and an attempt to compel the conscience; but those who have known the truth will be afraid to yield to the powers of darkness. God has a people who will not receive the mark of the beast in their right hand or in their forehead....
"But when the decree shall go forth enforcing the counterfeit sabbath, and the loud cry of the third angel shall warn men against the worship of the beast and his image, the line will be clearly drawn between the false and the true. Then those who still continue in transgression will receive the mark of the beast.
"With rapid steps we are approaching this period. When Protestant churches shall unite with the secular power to sustain a false religion, for opposing which their ancestors endured the fiercest persecution, then will the papal sabbath be enforced by the combined authority of church and state. There will be a national apostasy, which will end only in national ruin."[122]

---

[119] Revelation 22:14

[120] James 2:20

[121] E. G. White, *Last Day Events* (1992), p. 224.6.

[122] E. G. White, *Evangelism* (1946), p. 234.2-234.1.

Revelation 14:11 And the smoke of their torment ascendeth up for ever and ever: and they have no rest day nor night, who worship the beast and his image, and whosoever receiveth the mark of his name.

It may seem, at first, that this verse is telling us that the wicked will be tormented for all eternity. It is important not to build an entire doctrine on one or two verses, but rather look at the entire tenor of Scripture relating to the subject. If you put up a fence in a straight line, only to see later that one post is out of line, do you move the fence to be in line with the post? No! You move the post to come into line with the fence. But many times, with Scripture we like to move the whole fence to conform to our idea of what we think a single verse is saying rather than letting the rest of Scripture help us understand the difficult verse.

It is very clear from the rest of Scripture that people are not tormented for all the ceaseless ages of eternity. Often, to understand what a verse is saying, it is helpful to consider what the verse is not saying. This verse does not say that they are tormented forever and ever. Rather, it says that "**the smoke of their torment ascendeth up for ever and ever.**"

Let's say you live in a dry area of the country, where you are not supposed to build fires during the summer. Despite this you still build a big bonfire. Then you realize that it is making a lot of smoke and that the smoke jumpers, and helicopters, and Department of Natural Resources will soon be descending on you. So, you immediately put your fire out. The question is: does that stop the smoke from rising? The answer is that extinguishing the fire eventually stops the creation of more smoke, but the smoke that has already ascended will continue to rise forever. The Bible is simply telling us that sinners will vanish into smoke and that the evidence of that judgment; the memory of the price of sin, will always exist. Though the tears of sadness will be wiped away, though the pang of sorrow for a loved one not saved will fade; through all eternity there will be an intelligent knowledge of what sin has cost, preventing sin from occurring again.

"And ye shall tread down the wicked; for they shall be ashes under the soles of your feet in the day that I shall do this, saith the LORD of hosts."[123] How could we possibly tread down the ashes of the wicked, in the day that he does it, if the fire is burning for all eternity? "The theory of the immortality of the soul was one of those false doctrines that Rome, borrowing from paganism, incorporated into the religion of Christendom. Martin Luther classed it with the 'monstrous fables that form part of the Roman dunghill of decretals.' "Commenting on the words of Solomon in Ecclesiastes, that the dead know not anything, the Reformer says: 'Solomon judgeth that the dead are asleep, and feel nothing at all. For the dead lie there, accounting neither days nor years, but when they are awakened, they shall seem to have slept scarce one minute.'"[124] "Behold, they shall be as stubble; the fire shall burn them; they shall not deliver themselves from the power of the flame: there shall not be a coal to warm at, nor fire to sit before it."[125] This fire cannot be quenched—nobody can put it out—but when it is done burning, it will go out by itself; it will be so out that there will not even be so much as a "coal to warm at."

Speaking of Satan, under the metaphor of the king of Tyre, Ezekiel says, "...therefore will I bring forth a fire from the midst of thee, it shall devour thee, and I will bring thee to ashes upon the earth in the sight of all them that behold thee. All they that know thee among the people shall be astonished at thee: thou shalt be a terror, and never shalt thou be any more."[126] Will Satan be down there poking, prodding and torturing people throughout all the ceaseless ages of eternity? No. Scripture says he will be burned up and never be anymore. "For yet a little while, and the wicked shall not be: yea, thou shalt diligently consider his place, and it shall not be. But the wicked shall perish, and the enemies of the LORD shall be as the fat of lambs: they shall consume; into smoke shall they consume away."[127] The wicked will be smoke; they will be gone, consumed completely and eternally dead.

God asks in Nahum 1:9, "What do ye imagine against the LORD? he will make an utter end: affliction shall not rise up the second time." God wants to restore the universe to its Edenic state as it was before

---

[123] Malachi 4:3

[124] E. G. White, *The Faith I Live By* (1958), p. 175.2.

[125] Isaiah 47:14

[126] Ezekiel 28:18-19

[127] Psalms 37:10, 20

sin. This whole plan of salvation is because a loving God wants to allow perfectly free choice and at the same time, make it very clear that Satan's accusations are false and his ideas of how to run a government do not work. But God will not allow sin to be immortalized through all the ceaseless ages of eternity by the shrieks and cursing of people in hellfire. God will bring an end to sin: and affliction shall not rise the second time. Amen!

"I saw a new heaven and a new earth: for the first heaven and the first earth were passed away."[128] "The fire that consumes the wicked purifies the earth. Every trace of the curse is swept away. No eternally burning hell will keep before the ransomed the fearful consequences of sin.
"One reminder alone remains: Our Redeemer will ever bear the marks of His crucifixion. Upon His wounded head, upon His side, His hands and feet, are the only traces of the cruel work that sin has wrought. Says the prophet, beholding Christ in His glory: 'He had bright beams coming out of His side: and there was the hiding of His power.' Habakkuk 3:4, margin. That pierced side whence flowed the crimson stream that reconciled man to God—there is the Saviour's glory, there 'the hiding of His power.' 'Mighty to save,' through the sacrifice of redemption, He was therefore strong to execute justice upon them that despised God's mercy. And the tokens of His humiliation are His highest honor; through the eternal ages the wounds of Calvary will show forth His praise and declare His power."[129]

Revelation 14:12 Here is the patience of the saints: here are they that keep the commandments of God, and the faith of Jesus.

The culmination of the third angel's message points to the saints of God, his remnant church, who **"keep the commandments of God, and the faith of Jesus."**

"The third angel of Revelation 14 is represented as flying swiftly through the midst of heaven crying: '**Here are they that keep the commandments of God, and the faith of Jesus.**' Here is shown

---

[128] Revelation 21:1

[129] E. G. White, *The Great Controversy* (1911), p. 674.2.

the nature of the work of the people of God. They have a message of so great importance that they are represented as flying in the presentation of it to the world. They are holding in their hands the bread of life for a famishing world. The love of Christ constraineth them. This is the last message. There are no more invitations of mercy to be given after this message shall have done its work. What a trust! What a responsibility is resting upon all to carry the words of the gracious invitation: 'And the Spirit and the bride say, Come. And let him that heareth say, Come. And let him that is athirst come. And whosoever will, let him take the water of life freely.'"[130]

"These truths, as presented in Revelation 14 in connection with 'the everlasting gospel,' will distinguish the church of Christ at the time of His appearing. For as the result of the threefold message it is announced: 'Here are they that keep the commandments of God, and the faith of Jesus.' And this message is the last to be given before the coming of the Lord. Immediately following its proclamation the Son of man is seen by the prophet, coming in glory to reap the harvest of the earth."[131]

It is going to take patience to go through these last days, for it will be a trying time, in which our faith will be severely tried. "'God is faithful, who will not suffer you to be tempted above that ye are able; but will with the temptation also make a way to escape, that ye may be able to bear it.'
"Those who have weighty responsibilities to bear in connection with the work of God are the ones that will be beset with the strongest temptations. If Satan can cause them to waver from the right, he not only takes away their own strength, but he destroys their influence for good over others.... Acting upon the principle that Christ presented in his prayer, 'I sanctify myself, that they also might be sanctified through the truth,' they should take the position that they will be steadfast to God under every circumstance, that they may exert an influence to make others steadfast.
"The temptations of Satan are manifold; but those to which our attention is called in the text are unbelief and impatience. 'Knowing this, that the trying of your faith worketh patience.' Impatience, then, is the result of a lack of faith. 'But let patience have her perfect work, that ye may be perfect and entire, wanting nothing.' If we do not

---

[130] E. G. White, *Testimonies for the Church*, Vol. 5 (1889), p. 206.3.

[131] E. G. White, *The Great Controversy* (1911), p. 453.3.

maintain the grace of patience, we shall never reach a state of perfection. Some of us have a nervous temperament, and are naturally as quick as a flash to think and to act; but let no one think that he cannot learn to become patient. Patience is a plant that will make rapid growth if carefully cultivated. By becoming thoroughly acquainted with ourselves, and then combining with the grace of God a firm determination on our part, we may be conquerors, and become perfect in all things, wanting in nothing."[132]

"'The faith of Jesus.' It is talked of, but not understood. What constitutes the faith of Jesus, that belongs, to the third angel's message? Jesus becoming our sin-bearer that He might become our sin-pardoning Saviour. He was treated as we deserve to be treated. He came to our world and took our sins that we might take His righteousness. Faith in the ability of Christ to save us amply and fully and entirely is the faith of Jesus.

"The only safety for the Israelites was blood upon the doorposts. God said, 'When I see the blood, I will pass over you' (Exodus 12:13). All other devices for safety would be without avail. Nothing but the blood on the doorposts would bar the way that the angel of death should not enter. There is salvation for the sinner in the blood of Jesus Christ alone, which cleanseth us from all sin. The man with a cultivated intellect may have vast stores of knowledge, he may engage in theological speculations, he may be great and honored of men and be considered the repository of knowledge, but unless he has a saving knowledge of Christ crucified for him, and by faith lays hold of the righteousness of Christ, he is lost. Christ 'was wounded for our transgressions, he was bruised for our iniquities: the chastisement of our peace was upon him; and with his stripes we are healed' (Isaiah 53:5). 'Saved by the blood of Jesus Christ,' will be our only hope for time and our song throughout eternity."[133]

Revelation 14:13 And I heard a voice from heaven saying unto me, Write, Blessed are the dead which die in the Lord from henceforth: Yea, saith the Spirit, that they may rest from their labours; and their works do follow them.

---

[132] E. G. White, *Historical Sketches of the Foreign Missions of the Seventh-day Adventists* (1886), p.134.1-3.

[133] E. G. White, *1888 Materials* (1987), p. 217.2-218.1.

God wants to comfort us with these words, for though he wants us to strive to be among the 144,000 who live to see him come, we realize that perhaps we will die before that time. Therefore, God gives a special blessing to those who die in the Lord from henceforth. The Saviour gently reminds them that they will rest from their labors— sleeping in the grave, just as he promised, until he comes in the clouds of heaven and calls them forth at his glorious appearing. This is the promise in Daniel 12:2, of the special resurrection to those who die under the third angel's message, keeping the sabbath.

Revelation 14:14 And I looked, and behold a white cloud, and upon the cloud one sat like unto the Son of man, having on his head a golden crown, and in his hand a sharp sickle.

Revelation 14:15 And another angel came out of the temple, crying with a loud voice to him that sat on the cloud, Thrust in thy sickle, and reap: for the time is come for thee to reap; for the harvest of the earth is ripe.

Revelation 14:16 And he that sat on the cloud thrust in his sickle on the earth; and the earth was reaped.

Jesus will reap the harvest of the earth when every decision has been made. Once every person has decided either for or against him, there is no sense in prolonging the great controversy any longer. For this reason, God allows things to come to such a crisis as legislation that tries to force people, on pain of death or economic sanction, to violate God's law. In this, God is separating the wheat from the tares; the line is drawn in the sand; the muddied waters are made clear; allowing every person on the planet to have an opportunity to make an intelligent decision for or against God. Once this occurs, he will reap the earth, for the harvest is ripe.

Revelation 14:17 And another angel came out of the temple which is in heaven, he also having a sharp sickle.

Revelation 14:18 And another angel came out from the altar, which had power over fire; and cried with a loud cry to him that had the sharp sickle, saying, Thrust in thy sharp sickle, and gather the clusters of the vine of the earth; for her grapes are fully ripe.

In these metaphors, the grain of the earth represents the righteous, whom Jesus gathers to himself. The grapes represent the wicked who will be gathered by the angel of destruction.

Revelation 14:19 And the angel thrust in his sickle into the earth, and gathered the vine of the earth, and cast it into the great winepress of the wrath of God.

In this solemn pronouncement the wine press of the wrath of God represents that wrath that God will pour out, unmixed with mercy, upon those that have the mark of the beast.

Revelation 14:20 And the winepress was trodden without the city, and blood came out of the winepress, even unto the horse bridles, by the space of a thousand and six hundred furlongs.

"In the battle of Armageddon, blood shall flow for 1600 furlongs, to the bits of the horses' bridles. It is remarkable, that this 1600 furlongs make exactly the whole extent of the State of Rome, which the popes have so long held. From the Tiber to the Po [Rome's two rivers] is just 200 miles or 1600 furlongs."[134]

"Christ felt much as sinners will feel when the vials of God's wrath shall be poured out upon them. Black despair, like the pall of death, will gather about their guilty souls, and then they will realize to the fullest extent the sinfulness of sin. Salvation has been purchased for them by the suffering and death of the Son of God. It might be theirs, if they would accept of it willingly, gladly; but none are compelled to yield obedience to the law of God. If they refuse the heavenly benefit and choose the pleasures and deceitfulness of sin, they have their choice, and at the end receive their wages, which is the wrath of God and eternal death. They will be forever separated from the presence of Jesus, whose sacrifice they had despised. They will have lost a life of happiness and sacrificed eternal glory for the pleasures of sin for a season." [135]

---

[134] Alexander Campbell, *A Debate on the Roman Catholic Religion* (Cincinnati: J. A. James & Co., 1837), p. 232.

[135] E. G. White, *Testimonies for the Church,* Vol. 2 (1871), p. 210.1.

"When the storm of God's wrath breaks upon the world, it will be a terrible revelation for souls to find that their house is being swept away because it is built upon the sand. Let the warning be given them before it is too late. We should now feel the responsibility of laboring with intense earnestness to impart to others the truths that God has given for this time. We cannot be too much in earnest.

"The heart of God is moved. Souls are very precious in His sight. It was for this world that Christ wept in agony; for this world He was crucified. God gave His only-begotten Son to save sinners, and He desires us to love others as He has loved us. He desires to see those who have a knowledge of the truth imparting this knowledge to their fellow men.

"Now is the time for the last warning to be given. There is a special power in the presentation of the truth at the present time; but how long will it continue? Only a little while. If there was ever a crisis, it is now.

"All are now deciding their eternal destiny. Men need to be aroused to realize the solemnity of the time, the nearness of the day when human probation shall be ended. Decided efforts should be made to bring the message for this time prominently before the people. The third angel is to go forth with great power. Let none ignore this work or treat it as of little importance."[136]

"Cry aloud, spare not, lift up thy voice like a trumpet, and show My people their transgression, and the house of Jacob their sins."[137] Amen.

---

[136] E. G. White, *Testimonies for the Church,* Vol. 6 (1901), p. 16.1-4.

[137] Isaiah 58:1

Revelation 15

SUMMARY:
Revelation 15 introduces the seven last plagues to be poured out on those that receive the mark of the beast at the very end of time. These are to be the most terrible judgments ever visited upon the earth. John begins this description by relating what he saw in vision:

Revelation 15:1 And I saw another sign in heaven, great and marvelous, seven angels having the seven last plagues; for in them is filled up the wrath of God.

This heavenly vision portrays, to the astonished gaze of the aged Apostle, the culmination of God's wrath against sin—no longer mingled with mercy.

Revelation 15:2 And I saw as it were a sea of glass mingled with fire; and them that had gotten the victory over the beast, and over his image, and over his mark, and over the number of his name, stand on the sea of glass, having the harps of God.

Here we see the love and the mercy of God. Even as he reveals the terrible plagues that will be poured out, he wants to make sure that his people do not lose hope. Therefore, as soon as John begins to see the seven angels with these seven last plagues, God immediately shows him a future heavenly scene of the people who have obtained the victory over the beast and over his image, and over the number of his name, standing on the sea of glass.

It is as if he is pleading with us—look, this might seem terrible; this might seem amazing; perhaps, to some, it might even seem harsh, but in my mercy, I have given every opportunity—every possible warning to avoid the wrath to come. God wants you to realize you can be one of those who gains the victory. You can be standing on the sea of glass. There is hope.

Revelation 15:3 And they sing the song of Moses the servant of God, and the song of the lamb, saying, Great and marvelous are

thy works, Lord God Almighty; just and true are thy ways, thou king of saints.

Still, in case some might misunderstand these plagues, God wants to demonstrate that after those who have suffered persecution from the beast have gained the victory, all will agree and testify that God's works are great and marvelous, just and true.

Revelation 15:4 Who shall not fear thee, O Lord, and glorify thy name? For thou only art holy; for all nations shall come and worship before thee; for thy judgments are made manifest.

The song of Moses and of the Lamb continues to affirm that the judgments of God are open for all to see. Justice requires judgment. After God's mercy has done everything it possibly can; after it is clear that no one else will ever again accept God, he closes the investigative judgment and brings the promised punishment on the wicked. He does not close the door of mercy while there are still those trying to enter. Only when each individual has made their final choice, for or against God, in full knowledge of the issues at stake, will he bring the close of probation and pour out the final plagues.[1]

Revelation 15:5 And after that I looked, and, behold, the temple of the tabernacle of testimony in heaven was opened.

The door of mercy lingers open to the last possible moment. With the departure of the destroying angels from the heavenly court room, the angel of mercy takes her flight to return no more.[2] The last case has been decided. Every person on earth has made their choice. Probation has closed for the human race. "He that is unjust, let him be unjust still: and he which is filthy, let him be filthy still: and he that is righteous, let him be righteous still: and he that is holy, let him be holy still."[3]

---

[1] "It is no arbitrary decree on the part of God that excludes the wicked from heaven; they are shut out by their own unfitness for its companionship. The glory of God would be to them a consuming fire. They would welcome destruction, that they might be hidden from the face of Him who died to redeem them."
E. G. White, *Heaven* (2003), p. 66.1.

[2] E. G. White, *Testimonies to the Church*, Vol. 5 (1889), p. 451.2.

[3] Revelation 22:11

Revelation 15:6 And the seven angels came out of the temple, having the seven plagues, clothed in pure and white linen, and having their breasts girded with golden girdles.

Because they come out of the temple, and are clothed in white linen, these seven angels are clearly holy, heavenly, angels, sent by God, commissioned to pour the seven last plagues upon the earth.

Revelation 15:7 One of the four beasts gave unto the seven angels seven golden vials full of the wrath of God, who liveth forever and ever.

As we saw in Revelation 4, these four beasts are seraphs, an order of angelic being. But, they are also described as having attributes symbolizing the word of God. In particular, the four beasts represent the portion of the word of God recorded in the four gospels. These gospels are the segment of Scripture that document the life of Jesus on this earth, when he physically walked among us as a man, speaking words directly to the children of men. Jesus told us that these Words would judge us at the last day. "He that rejecteth me, and receiveth not my words, hath one that judgeth him: the word that I have spoken, the same shall judge him in the last day."[4] And so it is that one of the four beasts, which represents the Words that Jesus spoke on earth, is the one who delivers the seven last judgments to the seven angels to be poured upon the earth.

Revelation 15:8 And the temple was filled with smoke from the glory of God, and from his power; and no man was able to enter into the temple, till the seven plagues of the seven angels were fulfilled.

The glory of God streams out of the temple; that glory which is a consuming fire to sin, "For our God is a consuming fire."[5] Amen.

---

[4] John 12:48

[5] Hebrews 12:29

Revelation 16

SUMMARY:
Revelation 16 enumerates the devastation that occurs as each of the seven last plagues is poured upon the earth. The first plague causes grievous sores upon those who have the mark of the beast. In the second, the sea is turned to blood and every living thing in the sea dies. The third plague causes the fresh water to turn to blood. In the fourth, men are scorched with the heat of the sun. The fifth brings darkness on the seat of the beast—darkness so deep that it is painful. "The sixth angel poured out his vial upon the great river Euphrates; and the water thereof was dried up, that the way of the kings of the east might be prepared." The seventh angel pours his vial in the air and a voice announces, "It is done." The worst earthquake of all history occurs, and giant hail stones, weighing about sixty pounds each, fall on the earth.

Revelation 16:1 And I heard a great voice out of the temple saying to the seven angels, Go your ways, and pour out the vials of the wrath of God upon the earth.

The vials are that which contain the seven last plagues. The instruction for the angels to pour out the vials comes from the temple. This is because the investigative judgment has come to an end and Jesus has just finished that process in the most holy place. Probation has closed; the door of mercy is shut; and the plagues are commissioned to be poured out.

Revelation 16:2 And the first went, and poured out his vial upon the earth; and there fell a noisome and grievous sore upon the men which had the mark of the beast, and upon them which worshipped his image.

These plagues fall only on the wicked. When the plagues fell on Egypt, just prior to the exodus of the children of Israel, there were ten plagues, the first three of which affected everyone, including the children of Israel; and the last seven of which fell only on the Egyptians. At the end of time there are just seven plagues, which fall only on those who have the mark of the beast and worship his image. This indicates that probation closes before the seven last plagues are poured out. Every individual will either have the mark of the beast or the seal of God. Every choice has been made, and no one will change their mind.

According to modern occultists, boils are a sign of contact with demons. One of the comic industry's biggest names, who has written for Superman, is Grant Morrison, who is deeply involved in magic and the occult. In his book *Super gods*, Grant states, "I came out in boils, traditional signs of demon contact."[1] This fits with the Biblical testimony, for when Satan was given permission to physically afflict Job, he was afflicted with boils. The plague of boils is another evidence that the men with the mark of the beast have had direct contact with demonic spirits during the fifth and sixth trumpets.

Revelation 16:3 And the second angel poured out his vial upon the sea; and it became as the blood of a dead man; and every living soul died in the sea.

Just as in the second trumpet, the sea turns to blood, only this time every living thing dies, rather than just one third being affected. The language states that the sea became "**as the blood of a dead man**." The word "as" means: like. Therefore, the language of the passage does not demand that the sea turns into actual biological blood. Scripture often uses metaphoric language when it is not necessarily using symbolism. A good example of this is in Joel 2:31, "The sun shall be turned into darkness, and the moon into blood, before the great and the terrible day of the LORD come." Here we can clearly see that the moon is said to turn into blood. The fulfillment of this has already happened historically, and the moon did not literally turn into real blood; the moon simply turned the color of blood. The passage is describing a literal event, using metaphoric language. It is not necessary to be over-literal with a metaphor in order for a passage to be understood literally.

"These plagues are not universal, or the inhabitants of the earth would be wholly cut off. Yet they will be the most awful scourges that have ever been known to mortals. All the judgments upon men, prior to the close of probation, have been mingled with mercy. The

---

[1] Grant Morrison, *Super gods* (New York: Spiegel & Grau, 2010), p. 281.

pleading blood of Christ has shielded the sinner from receiving the full measure of his guilt; but in the final Judgment, wrath is poured out unmixed with mercy."[2]

Revelation 16:4 And the third angel poured out his vial upon the rivers and fountains of waters; and they became blood.

Under the second vial, the sea is affected by the plague of blood, but under the third the fresh water becomes affected making it difficult to find drinking water.

"Though the people of God endure privation, and even suffer for want of food, they are not left to perish. While God's judgments are visited upon the earth, and the wicked are dying from hunger and thirst, angels provide the righteous with food and water."[3]

The Lord gives this promise to the righteous during this time: "He shall dwell on high: his place of defence shall be the munitions of rocks: bread shall be given him; his waters shall be sure."[4]

Revelation 16:5 And I heard the angel of the waters say, Thou art righteous, O Lord, which art, and wast, and shalt be, because thou hast judged thus.

Even as these terrible plagues are delineated, the angel who has watched the dealings of God with humans from the beginning, acknowledges his mercy and justice. Punishment must come on the wicked; otherwise God could not be just. Yet multiple times throughout this chapter, heavenly witnesses testify to God's righteousness in judgment. The angel that is pouring out this plague gives testimony that it is a righteous judgment.

---

[2] E. G. White, *The Great Controversy* (1911), p. 628.2.

[3] E. G. White, *The Spirit of Prophecy* (1884), Vol. 4, p. 446.1.

[4] Isaiah 33:16

Revelation 16:6 For they have shed the blood of saints and prophets, and thou hast given them blood to drink; for they are worthy.

This judgment is especially for the wicked who have shed the blood of the righteous.

"Terrible as these inflictions are, God's justice stands fully vindicated. The angel of God declares: 'Thou art righteous, O Lord,... because Thou hast judged thus. For they have shed the blood of saints and prophets, **and Thou hast given them blood to drink; for they are worthy.**' Revelation 16:2-6. By condemning the people of God to death, they have as truly incurred the guilt of their blood as if it had been shed by their hands. In like manner Christ declared the Jews of His time guilty of all the blood of holy men which had been shed since the days of Abel; for they possessed the same spirit and were seeking to do the same work with these murderers of the prophets.... "Could men see with heavenly vision, they would behold companies of angels that excel in strength stationed about those who have kept the word of Christ's patience. With sympathizing tenderness, angels have witnessed their distress and have heard their prayers. They are waiting the word of their Commander to snatch them from their peril. But they must wait yet a little longer. The people of God must drink of the cup and be baptized with the baptism. The very delay, so painful to them, is the best answer to their petitions. As they endeavor to wait trustingly for the Lord to work they are led to exercise faith, hope, and patience, which have been too little exercised during their religious experience. Yet for the elect's sake the time of trouble will be shortened. 'Shall not God avenge His own elect, which cry day and night unto Him?... I tell you that He will avenge them speedily.' Luke 18:7, 8. The end will come more quickly than men expect. The wheat will be gathered and bound in sheaves for the garner of God; the tares will be bound as fagots for the fires of destruction."[5]

Revelation 16:7 And I heard another out of the altar say, Even so, Lord God Almighty, true and righteous are thy judgments.

Spontaneously, heavenly beings are breaking forth with the declaration that these judgments are true and righteous. This is a

---

[5] E. G. White, *The Great Controversy* (1911), p. 627.3-630.2.

comfort for us today, especially if some tend to think that the plagues seem severe. God has done everything that infinite love can do. He has sent this message of mercy so that everyone may have the opportunity of knowing how to avoid these plagues. But He has promised that sooner or later, punishment will be visited if the wicked cling to their sins.

Revelation 16:8 And the fourth angel poured out his vial upon the sun; and power was given unto him to scorch men with fire.

Modern society has descended into pagan worship. Pagan worship is characterized primarily by sun worship. God simply gives them what they desire.

Revelation 16:9 And men were scorched with great heat, and blasphemed the name of God, which hath power over these plagues: and they repented not to give him glory.

Despite the plagues, the wicked do not change their minds. They charge the consequences of their own choice on God, blaspheming his name. Many of the people on whom the plagues are falling do not even believe in God, yet they blame the God they claim does not exist.

"It is often the case that trouble is greater in anticipation than in reality; but this is not true of the crisis before us. The most vivid presentation cannot reach the magnitude of the ordeal."[6]

Revelation 16:10 And the fifth angel poured out his vial upon the seat of the beast; and his kingdom was full of darkness; and they gnawed their tongues for pain,

Fascination with the darkness of the occult has become almost universal, with the Harry Potter and vampire craze. Modern culture is fascinated with blood, darkness, vampires, violence and death. God gives them a taste of the evil that they worship.

---

[6] E. G. White, *The Great Controversy* (1911), p. 621-622.

Apparently, this darkness is so oppressive that it actually causes them pain. This darkness is similar to what happened in Egypt. Deuteronomy 10:22-23 says, "And Moses stretched forth his hand toward heaven; and there was a thick darkness in all the land of Egypt three days: They saw not one another, neither rose any from his place for three days: but all the children of Israel had light in their dwellings."

As in the exodus of Egypt, God makes a distinction between his people and the wicked. This plague falls on the seat of the beast. Because so much deception has been propagated, God will make a clear distinction between the righteous and the wicked; between those that are serving God and those that are serving Satan. The seat of the beast is the throne of the scarlet beast of Revelation 17. God will show specifically where his displeasure is focused.

Revelation 16:11 And blasphemed the God of heaven because of their pains and their sores, and repented not of their deeds.

Still, the wicked do not change their minds—they do not repent. The sores received in the first plague have not abated by the fifth.

Revelation 16:12 And the sixth angel poured out his vial upon the great river Euphrates; and the water thereof was dried up, that the way of the kings of the east might be prepared.

The history of the River Euphrates goes all the way back to the Garden of Eden as described in the book of Genesis. It was one of the four rivers that watered Eden. Obviously, the current River Euphrates is not the same as the one as in the Garden of Eden, which was completely destroyed by the flood. The Euphrates of today is the longest river in Western Asia, being almost 2000 miles in length. In Scripture the Euphrates assumes symbolic meaning, especially since it is associated with Babylon.

Babylon traces its origins to the Tower of Babel, built in the plain of Shinar, on the banks of the Euphrates River, right after the flood. This tower became the symbol of defiance against God. When Babylon became a world empire under Nebuchadnezzar and later his grandson Belshazzar, the River Euphrates flowed through the city. The Medes and Persians overcame Babylon by diverting the Euphrates, and marching under the wall of the city.

Although Babylon was used by God through Nebuchadnezzar's conversion,[7] to distribute the message of salvation to the entire world, in two generations it quickly descended into apostasy, to the extent that in Scripture Babylon came to symbolize the false kingdom and religion set up by Satan throughout all history to war against the kingdom and religion of God. The word Babel, from which comes the name Babylon, means confusion; referring to the confusion resulting from God confounding the language at the tower. Specifically, prophetic Babylon came to symbolize Rome.[8]

The river Euphrates[9] was corrupted from its originally intended purpose in the Garden of Eden. Abraham came from the land of the Chaldeans, where the Euphrates river flowed. God called him out of Babylon to establish his true church.

Waters, as we have seen in prophetic symbolism, represent peoples, and multitudes, and nations, and tongues.[10] The drying up of the Euphrates indicates the evaporation of support for the false religious system of Babylon in preparation for the second coming of Jesus. According to this passage, Rome loses support from all peoples, nations and tongues. This is described further in Revelation 17. The reason given for the loss of resources is that "**the water thereof was dried up, that the way of the kings of the east might be prepared**."

This, of course, brings us to the question, who are "**the kings of the east**?"

"Who raised up the righteous man from the east, called him to his foot, gave the nations before him, and made him rule over kings? He gave them as the dust to his sword, and as driven stubble to his bow.

---

[7] See comments on Revelation 6:2-4.

[8] Even Roman Catholic annotators admit that Babylon refers to Rome:
"'Babylon,' from which Peter addresses his first Epistle, is understood by learned annotators, Protestant and Catholic, to refer to Rome."
James Cardinal Gibbons, *The Faith of Our Fathers,* p.87.6; 111th printing. ISBN 0-89555-158-6.

[9] Genesis 2:14

[10] Revelation 17:15

He pursued them, and passed safely; even by the way that he had not gone with his feet. Who hath wrought and done it, calling the generations from the beginning? I the LORD, the first, and with the last; I am he."[11]

The righteous man from the east is none other the Lord himself— Jesus Christ, the first and the last. Jesus is the one who came to this earth and returned to heaven from earth by a way that he had not gone with his feet. Jesus is the king of the east.

Why then, does Revelation 16:12 say "kings of the east?" Frequently, the Bible refers to the one and only God in plural form to designate the three persons of the Godhead. For example, Genesis 1:26, says "And God {singular} said, Let us {plural} make man in our {plural} image, after our {plural} likeness:"

The coming of the kings of the east is the Godhead, descending to this earth at the second coming of Jesus. Support for Satan's kingdom, headquartered in Rome, dries up in preparation for the second coming of Jesus.

Revelation 16:13 And I saw three unclean spirits like frogs come out of the mouth of the dragon, and out of the mouth of the beast, and out of the mouth of the false prophet.

The dragon, we know from Revelation 12, is Satan, who is the direct source of spiritualism and the occult. The beast we know from Revelation 13, is the papal power—the Roman Catholic Church.

A true prophet speaks as the mouthpiece of God.[12] A false prophet then would be one who claims to present a prophetic message from God, but speaks deception. The false prophet is the earth beast, that we encountered in Revelation 13, which once knew the truth but turned away from it. The earth beast spoke initially for Christ, as a lamb, but then began to speak like the great deceiver—the dragon. This power was identified, in Revelation 13, as Protestant America.

---

[11] Isaiah 41:2-4

[12] Exodus 7:1-2

"When Protestantism shall stretch her hand across the gulf to grasp the hand of the Roman power, when she shall reach over the abyss to clasp hands with Spiritualism, when, under the influence of this threefold union, our country shall repudiate every principle of its Constitution as a Protestant and Republican government, and shall make provision for the propagation of papal falsehoods and delusions, then we may know that the time has come for the marvelous working of Satan, and that the end is near."[13]

Scripture portrays three unclean spirits like frogs, one coming out of each of their mouths. Involvement with unclean spirits is now the defining characteristic of all three entities—the papacy, Protestant America, and spiritualism. The sixth plague includes the full accomplishment of Satan's designs in the development of spiritualism. These three evil spirits prepare the world for Satan's final impersonation of Christ.

"Satan has long been preparing for his final effort to deceive the world. The foundation of his work was laid by the assurance given to Eve in Eden: "Ye shall not surely die." "In the day ye eat thereof, then your eyes shall be opened, and ye shall be as gods, knowing good and evil." Genesis 3:4, 5. Little by little he has prepared the way for his masterpiece of deception in the development of spiritualism. He has not yet reached the full accomplishment of his designs; but it will be reached in the last remnant of time. Says the prophet: "I saw three unclean spirits like frogs;... they are the spirits of devils, working miracles, which go forth unto the kings of the earth and of the whole world, to gather them to the battle of that great day of God Almighty." Revelation 16:13, 14. Except those who are kept by the power of God, through faith in His word, the whole world will be swept into the ranks of this delusion. The people are fast being lulled to a fatal security, to be awakened only by the outpouring of the wrath of God."[14]

"As spiritualism more closely imitates the nominal Christianity of the day, it has greater power to deceive and ensnare. Satan himself is converted, after the modern order of things. He will appear in the character of an angel of light. Through the agency of spiritualism, miracles will be wrought, the sick will be healed, and many

---

[13] E. G. White, *Testimonies for the Church*, Vol. 5 (1889), p. 451.

[14] E. G. White, *The Great Controversy* (1911), p. 561.2.

undeniable wonders will be performed. And as the spirits will profess faith in the Bible and manifest respect for the institutions of the church, their work will be accepted as a manifestation of divine power.

"The line of distinction between professed Christians and the ungodly is now hardly distinguishable. Church members love what the world loves and are ready to join with them, and Satan determines to unite them in one body and thus strengthen his cause by sweeping all into the ranks of spiritualism. Papists, who boast of miracles as a certain sign of the true church, will be readily deceived by this wonder-working power; and Protestants, having cast away the shield of truth, will also be deluded. Papists, Protestants, and worldlings will alike accept the form of godliness without the power, and they will see in this union a grand movement for the conversion of the world and the ushering in of the long-expected millennium."[15]

Revelation 16:14 For they are the spirits of devils, working miracles, which go forth unto the kings of the earth and of the whole world, to gather them to the battle of that great day of God Almighty.

These are spirits of devils working through the coalition of Catholicism, Protestantism, and spiritualism to unite the world under demonic control. "For such are false apostles, deceitful workers, transforming themselves into the apostles of Christ. And no marvel; for Satan himself is transformed into an angel of light. Therefore it is no great thing if his ministers also be transformed as the ministers of righteousness; whose end shall be according to their works."[16]

"The Protestants of the United States will be foremost in stretching their hands across the gulf to grasp the hand of spiritualism; they will reach over the abyss to clasp hands with the Roman power; and under the influence of this threefold union, this country will follow in the steps of Rome in trampling on the rights of conscience."[17]

The plagues cause the wicked to blame all their trouble on the few who refuse to violate God's law, and they finally pronounce the death

---

[15] E. G. White, *The Great Controversy* (1911), p. 588.2-3.

[16] 2 Corinthians 11:13-15

[17] E. G. White, *The Great Controversy* (1911), p. 588.1.

penalty for anyone who refuses to honour Sunday and refuses to desecrate the sabbath of the fourth commandment.

"As men depart further and further from God, Satan is permitted to have power over the children of disobedience. He hurls destruction among men. There is calamity by land and sea. Property and life are destroyed by fire and flood. Satan resolves to charge this upon those who refuse to bow to the idol which he has set up. His agents point to Seventh-day Adventists as the cause of the trouble. 'These people stand out in defiance of law,' they say. 'They desecrate Sunday. Were they compelled to obey the law for Sunday observance, there would be a cessation of these terrible judgments.'"[18]

"These plagues enraged the wicked against the righteous; they thought that we had brought the judgments of God upon them, and that if they could rid the earth of us, the plagues would then be stayed. A decree went forth to slay the saints, which caused them to cry day and night for deliverance. This was the time of Jacob's trouble. Then all the saints cried out with anguish of spirit, and were delivered by the voice of God. The 144,000 triumphed. Their faces were lighted up with the glory of God."[19]

Revelation 16:15 Behold, I come as a thief. Blessed is he that watcheth, and keepeth his garments, lest he walk naked, and they see his shame.

"Jesus says, '**Behold, I come as a thief. Blessed is he that watcheth, and keepeth his garments, lest he walk naked, and they see his shame**' [Revelation 16:15]. Here is the great burden to be carried away by every individual. Are my sins forgiven? Has Christ, the Burden-bearer, taken away my guilt? Have I a clean heart, the righteousness of Jesus Christ, by faith? Woe be to any soul who is not seeking a refuge in Christ, and conforming the character to the character of Christ. Woe be to all who shall in anywise divert the mind from this work, and cause any soul to be less vigilant now."[20]

---

[18] E. G. White, *The Great Controversy* (1911), p. 176.2.

[19] E. G. White, *Early Writings* (1882), p. 36.2.

[20] E. G. White, *Manuscript Releases,* Vol. 18 (1990), p. 62.3.

The coming of Jesus will be as a surprise to the wicked. He will not come as a thief to those who are righteous, those who are watching and waiting for his coming. He only comes as a thief to the wicked.

Some use this text to support the claim that there will be a secret rapture; that suddenly the righteous will be gone, and their car will be left going down the road without a driver or an airplane will be left flying through the sky without a pilot. The Bible teaches no such thing.

"For this we say unto you by the word of the Lord, that we which are alive and remain unto the coming of the Lord shall not prevent[21] them which are asleep. For **the Lord himself shall descend from heaven with a shout, with the voice of the archangel, and with the trump of God**: and **the dead in Christ shall rise first**: Then we which are alive and remain shall be caught up together with them in the clouds, to meet the Lord in the air: and so shall we ever be with the Lord. Wherefore comfort one another with these words."[22] This is most certainly not describing a secret rapture. There is the voice of the archangel, which is the Lord himself, that shakes heaven and earth. There is the trump of God. There is a resurrection with all the righteous dead coming out of their graves. Does this sound like something that is secret? Absolutely not.

"Behold, he cometh with clouds; and every eye shall see him, and they also which pierced him: and all kindreds of the earth shall wail because of him. Even so, Amen."[23]

Every eye shall see him. That does not except anyone. The second coming of Christ is not a secret rapture where all of a sudden people are caught up unexpectedly and everybody else is looking around wondering what happened. When Jesus comes everyone will see the entire, glorious and thunderous event—even the wicked. "For as the lightning cometh out of the east, and shineth even unto the west; so shall also the coming of the Son of man be."[24]

---

[21] The word prevent used to mean precede.

[22] 1 Thessalonians 4:15-18

[23] Revelation 1:7

[24] Matthew 24:27

He comes as a thief because his coming will be to the wicked, unexpected. But when he comes everyone will know and see.

Revelation 16:16 And he gathered them together into a place called in the Hebrew tongue Armageddon.

This is another verse that contains a famous word that everyone has heard, but few know its Biblical meaning—Armageddon. People search and speculate over its physical location.

The word comes from two Hebrew words:
Har, which is translated: a mountain, mount, or hills
Megiddô, which is the valley of Megiddo in Palestine

Armageddon would then mean "mount Megiddo." There is only one problem, Megiddo is a valley—not a mountain. Piercing the horizon of the Valley of Megiddo is Mount Carmel, the location of the battle between God and Baal. This is where the showdown between the God of Israel with his prophet Elijah, and Baal and his 850 prophets took place. The Kishon river, which flows through the valley of Megiddo and empties into the Mediterranean Sea on the north side of mount Carmel, is where the prophets of Baal were slain by the command of Elijah after it was unequivocally shown who was the true God.

Armageddon will not be a battle in the physical valley of Megiddo, but the worldwide martial of the forces of darkness to a showdown with the forces of light.

"We need to study the pouring out of the seventh vial. The powers of evil will not yield up the conflict without a struggle. But Providence has a part to act in the battle of Armageddon. When the earth is lighted with the glory of the angel of Revelation eighteen, the religious elements, good and evil, will awake from slumber, and the armies of the living God will take the field."[25] "The Captain of the Lord's host will stand at the head of the angels of heaven to direct the battle."[26]

---

[25] E. G. White, *Maranatha* (1976), p. 257.2.

[26] *Ibid.*, p. 297.5-6.

In the final battle the wicked demonstrate their intention to murder Christ in the person of his saints. For a time, the saints cry day and night for deliverance. Then God interposes to save his people by arriving personally at the battlefield. This is Armageddon, the battle of the great day of God Almighty, where it will be shown to the whole world who is the true God.

Revelation 16:17 And the seventh angel poured out his vial into the air; and there came a great voice out of the temple of heaven, from the throne, saying, It is done.

When all the forces of Satan are arrayed against the truth and the people of God, then the pronouncement is made, "**It is done**." It is at the very last that God declares the battle over and comes to deliver his faithful people.

"He [God] has always chosen extremities, when there seemed no possible chance for deliverance from Satan's workings, for the manifestation of His power.
"It is at midnight that God manifests His power for the deliverance of His people. The sun appears, shining in its strength. Signs and wonders follow in quick succession. The wicked look with terror and amazement upon the scene, while the righteous behold with solemn joy the tokens of their deliverance. Everything in nature seems turned out of its course. The streams cease to flow. Dark, heavy clouds come up and clash against each other. In the midst of the angry heavens is one clear space of indescribable glory, whence comes the voice of God like the sound of many waters, saying: '**It is done**.' Revelation 16:17."[27]

Revelation 16:18 And there were voices, and thunders, and lightnings; and there was a great earthquake, such as was not since men were upon the earth, so mighty an earthquake, and so great.

After this pronouncement there occurs the greatest earthquake ever known to humans. Earth has survived some big quakes, but this earthquake will be like nothing we have ever experienced.

---

[27] E. G. White, *Maranatha* (1976), p. 279.2-3.

"That voice shakes the heavens and the earth. There is a mighty earthquake, 'such as was not since men were upon the earth, so mighty an earthquake, and so great.' Verses 17, 18. The firmament appears to open and shut. The glory from the throne of God seems flashing through. The mountains shake like a reed in the wind, and ragged rocks are scattered on every side. There is a roar as of a coming tempest. The sea is lashed into fury. There is heard the shriek of a hurricane like the voice of demons upon a mission of destruction. The whole earth heaves and swells like the waves of the sea. Its surface is breaking up. Its very foundations seem to be giving way. Mountain chains are sinking. Inhabited islands disappear. The seaports that have become like Sodom for wickedness are swallowed up by the angry waters…. The proudest cities of the earth are laid low. The lordly palaces, upon which the world's great men have lavished their wealth in order to glorify themselves, are crumbling to ruin before their eyes. Prison walls are rent asunder, and God's people, who have been held in bondage for their faith, are set free."[28]

The greatest earthquake this earth has ever seen was probably just after the flood during the separation of the continents. The Bible tells us that Peleg was so named because in the year he was born, the earth was divided. Some think that this is a reference to the continents dividing. Examining the geology of the continents gives significant evidence for such movement. For example, the continental shelves of the East coast of North and South America have a very similar contour to the West coast of Africa. It also appears as though North and South America moved West, away from Africa, because what would have been their leading edge—their western coastline—is shoved up into a mountain range extending from Canada to South America. This would be expected if the two continents were shifting to the west. Peleg was apparently born in the year this occurred.

We are told that during the flood, the breaking up of the earth's crust and the opening of the fountains of the deep, were so terrible that

---

[28] E. G. White, *The Great Controversy* (1911), p. 636.3.

Satan feared for his life.[29] These must have been terrific earthquakes, happening over 4,000 years ago. Yet this verse in Revelation portrays an earthquake that will be even greater. What could cause an earthquake greater than the continents shifting apart halfway around the globe from each other? Perhaps, the only thing that could cause a greater earthquake would be the shifting of those continents back around to meet each other again.[30]

It is interesting to compare the seven trumpets and the seven vials. The seven trumpets are very similar to the seven vials, with the seven vials affecting the whole earth rather than only one third.

---

[29] "As the violence of the storm increased, trees, buildings, rocks, and earth were hurled in every direction. The terror of man and beast was beyond description. Above the roar of the tempest was heard the wailing of a people that had despised the authority of God. Satan himself, who was compelled to remain in the midst of the warring elements, feared for his own existence." E. G. White, *Patriarchs and Prophets* (1890), p. 99.3.

[30] See also Revelation 16:20.

SIMILARITIES BETWEEN THE SEVEN TRUMPETS AND THE SEVEN LAST PLAGUES:

Seven Trumpets	Seven Vials
1. Hail, blood, fire—1/3 of trees and all grass burnt up.	1. Sores on those with the mark of the beast.
2. Mountain of fire cast in sea—1/3 of sea turns blood; 1/3 of sea life dies; 1/3 ships destroyed.	2. Sea turns to blood—everything in the sea dies.
3. Star falls on 1/3 of rivers & springs: many men die because of resulting bitter water	3. Rivers & springs turn to blood.
4. 1/3 of sun, moon, stars darkened to 1/3 of the day.	4. Sun scorches men with fire.
5. Star falls from heaven: given key to bottomless pit; unlocks it and smoke/locusts come out and torment men (only those who don't have the seal of God) for 5 months.	5. The kingdom of the beast is full of darkness; men gnaw their tongues for their pains and sores.
6. Four angels are loosed and slay 1/3 of men; along with 200 million horsemen. Three types of fire.	6. Euphrates dried up—battle of Armageddon; spirits of devils go out to deceive. Three spirits like frogs that will be destroyed by fire.
7. Kingdom becomes Christ's; temple of God was opened and there were lightnings and voices and thunderings, and an earthquake, and great hail.	7. Voice from the temple. "it is done!" Voices, and thunders, and lightnings: and greatest earthquake ever and hail.

Though the seven trumpets[31] and seven vials do not share the same point of commencement, they do share the same point of termination. When the seventh trumpet blows, there are lightnings, voices, thunderings, and an earthquake and great hail. When the seventh vial is poured out, there are voices, thunders, lightnings, and the greatest earthquake in history, with hail; showing that the seventh trumpet and the seventh plague are the same event. The trumpets come first, as the warning plagues, and extend over a longer period of time. The sixth trumpet sounds at the close of probation, initiating the seven last plagues, with six of the seven last plagues occurring during the sixth trumpet. Finally, the seventh trumpet sounds simultaneous to the outpouring of the seventh vial.

---

[31] See comments on Revelation 8, 9.

Revelation 16:19 And the great city was divided into three parts, and the cities of the nations fell: and great Babylon came in remembrance before God, to give unto her the cup of the wine of the fierceness of his wrath.

Again, the wrath is being focused on Babylon—spiritual Babylon—that is Rome. The great city will be divided in three parts. God will pour special, specific plagues on Rome because of the part that she has played in the deception of all nations.

Revelation 16:20 And every island fled away, and the mountains were not found.

"Greater wonders than have yet been seen will be witnessed by those upon the earth a short period previous to the coming of Christ. 'And I will show wonders in the heavens above, and signs in the earth beneath, blood and fire and vapour of smoke.' 'And there were voices and thunders and lightnings, and there was a great earthquake, such as was not since men were upon the earth, so mighty an earthquake and so great. And every island fled away, and the mountains were not found....'

"The bowels of the earth were the Lord's arsenal, from which he drew forth the weapons he employed in the destruction of the old world. Waters in the bowels of the earth gushed forth, and united with the waters from Heaven, to accomplish the work of destruction. Since the flood, God has used both water and fire in the earth as his agents to destroy wicked cities.

"In the day of the Lord, just before the coming of Christ, God will send lightnings from Heaven in his wrath, which will unite with fire in the earth. The mountains will burn like a furnace, and will pour forth terrible streams of lava, destroying gardens and fields, villages and cities; and as they pour their melted ore, rocks and heated mud into the rivers, will cause them to boil like a pot, and send forth massive rocks and scatter their broken fragments upon the land with indescribable violence. Whole rivers will be dried up. The earth will be convulsed, and there will be dreadful eruptions and earthquakes everywhere. God will plague the wicked inhabitants of the earth until they are destroyed from off it."[32]

---

[32] E. G. White, *Spiritual Gifts*, Vol. 3 (1864), p. 82.1-3.

"John also had been a witness of this most startling revelation. He saw the sea and the waves roaring, and men's hearts failing them for fear. He beheld the earth moved, and the mountains carried into the midst of the sea, the water thereof roaring and troubled, and the mountains shaking with the swelling thereof. He was shown plagues, pestilence, famine, and death performing their terrible mission."[33]

When this earthquake occurs, every island flees away and the mountains are not found, implying that everything is moving on the planet. It will indeed be the greatest earthquake ever to occur on planet earth.

Revelation 16:21 And there fell upon men a great hail out of heaven, every stone about the weight of a talent: and men blasphemed God because of the plague of the hail; for the plague thereof was exceeding great.

"At His own will God summons the forces of nature to overthrow the might of His enemies—'fire, and hail; snow, and vapor; stormy wind fulfilling His word.' Psalm 148:8. When the heathen Amorites had set themselves to resist His purposes, God interposed, casting down 'great stones from heaven' upon the enemies of Israel. We are told of a greater battle to take place in the closing scenes of earth's history, when 'Jehovah hath opened His armory, and hath brought forth the weapons of His indignation.' Jeremiah 50:25. 'Hast thou,' he inquires, 'entered into the treasures of the snow? or hast thou seen the treasures of the hail, which I have reserved against the time of trouble, against the day of battle and war?' Job 38:22, 23.
"The revelator describes the destruction that is to take place when the 'great voice out of the temple of heaven' announces, 'It is done.' He says, '**There fell upon men a great hail out of heaven, every stone about the weight of a talent**.'[34] Revelation 16:17, 21."[35]

The wicked do not repent of their deeds because of these plagues; rather they proceed to blaspheme God for the plagues that are falling

---

[33] E. G. White, *Testimonies to Ministers and Gospel Workers* (1923) p. 445.2.

[34] A talent weighs over 60 pounds.

[35] E. G. White, *Patriarchs and Prophets* (1890), p. 509.3-4.

upon them. God was blamed by the wicked before there were plagues, and God gets blamed when the plagues fall.

This chapter shows what will fall on those who have disregarded God's warnings, "trodden under foot the Son of God," "counted the blood of the covenant, wherewith he was sanctified, an unholy thing, and hath done despite unto the Spirit of grace?"[36] God had given them ample opportunity, ample information, to be able to turn toward him, and avoid the plagues that are coming, but they rejected his mercy.

I pray that as you read his word, you will realize the amazing love of God and how Jesus is giving us this message of love. But in love for his children he must also bring mercy to an end and initiate justice and judgment. When we see injustice in this world we wish for justice. Why should we think that God would have any less of a desire for justice?

Will you accept the gift that he is offering—the forgiveness of your sins, that they may be blotted out of the heavenly sanctuary? Will you accept his righteous life so that when these things come on the earth, you do not receive these plagues? "Watch ye therefore, and pray always, that ye may be accounted worthy to escape all these things that shall come to pass, and to stand before the Son of man."[37] Amen.

---

[36] Hebrews 10:29

[37] Luke 20:35

Revelation 17

SUMMARY:

In Revelation 17 John sees a harlot woman sitting on a scarlet beast which has seven heads and ten horns. The harlot's name is: MYSTERY, BABYLON THE GREAT, THE MOTHER OF HARLOTS AND ABOMINATIONS OF THE EARTH. Seven kings are brought to view—five fallen, one who is, and one who is not yet come. Then an eighth appears who is not counted among the seven. Ten additional kings unite and give their power and strength unto the beast, and make war with the Lamb, who overcomes them. The ten kings eventually hate the whore, eat her flesh and burn her with fire. Revelation 17 is one of the most astonishing chapters in all of Revelation, and perhaps even the entire Bible. With dramatic imagery it carries us forward to the final destruction of Rome—the judgment of the great whore that sits on many waters.

Revelation 17:1 And there came one of the seven angels which had the seven vials, and talked with me, saying unto me, Come hither; I will show unto thee the judgment of the great whore that sitteth upon many waters:

The angel speaking to John in this vision, already holds one of the vials—or seven last plagues—in his hand. Therefore, the context for the things to be revealed in this chapter is just prior to the close of probation. The angel also tells us exactly what he will reveal: "**I will show unto thee the judgment of the great whore that sitteth upon many waters**." This judgment is clearly still a future and very end-time event.

In Bible prophecy a woman represents a church. A pure woman represents God's true church. "I have likened the daughter of Zion to a comely and delicate woman."[1] "And say unto Zion, Thou art my people."[2] Zion is God's people, who he compares to a beautiful, pure woman. The daughter of Zion is spiritual Israel, God's remnant church. "For I am jealous over you with godly jealousy: for I have

---

[1] Jeremiah 6:2

[2] Isaiah 51:15

espoused you to one husband, that I may present you as a chaste virgin to Christ."[3] On the other hand, Isaiah 1:21 tells us, "How is the faithful city become an harlot! it was full of judgment; righteousness lodged in it; but now murderers." Jerusalem represented God's church in the Old Testament. How can this once faithful city—previously a pure woman—have abandoned her husband and become an harlot? "Babylon is also charged with the sin of unlawful connection with 'the kings of the earth.' It was by departure from the Lord, and alliance with the heathen, that the Jewish church became a harlot; and Rome, corrupting herself in like manner by seeking the support of worldly powers, receives a like condemnation."[4]

The whore of Revelation 17 sits on many waters. The verse that defines the meaning of waters as a prophetic symbol is found in Revelation 17:15, "And he saith unto me, The waters which thou sawest, where the whore sitteth, are peoples, and multitudes, and nations, and tongues." The prophetic symbols portray an apostate church committing spiritual fornication to control peoples, multitudes, nations and languages.

Revelation 17:2 With whom the kings of the earth have committed fornication, and the inhabitants of the earth have been made drunk with the wine of her fornication.

This harlot church has formed an illicit relationship with the political powers, or kings of the earth. The harlot is portrayed as committing fornication with the heads of state of the world's empires. In God's eyes it is illegitimate to combine church and state, for whenever this occurs, coercion of conscience and persecution inevitably follows.

The inhabitants of the earth are drunk with the wine of her fornication. "The great sin charged against Babylon is that she 'made all nations drink of the wine of the wrath of her fornication.' This cup of intoxication which she presents to the world represents the false doctrines that she has accepted as the result of her unlawful connection with the great ones of the earth. Friendship with the world corrupts her faith, and in her turn she exerts a corrupting influence

---

[3] 2 Corinthians 11:2

[4] E. G. White, *The Great Controversy* (1911), p. 382.2.

upon the world by teaching doctrines which are opposed to the plainest statements of Holy Writ."[5] Alcohol removes a person's inhibitions and causes confusion. Yet the individual is unaware of the impairment. If one has ever tried to reason with a person who is drunk, you quickly find it is almost impossible. This apostate church is making the kings of the earth drunk with her false doctrine. They become confused yet believe that they are not.

"When faithful teachers expound the word of God, there arise men of learning, ministers professing to understand the Scriptures, who denounce sound doctrine as heresy, and thus turn away inquirers after truth. Were it not that the world is hopelessly intoxicated with the wine of Babylon, multitudes would be convicted and converted by the plain, cutting truths of the word of God. But religious faith appears so confused and discordant that the people know not what to believe as truth. The sin of the world's impenitence lies at the door of the church."[6]

Revelation 17:3 So he carried me away in the spirit into the wilderness: and I saw a woman sit upon a scarlet coloured beast, full of names of blasphemy, having seven heads and ten horns.

To view the events of this vision John is carried into the wilderness. Waters, as we saw, represent peoples, nations, tongues, and multitudes. By contrast therefore, wilderness areas (earth) represent relatively unpopulated places of the world. Specifically, as we have seen, in Revelation 13, the earth represents the land of America in which arose the world power with two horns like a lamb. John is shown the events about to transpire from the perspective of America, which rises to world prominence from 1776 to World War I (which fully established the new nation as a world power). This corresponds roughly to the time period of the deadly wound—1798-1929. Therefore, we should expect the things revealed in this passage to occur after America becomes a world power, and climax just before the close of probation.

---

[5] E. G. White, *The Great Controversy* (1911), p. 388.2.

[6] *Ibid.,* p. 339.1.

Just as the sea beast of Revelation 13 was a blasphemous power:[7] so the scarlet beast is "full of names of blasphemy." The "name of the beast" is located on his heads,[8] and is directly associated with "the number of his name,"[9] which number is 666.[10]

This scarlet beast has seven heads and tens horns—identical characteristics to the dragon[11] of Revelation 12 and the leopard-like beast (sea beast)[12] of Revelation 13. Its scarlet color indicates that it has become even more satanic, fully taking on the appearance of the dragon (or Satan) of chapter twelve.

---

[7] "and he opened his mouth in blasphemy against God," Revelation 13:6

[8] Revelation 13:1

[9] Revelation 13:17

[10] Revelation 13:18

[11] Revelation 12:3

[12] Revelation 13:1

Revelation 17:4 And the woman was arrayed in purple and scarlet colour, and decked with gold and precious stones and pearls, having a golden cup in her hand full of abominations and filthiness of her fornication:

The colors that the woman is wearing are sanctuary colors—used in the wilderness tabernacle, and in Solomon's temple. Besides white, there is a color that is conspicuous in its absence. In the sanctuary there were three primary colors used—purple, scarlet, and blue.

The first color, purple, represents royalty. When Jesus was about to be crucified, a purple robe was placed on him and they mocked him saying, "Hail, king of the Jews." The power portrayed by the harlot has no problem claiming the attributes of royalty.

The second color is scarlet. Scarlet depicts the color of sacrifice: "the blood of Jesus Christ... cleanseth us from all sin."[13] This ecclesiastical power claims to have the ability to forgive sins, and has no problem with claiming to be a substitute for the sacrifice of Christ, or with the sacrifice of millions of martyrs under the name of Christianity.

The color that is missing is blue, which represents obedience and the law of God. The harlot claims to be above God's law, so obedience is not a part of the garments of this defiled woman. Numbers 15:38-40 says, "Speak unto the children of Israel, and bid them that they make them fringes in the borders of their garments throughout their generations, and that they put upon the fringe of the borders a ribband of blue: And it shall be unto you for a fringe, that ye may look upon it, and remember all the commandments of the LORD, and do them; and that ye seek not after your own heart and your own eyes, after which ye use to go a whoring: That ye may remember, and do all my commandments, and be holy unto your God." This woman is committing whoredoms by transgressing God's law and thinking to change God's times and laws.[14] For this reason Paul refers to this power as the "man of sin," "the mystery of iniquity," and "that wicked."[15] Indeed, it is the Catholic Church that claims, as its mark of

---

[13] 1 John 1:7

[14] Daniel 7:25

[15] 2 Thessalonians 2:2-12

authority, to have changed the only commandment of God that deals with time.[16] "Colors for the Catholic church on official occasions are purple and scarlet. God went so far as to describe even the physical appearances of this power. Clearly, by providing all these detailed identifying characteristics, God wanted to leave no question as to the power he was describing."[17]

Considering the meaning that the Bible gives to this blue color, and the description in Exodus of Moses' and the seventy-elder's view of the majesty of God, it is possible that the stones that God initially gave Moses with the ten commandments carved on them were made from the blue sapphire stone composing the base of God's throne. "And they saw the God of Israel: and there was under his feet as it were a paved work of a sapphire stone, and as it were the body of heaven in his clearness. And the LORD said unto Moses, Come up to me into the mount, and be there: and I will give thee tables of stone, and a law, and commandments which I have written; that thou mayest teach them."[18]

This impure woman counterfeits the position and ministry of the true high priest—Jesus Christ. "He magnified himself even to the prince of the host, and by him... the place of his sanctuary was cast down."[19] In the Old Testament types and symbols, the high priest (representing Christ) was dressed in blue, purple and scarlet,[20] which this counterfeit power seeks to copy—except for the blue. There is but one church on this earth, that at the highest levels, clothes itself in these two colors—purple and scarlet.

The scarlet harlot holds a golden cup in her hand full of abominations. Scripture identifies what we should expect to find if we glimpse the abominations emanating from this cup. Turning to the book of Ezekiel we find a fascinating passage.[21] Ezekiel describes a strange experience where Jesus takes the prophet into vision by a lock of his hair. He is carried to the temple, where he is told to dig in

---

[16] See comments on Revelation 13:12.

[17] Martin Klein, *Thou Hast Magnified Thy Word Above All Thy Name* (2016), p. 53.

[18] Exodus 24:10, 12

[19] Daniel 8:11

[20] Exodus 28:4-6

[21] Ezekiel 8:14-15

a hole in the wall, to find a door into the temple. He is then shown abomination after abomination occurring in the very temple of God. Every time the angel shows him an abomination, he says, in essence: wait, I will show you greater abominations than these. If we contemplate the last two abominations we see what God considers to be the very greatest of all abominations.

"Then he brought me to the door of the gate of the LORD's house which was toward the north; and, behold, there sat women weeping for Tammuz. Then said he unto me, Hast thou seen this, O son of man? turn thee yet again, and thou shalt see greater abominations than these." Tammuz is a mythical pagan deity that is the illegitimate son of the sun god, and had become somewhat of a sex symbol in this ancient culture. These women are weeping over Tammuz, a mythical character, in the same manner as women of today weep over media sex symbols. This abomination is associated with sun worship, but Christ tells Ezekiel, "I will show you greater abominations yet than these. And he brought me into the inner court of the LORD's house, and, behold, at the door of the temple of the LORD, between the porch and the altar, were about five and twenty men, with their backs toward the temple of the LORD, and their faces toward the east; and they worshipped the sun toward the east."

The greatest of all abominations, in God's eyes, is sun worship; particularly sun worship that is masquerading as God's true worship. Sun worship, claiming to be Christianity, is what God says is the greatest abomination. Why is this?

The name of Satan before he fell from heaven was Lucifer, which means "son of the morning" or "light bearer."[22] This name, Satan has now twisted, and is claiming to be the spiritual light-bearer to the planet, just as the sun brings physical light to the earth. For this reason, Satan has chosen the sun to represent himself. Therefore, sun worship, in the place of God's true worship, is really Satan worship.[23] In this manner Satan, through deception, gains the worship that is due to God alone. This is the reason why God says it is the greatest abomination of all.

---

[22] Lucifer does not mean "morning star," as it is rendered in some modern translations. "Morning star" is a term that refers to Jesus (see Revelation 22:16). "Son of the morning" as in the KJV is correct, as Lucifer was a son of the Morning Star, Jesus.

[23] This is why every pagan religion worships the sun in some way.

The great whore is said to have a cup full of abominations. Therefore, its contents would include the greatest of all abominations—sun worship. The only church in the world to use a woman with a golden cup in her hand as one of its symbols is the Roman Catholic Church.

Here we see on the back of these Vatican coins, the woman holding a cup, or the cup alone, with the solar disk of Lucifer emanating from the chalice.

Notice that the woman is labeled Fides. The pagan Roman deity named Fides was the goddess of fidelity. The cup is held in the right hand. Albert G. Mackey, 33° Freemason, in his book, *A Manual of the Lodge*, tells us what this word and symbolism means: "The right hand has in all ages been deemed an emblem of fidelity, and our ancient brethren worshipped Deity under the name Fides or Fidelity... Numa was the first who erected an altar to Fides, under which name the goddess of oaths and honesty was worshipped."[24] We see this goddess portrayed in other places in our culture today, most notably in the "Semper fidelis" of the U.S. Marine Corps.

On the back of certain official Vatican coins is found the phrase, "Citta del Vaticano"—City of the Vatican. What is the meaning of the word Vatican? In the Latin vulgate, which is the Catholic Bible in the official church language, we find in Nehemiah 6:12, "Et intellexi quod deus non misisset eum sed quasi **vaticinans** locutus esset ad me et tobia et sanaballat conduxissent eum." In the middle of the verse we find the word vaticinans, which is derived from the same root word as Vatican—vaticinas. To find the meaning of the word in English, we turn to Nehemiah 6:12, "And, lo, I perceived that God had not sent him; but that he pronounced this **prophecy** against me: for Tobiah and Sanballat had hired him." Therefore, Citta del Vaticano literally means the "City of Prophecy."

[24] Albert G. Mackey, M.D. *A Manual of the Lodge*, (New York: Effingham Maynard & Co., 1891), p. 40-41.

Revelation 17:5 And upon her forehead was a name written, MYSTERY, BABYLON THE GREAT, THE MOTHER OF HARLOTS AND ABOMINATIONS OF THE EARTH.

This woman is shrouded in mystery and secrecy. When Jesus was on earth he said, "I spake openly to the world; I ever taught in the synagogue, and in the temple, whither the Jews always resort; and in secret have I said nothing."[25] Jesus' doctrine is not one of mystery; not one shrouded in obscurity, or clothed in secrecy. But Babylon clothes its doctrines and movements in mystery, and secrecy.

That "**Babylon the great**" refers to Rome is even admitted by Catholic apologists. James Cardinal Gibbons in his *Faith of our Fathers* writes: "'Babylon,' from which Peter addresses his first Epistle, is understood by learned annotators, Protestant and Catholic, to refer to Rome."[26] In every detail Rome conforms to the Bible's predictions, even verifying in their own words the marks that identify them as the anti-Christ power of Bible prophecy.

She is also said to be a **mother** of harlots. First, this implies that she has children. Second, as she is the mother of **harlots**, it implies that her children are daughters. Third, as she is the "**mother of harlots**," her daughters have taken up the same profession as their mother. Cardinal Ratzinger, on September 4, 2000, using Biblical language, said, "It must always be clear, when the expression sister Churches is used in this proper sense, that the one, holy, catholic and apostolic Universal Church is not sister but mother of all the particular Churches."[27]

During the Reformation many daughter churches formed, as people left Babylon—yet not harlot daughters, for they were initially pure. They were seeking to follow the word of God and reform the evils that they saw in the church of Rome. They were calling people back to the Bible and the Bible only. Unfortunately, most of these churches eventually began to return to their mother's confusing

---

[25] John 18:20

[26] James Cardinal Gibbons, *The Faith of Our Fathers*, p.87.6; 111th printing. ISBN 0-89555-158-6.

[27] Joseph Cardinal Ratzinger, LETTER TO THE PRESIDENTS OF THE CONFERENCES OF BISHOPS, Rome, from the Offices of the Congregation for the Doctrine of the Faith, June 30, 2000, the Solemnity of the Sacred Heart of Jesus.
http://www.vatican.va/roman_curia/congregations/cfaith/documents/rc_con_cfaith_doc_20000630_chiese-sorelle_en.html Retrieved 12-13-2016.

doctrines, and to imbibe in the intoxicating wine of Babylon. As they began to apostatize they became harlots like their mother. They forsook their husband and went whoring after the kings of the earth and began to form political relationships with the powers of the world. The apostate Protestant churches began to forsake pure Bible doctrine, and the law of God, joining once again with the mother church. This verse indicates unequivocally that John is being shown the post-reformation events, rather than ancient history.

"Babylon is said to be 'the mother of harlots.' By her daughters must be symbolized churches that cling to her doctrines and traditions, and follow her example of sacrificing the truth and the approval of God, in order to form an unlawful alliance with the world. The message of Revelation 14, announcing the fall of Babylon, must apply to religious bodies that were once pure and have become corrupt. Since this message follows the warning of the judgment, it must be given in the last days; therefore it cannot refer to the Roman Church alone, for that church has been in a fallen condition for many centuries. Furthermore, in the eighteenth chapter of the Revelation the people of God are called upon to come out of Babylon. According to this scripture, many of God's people must still be in Babylon. And in what religious bodies are the greater part of the followers of Christ now to be found? Without doubt, in the various churches professing the Protestant faith....

"Many of the Protestant churches are following Rome's example of iniquitous connection with 'the kings of the earth'—the state churches, by their relation to secular governments; and other denominations, by seeking the favor of the world. And the term 'Babylon'—confusion—may be appropriately applied to these bodies, all professing to derive their doctrines from the Bible, yet divided into almost innumerable sects, with widely conflicting creeds and theories."[28]

Revelation 17:6 And I saw the woman drunken with the blood of the saints, and with the blood of the martyrs of Jesus: and when I saw her, I wondered with great admiration.

---

[28] E. G. White, *The Great Controversy* (1911), p. 382.3-383.1.

For this woman to be drunken with the blood of the saints, that blood must have already been shed. She shed the blood of the saints primarily during the dark ages. Indeed, Revelation 18 goes even further to say that not only is the blood of the saints and prophets found in her, but the blood of all that are slain on the earth.[29] Once again, the context indicates a post-dark-ages church, as she is drunk with the blood which has already been shed.

Abraham Lincoln recognized this when he said, "For it is a fact, which is now evident to me, that, with very few exceptions, every priest and every true Roman Catholic is a determined enemy of liberty.... if the American people could learn what I know of the fierce hatred of the generality of the priests of Rome against our institutions, our schools, our most sacred rights, and our so dearly bought liberties, they would drive them away, to-morrow, from among us, or they would shoot them as traitors.... This war would never have been possible without the sinister influence of the Jesuits. We owe it to Popery that we now see our land reddened with the blood of her noblest sons."[30]

"The Roman Church now presents a fair front to the world, covering with apologies her record of horrible cruelties. She has clothed herself in Christlike garments; but she is unchanged. Every principle of the papacy that existed in past ages exists today. The doctrines devised in the darkest ages are still held. Let none deceive themselves. The papacy that Protestants are now so ready to honor is the same that ruled the world in the days of the Reformation, when men of God stood up, at the peril of their lives, to expose her iniquity. She possesses the same pride and arrogant assumption that lorded it over kings and princes, and claimed the prerogatives of God. Her spirit is no less cruel and despotic now than when she crushed out human liberty and slew the saints of the Most High.
"The papacy is just what prophecy declared that she would be, the apostasy of the latter times. 2 Thessalonians 2:3, 4. It is a part of her policy to assume the character which will best accomplish her purpose; but beneath the variable appearance of the chameleon she conceals the invariable venom of the serpent. 'Faith ought not to be kept with heretics, nor persons suspected of heresy' (Lenfant,

---

[29] Revelation 18:24

[30] Charles Chiniquy, *Fifty Years in the Church of Rome* (Cleveland, OH: Geo. M. Rewell & Co., 1890), p. 697, 699.

volume 1, page 516), she declares. Shall this power, whose record for a thousand years is written in the blood of the saints, be now acknowledged as a part of the church of Christ?

"It is not without reason that the claim has been put forth in Protestant countries that Catholicism differs less widely from Protestantism than in former times. There has been a change; but the change is not in the papacy. Catholicism indeed resembles much of the Protestantism that now exists, because Protestantism has so greatly degenerated since the days of the Reformers."[31]

"The Roman Catholic Church, with all its ramifications throughout the world, forms one vast organization under the control, and designed to serve the interests, of the papal see. Its millions of communicants, in every country on the globe, are instructed to hold themselves as bound in allegiance to the pope. Whatever their nationality or their government, they are to regard the authority of the church as above all other. Though they may take the oath pledging their loyalty to the state, yet back of this lies the vow of obedience to Rome, absolving them from every pledge inimical to her interests."[32]

"Says the prophet: 'I saw the woman drunk with the blood of the saints, and with the blood of the martyrs of Jesus.' Babylon is further declared to be 'that great city, which reigneth over the kings of the earth.' Revelation 17:4-6, 18. The power that for so many centuries maintained despotic sway over the monarchs of Christendom is Rome. The purple and scarlet color, the gold and precious stones and pearls, vividly picture the magnificence and more than kingly pomp affected by the haughty see of Rome. And no other power could be so truly declared 'drunken with the blood of the saints' as that church which has so cruelly persecuted the followers of Christ."[33] "In the thirteenth century was established that most terrible of all the engines of the papacy—the Inquisition. The prince of darkness wrought with the leaders of the papal hierarchy. In their secret councils Satan and his angels controlled the minds of evil men, while unseen in the midst stood an angel of God, taking the fearful record of their iniquitous decrees and writing the history of deeds too horrible to appear to human eyes. 'Babylon the great' was

---

[31] E. G. White, *The Great Controversy* (1911), p. 571.1-3.

[32] E. G. White, *The Great Controversy* (1911), p. 580.2.

[33] *Ibid.*, p. 382.2.

'drunken with the blood of the saints.' The mangled forms of millions of martyrs cried to God for vengeance upon that apostate power."[34]

"The first triumphs of the Reformation past, Rome summoned new forces, hoping to accomplish its destruction. At this time, the order of the Jesuits was created, the most cruel, unscrupulous, and powerful of all the champions of popery. Cut off from every earthly tie and human interest, dead to the claims of natural affection, reason and conscience wholly silenced, they knew no rule, no tie, but that of their order, and no duty but to extend its power. The gospel of Christ had enabled its adherents to meet danger and endure suffering, undismayed by cold, hunger, toil, and poverty, to uphold the banner of truth in face of the rack, the dungeon, and the stake. To combat these forces, Jesuitism inspired its followers with a fanaticism that enabled them to endure like dangers, and to oppose to the power of truth all the weapons of deception. There was no crime too great for them to commit, no deception too base for them to practice, no disguise too difficult for them to assume. Vowed to perpetual poverty and humility, it was their studied aim to secure wealth and power, to be devoted to the overthrow of Protestantism, and the re-establishment of the papal supremacy."[35]

The Jesuits, a powerful secret order in the Catholic Church apparently make the following oath when initiated to the order: "I _____, now in the presence of Almighty God, the Blessed Virgin Mary, the Blessed Michael the Archangel, the Blessed St. John the Baptist, the Holy Apostles, Peter and Paul, and all the Saints, sacred hosts of Heaven, and to you, my ghostly Father, the Superior General of the Society of Jesus, founded by St. Ignatius Loyola, in the Pontification of Paul the Third, and continued to the present, do by the womb of the virgin, the matrix of God, and the rod of Jesus Christ, declare and swear that his holiness, the Pope, is Christ's Vice-regent, and is the true and only head of the Catholic or Universal Church throughout the earth; and that by the virtue of the keys of binding and loosing, given to his Holiness by my Savior, Jesus Christ, he hath power to depose heretical kings, princes, states, commonwealths and governments, all being illegal without his sacred confirmation, and that they may be safely destroyed.

---

[34] E. G. White, *The Great Controversy* (1911), p. 59.3.

[35] *Ibid.,* p. 234.2.

"I do further declare, that I will help and assist and advise all or any of his Holiness' agents in any place wherever I shall be, and do my utmost to extirpate the heretical Protestant or Liberal doctrines and to destroy all their pretended powers, legal or otherwise.

"I do further promise and declare, that notwithstanding I am dispensed with to assume any religion heretical, for the propagating of the Mother Church's interest, to keep secret and private all her agents' counsels, from time to time as they may instruct me, and not to divulge directly or indirectly, by word, writing, or circumstances whatever; but to execute all that shall be proposed given in charge or discovered unto me, by you, my ghostly father...

"I do further promise and declare, that I will have no opinion or will of my own, or any mental reservation whatever, even as a corpse or cadaver but unhesitatingly obey each and every command that I may receive from my superiors in the Militia of the Pope and Jesus Christ.

"That I will go to any part of the world, whatsoever, without murmuring and will be submissive in all things whatsoever communicated to me.... I do further promise and declare, that I will, when opportunity presents, make and wage relentless war, secretly or openly, against all heretics, Protestants and Liberals, as I am directed to do to extirpate and exterminate them from the face of the whole earth, and that I will spare neither sex, age nor condition, and that I will hang, waste, boil, flay, strangle and bury alive these infamous heretics; rip up the stomachs and wombs of their women and crush their infants heads against the wall, in order to annihilate forever their execrable race.

"That when the same cannot be done openly, I will secretly use the poison cup, the strangulation cord, the steel of the poniard, or the leaden bullet, regardless of the honor, rank, dignity or authority of the person or persons whatsoever may be their condition in life, either public or private, as I at any time may be directed so to do by any agent of the Pope or superior of the Brotherhood of the Holy Faith of the Society of Jesus."[36]

"You have been taught to insidiously plant the seeds of jealousy and hatred between communities, provinces, and states that were at peace, and incite them to deeds of blood, involving them in war with each other, and to create revolutions, and civil war in countries that were independent and prosperous, cultivating the arts and sciences

---

[36] The Jesuit Extreme Oath of Induction as recorded in the Journals of the 62nd U.S. Congress, 3rd Session, House Calendar No. 397, House Bill 1523, Contested election case of Eugene C. Bonniwell, against Thos. S. Butler, Feb. 15, 1913, pp. 3215-3216.

and enjoying the blessings of peace. To take sides with the combatants and to act secretly in concert with your brother Jesuit, who might be engaged on the other side, but openly opposed to that with which you might be connected; only that the church might be the gainer in the end, in the conditions fixed in the treaties for peace and that the end justifies the means."[37]

So, neither Abraham Lincoln, nor the spirit of prophecy, nor the Jesuits themselves, seem to think that the Bible is exaggerating when it says, she is **"drunken with the blood of the saints, and with the blood of the martyrs of Jesus"** and **"in her was found the blood of prophets, and of saints, and of all that were slain upon the earth."** [38]

When John sees her, he wonders with great admiration. The angel takes exception to this and asks John why he marvels.

Revelation 17:7 And the angel said unto me, Wherefore didst thou marvel? I will tell thee the mystery of the woman, and of the beast that carrieth her, which hath the seven heads and ten horns.

The angel's question alerts John that he must not wonder after this power. In Revelation 13 we saw that the whole world will wonder after this beast except those who have the seal of God in their foreheads and their names written in the book of life. If your name is to be in that book of life, you cannot wonder after this beast. The angel then states that he will explain to John the meaning of what he has seen.

Revelation 17:8 The beast that thou sawest was, and is not; and shall ascend out of the bottomless pit, and go into perdition: and they that dwell on the earth shall wonder, whose names were not written in the book of life from the foundation of the world, when they behold the beast that was, and is not, and yet is.

---

[37] Library of Congress, Catalog Card Number, 66-43354.

[38] Revelation 18:24

When the papal beast ascends from the bottomless pit at the healing of the wound, a new "power of satanic origin and character,"[39] would inhabit the old leopard-like body, giving it a new color. Only the Jesuit order, who delivered the deadly wound to the Papacy, in 1798, as punishment for attempting to suppress their order (in 1773), would be able to reinvigorate the Papacy's political power—this time, under the control of the order. This is clearly signaled on the coin minted to commemorate the 1929 Lateran Treaty, with the Jesuit letters IHS emblazoned on the solar disk emanating from the chalice.

The phrases "**was, and is not, and shall ascend**,..." and "**they that dwell on the earth shall wonder**" are directly parallel to Revelation 13:3, "I saw one of his heads... wounded to death; and his deadly wound was healed: and **all the world wondered after the beast**."

Revelation 17:8	Revelation 13:3
"was"	"I saw one of his heads"
"and is not"	"wounded to death"
"and shall ascend"	"and his deadly wound was healed"
"and they that dwell on the earth shall wonder"	"and all the world wondered after the beast"

Revelation 17:8 is describing the very same wound and healed wound as Revelation 13. This demonstrates that the sea beast of Revelation 13 and the scarlet beast of Revelation 17 externally appear to be the same political entity (they also each have seven heads and ten horns). Yet, as the beast ascends in Revelation 17, with its wound healed, it has become even more satanic than before, now sharing the color of the great red dragon of Revelation 12, being transformed into the beast from the bottomless pit.[40] The context of this verse indicates that the wondering occurs as a result of the healing of the wound and therefore must follow the healing.

---

[39] E. G. White, *The Great Controversy* (1911), p. 269.3.

[40] See comments on Revelation 11:7-8.

Revelation 17:8			
1st Phrase	was	is not	shall ascend	go into perdition
2nd Phrase	was	and is not	yet is	
Time Frame	538 - 1798	1798 - 1929	1929 - now	Second Coming

Inserting the predicted prophetic dates shows the chronology of the wording. The "was" stage refers to the papacy during its predicted political supremacy from A.D. 538-1798. The "is not" stage refers to the period during which it sustained its deadly wound A.D. 1798-1929. The "shall ascend" stage refers to the time period beginning with the restoration of political status in 1929[41] until just prior to the second coming when God pours his judgment on her, implementing the "go into perdition" stage.

Notice that the angel repeats these stages of the Papal power a second time in this verse, changing the tense of the third stage from future to present. Instead of "**shall ascend**," he now says, "**yet is**."

"The beast that thou sawest **was**, and **is not**; and **shall ascend** out of the bottomless pit, and **go into perdition**: and they that dwell on the earth shall wonder, whose names were not written in the book of life from the foundation of the world, when they behold the beast that **was**, and **is not**, and **yet is**."

This change of tenses is directly connected to the world wondering after the beast, showing that the angel has taken John further into the future[42] to view this phenomenon. In Revelation 17:8 the angel takes John from the time when the ascending is yet in the future ("shall ascend"), and transports him to the time when that period is in the present ("yet is"). In this manner John's attention is directed to the days in which we live; to the period of time between 1929 and the second coming for the events that follow. It is during this period that the angel says that all the people in the world, whose names are not

---

[41] See comments on Revelation 13:3-4.

[42] There is Biblical precedent for a prophet being taken in vision to a point of time in the future, viewing events from that position in the future. In Daniel 8:1 the prophet tells us clearly that the vision occurs in the third year of the reign of king Belshazzar. This is still during the empire of Babylon and Daniel would have been physically located at the city of Babylon. Yet in his vision he sees himself in another palace at a future point in time: "And I saw in a vision; and it came to pass, when I saw, that I was at Shushan in the palace..." Daniel 8:2. In vision, Daniel sees that he will be serving in the palace at Shushan, the capital of the Medo-Persian empire; a future event that had not yet occurred.

written in the book of life, wonder after the beast. Therefore, the angel is about to tell us of the events from 1929 to the second coming.

Revelation 17:9 And here is the mind which hath wisdom. The seven heads are seven mountains, on which the woman sitteth.

This is the second of only two places in the Bible where this phrase is used: "**Here is** the mind that hath **wisdom**." The other place is in Revelation 13:18, where it is abbreviated to: "Here is wisdom." The first "here is wisdom" identifies the man at the head of the papal church. The second "here is wisdom" identifies the capital city of the papal church with the simple statement, "**The seven heads are seven mountains, on which the woman sitteth**."

The papal church is situated on seven mountains. Rome has for millennia been known as the "city of seven hills."[43] The angel is making sure, before continuing, that the identity of the woman is exposed, despite his cryptic words. Once the angel established the time frame of what he will reveal, and verifies the power of which he is speaking, he begins to introduce his main point: "And there are seven kings...."

Revelation 17:10 And there are seven kings: five are fallen, and one is, and the other is not yet come; and when he cometh, he must continue a short space.

Since the angel has clearly established that he is referring to the political power headquartered at the Vatican, what can be considered to be the king of this power other than the pope? This verse is revealing that there will be seven popes after 1929, and at the point in time to which John has been transported in vision, five would have fallen, one would be in power, and another would reign for a short time.

---

[43] Historical references to Rome as the city of seven hills or mountains:
- Horace Carmen Saeculare 7.
- Virgil *Aeneid VI*. 782-784.
- Georgics II. 534, 535.
- Martial *Epigrams IV*. 64, 11, 12.
- Cicero Letters to Atticus VI. 5.
- Propertius *Elegies III*. 11; etc.

Popes since 1929:
Five are fallen:

260	•	Pius XI (1922-39)
261	•	Pius XII (1939-58)
262	•	Blessed John XXIII (1958-63)
263	•	Paul VI (1963-78)
264	•	John Paul I (1978)

One is:

265	•	John Paul II (1978-2005)

The Other is Not yet come:

266	•	Benedict XVI (2005-2013)

Revelation 13:1 reveals that each of the seven heads has the name of blasphemy. The name that occurs on each head of the beast is the name of the beast, which is the number of a man and adds up to 666.[44] The name of the beast, as shown in Revelation 13:18, is the pope's title Vicarius Filii Dei, or Vicarius Christi. Both titles are the same, meaning Vicar of the Son of God or Vicar of Christ.[45] Vicar means: substitute for, in place of, or against. Thus, Vicar of Christ literally means: in place of Christ, against Christ, or anti-Christ. The Bible says of this power that he "opposeth and exalteth himself above all that is called God, or that is worshipped; so that he as God sitteth in the temple of God, showing himself that he is God."[46] The title is blasphemous because he is claiming to be in the place of God. This title is placed on the mitre of the pope. Therefore, since 666 is the number of the man at the head of the beast; and since that number is the number of the name of the beast; and since the name of the beast is on each head of the beast; therefore, according to Scripture, the heads of the beast represent heads of the papacy[47] who wear the blasphemous name of the beast on their head.

The spirit of prophecy indicates that the heads of the beast represent popes: "We looked upon the bust of Pius VI. The marble statue beneath the bust contained the heart of the pope. This is the pope

---

[44] Revelation 13:17-18

[45] See comments on Revelation 13:18.

[46] 2 Thessalonians 2:4

[47] Heads in symbolic Bible prophecy represent kings. The head of the image of Daniel 2 represents Nebuchadnezzar (Daniel 2:38); the four heads on the leopard in Daniel 7 represent the four generals who divided the Greek empire.

specified in prophecy, which received the deadly wound."[48] Revelation 13:3 tells us that it was one of the heads that was wounded. This passage reveals that it is a pope that received the deadly wound, therefore the heads represent popes.

During the period between 1798 and 1929, the papacy had lost its political power; therefore, they did not have a king. The popes that were elected during that time served as bishop, not as king. Even since the healing of the wound in 1929, they still style themselves as clergy, with the ecclesiastical form most prominent. Yet their political status has returned, again making them kings. The woman (church) now controls the beast (state). This church/state relationship is the feature to which the earth beast (chapter 13) creates an image.

Even the Vatican shows us that "**there are seven kings**."

49

This set of official Vatican stamps commemorates the popes from 1929 to the reign of Benedict XVI. Behind their heads on the different colored backgrounds are two repeating numbers—1929 and 2009. These are the kings since 1929 up until 2009 when the set of stamps was printed.

Why would John Paul II be the one that is? This makes perfect sense, because he was in power for almost three decades. Newt Gingrich's documentary on Pope John Paul II, states, "Throughout the 2000-year history of the papacy, only two popes served longer than John Paul II. From his humble roots in Krakow, he became the leader of a billion Catholics, the most recognized and possibly the most influential man of our lifetime."[50] This statement was made in 2010, well after John Paul II had died, and well into the reign of Benedict XVI. It only makes sense that it was John Paul II's pivotal reign to which the angel points John the Revelator as the one who is.

---

[48] E. G. White, *Manuscript Releases*, Vol. 5 (1990), p. 318.1

[49] http://biblelight.net/wound.htm

[50] http://www.ninedaysthatchangedtheworld.com/

The angel informed John that when the seventh comes, he will reign but a short time. In an article on CNN.com, April 20, 2005, entitled, "New pope suffered 1991 brain hemorrhage," Ratzinger tells why he choose the name Benedict. "When Ratzinger told cardinals in the conclave why he wanted to take on the name Benedict XVI, 'one of the things he alluded to was the fact that Benedict XV, the last pope to have that name, had one of the shortest pontificates of the 20th century...'"

"April 21, 2005, VATICAN CITY, Pope Benedict XVI predicted a 'short reign' in comments to cardinals just after his election, and his brother said Wednesday he was worried about the stress the job would put on the 78-year-old pontiff. Joseph Ratzinger has had ailments in the past, including a 1991 hemorrhagic stroke, that raise questions about how long his papacy will last and whether the world will watch another pope slowly succumb to age and ailments on a very public stage. Pope Benedict was the oldest pontiff elected in 275 years.... Chicago Cardinal Francis George said Ratzinger, who had repeatedly asked John Paul to let him retire, told the cardinals, 'I too hope in this short reign to be a man of peace.'"[51]

Just as the Bible predicted, Benedict XVI indeed had a short reign. Now we are at a point in history where we are beyond both the one that is and the one that reigned but a **"short space."** On March 13, 2013 the world watched as pope Francis took the stage, as a result of his living predecessor's resignation.

Revelation 17:11 And the beast that was, and is not, even he is the eighth, and is of the seven, and goeth into perdition.

The eighth king is referred to as the beast that **"was and is not,"** indicating that he would represent all the political power of the papacy and of the Jesuits, in one man. Note that it is the beast that is associated with the eighth king, not the woman. Therefore, political power would be concentrated in the eighth king—the power to punish dissenters, with the restoration of persecution.

---

[51] Nicole Winfield, "Elderly pontiff predicts 'short reign,'" Associated Press, *Chicago Tribune*, April 21, 2005.

The eighth is also said to be of the seven. The eighth is a Jesuit pope, of the order that delivered the deadly wound [52] in 1798, and allowed the temporal reign of the popes since 1929.

Notice it says that "**he is the eighth, and is of the seven, and goeth into perdition.**" There are seven heads which correspond to seven mountains, and there are seven kings. Seven of the kings correspond to each of seven mountains, which indicates that this eighth one does not have a corresponding mountain.

There is an interesting ecclesiastical term that is used in the Catholic church called ultramontanism. Ultramontanism literally means beyond the mountains. "The term originates in ecclesiastical language from the Middle Ages: when a non-Italian man was elected

---

[52] Another beast that received a deadly wound which was healed was the Jesuit order, the beast from the bottomless pit, which made war against the Bible in the streets of France (see comments on Revelation 11). The Jesuits ran the inquisition, the engine of persecution of the papacy. The Testimony of Jesus gives 1773 as the date for the cessation of persecution (see E. G. White, *The Great Controversy*, p. 306.1). "Should our nation abjure the principles of Protestantism, to give countenance and sanction to the Sunday law, they will in this act join hands with popery; for it will be nothing else than giving life to the tyranny which has been eagerly waiting and watching its opportunity to spring into active despotism."
E. G. White, *The Review and Herald*, December 11, 1888, par. 4.

"As the Inquisition was the tribulum by which the Papacy inflicted such sore tribulation upon the church, and as the Order of the Jesuits was the strength of the Inquisition, therefore we believe that the abolition of the Order of the Jesuits is the event that marks the end of the tribulation. They had been expelled from Portugal in 1753, from France in 1761, and from Spain in 1767; but these decrees could not be permanently successful as long as the Jesuits retained their Order intact, and had the support of the Pope. But it was not long before the Pope was forced to turn against them, and the final crash came. Of this event we give the following narrative: 'At last came the final blow that was to shatter into pieces the great army of Loyola. For more than two centuries the Jesuits had been fighting the battles of Rome. To exalt the supremacy of the Pope, they had died by thousands in English jails and Indian solitudes, had pierced land and sea to carry the strange story of the primacy to heathen millions, and to build anew the medieval church in the heart of Oriental idolatry. And now it was the Pope and Rome that were to complete their destruction. By a cruel ingratitude, the deity on earth whom they had worshiped with a fidelity unequaled among men, was to hurl his anathemas against his most faithful disciples. France and Spain elected Pope Clement XIV. upon his pledge that he would dissolve the Order. **He issued his bull July 21, 1773, directing that, for the welfare of the church and the good of mankind, the institution of Loyola should be abolished.**' —Historical Studies, Id.
"**For these reasons we believe that the abolition of the Order of Jesuits is the event, and July 21, 1773, is the date, when 'the tribulation of those days' ended.**
"NOTE.—The Jesuits were restored in 1814, by Pope Pius VII.; but not to their persecuting power. In the different countries of Europe since that time the Order has been expelled and restored several times, and even by the Papacy once. But Pius IX., after his return from Gaeta in 1849, gave them its entire confidence till the day of his death, and **in his Vatican decrees is seen the crowning triumph of Jesuit Ultramontanism.**"
A. T. Jones, "The End of the Tribulation of Those Days," *Signs of the Times*, August 12, 1886, p. 487.13.

to the papacy, he was said to be papa ultramontano, that is, a Pope from beyond the mountains (referring to the Alps).

"From the 17th century, ultramontanism became closely associated with the Jesuits, who defended the superiority of Popes over councils and kings, even in temporal questions."[53]

Perhaps the Bible is revealing to us that the eighth king will indeed be a non-Italian, Jesuit pope. Let us see what else ultramontanism means, and if the additional definitions also apply, exactly, to the current pope.

"It is indisputably legitimate to speak of Ultramontanism as a distinct policy, but it is very difficult to define its essential character.

"There is something chameleon-like in its appearances; its genuine views are kept in the background from tactical considerations, and first one aspect, then another, comes into prominence.

"The first and fundamental characteristic of Ultramontanism is its championship of a logical carrying out of the so-called 'papalistic system,' the concentration, that is, of all ecclesiastical power in the person of the Roman bishop.

"A second peculiarity of Ultramontanism is its confusion of religion with politics; it claims for the Roman Catholic Church the functions of a political power, and asserts that it is the duty of the secular state to carry out its instructions and wishes.

"...this endeavour is the third great characteristic of Ultramontanism. Wherever its operations can be traced, they are dominated by the conviction that all stirrings of independence must be repressed....

"In the fourth place, Ultramontanism is the embodiment of intolerance towards other creeds.

"Thus Ultramontanism is not to be conceived as a theological movement, but as the programme of a party whose principles are in fundamental opposition to modern culture, modern education, modern tolerance and the modern state... The hierophants of this Ultramontane system are to be found in the Society of Jesus [Jesuits]. In fact, **the terms jesuitical and ultramontane may, in numerous cases, be regarded as equivalent**."[54]

---

[53] http://en.wikipedia.org/wiki/Ultramontanism Retrieved 3-24-13.

[54] 1911 Encyclopædia Britannica - Ultramontanism
http://en.wikisource.org/wiki/1911_Encyclopædia_Britannica/Ultramontanism Retrieved 4-7-2013.

The definition of the term ultramontanism, is an exact description of Pope Francis. In summary, ultramontane or "Pope beyond the mountains" is defined as:
1. a non-Italian pope
2. a Jesuit pope
3. insisting that the pope has all ecclesiastical powers
4. insisting on church control of the state, which will lead to
5. repressing freedom of conscience, and
6. revival of religious intolerance, which inevitably leads to
7. persecution

Verse 8 informed us that the beast goes into perdition and this verse says this eighth king will go into perdition. This refers to their destruction at the second coming of Christ and alludes to the judgment of the great whore, which the angel informed John was what the vision would reveal. The punishments from God that fall on the beast power will fall likewise on the eighth king. The eighth lives until the second coming of Jesus. If this is the case, we are living during the reign of the world's last pope. It seems indeed that we are on the very verge of the final events of earth's history.

Revelation 17:12 And the ten horns which thou sawest are ten kings, which have received no kingdom as yet; but receive power as kings one hour with the beast.

Revelation 17:13 These have one mind, and shall give their power and strength unto the beast.

Notice that these ten horns are not the same as the ten horns on the beast of Daniel 7, for it says that these **"have received no kingdom as yet."** Revelation 17 outlines the deadly wound and its healing, the eight kings that follow, and at that time, these ten kings still have not received their kingdom. This is not true of the ten tribes of Europe, which were delineated on the fourth beast of Daniel 7. Further, three of the ten tribes of Western Europe were uprooted, leaving only seven. Therefore, these ten kings are not the ten kings of Europe.

The ten kings of this chapter receive power for one hour with the beast. Using symbolic prophetic time in which a day represents a year,[55] we could say that an hour is 1/24 of a day, and thus could represent 1/24 of a year. Thus, if we divide 360 days (a Biblical year) by 24, we find that an hour would be equal to 15 days or just over two weeks. Apparently these ten political powers reign with the beast for 15 days.

Who then are these ten kings? **"In the seventeenth of Revelation is foretold the destruction of all the churches who corrupt themselves by idolatrous devotion to the service of the papacy**, those who have drunk of the wine of the wrath of her fornication.

"Thus is represented the papal power, which with all deceivableness of unrighteousness, by outside attraction and gorgeous display, deceives all nations; promising them, as did Satan our first parents, all good to those who receive its mark, and all harm to those who oppose its fallacies. The power which has the deepest inward corruption will make the greatest display, and will clothe itself with the most elaborate signs of power.

"The Bible plainly declares that this covers a corrupt and deceiving wickedness. 'Upon her forehead was a name written, Mystery, Babylon the Great, The Mother of Harlots and Abominations of the Earth.'

"What is it that gives its kingdom to this power? **Protestantism**, a power which, while **professing to have the temper and spirit of a lamb** and to be allied to Heaven, **speaks with the voice of a dragon**. It is moved by a power from beneath."[56]

Revelation 13 outlined a nation that would commence with the temper and spirit of a lamb but eventually speak like a dragon—the United States of America. "One nation, and only one, meets the specifications of this prophecy; it points unmistakably to the United States of America."[57] "Here is a striking figure of the rise and growth of our own nation. And the lamb-like horns, emblems of innocence and gentleness, well represent the character of our government, as expressed in its two fundamental principles, Republicanism and Protestantism."[58]

---

[55] Ezekiel 4:6; Numbers 14:24; See also Daniel 7-8.

[56] E. G. White, *The Seventh-day Adventist Bible Commentary,* Vol. 7, (1955) p. 983.5.

[57] E. G. White, *The Great Controversy* (1911), p. 440.2.

[58] E. G. White, *The Spirit of Prophecy* (1884), Vol. 4, p. 277.1.

Protestant America will give its power and strength to the beast, in return for a share in power—ten kings who reign one hour with the beast. Perhaps they make some kind of unusual coalition; so unusual that it lasts for only a very short period of time, before it begins to fall apart. The Bible continues describing this relationship.

Revelation 17:14 These shall make war with the Lamb, and the Lamb shall overcome them: for he is Lord of lords, and King of kings: and they that are with him are called, and chosen, and faithful.

In the midst of these momentous, earth-shaking, perhaps frightening events that Scripture reveals will come upon this planet, God reassures us that when persecution kindles, the war is really against Christ. Sometimes Christians get worried about anticipated persecution. But, we have the privilege to remember that it is the lamb they are making war with when they persecute God's people— and the Lamb shall overcome them! This is why the Revelation of Jesus Christ is an amazing message of who Jesus is and what he will accomplish. He will overcome all these powers and peoples who are allied with the beast, for he is Lord of lords and King of kings. Here, in the middle of the dramatic description of the crisis of the ages he presents a most precious promise: "**And they that are with him are called, and chosen, and faithful.**" The Lord Jesus has "called you out of darkness into his marvellous light."[59] "Faithful is he that calleth you, who also will do it."[60] "He hath chosen us in him before the foundation of the world, that we should be holy and without blame before him in love:"[61] May we each be among this special group.

"All that have put on the robe of Christ's righteousness will stand before Him as chosen and faithful and true. Satan has no power to pluck them out of the hand of Christ. Not one soul that in penitence and faith has claimed His protection will Christ permit to pass under the enemy's power. His word is pledged: 'Let him take hold of My strength, that he may make peace with Me; and he shall make peace

---

[59] 1 Peter 2:9

[60] 1 Thessalonians 5:24

[61] Ephesians 1:4

with Me.' Isaiah 27:5. The promise given to Joshua is made to all: 'If thou wilt keep My charge,... I will give thee places to walk among these that stand by.' Zechariah 3:7. Angels of God will walk on either side of them, even in this world, and they will stand at last among the angels that surround the throne of God."[62]

"Let us hold fast the profession of our faith without wavering; (for he is faithful that promised;)"[63] "who shall stablish you, and keep you from evil."[64] Will you believe his Word? No matter what is said, no matter what is done, no matter what inducements or threatenings are made against us, we have been called and chosen and by God's grace we can be faithful to him for he is faithful who gave us this amazing promise.

Revelation 17:15 And he saith unto me, The waters which thou sawest, where the whore sitteth, are peoples, and multitudes, and nations, and tongues.

This verse defines what waters symbolize in Bible prophecy.

Revelation 17:16 And the ten horns which thou sawest upon the beast, these shall hate the whore, and shall make her desolate and naked, and shall eat her flesh, and burn her with fire.

Something happens after an hour of power with the beast, and these ten kings turn on the whore "**and shall make her desolate and naked, and shall eat her flesh, and burn her with fire.**" Jesus reveals that Protestant America will burn Rome.

A woman who committed adultery in Bible times was to be executed by stoning. "If a damsel that is a virgin be betrothed unto an husband, and a man find her in the city, and lie with her... ye shall stone them with stones that they die; the damsel, because she cried not, being in the city; and the man, because he hath humbled his neighbour's wife: so thou shalt put away evil from among you. But if

---

[62] E. G. White, *Counsels for the Church* (1991), p. 351.3.

[63] Hebrews 10:23

[64] 2 Thessalonians 3:3

a man find a betrothed damsel in the field, and the man force her, and lie with her: then the man only that lay with her shall die: But unto the damsel thou shalt do nothing; there is in the damsel no sin worthy of death: for as when a man riseth against his neighbour, and slayeth him, even so is this matter: For he found her in the field, and the betrothed damsel cried, and there was none to save her."[65]

However, there was a different punishment for a woman who was a daughter of a priest. "And the daughter of any priest, if she profane herself by playing the whore, she profaneth her father: she shall be burnt with fire."[66] The common person would be stoned for committing adultery, but the daughter of a priest who committed harlotry was to be burned with fire. Babylon, the mother of harlots, is to be burned with fire. She claims to be the daughter of a priest. She claims to be the voice of God on earth. Because of her claim to purity while playing the whore, God decrees that she is to be burned with fire.

Revelation 17:17 For God hath put in their hearts to fulfil his will, and to agree, and give their kingdom unto the beast, until the words of God shall be fulfilled.

Once the ultimate political One World Order is finally achieved, with the world's greatest powers uniting in opposition against God, those holding the power have no further need of the Catholic church—it only served as a means to their political ends. Therefore, just days after betraying their national sovereignty to the papal beast, the ten kings find themselves fulfilling the word of God by destroying the papal woman. This destabilization of world religion will open the way for the final development of spiritualism. "Satan has long been preparing for his final effort to deceive the world.... Little by little he has prepared the way for his masterpiece of deception in the development of spiritualism. He has not yet reached the full accomplishment of his designs; but it will be reached in the last remnant of time."[67]

---

[65] Deuteronomy 22:23-27

[66] Leviticus 21:9

[67] E. G. White, *The Great Controversy* (1911), p. 561.2.

"As the crowning act in the great drama of deception, Satan himself will personate Christ. The church has long professed to look to the Saviour's advent as the consummation of her hopes. Now the great deceiver will make it appear that Christ has come. In different parts of the earth, Satan will manifest himself among men as a majestic being of dazzling brightness, resembling the description of the Son of God given by John in the Revelation... The glory that surrounds him is unsurpassed by anything that mortal eyes have yet beheld. The shout of triumph rings out upon the air: 'Christ has come! Christ has come!' The people prostrate themselves in adoration before him, while he lifts up his hands and pronounces a blessing upon them, as Christ blessed His disciples when He was upon the earth. His voice is soft and subdued, yet full of melody. In gentle, compassionate tones he presents some of the same gracious, heavenly truths which the Saviour uttered; he heals the diseases of the people, and then, in his assumed character of Christ, he claims to have changed the Sabbath to Sunday, and commands all to hallow the day which he has blessed. He declares that those who persist in keeping holy the seventh day are blaspheming his name by refusing to listen to his angels sent to them with light and truth. This is the strong, almost overmastering delusion....

"But the people of God will not be misled. The teachings of this false christ are not in accordance with the Scriptures. His blessing is pronounced upon the worshipers of the beast and his image, the very class upon whom the Bible declares that God's unmingled wrath shall be poured out.

"And, furthermore, Satan is not permitted to counterfeit the manner of Christ's advent. The Saviour has warned His people against deception upon this point, and has clearly foretold the manner of His second coming.... 'Wherefore if they shall say unto you, Behold, He is in the desert; go not forth; behold, He is in the secret chambers; believe it not. For as the lightning cometh out of the east, and shineth even unto the west; so shall also the coming of the Son of man be.'... This coming there is no possibility of counterfeiting. It will be universally known—witnessed by the whole world.

"Only those who have been diligent students of the Scriptures and who have received the love of the truth will be shielded from the powerful delusion that takes the world captive."[68]

---

[68] E. G. White, *The Great Controversy* (1911), p. 625.1-3

Revelation 17:18 And the woman which thou sawest is that great city, which reigneth over the kings of the earth.

In case there is any doubt over who this woman represents, the angel gives one last identifying mark. There is no city on earth which can be said to reign over the kings of the earth besides Rome—the Vatican. We still use an old saying today, "All roads lead to Rome." God does not want us to partake of the plagues that will be visited upon the woman and her beast. So, he has provided the details for the escape plan and evidence for its authenticity.

In the next chapter, God reveals the plagues to be poured upon the harlot city and her empire. God decrees that one final call will be made, at the very last hour of earth's history; the last warning message to go to this planet, a message that calls his people to come out of Babylon, before it is forever too late. It is a message from a loving God with a broken heart who longs to be reconciled with his people: A God who longs for a people that will allow him to reproduce himself in their lives; that will trust him enough to love not their lives unto death. Our prayer, in preparation for these final events of earth's history, should be that God will loose us from any ties that still bind us to Babylon, and keep us faithful. Amen.

Revelation 18

SUMMARY:

Revelation 18 outlines the plagues that will fall on the harlot, after the call is given (by a fourth angel) for God's people to come out of Babylon that they be not partakers of her sins and receive not of her plagues. Babylon's connection to every aspect of the economy at the end of time is unmasked. The merchants of the earth weep and wail when they see her destruction.

"The mercy of God is shown by his long forbearance. He is holding back his judgments, waiting for the message of warning to be sounded to all. There are many who have not yet heard the testing truths for this time. The last call of mercy is to be given more fully to our world. The truths of the eighteenth and nineteenth chapters of Revelation should be read and understood by all."[1]

Revelation 18:1 And after these things I saw another angel come down from heaven, having great power; and the earth was lightened with his glory.

As with the three angels of Revelation 14, this fourth angel, "**having great power**," represents a message that is taken to the whole world by God's people. "The three angels' messages are to be combined, giving their threefold light to the world. In the Revelation, John says, '**I saw another angel come down from heaven, having great power; and the earth was lightened with his glory**....' This represents the giving of the last and threefold message of warning to the world."[2]

The extent of the message is shown by the fact that "**the earth was lightened with his glory**." "For mine eyes have seen thy **salvation**, Which thou hast prepared before the face of all people; **A light to lighten** the Gentiles, and **the glory** of thy people Israel."[3] The blazing light of salvation; the magnificent message of the everlasting gospel, is to lighten the Gentiles, and is to be the glory of God's

---

[1] E. G. White, *Review and Herald,* July 5, 1906 par. 37.

[2] E. G. White, *Maranatha* (1976), p. 173.5.

[3] Luke 2:30-32

people—spiritual Israel. When the remnant of God give this message with a loud voice; the light of the glory of God illuminates the whole earth.

"And the **glory of the LORD shall be revealed**, and all flesh shall see it together: for the mouth of the LORD hath spoken it. The voice said, Cry. And he said, What shall I cry? All flesh is grass, and all the goodliness thereof is as the flower of the field: The grass withereth, the flower fadeth: **because the spirit of the LORD bloweth upon it:** surely the people is grass. The grass withereth, the flower fadeth: but the word of our God shall stand for ever."[4] Another passage states this very clearly again: Peter quotes the above passage in the New Testament: "For all flesh is as grass, and all the glory of man as the flower of grass. The grass withereth, and the flower thereof falleth away: But the word of the Lord endureth for ever. And this is the word which by the gospel is preached unto you."[5]

The glory of the Lord's character[6] will be revealed in the people of God, which illuminates the earth. The cry is to be given that all flesh is grass. All of man's glory; all of our goodness and righteousness is as the grass and flower of the field that withers and fades away. We can only trust to the righteousness of Christ to overcome the deceptions of Babylon and escape the plagues that will fall on the wicked.

It is the Spirit of God that causes this message to go forth with power, for the "spirit of the LORD bloweth upon"[7] man. "But we all, with open face beholding as in a glass the **glory of the Lord**, are changed into the same image **from glory to glory**, even as **by the Spirit of the Lord**."[8]

The everlasting gospel, the doctrine of Jesus Christ, as given by this angel, is likened to the dew and rain. "Give ear, O ye heavens, and I will speak; and hear, O earth, the words of my mouth.

---

[4] Isaiah 40:5-10; emphasis added.

[5] 1 Peter 1:24-25

[6] See Exodus 33, 18, 19; 34:5-7; see also comments on Revelation 14:1.

[7] Isaiah 40:7

[8] 2 Corinthians 3:18

My doctrine shall drop as the rain, my speech shall distill as the dew, as the small rain upon the tender herb, and as the showers upon the grass:"[9] The rain represents the Holy Spirit which brings new life to the grass.

When the Holy Spirit was poured out on the day of Pentecost upon the disciples, they "spake the word of God with boldness... and with great power gave...witness of the resurrection of the Lord Jesus: and great grace was upon them all."[10] Some mocked the message, saying that the disciples were drunk, and Peter, filled with the Holy Spirit said with a loud voice, " these are not drunken, as ye suppose, seeing it is but the third hour of the day. But this is that which was spoken by the prophet Joel; And it shall come to pass in the last days, saith God, I will pour out of my Spirit upon all flesh: and your sons and your daughters shall prophesy, and your young men shall see visions, and your old men shall dream dreams: And on my servants and on my handmaidens I will pour out in those days of my Spirit; and they shall prophesy: And I will show wonders in heaven above, and signs in the earth beneath; blood, and fire, and vapour of smoke: The sun shall be turned into darkness, and the moon into blood, before that great and notable day of the Lord come: And it shall come to pass, that whosoever shall call on the name of the Lord shall be saved."[11] Peter then commenced to preach unto them the gospel, calling for repentance and confession of sins and acceptance of the Lord Jesus. The prophet Joel had prophesied of the outpouring of the Holy Spirit on Pentecost. A few verses before, the outpouring of God's spirit at the end of time is predicted. "Be glad then, ye children of Zion, and rejoice in the LORD your God: for he hath given you the former rain moderately, and he will cause to come down for you the rain, the former rain, and the latter rain in the first month."[12]

The former rain is the first outpouring of God's Spirit in large measure at Pentecost, while the latter rain is the mighty outpouring just before Jesus comes, when this fourth angel proclaims his message with great power and the earth is lightened with his glory.

---

[9] Deuteronomy 32:1-2

[10] Acts 4:31-33

[11] Acts 2:16:21; See Joel 2:28-32.

[12] Joel 2:23

"It is true that in the time of the end, when God's work in the earth is closing, the earnest efforts put forth by consecrated believers under the guidance of the Holy Spirit are to be accompanied by special tokens of divine favor. Under the figure of the early and the latter rain, that falls in Eastern lands at seedtime and harvest, the Hebrew prophets foretold the bestowal of spiritual grace in extraordinary measure upon God's church. The outpouring of the Spirit in the days of the apostles was the beginning of the early, or former, rain, and glorious was the result. To the end of time the presence of the Spirit is to abide with the true church.

"But near the close of earth's harvest, a special bestowal of spiritual grace is promised to prepare the church for the coming of the Son of man. This outpouring of the Spirit is likened to the falling of the latter rain; and it is for this added power that Christians are to send their petitions to the Lord of the harvest 'in the time of the latter rain.' In response, 'the Lord shall make bright clouds, and give them showers of rain.' 'He will cause to come down . . . the rain, the former rain, and the latter rain,' Zechariah 10:1; Joel 2:23."[13]

This fourth angel's message goes forth with great power and combines with the three angels' messages, swelling into a loud cry.[14] "As the third angel's message swells into a loud cry, great power and glory will attend its proclamation. The faces of God's people will shine with the light of heaven."[15]

Revelation 18:2 And he cried mightily with a strong voice, saying, Babylon the great is fallen, is fallen, and is become the habitation of devils, and the hold of every foul spirit, and a cage of every unclean and hateful bird.

The declaration that Babylon has fallen is a repetition of the second angel's message in Revelation 14, with a specific call that Babylon has now become even more corrupt than before; it is now filled with demonic activity, influenced by spiritualism like never before and has

---

[13] E. G. White, *Acts of the Apostles* (1911), p. 54.2-55.1. See also Proverbs 16:15; Hosea 6:3; James 5:7-8.

[14] "'After these things,' said John, 'I saw another angel come down from heaven, having great power, and the earth was lightened with his glory.' In this illumination, the light of all the three messages is combined."
E. G. White, 1888 Materials, p. 804.3.

[15] E. G. White, *Testimonies for the Church,* Vol. 1 (1868), p. 17.1.

become "**the hold of every foul spirit, and a cage of every unclean and hateful bird**."

"This scripture points forward to a time when the announcement of the fall of Babylon, as made by the second angel of Revelation 14 (verse 8), is to be repeated, **with the additional mention of the corruptions which have been entering the various organizations that constitute Babylon, since that message was first given**, in the summer of 1844. A terrible condition of the religious world is here described. With every rejection of truth the minds of the people will become darker, their hearts more stubborn, until they are entrenched in an infidel hardihood. In defiance of the warnings which God has given, they will continue to trample upon one of the precepts of the Decalogue, until they are led to persecute those who hold it sacred. Christ is set at nought in the contempt placed upon His word and His people. As the teachings of spiritualism are accepted by the churches, the restraint imposed upon the carnal heart is removed, and the profession of religion will become a cloak to conceal the basest iniquity. **A belief in spiritual manifestations opens the door to seducing spirits and doctrines of devils, and thus the influence of evil angels will be felt in the churches**."[16]

There are now various organizations constituting Babylon which have become a conglomeration of false doctrine. Babylon specifically represents Rome and the false doctrines that originate from Rome. At the very end of time it also is comprised of all the daughter churches that have accepted the pagan doctrines of the mother harlot. Babylon now includes financial and economic institutions, media and entertainment organizations, educational systems, and much more—as the rest of this chapter will demonstrate. The mighty call that Babylon is fallen, with the mention of the corruptions entering these organizations, is necessary to alert the true-hearted with an awareness that provides the motivation for leaving Babylon. The Spiritualism that has entered these organizations has made them the habitation of devils.

"A prayerful study of the Bible would show Protestants the real character of the papacy and would cause them to abhor and to shun it; but many are so wise in their own conceit that they feel no need of humbly seeking God that they may be led into the truth. Although

---

[16] E. G. White, *The Great Controversy* (1911), p. 603.2.

priding themselves on their enlightenment, they are ignorant both of the Scriptures and of the power of God. They must have some means of quieting their consciences, and they seek that which is least spiritual and humiliating. What they desire is a method of forgetting God which shall pass as a method of remembering Him. The papacy is well adapted to meet the wants of all these. It is prepared for two classes of mankind, embracing nearly the whole world—those who would be saved by their merits, and those who would be saved in their sins. Here is the secret of its power."[17]

"The church that holds to the word of God is irreconcilably separated from Rome. Protestants were once thus apart from this great church of apostasy, but they have approached more nearly to her, and are still in the path of reconciliation to the Church of Rome. Rome never changes. Her principles have not altered in the least. She has not lessened the breach between herself and Protestants; they have done all the advancing. But what does this argue for the Protestantism of this day? It is the rejection of Bible truth which makes men approach to infidelity. It is a backsliding church that lessens the distance between itself and the Papacy."[18]

"Revelation 18 points to the time when, as the result of rejecting the threefold warning of Revelation 14:6-12, the church will have fully reached the condition foretold by the second angel, and the people of God still in Babylon will be called upon to separate from her communion. This message is the last that will ever be given to the world; and it will accomplish its work."[19]

Revelation 18:3 For all nations have drunk of the wine of the wrath of her fornication, and the kings of the earth have committed fornication with her, and the merchants of the earth are waxed rich through the abundance of her delicacies.

All the nations have drunk of her false doctrines. The kings of the earth have entered an illegitimate alliance with her—combining church and state. The merchants of the earth are gaining riches through her systems.

---

[17] E. G. White, *The Great Controversy* (1911), p. 572.2.

[18] E. G. White, *The Signs of the Times*, February 19, 1894 par. 4.

[19] E. G. White, *The Great Controversy* (1911), p. 390.2.

"The fallen denominational churches are Babylon. Babylon has been fostering poisonous doctrines, the wine of error. This wine of error is made up of false doctrines, such as the natural immortality of the soul, the eternal torment of the wicked, the denial of the pre-existence of Christ prior to His birth in Bethlehem, and advocating and exalting the first day of the week above God's holy and sanctified day. These and kindred errors are presented to the world by the various churches, and thus the Scriptures are fulfilled that say, 'For all nations have drunk of the wine of the wrath of her fornication.' It is a wrath which is created by false doctrines, and when kings and presidents drink this wine of the wrath of her fornication, they are stirred with anger against those who will not come into harmony with the false and satanic heresies which exalt the false sabbath, and lead men to trample underfoot God's memorial."[20]

Revelation 18:4 And I heard another voice from heaven, saying, Come out of her, my people, that ye be not partakers of her sins, and that ye receive not of her plagues.

This is the final warning message, pleading with God's people to come out of Babylon. "**Come out of her, my people**." God has his people in all these different corrupt organizations that have not yet heard the full presentation of the truth and do not realize how infiltrated every aspect of society has become with the maddening influence of Babylon.

"Of Babylon, at the time brought to view in this prophecy, it is declared: 'Her sins have reached unto heaven, and God hath remembered her iniquities.' Revelation 18:5. She has filled up the measure of her guilt, and destruction is about to fall upon her. But God still has a people in Babylon; and before the visitation of His judgments these faithful ones must be called out, that they partake not of her sins and 'receive not of her plagues.' Hence the movement symbolized by the angel coming down from heaven, lightening the earth with his glory and crying mightily with a strong voice, announcing the sins of Babylon. In connection with his message the call is heard: 'Come out of her, My people.' These announcements,

---

[20] E. G. White, *Testimonies to Ministers and Gospel Workers* (1923) p. 61.3.

uniting with the third angel's message, constitute the final warning to be given to the inhabitants of the earth."[21]

"Furthermore, in the eighteenth chapter of the Revelation the people of God are called upon to come out of Babylon. According to this scripture, many of God's people must still be in Babylon. And in what religious bodies are the greater part of the followers of Christ now to be found? Without doubt, in the various churches professing the Protestant faith."[22]

This is a message for all that are true-hearted. All that are still responsive to the Spirit of God will be called out of Babylon, so that there may be one fold and one shepherd. This is a special message of love that Jesus is giving, for he says, "**That ye receive not of her plagues**." The plagues of God will be poured on Babylon. God wants to save his people from destruction. So he gives a final opportunity to avoid the plagues, soon to be poured out, by separating from everything that is associated with Babylon; separating from the world's customs and habits.

"Calamities by land and sea, by fire and flood, by pestilence and famine, by horrible accidents, by earthquakes in divers places, all testify in unmistakable language that the end of all things is at hand, and that great Babylon is coming into remembrance before God. The Lord is even at the door, and men's hearts are failing them for fear, and for looking after those things which shall come upon the earth; for the powers of heaven shall be shaken. But there is a defense for those who keep the commandments of God and the faith of Jesus. The prophet declares, 'Thy righteousness shall go before thee.' Whose righteousness?—The righteousness of Christ. And he continues, 'The glory of the Lord shall be thy rearward.'"[23]

"Angels were sent to aid the mighty angel from heaven, and I heard voices which seemed to sound everywhere, 'Come out of her, My people, that ye be not partakers of her sins, and that ye receive not of her plagues. For her sins have reached unto heaven, and God hath remembered her iniquities.'...

---

[21] E. G. White, *The Great Controversy* (1911), p. 604.1.

[22] *Ibid.*, p. 382.3.

[23] E. G. White, *Signs of the Times*, October 1, 1894 par. 10.

"The light that was shed upon the waiting ones penetrated everywhere, and those in the churches who had any light, who had not heard and rejected the three messages, obeyed the call and left the fallen churches. Many had come to years of accountability since these messages had been given, and the light shone upon them, and they were privileged to choose life or death. Some chose life and took their stand with those who were looking for their Lord and keeping all His commandments. The third message was to do its work; all were to be tested upon it, and the precious ones were to be called out from the religious bodies. A compelling power moved the honest, while the manifestation of the power of God brought a fear and restraint upon their unbelieving relatives and friends so that they dared not, neither had they the power to, hinder those who felt the work of the Spirit of God upon them. The last call was carried even to the poor slaves, and the pious among them poured forth their songs of rapturous joy at the prospect of their happy deliverance. Their masters could not check them; fear and astonishment kept them silent. Mighty miracles were wrought, the sick were healed, and signs and wonders followed the believers. God was in the work, and every saint, fearless of consequences, followed the convictions of his own conscience and united with those who were keeping all the commandments of God; and with power they sounded abroad the third message. I saw that this message will close with power and strength far exceeding the midnight cry.

"Servants of God, endowed with power from on high with their faces lighted up, and shining with holy consecration, went forth to proclaim the message from heaven. Souls that were scattered all through the religious bodies answered to the call, and the precious were hurried out of the doomed churches, as Lot was hurried out of Sodom before her destruction. God's people were strengthened by the excellent glory which rested upon them in rich abundance and prepared them to endure the hour of temptation. I heard everywhere a multitude of voices saying, 'Here is the patience of the saints: here are they that keep the commandments of God, and the faith of Jesus.'"[24]

Revelation 18:5 For her sins have reached unto heaven, and God hath remembered her iniquities.

---

[24] E. G. White, *Early Writings* (1882), p. 277.2-277.2.

Babylon's cup is now so full of iniquities that God will keep silent no longer.

Revelation 18:6 Reward her even as she rewarded you, and double unto her double according to her works: in the cup which she hath filled fill to her double.

Chapter 18 is a continuation of Revelation 17, and the judgments of the great whore referred to there are now to be revealed. The plagues and punishments are to be poured out on this power for the part that she has played in killing the saints, deceiving people throughout the world, and causing the eternal ruin of multitudes.

Revelation 18:7 How much she hath glorified herself, and lived deliciously, so much torment and sorrow give her: for she saith in her heart, I sit a queen, and am no widow, and shall see no sorrow.

Despite her boasting, all her glory and luxury will crumble before her eyes.

Revelation 18:8 Therefore shall her plagues come in one day, death, and mourning, and famine; and she shall be utterly burned with fire: for strong is the Lord God who judgeth her.

The punishment has been specified that is to fall on this harlot woman—who claims to be a follower of Christ and the representative of God on the earth—therefore she must be burned with fire.[25] This begins the expanded description of the retribution mentioned in Revelation 17.

Revelation 18:9 And the kings of the earth, who have committed fornication and lived deliciously with her, shall bewail her, and lament for her, when they shall see the smoke of her burning,

---

[25] See comments on Revelation 17:16.

The kings of the earth recognize the power and prestige that they have gained from this unlawful alliance, and they lament that she is burning.

Revelation 18:10 Standing afar off for the fear of her torment, saying, Alas, alas that great city Babylon, that mighty city! for in one hour is thy judgment come.

Why do they stand afar off for fear of her torment? Nuclear weapons would have the capability of making a stone city burn, and would give a reason for them to stand "**afar off for the fear of her torment**." Time will tell exactly how God's word will be fulfilled. God has pronounced that her plagues will come very quickly with no recourse—"**in one hour is thy judgment come.**"

Revelation 18:11 And the merchants of the earth shall weep and mourn over her; for no man buyeth their merchandise any more:

As a result of the burning of Rome, the merchants of the earth no longer have customers buying their merchandise. The judgment on Rome triggers a massive collapse of the world's economy. All the merchants are weeping and mourning the loss of their revenues because of her destruction. This shows that the papacy controls the world's economy. What kinds of industries are connected to and controlled by the papacy?

Revelation 18:12 The merchandise of gold, and silver, and precious stones, and of pearls, and fine linen, and purple, and silk, and scarlet, and all thyine wood, and all manner vessels of ivory, and all manner vessels of most precious wood, and of brass, and iron, and marble,

The merchandise of gold, and silver, and precious stones specifies the mining and banking industry. She has control of the money. Pearls signify the jewelry industry. She controls the fine linen, purple, silk, and scarlet fabrics—manipulating at will the textile, fashion and clothing industry. Thyine wood is a type of evergreen coniferous in the cyprus family, having burls at the base of the trunk used for decorative woodwork. This represents the logging, milling, and lumber industries and their craftsmen. "**All manner of vessels of ivory**"—she controls the poaching industry. It is illegal to kill elephants, yet the world trade in ivory continues to climb. She controls all manner of vessels of precious wood, and brass, and iron, and marble, and the artisans and manufacturers who make things out of these natural resources. All this is connected to Babylon, and it all begins to crumble. The economic web commences to unravel as these judgments fall.

Revelation 18:13 And cinnamon, and odours, and ointments, and frankincense, and wine, and oil, and fine flour, and wheat, and beasts, and sheep, and horses, and chariots, and slaves, and souls of men.

Babylon is connected to the "**cinnamon, and odours, and ointments, and frankincense**," controlling the perfume and spice industry. She is over the wine, and oil, and fine flour, and wheat; she has control of the food industry, the farming and agriculture. She controls the animal husbandry and meat industry. Babylon has the supremacy with the chariots—the automobile and transportation industries. Babylon controls the empires of oil and coal.

Sadly, she controls the slave market—the illegal trade of human beings. Is there really still slavery? *National Geographic* did a 24-page story in September, 2003, titled *21st Century Slaves*. In this article they listed 116 countries in which more than 100 slaves were sold in 2002. The article described six cases of slavery uncovered in Florida recently. In one case, the Ramos family used about 700 slaves to run their citrus operation. Three members of their family are in prison for 35 years for participation in this traffic. The United States Justice Department held a national training conference on combating slavery and released a statement on July 16, 2004, "Trafficking in persons, a modern day form of slavery, is a serious problem in the United States and throughout the world. Each year, an estimated 600,000-800,000 men, women, and children are trafficked against their will across international borders. Of those, 14,500-17,500 are trafficked into America. Victims are forced into prostitution, or to work in sweatshops, quarries, as domestic labor, or child soldiers, and in many forms of involuntary servitude."[26]

Estimates of the Africans exported during the years of open slavery range from 10 million to 100 million over the 450 years before its outlaw. This would be a rate between 20,000 and 200,000 per year. Compare this number to the Justice Department's current estimate of 600,000-800,000 slaves traded per year. This means the current slave trade is 3-40 times worse than during the years of slavery. Slavery is not the only way that Babylon traffics in the souls of men. Babylon makes merchandize of things that are completely destroying people's lives and souls; such as illegal drugs, tobacco, alcohol, marijuana, music, media, gambling, pornography, prostitution and spiritualistic materials and activities.

"Houses of prostitution, dens of vice, criminal courts, prisons, almshouses, insane asylums, hospitals, all are, to a great degree, filled as a result of the liquor seller's work. Like the mystic Babylon of the Apocalypse, he is dealing in '**slaves, and souls of men.**' Behind the liquor seller stands the mighty destroyer of souls, and every art which earth or hell can devise is employed to draw human beings under his power. In the city and the country, on the railway trains, on the great steamers, in places of business, in the halls of pleasure, in the medical dispensary, even in the church, on the sacred Communion table, his traps are set. Nothing is left undone to create and to foster the desire for intoxicants. On almost every corner stands the public house, with its brilliant lights, its welcome and good cheer, inviting the working man, the wealthy idler, and the unsuspecting youth."[27]

"Appetite is indulged without restraint. Professed followers of Christ are today eating and drinking with the drunken, while their names stand in honored church records. Intemperance benumbs the moral and spiritual powers and prepares the way for indulgence of the lower passions. Multitudes feel under no moral obligation to curb their sensual desires, and they become the slaves of lust. Men are living for the pleasures of sense; for this world and this life alone. Extravagance pervades all circles of society. Integrity is sacrificed for luxury and display. They that make haste to be rich pervert justice

---

[26] https://www.justice.gov/archive/opa/pr/2004/July/04_ag_489.htm retrieved 1-3-2017.

[27] E. G. White, *Ministry of Healing* (1905), p. 338.3.

and oppress the poor, and **'slaves and souls of men'** are still bought and sold. Fraud and bribery and theft stalk unrebuked in high places and in low. The issues of the press teem with records of murder—crimes so cold-blooded and causeless that it seems as though every instinct of humanity were blotted out. And these atrocities have become of so common occurrence that they hardly elicit a comment or awaken surprise. The spirit of anarchy is permeating all nations, and the outbreaks that from time to time excite the horror of the world are but indications of the pent-up fires of passion and lawlessness that, having once escaped control, will fill the earth with woe and desolation. The picture which Inspiration has given of the antediluvian world represents too truly the condition to which modern society is fast hastening. Even now, in the present century, and in professedly Christian lands, there are crimes daily perpetrated as black and terrible as those for which the old-world sinners were destroyed."[28]

Revelation 18:14 And the fruits that thy soul lusted after are departed from thee, and all things which were dainty and goodly are departed from thee, and thou shalt find them no more at all.

Revelation 18:15 The merchants of these things, which were made rich by her, shall stand afar off for the fear of her torment, weeping and wailing,

"Such are the judgments that fall upon Babylon in the day of the visitation of God's wrath. She has filled up the measure of her iniquity; her time has come; she is ripe for destruction.
"When the voice of God turns the captivity of His people, there is a terrible awakening of those who have lost all in the great conflict of life. While probation continued they were blinded by Satan's deceptions, and they justified their course of sin. The rich prided themselves upon their superiority to those who were less favored; but they had obtained their riches by violation of the law of God. They had neglected to feed the hungry, to clothe the naked, to deal justly, and to love mercy. They had sought to exalt themselves and to obtain the homage of their fellow creatures. Now they are stripped of all that made them great and are left destitute and defenseless. They look with terror upon the destruction of the idols which they

---

[28] E. G. White, *Patriarchs and Prophets* (1890), p. 101.3.

preferred before their Maker. They have sold their souls for earthly riches and enjoyments, and have not sought to become rich toward God. The result is, their lives are a failure; their pleasures are now turned to gall, their treasures to corruption. The gain of a lifetime is swept away in a moment. The rich bemoan the destruction of their grand houses, the scattering of their gold and silver. But their lamentations are silenced by the fear that they themselves are to perish with their idols.

"The wicked are filled with regret, not because of their sinful neglect of God and their fellow men, but because God has conquered. They lament that the result is what it is; but they do not repent of their wickedness. They would leave no means untried to conquer if they could."[29]

Revelation 18:16 And saying, Alas, alas, that great city, that was clothed in fine linen, and purple, and scarlet, and decked with gold, and precious stones, and pearls!

Here we see a direct reference to the same attire that she clothed herself with in Revelation 17. "The power that for so many centuries maintained despotic sway over the monarchs of Christendom is Rome. The purple and scarlet color, the gold and precious stones and pearls, vividly picture the magnificence and more than kingly pomp affected by the haughty see of Rome."[30]

Revelation 18:17 For in one hour so great riches is come to nought. And every shipmaster, and all the company in ships, and sailors, and as many as trade by sea, stood afar off,

For the second time it is stated that her destruction comes in one hour. Now every shipmaster is bewailing her. Babylon is connected to and controls the shipping of the world. The whole world's economy crumbles when she is destroyed. The riches the world trusted in and lusted after vanish as a vapor.

---

[29] E. G. White, *The Great Controversy* (1911), p. 653.3-654.2.

[30] *Ibid.*, p. 382.2.

Revelation 18:18 And cried when they saw the smoke of her burning, saying, What city is like unto this great city!

They weep over her because their riches have vanished with her. Though these judgments are falling on a city, the effects transmit to all the merchants of the earth for they are all connected to and controlled by her whoredoms with the kings of the earth.

Revelation 18:19 And they cast dust on their heads, and cried, weeping and wailing, saying, Alas, alas, that great city, wherein were made rich all that had ships in the sea by reason of her costliness! for in one hour is she made desolate.

Revelation 18 is simply an expansion of what the previous chapter already revealed. The ten kings after giving their power to reign with the beast for an hour, hate the whore, eat her flesh, and burn her with fire. Here is the third mention of her destruction coming in one hour.

Revelation 18:20 Rejoice over her, thou heaven, and ye holy apostles and prophets; for God hath avenged you on her.

God's people are instructed to praise the Lord for these destructions, for throughout history they have had to suffer under this power. Apostles, prophets, and saints of God have been persecuted and killed by her lust for blood. Finally, the Bible gives testimony that God's people are able to rejoice because God has brought judgment on this masterpiece of Satan.[31]

Revelation 18:21 And a mighty angel took up a stone like a great millstone, and cast it into the sea, saying, Thus with violence

---

[31] The Catholic Bishop Henry Edward Manning, who was at the time Archbishop of Westminster, states the facts in the most stark terms possible: "Now a system like this [Roman Catholicism] is so unlike anything human, it has upon it notes, tokens, marks so altogether supernatural that men now acknowledge it to be either Christ or Antichrist. There is nothing between these extremes. Most true is this alternative. The Catholic church is either the masterpiece of Satan or the kingdom of the Son of God."
James Cardinal Gibbons, *The Faith of Our Fathers*, p.87.6; 111th printing. ISBN 0-89555-158-6.

shall that great city Babylon be thrown down, and shall be found no more at all.

The angel revealed that this city would be burned with fire. Then with great violence the angel casts the millstone into the sea to demonstrate the violence of the overthrow of Babylon. Jesus said, "But whoso shall offend one of these little ones which believe in me, it were better for him that a millstone were hanged about his neck, and that he were drowned in the depth of the sea."[32]

Revelation 18:22 And the voice of harpers, and musicians, and of pipers, and trumpeters, shall be heard no more at all in thee; and no craftsman, of whatsoever craft he be, shall be found any more in thee; and the sound of a millstone shall be heard no more at all in thee;

Babylon controls the music industry.[33] "The introduction of music into their homes, instead of inciting to holiness and spirituality, has been the means of diverting their minds from the truth. Frivolous songs and the popular sheet music of the day seem congenial to their taste. The instruments of music have taken time which should have been devoted to prayer. Music, when not abused, is a great blessing; but when put to a wrong use, it is a terrible curse. It excites, but does not impart that strength and courage which the Christian can find only at the throne of grace while humbly making known his wants and, with strong cries and tears, pleading for heavenly strength to be fortified against the powerful temptations of the evil one. Satan is leading the young captive. Oh, what can I say to lead them to break his power of infatuation! He is a skillful charmer luring them on to perdition."[34]

"Many Protestants suppose that the Catholic religion is unattractive and that its worship is a dull, meaningless round of ceremony. Here they mistake. While Romanism is based upon deception, it is not a coarse and clumsy imposture. The religious service of the Roman Church is a most impressive ceremonial.... The ear also is captivated. The music is unsurpassed. The rich notes of the deep-

---

[32] Matthew 18:6

[33] See, *Media on the Brain*, directed by Scott Ritsema (Belt of Truth Ministries, 2013), and *Battlefield Hollywood*, directed by Scott and Thom Mayer (Little Light Studios, 2009).

[34] E. G. White, *The Adventist Home* (1952), p. 407.4.

toned organ, blending with the melody of many voices as it swells through the lofty domes and pillared aisles of her grand cathedrals, cannot fail to impress the mind with awe and reverence.

"This outward splendor, pomp, and ceremony, that only mocks the longings of the sin-sick soul, is an evidence of inward corruption. The religion of Christ needs not such attractions to recommend it. In the light shining from the cross, true Christianity appears so pure and lovely that no external decorations can enhance its true worth. It is the beauty of holiness, a meek and quiet spirit, which is of value with God.

"Brilliancy of style is not necessarily an index of pure, elevated thought. High conceptions of art, delicate refinement of taste, often exist in minds that are earthly and sensual. They are often employed by Satan to lead men to forget the necessities of the soul, to lose sight of the future, immortal life, to turn away from their infinite Helper, and to live for this world alone.

"A religion of externals is attractive to the unrenewed heart. The pomp and ceremony of the Catholic worship has a seductive, bewitching power, by which many are deceived; and they come to look upon the Roman Church as the very gate of heaven."[35]

All the activity in the city is gone; everything is silent. It will be deadly still when these judgments fall.

Revelation 18:23 And the light of a candle shall shine no more at all in thee; and the voice of the bridegroom and of the bride shall be heard no more at all in thee: for thy merchants were the great men of the earth; for by thy sorceries were all nations deceived.

Roman Catholicism is particularly associated with the use of candles. The wedding industry, and all that is associated with brides and bridegrooms will collapse.

It is by her **"sorceries"** that all nations are deceived. Certainly, the occult activities of Rome have been a primary influence for deceiving the whole world. It is well known that the Vatican routinely communicates directly with demons and worships Satan. In a radio interview, famed Jesuit author Malachi Martin revealed some of the

---

[35] E. G. White, *The Great Controversy* (1911), p. 566.2-567.2.

darkness of Rome, "'Father, uh, I've got an article here, entitled, Two Eminent Churchmen Agree,'

"'Yes.'

"'Uh, that there actually is—this is a shocker to a lot of people. That there is, there are, Satanic practices going on at the Vatican—could that be true?'

"'Yes. Now, when we say in the Vatican, it's at a certain level, and there's no doubt about it that there have been and still are practices that are, uh, formally, uh, venerating Lucifer, the prince of this world.'"[36]

Clearly the primary meaning of "**sorceries**" is the occult practices and spiritualistic doctrines of Rome. However, the Greek word translated sorceries actually has another meaning that gives us a very important insight.

The word for sorceries in the Greek is: φαρμακεία (pharmakeia), from which we get the English word pharmacy. By their pharmaceuticals; by their drugs, all nations are deceived. Babylon controls the pharmaceutical and medical industries.

Up to 30% of hospitalizations are due to adverse drug events.[37] According to the Centers for Disease Control there were 715,000 in-patient hospital deaths in 2010. This means that approximately 214,000 of those deaths may have been due to adverse drug reactions (ADR). This number corresponds almost exactly to other published data. The *Journal of American Medical Association* published a review of 39 studies from the previous thirty years and stated, "The incidence of serious and fatal ADRs in US hospitals was found to be extremely high."[38] They found the incidence of fatal adverse drug reaction to be 0.32%, which represented 106,000 deaths per year. The review was only counting deaths from properly prescribed and administered medications, in the hospital. If you add to that the 80,000 deaths caused by improperly prescribed medications, adverse drug reactions become the third leading cause

---

[36] *Tares Among the Wheat*, directed by Christian J. Pinto (Adullam Films, LLC, 2012), 2:50:10.

[37] *J Pharmacol Pharmacother*. 2013 December; 4(Suppl1): S73–S77.

[38] J. Lazarou, et. al., "Incidence of Adverse Drug Reactions in Hospitalized Patients," *JAMA*, April 15, 1998, Vol. 279, No. 15.

of death in the United States.[39] Prescriber error, medication error, and adverse events from drugs or surgery kill 225,400 people per year in the U.S., according to data presented in the Journal of American Medical Association.[40] These deaths represent only those deaths that are reported to be caused by the medication. Estimates of reporting rates in published medical literature range from 1% to 15%.[41] Using a conservative 200,000 average annual death rate for reported ADRs and using the most conservative reporting percentage (15%[42]) yields an estimate of total deaths due to drug medication, including those that go unreported, to be 1,320,000 for 2010. Since there were 2,468,435 deaths[43] in 2010, this means that the most conservative estimate for total deaths due to drug medications was 53.5% of deaths for 2010—more than all other causes combined. God already revealed this more than 150 years ago: "I was shown that **more deaths have been caused by drug-taking than from all other causes combined**. If there was in the land one physician in the place of thousands, a vast amount of premature mortality would be prevented. Multitudes of physicians, and multitudes of drugs, have cursed the inhabitants of the earth, and have carried thousands and tens of thousands to untimely graves."[44]

Revelation 18:24 And in her was found the blood of prophets, and of saints, and of all that were slain upon the earth.

This is a very sobering verse. Is this being overstated? Is Babylon really responsible for all the wars, and all the murders that have happened on the earth?

---

[39] Ray Strand, M.D. *Death by Prescription* (Nashville, TN: Thomas Nelson, 2003), p. 8.

[40] Starfield B., "Is U.S. Health Really the Best in the World?," *JAMA* 284 (2000): 483-485.

[41] Quarter Watch, *Monitoring FDA MedWatch Reports*, May 31, 2012. http://www.ismp.org/quarterwatch/pdfs/2011Q4.pdf

[42] The higher fifteen percent reporting rate means the estimated unreported percentage is much lower (85%); therefore, the higher estimated reporting rate is the more conservative figure for estimating the total ADRs. The lower 1% reporting rate would mean that 99% of adverse reaction are unreported. If the 1% reporting estimate was used, we would expect 20,000,000 deaths, which exceeds the total deaths in 2010 by a wide margin. Therefore, the 15% reporting rate is probably much closer to the actual figure.

[43] http://www.cdc.gov/nchs/fastats/deaths.htm

[44] E. G. White, *Spiritual Gifts*, Vol. 4a (1864), p.133.1.

If we go back to the first martyr ever slain, Abel, who was killed by his brother Cain, we find the same system of false doctrine—trusting in the works of man to gain salvation. This has been the system of Babylon throughout all history. Those who built the tower of Babel (from where we get the name Babylon) were trusting in their own works to save them from another flood, since they did not believe God's promise. This tower led to the formalization of the system of Babylon. A careful study of history reveals that the Catholic Church, the inheritor of the mysteries of Babylon,[45] has been responsible for many (all, according to Scripture) of the wars that have plagued the planet since her establishment.

Charles Chiniquy in his book, *Fifty Years in the Church of Rome*, documents Abraham Lincoln's knowledge of the Jesuit involvement in the American civil war: "For it is a fact, which is now evident to me, that, with very few exceptions, every priest and every true Roman Catholic is a determined enemy of liberty... if the American people could learn what I know of the fierce hatred of the generality of the priests of Rome against our institutions, our schools, our most sacred rights, and our so dearly bought liberties, they would drive them away, to-morrow, from among us, or they would shoot them as traitors. This war would never have been possible without the sinister influence of the Jesuits. We owe to Popery that we now see our land reddened with the blood of her noblest sons."[46]

God has promised that because of her terrible wickedness this indictment and these judgments will come upon this Babylonian harlot. We need justice, and a loving God must implement that justice. As necessary as his love and mercy, is punishment for those who are unrepentant and those who continue to perpetrate these evils upon society. Without punishment for evil, there could be no justice. Without justice there could be no love and mercy.

We long for the day when God finishes this difficult work; when he brings to an end sin and suffering; when he terminates deception. May we plead with the Lord to give us strength to make it through these final difficult hours of earth's history and be faithful unto death that he might give us a crown of life.[47] Amen.

---

[45] See the excellent historical work *The Two Babylons; or The Papal Worship Proved to be the Worship of Nimrod and His Wife*, by Alexander Hislop.

[46] Charles Chiniquy, *Fifty Years in the Church of Rome* (1890), p. 697, 699.

[47] Revelation 2:10

Revelation 19

SUMMARY:
Revelation 19 represents the second coming of Jesus as Christ riding on a white horse with a sharp two-edged sword proceeding from his mouth. The wicked are slain, and the fowls feast on their flesh.

Revelation 19:1 And after these things I heard a great voice of much people in heaven, saying, Alleluia; Salvation, and glory, and honour, and power, unto the Lord our God:

"The words will soon be spoken, 'Go your ways, and pour out the vials of the wrath of God upon the earth.' One of the ministers of vengeance declares. 'And I heard the angel of the waters say, Thou art righteous, O Lord, which art, and wast, and shalt be, because Thou hast judged thus.' These heavenly beings, in executing the mandate of God, ask no questions, but do as they are bid. Jehovah of hosts, the Lord God Almighty, the just, the true, and the holy, has given them their work to do. With unswerving fidelity they go forth panoplied in pure white linen, having their breasts girded with golden girdles. And when their task is done, when the last vial of God's wrath is poured out, they return and lay their emptied vials at the feet of the Lord.

"And the next scene is recorded, 'After these things... I heard as it were the voice of a great multitude, and as the voice of many waters, and as the voice of mighty thunderings, saying, Alleluia: for the Lord God Omnipotent reigneth.' They sing the song of Moses and the song of the Lamb. [Revelation 19:1-6]"[1]

"The sinner could not be happy in the companionship of the saints in light, with Jesus, with the Lord of hosts; for on every side will be heard the song of praise and thanksgiving; and honor will be ascribed to the Father and the Son. A song will be raised that the unsanctified, unholy ones have never learned, and it will be out of harmony with their depraved tastes and desires. It will be unbearable to them. The apostle John heard this song. He says, '**I heard a great voice of much people in heaven, saying, Alleluia; Salvation, and**

---

[1] E. G. White, *Testimonies to Ministers and Gospel Workers* (1923), p. 432.1-2.

**glory, and honor, and power, unto the Lord our God: for true
and righteous are his judgments**: ...' It is impossible for the sinner
to enjoy the bliss of heaven."[2]

This verse gives us a preview of the righteous after the second
coming occurs and Jesus has already taken them to heaven.

*Revelation 19:2 For true and righteous are his judgments: for he
hath judged the great whore, which did corrupt the earth with
her fornication, and hath avenged the blood of his servants at
her hand.*

Praise the Lord for this great promise. It is assuring us that even in
our glorified state we will still see the judgments of God against the
great whore, as **"true and righteous."**

*Revelation 19:3 And again they said, Alleluia. And her smoke
rose up for ever and ever.*

The smoke that is rising is the smoke from the burning of
Babylon. The judgments of God have fallen on her, and her
destruction is complete; she will never come to life again.[3] The
passage does not intend eternal torment. How do we know?

First, the verse does not say that she will be tortured throughout
eternity. How could an organization be tortured in this manner?

Second, the time frame encompassed by the words "for ever," in
Scripture, is determined by the context and the testimony of the rest
of Scripture. The same is true in English today. Forever could mean
for all eternity, but we also use it metaphorically. We might say it took
forever to drive from point A to point B, when we do not really mean
all eternity. Scripture also does not always mean eternity when
speaking of forever or eternal. For example, "Even as Sodom and
Gomorrha, and the cities about them in like manner, giving
themselves over to fornication, and going after strange flesh, are set

---

[2] E. G. White, *Review and Herald,* February 17, 1891 par. 5.

[3] See comments on Revelation 14:11.

forth for an example, suffering the vengeance of eternal fire."[4] Sodom and Gomorrah are obviously not still burning today. The Bible here does not intend to mean burning throughout the ceaseless ages of eternity. The words that are used in both Greek and Hebrew translated forever actually mean until the point of disappearance, or until the horizon, which gives the idea that it is a long time but does not always mean for eternity. Further, the fire that consumed them is eternal because it came from God, and God is a consuming fire,[5] but the people themselves are not continuing to burn and suffer. The consequences of the fire are eternal.

Third, this verse is using symbolic language; the smoke rising forever is symbolic of the finality of her punishment.

Revelation 19:4 And the four and twenty elders and the four beasts fell down and worshipped God that sat on the throne, saying, Amen; Alleluia.

Everyone in heaven agrees with the proclamation that God has been just and faithful, and they fall in worship before God as a result of the justice of his judgments. The universe acknowledges the consistency and the justice of God and is bearing testimony to the fact.

Revelation 19:5 And a voice came out of the throne, saying, Praise our God, all ye his servants, and ye that fear him, both small and great.

Revelation 19:6 And I heard as it were the voice of a great multitude, and as the voice of many waters, and as the voice of mighty thunderings, saying, Alleluia: for the Lord God omnipotent reigneth.

"God has given us His holy precepts, because He loves mankind....The law is an expression of the thought of God; when received in Christ, it becomes our thought.... He gave us the precepts of the law that in obeying them we might have joy. When at

---

[4] Jude 1:7

[5] Deuteronomy 4:24; 9:3; Hebrews 12:29

Jesus' birth the angels sang, — 'Glory to God in the highest, And on earth peace, good will toward men' (Luke 2:14), they were declaring the principles of the law which He had come to magnify and make honorable."[6]

"Oh that today the human family could recognize that song! The declaration then made, the note then struck, will swell to the close of time, and resound to the ends of the earth. When the Sun of Righteousness shall arise, with healing in His wings, that song will be re-echoed by the voice of a great multitude, as the voice of many waters, saying, 'Alleluia: for the Lord God omnipotent reigneth.' Revelation 19:6."[7] When does the Sun of Righteousness arise? "The Lord is soon to come; there must be a refining, winnowing process in every church, for there are among us wicked men who do not love the truth. There is need of a transformation of character. Will the church arise and put on her beautiful garments, the righteousness of Christ? It is soon to be seen who are vessels unto honor. 'And after these things I saw another angel come down from heaven, having great power; and the earth was lightened with his glory. And he cried mightily with a strong voice, saying, Babylon the great is fallen, is fallen, and is become the habitation of devils, and the hold of every foul spirit, and a cage of every unclean and hateful bird.' 'Then shall ye return, and discern between the righteous and the wicked, between him that serveth God and him that serveth him not. For, behold, the day cometh, that shall burn as an oven; and all the proud, yea, and all that do wickedly, shall be stubble; and the day that cometh shall burn them up, saith the Lord of hosts, that it shall leave them neither root nor branch. But unto you that fear my name shall the Sun of Righteousness arise with healing in his wings.' "Here are brought plainly to view those who will be vessels unto honor; for they will receive the latter rain. Every soul that continues in sin in the face of the light now shining upon our pathway, will be blinded and accept the delusions of Satan. We are now nearing the close of this world's history. Where are the faithful watchmen on the walls of Zion, who will not slumber, but faithfully declare the time of night? Christ is coming to be admired in all them that believe. How painful it is to contemplate the fact that the Lord Jesus is being kept in the background. How few magnify his grace and exalt his infinite

---

[6] E. G. White, *The Desire of Ages* (1898), p. 308.1.

[7] *Ibid.*, p. 48.1.

compassion and love. There will be no envy, no jealousy, in the hearts of those who seek to be like Jesus in character."[8]

"If we keep our minds stayed upon Christ, he will come unto us as the rain, as the former and latter rain upon the earth. As the Sun of Righteousness, He will arise with healing in His wings. We may grow as the lily, revive as the corn, and grow as the vine."[9]

The Sun of Righteousness arises at the time of the latter rain; the time of the final call to the world portrayed in Revelation 18. There will be a great multitude proclaiming this message with a loud cry. "The third angel proclaims his message in no whispered tones, in no hesitant manner. He cries with a loud voice, while flying swiftly through the midst of heaven. This shows that the work of God's servants is to be earnest and rapidly performed. They must be brave witnesses for the truth. With no shame upon their countenances, with uplifted heads, with the bright beams of the Sun of Righteousness shining upon them, with rejoicing that their redemption draweth nigh, they go forth declaring the last message of mercy to the world."[10]

Revelation 19:7 Let us be glad and rejoice, and give honour to him: for the marriage of the Lamb is come, and his wife hath made herself ready.

"The coming of Christ as our high priest to the most holy place, for the **cleansing of the sanctuary**, brought to view in Daniel 8:14; the coming of the Son of man to the Ancient of Days, as presented in Daniel 7:13; and the coming of the Lord to His temple, foretold by Malachi, are descriptions of the same event; and this is also represented by the **coming of the bridegroom to the marriage**, described by Christ in the parable of the ten virgins, of Matthew 25. "The proclamation, 'Behold, the Bridegroom cometh,' in the summer of 1844, led thousands to expect the immediate advent of the Lord. At the appointed time the Bridegroom came, not to the earth, as the people expected, but to the Ancient of Days in heaven, to the marriage, the reception of His kingdom. 'They that were ready went in with Him to the marriage: and the door was shut.' They were not to

---

[8] E. G. White, *Review and Herald,* March 19, 1895 par. 5-6.

[9] E. G. White, *Selected Messages,* Book 3 (1980), p.204.3.

[10] E. G. White, *Reflecting Christ* (1985), p.347.3.

be present in person at the marriage; for it takes place in heaven, while they are upon the earth. The followers of Christ are to 'wait for their Lord, when He will return from the wedding.' Luke 12:36. But they are to understand His work, and to follow Him by faith as He goes in before God. It is in this sense that they are said to go in to the marriage.

"In the parable it was those that had oil in their vessels with their lamps that went in to the marriage.... And all who through the testimony of the Scriptures accept the same truths, following Christ by faith as He enters in before God to perform the last work of mediation, and at its close to receive His kingdom—all these are represented as going in to the marriage.

"In the parable of Matthew 22 the same figure of the marriage is introduced, and the investigative judgment is clearly represented as taking place before the marriage. Previous to the wedding the king comes in to see the guests, to see if all are attired in the wedding garment, the spotless robe of character washed and made white in the blood of the Lamb. Matthew 22:11; Revelation 7:14. He who is found wanting is cast out, but all who upon examination are seen to have the wedding garment on are accepted of God and accounted worthy of a share in His kingdom and a seat upon His throne. This work of examination of character, of determining who are prepared for the kingdom of God, is that of the investigative judgment, the closing of work in the sanctuary above.

"When the work of investigation shall be ended, when the cases of those who in all ages have professed to be followers of Christ have been examined and decided, then, and not till then, probation will close, and the door of mercy will be shut. Thus in the one short sentence, 'They that were ready went in with Him to the marriage: and the door was shut,' we are carried down through the Saviour's final ministration, to the time when the great work for man's salvation shall be completed."[11]

"By the marriage is represented the union of humanity with divinity; the wedding garment represents the character which all must possess who shall be accounted fit guests for the wedding."[12]

---

[11] E. G. White, *The Great Controversy* (1911), p. 426.1-428.2.

[12] E. G. White, *Christ's Object Lessons* (1900), p. 307.1.
See comments on Revelation 11:15.

Revelation 19:8 And to her was granted that she should be arrayed in fine linen, clean and white: for the fine linen is the righteousness of saints.

The wife of the lamb is the New Jerusalem.[13] The New Jerusalem is the church of heaven, which is to be united with the church on earth.

"The Holy City, the New Jerusalem, which is the capital and representative of the kingdom, is called 'the bride, the Lamb's wife.' Said the angel to John: 'Come hither, I will show thee the bride, the Lamb's wife.' 'He carried me away in the spirit,' says the prophet, 'and showed me that great city, the holy Jerusalem, descending out of heaven from God.' Revelation 21:9, 10. Clearly, then, the bride represents the Holy City, and the virgins that go out to meet the bridegroom are a symbol of the church on earth. In the Revelation the people of God are said to be the guests at the marriage supper. Revelation 19:9. If guests, they cannot be represented also as the bride."[14]

"By the wedding garment in the parable is represented the pure, spotless character which Christ's true followers will possess. To the church it is given '**that she should be arrayed in fine linen, clean and white**,' 'not having spot, or wrinkle, or any such thing.' Revelation 19:8; Ephesians 5:27. The fine linen, says the Scripture, 'is the righteousness of saints.' Revelation 19:8. It is the righteousness of Christ, His own unblemished character, that through faith is imparted to all who receive Him as their personal Saviour."[15]

Revelation 19:9 And he saith unto me, Write, Blessed are they which are called unto the marriage supper of the Lamb. And he saith unto me, These are the true sayings of God.

"I saw that while Jesus was in the most holy place He would be **married** to the New Jerusalem; and after His work should be accomplished in the holiest, He would descend to the earth in kingly

---

[13] Revelation 21:2

[14] E. G. White, *The Great Controversy* (1911), p. 426.2.

[15] E. G. White, *Christ's Object Lessons* (1900), p. 310.1.

power and take to Himself the precious ones who had patiently waited His return."[16] "Having received the kingdom, He will come in His glory, as King of kings and Lord of lords, for the redemption of His people, who are to 'sit down with Abraham, and Isaac, and Jacob,' at His table in His kingdom (Matthew 8:11; Luke 22:30), to partake of **the marriage supper of the Lamb**."[17]

"It is impossible for man to save himself. He may deceive himself in regard to this matter, but he cannot save himself. Christ's righteousness alone can avail for his salvation, and this is the gift of God. **This is the wedding garment in which you may appear as a welcome guest at the marriage supper of the Lamb**. Let faith take hold of Christ without delay, and you will be a new creature in Jesus, a light to the world.[18]

Through the prophetic gift we gain glimpses of the open gates of heaven and a vision of the marriage supper of the lamb, "This temple was supported by seven pillars, all of transparent gold, set with pearls most glorious. The wonderful things I there saw, I cannot describe. Oh, that I could talk in the language of Canaan, then could I tell a little of the glory of the better world. I saw there tables of stone in which the names of the 144,000 were engraved in letters of gold. "After beholding the glory of the temple, we went out, and Jesus left us and went to the city. Soon we heard His lovely voice again, saying: 'Come, My people, you have come out of great tribulation, and done My will, suffered for Me, **come in to supper**; for I will gird Myself and serve you.' We shouted, 'Alleluia, glory,' and entered the city. Here I saw a table of pure silver; it was many miles in length, yet our eyes could extend over it. I saw the fruit of the tree of life, the manna, almonds, figs, pomegranates, grapes, and many other kinds of fruit. I asked Jesus to let me eat of the fruit. He said: 'Not now. Those who eat of the fruit of this land, go back to earth no more. But in a little while, if faithful, you shall both eat of the fruit of the tree of life and drink of the water of the fountain. And,' said He, 'you must go back to the earth again, and relate to others what I have revealed to you.' Then an angel bore me gently down to this dark world. Sometimes I think I can stay here no longer, all things of earth look

---

16 E. G. White, *Early Writings* (1882), p.251.1.

17 E. G. White, *The Great Controversy* (1911), p.426.2.

18 E. G. White, *Selected Message*, Book 1 (1958), p. 331.1.

so dreary. I feel very lonely here, for I have seen a better land. Oh that I had wings like a dove, then would I fly away and be at rest."[19]

A blessing is pronounced on those who are called to the marriage supper of the Lamb. What a supper it will be!

This is the first of two suppers in Revelation. All are invited to this supper, but not all will come. The second supper, the supper of the birds,[20] is not a meal one would wish to attend.

"**'These are the true sayings of God,'**.... Why is this statement made?—Because it is in contradiction to the statements made by the world that Christ changed the seventh-day Sabbath to the first day of the week. There are thousands upon thousands who bear aloft the standard of the world's sabbath, exalting the image of the papacy created by the man of sin. The church[es] worship the image of the beast, and receive his mark, even as the inhabitants of Babylon worshiped the golden image which Nebuchadnezzar set up in the Plain of Dura."[21]

Revelation 19:10 And I fell at his feet to worship him. And he said unto me, See thou do it not: I am thy fellowservant, and of thy brethren that have the testimony of Jesus: worship God: for the testimony of Jesus is the spirit of prophecy.

As John sees this heavenly being, he is overcome with his glory and majesty and falls down at his feet to worship him. But this is an angel that is a created being. There are places in the Bible where an angel accepts worship, but when that happens we know that angel is actually God. No created angel loyal to God would accept worship. This angel is obviously a created being, because he firmly reproves John, saying, "**See thou do it not: I am thy fellowservant, and of thy brethren that have the testimony of Jesus: worship God.**"

The angel then defines the "**testimony of Jesus**" as "**the spirit of prophecy.**" Jesus has given a special message to his servants the

---

[19] E. G. White, *Testimonies for the Church*, Vol. 1 (1868), p.69.1-2.

[20] Revelation 19:17

[21] E. G. White, General Conference Daily Bulletin, March 7, 1899 par. 5.

prophets through the spirit of prophecy. If we want to labor with him, we are to accept that testimony of Jesus. We are to accept the things that God reveals to us, through his servants the prophets, and follow them.[22] "Believe in the LORD your God, so shall ye be established; believe his prophets, so shall ye prosper."[23]

Revelation 19:11 And I saw heaven opened, and behold a white horse; and he that sat upon him was called Faithful and True, and in righteousness he doth judge and make war.

Who is this man on the white horse? In these few verses there are over twelve identifying marks that tell us that this is Jesus Christ himself.

He is **"called Faithful and True:"** "Jesus Christ, who is the faithful witness...."[24] "and hath given us an understanding, that we may know him that is true, and we are in him that is true, even in his Son Jesus Christ. This is the true God, and eternal life."[25]

Jesus Christ is the judge, **"for in righteousness he doth judge and make war:"** "For the Father judgeth no man, but hath committed all judgment unto the Son."[26]

Revelation 19:12 His eyes were as a flame of fire, and on his head were many crowns; and he had a name written, that no man knew, but he himself.

In the description of Christ in Revelation 1:13-16, **"his eyes were as a flame of fire."**

---

[22] For more on the spirit of prophecy see comments on Daniel 10:17.

[23] 2 Chronicles 20:20

[24] Revelation 1:5

[25] 1 John 5:20

[26] John 5:22

Jesus is the one "crowned with glory and honor"[27] No longer is he crowned with the crown of thorns as when he was sacrificed for man, but now he wears the crowns of victory.

Revelation 19:13 And he was clothed with a vesture dipped in blood: and his name is called The Word of God.

He whose vesture was dipped in blood for you and me is none other than the Lord Jesus.

One of the most obvious identifying marks is his name: "**His name is called The Word of God.**" "In the beginning was the Word, and the Word was with God, and the Word was God. The same was in the beginning with God. All things were made by him; and without him was not any thing made that was made. And the Word was made flesh, and dwelt among us, (and we beheld his glory, the glory as of the only begotten of the Father,) full of grace and truth."[28]

The Lord Jesus Christ, "God... manifest in the flesh... received up into glory,"[29] promised us almost 2,000 years ago that he would come again to take us home with him. In these verses he is on his way to rescue his people. This is the blessed hope; long talked of, long hoped for—this day has been contemplated with eager anticipation by sons and daughters of God throughout the ages.

Revelation 19:14 And the armies which were in heaven followed him upon white horses, clothed in fine linen, white and clean.

The entire army of heaven, clothed in the perfection of Christ, is on its way to this earth. Not one would miss this event for anything.

Revelation 19:15 And out of his mouth goeth a sharp sword, that with it he should smite the nations: and he shall rule them

---

[27] Hebrews 2:9

[28] John 1:1-3, 14

[29] 1 Timothy 3:16

***with a rod of iron: and he treadeth the winepress of the
fierceness and wrath of Almighty God.***

In the description of Jesus in Revelation 1, we read "out of his mouth
went a sharp twoedged sword."[30] Ephesians 6:17 defines the
symbolism of the sword, "And take the helmet of salvation, and the
sword of the Spirit, which is the word of God." The sword is the word
of God and it is the word of God that smites the nations. Jesus said
"And if any man hear my words, and believe not, I judge him not: for I
came not to judge the world, but to save the world. He that rejecteth
me, and receiveth not my words, hath one that judgeth him: **the
word that I have spoken, the same shall judge him in the last
day**."[31] "For the word of God is quick, and powerful, and sharper than
any twoedged sword, piercing even to the dividing asunder of soul
and spirit, and of the joints and marrow, and is a discerner of the
thoughts and intents of the heart."[32] If we do not let that sword do its
work in our lives now to take away sin, we will be slain by the same
sword when Jesus comes in the clouds of heaven.

Ruling "**with a rod of iron**" is the pouring out of his final judgment
and punishment. "Thou shalt break them with a rod of iron; thou shalt
dash them in pieces like a potter's vessel."[33] "And she brought forth a
man child, who was to rule all nations with a rod of iron: and her child
was caught up unto God, and to his throne."[34]

***Revelation 19:16 And he hath on his vesture and on his thigh a
name written, KING OF KINGS, AND LORD OF LORDS.***

"The heavenly gates are again to be lifted up, and with ten thousand
times ten thousand and thousands of thousands of holy ones, our
Saviour will come forth as **King of kings and Lord of lords**.
Jehovah Immanuel 'shall be king over all the earth: in that day shall
there be one Lord, and His name one.' 'The tabernacle of God' shall
be with men, 'and He will dwell with them, and they shall be His

---

[30] Revelation 1:16

[31] John 12:47-48

[32] Hebrews 4:12

[33] Psalms 2:9

[34] Revelation 12:5

people, and God Himself shall be with them, and be their God.'
Zechariah 14:9; Revelation 21:3."[35]

*Revelation 19:17 And I saw an angel standing in the sun; and he
cried with a loud voice, saying to all the fowls that fly in the
midst of heaven, Come and gather yourselves together unto the
supper of the great God;*

This is the second supper mentioned in Revelation. Those who do
not accept the invitation to the supper of the Lamb will be at the
supper of the birds—as the menu.

A type of this event occurred when David faced the giant. When
young David arrived at the battle against the Philistines, and heard
the outrage of Goliath's threats against Israel, he said, "Who is this
uncircumcised Philistine, that he should defy the armies of the living
God?" David offered to fight the Philistine and as he neared Goliath
he said, "Thou comest to me with a sword, and with a spear, and
with a shield: but I come to thee in the name of the LORD of hosts,
the God of the armies of Israel, whom thou hast defied. This day will
the LORD deliver thee into mine hand; and I will smite thee, and take
thine head from thee; and I will give the carcases of the host of the
Philistines this day unto the fowls of the air, and to the wild beasts of
the earth; that all the earth may know that there is a God in Israel.
And all this assembly shall know that the LORD saveth not with
sword and spear: for the battle is the LORD's, and he will give you
into our hands."[36]

*Revelation 19:18 That ye may eat the flesh of kings, and the
flesh of captains, and the flesh of mighty men, and the flesh of
horses, and of them that sit on them, and the flesh of all men,
both free and bond, both small and great.*

This supper will be a gruesome supper for the birds who are invited
to eat the flesh of the wicked—those who are slain by the brightness
of the coming of the Son of David.

---

[35] E. G. White, *Thoughts from the Mount of Blessings* (1896), p. 108.2.

[36] 1 Samuel 17:26, 45-47

"Doth the eagle mount up at thy command, and make her nest on high? She dwelleth and abideth on the rock, upon the crag of the rock, and the strong place. From thence she seeketh the prey, and her eyes behold afar off. Her young ones also suck up blood: and where the slain are, there is she."[37] "And he said unto them, Wheresoever the body is, thither will the eagles be gathered together."[38]

"I then beheld the earth. The wicked were dead, and their bodies were lying upon the face of the earth. The inhabitants of earth had suffered the wrath of God in the seven last plagues. They had gnawed their tongues for pain and had cursed God. The false shepherds were signal objects of Jehovah's wrath. Their eyes had consumed away in their holes, and their tongues in their mouths, while they stood upon their feet.[39] After the saints were delivered by the voice of God, the rage of the wicked multitude was turned upon each other. The earth seemed to be deluged with blood, and dead bodies were from one end of the earth to the other."[40]

Revelation 19:19 And I saw the beast, and the kings of the earth, and their armies, gathered together to make war against him that sat on the horse, and against his army.

At this point the woman was already punished when the ten kings hated the whore, ate her flesh, and burned her with fire.[41] They destroyed the women, or the Roman Catholic church,[42] but the beast from the bottomless pit is still in existence. Apostate Protestantism who had made a coalition with the papacy and with the kings of the earth and their armies, are now going to make war against Jesus Christ and his army when he comes. As you can imagine, this will be a fruitless endeavor. Almost all the world will prepare to fight against the king of glory as he comes in the clouds of heaven. "These shall make war with the Lamb, and the Lamb shall overcome them: for he

---

[37] Job 39:27

[38] Luke 17:34-37

[39] Zechariah 14:12

[40] E. G. White, *Spiritual Gifts*, Vol. 1 (1858), p. 211.1.

[41] See comments on Revelation 17:16; 18.

[42] Revelation 17:13-18

is Lord of lords, and King of kings: and they that are with him are called, and chosen, and faithful."[43]

The same battle is outlined in Revelation 16:14-16, "For they are the spirits of devils, working miracles, which go forth unto the kings of the earth and of the whole world, to gather them to the battle of that great day of God Almighty. And he gathered them together into a place called in the Hebrew tongue Armageddon."

The kings of the earth and the spirits of devils are actually cooperating together for this battle. This is the great battle of Armageddon.[44]

"A terrible conflict is before us. We are nearing the battle of the great day of God Almighty. That which has been held in control is to be let loose. The angel of mercy is folding her wings, preparing to step down from the throne and leave the world to the control of Satan. The principalities and powers of earth are in bitter revolt against the God of heaven. They are filled with hatred against those who serve Him, and soon, very soon, will be fought the last great battle between good and evil. The earth is to be the battle field—the scene of the final contest and the final victory. Here, where for so long Satan has led men against God, rebellion is to be forever suppressed."[45]

Revelation 19:20 And the beast was taken, and with him the false prophet that wrought miracles before him, with which he deceived them that had received the mark of the beast, and them that worshipped his image. These both were cast alive into a lake of fire burning with brimstone.

The fire that burns the beast and the false prophet was prophesied in 2 Thessalonians 2:8, "And then shall that Wicked be revealed, whom the Lord shall consume with the spirit of his mouth, and shall destroy with the brightness of his coming."

---

[43] Revelation 17:14

[44] See comments on Revelation 16.

[45] E. G. White, *Last Day Events* (1992), p. 250.1.

The beast is the political power of the papacy. The false prophet is apostate Protestant America—a country that claimed to have the principles and characteristics of Christ himself, but began to speak as a dragon. These two are cast alive into a lake of fire burning with brimstone. There will be some fire and brimstone at the time of the second coming, which will burn these two powers. But this is not the final lake of fire called hellfire.[46]

Revelation 19:21 And the remnant were slain with the sword of him that sat upon the horse, which sword proceeded out of his mouth: and all the fowls were filled with their flesh.

The wicked are slain by the word of God. While Jesus is catching up the righteous into the clouds, to meet him in the air, the wicked are slain with the brightness of his coming. Then begins the supper of the birds.

"At the coming of Christ the wicked are blotted from the face of the whole earth—consumed with the spirit of His mouth and destroyed by the brightness of His glory. Christ takes His people to the City of God, and the earth is emptied of its inhabitants. 'Behold, the Lord maketh the earth empty, and maketh it waste, and turneth it upside down, and scattereth abroad the inhabitants thereof.' 'The land shall be utterly emptied, and utterly spoiled: for the Lord hath spoken this word.' 'Because they have transgressed the laws, changed the ordinance, broken the everlasting covenant. Therefore hath the curse devoured the earth, and they that dwell therein are desolate: therefore the inhabitants of the earth are burned.' Isaiah 24:1, 3, 5, 6. The whole earth appears like a desolate wilderness. The ruins of cities and villages destroyed by the earthquake, uprooted trees, ragged rocks thrown out by the sea or torn out of the earth itself, are scattered over its surface, while vast caverns mark the spot where the mountains have been rent from their foundations."[47]

Now the earth is in complete destruction and desolate. "I beheld the earth, and, lo, it was without form, and void; and the heavens, and they had no light. I beheld the mountains, and, lo, they trembled, and all the hills moved lightly. I beheld, and, lo, there was no man, and all

---

[46] Hellfire will be covered in more detail in chapter 20.

[47] E. G. White, *The Great Controversy* (1911), p. 657.1-2.

the birds of the heavens were fled. I beheld, and, lo, the fruitful place was a wilderness, and all the cities thereof were broken down at the presence of the LORD, and by his fierce anger. For thus hath the LORD said, The whole land shall be desolate; yet will I not make a full end."[48]

This is not yet the full end. God is not completely finished with the plan of redemption. He has rescued his faithful people who have accepted his righteousness in place of their filthy rags, but the wicked are slain and the earth lies in ruins awaiting the full end and a new beginning. Amen.

---

[48] Jeremiah 4:23-27

Revelation 20

SUMMARY:
Revelation 20 outlines the one thousand years, or millennium, in which all the wicked are dead on the earth, the righteous have been taken to heaven at the second coming of Jesus, and Satan and his angels are restricted to earth with nothing to do but think about the ruin they have caused. Then the righteous participate in the final sentencing of the wicked (verse 4). At the end of the millennium, the New Jerusalem comes down from God out of heaven, the wicked dead are raised to life to receive their punishment, and the wicked prepare to take the city by force. Once they march on the city, the final battle of the universe is fought—Gog and Magog. Fire comes down from God out of heaven and devours the wicked with Satan and his angels. Death and hell are the final enemies to be forever destroyed.

Revelation 20:1 And I saw an angel come down from heaven, having the key of the bottomless pit and a great chain in his hand.

This is a holy angel as he comes "**down from heaven**." In Revelation 9 the star that fell from heaven was given the key to the bottomless pit. Coming down from heaven and falling from heaven are distinctly different terms. An angel that comes down is being sent on a mission by God. An angel that falls from heaven is an angel that has been evicted. Notice the wording regarding the fallen angel, "And the fifth angel sounded, and I saw a star fall from heaven unto the earth: and to him was given the key of the bottomless pit. And they had a king over them, which is the angel of the bottomless pit, whose name in the Hebrew tongue is Abaddon, but in the Greek tongue hath his name Apollyon."[1] Abaddon and Apollyon both mean destroyer, which is a fit name for Satan. Satan is given liberty from the bottomless pit for a short time.[2]

---

[1] Revelation 9:1, 11

[2] See comments on Revelation 9.

Now a heavenly angel has the key to the bottomless pit, indicating that it has been removed from Satan's possession. God is in the process of conquering every aspect of Satan's dominion.

What is the bottomless pit? "And when he was come to the other side into the country of the Gergesenes, there met him two possessed with devils, coming out of the tombs, exceeding fierce, so that no man might pass by that way. And, behold, they cried out, saying, What have we to do with thee, Jesus, thou Son of God? art thou come hither to torment us before the time?"[3] Luke 8:29, 31 relating the same story says "For he had commanded the unclean spirit to come out of the man... And they besought him that he would not command them to go out into the deep." After possessing a human, the devils did not want to be returned to their state of restriction.

The word translated 'deep' in Luke is the same Greek word 'ἀβυσσος - abussos' translated bottomless pit in Revelation 20:1.

"That the expression 'bottomless pit' represents the earth in a state of confusion and darkness is evident from other scriptures. Concerning the condition of the earth 'in the beginning,' the Bible record says that it 'was without form, and void; and darkness was upon the face of the deep.' Genesis 1:2. Prophecy teaches that it will be brought back, partially at least, to this condition. Looking forward to the great day of God, the prophet Jeremiah declares: 'I beheld the earth, and, lo, it was without form, and void; and the heavens, and they had no light. I beheld the mountains, and, lo, they trembled, and all the hills moved lightly. I beheld, and, lo, there was no man, and all the birds of the heavens were fled. I beheld, and, lo, the fruitful place was a wilderness, and all the cities thereof were broken down.' Jeremiah 4:23-26."[4]

Revelation 20:2 And he laid hold on the dragon, that old serpent, which is the Devil, and Satan, and bound him a thousand years,

---

[3] Matthew 8:28-29

[4] E. G. White, *The Great Controversy* (1911), p. 658.3.

One of God's angels who now has the key to the bottomless pit places Satan under lock and key for a thousand years—this is the millennium. Satan and his angels will be incarcerated on earth during this thousand-year period.

"Now the event takes place foreshadowed in the last solemn service of the Day of Atonement. When the ministration in the holy of holies had been completed, and the sins of Israel had been removed from the sanctuary by virtue of the blood of the sin offering, then the scapegoat was presented alive before the Lord; and in the presence of the congregation the high priest confessed over him 'all the iniquities of the children of Israel, and all their transgressions in all their sins, putting them upon the head of the goat.' Leviticus 16:21. In like manner, when the work of atonement in the heavenly sanctuary has been completed, then in the presence of God and heavenly angels and the hosts of the redeemed the sins of God's people will be placed upon Satan; he will be declared guilty of all the evil which he has caused them to commit. And as the scapegoat was sent away into a land not inhabited, so Satan will be banished to the desolate earth, an uninhabited and dreary wilderness."[5]

Revelation 20:3 And cast him into the bottomless pit, and shut him up, and set a seal upon him, that he should deceive the nations no more, till the thousand years should be fulfilled: and after that he must be loosed a little season.

Satan will be incarcerated on earth for one thousand years, with no one to tempt, deceive, harass or destroy. At the end of the thousand years he will be loosed a little season. One final opportunity will be granted for Satan to deceive the nations again.

"At the coming of Christ the wicked are blotted from the face of the whole earth—consumed with the spirit of His mouth and destroyed by the brightness of His glory. Christ takes His people to the City of God, and the earth is emptied of its inhabitants. 'Behold, the Lord maketh the earth empty, and maketh it waste, and turneth it upside down, and scattereth abroad the inhabitants thereof.' 'The land shall be utterly emptied, and utterly spoiled: for the Lord hath spoken this word.' 'Because they have transgressed the laws, changed the

---

[5] E. G. White, *The Great Controversy* (1911), p. 658.1.

ordinance, broken the everlasting covenant. Therefore hath the curse devoured the earth, and they that dwell therein are desolate: therefore the inhabitants of the earth are burned.' Isaiah 24:1, 3, 5, 6. "The whole earth appears like a desolate wilderness. The ruins of cities and villages destroyed by the earthquake, uprooted trees, ragged rocks thrown out by the sea or torn out of the earth itself, are scattered over its surface, while vast caverns mark the spot where the mountains have been rent from their foundations...

"The revelator foretells the banishment of Satan and the condition of chaos and desolation to which the earth is to be reduced, and he declares that this condition will exist for a thousand years. After presenting the scenes of the Lord's second coming and the destruction of the wicked, the prophecy continues: 'I saw an angel come down from heaven, having the key of the bottomless pit and a great chain in his hand. And he laid hold on the dragon, that old serpent, which is the devil, and Satan, and bound him a thousand years, and cast him into the bottomless pit, and shut him up, and set a seal upon him, that he should deceive the nations no more, till the thousand years should be fulfilled: and after that he must be loosed a little season.' Revelation 20:1-3....

"For six thousand years, Satan's work of rebellion has 'made the earth to tremble.' He had 'made the world as a wilderness, and destroyed the cities thereof.' And he 'opened not the house of his prisoners.' For six thousand years his prison house has received God's people, and he would have held them captive forever; but Christ had broken his bonds and set the prisoners free.

"Even the wicked are now placed beyond the power of Satan, and alone with his evil angels he remains to realize the effect of the curse which sin has brought. 'The kings of the nations, even all of them, lie in glory, everyone in his own house [the grave]. But thou art cast out of thy grave like an abominable branch.... Thou shalt not be joined with them in burial, because thou hast destroyed thy land, and slain thy people.' Isaiah 14:18-20.

"For a thousand years, Satan will wander to and fro in the desolate earth to behold the results of his rebellion against the law of God. During this time his sufferings are intense. Since his fall his life of unceasing activity has banished reflection; but he is now deprived of his power and left to contemplate the part which he has acted since first he rebelled against the government of heaven, and to look forward with trembling and terror to the dreadful future when he must suffer for all the evil that he has done and be punished for the sins that he has caused to be committed.

"To God's people the captivity of Satan will bring gladness and rejoicing. Says the prophet: 'It shall come to pass in the day that Jehovah shall give thee rest from thy sorrow, and from thy trouble, and from the hard service wherein thou wast made to serve, that thou shalt take up this parable against the king of Babylon here representing Satan, and say, How hath the oppressor ceased! . . . Jehovah hath broken the staff of the wicked, the scepter of the rulers; that smote the peoples in wrath with a continual stroke, that ruled the nations in anger, with a persecution that none restrained.'"[6]

Revelation 20:4 And I saw thrones, and they sat upon them, and judgment was given unto them: and I saw the souls of them that were beheaded for the witness of Jesus, and for the word of God, and which had not worshipped the beast, neither his image, neither had received his mark upon their foreheads, or in their hands; and they lived and reigned with Christ a thousand years.

These souls are the redeemed. They are not disembodied spirits, they are souls—real live people.[7] They live and reign with Christ for a thousand years and "**judgment was given unto them.**" Scripture elsewhere tells us that the righteous will participate in the judgment of the wicked and the evil angels. "Do ye not know that the saints shall judge the world? and if the world shall be judged by you, are ye unworthy to judge the smallest matters? Know ye not that we shall judge angels? how much more things that pertain to this life?"[8]

The saints will judge the world and even angels—the fallen angels, who joined Satan's rebellion. The judgment the righteous participate in is not deciding who are saved and lost, for this is already done when Jesus comes.[9] The saints participate in the sentencing—the

---

[6] E. G. White, *The Great Controversy* (1911), p. 657.1-660.2.

[7] Genesis 2:7

[8] 1 Corinthians 6:2-3

[9] Revelation 22:11-12 "He that is unjust, let him be unjust still: and he which is filthy, let him be filthy still: and he that is righteous, let him be righteous still: and he that is holy, let him be holy still. And, behold, I come quickly; and my reward is with me, to give every man according as his work shall be."
When Jesus comes he brings his reward with him; the decisions of destiny have been made based on the evidence of deeds committed. Any sins not covered with the blood of Jesus will be born by the guilty individual.

decision regarding the severity of punishment each of the wicked is to suffer. God involves the redeemed in this process of judgment so they are satisfied with the mercy and justice of the decisions made. God will not make these decisions by himself.

"Praise ye the LORD. Sing unto the LORD a new song, and his praise in the congregation of saints... For the LORD taketh pleasure in his people: he will beautify the meek with salvation. Let the saints be joyful in glory: let them sing aloud upon their beds. Let the high praises of God be in their mouth, and a twoedged sword in their hand; To execute vengeance upon the heathen, and punishments upon the people; To bind their kings with chains, and their nobles with fetters of iron; To execute upon them the judgment written: this honour have all his saints. Praise ye the LORD."[10]

The saints have twoedged swords in their hands. The word of God is the twoedged sword.[11] And Jesus said: "And if any man hear my words, and believe not, I judge him not: for I came not to judge the world, but to save the world. He that rejecteth me, and receiveth not my words, hath one that judgeth him: the word that I have spoken, the same shall judge him in the last day."[12]

It is by the word of God that the saints execute vengeance on the heathen, and decide the punishment that each of the wicked will face at the end of the millennium.

"Then I saw thrones, and Jesus and the redeemed saints sat upon them; and the saints reigned as kings and priests unto God. Christ, in union with His people, judged the wicked dead, comparing their acts with the statute book, the word of God, and deciding every case according to the deeds done in the body. Then they meted out to the wicked the portion which they must suffer, according to their works; and it was written against their names in the book of death. Satan also and his angels were judged by Jesus and the saints. Satan's punishment was to be far greater than that of those whom he had deceived. His suffering would so far exceed theirs as to bear no

---

[10] Psalm 149:1-9

[11] Ephesians 6:17; Hebrews 4:12

[12] John 12:47-48

comparison with it. After all those whom he had deceived had perished, Satan was still to live and suffer on much longer."[13]

Revelation 20:5 But the rest of the dead lived not again until the thousand years were finished. This is the first resurrection.

If the wicked dead do not live again **until** the thousand years are finished this means that they are to be brought back to life at the end of the thousand years. God will resurrect the wicked from death.

The first sentence of this verse is a parenthetical statement. The last sentence of this verse: **"This is the first resurrection,"** does not refer to the sentence immediately preceding, rather it refers to everything that has been previously outlined about the judgment and the fact that the righteous are living and reigning with Christ. The flow of the previous verses in relation to this parenthesis is that Satan is bound to the earth during the thousand years, that the redeemed are in heaven judging him and the wicked, and they reign with Christ a thousand years "**(but the rest of the dead lived not again until the thousand years were finished); this is the first resurrection.**"

Between explaining what the righteous are doing during the thousand years and the stating that those who are in heaven are a part of the first resurrection, the angel inserts a parenthetical statement to tell us that, by the way, the wicked during this thousand years are dead on the earth. It becomes very clear that this is the case in the next verse.

Revelation 20:6 Blessed and holy is he that hath part in the first resurrection: on such the second death hath no power, but they shall be priests of God and of Christ, and shall reign with him a thousand years.

Those that have a part in the first resurrection are those who reign with Christ a thousand years; they are the redeemed of the earth. This is that resurrection we want to be part of, for then the second death will have no power over us.

---

[13] E. G. White, *Early Writings* (1882), p. 290.3.

The second resurrection occurs at the end of the millennium after the saints have finished the process of judgment in heaven. It is the resurrection of the wicked.

Revelation 20:7 And when the thousand years are expired, Satan shall be loosed out of his prison,

Repeated[14] are those revealing words that Satan will "**be loosed out of his prison**." Bound by circumstances for a thousand years Satan has been in the virtual prison of the desolated earth. The resurrection of the wicked, by Christ, provides Satan with subjects for one final battle. Satan and his angels are now released from their solitary confinement.

"After the judgment of the wicked dead had been finished, at the end of the one thousand years, Jesus left the city, and the saints and a train of the angelic host followed Him. Jesus descended upon a great mountain, which as soon as His feet touched it, parted asunder and became a mighty plain. Then we looked up and saw the great and beautiful city.... And it came down in all its splendor and dazzling glory and settled in the mighty plain which Jesus had prepared for it. "Then Jesus and all the retinue of holy angels, and all the redeemed saints, left the city. The angels surrounded their Commander and escorted Him on His way, and the train of redeemed saints followed. **Then, in terrible, fearful majesty, Jesus called forth the wicked dead**; and they came up with the same feeble, sickly bodies that went into the grave. What a spectacle! what a scene! At the first resurrection all came forth in immortal bloom; but at the second the marks of the curse are visible on all. The kings and noblemen of the earth, the mean and low, the learned and unlearned, come forth together. All behold the Son of man; and those very men who despised and mocked Him, who put the crown of thorns upon His sacred brow, and smote Him with the reed, behold Him in all His kingly majesty. Those who spit upon Him in the hour of His trial now turn from His piercing gaze and from the glory of His countenance. Those who drove the nails through His hands and feet now look upon the marks of His crucifixion. Those who thrust the spear into His side behold the marks of their cruelty on His body. And they know that He is the very one whom they crucified and derided in His

---

[14] Revelation 20:3

expiring agony. And then there arises one long protracted wail of agony, as they flee to hide from the presence of the King of kings and Lord of lords.

"All are seeking to hide in the rocks, to shield themselves from the terrible glory of Him whom they once despised. And, overwhelmed and pained with His majesty and exceeding glory, they with one accord raise their voices, and with terrible distinctness exclaim, 'Blessed is He that cometh in the name of the Lord!'

"Then Jesus and the holy angels, accompanied by all the saints, again go to the city, and the bitter lamentations and wailings of the doomed wicked fill the air...."[15]

Revelation 20:8 And shall go out to deceive the nations which are in the four quarters of the earth, Gog and Magog, to gather them together to battle: the number of whom is as the sand of the sea.

Satan goes forth to deceive the nations for the last time. He gathers them together for a second battle. The battle of Armageddon occurred at the second coming. This battle, Gog and Magog, occurs after God resurrects the wicked at the end of the 1,000 years. Satan rallies them together and convinces them that they can kill God and the righteous and take the glories of the New Jerusalem by force.

"Now Satan prepares for a last mighty struggle for the supremacy. While deprived of his power and cut off from his work of deception, the prince of evil was miserable and dejected; but as the wicked dead are raised and he sees the vast multitudes upon his side, his hopes revive, and he determines not to yield the great controversy. He will marshal all the armies of the lost under his banner and through them endeavor to execute his plans. The wicked are Satan's captives. In rejecting Christ they have accepted the rule of the rebel leader. They are ready to receive his suggestions and to do his bidding. Yet, true to his early cunning, he does not acknowledge himself to be Satan. He claims to be the prince who is the rightful owner of the world and whose inheritance has been unlawfully wrested from him. He represents himself to his deluded subjects as a redeemer, assuring them that his power has brought them forth from their graves and that he is about to rescue them from the most cruel

---

[15] E. G. White, *Early Writings* (1882), p. 291.1-292.3.

tyranny. The presence of Christ having been removed, Satan works wonders to support his claims. He makes the weak strong and inspires all with his own spirit and energy. He proposes to lead them against the camp of the saints and to take possession of the City of God. With fiendish exultation he points to the unnumbered millions who have been raised from the dead and declares that as their leader he is well able to overthrow the city and regain his throne and his kingdom.

"In that vast throng are multitudes of the long-lived race that existed before the Flood; men of lofty stature and giant intellect, who, yielding to the control of fallen angels, devoted all their skill and knowledge to the exaltation of themselves; men whose wonderful works of art led the world to idolize their genius, but whose cruelty and evil inventions, defiling the earth and defacing the image of God, caused Him to blot them from the face of His creation. There are

kings and generals who conquered nations, valiant men who never lost a battle, proud, ambitious warriors whose approach made kingdoms tremble. In death these experienced no change. As they come up from the grave, they resume the current of their thoughts just where it ceased. They are actuated by the same desire to conquer that ruled them when they fell.

"Satan consults with his angels, and then with these kings and conquerors and mighty men. They look upon the strength and numbers on their side, and declare that the army within the city is small in comparison with theirs, and that it can be overcome. They lay their plans to take possession of the riches and glory of the New Jerusalem. All immediately begin to prepare for battle. Skillful artisans construct implements of war. Military leaders, famed for their success, marshal the throngs of warlike men into companies and divisions."[16]

The Scriptures speak of Magog in Ezekiel 39:6 "And I will send a fire on Magog, and among them that dwell carelessly in the isles: and they shall know that I am the LORD." "It is no arbitrary decree on the part of God that excludes the wicked from heaven; they are shut out by their own unfitness for its companionship. The glory of God would be to them a consuming fire. They would welcome destruction, that they might be hidden from the face of Him who died to redeem them."[17]

God in his great loving kindness and mercy, allows the righteous to see that the wicked would not choose anything else even if they were given a second chance. This is one of the most amazing parts of the plan of salvation. After all that we have put God through, after all the sorrow and suffering we have caused our fellow human beings, once he rescues us from sin and takes us to heaven, he could just say, I am God. The wicked were bad. You just should be happy to be here and believe what I say because I said so. But God does not do this. He is loving and merciful, and desires that all his beings have an intelligent knowledge of his purposes and judgments.

If God did not raise the wicked and allow the righteous to see how wicked they really are and that they still do not desire to follow God, some might still have questions. Perhaps ten million years into

---

16 E. G. White, *The Great Controversy* (1911), p. 663.1-664.2.

17 E. G. White, *Heaven* (2003), p. 66.1.

eternity, someone might begin pondering: I know God is righteous, and just, and he makes the right decisions; I am sure he did the right thing; I had a chance to look at all the books of record and see why some of the people who I thought would be here, are not here; but I wonder... I just wonder what would have happened if that person would have been raised to life again; I wonder if they really would have been like the books say they were; I wonder if maybe they would have changed their minds. If someone started to think these kinds of thoughts ten million years into eternity, the entire safety of the universe would be in danger of sin occurring a second time. But Scripture assures us that "affliction shall not rise up the second time."[18] There will be so much evidence provided that no one will ever have any kind of doubt regarding God's justice. Each of the righteous will be able to see that their loved ones who are not in the city have most certainly chosen Satan as their leader. The righteous will behold with their own eyes that person, whom they thought would be in heaven, preparing to kill God!

There will be tears in heaven. The promise that God will wipe away all tears does not come until all this is finished. There will be tears during the thousand years as we review the books of record. There will be tears as we realize that the wicked want to kill us and to kill God. But once the wicked are forever destroyed, God will wipe the tears away, forever.

Revelation 20:9 And they went up on the breadth of the earth, and compassed the camp of the saints about, and the beloved city: and fire came down from God out of heaven, and devoured them.

The New Jerusalem, has come down out of heaven and is upon earth. With Satan as their leader the wicked surround the city, preparing to take its fabulous wealth by force. This means that they are prepared to kill God and everyone in the city. All the righteous will be able to see who the wicked really are; the hate in their eyes against God; and that they have fully committed to the leadership of Satan. All will see that God's judgments are righteousness.

---

[18] Nahum 1:9

The wicked **"compassed the camp of the saints about, and the beloved city: and fire came down from God out of heaven, and devoured them.**" This is hellfire—the final punishment that causes the eternal oblivion of the wicked.

There is no hellfire burning right now. The Bible explicitly tells us that hellfire burns the wicked **after** they try to attack the New Jerusalem. This clearly has not yet happened, as the New Jerusalem is not yet on earth. Therefore, hellfire is still in the future from our day. In fact, hellfire burns for a finite period of time.

God will completely eradicate sin. If the wicked were cursing in hell for the ceaseless ages of eternity, because of their torment, there would be an exponential accumulation of guilt throughout eternity, and sin would never be eradicated. God does not take pleasure in the death of the wicked. This will be a sad day for him. He gave his life to save them, yet they rejected him, and now he must destroy them with their sin. "As I live, saith the Lord GOD, I have no pleasure in the death of the wicked; but that the wicked turn from his way and live: turn ye, turn ye from your evil ways; for why will ye die…?"[19] "For the LORD shall rise up as in mount Perazim, he shall be wroth as in the valley of Gibeon, that he may do his work, his strange work; and bring to pass his act, his strange act."[20] The fact that God says that the destruction of the wicked is his act—his strange act—shows that it is, in fact, his act.

Revelation 20:10 And the devil that deceived them was cast into the lake of fire and brimstone, where the beast and the false prophet are, and shall be tormented day and night for ever and ever.

This is the one verse in the Bible which seems, when taken without the rest of the Scriptural evidence, to be saying that there will be eternal torment, at least for Satan. But let us take a closer look at this subject. What happens to people when they die and what is hellfire? This is an important Biblical doctrine that is almost universally misunderstood because of the deceptions of Satan, and the doctrines of the anti-Christ power.

---

[19] Ezekiel 33:11

[20] Isaiah 28:21

"The majority of the Christian world believes that at death the soul goes either to heaven or to hell. The prevailing belief about hell fire is that the unfortunate souls that end up there will be tortured throughout the ceaseless ages of eternity. These beliefs are held without respect to their origin, and without considering all the evidence of Scripture. This Catholic doctrine of hell has trickled into most Protestant churches of today. By portraying God as a sadistic tyrant, its horrific cruelty has caused many people to become atheists."[21]

"The theory of the immortality of the soul was one of those false doctrines that Rome, borrowing from paganism, incorporated into the religion of Christendom. Martin Luther classed it with the 'monstrous fables that form part of the Roman dunghill of decretals.' Commenting on the words of Solomon in Ecclesiastes, that the dead know not anything, the Reformer says: '...Solomon judgeth that the dead are asleep, and feel nothing at all. For the dead lie there, accounting neither days nor years, but when they are awakened, they shall seem to have slept scarce one minute.'"[22]

"An eternally-burning hell preached from the pulpit, and kept before the people, does injustice to the benevolent character of God. It presents him as the veriest tyrant in the universe. This wide-spread dogma has turned thousands to Universalism, infidelity, and atheism.
"The word of God is plain. It is a straight chain of truth. It will prove an anchor to those who are willing to receive it, even if they have to sacrifice their cherished fables. It will save them from the terrible delusions of these perilous times.
"Satan has led the minds of the ministers of different churches to adhere as tenaciously to their popular errors, as he led the Jews in their blindness to cling to their sacrifices, and crucify Christ."[23]

Catholic paintings depict their idea of what happens in hell. In paintings, such as *Hortus deliciarum*, you see people being tortured by flames, thrown into burning pots of oil, hung upside down and stabbed through and held over the flames by demons. Lucifer, himself chained in the fire, is torturing victims. There is a priest at the bottom left who is presiding over the whole thing. It is really quite a

---

[21] Martin Klein, *Thou Hast Magnified Thy Word Above All Thy Name* (2016), p. 178.

[22] E. G. White, *The Great Controversy* (1911), p. 549.2.

[23] E. G. White, *Spiritual Gifts*, Vol. 4b (1864), p. 104.2-4.

horrific picture. This idea absolutely does not come from the Bible. The Bible presents no such doctrine. This was dreamed up and brought into the Christian religion directly from pagan philosophy.

"In Greek mythology, Tartarus was a prison of the Tartan gods. Tartarus was considered the place where the Tartan gods must suffer. Plato and Homer concocted these legendary myths. Plato wrote that souls were judged after death and those who received punishment were sent to Tartarus. Homer, in the *Iliad*, speaks of the underworld. The ghosts of the suitors who have died are herded there by Hermes. Then they had the Greek god Hades, oldest male child of Cronus and Rhea, with the brothers named Zeus and Poseidon. In fact, this Greek mythology so permeated the culture of Biblical times that the Greek word for hell is hades. The name of this Greek god became a common word to refer to the place of burning. It is Greek mythology which originated the idea of an eternally burning hell. This is the source of the popular Christian belief that somewhere hellfire is burning today. The hellfire of the Bible is totally different than the hellfire of Greek mythology."[24]

As we saw earlier, the Bible tells us in Revelation 20:9 when hellfire burns: "And they went up on the breadth of the earth, and compassed the camp of the saints about, and the beloved city: and fire came down from God out of heaven, and devoured them."

"Not until the saved have been taken to heaven for 1,000 years, to review the books of record, and the holy city has come down to the earth from God out of heaven, are the wicked resurrected to face their final punishment by fire. In one final demonstration to the universe that God's judgments were just, the wicked try to attack the city of God, and fire from God devours them....
"Therefore hellfire is not burning at this time. It is the final destruction of sin and sinners—the final punishment that was only "prepared for the devil and his angels."[25] The question then arises as to how long hellfire burns. A few verses speak of "everlasting fire" and Revelation 20:10 says that the beast and false prophet are **"tormented day and night for ever and ever."** Therefore, some find it an easy matter to jump from these one or two verses to a belief in Greek mythology.

---

[24] Martin Klein, *Thou Hast Magnified Thy Word Above All Thy Name* (2016), p. 179.

[25] Matthew 25:41

"One principal of sound Biblical interpretation is that no doctrine may be built around one or two verses.[26] In order to get a clear view of what the Bible says on a particular subject, one must examine all the evidence. If there are verses that seem to be contradictory, you would always go with the weight of evidence and establish doctrine with the majority of texts on the subject rather than basing a doctrine on just one text. It is easy to twist or misunderstand one or two texts, but when you look at the whole overview, it is much more difficult to do so. The bulk of evidence can then give a framework for understanding the few verses that may at first seem contradictory."[27]

So, let us ask ourselves, initially, if when the Bible says the devil, the beast, and the false prophet are tormented "for ever and ever," the phrase by definition must always mean throughout the ceaseless ages of eternity? Turning to Jonah 2:6 we read the description of his experience going down in the belly of the whale: "I went down to the bottoms of the mountains; the earth with her bars was about me **for ever**: yet hast thou brought up my life from corruption, O LORD my God." It certainly might have seemed forever, yet, the Bible tells us Jonah was only there three days and three nights.[28]

"In the same manner, the word that is used for forever in the New Testament means, 'until the horizon,' or 'for an age.' It is a word that can mean something a long way off in the future, or it can mean something relatively short, depending on the context. Therefore, it does not demand the meaning of 'through all ceaseless ages of eternity,' but can mean 'until it is out of sight,' or 'until it is forgotten.' So, in the case of Jonah going down in the whale, the idea of forever was not really for all eternity; rather what seemed like a long time for the situation.[29] We commonly do this in English, we might say that it

---

[26] An extreme example of building a doctrine with just two texts would be to combine part of Matthew 27:5, [Judas] "...departed, and went and hanged himself," with part of Luke 10:37 "...Go, and do thou likewise," and claim that the Bible is teaching us to commit suicide. This, of course would be absolutely absurd. But, it illustrates the fact that single verses, or portions of verses, or even a couple verses, taken out of context, and without regard to the rest of the teachings of Scripture can easily be misconstrued. Satan himself did this when quoting Scripture to Christ in the wilderness of temptation.

[27] Martin Klein, *Thou Hast Magnified Thy Word Above All Thy Name* (2016), p. 179-180.

[28] Jonah 1:17

[29] This way of looking at these expressions of forever is, of course, dependent on additional Biblical evidence for a finite hell fire.

took forever to get from one town to the next, and we certainly do not mean to say it took all eternity.

"If it is true that God is a God of love, fairness, and justice, then it would not make sense for God to punish people for a short life of sin, of perhaps 70 years or even less, through billions of years of eternity. This would not be a God of love. Heaven would not be a pleasant place for those righteous who had loved ones burning on through all eternity."[30]

Let us examine the Scriptural evidence, and allow the Bible to interpret itself.

Ezekiel 28:18, 36 uses the metaphor of the king of Tyre[31] to describe Satan; the Bible says, "Thou hast defiled thy sanctuaries by the multitude of thine iniquities, by the iniquity of thy traffic; therefore will I bring forth a fire from the midst of thee, it shall devour thee, and I will bring thee to ashes upon the earth in the sight of all them that behold thee.... thou shalt be a terror, and never shalt be any more."

According to Scripture, Satan will be consumed once and for all. He will not continue torturing people, throughout eternity, but will cease to exist!

Is there more evidence? Psalms 37:10: "For yet a little while, and the wicked shall not be: yea, thou shalt diligently consider his place, and it shall not be." The place of the wicked cannot even be discovered. Verse 20 says that the wicked "shall be as the fat of lambs: they shall consume; into smoke shall they consume away."

Psalms 9:5-6 says, "Thou hast rebuked the heathen, thou hast destroyed the wicked, thou hast put out their name for ever and ever. O thou enemy, destructions are come to a perpetual end: and thou hast destroyed cities; their memorial is perished with them."

They are destroyed and even the memory of them has perished. Obviously, if they were being tortured in hell for all eternity, this

---

[30] Martin Klein, *Thou Hast Magnified Thy Word Above All Thy Name* (2016), p. 180-181.

[31] Some have claimed the passage in Ezekiel 28 is speaking only of the literal king of Tyre. This is impossible because it says he was in Eden, the garden of God, that he was the anointed covering cherub, walked in the stones of fire, and was on the holy mountain of God. The passage describes the heavenly throne room, and can only apply to Lucifer before he fell.

would not be the case. You would be able to remember them. You would be able to find their names.

Malachi 4:3 speaks to this, "And ye shall tread down the wicked; for they shall be ashes under the soles of your feet in the day that I shall do this, saith the LORD of hosts." The Bible is telling us that we will actually walk on the ashes of those who have completely consumed away. This certainly does not sound like they are still writhing in the flames of hell. This is not Greek mythology, but the Bible doctrine of what happens when hellfire burns.

Scripture tells us how hot the fire will be after it has completed its work of cleansing the earth, in Isaiah 47:14, "Behold, they shall be as stubble; the fire shall burn them; they shall not deliver themselves from the power of the flame: there shall not be a coal to warm at, nor fire to sit before it."

Yes, the fire will be hot. Yes, the fire will burn the wicked. Yes, it will devour them. No one can deliver the wicked from the power of this fire. But, once it has completed its work, it will go out, so cold, that there will not even be a coal to warm at or a little campfire by which to sit.

Considering text after text of harmonious Biblical doctrine allows us to see the true picture of hellfire, and gives a framework for interpreting the few texts that seem in contradiction.

Interestingly enough, there is someone who will live in eternal fire, but, it is not the wicked, as you may think. "The sinners in Zion are afraid; fearfulness hath surprised the hypocrites. Who among us shall dwell with the devouring fire? who among us shall dwell with everlasting burnings? He that walketh righteously, and speaketh uprightly; he that despiseth the gain of oppressions, that shaketh his hands from holding of bribes, that stoppeth his ears from hearing of blood, and shutteth his eyes from seeing evil."[32]

The righteous will dwell in everlasting burnings, not the wicked, because the Bible tells us that God is a consuming fire. Sin cannot exist in the presence of God, as he is a consuming fire to sin. Thus, at the end of time, when God will put an end to sin for all eternity,

---

[32] Isaiah 33:14-15

God must destroy sin and sinners forever. He will destroy sin, and anyone who continues to hold onto their sins will be consumed with them. He has made abundant provision for us to have forgiveness and victory over our sin. That consuming fire of God's presence will not hurt those who are righteous. They will be able to live in the presence of that everlasting burning, just like Daniel's three friends who walked with Jesus in the fiery furnace. So, the righteous will walk in the eternal fire of God's presence without being hurt or consumed; but the wicked will be destroyed by the same fire.

Linked with the idea of an eternally burning hellfire is the idea of what actually happens when people die. According to the Greek mythology, and also according to Catholic doctrine, as soon as someone dies, their spirit is separated from their body. The spirit is thought to be some kind of a conscious living entity which goes either to heaven or to hell. According to this idea there is some kind of consciousness for all eternity, in the hot place or in the good place.

This theory also does not come from the Bible. "For the living know that they shall die: but the dead know not any thing, neither have they any more a reward; for the memory of them is forgotten. Also their love, and their hatred, and their envy, is now perished; neither have they any more a portion for ever in any thing that is done under the sun."[33]

God tells us that when you die, you do not know anything. You are not a conscious living entity up in heaven or in hell. You go to sleep and return to the dust of the earth. This is what the Bible teaches.

Jesus calls death a sleep over and over again. When he went to resurrect Lazarus, he said, "Lazarus, come forth."[34] He did not tell him to come down. Think how ridiculous it would have been if, at the point of death, Lazarus's spirit had gone to heaven and Jesus had called him back down to the earth. If he were up there enjoying the bliss of heaven, would it not be a rude trick to play on him, to call him back down into his body to continue his suffering on this sinful earth? Jesus told his disciples he was going to awaken Lazarus. Lazarus

---

[33] Ecclesiastes 9:5-6

[34] John 11:43

did not come out of the grave with any stories of heaven or of hell. He simply woke up.

The Bible tells us in Job, "But man dieth, and wasteth away: yea, man giveth up the ghost, and where is he? As the waters fail from the sea, and the flood decayeth and drieth up: So man lieth down, and riseth not: till the heavens be no more, they shall not awake, nor be raised out of their sleep."[35]

Job goes on to describe the resurrection in verse 13 and 14, "O that thou wouldest hide me in the grave, that thou wouldest keep me secret, until thy wrath be past, that thou wouldest appoint me a set time, and remember me! If a man die, shall he live again? all the days of my appointed time will I wait, till my change come." Job understood what happens to men when they die. They go into the grave, they become no more. They are hid there—kept secret, but God remembers them. They do not know anything until the appointed time and their change comes. At the resurrection of the second coming, Jesus awakens those that are righteous from their dusty beds. He remembers where they were, who they were, and he makes them alive again. But, the dead are not some kind of conscious entity somewhere else outside their body.

"The dead praise not the LORD, neither any that go down into silence."[36] Surely, if some people went straight to heaven when they died, they would be praising God, would they not? If you were in heaven, would you not be praising God? But here the Bible tells us that the dead do not praise the Lord. They go down into silence, into the sleep of the grave.

"His breath goeth forth, he returneth to his earth; in that very day his thoughts perish."[37] It is the breath, or the power of God, that returns to the One who gave it. It is not some kind of conscious living entity, but just the power, that electricity that keeps the light bulb going. When you turn off the light, what happens to the electricity? What happens to the light? The light is simply gone. Without the power from the electricity, the light just is not there. It is the same way with the breath of God. When he gives the breath of life, it gives life.

---

[35] Job 14:10-12

[36] Psalms 115:17

[37] Psalms 146:4

When we die, that breath of life goes back to God. Our bodies go into the dust until God returns and resurrects us at the second coming.

"For David is not ascended into the heavens: but he saith himself, The Lord said unto my Lord, Sit thou on my right hand, Until I make thy foes thy footstool."[38] The Bible says that David was a man after God's own heart. Surely, if people go to heaven as soon as they die, David would be in heaven. But the Bible states plainly that he is not in heaven. This is because he is sleeping in the grave, awaiting the resurrection, just like everyone else. What a comfort it is to know that our loved ones who have died are not up in heaven enduring the sight of the pain and suffering we are still experiencing on this earth. Our loved ones are sleeping in the grave, awaiting the resurrection call. What sense would it make to have a resurrection if everyone is already in heaven or in hell? There would be no point of a judgment if everyone received their reward at death.

One of Satan's two original lies in the Garden of Eden was that the dead do not really die: "Ye shall not surely die"[39]—maybe you'll die, but you will not be completely dead; you will continue to live on. That original lie opened the whole realm of possibility of necromancy or speaking to the dead. The Bible explicitly condemns this practice,[40] because if you speak to the dead, you are really speaking with demons. You are not speaking to your dead loved one, for the Bible says your dead loved one knows nothing. "For such are false apostles, deceitful workers, transforming themselves into the apostles of Christ. And no marvel; for Satan himself is transformed into an angel of light."[41]

"They are dead, they shall not live; they are deceased, they shall not rise: therefore hast thou visited and destroyed them, and made all their memory to perish."[42]

---

[38] Acts 2:34-35

[39] Genesis 3:4

[40] Deuteronomy 18:10-12 "There shall not be found among you any one that maketh his son or his daughter to pass through the fire, or that useth divination, or an observer of times, or an enchanter, or a witch, Or a charmer, or a consulter with familiar spirits, or a wizard, or a necromancer. For all that do these things are an abomination unto the LORD: and because of these abominations the LORD thy God doth drive them out from before thee."

[41] 2 Corinthians 11:13-14

[42] Isaiah 26:14

Again, and again the Bible is consistent with this precious doctrine of what happens when you die.

"But I would not have you to be ignorant, brethren, **concerning them which are asleep**, that ye sorrow not, even as others which have no hope. For if we believe that Jesus died and rose again, even so **them also which sleep in Jesus** will God bring with him. For this we say unto you by the word of the Lord, that we which are alive and remain unto the coming of the Lord shall not prevent {precede} **them which are asleep.** For the Lord himself shall descend from heaven with a shout, with the voice of the archangel, and with the trump of God: and **the dead in Christ shall rise** first: Then we which are alive and remain shall be caught up together with them in the clouds, to meet the Lord in the air: and so shall we ever be with the Lord. "**Wherefore comfort one another with these words.**"[43]

 Once gain, the Bible describes the dead as being asleep and rising from their graves. Comforting words, precious promise!

Revelation 20:11 And I saw a great white throne, and him that sat on it, from whose face the earth and the heaven fled away; and there was found no place for them.

Revelation 20:1-6 describes the events during the millennium and Revelation 20:7-15 reveals the events after the millennium. This chapter contains a Hebrew parallelism. Verses 7-11 cover the events in chronological order, then verses 12-15 skip back, reviewing some of the events again. Verses 12-13 replay the judgment scene when the wicked are given their sentence; verses 14-15 re-describe the the hellfire that destroys them.

Just as Satan orders the wicked surrounding the city to advance against it, the great white throne is seen.

"At last the order to advance is given, and the countless host moves on—an army such as was never summoned by earthly conquerors, such as the combined forces of all ages since war began on earth could never equal. Satan, the mightiest of warriors, leads the van, and his angels unite their forces for this final struggle. Kings and

---

[43] 1 Thessalonians 4:13-18

warriors are in his train, and the multitudes follow in vast companies, each under its appointed leader. With military precision the serried ranks advance over the earth's broken and uneven surface to the City of God. By command of Jesus, the gates of the New Jerusalem are closed, and the armies of Satan surround the city and make ready for the onset.

"Now Christ again appears to the view of His enemies. Far above the city, upon a foundation of burnished gold, is a throne, high and lifted up. Upon this throne sits the Son of God, and around Him are the subjects of His kingdom. The power and majesty of Christ no language can describe, no pen portray. The glory of the Eternal Father is enshrouding His Son. The brightness of His presence fills the City of God, and flows out beyond the gates, flooding the whole earth with its radiance."[44]

"Before the universe has been clearly presented the great sacrifice made by the Father and the Son in man's behalf. The hour has come when Christ occupies His rightful position and is glorified above principalities and powers and every name that is named. It was for the joy that was set before Him—that He might bring many sons unto glory—that He endured the cross and despised the shame. And inconceivably great as was the sorrow and the shame, yet greater is the joy and the glory. He looks upon the redeemed, renewed in His own image, every heart bearing the perfect impress of the divine, every face reflecting the likeness of their King. He beholds in them the result of the travail of His soul, and He is satisfied. Then, in a voice that reaches the assembled multitudes of the righteous and the wicked, He declares: 'Behold the purchase of My blood! For these I suffered, for these I died, that they might dwell in My presence throughout eternal ages.'...."[45]

---

[44] E. G. White, *The Great Controversy* (1911), p. 664.3-665.1.
"Nearest the throne are those who were once zealous in the cause of Satan, but who, plucked as brands from the burning, have followed their Saviour with deep, intense devotion. Next are those who perfected Christian characters in the midst of falsehood and infidelity, those who honored the law of God when the Christian world declared it void, and the millions, of all ages, who were martyred for their faith. And beyond is the 'great multitude, which no man could number, of all nations, and kindreds, and people, and tongues'.... Their warfare is ended, their victory won. They have run the race and reached the prize. The palm branch in their hands is a symbol of their triumph, the white robe an emblem of the spotless righteousness of Christ which now is theirs."
E. G. White, *The Great Controversy* (1911), p. 665.2.

[45] E. G. White, *The Great Controversy* (1911), p. 671.1.

Revelation 20:12 And I saw the dead, small and great, stand before God; and the books were opened: and another book was opened, which is the book of life: and the dead were judged out of those things which were written in the books, according to their works.

"As soon as the books of record are opened, and the eye of Jesus looks upon the wicked, they are conscious of every sin which they have ever committed. They see just where their feet diverged from the path of purity and holiness, just how far pride and rebellion have carried them in the violation of the law of God. The seductive temptations which they encouraged by indulgence in sin, the blessings perverted, the messengers of God despised, the warnings rejected, the waves of mercy beaten back by the stubborn, unrepentant heart—all appear as if written in letters of fire.

"Above the throne is revealed the cross; and like a panoramic view appear the scenes of Adam's temptation and fall, and the successive steps in the great plan of redemption. The Saviour's lowly birth; His early life of simplicity and obedience; His baptism in Jordan; the fast and temptation in the wilderness; His public ministry, unfolding to men heaven's most precious blessings; the days crowded with deeds of love and mercy, the nights of prayer and watching in the solitude of the mountains; the plottings of envy, hate, and malice which repaid His benefits; the awful, mysterious agony in Gethsemane beneath the crushing weight of the sins of the whole world; His betrayal into the hands of the murderous mob; the fearful events of that night of horror—the unresisting prisoner, forsaken by His best-loved disciples, rudely hurried through the streets of Jerusalem; the Son of God exultingly displayed before Annas, arraigned in the high priest's palace, in the judgment hall of Pilate, before the cowardly and cruel Herod, mocked, insulted, tortured, and condemned to die—all are vividly portrayed.

"And now before the swaying multitude are revealed the final scenes—the patient Sufferer treading the path to Calvary; the Prince of heaven hanging upon the cross; the haughty priests and the jeering rabble deriding His expiring agony; the supernatural darkness; the heaving earth, the rent rocks, the open graves, marking the moment when the world's Redeemer yielded up His life.

"The awful spectacle appears just as it was. Satan, his angels, and his subjects have no power to turn from the picture of their own work. Each actor recalls the part which he performed. Herod, who slew the innocent children of Bethlehem that he might destroy the King of Israel; the base Herodias, upon whose guilty soul rests the blood of

John the Baptist; the weak, timeserving Pilate; the mocking soldiers; the priests and rulers and the maddened throng who cried, 'His blood be on us, and on our children!'—all behold the enormity of their guilt. They vainly seek to hide from the divine majesty of His countenance, outshining the glory of the sun, while the redeemed cast their crowns at the Saviour's feet, exclaiming: 'He died for me!'

"Amid the ransomed throng are the apostles of Christ, the heroic Paul, the ardent Peter, the loved and loving John, and their truehearted brethren, and with them the vast host of martyrs; while outside the walls, with every vile and abominable thing, are those by whom they were persecuted, imprisoned, and slain. There is Nero, that monster of cruelty and vice, beholding the joy and exaltation of those whom he once tortured, and in whose extremest anguish he found satanic delight. His mother is there to witness the result of her own work; to see how the evil stamp of character transmitted to her son, the passions encouraged and developed by her influence and example, have borne fruit in crimes that caused the world to shudder.

"There are papist priests and prelates, who claimed to be Christ's ambassadors, yet employed the rack, the dungeon, and the stake to control the consciences of His people. There are the proud pontiffs who exalted themselves above God and presumed to change the law of the Most High. Those pretended fathers of the church have an account to render to God from which they would fain be excused. Too late they are made to see that the Omniscient One is jealous of His law and that He will in no wise clear the guilty. They learn now that Christ identifies His interest with that of His suffering people; and they feel the force of His own words: 'Inasmuch as ye have done it unto one of the least of these My brethren, ye have done it unto Me.' Matthew 25:40...

"As if entranced, the wicked have looked upon the coronation of the Son of God. They see in His hands the tables of the divine law, the statutes which they have despised and transgressed... the multitudes without the city, all with one voice exclaim, 'Great and marvelous are Thy works, Lord God Almighty; just and true are Thy ways, Thou King of saints' (Revelation 15:3); and, falling prostrate, they worship the Prince of life."[46]

The wicked are judged according to what is written in the books. They too will see the fairness of God and every knee will bow and

---

[46] E. G. White, *The Great Controversy* (1911), p. 666.2-668.4.

acknowledge that God's judgments are just. Even the wicked, at this point, recognize that his judgments are righteous. Satan himself admits the justice of God.

"Satan seems paralyzed as he beholds the glory and majesty of Christ. He who was once a covering cherub remembers whence he has fallen...
"Memory recalls the home of his innocence and purity, the peace and content that were his until he indulged in murmuring against God, and envy of Christ. His accusations, his rebellion, his deceptions to gain the sympathy and support of the angels, his stubborn persistence in making no effort for self-recovery when God would have granted him forgiveness—all come vividly before him. He reviews his work among men and its results—the enmity of man toward his fellow man, the terrible destruction of life, the rise and fall of kingdoms, the overturning of thrones, the long succession of tumults, conflicts, and revolutions. He recalls his constant efforts to oppose the work of Christ and to sink man lower and lower. He sees that his hellish plots have been powerless to destroy those who have put their trust in Jesus. As Satan looks upon his kingdom, the fruit of his toil, he sees only failure and ruin....
"For thousands of years this chief of conspiracy has palmed off falsehood for truth. But the time has now come when the rebellion is to be finally defeated and the history and character of Satan disclosed. In his last great effort to dethrone Christ, destroy His people, and take possession of the City of God, the archdeceiver has been fully unmasked. Those who have united with him see the total failure of his cause. Christ's followers and the loyal angels behold the full extent of his machinations against the government of God. He is the object of universal abhorrence.
"Satan sees that his voluntary rebellion has unfitted him for heaven. He has trained his powers to war against God; the purity, peace, and harmony of heaven would be to him supreme torture. His accusations against the mercy and justice of God are now silenced. The reproach which he has endeavored to cast upon Jehovah rests wholly upon himself. And now Satan bows down and confesses the justice of his sentence."[47]

[47] E. G. White, *The Great Controversy* (1911), p. 669.1-670.2.

Revelation 20:13 And the sea gave up the dead which were in it; and death and hell delivered up the dead which were in them: and they were judged every man according to their works.

The Bible says they will be judged **"according to their works."** Since we are not saved by our works,[48] how are the wicked judged by their works?[49]

God "so loved sinful people that He gave Himself in His Son, that they might have another opportunity, another trial, another chance to show their obedience. He so loved men and women that in order to save them He gave His Son to the world, and in that gift He gave all heaven! This was the only provision God could make. By this gift a way was provided for sinners to return to their loyalty."[50]

God risked the entire universe to become a man and pour out his own blood to rescue those whom he calls his friends.[51] "Wherefore Jesus also, that he might sanctify the people with his own blood, suffered without the gate."[52] "And without controversy great is the mystery of godliness: God was manifest in the flesh, justified in the Spirit, seen of angels, preached unto the Gentiles, believed on in the world, received up into glory."[53]

God did this while we were his enemies. "For if, when we were enemies, we were reconciled to God by the death of his Son, much more, being reconciled, we shall be saved by his life."[54] This means that the sacrifice of Jesus paid the penalty of your sins before you even knew who he was. Whether you are an Atheist, Muslim, Buddhist, Hindu, Jew, New-ager, hippie, Catholic, Agnostic, Christian; man, woman, or child, Christ accomplished something for

---

[48] Romans 3:28; Galatians 2:16; Titus 3:5; 2 Timothy 1:9.

[49] See also Job 34:10-12; Psalm 62:12; Proverbs 24:12; Jeremiah 25:14; 32:19; Matthew 16:27; 1 Peter 1:17; Revelation 2:23; 22:12.

[50] E. G. White, *Christ Triumphant* (1999), p. 279.4.

[51] John 15:15 Henceforth I call you not servants; for the servant knoweth not what his lord doeth: but I have called you friends; for all things that I have heard of my Father I have made known unto you.

[52] Hebrews 13:12

[53] 1 Timothy 3:16

[54] Romans 5:10

you, whether you like it, know it, believe it, accept it, or not. He accomplished this for the whole world. "To wit, that God was in Christ, **reconciling the world unto himself**, not imputing their trespasses unto them; and hath committed unto us the word of reconciliation."[55] "Therefore as by the offence of one judgment came upon all men to condemnation; even so by the righteousness of one the free gift came upon **all men** unto justification of life."[56]

His death made atonement for the sins of the world, freed you from the condemnation of your sin, and gave you an opportunity for a second probation. This is what the Bible calls **justification of life**— you were not executed as soon as you were guilty of death, for he knew that in yourself you had no power to resist sin. "The wages of sin is death; but the gift of God is eternal life through Jesus Christ our Lord."[57] Justification of life is not enough to save you eternally, however. He values your freedom of choice more than he values your salvation! He will not save you against your will. Therefore, to be saved, you must accept his life and righteousness in place of yours; you must accept the infinite sacrifice of his death on your behalf. "For if, when we were enemies, we were reconciled to God by the death of his Son, much more, being reconciled, we shall be **saved by his life**."[58] This is called **justification by faith**. "Therefore being justified by faith, we have peace with God through our Lord Jesus Christ."[59]

If you do not accept his life and death for yours, then those sins he already paid for, will eventually be imputed back to you. "Blessed is the man to whom the Lord will not impute sin."[60] Since there is a man who is blessed because the Lord does not impute sin to him, that means there is also a man who is cursed because the Lord does impute sin unto him. God has provided everything for our salvation, but if we reject all that he has done and cling to our sins he cannot save us. Those who reject Christ's payment for their debt will have

---

[55] 2 Corinthians 5:19

[56] Romans 5:18

[57] Romans 6:23

[58] Romans 5:10

[59] Romans 5:1

[60] Romans 4:8; Matthew 18:23-35

their debt reinstated, they will be judged according to their works of sin, and will be delivered to the tormentors, till they pay their debt of sin.[61]

"The whole wicked world stand arraigned at the bar of God on the charge of high treason against the government of heaven. They have none to plead their cause; they are without excuse; and the sentence of eternal death is pronounced against them.

"It is now evident to all that the wages of sin is not noble independence and eternal life, but slavery, ruin, and death. The wicked see what they have forfeited by their life of rebellion. The far more exceeding and eternal weight of glory was despised when offered them; but how desirable it now appears. 'All this,' cries the lost soul, 'I might have had; but I chose to put these things far from me. Oh, strange infatuation! I have exchanged peace, happiness, and honor for wretchedness, infamy, and despair.' All see that their exclusion from heaven is just. By their lives they have declared: 'We will not have this Man Jesus to reign over us.'"[62]

"In heaven it is said by the ministering angels: The ministry which we have been commissioned to perform we have done. We pressed back the army of evil angels. We sent brightness and light into the souls of men, quickening their memory of the love of God expressed in Jesus. We attracted their eyes to the cross of Christ. Their hearts were deeply moved by a sense of the sin that crucified the Son of God. They were convicted. They saw the steps to be taken in conversion; they felt the power of the gospel; their hearts were made tender as they saw the sweetness of the love of God. They beheld the beauty of the character of Christ. But with the many it was all in vain. They would not surrender their own habits and character. They would not put off the garments of earth in order to be clothed with the robe of heaven. Their hearts were given to covetousness. They loved the associations of the world more than they loved their God.

"Solemn will be the day of final decision. In prophetic vision the apostle John describes it: 'I saw a great white throne, and Him that sat on it, from whose face the earth and the heaven fled away; and there was found no place for them. And I saw the dead, small and great, stand before God; and the books were opened; and another

---

[61] Matthew 18:23-35. For more on the subject of justification see Martin Klein, *The Most Precious Message*.

[62] E. G. White, *The Great Controversy* (1911), p. 668.2-3.

book was opened, which is the book of life; and the dead were judged out of those things which were written in the books, according to their works.' Revelation 20:11, 12.

"Sad will be the retrospect in that day when men stand face to face with eternity. The whole life will present itself just as it has been. The world's pleasures, riches, and honors will not then seem so important. Men will then see that the righteousness they despised is alone of value. They will see that they have fashioned their characters under the deceptive allurements of Satan. The garments they have chosen are the badge of their allegiance to the first great apostate. Then they will see the results of their choice. They will have a knowledge of what it means to transgress the commandments of God.

"There will be no future probation in which to prepare for eternity. It is in this life that we are to put on the robe of Christ's righteousness. This is our only opportunity to form characters for the home which Christ has made ready for those who obey His commandments."[63]

Revelation 20:14 And death and hell were cast into the lake of fire. This is the second death.

Praise the Lord for this promise. Perhaps we will be called to give our life for the truth, but God gives us this precious promise, that finally death, hell, sin, and Satan will be cast into the lake of fire and destroyed once and for all. This is the second death.

Revelation 20:15 And whosoever was not found written in the book of life was cast into the lake of fire.

"Notwithstanding that Satan has been constrained to acknowledge God's justice and to bow to the supremacy of Christ, his character remains unchanged. The spirit of rebellion, like a mighty torrent, again bursts forth. Filled with frenzy, he determines not to yield the great controversy. The time has come for a last desperate struggle against the King of heaven. He rushes into the midst of his subjects and endeavors to inspire them with his own fury and arouse them to instant battle. But of all the countless millions whom he has allured into rebellion, there are none now to acknowledge his supremacy.

---

[63] E. G. White, *Christ's Object Lessons* (1900), p. 318.1-319.1.

His power is at an end. The wicked are filled with the same hatred of God that inspires Satan; but they see that their case is hopeless, that they cannot prevail against Jehovah. Their rage is kindled against Satan and those who have been his agents in deception, and with the fury of demons they turn upon them.

"Saith the Lord: 'Because thou hast set thine heart as the heart of God; behold, therefore I will bring strangers upon thee, the terrible of the nations: and they shall draw their swords against the beauty of thy wisdom, and they shall defile thy brightness. They shall bring thee down to the pit.' 'I will destroy thee, O covering cherub, from the midst of the stones of fire.... I will cast thee to the ground, I will lay thee before kings, that they may behold thee.... I will bring thee to ashes upon the earth in the sight of all them that behold thee.... Thou shalt be a terror, and never shalt thou be any more.' Ezekiel 28:6-8, 16-19.

"'Every battle of the warrior is with confused noise, and garments rolled in blood; but this shall be with burning and fuel of fire.' 'The indignation of the Lord is upon all nations, and His fury upon all their armies: He hath utterly destroyed them, He hath delivered them to the slaughter.' 'Upon the wicked He shall rain quick burning coals, fire and brimstone and an horrible tempest: this shall be the portion of their cup.' Isaiah 9:5; 34:2; Psalm 11:6, margin. Fire comes down from God out of heaven. The earth is broken up. The weapons concealed in its depths are drawn forth. Devouring flames burst from every yawning chasm. The very rocks are on fire. The day has come that shall burn as an oven. The elements melt with fervent heat, the earth also, and the works that are therein are burned up. Malachi 4:1; 2 Peter 3:10. The earth's surface seems one molten mass—a vast, seething lake of fire. It is the time of the judgment and perdition of ungodly men—'the day of the Lord's vengeance, and the year of recompenses for the controversy of Zion.' Isaiah 34:8."[64]

"Satan and his angels try to encourage the wicked multitude to action; but fire descends from Heaven, and unites with the fire in the earth, and aids in the general conflagration.

"Those majestic trees which God had caused to grow upon the earth, for the benefit of the inhabitants of the old world, and which they had used to form into idols, and to corrupt themselves with, God has reserved in the earth, in the shape of coal and oil to use as agencies in their final destruction. As he called forth the waters in the earth at

---

[64] E. G. White, *The Great Controversy* (1911), p. 671.2-672.2

the time of the flood, as weapons from his arsenal to accomplish the destruction of the antediluvian race, so at the end of the one thousand years he will call forth the fires in the earth as his weapons which he has reserved for the final destruction, not only of successive generations since the flood, but the antediluvian race who perished by the flood.

"When the flood of waters was at its height upon the earth, it had the appearance of a boundless lake of water. When God finally purifies the earth, it will appear like a boundless lake of fire. As God preserved the ark amid the commotions of the flood, because it contained eight righteous persons, he will preserve the New Jerusalem, containing the faithful of all ages, from righteous Abel down to the last saint which lived. Although the whole earth, with the exception of that portion where the city rests, will be wrapped in a sea of liquid fire, yet the city is preserved as was the ark, by a miracle of Almighty power. It stands unharmed amid the devouring elements."[65]

Friend, you will be there that day—either in the city, or outside. God does not want you to be cast in that lake of fire. He loves every one of us with an everlasting love.

"Christ is able to save to the uttermost all who come to Him in faith. He will cleanse them from all defilement if they will let Him. But if they **cling to their sins**, they cannot possibly be saved; for Christ's righteousness covers no sin unrepented of. God has declared that those who receive Christ as their Redeemer, accepting Him as the One who takes away all sin, will receive pardon for their transgressions. These are the terms of our election. Man's salvation depends upon his receiving Christ by faith. Those who will not receive Him lose eternal life because they refused to avail themselves of the only means provided by the Father and the Son for the salvation of a perishing world."[66]

"Therefore I will judge you, O house of Israel, every one according to his ways, saith the Lord GOD. Repent, and turn yourselves from all your transgressions; so iniquity shall not be your ruin. Cast away from you all your transgressions, whereby ye have transgressed; and

---

[65] E. G. White, *Spiritual Gifts,* Vol. 3 (1864), p. 86.1-87.2.

[66] E. G. White, *The Seventh-day Adventist Bible Commentary,* Vol. 7, (1955), p. 931.1.

make you a new heart and a new spirit: for why will ye die, O house of Israel? For I have no pleasure in the death of him that dieth, saith the Lord GOD: wherefore turn yourselves, and live ye."[67]

Christ is pleading with us while probation still lingers to turn to him will all our heart.[68] He longs to save us. God poured out all his blood on this planet, because he loved us so much. He has done everything he can possibly do, but he will not violate your power of choice.

"The Lord is proving and testing His people. Angels of God are watching the development of character and weighing moral worth. Probation is almost ended.... Oh, that the word of warning might burn into your souls! Get ready! get ready! Work while the day lasts, for the night cometh when no man can work. The mandate will go forth: He that is holy, let him be holy still; and he that is filthy, let him be filthy still. The destiny of all will be decided. A few, yes, only a few, of the vast number who people the earth will be saved unto life eternal, while the masses who have not perfected their souls in obeying the truth will be appointed to the second death. O Saviour, save the purchase of Thy blood! is the cry of my anguished heart."[69] Amen.

---

[67] Ezekiel 18:30-32

[68] Joel 2:12

[69] E. G. White, *Testimonies for the Church,* Vol. 2 (1871), p. 401.1.

Revelation 21

SUMMARY:
The final two chapters of Revelation show us an amazing picture of
the end of sin and suffering. God creates the earth anew, and wipes
away all tears, forever. The book of Genesis presents Eden lost. The
book of Revelation unveils Eden restored. The description of the
New Jerusalem follows, with twelve gates made of twelve pearls,
streets of gold, and twelve foundations each of a different precious
stone. "Sin and sinners are no more. The entire universe is clean.
One pulse of harmony and gladness beats through the vast
creation."[1]

*Revelation 21:1 And I saw a new heaven and a new earth: for
the first heaven and the first earth were passed away; and there
was no more sea.*

As a result of the flood, vast oceans cover the majority of our planet,
but when God makes all things new there will be no more sea. This
does not mean that God will not have a place for the whales to swim,
but earth will be restored to Edenic conditions without huge oceans
separating continents.

"The sea divides friends. It is a barrier between us and those whom
we love. Our associations are broken up by the broad, fathomless
ocean. In the new earth there will be no more sea, and there shall
pass there 'no galley with oars.' In the past many who have loved
and served God have been bound by chains to their seats in galleys,
compelled to serve the purpose of cruel, hardhearted men. The Lord
has looked upon their suffering in sympathy and compassion. Thank
God, in the earth made new there will be no fierce torrents, no
engulfing ocean, no restless, murmuring waves."[2]

God will make everything new; sin and sinners are no more.

In Micah 7:18-19 the Bible gives an amazing description of how he
forgives: "Who is a God like unto thee, that pardoneth iniquity, and
passeth by the transgression of the remnant of his heritage? he

---

[1] E. G. White, *The Great Controversy* (1911), p. 678.3.

[2] E. G. White, *Maranatha* (1976), p. 351.5.

retaineth not his anger for ever, because he delighteth in mercy. He will turn again, he will have compassion upon us; he will subdue our iniquities; and thou wilt cast all their sins into the depths of the sea."

And here we are told there will be no more sea. Not only will there not be any more large oceans to bring separation, but there will be no more sin. Our sins hidden in the ocean depths will be gone with the ocean.

"'I saw a new heaven and a new earth: for the first heaven and the first earth were passed away.' Revelation 21:1. The fire that consumes the wicked purifies the earth. Every trace of the curse is swept away. No eternally burning hell will keep before the ransomed the fearful consequences of sin.

"One reminder alone remains: Our Redeemer will ever bear the marks of His crucifixion. Upon His wounded head, upon His side, His hands and feet, are the only traces of the cruel work that sin has wrought. Says the prophet, beholding Christ in His glory: 'He had bright beams coming out of His side: and there was the hiding of His power.' Habakkuk 3:4, margin. That pierced side whence flowed the crimson stream that reconciled man to God—there is the Saviour's glory, there 'the hiding of His power.' 'Mighty to save,' through the sacrifice of redemption, He was therefore strong to execute justice upon them that despised God's mercy. And the tokens of His humiliation are His highest honor; through the eternal ages the wounds of Calvary will show forth His praise and declare His power."[3]

Revelation 21:2 And I John saw the holy city, new Jerusalem, coming down from God out of heaven, prepared as a bride adorned for her husband.

The new Jerusalem comes down to this earth before the destruction of the wicked, for in Revelation 20:9 we see that Satan and the wicked "went up on the breadth of the earth, and compassed the camp of the saints about, and the beloved city: and fire came down from God out of heaven, and devoured them."

---

[3] E. G. White, *The Great Controversy* (1911), p. 674.1-2.

"Christ descends upon the Mount of Olives, whence, after His resurrection, He ascended, and where angels repeated the promise of His return. Says the prophet: 'The Lord my God shall come, and all the saints with Thee.' 'And His feet shall stand in that day upon the Mount of Olives, which is before Jerusalem on the east, and the Mount of Olives shall cleave in the midst thereof,... and there shall be a very great valley.' 'And the Lord shall be king over all the earth: in that day shall there be one Lord, and His name one.' Zechariah 14:5, 4, 9. As the New Jerusalem, in its dazzling splendor, comes down out of heaven, it rests upon the place purified and made ready to receive it, and Christ, with His people and the angels, enters the Holy City."[4]

After the new Jerusalem descends, the wicked are destroyed and the earth is purified of sin. The new Jerusalem, his church, is the bride of Christ—a symbol of the love he has for his people.

Revelation 21:3 And I heard a great voice out of heaven saying, Behold, the tabernacle of God is with men, and he will dwell with them, and they shall be his people, and God himself shall be with them, and be their God.

In the sanctuary services in the wilderness that outlined the plan of salvation and pointed forward to Christ's sacrifice, the calendar of ceremonies was representative of various aspects of the plan of salvation. The culmination of that yearly cycle was the Feast of Tabernacles.[5] As the Passover foreshadowed Jesus' first coming and his sacrifice as the Passover lamb, so the Feast of Tabernacles indicates the culmination of the plan of salvation, when God will dwell with us.

"These types were fulfilled, not only as to the event, but as to the time. On the fourteenth day of the first Jewish month, the very day and month on which for fifteen long centuries the Passover lamb had been slain, Christ, having eaten the Passover with His disciples, instituted that feast which was to commemorate His own death as 'the Lamb of God, which taketh away the sin of the world.' That same night He was taken by wicked hands to be crucified and slain. And

---

[4] E. G. White, *The Great Controversy* (1911), p. 662.3.

[5] See comments on Daniel 8, 9.

as the antitype of the wave sheaf our Lord was raised from the dead on the third day, 'the first fruits of them that slept,' a sample of all the resurrected just, whose 'vile body' shall be changed, and 'fashioned like unto His glorious body.' 1 Corinthians 15:20; Philippians 3:21. "In like manner the types which relate to the second advent must be fulfilled at the time pointed out in the symbolic service."[6]

The second coming of Jesus, which is the commencement of the Feast of Tabernacles, will be at the time pointed out in the symbolic service. In other words, the day of Tabernacles, which occurs in the late fall, will be the time of year when Jesus comes.[7] Tabernacles is also symbolic of the fact that the monarch of the universe will move his capital and his throne, his city and his mansion, to this earth, forever to dwell with his human family.

"The Feast of Tabernacles was not only commemorative but typical. It not only pointed back to the wilderness sojourn, but, as the feast of harvest, it celebrated the ingathering of the fruits of the earth, and pointed forward to the great day of final ingathering, when the Lord of the harvest shall send forth His reapers to gather the tares together in bundles for the fire, and to gather the wheat into His garner… "The people of Israel praised God at the Feast of Tabernacles, as they called to mind His mercy in their deliverance from the bondage of Egypt and His tender care for them during their pilgrim life in the wilderness. They rejoiced also in the consciousness of pardon and acceptance, through the service of the day of atonement, just ended. But when the ransomed of the Lord shall have been safely gathered into the heavenly Canaan, forever delivered from the bondage of the

---

[6] E. G. White, *The Great Controversy* (1911), p. 399.3-4.

[7] This does not mean we can figure out the day and hour of Jesus' coming.

Matthew 25:13 "Watch therefore, for ye know neither the day nor the hour wherein the Son of man cometh."

Mathew 24:30-33 "And then shall appear the sign of the Son of man in heaven: and then shall all the tribes of the earth mourn, and they shall see the Son of man coming in the clouds of heaven with power and great glory... So likewise ye, when ye shall see all these things, know that it is near, even at the doors."

For convenience modern Jewish calendars do not order the feasts on the correct day, Biblically. In the Biblical Jewish calendar, one would not know when the feasts are to occur until the first day of that calendar year. The first day of the new year was determined by the ripening of the barley harvest in Palestine, which was inspected by the high priest. Once a particular year had started, then you would know on what day each one of those feasts would occur. Consequently, one could not predict two or three years ahead of time what day the feast of Tabernacles would be on.

curse... they will rejoice with joy unspeakable and full of glory. Christ's great work of atonement for men will then have been completed, and their sins will have been forever blotted out."[8]

"In Christ the family of earth and the family of heaven are bound together. Christ glorified is our brother. Heaven is enshrined in humanity, and humanity is enfolded in the bosom of Infinite Love. "...The exaltation of the redeemed will be an eternal testimony to God's mercy. 'In the ages to come,' He will 'show the exceeding riches of His grace in His kindness toward us through Christ Jesus.'...

"Through Christ's redeeming work the government of God stands justified. The Omnipotent One is made known as the God of love. Satan's charges are refuted, and his character unveiled. Rebellion can never again arise. Sin can never again enter the universe. Through eternal ages all are secure from apostasy. By love's self-sacrifice, the inhabitants of earth and heaven are bound to their Creator in bonds of indissoluble union.

"The work of redemption will be complete. In the place where sin abounded, God's grace much more abounds. The earth itself, the very field that Satan claims as his, is to be not only ransomed but exalted. Our little world, under the curse of sin the one dark blot in His glorious creation, will be honored above all other worlds in the universe of God. Here, where the Son of God tabernacled in humanity; where the King of glory lived and suffered and died, — here, when He shall make all things new, the tabernacle of God shall be with men, 'and He will dwell with them, and they shall be His people, and God Himself shall be with them, and be their God.' And through endless ages as the redeemed walk in the light of the Lord, they will praise Him for His unspeakable Gift, — Immanuel, 'God with us.'"[9]

Revelation 21:4 And God shall wipe away all tears from their eyes; and there shall be no more death, neither sorrow, nor crying, neither shall there be any more pain: for the former things are passed away.

---

[8] E. G. White, *Patriarchs and Prophets* (1890), p. 541.2-542.1.

[9] E. G. White, *The Desire of Ages* (1898), p. 25.3-26.3.

A precious promise indeed! This is the culmination of all Scripture and the climax of the Revelation of Jesus Christ. Everything points to the day in which God can finally wipe away all tears from all our eyes, and make all things new.

God does not wipe away the tears from our eyes until after the millennium, when sin and sinners are no more. Even though everyone has agreed that the punishments are just, the day of judgment will still be a day of sadness, knowing that those outside could have been in the city with God's people had they chosen Christ. But once that is all finished, God says, the former things will be forgotten: "For, behold, I create new heavens and a new earth: and the former shall not be remembered, nor come into mind."[10]

Revelation 21:5 And he that sat upon the throne said, Behold, I make all things new. And he said unto me, Write: for these words are true and faithful.

In the beginning when God created the world everything was in place and completely finished before he created Adam and Eve. Adam did not see any of the process of creation. When God recreates the world we will have the privilege of watching God create the new heavens and the new earth. Imagine what it will be like when God speaks these things into existence. Suddenly you see the green flush rush over the face of the brown earth; followed by the blush of flowers spreading rapidly around the globe; then a word brush of trees painting across the hills; finally the roar of the lion and the song of the thrush. "**Behold**," God says—watch this! God has infinite things that he can hardly wait for us to see.

Revelation 21:6 And he said unto me, It is done. I am Alpha and Omega, the beginning and the end. I will give unto him that is athirst of the fountain of the water of life freely.

Jesus, who is the Alpha and Omega, the beginning and end, pronounces the rescue of his people complete.[11]

---

[10] Isaiah 65:17

[11] See comments on Revelation 1.

"The flowing of the water from the rock in the desert was celebrated by the Israelites, after their establishment in Canaan, with demonstrations of great rejoicing. In the time of Christ this celebration had become a most impressive ceremony. It took place on the occasion of the Feast of Tabernacles, when the people from all the land were assembled at Jerusalem. On each of the seven days of the feast the priests went out with music and the choir of Levites to draw water in a golden vessel from the spring of Siloam. They were followed by multitudes of the worshipers, as many as could get near the stream drinking of it, while the jubilant strains arose, 'With joy shall ye draw water out of the wells of salvation.' Isaiah 12:3. Then the water drawn by the priests was borne to the temple amid the sounding of trumpets and the solemn chant, 'Our feet shall stand within thy gates, O Jerusalem.' Psalm 122:2. The water was poured out upon the altar of burnt offering, while songs of praise rang out, the multitudes joining in triumphant chorus with musical instruments and deep-toned trumpets.

"The Saviour made use of this symbolic service to direct the minds of the people to the blessings that He had come to bring them. 'In the last day, that great day of the feast,' His voice was heard in tones that rang through the temple courts, 'If any man thirst, let him come unto Me, and drink. He that believeth on Me, as the Scripture hath said, out of his belly shall flow rivers of living water.' 'This,' said John, 'spake He of the Spirit, which they that believe on Him should receive.' John 7:37-39. The refreshing water, welling up in a parched and barren land, causing the desert place to blossom, and flowing out to give life to the perishing, is an emblem of the divine grace which Christ alone can bestow, and which is as the living water, purifying, refreshing, and invigorating the soul. He in whom Christ is abiding has within him a never-failing fountain of grace and strength. Jesus cheers the life and brightens the path of all who truly seek Him. His love, received into the heart, will spring up in good works unto eternal life. And not only does it bless the soul in which it springs, but the living stream will flow out in words and deeds of righteousness, to refresh the thirsting around him....

"Isaiah... records the precious promise, bringing vividly to mind the living stream that flowed for Israel: 'When the poor and needy seek water, and there is none, and their tongue faileth for thirst, I the Lord will hear them, I the God of Israel will not forsake them.' 'I will pour water upon him that is thirsty, and floods upon the dry ground;' 'in the wilderness shall waters break out, and streams in the desert.' The invitation is given, 'Ho, every one that thirsteth, come ye to the waters.' Isaiah 41:17; 44:3; Isaiah 35:6; 55:1. And in the closing pages of the Sacred Word this invitation is echoed. The river of the water of life, 'clear as crystal,' proceeds from the throne of God and the Lamb; and the gracious call is ringing down through the ages, '**Whosoever will, let him take the water of life freely**.'"[12] "This promise is only to those that thirst. None but those who feel their need of the water of life, and seek it at the loss of all things else, will be supplied. 'He that overcometh shall inherit all things; and I will be his God, and he shall be My son.' Verse 7. Here, also, conditions are specified. In order to inherit all things, we must resist and overcome sin."[13]

Revelation 21:7 He that overcometh shall inherit all things; and I will be his God, and he shall be my son.

"The world's Redeemer was treated as we deserve to be treated, in order that we might be treated as he deserved to be treated. He came to our world and took our sins upon his own divine soul, that we might receive his imputed righteousness. He was condemned for our sins, in which he had no share, that we might be justified by his righteousness, in which we had no share. The world's Redeemer gave himself for us. Who was he?—The Majesty of heaven, pouring out his blood upon the altar of justice for the sins of guilty man. We should know our relationship to Christ and his relationship to us."[14]

God proposes to make us sons and daughters of the King of Kings. All who overcome by the power of Christ will be a part of his family. There is some overcoming to do. God will not save us in our sins, but from our sins.

"Sanctification is not the work of a moment, an hour, a day, but of a lifetime. It is not gained by a happy flight of feeling, but is the result of constantly dying to sin, and constantly living for Christ. Wrongs cannot be righted nor reformations wrought in the character by feeble, intermittent efforts. It is only by long, persevering effort, sore discipline, and stern conflict, that we shall overcome. We know not one day how strong will be our conflict the next. So long as Satan reigns, we shall have self to subdue, besetting sins to overcome; so

---

[12] E. G. White, *Patriarchs and Prophets* (1890), p. 412.1-413.2.

[13] E. G. White, *The Great Controversy* (1911), p. 540.2.

[14] E. G. White, *Review and Herald,* March 21, 1893, par. 6.

long as life shall last, there will be no stopping place, no point which we can reach and say, I have fully attained. Sanctification is the result of lifelong obedience.

"...The nearer we come to Jesus, and the more clearly we discern the purity of His character, the more clearly shall we see the exceeding sinfulness of sin, and the less shall we feel like exalting ourselves. There will be a continual reaching out of the soul after God, a continual, earnest, heartbreaking confession of sin and humbling of the heart before Him. At every advance step in our Christian experience our repentance will deepen. We shall know that our sufficiency is in Christ alone and shall make the apostle's confession our own: 'I know that in me (that is, in my flesh,) dwelleth no good thing.' 'God forbid that I should glory, save in the cross of our Lord Jesus Christ, by whom the world is crucified unto me, and I unto the world.' Romans 7:18; Galatians 6:14."[15]

Revelation 21:8 But the fearful, and unbelieving, and the abominable, and murderers, and whoremongers, and sorcerers, and idolaters, and all liars, shall have their part in the lake which burneth with fire and brimstone: which is the second death.

Jesus says, I have invited all to come and drink of the fountain of everlasting life; to those who overcome I have given to inherit all things, but those who will not come and enter in are those who are listed here. It is quite a list, let us examine it a little more closely.

THE FEARFUL:

Sometimes we fear persecution, we fear disapproval from humans. We often fear, but God says: "There is no fear in love; but perfect love casteth out fear: because fear hath torment. He that feareth is not made perfect in love."[16]

"Those outside of the city are among the most confident, boastful, and apparently zealous ones who love in word, but not in deed and in truth. Their hearts are not right with God. His fear is not before them. The fearful and unbelieving, who are punished with the second death, are of that class who are ashamed of Christ in this world.

---

[15] E. G. White, *Acts of the Apostles* (1911), p. 560.3-560.2.

[16] 1 John 4:18.

They are afraid to do right and follow Christ, lest they should meet with pecuniary loss. They neglect their duty, to avoid reproach and trials, and to escape dangers. Those who dare not do right because they will thus expose themselves to trials, persecution, loss, and suffering are cowards, and, with idolaters, liars, and all sinners, they are ripening for the second death."[17]

THE UNBELIEVING:

Doubt is rampant in churches today, especially among the most educated people. It is fashionable to doubt, question, and cavil regarding the Scriptures.

"Brethren, cling to your Bible, as it reads, and stop your criticisms in regard to its validity, and obey the Word, and not one of you will be lost. The ingenuity of men has been exercised for ages to measure the Word of God by their finite minds and limited comprehension. If the Lord, the Author of the living oracles, would throw back the curtain and reveal His wisdom and His glory before them, they would shrink into nothingness and exclaim as did Isaiah, 'I am a man of unclean lips, and I dwell in the midst of people of unclean lips' (Isaiah 6:5)."[18]

"If he [the enemy of God and man] can control minds so that doubt and unbelief and darkness shall compose the experience of those who claim to be the children of God, he can overcome them with temptation. That simple faith that takes God at his word should be encouraged. God's people must have that faith which will lay hold of divine power; 'for by grace are ye saved through faith; and that not of yourselves: it is the gift of God.' [Ephesians 2:8.] Those who believe that God for Christ's sake has forgiven their sins should not, through temptation, fail to press on to fight the good fight of faith. Their faith should grow stronger until their Christian life, as well as their words, shall declare, 'The blood of Jesus Christ cleanseth us from all sin.'"[19]

---

[17] E. G. White, *Testimonies for the Church,* Vol. 2 (1871), p. 360.1-361.1.

[18] E. G. White, *Selected Messages,* Book 1 (1858), p. 18.1.

[19] E. G. White, *Gospel Workers,* (1892) p. 103.2.

THE MURDERERS:

Some might be thinking I am not a murderer. I have not killed anybody. Do not be too sure. Scripture says, "Whosoever hateth his brother is a murderer: and ye know that no murderer hath eternal life abiding in him."[20]

It is our sins that killed the Son of God.

WHOREMONGERS:

Some might reason, I have never visited a whore, so I am doing pretty good.

"Ye have heard that it was said by them of old time, Thou shalt not commit adultery: But I say unto you, That whosoever looketh on a woman to lust after her hath committed adultery with her already in his heart."[21]

THE SORCERERS AND IDOLATERS:

Perhaps you are thinking, I would not do anything like that; I am a Christian; I would never do sorcery or worship an idol.

Before inflating with self-righteousness, see how God considers these things.

"For rebellion is as the sin of witchcraft, and stubbornness is as iniquity and idolatry..."[22] Are we sometimes rebellious? Are we often stubborn? We are proud of these characteristics.

---

[20] 1 John 3:15

[21] Matthew 5:27-28
An excellent resource for finding purity and gaining victory over lust is the video series, *A Greater Lust*, by Scott Ritsema. www.beltoftruthministries.org

[22] 1 Samuel 5:23

ALL LIARS:

"Falsehood and deception of every cast is sin against the God of truth and verity. The word of God is plain upon these points. Ye shall not 'deal falsely, neither lie one to another.' 'All liars shall have their part in the lake which burneth with fire and brimstone: which is the second death.' God is a God of sincerity and truth. The word of God is a book of truth. Jesus is a faithful and true witness. The church is the witness and ground of the truth. All the precepts of the Most High are true and righteous altogether. How, then, must prevarication and any exaggeration or deception appear in His sight? For the falsehood he uttered because he coveted the gifts which the prophet refused, the servant of Elisha was struck with leprosy, which ended only with death."[23]

This list is talking about every one of us. We are sinners in need of a Saviour. Even our righteousness is as filthy rags. We need only to think about how it applies to us, and we will be on our knees asking God for grace and power to overcome. God is going to have to deliver us from these things, or we will not be in heaven. God has promised to give us the strength and power to overcome all besetting sins.

Revelation 21:9 And there came unto me one of the seven angels which had the seven vials full of the seven last plagues, and talked with me, saying, Come hither, I will show thee the bride, the Lamb's wife.

This is apparently the same angel who talked to John in Revelation 17 when he was shown the harlot on the scarlet beast. Now he will show John the bride, the lamb's wife.

Revelation 21:10 And he carried me away in the spirit to a great and high mountain, and showed me that great city, the holy Jerusalem, descending out of heaven from God,

Revelation 21:11 Having the glory of God: and her light was like unto a stone most precious, even like a jasper stone, clear as crystal;

---

[23] E. G. White, *Testimonies for the Church*, Vol. 4 (1881), p. 336.1.

The city is transparent, she has the glory of God, and the light of his glory is shining through the city. Imagine what that will look like.

Revelation 21:12 And had a wall great and high, and had twelve gates, and at the gates twelve angels, and names written thereon, which are the names of the twelve tribes of the children of Israel:

Revelation 21:13 On the east three gates; on the north three gates; on the south three gates; and on the west three gates.

Revelation 21:14 And the wall of the city had twelve foundations, and in them the names of the twelve apostles of the Lamb.

The city has twelve gates with the names of the twelve tribes of Israel written on them and twelve foundations with the names of the twelve apostles. The number twelve is symbolic of leadership. Jesus has listed the leaders of the Old Testament church and the leaders of the New Testament church on the gates and on the foundations.

Ezekiel specifies which tribe will be on each side.

"And these are the goings out of the city on the north side, four thousand and five hundred measures. And the gates of the city shall be after the names of the tribes of Israel: three gates northward; one gate of Reuben, one gate of Judah, one gate of Levi. And at the east side four thousand and five hundred: and three gates; and one gate of Joseph, one gate of Benjamin, one gate of Dan. And at the south side four thousand and five hundred measures: and three gates; one gate of Simeon, one gate of Issachar, one gate of Zebulun. At the west side four thousand and five hundred, with their three gates; one gate of Gad, one gate of Asher, one gate of Naphtali."[24]

Revelation 21:15 And he that talked with me had a golden reed to measure the city, and the gates thereof, and the wall thereof.

---

[24] Ezekiel 48:34

737

Revelation 21:16 And the city lieth foursquare, and the length is as large as the breadth: and he measured the city with the reed, twelve thousand furlongs. The length and the breadth and the height of it are equal.

The angel does not measure one side with the reed, but rather he measures the city. This means he measures all the way around the city.[25] The measurement of the city is 12,000 furlongs. It has four sides, all of which are equal, therefore 12,000 furlongs divided by 4 is 3,000 furlongs per side.

How long is a furlong? Some have calculated the size using an English furlong, but since the English furlongs did not exist when John wrote Revelation, a Roman furlong is preferred. A Roman furlong is 606.75 feet,[26] which if we multiply by 3,000 furlongs and then divide it by 5,280 feet per mile, we find that the city measures 344.74432 miles per side. This is 118,849 square miles, at the base. By comparison, New Mexico is 121,589 square miles and Arizona is 113,998 square miles. This is a city that is the size of an entire Western state.

The height is equal to the width, which means the city is 344.7 miles high. This is as high as our current thermosphere, the last layer before the exosphere, which is essentially outer space. The pinnacle would be 100 miles above the orbit of the International Space Station. We have no reference to fathom a city like this. No wonder the Bible says, "Eye hath not seen, nor ear heard, neither have entered into the heart of man, the things which God hath prepared for them that love him."

Many, when reading that the length and the breadth and height are equal, assume that this city is a cube. But a cube is not the only shape to meet those specifications, nor is it an architecturally appealing structure. The next verse proves that it is not a cube.

---

[25] This agrees with Ezekiel's method of measuring a city with an angel. See Ezekiel 48:30-34. Ezekiel 48:35 "It was **round about** eighteen thousand measures: and the name of the city from that day shall be, The LORD is there."

[26] James Orr, M.A., D.D., (editor) *The International Standard Bible Encyclopædia*, Vol. 2, (Chicago: Howard-Severance Co., 1915) p. 1149.

Revelation 21:17 And he measured the wall thereof, an hundred and forty and four cubits, according to the measure of a man, that is, of the angel.

If the city was a cube the wall would be 3,000 furlongs high. But the wall is not 3,000 furlongs high; rather it is 144 cubits. One cubit is 18 inches, which makes the wall 216 feet high.

The city is 344.7 miles high, long, and wide, while the height of the wall is only 216 feet, therefore the city is not a cube. There is another shape with height, length, and width equal—that is a pyramid. The wall goes straight up for 216 feet, with the city rising from there in the shape of a pyramid, with the pinnacle reaching 344.7 miles into the sky.

Perhaps this is why Satan has caused the pyramid to have occult connotations and to be revered in pagan worship. He was once in heaven and fell from the courts of glory. He knows better than anyone on this planet, what that city looked like. In the occult world a pyramid is often depicted with one all-seeing eye in the tip of the pyramid, hovering above the lower part. Perhaps Satan is trying to imitate the throne of God, that he attempted to overthrow, with the temple above the city.[27]

It is interesting that John says of the cubit used to measure the wall that it is **"according to the measure of a man,"** and then adds, **"that is, of the angel."** In other words, he is saying that it is a cubit, just like a cubit is normally the measurement from the elbow to the tips of the finger, but then he clarifies that it is really the cubit of the angel. The angel was likely much taller than John, so perhaps we do not know the exact length of 144 angel cubits.

---

[27] **"Far above the city, upon a foundation of burnished gold, is a throne, high and lifted up.** Upon this throne sits the Son of God, and around Him are the subjects of His kingdom. The power and majesty of Christ no language can describe, no pen portray. The glory of the Eternal Father is enshrouding His Son. The brightness of His presence fills the City of God, and flows out beyond the gates, flooding the whole earth with its radiance."
E. G. White, *The Great Controversy* (1911), p. 665.1.

The city that John sees in vision is square at the base, with twelve gates,[28] with a river of life,[29] and a tree of life.[30] The prophet Ezekiel was also given a vision of a city that is square at the base,[31] with twelve gates,[32] with a river of life,[33] and a tree of life.[34] "The name of the city from that day shall be, The LORD is there."[35] There is only one city that can be called by this name—the New Jerusalem.

Ezekiel also provides the measurements of the city he is shown: "And these shall be the measures thereof; the north side four thousand and five hundred, and the south side four thousand and five hundred, and on the east side four thousand and five hundred, and the west side four thousand and five hundred."[36] "It was round about eighteen thousand measures."[37]

However, Ezekiel gives the size of the city as 18,000 measures instead of John's 12,000 furlongs. How large is 18,000 measures? Ezekiel was shown a measurement which he called a cubit, but which he clarified to be a cubit and a handbreadth.[38] This special cubit, or "measure," consisted of eighteen inches for the regular cubit plus three inches for the handbreadth, equaling twenty-one inches. Therefore, the city is 1.5 miles on a side and 6 miles around. This is a very small "city," with suburbs of 438 feet.[39]

Are these two cities connected, and why such a difference in size? The Bible gives a precedent for a small-scale model of the heavenly sanctuary. Speaking of the tabernacle that was built by Moses, as given by God's direction in the wilderness, the Bible records in

---

[28] Revelation 21:21

[29] Revelation 22:1

[30] Revelation 22:2

[31] Ezekiel 48:16, 35

[32] Ezekiel 48:31-34

[33] Ezekiel 47:1-12

[34] Ezekiel 47:12; Compare Revelation 22:2.

[35] Ezekiel 48:35

[36] Ezekiel 48:16

[37] Ezekiel 48:35

[38] Ezekiel 40:5; 43:13

[39] Ezekiel 48:17

Hebrews 8:5 "Who serve unto the example and shadow of heavenly things, as Moses was admonished of God when he was about to make the tabernacle: for, See, saith he, that thou make all things according to the pattern showed to thee in the mount." The tabernacle in the wilderness was to follow the pattern of something much larger; it was a shadow of heavenly things.

In Hebrews 9:23, speaking of the sacrifices of the goats and calves offered in the earthly tabernacle, the Bible compares these with the heavenly: "It was therefore necessary that the patterns of things in the heavens should be purified with these; but the heavenly things themselves with better sacrifices than these."

The earthly tabernacle was the pattern of the heavenly sanctuary. The sacrifice of Jesus on the cross was the sacrifice better than goats and calves, which was to purify the heavenly sanctuary. The inner compartment, or most holy place, of the wilderness tabernacle was not quite fifteen feet by fifteen feet.[40] When Solomon built the permanent temple, to replace the mobile tent, he followed the same pattern, but made it larger with the most holy place thirty by thirty feet.[41] When John was shown the heavenly sanctuary, he saw millions of angels in the throne[42] room of God.[43] Millions of angels cannot fit in a thirty by thirty foot space much less a fifteen by fifteen foot room. Clearly the heavenly sanctuary is much larger than the earthly tabernacle.

Could it be that when Ezekiel sees in his vision a city only 1.5 miles on a side, that God showed him a small-scale model of the city to which John received the life-sized measurements? What if Ezekiel was given to-scale measurements of a map, from which we can extrapolate to the size of John's city, revealing more detail about the heavenly city and its temple?

---

[40] Exodus 26:16, 22 (The most holy was enclosed by six vertical boards per side, with each board measuring a cubit and a half wide, making the room about 9 by 9 cubits. The holy place was the same width and twice the length.)

[41] 1 Kings 6:2

[42] The throne of God was represented in the earthly model by the mercy seat in the most holy place of the sanctuary. Therefore, the most holy place is the throne room of the universe.

[43] See comments on Revelation 5:11.

In the book of Ezekiel, from chapters 40-48, is given a description of strips of land around a city and detailed measurements of the temple. Two strips of land are described that are 25,000 by 10,000 cubits, the first being for the priests,[44] which contained the temple, and the second for the Levites.[45] The city, which is 4,500 cubits on a side, has a 250-cubit wide suburb, which is less than 500 feet, making a very small suburb if this is the city's literal size. On either side of the city are two strips of land that are 10,000 by 5,000 cubits, which are the gardens to grow the food to feed the city.[46] Ezekiel goes on to describe 13 strips of land,[47] one of which would contain the temple: Ezekiel 48:8 "And by the border of Judah, from the east side unto the west side, shall be the offering which ye shall offer of five and twenty thousand reeds in breadth, and in length as one of the other parts, from the east side unto the west side: and the sanctuary shall be in the midst of it."

One strip of land is designated for each of the twelve tribes, and one strip contains the sanctuary and the city, with the remaining land of that strip for "the prince"[48]—Emmanuel.

If the city Ezekiel saw is a small-scale pattern of the full-sized city John saw, then if we were to compare the ratio of Ezekiel's city to Ezekiel's land, with the size of John's city, and scale up the land proportionally, we would know the size of the land on John's scale of measurement.

Assuming the width for each tribe's land is the same as that of the strip containing the sanctuary (since the sanctuary strip, we are told, is "in length as one of the other parts," Ezekiel 48:8), the 13 strips of

---

[44] Ezekiel 48:10

[45] Ezekiel 48:13

[46] Ezekiel 48:18

[47] Ezekiel 48:2-8; 23-27

[48] Ezekiel 48:21

Dan
Asher
Naphtali
Manasseh
Ephraim
Reuben
Judah

The Prince	▪ Temple & City

Benjamin
Simeon
Issachar
Zebulun
Gad

[49]

land multiplied by 25,000 cubits equal 325,000 cubits for the total width of the land. If we then take the 325,000 cubits and divide it by the size of Ezekiel's city or 4,500 cubits and multiply that ratio by the size of John's city (344.74432 miles), we would know the size of the land on John's scale of measurement.

325,000/4,500 X 344.74432 miles = 24,898 miles.

---

[49] http://www.pickle-publishing.com

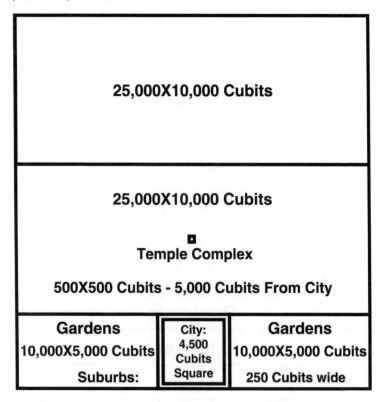

The land, on John's scale, is 24,898 miles wide. Modern science tells us that the circumference of the earth at the equator is 24,901 miles.[50] Almost millennia ago these prophecies were written, revealing the circumference of our globe, long before modern science measured the planet.

The Bible says, "But the meek shall inherit the earth..."[51] "For the promise, that he should be the heir of the world, was not to Abraham, or to his seed, through the law, but through the righteousness of faith."[52] "For they are not all Israel, which are of Israel: Neither, because they are the seed of Abraham, are they all children: but, In Isaac shall thy seed be called. That is, They which are the children of

---

[50] This yields a margin of error of only 0.012%.

[51] Psalms 37:11

[52] Romans 4:13

the flesh, these are not the children of God: but the children of the promise are counted for the seed."[53]
God is telling us that the children of promise, or spiritual Israel will inherit the earth. And buried in his Word, like a diamond awaiting discovery, is a prophecy revealing the dimensions of the globe—a map of the new earth.[54]

Applying the same ratio[55] to the other measurements of Ezekiel's temple reveals the actual size of the temple according to John's scale of measurement. Suddenly, our wildest imaginations can hardly grasp the glory that is revealed.[56] We see gates that are ¾ mile wide;[57] four miles from the face of the outer gate to the porch of the inner gate;[58] arches that are 0.4 miles wide and two miles long;[59] and pillars that are half a mile thick and four and a half miles high,[60] with palm trees on top.[61]

God tells us the purpose of giving Ezekiel all these measurements. Ezekiel 43:10 says, "Thou son of man, show the house to the house of Israel, that they may be ashamed of their iniquities: and let them measure the pattern."

Ezekiel is to show the house (the temple) to Israel, that they may be ashamed of their iniquities. If Ezekiel's measurements are taken literally, there is nothing that would make us ashamed of our iniquities. But, if we understand Ezekiel's city to be a small-scale

---

[53] Romans 9:7-8

[54] For more on Israel and spiritual Israel see see comments on Daniel 9, 4b.

[55] The formula, y/4,500 cu. X 344.74 mi. = x, yields a full-scale measurement in miles, where y is one of Ezekiel's measurements in cubits.

[56] To glimpse some of the glories to be home of the redeemed, see *Full Disclosure: The Coming New World Order*, Martin Klein (Savannah Pictures, 2012), www.savannahpictures.com.

[57] Ezekiel 40:11

[58] Ezekiel 40:15

[59] Ezekiel 40:30

[60] Ezekiel 41:1; 40:14

[61] Ezekiel 40:16

replica of John's city, we can decode[62] the rest of Ezekiel's measurements, revealing a glimpse of the stunning magnificence of this temple. With this vision of glory, we fall on our knees, ashamed of our iniquities. Jesus is the "lamb slain from the foundation of the world."[63] Therefore God's eternal throne, and the temple that houses it, is a sculpture of the plan in place from all eternity, to save his creatures should they sin.

Revelation 21:18 And the building of the wall of it was of jasper: and the city was pure gold, like unto clear glass.

Imagine the glory of God streaming through the streets, radiating right down through the city, and shining through those transparent walls.

Revelation 21:19 And the foundations of the wall of the city were garnished with all manner of precious stones. The first foundation was jasper; the second, sapphire; the third, a chalcedony; the fourth, an emerald;

Revelation 21:20 The fifth, sardonyx; the sixth, sardius; the seventh, chrysolyte; the eighth, beryl; the ninth, a topaz; the tenth, a chrysoprasus; the eleventh, a jacinth; the twelfth, an amethyst.

These are not just little stones but twelve entire foundations of the city made from these precious stones.

Imagine the glory of God flooding through the streets, radiating down through the city, flashing through the transparent walls, and coming out as a prism like a rainbow through the foundations of the city. Nothing we can even comprehend would come close to this.

---

[62] Ezekiel is told to "measure the pattern," revealing that is a replica of something almost infinitely larger. When Ezekiel was shown this pattern, there was no way to know the real dimension that God had hidden in that message, until John was given the Revelation of Jesus Christ. Revealing Jesus reveals the glory and majesty of his throne.

[63] Revelation 13:8

Revelation 21:21 And the twelve gates were twelve pearls: every several gate was of one pearl: and the street of the city was pure gold, as it were transparent glass.

Each gate is made from one single pearl. With the city being 344 miles high having walls that are at least 216 feet in height, the gates must be enormous. Perhaps the tops of the gates extend higher than the top of the wall.
Pearls come from oysters. Try to comprehend the size of the oyster that could produce a pearl of this magnitude. "Eye hath not seen, nor ear heard, neither have entered into the heart of man, the things which God hath prepared for them that love him."[64]

"In my Father's house are many mansions: if it were not so, I would have told you. I go to prepare a place for you. And if I go and prepare a place for you, I will come again, and receive you unto myself; that where I am, there ye may be also."[65] Jesus has prepared a mansion for you. Your name is likely on the door of that mansion. Imagine the tears in his eyes and the quaver of his voice if he has to take your name down and say, I made this mansion especially for this person, but they chose not to be here with me; they chose not to follow my ways, and so unfortunately, they are not with us.

Revelation 21:22 And I saw no temple therein: for the Lord God Almighty and the Lamb are the temple of it.

John saw no temple in the city—the temple is outside the city (above it). "I saw also the Lord sitting upon a throne, high and lifted up, and his train filled the temple."[66]

"Far above the city, upon a foundation of burnished gold, is a throne, high and lifted up. Upon this throne sits the Son of God, and around Him are the subjects of His kingdom. The power and majesty of Christ no language can describe, no pen portray. The glory of the Eternal Father is enshrouding His Son. The brightness of His

---

[64] 1 Corinthians 2:9

[65] John 14:2-3

[66] Isaiah 6:1

presence fills the City of God, and flows out beyond the gates, flooding the whole earth with its radiance."[67]

Revelation 21:23 And the city had no need of the sun, neither of the moon, to shine in it: for the glory of God did lighten it, and the Lamb is the light thereof.

The Lamb, Jesus Christ, is the light of the city.

Revelation 21:24 And the nations of them which are saved shall walk in the light of it: and the kings of the earth do bring their glory and honour into it.

The God of the universe, who has all power and all creative ability, takes those who were once clothed in filthy rags, in complete rebellion, home to walk in the light of his house and city. Once he has clothed us with his righteousness he pronounces that we add glory and honor unto the New Jerusalem. How incomprehensibly exalted and honored will he make us?

Revelation 21:25 And the gates of it shall not be shut at all by day: for there shall be no night there.

Gates are no longer needed for protection—only for decoration—and to provide a symbol that points us to Jesus: "I am the door: by me if any man enter in, he shall be saved, and shall go in and out, and find pasture. The thief cometh not, but for to steal, and to kill, and to destroy: I am come that they might have life, and that they might have it more abundantly."[68]

Revelation 21:26 And they shall bring the glory and honour of the nations into it.

"All the treasures of the universe will be open to the study of God's redeemed. Unfettered by mortality, they wing their tireless flight to

---

[67] E. G. White, *The Great Controversy* (1911), p. 665.1.

[68] John 10:9-10

worlds afar—worlds that thrilled with sorrow at the spectacle of human woe and rang with songs of gladness at the tidings of a ransomed soul. With unutterable delight the children of earth enter into the joy and the wisdom of unfallen beings. They share the treasures of knowledge and understanding gained through ages upon ages in contemplation of God's handiwork. With undimmed vision they gaze upon the glory of creation—suns and stars and systems, all in their appointed order circling the throne of Deity. Upon all things, from the least to the greatest, the Creator's name is written, and in all are the riches of His power displayed.

"And the years of eternity, as they roll, will bring richer and still more glorious revelations of God and of Christ. As knowledge is progressive, so will love, reverence, and happiness increase. The more men learn of God, the greater will be their admiration of His character. As Jesus opens before them the riches of redemption and the amazing achievements in the great controversy with Satan, the hearts of the ransomed thrill with more fervent devotion, and with more rapturous joy they sweep the harps of gold; and ten thousand times ten thousand and thousands of thousands of voices unite to swell the mighty chorus of praise.

"'And every creature which is in heaven, and on the earth, and under the earth, and such as are in the sea, and all that are in them, heard I saying, Blessing, and honor, and glory, and power, be unto Him that sitteth upon the throne, and unto the Lamb for ever and ever.' Revelation 5:13.

"The great controversy is ended. Sin and sinners are no more. The entire universe is clean. One pulse of harmony and gladness beats through the vast creation. From Him who created all, flow life and light and gladness, throughout the realms of illimitable space. From the minutest atom to the greatest world, all things, animate and inanimate, in their unshadowed beauty and perfect joy, declare that God is love."[69]

Revelation 21:27 And there shall in no wise enter into it any thing that defileth, neither whatsoever worketh abomination, or maketh a lie: but they which are written in the Lamb's book of life.

---

[69] E. G. White, *The Great Controversy* (1911), p. 677.3-678.3.

"Who shall ascend into the hill of the LORD? or who shall stand in his holy place? He that hath clean hands, and a pure heart."[70] "Blessed are the pure in heart: for they shall see God."[71] "Create in me a clean heart, O God; and renew a right spirit within me."[72]

"Those who, through faith in the merits of the blood of Christ, have clean hands and pure heart, will receive the white robe, the crown of righteousness, and the life that will run parallel with the life of God."[73] Amen.

---

[70] Psalms 24:3-4

[71] Matthew 5:8

[72] Psalms 51:10

[73] E. G. White, "Pray Without Ceasing," *The Sign of the Times*, December 23, 1889 par. 3.

Revelation 22

SUMMARY:
Revelation 22 continues the description of heaven, including the tree of life—its twelve different fruits, each bearing in a different month—and the river of life from the throne of God. John is told not to seal up this prophecy for the time is at hand. Jesus promises that he is coming quickly, and pronounces a blessing on those that do his commandments that they may have a right to the tree of life, and may enter in through the gates into the city. A serious warning is pronounced on any who modify the prophecy, and Jesus repeats the promise that he is coming soon.

Revelation 22:1 And he showed me a pure river of water of life, clear as crystal, proceeding out of the throne of God and of the Lamb.

The throne of God is located in the most holy place of the temple; therefore, the river of life proceeds from the inner sanctuary, from the throne room of the Almighty. Water cleanses from sin, and the final cleansing of sin proceeds from the most holy place of the heavenly sanctuary.

Revelation 22:2 In the midst of the street of it, and on either side of the river, was there the tree of life, which bare twelve manner of fruits, and yielded her fruit every month: and the leaves of the tree were for the healing of the nations.

Ezekiel describes the same scene, "And by the river upon the bank thereof, on this side and on that side, shall grow all trees for meat, whose leaf shall not fade, neither shall the fruit thereof be consumed: it shall bring forth new fruit according to his months, because their waters they issued out of the sanctuary: and the fruit thereof shall be for meat, and the leaf thereof for medicine."[1]

The leaves will heal the effects of sin and suffering and the tree of life will perpetuate eternal life. The pain we have experienced will be wiped away. The tree of life will cause us to grow up into the stature of Adam. "As Adam came forth from the hand of his Creator he was of noble height and of beautiful symmetry. He was more than twice as tall as men now living upon the earth, and was well proportioned. His features were perfect and beautiful. His complexion was neither white nor sallow, but ruddy, glowing with the rich tint of health. Eve was not quite as tall as Adam. Her head reached a little above his shoulders. She, too, was noble, perfect in symmetry, and very beautiful."[2]

"Adam, who stands among the risen throng, is of lofty height and majestic form, in stature but little below the Son of God. He presents a marked contrast to the people of later generations; in this one respect is shown the great degeneracy of the race. But all arise with the freshness and vigor of eternal youth. In the beginning, man was created in the likeness of God, not only in character, but in form and feature. Sin defaced and almost obliterated the divine image; but

---

[1] Ezekiel 47:12

[2] E. G. White, *Spiritual Gifts*, Vol. 3 (1864), p. 33.2.

Christ came to restore that which had been lost. He will change our vile bodies and fashion them like unto His glorious body. The mortal, corruptible form, devoid of comeliness, once polluted with sin, becomes perfect, beautiful, and immortal. All blemishes and deformities are left in the grave. Restored to the tree of life in the long-lost Eden, the redeemed will 'grow up' (Malachi 4:2) to the full stature of the race in its primeval glory. The last lingering traces of the curse of sin will be removed, and Christ's faithful ones will appear in 'the beauty of the Lord our God,' in mind and soul and body reflecting the perfect image of their Lord. Oh, wonderful redemption! long talked of, long hoped for, contemplated with eager anticipation, but never fully understood."[3]

God has given a leaf of the tree of life that we may begin to partake of here and now. Jesus said, "As the living Father hath sent me, and I live by the Father: so he that eateth me, even he shall live by me. This is that bread which came down from heaven: not as your fathers did eat manna, and are dead: he that eateth of this bread shall live for ever. It is the spirit that quickeneth; the flesh profiteth nothing: **the words that I speak unto you, they are spirit, and they are life**."[4] The word of God is the bread of life. If we partake of the word of God we will live forever.

"In the Word the Saviour is revealed in all His beauty and loveliness. Every soul will find comfort and consolation in the Bible, which is full of promises concerning what God will do for the one who comes into right relation to Him. Especially will the sick be comforted by hearing the Word; for **in giving the Scriptures God has given to mankind a leaf from the tree of life**, which is for the healing of the nations. How can anyone who reads the Scriptures or who has heard them read, lose his interest in heavenly things, and find pleasure in amusements and enchantments of the world?"[5]

The tree of life bears a different type of fruit each month. We will never find the tree without fruit. Its' fruit is beyond anything we can comprehend on this earth.

---

[3] E. G. White, *The Great Controversy* (1911), p. 644.3.

[4] John 6:57-58, 63

[5] E. G. White, *The Seventh-day Adventist Bible Commentary*, Vol. 5 (1955), p. 1134.10.

Revelation 22:3 And there shall be no more curse: but the throne of God and of the Lamb shall be in it; and his servants shall serve him:

This is the most precious promise in all Scripture—**"There shall be no more curse."** Anyone, it seems, who has seen the sorrows, cares and death of this planet would desire this.

Service to Christ is not a burden; it will be our highest joy. "Come unto me, all ye that labour and are heavy laden, and I will give you rest. Take my yoke upon you, and learn of me; for I am meek and lowly in heart: and ye shall find rest unto your souls. For my yoke is easy, and my burden is light."[6] "It is a noble work to serve Jesus Christ, who gave his own life, his riches, his glory, in order to rescue us from the power of Satan. We are toiling for a precious, glorious crown and an inheritance that is immortal. The reward is promised: 'To him that overcometh will I grant to sit with me on my throne, even as I also overcame, and am set down with my Father in his throne.' "Will you serve God or Satan? Our Captain presents to us a crown of glory, a kingdom, mansions of bliss, and eternal life. What does Satan propose to give?—a life of sinful pleasure,—sin and its wages—death."[7]

Revelation 22:4 And they shall see his face; and his name shall be in their foreheads.

We will see the face of him who died for us. His character will have been implanted into our minds and hearts transforming us into his likeness that we will perfectly reflect the character of God. Thus his **"name is in our foreheads."**[8]

Revelation 22:5 And there shall be no night there; and they need no candle, neither light of the sun; for the Lord God giveth them light: and they shall reign for ever and ever.

---

[6] Matthew 11:28-30

[7] E. G. White, *The Youth's Instructor*, December 22, 1886 par. 7

[8] See comments on Revelation 7:2; 14:1.

"In the City of God **'there shall be no night.'** None will need or desire repose. There will be no weariness in doing the will of God and offering praise to His name. We shall ever feel the freshness of the morning and shall ever be far from its close. 'And they need no candle, neither light of the sun; for the Lord God giveth them light.' Revelation 22:5. The light of the sun will be superseded by a radiance which is not painfully dazzling, yet which immeasurably surpasses the brightness of our noontide. The glory of God and the Lamb floods the Holy City with unfading light. The redeemed walk in the sunless glory of perpetual day."[9]

"They shall reign for ever and ever": God took the form of "sinful flesh"[10] and became our brother[11] to rescue us from sin. The humans who have been redeemed will be members of the royal family of the universe. "By His life and His death, Christ has achieved even more than recovery from the ruin wrought through sin. It was Satan's purpose to bring about an eternal separation between God and man; but **in Christ we become more closely united to God than if we had never fallen. In taking our nature, the Saviour has bound Himself to humanity by a tie that is never to be broken.** Through the eternal ages He is linked with us. 'God so loved the world, that He gave His only-begotten Son.' John 3:16. He gave Him not only to bear our sins, and to die as our sacrifice; He gave Him to the fallen race. To assure us of His immutable counsel of peace, **God gave His only-begotten Son to become one of the human family, forever to retain His human nature.** This is the pledge that God will fulfill His word. 'Unto us a child is born, unto us a son is given: and the government shall be upon His shoulder.' God has adopted human nature in the person of His Son, and has carried the same into the highest heaven. It is the 'Son of man' who shares the throne of the universe. It is the 'Son of man' whose name shall be called, 'Wonderful, Counselor, The mighty God, The everlasting Father, The Prince of Peace.' Isaiah 9:6. The I AM is the Daysman between God and humanity, laying His hand upon both. He who is 'holy, harmless, undefiled, separate from sinners,' is not ashamed to call us brethren. Hebrews 7:26; 2:11. In Christ the family of earth and the family of heaven are bound together. Christ glorified is our brother. Heaven is

---

[9] E. G. White, *The Great Controversy* (1911), p. 676.3.

[10] Romans 8:3

[11] Hebrews 2:11

enshrined in humanity, and humanity is enfolded in the bosom of Infinite Love."[12] We reign with Christ forever as members of the royal family.

Revelation 22:6 And he said unto me, These sayings are faithful and true: and the Lord God of the holy prophets sent his angel to show unto his servants the things which must shortly be done.

These words are filled with urgency. The Revelation of Jesus Christ repeatedly reminds us that the things revealed are shortly to come to pass. Only God's power will keep us through the final events of earth's history. The words of Scripture, "**faithful and true**," hidden in our hearts will be our only safeguard.

Revelation 22:7 Behold, I come quickly: blessed is he that keepeth the sayings of the prophecy of this book.

Jesus reminds us, one final time, that he is coming soon. He pronounces a special blessing on those who keep the things that are written in the book of Revelation. Yet so many refuse or neglect to study this book. So called Christians cry, stop studying prophecy; study about Jesus.

Every prophecy in Scripture points to Jesus. "To John were opened scenes of deep and thrilling interest in the experience of the church. He saw the position, dangers, conflicts, and final deliverance of the people of God. He records the closing messages which are to ripen the harvest of the earth, either as sheaves for the heavenly garner or as fagots for the fires of destruction. Subjects of vast importance were revealed to him, especially for the last church, that those who should turn from error to truth might be instructed concerning the perils and conflicts before them. None need be in darkness in regard to what is coming upon the earth.
"Why, then, this widespread ignorance concerning an important part of Holy Writ? Why this general reluctance to investigate its teachings? It is the result of a studied effort of the prince of darkness to conceal from men that which reveals his deceptions. For this

---

[12] E. G. White, *The Desire of Ages* (1898), p. 25.3.

reason, Christ the Revelator, foreseeing the warfare that would be waged against the study of the Revelation, pronounced a blessing upon all who should read, hear, and observe the words of the prophecy."[13]

Revelation 22:8 And I John saw these things, and heard them. And when I had heard and seen, I fell down to worship before the feet of the angel which showed me these things.

Overcome with the glory and power of the angelic being speaking to him, John already once fell in worship and was told "See thou do it not: I am thy fellowservant."[14] Once more, upon seeing the glory of Gabriel, John is overwhelmed by his brightness and splendor, and in spite of himself, falls down in worship.

Revelation 22:9 Then saith he unto me, See thou do it not: for I am thy fellowservant, and of thy brethren the prophets, and of them which keep the sayings of this book: worship God.

"The words of the angel, 'I am Gabriel, that stand in the presence of God,' show that he holds a position of high honor in the heavenly courts. When he came with a message to Daniel, he said, 'There is none that holdeth with me in these things, but Michael Christ your Prince.' Daniel 10:21. Of Gabriel the Saviour speaks in the Revelation, saying that 'He sent and signified it by His angel unto His servant John.' Revelation 1:1. And to John the angel declared, 'I am a fellow servant with thee and with thy brethren the prophets.'[15] Revelation 22:9, Wonderful thought—that the angel who stands next in honor to the Son of God is the one chosen to open the purposes of God to sinful men."[16]

Gabriel tells John that he himself is one of those that keep the sayings of the book of Revelation—worship God. We have a gift in our hands—the book of God—that the highest angels of heaven

---

[13] E. G. White, *The Great Controversy* (1911), p. 341.4-342.1.

[14] Revelation 19:10

[15] RV

[16] E. G. White, *The Desire of Ages* (1898), p. 99.1.

study and keep. With this knowledge let us make every effort to read, study, and keep these words.

The message of the book of Revelation is to worship God alone. This book is a revelation of the character and glory of Jesus Christ—God "manifest in the flesh," dwelling among men to save us from our sins. Christ gives us a glimpse of the glory; a foretaste of what he has promised to those who love Him.

Revelation 22:10 And he saith unto me, Seal not the sayings of the prophecy of this book: for the time is at hand.

"Many have entertained the idea that the book of Revelation is a sealed book, and they will not devote time and study to its mysteries. They say that they are to keep looking to the glories of salvation, and that the mysteries revealed to John on the Isle of Patmos are worthy of less consideration than these.

"But God does not so regard this book.... The book of Revelation opens to the world what has been, what is, and what is to come; it is for our instruction upon whom the ends of the world are come. It should be studied with reverential awe. We are privileged in knowing what is for our learning....

"The Lord himself revealed to his servant John the mysteries of the book of Revelation, and he designs that they shall be open to the study of all. In this book are depicted scenes that are now in the past, and some of eternal interest that are taking place around us; other of its prophecies will not receive their complete fulfillment until the close of time, when the last great conflict between the powers of darkness and the Prince of heaven will take place."[17]

Revelation 22:11 He that is unjust, let him be unjust still: and he which is filthy, let him be filthy still: and he that is righteous, let him be righteous still: and he that is holy, let him be holy still.

This is the pronouncement of the close of probation for all mankind. When this proclamation is made, all cases will have been decided in the heavenly courts of the investigative judgment, and nothing else will stand in the way of Jesus returning.

---

[17] E. G. White, *Review and Herald,* August 31, 1897 par. 2-5.

"Oh, let us live wholly for the Lord and show by a well-ordered life and godly conversation that we have been with Jesus and are His meek and lowly followers. We must work while the day lasts, for when the dark night of trouble and anguish comes, it will be too late to work for God. Jesus is in His holy temple and will now accept our sacrifices, our prayers, and our confessions of faults and sins and will pardon all the transgressions of Israel, that they may be blotted out before He leaves the sanctuary. When Jesus leaves the sanctuary, then they who are holy and righteous will be holy and righteous still; for all their sins will then be blotted out, and they will be sealed with the seal of the living God. But those that are unjust and filthy will be unjust and filthy still; for then there will be no Priest in the sanctuary to offer their sacrifices, their confessions, and their prayers before the Father's throne. Therefore what is done to rescue souls from the coming storm of wrath must be done before Jesus leaves the most holy place of the heavenly sanctuary."[18]

Revelation 22:12 And, behold, I come quickly; and my reward is with me, to give every man according as his work shall be.

"'The great day of the Lord is near, it is near, and hasteth greatly.' Jesus says: '**Behold, I come quickly**.' We should keep these words ever in mind, and act as though we do indeed believe that the coming of the Lord is nigh, and that we are pilgrims and strangers upon the earth."[19]

The fact that Jesus has his reward with him when he comes, shows that the investigative judgment is completed before the second coming.

"The cleansing of the sanctuary therefore involves a work of investigation—a work of judgment. This work must be performed prior to the coming of Christ to redeem His people; for when He comes, His reward is with Him to give to every man according to his works. Revelation 22:12."[20]

---

[18] E. G. White, *Early Writings* (1882), p. 48.1.

[19] E. G. White, *Testimonies for the Church,* Vol. 5 (1889), p. 266.2.

[20] E. G. White, *The Great Controversy* (1911), p. 421.3.

While our works will not save us, we are judged according to our works. Christ will give his reward to every man "**according as his work shall be**."

"Although we have no merit in ourselves, in the great goodness and love of God we are rewarded as if the merit were our own. When we have done all the good we can possibly do, we are still unprofitable servants. We have done only what was our duty. What we have accomplished has been wrought solely through the grace of Christ, and no reward is due to us from God on the ground of our merit. But through the merit of our Saviour every promise that God has made will be fulfilled, and every man will be rewarded according to his deeds."[21]

Revelation 22:13 I am Alpha and Omega, the beginning and the end, the first and the last.

Jesus has written these things to us for our admonition because he is coming soon. He is the beginning; he is the end; he is God Almighty.

Revelation 22:14 Blessed are they that do his commandments, that they may have right to the tree of life, and may enter in through the gates into the city.

Multitudes of self-proclaimed Christians assert that we need not keep God's commandments. These are sadly mistaken and directly contradicting the plainest statements of Scripture. The Bible says **"blessed are they that do His commandments, that they may have a right to the tree of life**."

"The gifts of His grace through Christ are free to all. There is no election but one's own by which any may perish. God has set forth in His word the conditions upon which every soul will be elected to eternal life—obedience to His commandments, through faith in Christ. God has elected a character in harmony with His law, and

---

[21] E. G. White, *Welfare Ministry* (1952), p. 316.1.

anyone who shall reach the standard of His requirement will have an entrance into the kingdom of glory."[22]

The conditions for entering heaven are absolute perfect obedience to the law of God. How then will we enter there? We have already broken his law. In fact, the Bible says that "all have sinned, and come short of the glory of God;"[23] that "there is none righteous, no, not one… They are all gone out of the way, they are together become unprofitable; there is none that doeth good, no, not one"[24] and "the soul that sinneth, it shall die,"[25] "for the wages of sin is death."[26]

Those who keep the commandments perfectly are blessed and therefore have the right to enter into the gates. The problem is, none have kept and none can keep the commandments perfectly. "Since we are sinful, unholy, we cannot perfectly obey the holy law. We have no righteousness of our own with which to meet the claims of the law of God. But Christ has made a way of escape for us. He lived on earth amid trials and temptations such as we have to meet. He lived a sinless life. He died for us, and now He offers to take our sins and give us His righteousness. **If you give yourself to Him, and accept Him as your Saviour, then, sinful as your life may have been, for His sake you are accounted righteous.** Christ's character stands in place of your character, and **you are accepted before God just as if you had not sinned**."[27]

God promises to give us the robe of his righteousness. He proposes to remove the mess of our mistakes, and replace them with his perfect life. Then he has promised to give us the strength to overcome every inherited and cultivated tendency towards evil. Therefore, he tells us to do his commandments. "Whatever is to be

---

[22] E. G. White, *Patriarchs and Prophets* (1890), p. 207.4.

[23] Romans 3:23.

[24] Romans 3:10-12.

[25] Ezekiel 18:20.

[26] Romans 6:23.

[27] E. G. White, *Steps to Christ* (1892), p. 62.2.

done at His command may be accomplished in His strength. All His biddings are enablings."[28]

"The Lord...desires us to seek for a pure, clean soul, a soul washed and made white in the blood of the Lamb. It is the white robe of Christ's righteousness that gives the sinner admittance into the presence of the heavenly angels. Not the color of his hair, but his perfect obedience to all God's commandments, opens to him the gates of the Holy City."[29]

Revelation 22:15 For without are dogs, and sorcerers, and whoremongers, and murderers, and idolaters, and whosoever loveth and maketh a lie.

The holy city becomes the refuge of the redeemed from the dangers of the criminals outside, until the final cleansing of the earth by fire.[30]

"Falsehood and deception of every cast is sin against the God of truth and verity. The word of God is plain upon these points. Ye shall not 'deal falsely, neither lie one to another.' 'All liars shall have their part in the lake which burneth with fire and brimstone: which is the second death.' God is a God of sincerity and truth. The word of God is a book of truth. Jesus is a faithful and true witness. The church is the witness and ground of the truth. All the precepts of the Most High are true and righteous altogether. How, then, must prevarication and any exaggeration or deception appear in His sight? For the falsehood he uttered because he coveted the gifts which the prophet refused, the servant of Elisha was struck with leprosy, which ended only with death.
"Even life itself should not be purchased with the price of falsehood. By a word or a nod the martyrs might have denied the truth and saved their lives. By consenting to cast a single grain of incense upon the idol altar they might have been saved from the rack, the scaffold, or the cross. But they refused to be false in word or deed, though life was the boon they would receive by so doing. Imprisonment, torture, and death, with a clear conscience, were welcomed by them, rather than deliverance on condition of

---

[28] E. G. White, *Christ's Object Lessons* (1900), p. 333.1.

[29] E. G. White, *The Seventh-day Adventist Bible Commentary*, Vol. 7 (1955), p. 920.4.

[30] See comments on Revelation 20.

deception, falsehood, and apostasy. By fidelity and faith in Christ they earned spotless robes and jeweled crowns. Their lives were ennobled and elevated in the sight of God because they stood firmly for the truth under the most aggravated circumstances.

"Men are mortals. They may be sincerely pious and yet have many errors of understanding and many defects of character, but they cannot be Christ's followers and yet be in league with him who 'loveth and maketh a lie.' Such a life is a fraud, a perpetual falsehood, a fatal deception. It is a close test upon the courage of men and women to be brought to face their own sins and to frankly acknowledge them. To say, 'That mistake must be charged to my account,' requires a strength of inward principle that the world possesses in but a limited degree. But he who has the courage to say this in sincerity gains a decided victory over self and effectually closes the door against the enemy."[31]

Revelation 22:16 *I Jesus have sent mine angel to testify unto you these things in the churches. I am the root and the offspring of David, and the bright and morning star.*

Jesus is both the root and offspring of David. When he was on earth he asked the Pharisees how this could be: "While the Pharisees were gathered together, Jesus asked them, Saying, What think ye of Christ? whose son is he? They say unto him, The son of David. He saith unto them, How then doth David in spirit call him Lord, saying, The Lord said unto my Lord, Sit thou on my right hand, till I make thine enemies thy footstool? If David then call him Lord, how is he his son? And no man was able to answer him a word..."[32] Christ as Creator, is the root of David. Christ as redeemer, is David's son.

The morning star is the name of Jesus Christ himself.[33] Jesus, the Son of God, the Majesty of heaven, has sent heavenly witnesses to testify to us of these things.

---

[31] E. G. White, *Testimonies for the Church*, Vol. 4 (1902), p. 336.1-3.

[32] Matthew 22:41-46.

[33] Many modern bible versions, in Isaiah 14:12, which is a passage speaking of Lucifer, substitute "morning star" for the KJV's "son of the morning," effectively giving Satan the title of Jesus Christ. Certainly, Lucifer the "son of the morning" would be pleased to be called the "morning star." These versions drop the name Lucifer from the passage, so it becomes unclear of whom the passage is speaking. For more information on the reasons for this, and many other problems in modern versions, see: Martin Klein, *Thou Hast Magnified Thy Word Above All Thy Name* (2016).

"The Shekinah had departed from the sanctuary, but in the Child of Bethlehem was veiled the glory before which angels bow. This unconscious babe was the promised seed, to whom the first altar at the gate of Eden pointed. This was Shiloh, the peace giver. It was He who declared Himself to Moses as the I AM. It was He who in the pillar of cloud and of fire had been the guide of Israel. This was He whom seers had long foretold. He was the Desire of all nations, **the Root and the Offspring of David, and the Bright and Morning Star**. The name of that helpless little babe, inscribed in the roll of Israel, declaring Him our brother, was the hope of fallen humanity. The child for whom the redemption money had been paid was He who was to pay the ransom for the sins of the whole world. He was the true 'high priest over the house of God,' the head of 'an unchangeable priesthood,' the intercessor at 'the right hand of the Majesty on high.' Hebrews 10:21; 7:24; 1:3."[34]

Revelation 22:17 And the Spirit and the bride say, Come. And let him that heareth say, Come. And let him that is athirst come. And whosoever will, let him take the water of life freely.

In the closing verses of Scripture, God is presenting one final invitation to come to him. He invites you personally—please come, you may have the water of life, if you choose.

"**The Spirit and the bride say, come.**" The Spirit is calling, and the bride is calling. The bride is the new Jerusalem. The gates of pearl stand open as an invitation resounding through all creation—"come." Jesus says simply, "come." Why are you waiting to come to him? Are you trying to make yourself good enough? The Bible says your righteousness is as filthy rags.[35] "Satan will come to you, saying, 'You are a sinner;' but do not allow him to fill your mind with the thought that because you are sinful, God has cast you off. Say to him, Yes; I am a sinner, and for that very reason I need a Saviour. I need forgiveness and pardon, and Christ says that if I will come to him, I shall not perish. In his letter to me I read, 'If we confess our sins, he is faithful and just to forgive us our sins, and to cleanse us from all unrighteousness.' When Satan tells you that you are lost,

---

[34] E. G. White, *The Desire of Ages* (1898), p. 52.3.

[35] Isaiah 64:6

answer, Yes; but Jesus came to seek and to save that which was lost. 'A bruised reed shall he not break, and the smoking flax shall he not quench.' The greater my sin, the greater my need of a Saviour."[36]

"Christ is ready to pardon all who come to Him confessing their sins. To the tried, struggling soul is spoken the word, 'Let him take hold of My strength, that he may make peace with Me; and he shall make peace with Me.' Thank God, we have a High Priest who is touched with the feeling of our infirmities; for He was in all points tempted like as we are."[37] "Christ gave Himself to a shameful, agonizing death, showing His great travail of soul to save the perishing. Oh, Christ is able, Christ is willing, Christ is longing, to save all who will come unto Him!"[38]

To those who hear this invitation is given the command to invite others—"**let him that heareth say, Come.**" The Heavenly angels are anxious and waiting for us to cooperate with them in proclaiming this invitation.

"The call of the hour is answered by human agencies. Thus when the divine voice cries, 'Whom shall I send, and who will go for us?' the response will come, 'Here am I; send me.' ...We have no time to lose. We must encourage this work. ...To every man and woman who will co-operate with divine power, the Lord imparts a fitness for the work. All the requisite talent, courage, perseverance, faith, and tact will come as they put the armor on. A great work is to be done in our world, and human agencies will surely respond to the demand. The world must hear the warning. When the call comes, 'Whom shall I send, and who will go for us?' send back the answer, clear and distinct, 'Here am I; send me.'"[39]

"Our world is a vast lazar house, a scene of misery that we dare not allow even our thoughts to dwell upon. Did we realize it as it is, the burden would be too terrible. Yet God feels it all. In order to destroy sin and its results He gave His best Beloved, and He has put it in our power, through co-operation with Him, to bring this scene of misery

---

[36] E. G. White, *The Review and Herald*, September 15, 1896 par. 10.

[37] E. G. White, *Signs of the Times*, December 10, 1902 par. 9.

[38] E. G. White, *Heaven* (2003), p. 11.1.

[39] E. G. White, *Review and Herald*, January 22, 1901 par. 12.

to an end. 'This gospel of the kingdom shall be preached in all the world for a witness unto all nations; and then shall the end come.' Matthew 24:14."[40]

"It is the privilege of every Christian not only to look for but to hasten the coming of our Lord Jesus Christ, (2 Peter 3:12, margin). Were all who profess His name bearing fruit to His glory, how quickly the whole world would be sown with the seed of the gospel. Quickly the last great harvest would be ripened, and Christ would come to gather the precious grain."[41]

"The Duke of Wellington was once present where a party of Christian men were discussing the possibility of success in missionary effort among the heathen. They appealed to the duke to say whether in his judgment such efforts were likely to prove a success commensurate to the cost. The old soldier replied:
"'Gentlemen, what are your marching orders? Success is not the question for you to discuss. If I read your orders aright, they run thus, 'Go ye into all the world, and preach the gospel to every creature. Gentlemen, obey your marching orders.'
"My brethren, the Lord is coming, and we need to bend every energy to the accomplishment of the work before us. I appeal to you to give yourselves wholly to the work. Christ gave His time, His soul, His strength, to labor for the benefit and blessing of humanity."[42]

The condition of accepting the invitation and coming to Christ is that one must be athirst: "**Let him that is athirst, come.**" "Not by painful struggles or wearisome toil, not by gift or sacrifice, is righteousness obtained; but it is freely given to every soul who hungers and thirsts to receive it."[43] "**Whosoever will, let him take the water of life freely.**"
"He who seeks to quench his thirst at the fountains of this world will drink only to thirst again. Everywhere men are unsatisfied. They long for something to supply the need of the soul. Only One can meet that want. The need of the world, 'The Desire of all nations,' is Christ. The

---

[40] E. G. White, *Education* (1903), p. 263.2.

[41] E. G. White, *Christ's Object Lessons* (1900), p. 69.

[42] E. G. White, *Gospel Workers* (1915), p. 115.1-3.

[43] E. G. White, *Thoughts From the Mount of Blessings* (1896), p. 18.2.

divine grace which He alone can impart, is as living water, purifying, refreshing, and invigorating the soul."[44]

"Christ has opened a fountain for the sinful, suffering world, and the voice of divine mercy is heard: 'Come, all ye thirsting souls; come and drink.' You may take of the water of life freely. Let him that heareth say, Come; and whosoever will, let him come. Let every soul, women as well as men, sound this message. Then the work will be carried to the waste places of the earth."[45]

"Jesus prayed for His enemies, 'Father, forgive them; for they know not what they do.'...
"That prayer of Christ for His enemies embraced the world. It took in every sinner that had lived or should live, from the beginning of the world to the end of time. Upon all rests the guilt of crucifying the Son of God. To all, forgiveness is freely offered. 'Whosoever will' may have peace with God, and inherit eternal life."[46]

Revelation 22:18 For I testify unto every man that heareth the words of the prophecy of this book, If any man shall add unto these things, God shall add unto him the plagues that are written in this book:

Revelation 22:19 And if any man shall take away from the words of the book of this prophecy, God shall take away his part out of the book of life, and out of the holy city, and from the things which are written in this book.

---

[44] E. G. White, *The Desire of Ages* (1898), p. 187.2.

[45] E. G. White, *Testimonies for the Church*, Vol. 6 (1902), p. 86.2.

[46] E. G. White, *The Desire of Ages* (1898), p. 745.1.

This is a fearsome warning. God declares that if we tamper with this book; if we change it; if we make it say something that it does not say; adding to it, or taking from it, it is a matter of life or death.[47]

This is a warning that applies to all of Scripture, for Revelation is its completion, and this warning is repeated in other places in the Bible.[48]

Revelation 22:20 *He which testifieth these things saith, Surely I come quickly. Amen. Even so, come, Lord Jesus.*

"Knowing the time, that now it is high time to awake out of sleep: for now is our salvation nearer than when we believed."[49]

Revelation 22:21 *The grace of our Lord Jesus Christ be with you all. Amen.*

---

[47] Can you say with confidence that your faith is based on the infallible word of God? Were the Scriptures compiled by a messy group of councils and revised by a multitude of scribes? Is it true that there are errors and contradictions in the Bible and its manuscripts? Are there any corrupted copies of Scripture? Is there a secret scheme to tamper with the Word of God? Do you know for certain that the version of Scripture you read is a copy of God's preserved Word?

The facts and history of the preservation of Scripture are the foundation of our faith upon which depends our eternal destiny. Without His Word, the human race would have no knowledge of God. We must have full assurance that we are indeed reading the true and pure word of God.

For answers to these questions, and more, see Martin Klein, *Thou Hast Magnified Thy Word Above All Thy Name.*

[48] See Deuteronomy 4:2; Deuteronomy 12:32; Proverbs 30:5-6.

[49] Romans 13:11

Index

The Most Precious Message:
The Infinite Gift of Calvary

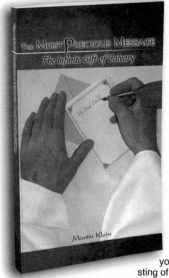

The most precious message ever given to mortals is the message that Jesus became our substitute, taking the penalty for our sins, that we might take his perfect righteousness and stand faultless in the judgement, appearing before the Father as if we had never sinned.
This is the message of righteousness by faith.

"'He was wounded for our transgressions, he was bruised for our iniquities: the chastisement of our peace was upon him; and with his stripes we are healed.' This penalty Christ bore for the sins of the transgressor; He has borne the punishment for every man and for this reason He can ransom every soul, however fallen his condition, if he will accept the law of God as his standard of righteousness."

"The same healing, life-giving message is now sounding. It points to the uplifted Saviour upon the shameful tree. Those who have been bitten by that old serpent, the devil, are bidden to look and live...
Look alone to Jesus as your righteousness and your sacrifice. As you are justified by faith, the deadly sting of the serpent will be healed."

"By pledging His own life Christ has made Himself responsible for every man and woman on the earth. He stands in the presence of God, saying, 'Father, I take upon Myself the guilt of that soul. It means death to him if he is left to bear it. If he repents he shall be forgiven. My blood shall cleanse him from all sin. I gave My life for the sins of the world.'"

"Jesus cares for each one as though there were not another individual on the face of the earth." "Come near... to Christ the Mighty Healer.... This wonderful manner of His love was evidenced at His crucifixion, and the light of His love is reflected in bright beams from the cross of Calvary. Now it remains for us to accept that love, to appropriate the promises of God to ourselves.
"Just repose in Jesus. Rest in Him as a tired child rests in the arms of its mother. The Lord pities you. He loves you. The Lord's arms are beneath you.... Wounded and bruised, just repose trust in God. A compassionate hand is stretched out to bind up your wounds. He will be more precious to your soul than the choicest friend, and all that can be desired is not comparable to Him. Only believe Him; only trust Him. Your friend in affliction—one who knows."

Paperback: 130 pages
Publisher: Savannah Pictures
ISBN: 978-0-9975897-4-0 (paperback)
Religion: Christian Life: Inspirational

Thou Hast Magnified Thy Word
Above All Thy Name

The Bible makes the claim to absolute truthfulness and infallibility.[1] It then provides the internal evidence to verify this claim. Complete harmony through sixty-six books by about forty different writers, spanning one and a half millennia, would be impossible if the author were not the Holy Spirit. In order for Scripture to make the claim of truthfulness, it must also contain the promise of preservation. God's promise to preserve his pure Word is dramatically fulfilled in the 1611 publication of the Authorized Version of the Bible, more commonly known today as the King James Version. The Bible's power, feared by its enemies, is the power to transform those who submit to its claims, and love its precepts. The written words of the King James translators have had a greater influence on this world than any other literary work the planet has ever seen. It has changed the course of nations, and altered history in a way the translators could not have fathomed. It has transmitted the precious gospel message to more souls than all other agencies combined. Only in eternity will its power be comprehended.

The King James translators of the Bible achieved what has never been accomplished before, or since. Although the translators are mostly unknown, and their masterpiece is either unappreciated or maligned; though the importance of their accomplishment is not comprehended; though every power of hell and demons has been arrayed against this book, yet their legacy survives as the living Word of God—the best-selling book of all time.

Though God promised to preserve his word, the stern facts of history and the unyielding testimony of Scripture prove that attempts have been made to pervert God's Word: "ye have perverted the words of the living God," Jeremiah 23:36.
Compare: KJV Job 19:26 "yet in my flesh shall I see God:"
        ASV Job 19:26 "then without my flesh shall I see God;"
Simple logic demands that two opposite statements cannot both be true. Therefore, one must be false. The one that is false cannot be God's pure, true, unperverted Word.

Thus, to fulfill the promise of preservation, the Scripture must contain a way to distinguish between the genuine and the counterfeit. With demonstrable and rather serious differences in so many current versions of the Bible, how can we be certain what is God's true and preserved Word? This book answers this question.

Paperback: 290 pages
Publisher: Savannah Pictures
ISBN: 978-0-9975897-5-7 (paperback—2nd Edition)
Religion: Christian Theology: Apologetics

The End